"You'll find [these] and several thousand other secrets, large and small, stuffed into a new book that ranks, quite simply, as the most important manuscript ever compiled on Colorado fishing. Perhaps the most difficult thing to grasp about Flyfisher's Guide to Colorado is that author Marty Bartholomew achieved this minor masterpiece in his very first attempt at serious writing.

"Never before has so much useful lore been presented under a single title. If Bartholomew tried to pack in another single morsel, it might pop through the cover."

— Charlie Meyers, *Denver Post* Outdoor Editor

"Veteran Colorado fly fishers and newcomers alike will be delighted with a new 512-page guidebook that explores the state's rich angling opportunities more comprehensively than any reference before it.

"Bartholomew, a fly-fishing instructor, fly tier and part-time fishing guide who lives in Aurora, didn't miss a thing. I tried to trip him up and couldn't find a single hole in his coverage of Colorado's fly-fishing waters.

"This is the only guidebook in many years that has attempted a statewide pilgrimage specifically for fly anglers, and it does it better than any other. It can help you plan a lifetime of fishing trips. Or drive you nuts with anticipation during the cabin-fever months.

— Ed Dentry, *Rocky Mountain News*

"Hot off the presses, this…guide is marketed as "the most comprehensive Colorado flyfishing guide available." Judging by the shelves in local bookstores, that very well could be true."

— *Boulder Daily Camera*

Flyfisher's Guide to™
Colorado

Titles Available in This Series

Flyfisher's Guide to™
Colorado

Marty Bartholomew

Introduction by A.K. Best

Warmwater Flyfishing
contributions by Barry Reynolds

Wilderness
Adventures
Press™

Belgrade, Montana

Published by Wilderness Adventures Press
45 Buckskin Road
Belgrade, MT 59714
800-925-3339
Website: www.wildadv.com
email: books@wildadv.com

10 9 8 7 6 5 4

Printed in the United States of America

Library of Congress Cataloging-in-Publication Data

Bartholomew, Marty, 1957–
    Flyfisher's guide to Colorado / Marty Bartholomew.
    p.   cm.
  ISBN 1–885106–56–4
    1. Fly fishing–Colorado–Guidebooks. 2. Colorado–Guidebooks.   I. Title.
SH475.B37   1998
799.1'757'09788–dc21   97–43890
                                                                          CIP

To the future of flyfishing,
my little anglers, Vanessa and Cole.

To my wife Ann
for allowing me the time and space
to complete this endeavor.

Your sacrifices are greatly appreciated.

Table of Contents

Acknowledgments

There are several people who helped me with this book, not only in the last year while working on this project, but in the many years of angling across Colorado with some of the best fishermen in the west. Their mentoring and insights into the sport have inspired me to pass along this knowledge to others in many different forms. This book was a great opportunity to share ideas and reach others whom I will never meet.

First, I would like to thank Barry Reynolds. If it were not for his introduction to Chuck and Blanche Johnson, I would have never had this opportunity to write a book. Also, thanks to Barry and John Berryman for their help with the warmwater section.

Second, thanks to Gus, Shannon, and Eric for sharing miles on the road and hours on the stream. Also to Eric Neufeld, I thank you for the footprints you have left in Rocky Mountain National Park and the valuable information you provided for that section.

Inside the four walls of Colorado, there are countless miles of stream and shoreline to flyfish; so much so that it would be nearly impossible for one person to scratch the surface of the available water. It was a great pleasure for me to have met, talked, and fished with people in the flyfishing business from across Colorado who shared that information with me, and in turn with you. There were also individuals such as Otto Shults, who has lived with the White River out his back door all his life and could have said, "Get lost, I don't want anyone to know about the White River," but willingly contributed information regardless. I found generosity around every corner. Everyone who provided information for this book is mentioned in some way, shape, or form. I want to thank each and every one of you for taking all the pestering phone calls, answering questionnaires, or allowing me to fish some of your favorite water with you.

One Saturday morning while putting together information for the maps in this book, I engaged in a phone call that opened my eyes to what we all should try to achieve. Paula Rea answered the phone, and after a quick introduction I started to quiz her about public fishing accesses on the Fryingpan River. Putting up resistance, she soon turned the discussion in another direction.

The table was turned and I was thrown questions like, What are we going to do to preserve this sport we love so much? How do we not love it to death? How do we collectively manage our resources and become stewards to protect it?

Whoa! This was getting too deep.

However, by keeping things simple, some good can be done by everyone who fishes. Tread lightly! Be gracious, not only to the land, but to the next angler. Leave the area better off than when you got there.

If everyone will keep these thoughts in mind and do just their small part, I'm sure the sport will reward you and future generations of anglers.

Introduction

I've known Marty Bartholomew for about 15 years as one of the finest fly tiers in the U.S. He is also a man who speaks from the heart. I've fished many of the lakes and streams Marty lists in this book, and I can tell you that he's right on! In fact, there is some information I secretly wish he hadn't shared with the rest of the world, because it's the stuff a few of us have learned by spending hundreds of hours in the water. But it's better to learn the whole truth from a man like Marty than it is to learn something less from others.

It doesn't matter if you've fished Colorado lakes and streams all your life or if you're planning to make your first flyfishing trip to the Colorado Rockies; this book is a must! Not only does it contain vital information on which road to turn on to find a brook trout feeder stream, it also tells you the phone number of the nearest locksmith in case you lose your keys—and I'll bet that's something a lot of locals don't know!

Motels, campgrounds, restaurants, fly shops, nearest airport, car rental agencies, hospitals, river and lake characteristics, special regulations, species and their average lengths, seasons, hatches by the month, recommended rod and leader lengths, line weights, which atlas to use and on which page to find your destination —they're all listed.

Seasonal stream flows, lake depths, boat ramp locations, weed bed placement, fly patterns and how to fish them are all treated in great detail. And there are Marty's tidbits of personal fishing experiences as well as comments from some of the guides and shop owners that he has fished with to round out this very informative book.

About the only thing he doesn't tell you (thankfully) is which rock to stand on. In short, if you own this book and can't catch trout in Colorado, only three things are possible: you can't read, all the trout are dead, or you're on the wrong planet.

Please treat these waters and the trout in them with the same love and respect that Marty so thoroughly does in writing and fishing and we'll all be able to enjoy them for many generations to come.

A.K. Best
Boulder, Colorado
July 1997

Major Roads and Rivers of Colorado

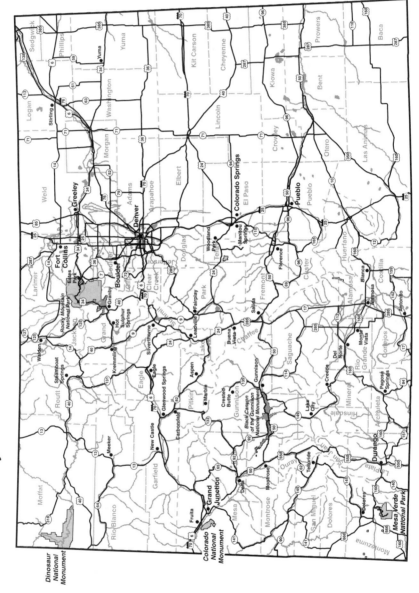

Colorado Facts

Eighth largest state in the union
104,100 square miles
66,624,000 acres
380 miles across
280 miles north to south

Elevations: 3,350 feet to 14,433 feet
Counties: 63
Towns and Cities:
Population (1990 census): 3,294,394
    2 Indian Reservations
    2 National Parks
    6 National Monuments
    2 National Grasslands
    2 National Recreation Areas
  11 National Forests
  23 State Recreation Areas
    1 State Forest
  24 Wilderness Areas
  11 State Parks

Primary Industries: Manufacturing, government, tourism, agriculture, aerospace, electronics equipment
Capital: Denver
Bird: Lark bunting
Flower: Rocky Mountain columbine
Tree: Colorado blue spruce
Animal: Bighorn sheep
Fish: Greenback cutthroat

Tips on Using This Book

You're planning to do some flyfishing in Colorado, and the big question is where to go. Well, that's a good question—in fact, I fish 90 percent of the time in Colorado, and I've asked the very same question. The options seem endless.

Colorado has more trout water than any one person could fish in a lifetime—world-famous waters such as the Fryingpan, Gunnison, and South Platte rivers, as well as little-known fisheries such as the Uncompahgre and San Miguel rivers. From the front range of the Rocky Mountains west to the Utah border, trout streams abound. With opportunities to hook pike, tiger muskie, and warmwater species such as large and smallmouth bass, wipers, carp, and numerous pan fish, an angler tossing flies here will have his hands full.

You will find the state divided into nine chapters with detailed information on all major river drainages and important stillwaters. There are also clear, concise maps and categorical hatch charts with proven fly patterns for every stage of a hatch. The best of these rivers and lakes do get a lot of angling pressure, so be prepared for crowds. There are some very good waters not covered due to their fragile environment.

Another great feature of this book is the hub city information. This includes hotels, restaurants, local fly shops and guide services, auto repair facilities, airports, and locksmiths (for those of us who have kicked our keys out along the river at one time or another). From anywhere in the United States, you should be able to open this book and make airline reservations, get a rental car, book a motel, and hire a top-notch flyfishing guide. There is also a section on Travel Tips, some of which I picked up from well-traveled anglers, flight attendants, and pilots, and personal experience.

I have done my best to maintain as accurate information as possible; however, fly shops may close, restaurants may board up the windows, and hotels may change their names. You will find a number for the local Chamber of Commerce or visitor information center when problems arise.

Motel Cost Key
$ — $30–$50 per night
$$ — $50–$70 per night
$$$ — $70 per night and up

Restaurant Cost Key
$ — $10 and under per meal
$$ — $10–$20 per meal
$$$ — $20 and up

Please read the section on Stream Etiquette to avoid unwanted conflicts with other anglers. There is good information for the beginning angler as well as for the most competent flyfisher. Rounding out the book, you will find descriptions and habits of fish species found in Colorado important to flyfishers. Along with the section on entomology, you will find out a little bit more about bugs and fish than you thought you really needed to know.

My goal throughout has been to make the daunting task of planning a successful flyfishing trip a little easier and to give you enough information to know what to do when you get there. My hope is that you hook ample numbers of fish, take home only memories, and enjoy "Colorful Colorado" to its fullest.

Fishing Regulations

These regulations are current as of printing and should remain current through the year 2000. However, always check current regulations for changes.

- Fishing license required for every person over 16 years of age.
- No license is transferable.

License Fees

Resident

Annual	$20.25
Five day	18.25
Daily	5.25
Senior, annual (64 years of age)	10.25
Combination fishing, small game	30.25
Second rod stamp	4.00

Nonresident

Annual	$40.25
Five day	18.25
Daily	5.25
Second rod stamp	4.00

Bag & Possession Limits

East of the Continental Divide except waters with special regulations:

Trout	8
Splake	8
Arctic char	8
Grayling	8

NEW for 1998—All streams and rivers west of the Continental Divide except waters with special regulations:

Trout	2
Splake	2
Arctic char	2
Grayling	2

All lakes, ponds, and reservoirs west of the Continental Divide except waters with special regulations:

Trout	4
Splake	4
Arctic char	4
Grayling	4

Note: On westslope waters, the total number of these species you can have in possession is **6**, providing that **2** came from streams and **4** came from lakes.

In addition to the above limits, you can take a full limit of each of the following fish species:

Brook trout, 8 inches or less 10
Kokanee salmon, angling 10
Walleye and saugeye 5
    Arkansas, South Fork Republican, & San Juan drainages 10
Largemouth, smallmouth, spotted bass 5
    Arkansas & South Fork Republican drainage 10
White bass and wiper 10
    Arkansas & South Fork Republican drainage 20
Crappie... 10
Northern pike 10
Tiger muskie, 30 inches or longer 1
Yellow perch, bluegill, sunfish, pumpkinseed, Sacramento perch 20

Colorado Division of Wildlife Offices

Denver Headquarters / 6060 Broadway, Denver 80216 / 303-297-1192
Northeast / 317 West Prospect Road, Ft. Collins 80526 / 970-484-2836
Northwest / 711 Independent Avenue, Grand Junction 81505 / 970-248-7175
Southeast / 2126 West Weber Street, Colorado Springs 80907 / 719-473-2945
Southwest / 2300 South Townsend Avenue, Montrose 81401 / 970-249-3431

24-hour recorded fishing information: 303-291-7533

Fishing Conditions Reports

Metro Denver & Foothills 303-291-7535
Northeast Colorado 303-291-7536
Northwest Colorado 303-291-7537
Southeast Colorado 303-291-7538
Southwest Colorado 303-291-7539

Information on Guides and Outfitters

Division of Regulatory Agencies 303-894-7778

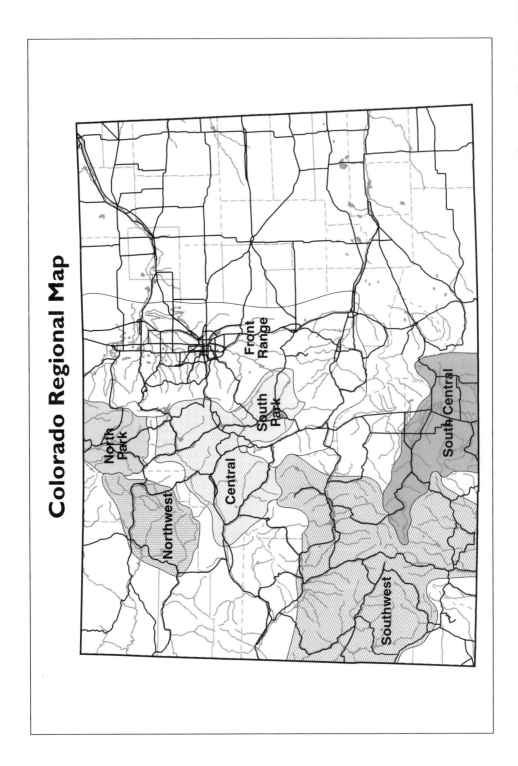

Colorado Regional Map

Front Range

Rising from the Great Plains, the Rocky Mountains dissect Colorado from north to south, right down the middle of the state. The snowcapped peaks of Mt. Evans, Longs Peak, and Pikes Peak form a monumental wall of 14,000-footers that dominate the western horizon—they are truly an incredible sight.

I've lived on the Front Range all my life and I'm still wildly impressed with them. It is no wonder that Denver, Ft. Collins and Colorado Springs became the size they are today. Eastern settlers must have considered the enormity of their task to cross those mountains and said, "Forget it, we're unpacking right here."

Today, the Front Range is easy to cross. Interstate 25, east of the Front Range, connects immense population centers with highway systems into and out of this great stretch of mountains. That doesn't mean that they are always easy to navigate. A tremendous amount of snowfall packs into the ponderosa pines and blue spruce forests during winter months, often in excess of 6 feet at high elevations.

When spring arrives, that snowpack finds its way into three main drainage basins: the South Platte, Arkansas, and the Cache la Poudre. Those drainages are known for their superb trout fishing. The world-renowned South Platte River offers the heart of the action. The lesser known Cache la Poudre River, Big Thompson River, and St. Vrain Creek are extremely productive tributaries of the South Platte. The Arkansas River carries the burden for the southern end of the Front Range.

The South Platte is the main water supply for the Denver Metro area and the agricultural demands of the plains. Existing in such great demand does have its pitfalls; the Platte has paid its dues with five dams holding back large bodies of water in its first 100 miles of existence. Lucky for us, the tailwaters below those dams have developed into wonderful fisheries. A quick note concerning the South Platte: its headwaters, including the water above and below Spinney Mountain Reservoir and the river below Elevenmile Reservoir, are covered in great detail in the chapter titled "South Park."

The Cache la Poudre, on the other hand, is a beautiful freestone river, one of the last in Colorado. Flowing through a tight, winding canyon, the Poudre is probably one of the best-kept secrets in the state. Mostly just locals know of its wonderful variety and productive hatches. The Arkansas River, in contrast, is a big brawling freestone with lots of room for flycasting. Numerous public accesses and free-rising brown trout make this a great getaway just about any day of the week. The Arkansas is best known for its Mother's Day caddis hatch, when zillions of those bugs come off.

Overall, the Front Range area of Colorado offers all kinds of flyfishing opportunity, whether you want to fish for small native trout on a creek or test the wide, challenging currents of a tailwater. All told, there is more angling to be done here than one could accomplish in a lifetime.

South Platte River
Below Cheesman Lake

N

Legend

— State/Cty Road
-- Trail
⚑ Campground
✖ Fishing Access
▬ Major River
▬ Minor River/Creek

Platte Canyon Res. 121

Waterton Canyon, 37 mi.

Kennedy Gulch   S. Foxton Road

Willow Creek

Resort Creek

Platte River

North Fork South

South Platte R. Rd.

Colorado Trail

Strontia Springs Res.

River

Bear Creek

Buffalo Creek

Buffalo Creek

Spring Creek

South Platte River Road

North Fork, 24 mi.

To Sedalia

Buffalo Creek Road

S. Deckers Road

FR 515

Platte

Pine Creek

Gunbarrel Creek

67

Willow Bend, 17 mi.

Scraggy View, 14 mi.

Sixmile Creek

Sugar Creek

Platte River Campground, 10 mi.

S. Deckers Road

Pine Creek

Trumbull, 6 mi.

Wigwam Cr. Rd.

Goose Cr. Rd.

Gill Trail

South

Deckers, 5 mi.

67

Gill Trail, Trailhead, 3 mi.

Cheesman Lake

Cheesman Dam, 0 mi.

Horse Creek

Turkey Creek

Fourmile Creek

© Wilderness Adventures Press

South Platte River

The difference between a good Colorado flyfisherman and a great Colorado fly-fisherman is one split shot. —Paul Brunn

Flyfishers from around the state, and hundreds from around the country, dodged a bullet (and possibly several tons of dynamite) in March 1990, when the EPA vetoed a permit that would have added yet another dam to the long list already impounding the South Platte River, possibly Colorado's best trout fishing locale.

That proposed dam, "Two Forks," would have drowned the premiere section on one of the finest trout streams in the nation.

A state biologist was quoted as saying, "One of the affected stretches of the South Platte, namely Cheesman Canyon, is among the nation's top 10 most productive trout streams." Dave Taylor, then a director for the state's Trout Unlimited organization, said, "Cheesman Canyon is a monument to the positive effects catch and release fishing can have on a rainbow fishery that receives tremendous angling pressure." John Gierach, a well known writer from Colorado, wrote in *The View from Rat Lake*, "This river is everything a trout stream should be."

The Two Forks project called for a 615-foot concrete wall to be built northeast of Deckers, just 30 air miles from Denver. The resulting reservoir would have flooded 30 miles of the South Platte River Valley, including Cheesman Canyon. Homes would have been lost, wildlife habitat would have been history. Fortunately, the EPA concluded that construction and operation of the dam would be a violation of the Clean-Water Act. A subsequent lawsuit, filed by eight suburban water districts in 1996, was tossed out by a federal judge.

The resounding blow of David knocking Goliath to his knees can still be heard in the canyon, amidst the dimpling trout and the swish of lines cast to them.

Cheesman Canyon and the Deckers Area

Even though it requires a minimum 20-minute walk up Gill Trail just to see the South Platte in Cheesman Canyon, that hike does not present much of a deterrent for anglers—the area gets pounded relentlessly—and for good reason: there are plenty of sizeable trout to be had.

Gill Trail starts with a makeshift series of logs, resembling steps, just off CR 126. To reach the trailhead from US 285, turn south at Pine Junction onto CR 126 and follow it 20 miles toward Deckers. From Colorado Springs, take US 24 west to Woodland Park. Turn right (north) on Colorado 67 to Deckers. Turn left (west) on CR 126 for 2.5 miles to the Gill Trail parking lot.

You can also access the canyon from the top of Gill Trail at Cheesman Reservoir. A day of fishing in the canyon can start here if you feel like a mountain goat. The trail down to the river is steep, and coming back out at the end of the day is a chore. However, if you must, take county road 211 to Cheesman Reservoir and then the trail from there. It's approximately a mile downhill to the river.

If you don't like to hike, the Deckers area is much easier to access. Parking and open fishing is plentiful right along the road north of Deckers. Stop by and see Dick Johnson at Flies & Lies in Deckers for the hot spots and hatch information.

Anglers who fish the canyon either pack their gear in and change on the bank of the river or slip the old waders on and trudge in ready for business. The latter has a tendency to break a good sweat, but it does reduce the haste of getting ready to fish with the stream right in front of you.

If you do hike into the canyon, expect heavy fishing pressure every day of the week. I often wonder if anyone ever works around here. Without an early start, expect all the best holes to be taken. The other option, especially if you arrive late, is to keep walking. You can easily cover 2 miles looking for solitude, but the struggle is usually worth it.

From Gill Trail, trout can be spotted in the pools and pockets the full length of the canyon, and there always seems to be room for another angler. Look for trout holding in all the typical places, but most often you'll find them at the tailout of riffles. Even in the fast water, the rainbows in the canyon are easy to spot; big, beautiful ruby red sides and gill plates stand out like sore thumbs.

Jim Cannon of Blue Quill Anglers in Evergreen refers to the "Canyon" as his favorite trip. I asked him, "When is the best time to fish Cheesman?"

"Any time," Cannon answered. "The canyon can be fished all year. The best reviews from our clients come in the spring. Blue-winged olives start to show themselves on a regular basis by late March and carry on into late May. Flows are perfect that time of year, 100 to 300 cfs."

The emerging stage of the olive hatch sparks the best action. Start by drifting a size 20 olive biot mayfly nymph under a size 20 or size 22 RS-2 CDC-winged emerger and pinch on enough weight to keep the flies near bottom. Strike indicators help detect subtle takes, but the flies must drift perfectly or the indicator will go undisturbed. I prefer a high stick, short line nymphing technique, without an indicator. That technique requires serious concentration and a little practice, but it's easier to control the speed and location of the fly in tricky currents. The strike is very obvious, and setting the hook is almost instantaneous.

When trout rise, take the weight off, dry the CDC wing on the RS-2, and fish the flies in the surface film. I like the CDC wing because it is easy to see and floats well. Trout in the canyon prefer feeding on nymphs, but they will switch to emergers and floating nymphs during a hatch when the volume of food is near the surface, so this is a perfect set up. However, sometimes those little gray sailboats start popping on the water and fish stop rising! Flyfishers just can't understand that scenario.

They might ask, "What is going on? Bugs everywhere, no action." The first place to look for an answer is up. If the sun is high and bright, trout avoid the surface. That's why overcast days produce the best olive hatches. Also, on cool days, mayflies drift longer as their wings dry and trout have more time to feed on them. During that time, one of the best adult blue-winged olive patterns is a size 18 or size 20 olive comparadun. Next best has to be an AK's olive quill. The key to success during

The South Platte below Cheesman Reservoir—prime hike-in water.

this stage of the hatch is casting to an individual riser—just don't flock shoot with those flies.

A word of caution: Pat Dorsey, a very knowledgeable flyfisherman and guide on the South Platte, warns, "Hatches on the South Platte below Cheesman and in the Deckers area are very sporadic. They'll hatch one day, then a couple days later, so it's really a hit and miss situation for dry fly action. However, that's not to say the nymph fishing won't be good."

Another piece of sage advice: Midge hatches often coincide with the Baetis emergences and trout often key in on the more diminutive insect. That situation fools many experienced anglers, myself included. When midges are the choice fly, tactics stay the same, but fly selection must be reevaluated.

A black beauty imitates the larvae while an olive or black palomino midge works in the film as the suspending pupae. A size 24 Griffith's gnat may also draw fish to the top.

Runoff may or may not affect the Canyon and Deckers area. Flows out of Cheesman Dam in June can reach 1,000 cfs, and those high flows reduce mobility and cloud the water for a day or two. However, that high water churns up alternate foods from this fertile environment, such as annelids (worms), stoneflies, and scuds. Heavier rods, stronger tippets and flies you can see without a microscope are in order.

After those high flows, the July caddis hatches begin, and they can be a kick in the butt. Emergences are not very heavy, and they usually happen in late afternoon and early evening. Dry fly action is possible during the day with size 16 olive or gray LaFontaine's sparkle pupa and a low riding size 14 or 16 tan CDC caddis. Again, trout prefer nymphs and emerging caddis, and a size 16 or 18 soft-hackle hare's ear, drifted in shallow pockets and at the edge of slow eddies should make you a believer.

When the sun goes out of sight, adult caddis wake from the willows and are seen fluttering over the water. Watch for rising snouts.

A small pale morning dun hatch also arrives in the canyon in July. Those flies hatch quickly, so there are usually more duns on the water than emergers. They rate about a size 18, but a size 20 PMD comparadun works best more often than not. Concentrate your efforts in the more aerated types of water, like riffles and swift runs, where PMD nymphs live. As nymphs go, a size 16 or 18 pheasant tail works well.

Trico hatches follow PMDs in August, and Dorsey tells me, "The Trico hatch in the canyon and below Deckers is one of the most reliable hatches on the South Platte. Look for the Trico activity in mid-August. Take note of your watch at 10 a.m. and tie on a size 22 spinner. The spinnerfall is about to happen."

I questioned Dorsey about the size 22 fly. "I've picked the naturals off the water, put them up against a size 24 and my fly looked like a gorilla." He answered, "A size 22 is a good starting point, and early in the spinnerfall it will fool a few. But changing to a smaller fly is not uncommon. The size of the actual insect changes throughout the hatch. Size 22s one day, size 26s the next. I tell all my clients there is no luck involved. It's pure technique and delicate presentations that catch these trout."

While caddis, PMDs and Trico hatches are all worth fishing, the South Platte's best hatch is the fall Baetis and Pseudocloeon.

The Pseudos are in the size 22 to 24 range. More commonly referred to as "the tiny blue-winged olive," these diminutive mayflies can present fly anglers with days of enjoyment from mid-September to the end of October. Pseudos have a tendency to be more active in the evenings, while the Baetis hatch at or near 11 a.m. When you find mayflies drifting and want to tell the difference between the two species, the Pseudos have two tails instead of the Baetis' three. Because of its large wings, the adult Pseudo looks big. But, when you see two tails, a size 22 is the biggest fly you should fish. The Baetis can go up to size 16, but most range between size 18 or 20.

During fall, be on the water by 9 AM to fish the Baetis hatch. The BWO nymphs are swimmers, and they get active about an hour to an hour and a half before they ascend. Pheasant-tail nymphs, olive biot mayfly nymphs, or sparse hare's ear nymphs in size 16 to 20 are productive imitations. The RS-2 is my fly of choice for an emerger pattern. I use the same tactics and leader setup during fall that I use in spring.

After a lull during midday, dry fly Pseudo action returns in the evening. I have a passion for a size 22 gray quill CDC spinner in September. Trout rise to that fly late in the day better than any other pattern I have used.

As I conclude this information on the Platte, I feel compelled to pass along one more bit of information. The threat of losing the South Platte to Two Forks Dam can

Nate Ridlen on the South Platte near Deckers. (Photo by Gus Ridlen)

be written to the history books. However, the South Platte has a new nemesis to deal with, as do many river basins in the West: whirling disease. At this writing, estimates claim losses of four, possibly five, years of wild trout in the South Platte due to WD.

And that's unfortunate, especially for such a highly visible water that represents the cornerstone of effective wild trout management. In 1976, the waters of Cheesman Canyon were the first in Colorado to become catch and release. In 1979, they had the prestige of being designated Wild Trout Water.

Wild Trout Water is managed as a wild fishery without intervention of a stocking program. The river has sustained itself wonderfully, until now. At one time, 700 pounds of trout per surface acre of water was normal. The number is well below half that at this time. There is talk of a restoration program by the Division of Wildlife that would stock 35,000 rainbows into the canyon. These trout are a strain from the Colorado River, and they are 5 inches long, which gives them a better chance of fighting off the disease.

I have faith in the DOW's ability to manage our fisheries, but I hope they don't jump the gun and do something stupid.

The South Platte has endured as a top-notch fishery, in spite of overuse, greed for more control over it, and now disease. I'm sure the fishing gods will look upon us with favor one more time.

Waterton Canyon

Waterton Canyon, just west of Denver, holds a special memory in my flyfishing career, one of those moments we flyfishermen rarely forget. Jim Wilborn, a neighbor of mine at the time, was telling me how great this flyfishing thing was. After a little coaxing and gathering up some gear, he talked me into going fishing with him.

A neat part about this initial trip was having to ride our bikes up the canyon. We jumped on C-470 west to Wadsworth Boulevard one late July afternoon after work, turned left (south) onto Wadsworth, and drove to the parking lot at the bottom of the canyon. Once there, we stowed our gear, hopped on the bikes, and rode the six miles to Strontia Springs Dam.

Putting on waders, stringing up a pole, tying on a fly—what a mess. Wilborn's simple suggestion: "Look around to see what is flying around and use a fly that looks like it."

Simple, right? Wrong! There was a yellow thing flying around, and with a meager selection of flies to choose from, it was anything but simple. I had this extended-body thing that was yellow, so I tried that. After thrashing around a while, I finally got the fly on the water and could see it. Then, all of a sudden, there it was: my first trout on a fly, a 12-inch brown! This was one of those sacred events in one's life from which there is no turning back. That was 12 years ago.

Later, I learned that the yellow insect flying that day was an adult cranefly, around a size 16, and that the fly I was using was an extended body mayfly about an inch long. Not quite what I would select today, but it certainly did its work then.

This tailwater is open throughout the year, but the access road may be a tough go on a bike during the winter months. A walk of a couple miles will get you into a decent fishing stretch of the canyon. Midges, small pheasant tails, and San Juan worms are good choices.

By late March, baetis activity picks up, and the trout will start to look up. Dry flies in sizes 16 to 20 imitating blue-winged olives will do the trick. Early spring is also a good time to try the river below the canyon before it flows into Chatfield Reservoir. Rainbows from the lake, some in the 5-pound range, can be taken on woolly buggers, halfbacks, scuds, and worms.

The flows from Strontia Springs Reservoir fluctuate quite a bit starting June 1. High flows over 500 cfs normally blow things out. Check local shops for flow rates.

Summer is the best time for biking and hiking into Waterton Canyon. Caddis, craneflies, and small stoneflies hatch sporadically throughout the summer. A late afternoon ride after work seems to be the best time to focus your energy on these fish. Work the edges of riffles, the tail ends of the runs, and the pockets along the banks with elk hair caddis, little yellow stoneflies, royal Wulffs, and Adams, all in sizes 14 to 18.

The canyon turns every shade of yellow, orange, and red in the fall. There is a very good chance of seeing bighorn sheep along the canyon walls, a truly amazing sight, considering the canyon is just a few minutes out of Denver. And when you're done sightseeing, the river could still provide outstanding dry-fly fishing as mayflies

A nice rainbow from Boxwood Gulch.

return to the water. September mornings around 10 AM are the time to start looking for baetis activity.

The North Fork of the South Platte

Heading west on Highway 285 from Denver leads to yet another opportunity to fish part of the South Platte drainage. The first public access to the North Fork is at the town of Pine. Turn left (south) onto Pine Valley Road (Highway 126) at the town of Pine Junction. Pine is about 5 miles from Highway 285. There is a recreational facility along the river with access in both directions.

A forest fire in the summer of 1996 burned hundreds of acres of timber southeast of this area near Buffalo Creek. The status of the river here is still in question. Check locally for updated information.

Other accesses can be found west of Bailey. Pullouts along the highway are numerous. However, there is private property throughout the valley, so pay close attention to signs indicating these stretches of water.

The North Fork is a small- to medium-sized stream with pocket water and riffles. Trout average 8 to 12 inches and can be caught with a wide variety of caddis and stonefly nymphs. Fishing is best after runoff, which usually occurs in early July.

Boxwood Gulch Ranch on the North Fork

Boxwood Gulch Ranch is quickly becoming a favorite flyfishing destination in Colorado. Boxwood is located at Shawnee on Highway 285 about 5 miles west of Bailey.

This is a place to come and pamper yourself for a day or two. It may sound a little unusual, but there's even a clubhouse located right on the banks of the stream for your convenience; inside, you can rest your bones, enjoy a cup of hot java or a cold refreshment, and shower at the end of the day if need be. Lunch is catered, and Barry Conyers will make sure that you enjoy your visit. Barry is the riverkeeper of this fine stretch of water and a long-time friend. The on-ranch guide service is supplied by Barry and his staff of professional guides, including John "Too Tall" Hagen and me.

Did I mention the fish here?

At last count, there could be as many as nine species of trout lurking in this stream. Rainbows, browns, cutthroat and cuttbows, brookies, palomino trout, and various species of steelhead can be caught. The stream at Boxwood has pocket water, whitewater, flats, fast runs, slow runs, and a very challenging diverted oxbow—stalking and making the perfect cast here can reward a flyfisher with a trout up to 10 pounds. Two stillwater ponds with steelhead and other trout in various stages of growth are also available.

Unlike most Colorado waters, the trout here feed on big flies with imposing names: Turk's Tarantula, Olive Death, Gold Prince Nymph, and the Bite Me; and don't forget a mouse pattern for the late summer months! Attractor dry flies like Trudes, royal Wulffs, stimulators, and hoppers up to size 8 are superb surface patterns. These fish do like to rise for their meals, so be prepared.

"The winter months can be the best time for nymph fishing here, and the most pleasant. The mild conditions we fish in here is referred to as the "Bailey Banana Belt," according to Barry. He adds that, "Dark stonefly nymphs in #8 and #6, woolly buggers, sculpins, spruce streamers, and beadhead caddis nymphs can reward a proficient angler with over 20 fish in a day. Big fish!"

The insect population is nothing to brag about. The hatches that do happen are minor and do not usually excite these guys. The competition between 1000 trout for food in a stretch of less than a mile of river can mean very aggressive feeding. That's why big flies work so well here.

Considering the small stream conditions, a 4- or 5-weight rod with a medium-fast action is preferred. A good disc-drag reel will be very important for handling these hefty trout. Nine- to 12-foot leaders tapered to 4X or 5X will take care of the working end of the stick. Most of the stream can be waded in waist-high waders. Flows reach 900 cfs during the month of June, but most of the time you're looking at something between 50 and 200 cfs.

Overnight lodging is arranged through the Mooredale Guest Ranch or The Silvertip Lodge. They are within two miles of Boxwood and very nice. Cost ranges from $60 to $70. Call Dan Mauritz, owner of Boxwood Gulch Ranch, to schedule a day on the river at 303-838-8818. Make a visit and sign the guest book for a great day of fishing.

Boxwood Gulch offers some very large rainbow trout. Here, the author shows off a good one. (Photo by Jim Neiberger)

Other Angling Opportunities Along the South Platte

Clear Creek

When all the rivers and streams seem to be overloaded with anglers, Clear Creek always has an empty hole to fish. Clear Creek parallels I-70 from just east of Idaho Springs to Georgetown. Idaho Springs is 32 miles west of Denver. For access to the stream, take exit 240 at Idaho Springs. Turn left, then turn right on old Highway 6. The stream is open to fishing most of its length.

I don't think I have ever casted a dry fly on this water; perhaps I haven't fished it at the right time. However, there are caddis, a few mayflies, and stoneflies here. Drifting Prince nymphs, golden stone nymphs, and beadhead hare's ears in the pocket water and deeper runs always produces a trout or two. The rainbows, browns, and Snake River cutthroat average between 8 and 12 inches.

The water can be swift, so care should be taken while wading. A basic 4- or 5-weight outfit is fine, but bring plenty of split shot.

Chicago Lakes

Also from Exit 240 at Idaho Springs, you can head south on Highway 103, then right on Highway 5 to the top of Mt. Evans at 14,264 feet. What a sight! The road is only open seasonally, and you'll draw on all your driving skills to get there.

At the intersection of 103 and 5 is Echo Lake. A trailhead at the southwest end of the lake leads you to the Chicago Lakes. The trail is in good shape by mid-July through September. It's a 4-mile walk into the lakes, and the round trip can be done in a day fairly easily if your legs are in decent shape. However, camping is allowed, and an overnight trip is not out of the question.

The trip is well worth the hike. The lower lake is the biggest of the two and is the best for overall numbers of trout. Cutthroat to 14 inches can be caught on elk hair caddis off and on throughout the day. Travel light as far as fishing goes: one box of flies should suffice, and be sure to include Adams, royal Wulffs, elk hair caddis, a few hare's ears, pheasant tail nymphs, and olive scuds in sizes ranging from 12 to 18. A 4- or 5-weight rod with a 9- to 12-foot leader and a spool of 5X tippet should fit in a shirt pocket. Presentation is straightforward: cast your flies in front of cruising or rising fish and hang on. If a quiet presentation does not get their attention, give the fly a series of short twitches, no more than 4 inches at a time.

There is one alternate route to the lakes. Near the top on Highway 5, if you look down to the west, you can see the Chicago Lakes. When I say down, I mean down—the lakes sit at the bottom of a massive rockslide. It is negotiable, but it's a tough go.

North Catamount Reservoir

West of Colorado Springs on Highway 24 are a few lakes worth investigating within an hour's drive. The first is North Catamount Reservoir near the base of Pike's Peak. Two miles west of Woodland Park on Highway 24, look for Edlowe Road (CR 28); turn left (south) and travel about 3 miles to the lake.

The cutthroat and rainbows start to chow down just after ice-out, so don't consider fishing the reservoir until mid-May. Midges will be hatching, and a number of fish will be rising. However, small subsurface flies are the most productive. When I say small, I'm not talking microscopic; dark biot midges in a size 16, soft-hackle peacock in sizes 14 to 16, and soft-hackle hare's ears in size 16 fished in the top foot of water will do the trick. Moving the flies with short, slow strips is most effective.

Covering two stages of the hatch is also a good plan of attack. Attach a #18 dry fly, such as a parachute Adams or a Griffith's gnat, to the end of a 9-foot leader tapered to 5X. From the bend of the hook, add a piece of 6X tippet 18 inches long. Tie on a biot midge for the trailing fly.

I would hate to fish ice-out conditions on any mountain lake without tossing a woolly bugger. It's a big meal for hungry trout and irresistible to many!

By June, other insect activity, including callibaetis mayflies and damselflies, begin to interest trout. The egg-laying, or spinner, stage of the mayfly hatch can be the most productive. Midmorning to early afternoon is the best time to catch this hatch. A #14 rusty spinner sitting on the surface is very productive.

Damsel migrations can happen any time during the summer months. An olive or brown swimming damsel nymph stripped toward the shore is always the best technique for presenting this bug to these aggressive 10- to 14-inch cutthroat.

Float-tubing is the flyfisherman's choice. There are many bays to slip into along the northwest side of the lake. A foot trail takes you around to the dam or the other side of the lake. This trail will also take you to South Catamount Reservoir. Kicking across this narrow lake is not out of the question, but it could end up being a lot of work if the wind decides to blow the wrong direction. Expect much the same from South Catamount as you would from North Catamount. You may find less people on the south lake because of the extra walk involved.

Four- and 5-weight rods are plenty of stick unless a sinktip or fullsink line is needed; in those cases, moving up to a 6-weight is best.

Crystal Creek Reservoir

This reservoir is located east of South Catamount Reservoir along the scenic Pike's Peak Road, which can be accessed from the town of Cascade, 4 miles west of Manitou Springs on Highway 24. Pike's Peak Road is a toll road, so be prepared with your fee.

This is a beautifully located lake with a great view of Pike's Peak. The lake is usually open by mid-May and fishes until late fall.

Rampart Reservoir

Rampart is located southeast of Woodland Park on Rampart Range Road. From Woodland Park, go north out of town on FR 393. Follow the signs to FR 300, Rampart Range Road. Turn right and travel about 5 miles to FR 306 where you should turn left. Follow this road to the reservoir.

Primarily a put-and-take reservoir, it is heavily stocked with rainbow trout. Many do not get caught and reach a very respectable size, up to 16 inches. Lake trout also inhabit this body of water and can be found in shallower water in May. Sinking lines loaded with a #4 white woolly bugger dressed with red flash is a good Mackinaw fly. Bunny flies in white, black, and natural gray also catch their share. If your float tube or boat is equipped with a depth and fish finder, all the better. Expect to fish in the 15- to 20-foot range.

Stream Facts: South Platte River

Seasons
- Fishing is open all year

Special Regulations
- From Cheesman Dam downstream to the upper Wigwam property line: Artificial flies and lures only. All fish must be released immediately.
- From the lower property line of the Wigwam Club to Scraggy View picnic ground: Artificial flies and lures only. Bag and possession limit for trout is 2 fish, 16 inches or longer.
- From Scraggy View downstream to dam at Strontia Springs Reservoir: Bag and possession limit for trout is 2 fish.
- From Strontia Springs Dam downstream to 300 yards upstream of the Denver Water Board's diversion structure (Waterton Canyon): Artificial flies and lures only. Bag and possession limit for trout is 2 fish, 16 inches or longer.

Trout
- Rainbow trout are highly colorful fish in Cheesman Canyon, averaging 14 to 17 inches, and hate the sting of a hook.
- Brown trout are vigorous fighters and very healthy.

River Miles
- Cheesman Dam—0
- Gill Trail—3
- Deckers—5
- Trumbull—6
- Platte River Campground—10
- Scraggy View—14
- Willow Bend—17
- North Fork—24
- Waterton Canyon—37

River Characteristics
- Tailwater fisheries below Cheesman, Strontia Springs, and Chatfield. Pocket water and deep pools make spotting fish the sport in Cheesman Canyon. Deckers area is more of a meandering stream, less gradient.

River Flows
- Winter flows rarely exceed 200 cfs
- Spring flows average 100 to 300 cfs
- June is usually the month for high flows. In 1995, a very high-water year, flows were over 2,000 cfs. The average flows are 400 to 800 cfs. Still fishable, but care must be taken.
- Summer and fall flows can fluctuate often, but they average 300 to 500 cfs tapering to 100 to 200 cfs.

Maps
- *Colorado Atlas & Gazetteer,* page 50
- Pike National Forest

SOUTH PLATTE RIVER (BELOW CHEESMAN) MAJOR HATCHES

Insect	A	M	J	J	A	S	O	N	Time	Flies
Midge			▓	▓	▓	▓	▓		M/E	Olive Biot Midge #16–#24; Brown Biot Midge #16–#24; Candy Kane #16–#24; Black Beauty #18–#24; Brassie #16–#24; Blood Midge #16–#24; Miracle Nymph #16–#20; AK's Midge Larva #16–#22; Feather Duster Midge #18–#20; Disco Midge #18–#24; Black Beauty Pupa #18–#24; CDC Biot Suspender Midge #18–#24; Griffith's Gnat #16–#22; Palomino Midge #18–#22; Serendipity #16–#24
Baetis		▓				▓			M/A	Olive Biot Nymph #18–#22; RS-2 #16–#24; Pheasant Tail Nymph #16–#20; Beadhead Pheasant Tail Nymph #16–#22; Flashback Pheasant Tail Nymph #16–#20 ; Olive Quill Emerger #18–#24; AK's Olive Quill #16–#22; Parachute Adams #12–#22; Olive Comparadun #16–#20; Gray Spinner #18–#24; Slate Thorax Dun #16–#22
Pseudocloeons							▓		A/E	Olive Biot Nymph #20–#24; RS-2 #20–#24; Olive Quill Emerger #20–#24; AK's Olive Quill #22; Olive CDC Comparadun #20–#24; Gray Spinner #22–#24; Slate Thorax Dun #22–#24
Trico								▓	M	Parachute Adams #20–#24; Trico Spinner #18–#26; Double Trico Spinner #18; Thorax Dun #16–#22; Poor's Witch #18–#22

HATCH TIME CODE: M = morning; A = afternoon; E = evening; D = dark; SF = spinner fall; / = continuation through periods.

SOUTH PLATTE RIVER (BELOW CHEESMAN) MAJOR HATCHES (CONT.)

Insect	A	M	J	J	A	S	O	N	Time	Flies
Caddis									A/E	Olive Caddis Nymph #10–#20; Breadcrust #10–#18; Buckskin #16–#20; LaFontaine's Sparkle Caddis Pupa #10–#20; Elk Hair Caddis #10–#22; CDC Tan Caddis #14–#20; Macramé Caddis #12–#16; Balloon Caddis #12–#16
Scud									M	Olive Scud #12–#16; Orange Scud #10–#16; 19½ Scud #12–#18; Tan Scud #12–#16; Flashback Scud #12–#16
Golden Stone									A	Sandy's Gold #6–#10; Gold-winged Prince Nymph #8–#10; Stimulator #8–#12
Terrestrials									A/E	Royal Wulff #10–#16; Humpy #10–#16; Renegade #10–#16; Black Ant #14–#20; Henry's Fork Hopper #8–#12
Pale Morning Duns									M/A	Biot PMD Nymph #16; Pheasant Tail Nymph #16–#22; Sparkle Dun #14–#18; Parachute PMD #14–#18; Dark Hare's Ear #14–#18

HATCH TIME CODE: M = morning; A = afternoon; E = evening; D = dark; SF = spinner fall; / = continuation through periods.

CACHE LA POUDRE RIVER

The Cache la Poudre is one of Colorado's most beautiful rivers, but glancing at the water while you drive along its banks could cause a wayward skid down a steep canyon. Not good.

Granted, it is difficult not to sneak a peak around each bend; the river cuts between colorful canyon walls, there is lots of wildlife to look at, including deer and bighorn sheep, and its pocket water is very tempting. However, I try to resist that temptation, especially on weekends and holidays when traffic crawls. Really, paying attention to the highway is a small price to pay when you have an entire day of prime flyfishing ahead of you. And, on the Cache la Poudre, that day could be your best of the year. This gorgeous freestone river offers lots of rainbow and brown trout that average 9 to 12 inches, with a few going 14 inches or more. Like most freestone rivers, there are only a few monster trout to be had, and they are extremely difficult to catch.

In a way, that can be a bonus. While most people are crowded around each other on the big-name rivers hunting hogs, you can visit the Poudre, fish in relative solitude, and catch some nice trout.

Your first glimpse of the upper Cache la Poudre occurs about 1.5 miles west of US 287 on Colorado 14 as it parallels this narrow two-lane road into Poudre Canyon. To reach the river from I-25 take exit 269 (Colorado 14) west toward Ft. Collins. Veer right (north) about 3.5 miles and stay on Colorado 14. Turn right on North College Avenue (US 287). Follow US 287 approximately 8 miles, turn left (west) on 14. Cruising Colorado 14 west out of Ft. Collins is among the most scenic drives in Colorado.

Two sections of the Poudre are designated Wild Trout Water, and they provide prime flyfishing. Signs mark these sections, and they are very obvious.

The first section starts at Pingree Park Road Bridge and continues upstream almost to the town of Rustic. The second section starts at the Black Hollow Creek confluence and runs upstream to Big Bend Campground. The upper section has a state trout hatchery next to it, and the river below the hatchery provides the best chance for a fish over 16 inches. And, if you are looking for a section of river with solid trout that doesn't get crowded, the lower stretch is it.

Special regulations permit a flyfisher to keep 2 fish over 16 inches, but catch and release is the normal practice—whack a fish on the head here and you're likely to get the evil eye. Most anglers realize that a 16-inch Poudre trout is about five or six years old. Killing it would be a dishonor to a fish that has survived the rigors of life, and it would also be a disservice to the next angler in line. Those fish are treasures, and they should be caught and released more than once.

The Poudre runs west to east, so most of the canyon is not exposed to the low angle of the sun during winter. Due to its geography, ice shelves remain on the river much later than they do in most of Colorado. As the ice exits in March, flyfishing perks up.

Nymph fishing with small midge and mayfly patterns is about the only option early in the year. Brassies, biot midges, gray may nymphs and pheasant-tails, no

Cache la Poudre River

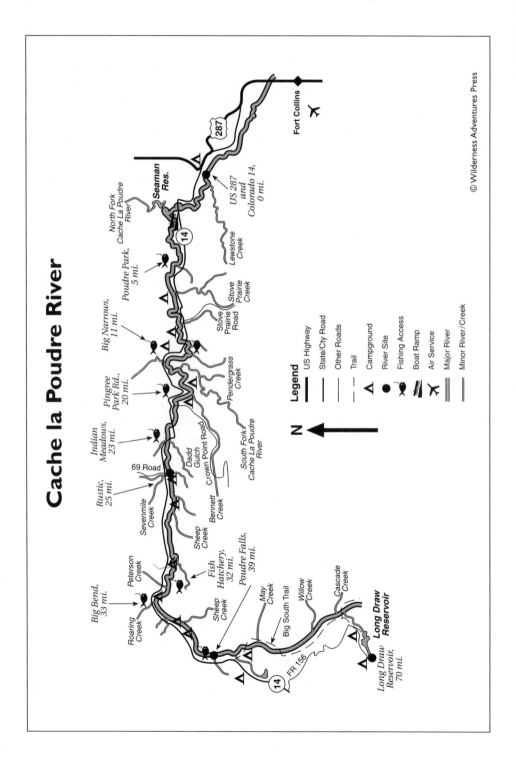

Legend

US Highway	
State/Cty Road	
Other Roads	
Trail	
Campground	
River Site	
Fishing Access	
Boat Ramp	
Air Service	
Major River	
Minor River/Creek	

N

Fort Collins

US 287 and Colorado 14, 0 mi.

287

Seaman Res.

North Fork Cache La Poudre River

14

Lewstone Creek

Poudre Park, 5 mi.

Stove Prairie Creek

Big Narrows, 11 mi.

Stove Prairie Road

Pingree Park Rd., 20 mi.

Pendergrass Creek

Indian Meadows, 23 mi.

Dadd Gulch

Crown Point Road

South Fork Cache La Poudre River

Rustic, 25 mi.

69 Road

Sevenmile Creek

Bennett Creek

Sheep Creek

Peterson Creek

Fish Hatchery, 32 mi.

Poudre Falls, 39 mi.

Big Bend, 33 mi.

Roaring Creek

Sheep Creek

May Creek

Big South Trail

Willow Creek

Cascade Creek

Long Draw Reservoir

FR 156

14

Long Draw Reservoir, 70 mi.

Shannon Skelton drifting to risers on the Cache la Poudre.

larger than a size 18, produce through March. Midges are seen sporadically, and the larvae or pupa patterns work best.

You will also want to carry a few buckskins. A size 16 or 18 buckskin is a favorite fly of mine from early spring through June 1. If I'm fishing two nymphs, a buckskin is sure to be one of them. A size 12 hare's ear or a Prince nymph do take trout on occasion and are good second flies.

By mid-April, Baetis mayflies hatch. And the Poudre's trout like to eat mayflies. Fishing emergers and floating nymphs along the banks, which hold trout early in the hatch, is your best tactic for moving fish to the surface. The shallow water and slow current along the banks give trout time to feed without fighting the heavy main current.

As the hatch progresses, more duns will be on the water, and you'll want to switch to an adult mayfly pattern. A well presented #18 parachute Adams, AK's olive quill, olive comparadun, or blue dun will draw strikes.

No matter which hatch is coming off or what time of the year you choose to fish the Poudre, you have to find good trout habitat to locate fish. The Poudre is a high gradient stream that begins in the mountains at 10,000 feet and drops to 5,000 feet within 50 miles. With that fast water, trout have to find specific habitats where they can feed, rest and, ultimately, survive. Trout do not like to recklessly expend energy, so they will take advantage of any obstruction to protect themselves from the current. On high-gradient streams like the Poudre, fish will hold in the pockets and eddies around large rocks and fallen timbers, inside corners near the bank, and in deep pools. Just remember this: if the water looks slow you'll probably find a fish living there. Basic riffles and runs, which are excellent trout habitat on tailwaters and low-gradient streams, do not hold many fish a large percentage of the time in the Poudre.

The Poudre and its faithful anglers are at the mercy of the runoff gods. The Poudre basin drains several small streams that race into the main river unrestricted. I've driven through the canyon in June, and I've been totally awestruck with the violence of the water. It amazes me that a stream that normally flows under 100 cfs could rise to 2,000 cfs. Kayakers and rafters take advantage of the rage, but fishermen say bye-bye until runoff recedes.

Fortunately, the water clears by mid-July when flows typically drop to 800 cfs. That flow is still quite heavy, but it's worth stringing up the rod. For the next month, hatches of all sorts keep the trout's attention. Most noted are the big green drakes and caddis.

The best area to fish those hatches, especially with a dry fly, is between Rustic and Big Bend, including the area below the fish hatchery. If you notice only a few *E. grandis* in the air or drifting on the water, tie on a size 12 Lawson parachute green drake, extended body. The action starts the instant the fly hits the water. They love those huge mayflies.

Caddis hatch throughout the river from July into September, and evenings are the best time to catch those bugs in action. A high riding size 14 or size 16 olive or gray elk hair caddis will take trout late in the day. However, if you experience caddis activity during the day, you must pay close attention to the way trout rise to them. If the trouts' noses are not visibly breaking the surface, figure they are taking emerging flies.

A favorite technique for caddis fishing is a two-fly setup. Tie an adult pattern to a 9- or 10-foot leader tapered to 4X. If flows are under 500 cfs, go with a 5X tippet. Add another piece of tippet, 12 to 18 inches long, to the bend of the hook. Tie a weighted soft hackle hare's ear to the end of that section. (A dirty yellow to light olive colored dubbing with a turn or two of partridge hackle on a 1X long, size 16 nymph hook works well as an emerging caddis.) The adult pattern, like an elk hair caddis or Goddard caddis, is used as a strike indicator, although it too will draw the occasional rise.

While flyfishers can usually fool trout with that setup, sometimes the fish become extremely selective. That happened to me one early August afternoon on the Poudre. In fact, trout were rising to everything but my fly! So, I dug flies out of an old box I didn't know I had. Fortunately, one scraggly looking fly came to the top, a zing-winged caddis. I'd never fished it before, but after a couple dozen casts I'd landed four brown trout, and I finally remembered where that fly originated.

The West Denver Trout Unlimited chapter has a fly tying clinic every February, which draws the best tiers in the Front Range. I was tying at the same table with Chuck Vestal. Vestal is a well-respected tier and always has something new up his sleeve. That year it was the zing-winged caddis.

"John Betts showed this to me and I've done real well with it," Vestal told me, just as he whipped one up. "The body is a tan synthetic dubbing chopped into small

Cache la Poudre River below the hatchery.

pieces. Wax your thread so it's real tacky, then touch dub the thread. John found the wing material—a thin, clear cellophane—in the trash and thought he could make something of it." Thanks for the fly, Chuck.

The pattern works well on the Poudre and other Colorado waters because it rides very low. It is difficult for the angler to see, but the trout can't refuse it, and I find that an acceptable tradeoff.

During summer months on the Poudre, you'll want to carry along some mayfly patterns to match a size 14 or 18 red quill and a size 14 or 16 blue-winged olive. And you definitely want a good terrestrial arsenal, too.

Flows generally taper to 400 cfs or lower by August 15 when terrestrial fishing peaks. A minuscule black ant produces fish when all other patterns go unnoticed. Fortunately, the type of water in which trout habitually seek shelter turns out to be the very same water ants end up getting knocked into. All the underbrush is at peak growth in August, and limbs overhang the banks. Ants, beetles, and stoneflies use that undergrowth for shelter and often fall into the water. Trout, which just love a crunchy terrestrial, lay in wait as chow from the heavens is delivered to them.

Dubbed ant patterns in black and cinnamon, deer-hair ants, and black flying ants are good choices when you see a fish rise under an overhanging limb, or if you're just blind-casting to likely spots. Sizes 16 through 22 should cover the gamut. A Peacock beetle, size 16, a black cricket, size 14, and a cream-colored size 10 Henry's Fork hopper should round out your terrestrial flies. Harbor a few of each in your box; you can lose them quickly in that brush.

Any river in Colorado that's worth its weight will have a fall hatch of Baetis, and the Poudre is no exception.

The late mayfly hatches on the Poudre occur in October, about the time brown trout start demonstrating their aggressive spawning behavior. Even the rainbows are aggressive during October as they attempt to put away as much food as possible before the long winter.

Although fishing can be fantastic during fall, there are some ethics to deal with. In my mind, trout that are actively feeding on Baetis are fair game. But, when you come across browns paired up on a spawning bed, please consider them off-limits. Colorado needs all the wild trout it can grow.

Whichever season you choose to fish the Poudre, enjoy your time on the river. This is truly one of the last wild Rocky Mountain freestone rivers not impeded by a dam. Left alone, it will stay a charming high country stream with many recreational opportunities for generations to come. Let's hope it stays that way.

Stream Facts: Cache la Poudre

Seasons
- Fishing is open all year.

Special Regulations
- Wild Trout Water: Artificial flies and lures. Possession limit, 2 trout, 16 inches or longer.
- From Rocky Mountain National Park downstream to Joe Wright Creek: Artificial flies and lures. Possession limit, 2 fish.
- Poudre River, North Fork, from Bull Creek upstream to Divide Creek: Artificial flies and lures. All trout must be returned to the water immediately.
- Poudre River, South Fork: Fishing prohibited from Rocky Mountain National Park downstream 1 mile.

Trout
- Rainbows
- Browns
- Cutthroat
- Brookies

River Miles
- US 287 and Colorado 14—0
- Poudre Park—5
- Big Narrows—11
- Pingree Park Road—20
- Indian Meadows—23
- Rustic—25
- Fish Hatchery—32
- Big Bend—33
- Poudre Falls—39
- Long Draw Reservoir—70

River Characteristics
- A freestone its entire length. Steep gradient in places, a few meadow sections. Lots of pocket water.

River Flows
- Late winter to early spring flows may reach 100 cfs, gradual increases until mid-May when flows reach 600–800 cfs. June is a blowout. It's worth a drive up the canyon just to see this monster water. July flows decline to 800 cfs and August drops the water to perfect conditions in the 300 cfs range. September and October fall below 200 cfs.

Maps
- *Colorado Atlas & Gazetteer*, pages 18, 19
- Roosevelt National Forest

CACHE LA POUDRE RIVER MAJOR HATCHES

Insect	A	M	J	J	A	S	O	N	Time	Flies
Midge		X	X	X	X	X	X		M/A	Olive Biot Midge #16–#24; Black Beauty #18–#24; Brassie #16–#24; AK's Midge Larva #16–#22; Feather Duster Midge #18–#20; Griffith's Gnat #16–#22; Palomino Midge #18–#22; Serendipity #16–#24
Baetis	X	X	X	X	X	X			M/A	Olive Biot Nymph #18–#22; RS–2 #16–#24; Pheasant Tail Nymph #16–#20; Beadhead Pheasant Tail Nymph #16–#22; Olive Quill Emerger #18–#24; AK's Olive Quill #16–#22; Parachute Adams #12–#22; Olive Comparadun #16–#20; Gray Spinner #18–#24
Green Drake			X	X	X				M/A	Green Drake Emerger #10–#12; Lawson's Parachute Green Drake #10–#12; Green Drake #10–#12; Adams #10–#12; Olive Hare's Ear #10–#12
Red Quill			X	X	X				M/A	AK's Red Quill #14–#18; Rusty Spinner #12–#20
Caddis	X	X	X	X	X	X			A/E	Olive Caddis Nymph #10–#20; Breadcrust #10–#18; Beadhead Breadcrust #10–#18; Buckskin #16–#20; LaFontaine's Sparkle Caddis Pupa #10–#20; Elk Hair Caddis #10–#22; CDC Caddis #14–#20; Z–Wing Caddis #14–#16; Macramé Caddis #12–#16

HATCH TIME CODE: M = morning; A = afternoon; E = evening; D = dark; SF = spinner fall; / = continuation through periods.

CACHE LA POUDRE RIVER MAJOR HATCHES (CONT.)

Insect	A	M	J	J	A	S	O	N	Time	Flies
Terrestrials			▓			▓			A/E	Rio Grande King Trude #8–#16; Royal Wulff #10–#16; Humpy #10–#16; Foam Madam X #8–#12; Renegade #10–#16; Black Ant #14–#20; Cinnamon Ant #14–#20; Gartside Hopper #8–#10; Henry's Fork Hopper #8–#12
Stoneflies			▓	▓	▓				M/A	Sandy's Gold #6–#10; Gold-winged Prince Nymph #8–#10; Kaufmann's Golden Stonefly #6–#12; Stimulator #8–#12; Foam Yellow Sally #12–#18; Half-back #4–#10; Prince Nymph #8–#16; Beadhead Prince Nymph #8–#16; Kaufmann's Brown Stonefly #4–#8; Sofa Pillow #6–#8; Stimulator #8–#12
Streamers	▓					▓		▓	M/E	Black Woolly Bugger #2–#10; Brown Woolly Bugger #4–#10; Platte River Special #4–#10; Spruce Fly #4–#10; Black-Nosed Dace #6–#8; Muddler Minnow #4–#10; Matuka Sculpin #4–#10

HATCH TIME CODE: M = morning; A = afternoon; E = evening; D = dark; SF = spinner fall; / = continuation through periods.

ARKANSAS RIVER

If you check out very much of the Arkansas River, you will soon realize it is the longest river in Colorado; you can follow it faithfully for hours.

Stretching 300 miles from its headwaters above Leadville to the Kansas state-line, the Arkansas parallels US 24 and gains momentum quickly as it flows south toward Salida. It turns east and follows US 50 to Pueblo.

It picks up speed from snowmelt off the Sawatch Mountains, which happen to be the highest range in Colorado. Looking west, those towering mountains grab your attention instantly. Mt. Elbert, the tallest peak in Colorado at 14,443 feet, is flanked to the north by Mt. Massive, which rates 14,421 feet. Thirteen more peaks over 14,000 feet and who knows how many in the 13,000-foot range add their snowpack to the brawling freestone drainage.

Some of that water is collected in Turquoise Lake, Twin Lakes Reservoir, and Clear Creek Reservoir. The outlets from those stillwaters provide a cool, clear, and con-trolled water supply for the Arkansas, and they provide excellent flyfishing options.

Bill Edrington, owner of Royal Gorge Anglers in Cañon City, has lived on the Arkansas River for years. He describes some changes made in the last couple of years to improve fishing conditions for the Mother's Day caddis hatch. "Flows are now being managed in order to allow more time for the caddis hatch to progress. Last year it lasted until May 18. Water storage is occurring in the winter so that releases can be held back well into May."

The Arkansas is maybe best known among flyfishers for its excellent Mother's Day caddis hatch, which many people rate "the best in the West." The most popular stretch of river runs from Buena Vista to Cañon City and the caddis progress upstream in April from Cañon City to Leadville at a rate of seven to 10 miles a day, depending on water temperature. The caddis species is *Brachycentrus,* and they hatch most actively when the water temperature reaches 50 to 55 degrees.

"When people come in wanting to know where the hatch is, we tell them to drive along the river until you can't see out of the windshield!" said Edrington.

The caddis hatch draws lots of anglers to the river, just hoping for a day of pure dry-fly fishing. Access sites along the river are well marked, and there are plenty of them. A word of caution: there are a few parking areas that require a permit. Make sure to put a couple bucks in the can if required. Rangers will ticket offenders.

Although having bugs on the water is a definite advantage during the caddis hatch, sometimes there can almost be too many. In fact, on the Arkansas your little size 16 elk hair caddis, floating among a carpet of grayish-tan wings, may seem insignificant. Spotting that elk hair in a maze of bugs is almost impossible. It doesn't help matters that you'll be peeling flies out from under your sunglasses, out of your ears and right out of your nose. If you're squeamish about bugs, don't bother visiting the Arkansas for this hatch.

Rod Patch at the Arkansas River Fly Shop in Salida told me, "This is definitely a breath through your teeth type of hatch."

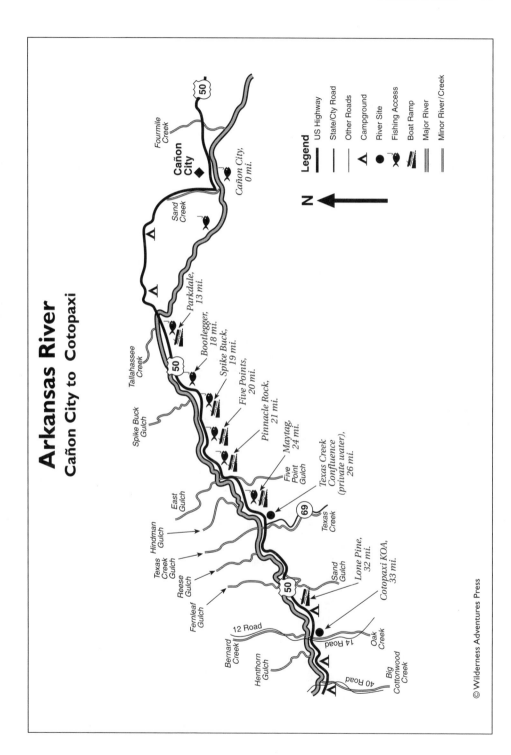

Arkansas River
Cañon City to Cotopaxi

Legend

| US Highway |
| State/Cty Road |
| Other Roads |
| Campground |
| River Site |
| Fishing Access |
| Boat Ramp |
| Major River |
| Minor River/Creek |

N

Fourmile Creek

Cañon City

Cañon City, 0 mi.

Sand Creek

Parkdale, 13 mi.

Bootlegger, 18 mi.

Spike Buck, 19 mi.

Five Points, 20 mi.

Pinnacle Rock, 21 mi.

Maytag, 24 mi.

Five Point Gulch

Texas Creek Confluence (private water), 26 mi.

Tallahassee Creek

Spike Buck Gulch

East Gulch

Hindman Gulch

Texas Creek Gulch

Reese Gulch

Fernleaf Gulch

Bernard Creek

12 Road

14 Road

40 Road

Henthorn Gulch

Big Cottonwood Creek

Oak Creek

Lone Pine, 32 mi.

Cotopaxi KOA, 33 mi.

Sand Gulch

Texas Creek

© Wilderness Adventures Press

Arkansas River
Cotopaxi to Salida

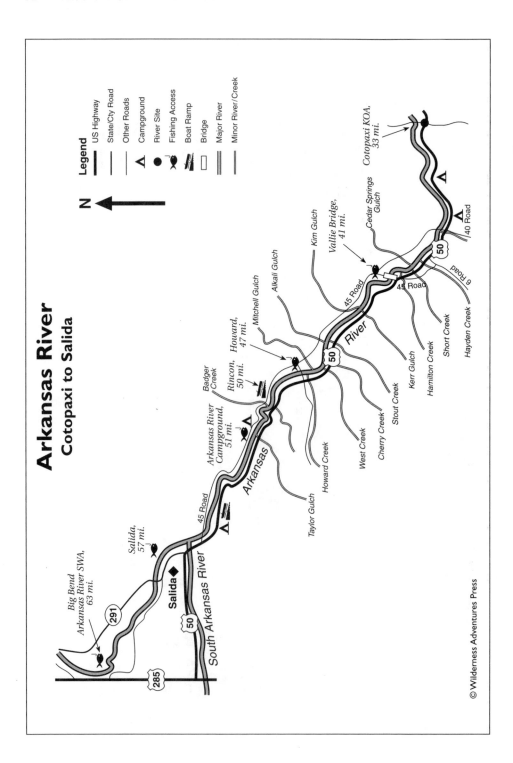

Legend

	US Highway
	State/Cty Road
	Other Roads
◣	Campground
●	River Site
🕮	Fishing Access
	Boat Ramp
▭	Bridge
	Major River
	Minor River/Creek

N

Cotopaxi KOA, 33 mi.

Cedar Springs Gulch

40 Road

Kim Gulch

Vallie Bridge, 41 mi.

45 Road

6 Road

45 Road

River

Short Creek

Hayden Creek

Hamilton Creek

Kerr Gulch

Stout Creek

Cherry Creek

West Creek

Mitchell Gulch

Alkali Gulch

Howard, 47 mi.

Rincon, 50 mi.

Badger Creek

Arkansas River Campground, 51 mi.

Howard Creek

Taylor Gulch

45 Road

Arkansas

Salida, 57 mi.

Big Bend Arkansas River SWA, 63 mi.

291

Salida ◆

50

South Arkansas River

285

© Wilderness Adventures Press

Arkansas River
Salida to Riverside

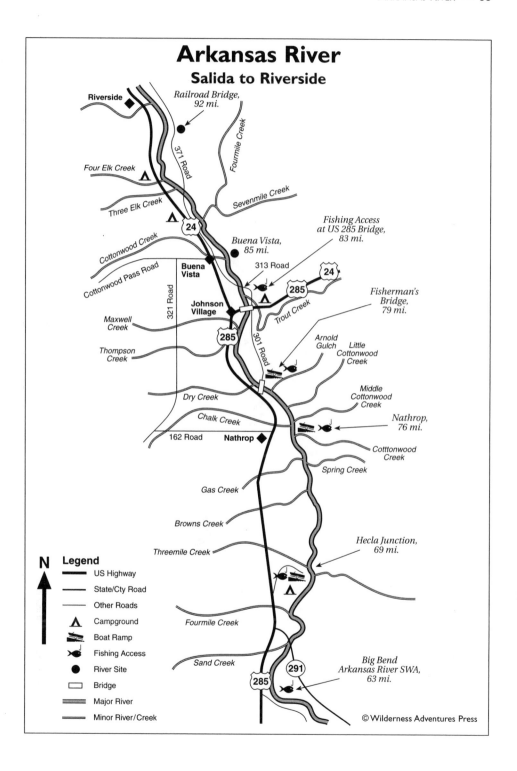

Riverside

Railroad Bridge,
92 mi.

Fourmile Creek

371 Road

Four Elk Creek

Three Elk Creek

Cottonwood Creek

Cottonwood Pass Road

24

Buena Vista,
85 mi.

Sevenmile Creek

Fishing Access
at US 285 Bridge,
83 mi.

313 Road

24

Buena
Vista

285

Johnson
Village

321 Road

285

Maxwell
Creek

Thompson
Creek

Trout Creek

Fisherman's
Bridge,
79 mi.

Arnold
Gulch   Little
Cottonwood
Creek

301 Road

Middle
Cottonwood
Creek

Dry Creek

Chalk Creek

162 Road   Nathrop

Nathrop,
76 mi.

Cotttonwood
Creek

Spring Creek

Gas Creek

Browns Creek

Threemile Creek

Hecla Junction,
69 mi.

N

Legend
— US Highway
— State/Cty Road
— Other Roads
Λ Campground
Boat Ramp
Fishing Access
● River Site
▭ Bridge
Major River
Minor River/Creek

Fourmile Creek

Sand Creek

285

291

Big Bend
Arkansas River SWA,
63 mi.

© Wilderness Adventures Press

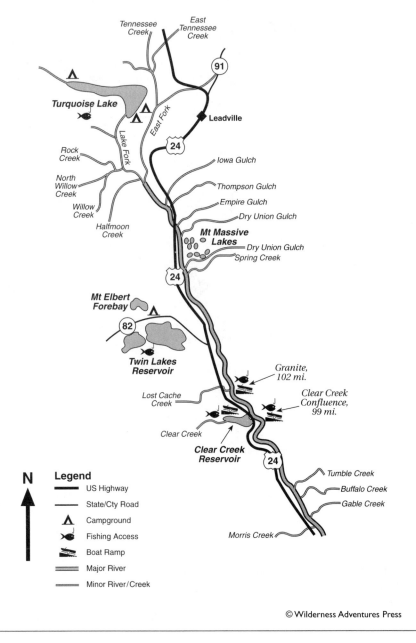

Arkansas River
Riverside to Leadville

Tennessee Creek

East Tennessee Creek

91

Turquoise Lake

East Fork

Leadville

24

Lake Fork

Rock Creek

North Willow Creek

Willow Creek

Halfmoon Creek

Iowa Gulch

Thompson Gulch

Empire Gulch

Dry Union Gulch

Mt Massive Lakes

Dry Union Gulch

Spring Creek

24

Mt Elbert Forebay

82

Twin Lakes Reservoir

Granite, 102 mi.

Lost Cache Creek

Clear Creek Confluence, 99 mi.

Clear Creek

Clear Creek Reservoir

24

Tumble Creek

Buffalo Creek

Gable Creek

Morris Creek

N

Legend
US Highway
State/Cty Road
Campground
Fishing Access
Boat Ramp
Major River
Minor River/Creek

© Wilderness Adventures Press

The Arkansas River at the mouth of Royal Gorge.

Recognizing a particular stage of the hatch is very important on the Arkansas. Nymph fishing with caddis patterns early in the morning is always a good bet if trout aren't rising already. A size 14 olive hare's ear, breadcrust, beadhead peacock, or LaFontaine deep pupa will hook up with browns averaging 10 to 14 inches. Browns definitely outnumber rainbows, but the 'bows are usually larger.

If fish are rising early, you'll see sipping rises, and that means it's a good bet they are feeding on dead or spent flies from the previous evening. Low-riding, no-hackle caddis patterns, like a size 16 partridge caddis, are the flies of choice. A size 16 rusty spinner is also a good pattern for early risers.

Just for fun, I have dredged a couple eager browns out of hiding with a size 6 black woolly bugger first thing in the morning. Hey, we didn't come down here to nymph or toss buggers all day, but sometimes you just got to do what you got to do.

If you want some serious dry fly action, wait until 11 AM—it's time! In fact, when the caddis hatch starts, it doesn't take long for an entire section of water to begin boiling with feeding trout; brown trout often end up completely out of the water chasing caddis pupa.

According to Patch, to be a successful dry-fly fisher during the caddis hatch, you must consider all of the elements, including basic setup.

"Tie a size 14 or 16 dry caddis—I prefer a black foam-bodied caddis tied by Don Puterbaugh—to the end of a 9-foot leader tapered to 4X or 5X," said Patch. "Then, from the bend of the hook add another 18- to 20-inch section of (5X) tippet material and tie a caddis pupa to that. The great thing about this setup is that you are covering two stages of the hatch at one time."

Once you're rigged, position yourself for a good presentation. That can be a difficult proposition when the Arkansas runs high and fast. Chest waders and good felt-soled boots are a must. And don't forget the wading belt—cinch it up unless you enjoy long skids along the bottom rocks.

Typically in flyfishing, a straight cast with an upstream mend is sufficient to take trout, but in tricky currents such as the ones you'll encounter on the Arkansas, a downstream presentation is best. A 9-foot, 5-weight rod is strong enough to make a long cast if necessary, and it will easily negotiate windy conditions, so it is a good choice during the caddis hatch. And that extra length makes mending easier.

When midday arrives, the caddis are so thick that fishing can become difficult. Most people say to hell with it and grab a beer and a sandwich—not a bad proposition all the way around. However, because I rarely eat lunch and am a glutton for punishment, I stay out there on the water and practice my casting.

During midday, I change tactics, although I continue to fish two flies. I use an elk hair caddis with a very light wing, mixed with CDC for visibility, and a big attractor pattern. A size 10 orange humpy setting on top of all those caddis has taken a number of trout for me. Royal Wulffs, Rio Grande trudes, and renegades are also in my bag of tricks.

The second most important time to be on the water is right after the sun goes over the last mountain peak; this magical time can provide incredible fishing. A word to the wise: know where your car is and how to get to it, because it will be dark before you quit for the day if you fish the hatch correctly. Carry a flashlight.

I must let you know that fishing the caddis hatch is not always difficult. There are days when the hatch is not heavy and a size 14 Troth elk hair caddis tied on 4X tippet will take 40 trout in a day. Dead-drifting, swinging, skating, dancing upside down, or just hanging at the end of a drift; it just doesn't matter, they take it.

If you're not into the caddis chaos, don't fret. There are other Arkansas River hatches that can provide excellent fishing.

"The blue-winged olives come off before the caddis in late March and early April, and that can provide some of the best fishing all year," said Edrington. "The weather can be cooler, which can be a plus for a Baetis hatch, and it does not draw the crowds the caddis hatch does."

Like the caddis hatch, a two-fly setup works well for Baetis, and Edrington's favorite flies are a size 18 parachute Adams with a pheasant tail nymph as a dropper.

"A slate thorax dun runs a close second in the dry fly category," he said. "I like a fly that rides low in the surface film in the cooler weather."

When fishing a spring Baetis hatch, timing can be everything. And during a season when winter and spring are locked in their annual tug of war, a window of prime Baetis opportunity may only last an hour or two.

To illustrate, a friend of mine took his father-in-law and another gentleman to the Arkansas the third week in April a few years back. He said he fished one of the best Baetis hatches ever. However, his fishing partners had gone back to the car for lunch around noon and missed the whole thing. Another reason to forgo lunch!

The Arkansas blows out of shape in late May, which kills all dry fly opportunities and makes it difficult to deal with an excellent golden stonefly hatch.

"It's too bad because the Arkansas is loaded with the big golden stones, *Acroneuria californica*," Edrington said. "Their migration is in late May, and by mid-June the river is flowing close to 4,000 cfs—just too difficult to manage."

However, when flows are high, you may be able to find trout close to the bank feeding on the stonefly nymphs. Occasionally, they may come up for the adults. Those big flies may get knocked out of the willows, or the wind might propel them across the surface. Stonefly nymphs like a Sandy's gold, Kaufmann's golden stone, and beadhead Prince in a size 6 are good. A size 8 yellow Kaufmann's stimulator is the only dry fly that you need to carry.

Late spring through summer is also "White Water" time, and 15-foot Avon no-hackles, as Edrington calls them, are found floating down the river in droves. In fact, until August 15, the minimum flow will be 750 cfs. Unless it rains. And rain storms can arrive quickly.

One time, the family and I were on Highway 50, headed west toward Cañon City in early August. We could see a storm brewing and quite a lightning show was going on.

We drove through a downpour just east of town, and when we arrived in Cañon City, we found the town literally under water. Ditches were full, streets were barely visible. Vehicles were stuck in the ditches. The Best Western Motel has a swimming pool converted to a trout pond—which overflowed. The fish, some to 25 inches, swam out of the pool and were finning along 19th street. The Arkansas remained a mess for a few days. Always be prepared for Colorado's wild weather. Weather in Colorado still amazes me, and I've lived here all my life.

Flows on the Arkansas remain in the 500 to 700 cfs category into September, so wading is a little tricky. But a skilled oarsman can float to areas of the river that are not fished most of the summer.

Mid-August through September is a great time to throw hoppers, crickets, beetles and ants. Dave's Hoppers, Wulffs, Shroeder's para-hopper, Letort crickets, beetles, and ants should all be fished along the banks. Float-fishing the river is a fast-paced affair when the water is up, so cast a fly downstream and let the boat catch up to it. That tactic allows for the longest drift. Pale morning duns and a variety of caddis may also be on the water in September. A high floating elk hair

High-stick nymphing methods produce nicely on the Arkansas.

caddis or a standard PMD pattern will do well. And access to the river is easy; boat ramps are located all along the river.

Excellent floats include Hecla Junction to Salida and Pinnacle Rock to Parkdale.

"Stonebride, just north of Salida to Howard, in my opinion, is the best section of the Arkansas," Patch said. "From the Stockyard Bridge to Badger Creek is the best 8 miles of the river. The brown trout thrive in that section, and they make up about 90 percent of the trout population."

Edrington, however, has another thought, "The water from Coaldale down to the Texas Creek area is now, perhaps, the best on the river in my opinion. I believe the quality water below Salida has taken a pounding over the past few years and is just not quite as productive as it once was. Fish have a habit of responding to pressure by relocating if they can. The Parkdale/Royal Gorge area is now better than ever. It's just harder to gain access.

Sounds to me like you can't go wrong wherever you decide to pull on the waders —I doubt you will be disappointed. If a wide-open, heavy-duty river with diverse water types and hatches appeals to you, the Arkansas is the place to be.

Other Places To Fish the Arkansas Above Buena Vista

The Arkansas River above Buena Vista is recovering nicely from years of abuse. Water quality has improved since the EPA installed a "Superfund" cleanup project at California Gulch near Leadville. In fact, the river is in the best shape it's been in for decades; insect populations and the size of fish are increasing each year.

Paul Seipel, a long-time friend and an Arkansas River angler since he was 17 (not to age you Paul, but people have to know you do have a few gray hairs for credibility), said, "Ten years ago, brown trout in the upper river averaged about 6 to 8 inches, and they may have only lived three to four years. Last year the average brown was in the 10- to 13-inch class."

Below Leadville, the fishing is good, too.

"All the caddis and mayflies that hatch on the lower river hatch here," Seipel said. "They are always later than the lower river and not as prolific, but the Baetis hatch from mid-April into May, and the caddis come off shortly after."

Below Pueblo Reservoir

If you would like to cure a case of cabin fever during winter, realize the Arkansas River below Pueblo Reservoir is one of the best kept secrets in the state! Hey, I got your attention, didn't I?

Xavier Duran, the owner of Xie's Fly Fishing Specialties in Pueblo, sure got my attention in a similar way when he shared his knowledge on this section of the Arkansas.

"November through March is the best time for a flyfisher," he said. "The water is low and clear, and the midge and Baetis hatches can be fantastic."

I was a little confused when Xie made a simple hatch chart for the river. I noticed the Baetis were listed as coming off from September through April. I questioned the mistake, and he insisted there was no mistake.

"It doesn't matter what winter month you visit," he said. "Given an overcast day, I would almost guarantee a blue-winged olive hatch. The first two miles of river below the dam are the best for rising browns and rainbows up to 16 inches. There are a few big browns in here, but they are more apt to take a streamer."

There are 8 to 9 miles of good fishing through Pueblo to the confluence with Fountain Creek. Access is about 95 percent public, so grabbing a spot to fish is easy. To reach the river below the dam from I-25, exit west on US 50 at the north end of Pueblo. Turn left (south) on Pueblo Boulevard to Nature Center Road. Turn right (west) to the parking areas.

The best leader setup for this stretch of river is no secret; a 10-footer tapered to 6X with a size 18 to 22 olive comparadun will do the trick for the olive hatch. For midge emergences, a Griffith's gnat is the fly of choice. When nymph fishing, a black

The Arkansas provides one of the West's best early-season caddis hatches.

midge or a chocolate hare's ear, size 18 to 24, is productive. A larger caddis nymph in light olive, tan, and green is a good choice, too.

"Flows of 100 to 300 cfs are best for producing hatches," Xie added. "Water level and clarity determine how well the fish will react to the ascending insects. However, flows do jump around a bit, and the water may be off-color for a day or two. The active feeding returns, just like nothing happened, when the water clears. That's why winter months are so good. By early April the water jumps to over a 1,000 cfs, and it can reach over 5,000 cfs."

There are a lot of popular Colorado tailwaters that are good winter fisheries, but this one is a real hoot: lots of open water, few anglers, easy access and a chance to dig out the dry fly box. What else could a feverish flyfisher ask for? In my mind, not much.

Other Angling Opportunities along the Arkansas

Grape Creek

From US 50 west of Cañon City, take CR 69 south to De Weese Reservoir. A dirt road leads you to Grape Creek below the dam. Fishing in the creek can be very good at times, depending on the water level. Some large browns to 20 inches are available to the angler who walks about two miles into the canyon. The average fish is a 12-inch brown. A few stocked rainbows and feisty brook trout can be caught. Typical Arkansas patterns like elk hair caddis, an Adams, slate BWOs, and hoppers work well here. A good hatch of golden stoneflies make June and July a great time to test this challenging little stream. De Weese Reservoir is pretty much filled with stocked trout.

Lake Fork

The Lake Fork of the Arkansas River flows out of Turquoise Lake and can provide opportunities to flyfish throughout the summer and fall. High water releases from Turquoise Lake in May and June find this stream unfishable.

Caddis, mayflies, and midges make up the main food sources for this stream. Expect to see trout rising to caddis in the afternoons and evenings. Standard elk hair caddis, CDC caddis, and emergent caddis in sizes 18 to 14 are good choices. A size 16 rusty spinner is also a great fly as daylight starts to dim.

Midges and mayflies may be on the water before noon. Parachute Adams, PMDs, and Lt. Cahills in sizes 18 to 14 are proven flies for this stream.

If the trout refuse to rise, nymphing is in order. Beadhead pheasant tails and hare's ears, biot midges, and the old reliable Prince nymph dead-drifted through the deeper runs will take fish. Don't forget the woolly bugger; it also works.

Camping is available at several locations around the lake.

Clear Creek

Above and below Clear Creek Reservoir, Clear Creek offers good fishing for browns and rainbows between 6 and 12 inches. Below the reservoir is always susceptible to water releases from the dam, while the stream above can be high with runoff in May and June. The stream directly above the reservoir is open to fishing, but upstream is riddled with private water, so please take heed to signs indicating private property.

All standard fly patterns, both nymphal and dry, produce on this stream. They are often stocked trout with an eye for anything that even remotely resembles food.

Stream Facts: Arkansas River

Seasons
- Fishing is open all year.

Special Regulations
- Artificial flies and lures only.
- Possession limit is 2 trout, 16 inches or longer.

Trout
- Browns are the predominant species. They average 10–14 inches. Rainbows and Snake River cutthroat are also present.

River Miles
The Arkansas River, starting just north of Leadville to Cañon City is approximately 120 miles long. The stretch from Buena Vista to Cañon City is most important to the flyfisher. Below Cañon City to Pueblo Reservoir is of least importance. Here are the distances between well-known landmarks:

- Cañon City—0
- Parkdale—13
- Five Points—20
- Pinnacle Rock—21
- Maytag—24
- Texas Creek—26
- Lone Pine—32
- Vallie Bridge—41
- Howard—47
- Arkansas River Campground—51
- Salida—57
- Arkansas River SWA—63
- Hecla Junction—69
- Nathrop—76
- Fisherman's Bridge—79
- Buena Vista—85
- Clear Creek—99

River Characteristics
- The Arkansas River is a true freestone until it runs into Pueblo Reservoir. Big pocket water, slick bottom in areas, so care should be taken. Heavy rafting during runoff and the summer months. It can be a little frustrating for the flyfisher.

River Flows
- Winter/Spring flows are always in the 300–500 cfs range.
- Runoff can begin around mid-May. There may be releases from Turquoise Lake, Twin Lakes and Clear Creek Reservoir for irrigation by May 1. The reason for these releases is due to the fact that this river carries nearly all of the ditch water allocated to Eastern Colorado and Kansas. Typical runoff flows peak by June 1. Flows up to 3,000 cfs are not uncommon. The river is left to the rafters at this time.
- By July 15 flows are down to below 1,000 cfs.
- Generally, flows reach 650 cfs by August 15.
- Fall flows are back in the 300–500 cfs range.

Boat Ramps

- Granite
- Railroad Bridge
- Buena Vista
- Fisherman's Bridge
- Ruby Mountain
- Hecla Junction
- Big Bend
- Salida
- Rincon
- Vallie Bridge
- Lone Pine
- Maytag
- Pinnacle Rock
- Spike Buck
- Bootlegger
- Parkdale
- Cañon City

Maps

- San Isabel National Forest
- *Colorado Atlas and Gazetteer*

ARKANSAS RIVER MAJOR HATCHES

Insect	A	M	J	J	A	S	O	N	Time	Flies
Caddis		▮	▮						M/A/E	Olive Caddis Nymph #10–#20; Breadcrust #10–#18; Beadhead Breadcrust #10–#18; Buckskin #16–#20; LaFontaine's Sparkle Caddis Pupa #10–#20; Elk Hair Caddis #10–#22; Don's Foam Caddis #12–#16; CDC Caddis #14–#20; Macramé Caddis #12–#16
Midge	▮	▮	▮	▮	▮			▮	M/A	Olive Biot Midge #16–#24; Brown Biot Midge #16–#24; Black Beauty #18–#24; Brassie #16–#24; AK's Midge Larva #16–#22; DC Biot Suspender Midge #18–#24; Griffith's Gnat #16–#22; Palomino Midge #18–#22
Baetis						▮	▮		M/A	Olive Biot Nymph #18–#22; RS-2 #16–#24; Pheasant Tail Nymph #16–#20; Beadhead Pheasant Tail Nymph #16–#22; AK's Olive Quill #16–#22; Parachute Adams #12–#22; Olive Comparadun #16–#20; Gray Spinner #18–#24; Slate Thorax Dun #16–#22
Pale Morning Duns				▮	▮				M/A	Biot PMD Nymph #16; Pheasant Tail Nymph #16–#22; Beadhead Pheasant Tail Nymph #14–#20; Sparkle Dun #14–#18; Parachute PMD #14–#18

HATCH TIME CODE: M = morning; A = afternoon; E = evening; D = dark; SF = spinner fall; / = continuation through periods.

ARKANSAS RIVER MAJOR HATCHES (CONT.)

Insect	A	M	J	J	A	S	O	N	Time	Flies
Golden Stone		▍	▍						M/A	Sandy's Gold #6–#10; Gold–winged Prince Nymph #8–#10; Kaufmann's Golden Stonefly #6–#12; Stimulator #8–#12; Halfback #4–#10; Prince Nymph #8–#16; Beadhead Prince Nymph #8–#16; Stimulator #8–#12; Bitch Creek Nymph #10
Terrestrials					▍	▍			A/E	Rio Grande King Trude #8–#16; Royal Wulff #10–#16; Humpy #10–#16; Foam Madam X #8–#12; Renegade #10–#16; Black Ant #14–#20; Henry's Fork Hopper #8–#12
Streamers		▍	▍			▍	▍	▍	M/E	Black Woolly Bugger #2–#10; Spruce Fly #4–#10; Black–Nosed Dace #6–#8; Muddler Minnow #4–#10; Matuka Sculpin #4–#10

HATCH TIME CODE: M = morning; A = afternoon; E = evening; D = dark; SF = spinner fall; / = continuation through periods.

St. Vrain Creek

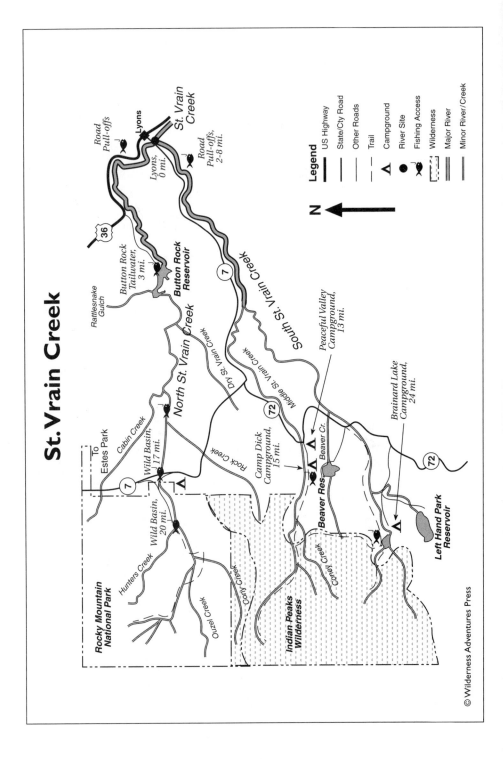

Legend

US Highway
State/Cty Road
Other Roads
Trail
Campground
River Site
Fishing Access
Wilderness
Major River
Minor River/Creek

N

St. Vrain Creek

Lyons

Road Pull-offs

Lyons, 0 mi.

Road Pull-offs, 2-8 mi.

36

Rattlesnake Gulch

Button Rock Tailwater, 3 mi.

Button Rock Reservoir

7

North St. Vrain Creek

Peaceful Valley Campground, 13 mi.

Dry St. Vrain Creek

Middle St. Vrain Creek

South St. Vrain Creek

72

Brainard Lake Campground, 24 mi.

To Estes Park

7

Cabin Creek

Wild Basin, 17 mi.

Rock Creek

Camp Dick Campground, 15 mi.

Beaver Cr.

Beaver Res

72

Left Hand Park Reservoir

Rocky Mountain National Park

Hunters Creek

Wild Basin, 20 mi.

Ouzel Creek

Cony Creek

Coney Creek

Indian Peaks Wilderness

© Wilderness Adventures Press

St. Vrain Creek

Some of you may recall St. Vrain Creek from John Gierach's books, such as *Trout Bum, Fly Fishing Small Streams* and *Even Brook Trout Get the Blues.*

John lives on the banks of St. Vrain Creek and has no intention of leaving anytime soon. For a flatlander who didn't have any idea what a Rocky Mountain trout stream looked like, he had a good eye for the picturesque; St. Vrain is a beautiful creek, everything a small stream in the Rockies should be.

The St. Vrain offers excellent flyfishing options on its main stem and forks, and a flyfisher can expect to catch several species of trout along the way.

Browns and rainbows dominate the lower reaches. As you ascend, cutthroat and brookies should tug at the end of your line.

Short, quick rods are ideal for small streams, including the St. Vrain. I prefer a rod that is 7 to 8 feet long, that casts a 3-, 4- or 5-weight line. For the creek, 7- to 9-foot leaders, tapered to 5X, are fine.

Flyfishing action begins in mid- to late April on the Vrain when sparse hatches of Baetis are present. A small brown stonefly also brings trout up at that time. To match the olives, I like to use a parachute Adams, or AK's olive quill. A size 18 dark elk hair caddis works for the small stoneflies. If you don't find rising fish, drift a size 18 pheasant-tail nymph, hare's ear, or a size 10 golden stone in the pockets behind the rocks or in the pools formed by fallen logs.

Fishing slows when runoff hits by June 1, leaving the St. Vrain unmanageable for the fly angler. When that happens, it's time to hit Lily Lake for greenback cutthroats or try one of the area's bass lakes.

Runoff, depending on the snowpack in any given year, lasts about a month. However, by July 1, expect the water to shape up, and get ready to enjoy some of the best fishing of the year.

For such a small stream, the St. Vrain's insect population is quite diverse.

Dale Darling, owner of St. Vrain Angler in Longmont, said that there may be more species of caddis in the Vrain than any other water he's fished. The best known caddis is a creamy yellow bug that hatches throughout the drainage.

"The best pattern for this hatch is the St. Vrain Caddis," Darling said. "It has a light yellow body, a wing of bleached elk or deer hair, and a ginger hackle. My favorite time to fish caddis is in the evenings when the sun is off the water. It's a nice relaxing time of the day, and the trout seem to rise freely. Pockets along the bank seem to be most productive."

Don't get the impression that these trout just jump into your net. Actually, fishing can be downright tough on the Vrain. Conditions are often tight due to thick vegetation growth, and precise drifts are a must. A delicate presentation can be difficult to achieve in those tight conditions; maddening, in fact. Perfecting a good dump cast is essential for success on the St. Vrain. To complicate matters, you may see multiple insect species hatching at the same time and will need to determine the insect and stage of hatch that is attracting the trout.

Typical pocket water found on the South Fork of the St. Vrain.

During early summer, the Western red quill, in sizes 14 and 16, is often seen on the Vrain, and the big golden stonefly, in sizes 6 to 10, is present, too.

Darling told me, "When I see a stonefly fluttering around, I immediately tie on a size 10 yellow stimulator. The trout grab it with no questions asked."

If you remain on the water late in the day, you will likely encounter a rusty colored mayfly spinner that comes back to the water in the evenings to lay eggs. The trout take notice. A delicately presented quill-bodied, spent-wing pattern, in sizes 14 through 18, is a good choice.

In August and September, a few green drakes will be present, but terrestrials become the most important food source. Size 12 Henry's Fork hoppers and size 14 flying black ants are productive.

Flows in late fall can become very low and when they are, the trout are very wary, extremely difficult to approach. Combine those conditions with tiny insects, like blue-winged olives and midges, and you need long leaders and fine tippets. Those who want to throw 7-foot, 3X leaders need not apply. A 10-foot, 5X or 6X leader is more like it. Small blue-winged olives, an Adams, and Griffith's gnats will match the Baetis and midge activity.

The three forks of the St. Vrain can be accessed from Colorado 7 between Lyons and Estes Park. Take US 36 north from Boulder to Lyons and turn left on Colorado 7. The South Fork of the St. Vrain parallels this well-maintained, two lane road for about 10 miles to its confluence with the Middle Fork of the St. Vrain. Fishing access along the highway is abundant.

The middle fork skirts the highway for four miles where you find Colorado 72. Turn left (south) toward Peaceful Valley. There is a trailhead for the middle fork at Peaceful Valley. This trail reaches the headwaters of the Middle Fork at St. Vrain glaciers, which rest at about 12,000 feet. The trail to the glaciers is over five miles long, but it should get you away from the crowds. Campgrounds at Peaceful Valley were refurbished in 1995 and provide good sites for overnighters.

A trailhead for the South Fork is located at County Road 96, another four miles south on Colorado 72. These trails are not for the timid or weak-legged; the St. Vrain drops about 6,000 feet in less than 30 miles. A day trip into these rugged streams takes some preparation. Food, water, and a first aid kit should be included in your gear. Another warning to those who visit the lower St. Vrain—RATTLESNAKES. They are seen in this area during summer and early fall, so use caution.

The North Fork of the St. Vrain is found north of Allenspark on Colorado 7. Turn left (west) at Wild Basin to find parking and access. A trail into Rocky Mountain National Park will lead you to the headwaters and many more opportunities to fish in a remote setting. Fishing downstream from Wild Basin is also possible. Slip on the hipwaders, grab a jug of water, and enjoy. Another access to the north fork is below Button Rock Reservoir. From Lyons, head north on US 36 toward Estes Park. Turn left (west) on CR 80 and follow to the base of the dam.

ST. VRAIN CREEK MAJOR HATCHES

Insect	A	M	J	J	A	S	O	N	Flies
Caddis		■	■	■	■	■			Olive Caddis Nymph #10–#20; Breadcrust #10–#18; Buckskin #16–#20; LaFontaine's Sparkle Caddis Pupa #10–#20; Elk Hair Caddis #10–#22; CDC Caddis #14–#20; St. Vrain Caddis #14–#16; Balloon Caddis #12–#16
Baetis		■					■		Olive Biot Nymph #18–#22; Pheasant Tail Nymph #16–#20; Beadhead Pheasant Tail Nymph #16–#22; Flashback Pheasant Tail Nymph #16–#20; Olive Quill Emerger #18–#24; AK's Olive Quill #16–#22; Parachute Adams #12–#22
Green Drake					■				Green Drake Emerger #10–#12; Lawson's Parachute Green Drake #10–#12; Green Drake #10–#12; Adams #10–#12; Olive Hare's Ear #10–#12
Red Quill				■					AK's Red Quill #14–#18; Rusty Spinner #12–#20
Golden Stone			■	■	■				Sandy's Gold #6–#10; Gold-winged Prince Nymph #8–#10; Beadhead Prince Nymph #8–#16; Sofa Pillow #6–#8; Stimulator #8–#12
Terrestrials				■	■	■			Rio Grande King Trude #8–#16; Royal Wulff #10–#16; Foam Madam X #8–#12; Renegade #10–#16; Black Ant #14–#20; Cinnamon Ant #14–#20; Gartside Hopper #8–#10; Henry's Fork Hopper #8–#12

THE BIG THOMPSON RIVER

Starting as a mere trickle on the east side of the Continental Divide, inside Rocky Mountain National Park, the Big Thompson flows from Forest Canyon Pass near the top of Trail Ridge Road through Forest Canyon. As small drainages offer additional snowmelt, the Big Thompson picks up volume, turning into one of Colorado's finest streams.

The Big Thompson becomes fishable at Moraine Park in Rocky Mountain National Park, about six miles downstream of its headwaters. It's there at Moraine Park, where the river splits into numerous braids and channels, that fishermen encounter the river's first public access. Trails leading up and down the river from that point will lead you to great flyfishing experiences.

To reach Moraine Park, head west out of Estes Park on US 34 and turn left (south) on US 36. Just over four miles later, find Bear Lake Road, and turn left again. Moraine Park is just down the road about a mile.

Moraine is a wide-open area, but the Big Thompson's banks are lined with willows. It's typical small stream conditions, and the river is filled with, you guessed it, brook, brown, and cutthroat trout in the 6- to 12-inch range. They'll readily take a variety of general attractor dry flies.

Although Rocky Mountain National Park gets pressured during summer, by lacing up the hiking boots or pulling on a pair of hip waders, you can get off the beaten path and into some solitude and fine fishing. A small box of dry flies, a short quick rod, a 7.5-foot leader, and a spool of 5X tippet should keep things interesting on the upper river.

Although it's a great trout fishery, the Big Thompson below Estes Lake is best known for enduring one of the worst floods in Colorado history.

After heavy rains in the high country in July 1976, a flash flood surprised the residents of the Big Thompson Canyon; in just hours, a 20-foot wall of water rushed down the canyon, destroying properties and taking over 100 lives. Again, in 1982, high water threatened the canyon's residents, but this time it took no lives, although it did heavily scar the river.

Today, the stream has improved, and trout habitat has been restored. Special regulations are in effect on the Big Thompson, and that helps preserve excellent opportunities for the flyfisher.

To reach the Big Thompson below Lake Estes, travel north from Denver on I-25 to the Loveland exit. Take US 34 west through Loveland. The Big Thompson parallels US 34 west to Estes Park.

There can be heavy pressure in that section during summer; however, most people head for Estes Park and Rocky Mountain National Park, so they don't spend adequate time working this stretch. Access to the river is good, and the fishing is favorable for trout in the 10- to 12-inch range.

From Waltonia upstream to Noel's Draw, fishing is restricted to flies and lures only, catch and release. Water types vary throughout the section's length, but riffles

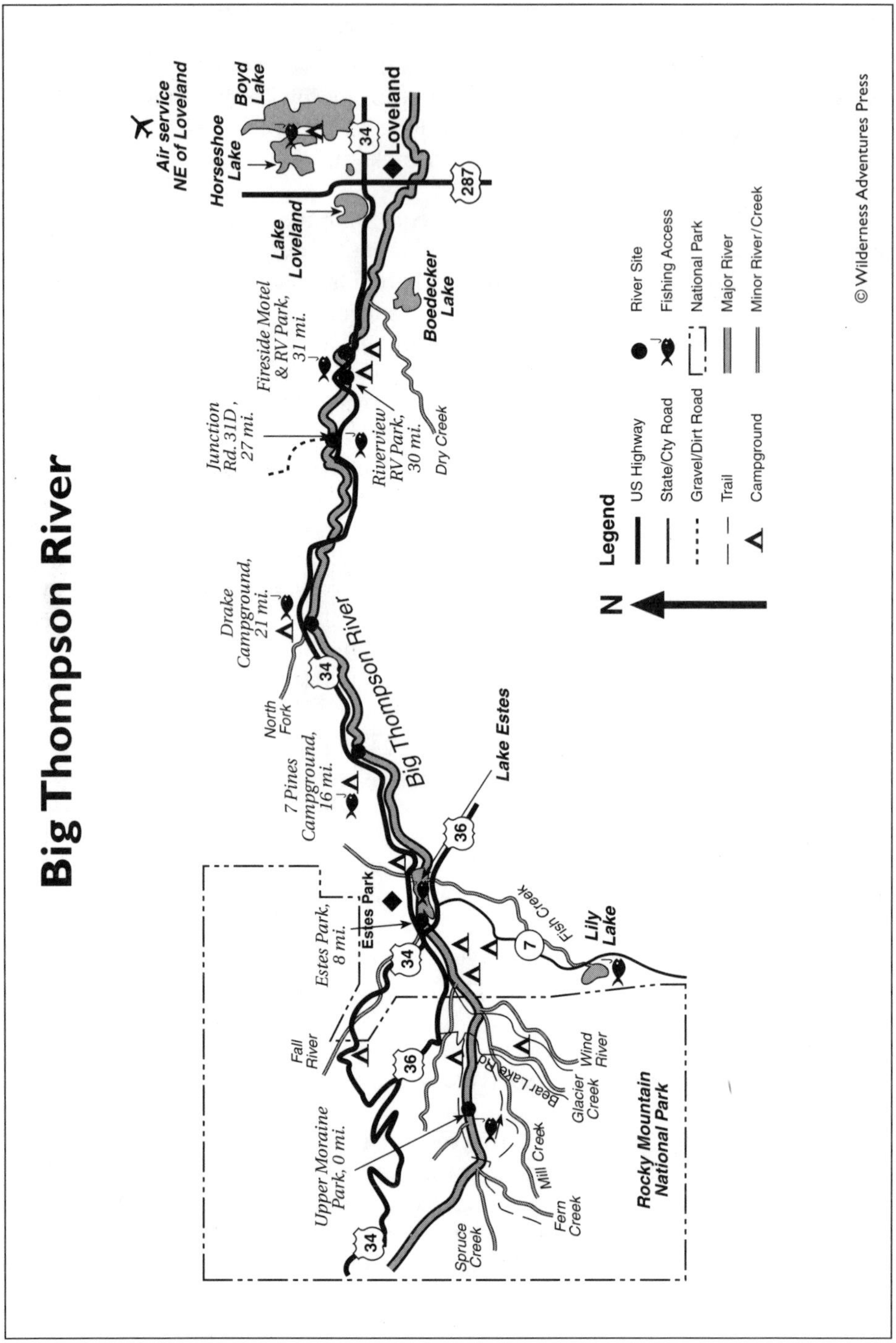

Big Thompson River

Horseshoe Lake

Boyd Lake

Air service NE of Loveland

Loveland

Lake Loveland

Boedecker Lake

Fireside Motel & RV Park, 31 mi.

Junction Rd. 31D, 27 mi.

Riverview RV Park, 30 mi.

Dry Creek

Drake Campground, 21 mi.

North Fork

Big Thompson River

7 Pines Campground, 16 mi.

Lake Estes

Estes Park

Estes Park, 8 mi.

Fish Creek

Lily Lake

Fall River

Upper Moraine Park, 0 mi.

Bear Lake Rd.

Glacier Creek

Wind River

Mill Creek

Fern Creek

Spruce Creek

Rocky Mountain National Park

Legend

N

—	US Highway	
—	State/Cty Road	
----	Gravel/Dirt Road	
--	Trail	
▲	Campground	

● River Site

🐟 Fishing Access

National Park

Major River

Minor River/Creek

© Wilderness Adventures Press

Releasing a rainbow on the Big Thompson.

and pocket water are the norm. Late summer, including July and August, is the best time to visit this stretch of the river. Flyfishers will find trout holding in the bankside pockets and behind midstream boulders, waiting for food to drift by. A size 12 humpy or royal Wulff, a size 16 little yellow stonefly, grasshoppers, Kaufmann's stimulators, and Rio Grande king trudes, up to size 10, will move those trout from their hiding places during the heat of the summer.

Midge and Baetis mayfly hatches gain the attention of feisty rainbow and brown trout as early as March and continue to do so until runoff pushes the river out of shape. Working the water with a small nymph tandem while waiting for surface action to begin is a flyfisher's best approach. Without getting fancy, brassies, pheasant tails, hare's ears, and biot midges from size 16 to 20 should imitate those Baetis and midges. Always drift those behind a beadhead Prince nymph. Dry flies, like a Griffith's gnat, size 16 to 22, a Parachute Adams and BWOs, size 16 to 20, work well when the hatch comes off.

Caddisflies and golden stoneflies are important insects after runoff. Working the pockets with stonefly nymphs is often effective, but why toss lead around when there are fish ready, willing, and able to get their food from the surface? Instead of those big, ugly nymphs, tie on a yellow stimulator and prepare to slay.

Caddis are equally important after runoff, and they can produce incredible surface action as they emerge. My experience shows that Big Thompson trout are not picky about fly patterns. Elk hair caddis, parachute caddis, and Goddard caddis, all in sizes 12 through 18, should draw strikes.

Sometimes the fish will rise to look at anything, but they often refuse to take. When that scenario happens, a smaller fly or a fly of a slightly different shape should consummate the stalk. For instance, if a fish refuses a size 16 elk hair caddis, switch to a size 18 parachute caddis, etc.

July and August offer the killer mayfly hatches, like green drakes, pale morning duns, and red quills, but their emergences can be sporadic. You may find them for a couple days here, a couple days there; consider yourself lucky to be at the right place at the right time if you encounter the hatches. Assuming your luck is good, go with a standard size 12 green drake when you encounter the big mayflies, try a size 16 PMD comparadun or a sparkle dun when you see the bread and butter mayflies, and try a size 14 or 16 AK's Western red quill or a rusty spinner in the same sizes when you encounter that tasty bug. Terrestrials are out in force during late summer, too, and hungry trout devour those offerings when they are presented.

When September and October arrive, you can tuck other patterns into your reserve fly box and whip out the blue-winged olives. On the cool, cloudy days, you have an excellent chance to take lots of fish on small flies. While the Big Thompson offers excellent opportunities on its public water, it would be a crime not to promote its potential on some of its private sections. Here goes:

Flyfishing Opportunities at Sylvan Dale Ranch

With all the comforts of home and true western hospitality, the Sylvan Dale Guest Ranch is a favorite destination for fly anglers and nonfishermen alike. With two chains of spring-fed trophy trout lakes and private access on the Big Thompson River, anglers can find solitude and an excellent chance to enter "The 24-Inch Club." All equipment, including float tubes, is available at the ranch.

Spring-Fed Lakes: The big attractions to Sylvan Dale are the lakes in the Big Valley. Ranch foreman Darlys Koschel told me, "The lakes are spring fed with water that runs 51 degrees Fahrenheit and (they) can be fished all year. Sylvan Dale has developed them into a unique experience, stocking different species in each lake."

Mother Lake offers rainbows and a few cutthroat to large proportions. Island Lake offers brown trout, and 20-inch fish are considered the children of the lot. Big Lake contains Donaldson trout, a fast-growing strain of rainbow.

All of the lakes in the Big Valley are managed as flyfishing only, catch and release with a maximum of four rods on them a day. Those regulations have paid off. Get this: each year approximately 50 trout over 24 inches are landed from the lakes.

Callibaetis hatch on the lakes starting in late May and the egg-laying stage offers possibly the best opportunity to catch one of those big trout feeding on the surface.

Start looking for Callibaetis on the water around noon. Rusty spinner patterns with natural hen tip wings and a reddish-brown quill body are good producers. However, if your eyesight is not what it used to be, or the wind has roughed up the surface, spentwings tied with Darlon or CDC will float better and will be easier to find on the surface.

Damselflies migrate to shore and hatch throughout summer, making them an available food source any day of the prime fishing season. Fortunately, the best time to catch damsels on the move is 10 AM to 2 PM—gentleman's hours. A size 12 swimming damsel nymph, twitched back to shore, is a great pattern when fish are feeding on damsels. However, you won't touch a fish unless you work that fly at the proper depth; vary the amount of weight or the amount of time you let the fly sink and make sure the nymph is not moving too fast. Three or 4-inch strips, with a second or two pause between, is perfect.

Casting adult damsel patterns from a float tube is also a blast. Locate the weed beds, drop a blue or olive Borger braided butt damsel over the edge of those beds and hang on. Avoid kicking directly over the beds, because it may spook trout out of the area.

Trico spinnerfalls in September and October round out the main fishing season on the lakes. And when the air fills with dancing Trico spinners, it's only a matter of time before the water boils with rising trout. A standard Trico spinner with a black body and white spent wings, size 20 to 24, is a great fly. Present those patterns off 6X or 7X tippet.

If dry-fly fishing is not your fancy, drag a woolly bugger around the lakes. Koschel, fishing a woolly bugger slowly along the bottom of Mother Lake, took a 29-inch rainbow in June 1994.

The Big Thompson River on Sylvan Dale Ranch: If you need a break from sitting in the float tube on those private lakes, two miles of private water on the Big Thompson might just take out a cramp or two.

Prime flyfishing on the river begins in April, as the weather warms. Midges and BWOs hatch sporadically through the month, with late April offering the best opportunities. AK's parachute olive quill and my olive biot emerger in sizes 16 to 20 will work for the mayfly hatch. While the river's trout average 12 to 14 inches, 16-inch fish are caught regularly.

Hatches of golden stones and caddis start when runoff subsides in July. Trout key on nymph patterns like a Kaufmann's golden stone, Sandy's gold, and gold-winged Prince nymphs, which imitate the stones. Stimulators and foam-bodied Madam-X's invite the trout to the surface when adults are fluttering around.

Caddisflies are also very important on this river during summer, and they are active every day. Forget the nymphs when caddis come off—this is dry fly fishing action only. Al Troth's elk hair caddis, LaFontaine's sparkle caddis emerger, greased up, and CDC caddis are proven patterns.

*Fishing the Big
Thompson's
pocket water.*

Pale evening duns are the prime midsummer mayfly. Fished in the evening with a size 14 rusty spinner, the river kicks out some nice trout.

In August, surface action peaks as hoppers, ants, and beetles frequent the water. Along with hatches of green drakes, PMDs, and red quills, flyfishing evenings on the river can be quite enjoyable.

The chilly mornings of September and October bring with them the best Baetis hatches of the year. Size 18 parachute blue-winged olives are the patterns of choice. Easy to see, yet offering a low-riding silhouette, that pattern best imitates the late-season mayflies.

Schools

If you're a novice who wants to learn more about flyfishing, regular schools are held at the ranch from April through October with excellent instructors like Mel Krieger, Barry Reynolds, and Chuck Prather. For fishing information and reservations call 970-667-3915.

Optional Angling Opportunities Near the Big Thompson River

Lake Estes

Located below Estes Park, Lake Estes gets its fair share of pressure due to easy access. However, it still provides good opportunities.

With 185 acres of surface area, the lake is best fished from a float tube in the evenings. After a long day tromping the streams, struggle into the tube and fins and cast dry flies to some agreeable, little, stocked trout. A parachute Adams, a renegade or palomino midge, all in sizes 14 to 18, will bring surface action.

Lily Lake

Located south of Estes Park, about six miles on Colorado 7, Lily Lake is visible on the west side of the road. With Longs Peak as a southwestern backdrop, Lily lake offers an excellent opportunity to hook up with greenback cutthroats in beautiful scenery. They average 10–14 inches, with cutts over 18 inches being caught once in a while.

The greenback is considered one of the most beautiful of all trout. Please let the fish spawn undisturbed. I know it's tempting to cast to fish you can see, but let's help maintain this great little lake for the future of the greenback.

Trolling damselfly nymphs behind a float tube is the norm during June and early July. Lily is shallow, so vegetation growth by late July can make fishing from a tube very difficult. However, casting a big foam-bodied hopper from the bank can be very productive.

A foot trail skirts the lake on both sides, making all areas accessible. Regulations require fishing with flies and lures only, catch and release.

Camping in the Big Thompson Drainage

Camping is available near Drake at Drake Campground. Sixty tent sites and 25 RV sites are offered.

About 2.5 miles upstream from Waltonia is 7 Pines Campground. They offer two tent sites and 22 RV sites.

Estes Park KOA Campground, located in Estes Park, has 26 tent sites and 70 RV sites.

Contact Arapahoe-Roosevelt National Forest at 970-498-2770 for more information on national forest campgrounds in the area. Several campgrounds exist in Rocky Mountain National Park. Call 970-586-2371 for availability.

Stream Facts: Big Thompson River

Seasons
• Fishing is open all year.

Special Regulations
• From bridge at Waltonia upstream 5.3 miles to bridge at Noel's Draw: Artificial flies and lures. All fish must be returned to the water immediately.

Trout
• Rainbows: stocked, average 10 to 13 inches.
• Browns: throughout the river, average 10 to 13 inches.
• Brook trout: above Lake Estes in the park.
• Cutthroat: above Lake Estes in the park.

River Miles
• Upper end of Moraine Park — 0
• Estes Park — 8
• 7 Pines Campground — 16
• Drake Campground — 21
• Intersection with Road 31D — 27

River Characteristics
• The part of the river most important to the flyfisherman is below Lake Estes. Although it would be considered a tailwater fishery, it fishes and looks like a freestone. Lots of nice pocket water with eager rainbows and browns to take dry flies.

River Flows
• Basically considered a small stream, flows can be well under 100 cfs during the winter and early spring. Runoff starts in late May with flows peaking in the 700 cfs range. Averaging 400 cfs to 500 cfs. Average summer flows are between 100 cfs and 200 cfs.

Side Roads
• Lily Lake south of Estes on Colorado 7. Flyfishing only, catch and release for greenback cutthroats.
• Devils Gulch Road parallels the North Fork Big Thompson. Turn north at the town of Drake.

Maps
• *Colorado Atlas & Gazetteer*, page 29
• Roosevelt National Forest

BIG THOMPSON RIVER MAJOR HATCHES

Insect	A	M	J	J	A	S	O	N	Flies
Midges		█						█	Olive Biot Midge #16–#24; Black Beauty #18–#24; Brassie #16–#24; AK's Midge Larva #16–#22; Feather Duster Midge #18–#20; CDC Biot Suspender Midge #18–#24; Griffith's Gnat #16–#22; Palomino Midge #18–#22
Baetis		█					█		Olive Biot Nymph #18–#22; RS-2 #16–#24; Pheasant Tail Nymph #16–#20; Beadhead Pheasant Tail Nymph #16–#22; Flashback Pheasant Tail Nymph #16–#20 ; Olive Quill Emerger #18–#24; AK's Olive Quill #16–#22; Parachute Adams #12–#22; Olive Comparadun #16–#20; Gray Spinner #18–#24; Slate Thorax Dun #16–#22
Green Drake			█	█					Green Drake Emerger #10–#12; Lawson's Parachute Green Drake #10–#12; Green Drake #10–#12; Adams #10–#12; Olive Hare's Ear #10–#12
Red Quill					█				AK's Red Quill #14–#18; Rusty Spinner #12–#20
Caddis			█		█	█			Olive Caddis Nymph #10–#20; Breadcrust #10–#18; Buckskin #16–#20; LaFontaine's Sparkle Caddis Pupa #10–#20; Elk Hair Caddis #10–#22; CDC Caddis #14–#20; St. Vrain Caddis #14–#16; Balloon Caddis #12–#16
Terrestrials				█	█				Rio Grande King Trude #8–#16; Royal Wulff #10–#16; Foam Madam X #8–#12; Renegade #10–#16; Black Ant #14–#20; Cinnamon Ant #14–#20; Gartside Hopper #8–#10; Henry's Fork Hopper #8–#12
Stoneflies			█		█				Sandy's Gold #6–#10; Gold-winged Prince Nymph #8–#10; Halfback #4–#10; Prince Nymph #8–#16; Beadhead Prince Nymph #8–#16; Kaufmann's Brown Stonefly #4–#8; Sofa Pillow #6–#8; Stimulator #8–#12; Bitch Creek Nymph #10
Streamers		█					█		Black Woolly Bugger #2–#10; Platte River Special #4–#10; Spruce Fly #4–#10; Muddler Minnow #4–#10; Matuka Sculpin #4–#10

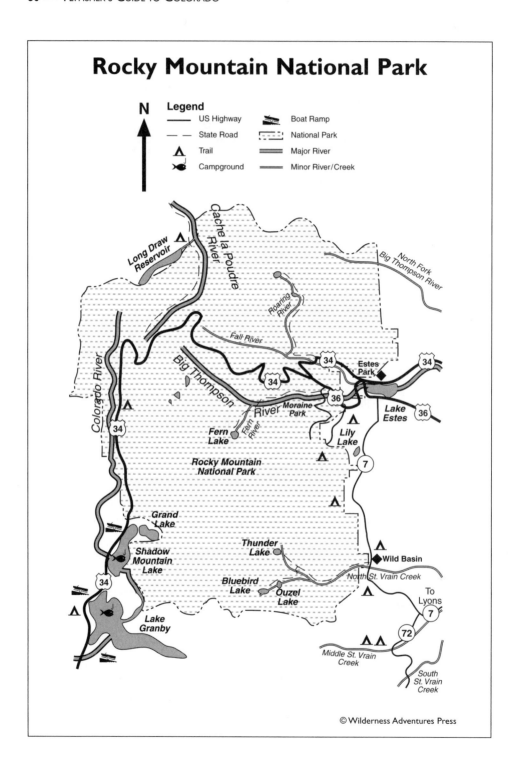

Rocky Mountain National Park

N

Legend

- —— US Highway
- – – – State Road
- ⛰ Trail
- 🐟 Campground
- 🛥 Boat Ramp
- National Park
- Major River
- Minor River/Creek

Long Draw Reservoir

Cache la Poudre River

North Fork Big Thompson River

Roaring River

Fall River

Colorado River

Big Thompson River

Moraine Park

Fern River

Fern Lake

Estes Park

Lake Estes

Lily Lake

Rocky Mountain National Park

Grand Lake

Shadow Mountain Lake

Thunder Lake

Wild Basin

North St. Vrain Creek

To Lyons

Bluebird Lake

Ouzel Lake

Lake Granby

Middle St. Vrain Creek

South St. Vrain Creek

© Wilderness Adventures Press

ROCKY MOUNTAIN NATIONAL PARK

Rocky Mountain National Park, a mountainous wonderland created in 1915, is located about 60 miles northwest of Denver. The park is a region of high peaks, deep canyons, waterfalls, lakes, glaciers, and forests. A preview can be seen from Trail Ridge Road, the highest continuous highway in the country. At 12,183 feet, the view at the top of Trail Ridge Road is spectacular. Today the park covers 265,727 acres and is an extraordinary place to explore. It is well known for its vast number of hiking trails. In fact, the park offers more than 355 miles of trails, which will keep even the most adamant hiker challenged.

Flyfishing in this magnificent park is also superb, yet often overlooked. There are four main species of fish to be found in the lakes and streams: rainbow, brown, cutthroat, and brook trout, with cutthroats providing the most interesting opportunities. You'll find the Colorado River cutthroat on the west side of the Continental Divide, while the east side is the stronghold of the native greenback cutthroat. Many of the streams and lakes are designated as greenback recovery areas.

The beautiful greenback thrives in the streams and lakes of the east side of the park, and it is great fun to catch. This fish, designated as the Colorado state fish, is managed under strict catch-and-release regulations. The greenback cutthroat should be returned to the water as quickly as possible and handled with great care.

Most of the streams in the park will be on the small side, with small fish living in them. However, that fact should not suggest that these fish are easy to catch. They can be as difficult to catch as the trout of Cheesman Canyon sipping midges, or the big rainbows on the Taylor River. On the flip side, these cutts can be very opportunistic feeders, and often they will eat a royal Wulff any chance they get.

Solitude is one of the park's flyfishing attributes. Unlike many of our more popular rivers and lakes, you can fish all day in the park without seeing or hearing another person. This is often true even for the streams along the roads, but even more so in the backcountry of the park.

The beauty of the park lies in its variety of water types; you can spend time on a meandering stream cutting its way through a meadow, dab a fly on a fast gradient stream filled with pocket water, or cast a line on an alpine lake in the high country. All in one day!

Trout live in places where an angler has a difficult time getting around. A good hike is usually required to reach the better streams and lakes and to find total solitude. To make things even more difficult, these spooky trout require a stealthy approach and usually a delicate cast is a must. Many of these tricky streams either feed a lake or are outlets. The lakes themselves provide excellent fishing and are easier to maneuver on than a brushy mountain stream.

When fishing these small streams and lakes take notice of the surroundings — they are magnificent.

I stopped by the St. Vrain Angler in Longmont, owned by Dale Darling, and chatted with him about Rocky Mountain National Park and the fishing opportunities there. As we were talking, a customer needed some help with her casting, so we walked across the street to a grassy area to proceed with the lesson. One of Dale's guides, Dave Mohr, walked over with us. Mohr said, "Rocky Mountain National Park is an area you can explore for a lifetime and find new opportunities every day."

My message to you is just that. Explore this wonderful corner of the world with a fly rod and a box of dry flies and find your own opportunities. Streams and lakes can be found along the main roads in the park, within an easy hour walk down a well-beaten path, or, for the serious backpacker, several miles back into the high country. Wherever you choose to travel, you will not be disappointed.

Portions of the St. Vrain Creeks and Big Thompson River in the park are covered in more detail in their respective sections. In this section you will find opportunities for other streams and lakes that provide good fishing. Remember, however, that there are many more that offer equal opportunity.

For more information on Rocky Mountain National Park contact the park at 303-586-1206.

Rocky Mountain National Park Rivers and Lakes

Colorado River

The Colorado River in Rocky Mountain National Park is much different than it is downstream (covered in the Central Colorado section).

The headwaters of the Colorado start here in the park, beginning the river's awesome journey across the western United States. Its characteristics are those of a small stream. Much of this stream runs through the Kawuneeche Valley with the Never Summer Mountain Range rising to the west. The upper river is impounded at Shadow Mountain Lake some 18 miles from its head.

The river is easily accessible off of US 34. From the west end of Granby, take US 34 northeast into Rocky Mountain National Park. You will drive around Lake Granby, skirt Shadow Mountain Lake, and head north another 4 miles before the river parallels the highway. US 34 is called Trail Ridge Road in the park and can provide a beautiful drive. This is an opportunity to experience beautiful high country without the usually difficult access.

The river can be accessed from many places off the highway or within a short walk. The Never Summer Ranch pulloff, about eight miles north of the park entrance, is a good stretch of water. Another mile north you will find Timber Creek Campground, another good access.

Near the campground, the stream meanders through the valley, forming classic shallow riffles and deep undercut banks. It is a great place to bring young anglers for their first experience with a fly rod. Expect to catch browns, rainbows and brook trout in the 8- to 12-inch range. A chance for a 16-inch brown is not out of the question.

Insect life is abundant in the valley, and any time after runoff is a good time to start fishing the river in the park. Mid-June is normally the time the river clears enough to fish.

Caddis and pale morning duns are present throughout summer. Elk hair caddis, a parachute Adams, and an AK's melon quill in sizes 12 to 18 should cover any surface action. A hare's ear, pheasant tail, beadhead or Prince nymph should draw strikes under the surface.

Eric Neufeld, a guide and employee at Front Range Anglers in Boulder, roams the park on a regular basis and finds this stretch of river quite enjoyable. "I like to walk the river here and fish any pocket water," he said. "I work into position for upstream casts, to obtain a drag-free drift. I fish behind any rocks and along any seam where slow water meets fast water. In the morning and evenings look for fish eating off the surface. Headhunting can be very exciting and productive. "For the most part, the stream is meandering, cutting its way through the valley. Fishing any undercut banks, letting a nymph swing underneath can produce aggressive takes."

There are several beaver ponds around the Never Summer Ranch worth fishing. It's common to see rising fish, and the stillwater presents some challenging opportunities.

Late August and September bring good blue-winged olive hatches. Standard patterns work well for most situations. Streamers and egg patterns are also good choices while the browns are spawning.

The Colorado River Trail follows the stream as it veers north from the main highway and leads you to the actual headwaters. This is a well defined foot trail for the angler who wants to see water that most people do not bother with—not for the lack of trout or quality of fishing, but because of the vigorous walk awaiting them.

About 3 miles up the trail you will find Lulu City, an old, abandoned mining site. The brook trout are aggressive here and willing to feed on flies such as elk hair caddis, stimulators, Rio Grande king trudes, and royal Wulffs.

As a reminder, the upper Colorado River is protected by park regulations. They should be checked before fishing.

Thunder Lake

Thunder Lake is one of many lakes accessible from the Wild Basin Area on the southeast end of the park. This is a good hike and will raise the heart rate of even the most fit outdoorsman due to an elevation gain of 2,074 feet in 6.8 miles. In fact, I usually give this trip 5 to 6 hours of hiking time with good weather conditions. Check the extended weather report with park authorities when making decisions on your length of stay.

There are four individual campsites and one group site available for overnight use. A backcountry permit is required for an overnight stay and can be acquired at the main Back Country office behind the visitors center or at the Wild Basin Ranger Station. The permit is $15. However, remember prices are always subject to change. Place the permit on the outside of your pack, visible to park rangers. Please observe the special regulations for the area, such as no fires, stoves only, and don't forget to bring a water filter, for there is no drinkable water at the campsites.

*Eric Neufeld shows
off a greenback cut
from Rocky
Mountain
National Park.*

This hike starts at the trailhead across from the Wild Basin Ranger Station and proceeds on the Thunder Lake Trail. This trail is maintained and marked extremely well with signs indicating mileage and direction. A trail map or topographical map of the area will help in answering any questions regarding direction. (I personally like the Trails Illustrated Map for Rocky Mountain National Park. It covers the entire park, shows mileage, camping, roads, elevation, and—most importantly for the flyfisherman—it's printed on plastic material that is water- and tear-proof.)

When approaching the lake, a wooden sign indicates your arrival. The individual sites are about 200 yards north of the sign. The trail to the individual sites follows a

It's tough to beat the scenery in Rocky Mountain National Park, but you have to put on the hiking boots and lose some sweat to reach its trout lakes.

small creek and is indicated by red arrowheads. Each site is marked with a silver arrowhead. The group site, which should be used particularly if you packed in on horse, is about 75 yards from the lake on the south side and is marked with a "G."

Down at the lake there is a Patrol Cabin which is not routinely staffed. It makes for a nice photo. Rising behind the lake is the Continental Divide.

For your first time fishing the lake I highly recommend taking a hike above it and looking down at its structure. If it can be done, this is good practice for fishing any new lake.

When fishing this lake, look for cruising fish foraging for food. Cast a good ways in front of them and watch for the take. This type of fishing can be done with a dry fly or with a nymph.

An Adams, elk hair caddis, Royal Wulff, rusty spinner, or a floating midge emerger in sizes 12 to 18 are good dry fly selections. I like to start with a size 14 Adams as a mayfly imitation. When I get refusals, it's time to go a couple sizes smaller or switch to an elk hair caddis. While these flies work well, don't forget one of Lee Wulff's creations, the Royal Wulff. The Royal Wulff is fun to fish and easy to see. Expect greenback cutthroats ranging from 10 to 14 inches to inspect your fly closely before accepting it as a meal.

Fishing streamers in the morning and evening can also be very productive. Find the ledges or submerged boulders and strip the streamers along the sides of them. This type of fishing can lead to above average fish and proves to be very exciting. Streamers such as woolly buggers, marabou muddler minnows, spruce flies, and leech patterns are good selections.

Nymphs in your fly box should include hare's ears, pheasant tails, olive scuds, and Carey specials. Sizes ranging from 10 to 18 should cover any situation.

The outlet of this lake forms North Saint Vrain Creek, a wonderful little stream. This is always a good place to look for fish. A nymph drifted drag-free will usually draw a strike. Nymphs such as zug bugs, Princes, hare's ear and poxyback scuds work well.

Ouzel Lake

Ouzel Lake is accessed from the same Wild Basin trailhead as Thunder Lake. While this hike is not quite as demanding as Thunder Lake, it will definitely raise the heart rate. The lake sits at about 10,000 feet, and the trail has an elevation gain of roughly 1,500 feet in 4.9 miles. Allow 3 or 4 hours of travel time to reach the lake.

Start your hike at the trailhead and hike for 1.8 miles to Calypso Cascades. Calypso Cascades is a scenic, tumbling waterfall that makes for some great photos. At Calypso Cascades, the trail forks; follow the west fork on the Bluebird Lake Trail. About a mile from Calypso Cascades is Ouzel Falls. Ouzel Falls is a beautiful waterfall that is at its peak in mid-June when snow is still melting. Ouzel Falls always makes for a pleasant water break or lunch stop. Keep an eye out for marmots running around.

Continue up the Bluebird Lake Trail for 2.2 miles to Ouzel Lake. On your way up to Ouzel Lake, take notice of the remains of the 1978 Ouzel Fire. The fire was started by lighting and burned more than 1,000 acres.

The lake has only one site, but it can accommodate up to seven people. There is another campsite just up the trail toward Bluebird Lake, called Upper Ouzel Creek. Both sites are marked with silver arrowheads. Please observe the special regulations that are printed on your Back Country Permit.

Ouzel Lake is full of native greenback cutthroat trout. This is catch-and-release only, so please be careful and return them to the water quickly and gently. Sight fishing to cruising fish is a great way to catch these incredible gems. As previously mentioned in the Thunder Lake description, cast well in front of the fish so you won't spook them.

Flies such as damsel nymphs, pheasant tails, and midge larva are good subsurface flies. Dry flies like a parachute Adams, no-hackle caddis, light Cahill, and the famous Royal Wulff work well.

Running out of Ouzel Lake toward Ouzel Falls is Ouzel Creek. This creek is a very nice meadow stream that offers some great fishing. Fishing this creek will take stealth and delicate presentations.

Fall River

Fall River is accessible from US 34, starting about a mile west of Estes Park as it parallels the highway. Once in the park you can fish Fall River from the Aspenglen Campground.

The river around Aspenglen Campground is fairly steep pocket water. Fish the seams and pools to the side of and behind the rocks with dry flies and nymphs, anticipating a quick strike. Use standard nymphs such as pheasant tails, hare's ears, Prince nymphs, and zug bugs, in sizes ranging from 12 to 18. Any of these in the beadhead versions are good choices. A 7- to 8-foot 4-weight is a favorite rod for these small stream conditions. A 7.5- to 9-foot leader with a strike indicator is an effective system.

Continuing west on US 34, traveling upstream, the river turns into a meadow stream as it meanders through Horseshoe Park. This stretch of water is absolutely gorgeous, with Ypsilon Mountain, Mount Chiquita, and Mount Chapin towering ahead. Herds of elk can be seen here just about any time of the year. And it's also a great place to do some fishing!

The fishing here is going to require the angler to be very quiet and patient. Typical cover that trout like, such as boulders and dead falls, are non-existent in this section. However, there are some very deep undercut banks holding trout. Fish these undercut banks with a quiet approach and a longer leader (approximately 10 to 13 feet). A well presented nymph or streamer drifting under these banks can produce solid hookups.

The streambed here is soft and silty. Look for any depression in the streambed for holding trout. Guaranteed, you will spook more than you spot, but I challenge you to drop a dry fly in front of one of these trout. This can be very difficult and often frustrating, but it is most rewarding.

Roaring River

Find the Lawn Lake Trailhead a couple miles west of the Fall River entrance on US 34, on the east side of the park. The trail is a mile-and-a-half to the best section of water and should be considered pretty difficult. You climb 800 feet in this short stint.

Roaring River is a typical high country small stream loaded with pocket water and a very good, self-sustaining population of greenback cutthroats. Forget the nymph box; carry some attractors, including Royal Wulffs, stimulators, humpies, and trudes, with a few caddis and parachute Adams in sizes 12 to 16.

This will be fast fishing. Cast your fly into all the pockets around the rocks and slow spots along the bank. Concentrate on one spot and cover it with as many casts as possible. Do not let the fly drift too far after it has passed through a spot. This practice only leads to problems with tangles and lost flies.

Fern Lake

From Moraine Park, take the Fern Lake Trail to find Fern Lake. The hike is 4 rugged miles, but well worth the trip. Considered one of the most successful greenback cutthroat recovery areas in the park, Fern Lake is a crystal clear body of water of about nine acres loaded with the Colorado state fish.

Consider using small flies ranging from sizes 16 to 20 that imitate midges and mayflies. Cast AK's olive quills, Griffith's gnats, palomino midges, rusty spinners, or parachute Adams to cruising trout near the shore. They are easy to spot as they make their way around the lake foraging for food. Just cast in front of them 10 to 20 feet and watch them rise to the fly as they pass under it.

Fern Creek, which flows into and out of the lake, can provide great dry fly fishing for the greenbacks as well. Tight surroundings make casting difficult, but these trout will take a dry fly as soon as it hits the water.

FRONT RANGE HUB CITIES
Denver
Elevation – 5,280 • Population – 467,610 • Area Code – 303

ACCOMMODATIONS
Listed here are a few of the many options in Denver:

Airport Budget Motel, I-70 and Chambers Road / 371-9102 / Near airport / $$

Holiday Inn, I-70 East / 15500 East 40th Avenue / 371-9494 / Near airport with 256 units / Dogs allowed / $$$

Best Western, 11595 West 6th Avenue, Lakewood / 238-7751 / West side of town with easy access to the mountains west of town / 200 units / Dogs allowed / $$$

La Quinta Inn, 3975 Peoria Street / 371-5640 / 112 units / Dogs allowed / $$$

BED AND BREAKFAST

Cliff House Country Inn, 121 Stone Street, Morrison / 697-9732 / Innkeeper: Peggy Hahn / Great place for couples, very nice accommodations / $$$$

RESTAURANTS (A FEW OF DENVER'S MANY OPTIONS)

Fresh Fish Company, 7800 East Hampden Avenue / 740-9556 / Open 5PM–11PM for dinner and cocktails / Great seafood / Reservations recommended / $$-$$$

The Chart House, 25908 Genesee Trail Road, Golden / 526-9813 / Open 5PM–10PM / Located in the foothills west of Denver / Great steaks / $$-$$$

Beau Jo's Pizza, Idaho Springs / 573-6924 / Home of the Colorado Mountain Pie / Awesome pizza / $$-$$$

Perkins Family Restaurant, 1495 Simms Street, Lakewood / 237-1339 / Open 24 hours / Good place to stop for breakfast before a day of fishing / $

Village Inn, 4775 Kipling Street, Wheatridge / 420-9792 / West side of town / Open 24 hours on Saturday and Sunday, 5AM–12AM weekdays / $

FLY SHOPS AND GUIDE SERVICES

All Pro Fish'n Sport, 6221 South Santa Fe Drive, Littleton 80120 / 795-3474 / Owner: Bob Hix / Full service, classes, guide service specializing in South Park

Alpine Angler, 2390 South Chambers Road, Aurora / 873-6997 / Owners: Bill and Billy Louthan / Full service fly shop, guide service, and classes

Anglers All, 5211 Santa Fe Drive, Littleton 80120 / 794-1104 / Owners: Bill Shappell, Terry Nicholson / Orvis, all tackle, full service, fly tying, casting lessons, rentals

Blue Quill Anglers, 1532 Highway 74, Evergreen 80439 / 674-4700 / Owner: Mark Harrington / Orvis schools, full service, guide service, rentals

Boxwood Gulch Ranch / 838-8818 / Owner: Dan Mauritz / Website: www.boxwood-gulch.com / Email: riverkeepr@aol.com / Private fishery on North Fork of South Platte; trophy trout / Call Barry Conyers at 816-0475 to book an approved guide

Colorado Angler Fly Shop, 1457 Nelson, Lakewood 80215 / 232-8298 / Owners: Ray and Ronda Sapp / Website: www.coloradoangler.com / Email: RioDS@aol.com / Full service, guide service, classes, rentals

The Complete Angler, 8547 East Arapahoe Road Unit D, Englewood / 694-2387 / Owner: Bill Grims

The Denver Angler, 5455 West 38th Avenue, Denver 80212 / 403-4512 / Owner: Rick Typher / Full service fly shop and guide service / Instructional classes in all phases of the sport

Diamond B Ranch / 569-2130 / Owner: Steve Barry / Private water on Clear Creek; trophy class rainbows, browns, and cutthroat; must use approved guide, call Steve Barry for information

Discount Fishing Tackle Inc., 2645 South Santa Fe Drive / Owner: Mike Gray / Free Saturday tying clinics, guide service, rentals

Discount Fishing Tackle Inc., 5550 Wadsworth Bypass, Arvada 80002; 4000 South Parker Road, Aurora 80015

The Flyfisher Ltd., 120 Madison Street, Denver 80206 / 322-5014 / Owner: Ren Cannon / Website: www.flyfisher.com / Orvis, full service, guide service, rentals

Flyfishing Services, Inc., 7925 West Layton #523, Littleton / 979-3077 / Owner : Chuck Prather / Guide service, private water; very reasonable, excellent guide

Flyfitters Inc., 8168 South Holly, Littleton 80122 / 850-7933 / Owner: John Baker / Full service

Master Angler, 8754 Cloverleaf Circle, Parker 80134 / 680-1004, 888-808-1004 / Owner: Pat Dorsey / Guide service for the South Platte, Williams Fork, Blue, and Colorado Rivers / Outstanding guide

Plum Creek Anglers, 981 North Park Street, Castle Rock 80104 / 814-0868 / Owner: Bill Scott / Full service

River and Stream Co., Southwest Plaza Mall / 979-7264 / Owner: Stan Pomeroy / Fly shop, clothing, and gifts

Rocky Mountain Angling Club, Creekside Suite 102, 6099 South Quebec, Englewood 80111 / 303-739-1993, 800-524-1814 / Private club with access to several stretches of water across the state; can recommend guides and particular types of water you wish to fish / Reasonable membership dues

Royal Stevens Ltd., 1610 East Girard Place Unit #1, Englewood 80110 / 788-0433 / Owner: Steve Johnson / Full service, private water, classes

St. Vrain Angler, 8951 Harlan Street, Westminster / 412-1111 / Manager: Mike Brisco / Website: www.peakpeak.com/~stvrain / Full service, guide service, classes, rentals

The Trout Fisher Inc., 2020 South Parker Road, Denver 80231 / 369-7970 / Owner: Dave Padilla / Website: www.thetroutfisher.com / Email: david@thetrout-fisher.com / Full service (3.8% tax), tying and flyfishing classes taught by Marty Bartholomew, largest tying material selection

Trout's Flyfishing, 1069 Old South Gaylord Street, Denver 80209 / 733-1434 / Manager: Greg Garcia / Full service, tying and flyfishing classes taught by Marty Bartholomew

The Gone Fishing Company, P.O. Box 440322 / 680-2430 or 800-352-4530 / Website: www.gone-fishing.com / Email: gnfishin@ix.netcom.com / Owner: Joe Butler / Guide service

Riverside Anglers, 499-9614 / Owner: Pete McNeil / Guide service for the Colorado River

The Hatch Fly Shop, 480 Sioux Trail Unit #50, Pine Junction 80470 / 816-0487 / Owner: Dan Hydinger

Uncle Milty's Tackle Box, 4811 South Broadway, Englewood / 789-3775 / Owner: Milt Poffel / All tackle store / In business 29 years

Beaverbuilt, 984 South Queen Way, Lakewood 80226 / 988-0200; Fax 988-0361 / Owner: Gary Barnhart / Custom rods, rod repairs, cane repairs, flies, and books

Angler Fine Arts & Gifts, Cherry Creek North, 201 Fillmore Street, Suite D, Denver 80206 / 333-6700 / Owner: Timothy Dinson / Website: www.anglerart.com

SPORTING GOODS

Alpenglow Mountain Sport Inc., 885 Lupine, Golden / 277-0133

Army and Navy Surplus Store, 3524 South Broadway, Englewood / 789-1827

Bait and Bullet Shop, 59 South 1 Avenue, Brighton / 659-3286

Colorado Sport and Tackle, 5385 Quebec, Commerce City / 287-2111

Jumbo Sports, 7848 County Line Road, Littleton / 792-3374 / Fly Fishing, backpacking, and departments

Gart Sports, 1000 Broadway / 861-1122

Grand West Outfitters, 801 Broadway / 825-0300

High Country Bass'n Shop, 1126 South Sheridan Boulevard / 934-4156

ICS Mountaineering, 278 Steele / 322-8646

REI, 4100 East Mexico Avenue / 756-3100

AIRPORTS

Denver International Airport, 342-2000, 342-0400 / United: 800-241-6522 / Delta: 800-221-1212 / American: 800-433-7300 / TWA: 800-221-2000

Arapahoe County Airport, 7800 South Peoria, Englewood / 790-0598 / Private planes

Front Range Airport, 5200 Front Range Parkway, Watkins / 261-9100 / Private planes

Jefferson County Airport, 466-2314 / Private planes

AUTO RENTAL

Avis Rent-A-Car, 342-5500, 800-831-2847

Enterprise Rent-A-Car, Denver International Airport / 342-7350, 800-325-8007

Thrifty Car Rental, Denver International Airport / 342-9400, 800-367-2277

FOR MORE INFORMATION

Aurora Chamber of Commerce
3131 South Vaughn Way
Aurora, CO 80014
755-5000

Denver Metro Chamber of Commerce
1445 Market Street
Denver, CO 80202
534-8500

Greater Englewood Chamber of Commerce
770 West Hampden Avenue
Englewood, CO 80110
789-4473

Wheatridge Chamber of Commerce
P.O. Box 280748
Wheatridge, CO 80228-0748
233-5555

Northwest Metro Chamber of Commerce
7305 Grandview Avenue
Arvada, CO 80002
424-0313

Colorado Springs
Elevation – 6,012 • Population – 281,140 • Area Code – 719

ACCOMMODATIONS

Antlers Hotel, 4 South Cascade Avenue / 473-5600, 800-222-8733 / 290 rooms / Dogs allowed / $$$

Broadmoor Hotel, 1 Lake Circle / 634-7711 / 700 rooms / World famous / $$$

Hampton Inn, 7245 Commerce Center Drive / 593-9700, 800-426-7866 / Dogs allowed / $$$

Town and Country Cottage, 123 Crystal Park Road, Manitou Springs 80829 / 685-5427 / Highly recommended / 10 rooms / $$$

Cascade Hills Motel, 7885 Highway 24, Cascade 80809 / 684-9977 / 14 rooms and 2 cabins / $$$

BED AND BREAKFAST

Black Bear Inn, 5250 Pikes Peak Highway / 684-0151 / Host: Christi Heidenrich / At the bottom of Pikes Peak Highway / Caters to float tubing and canoeing for the lakes on Pikes Peak / $$$

Gray's Avenue Hotel, 711 Manitou Avenue, Manitou Springs 80829 / 685-1277 / Inn Keepers: Tom and Lee Bray / $$$

CAMPING

Colorado Campground, 31013 Highway 67, Woodland Park / 687-0678

Lone Duck Campground, 8855 West Highway 24, Chipita Park / 684-9907

Travel Port Campground, 39284 Highway 24, Lake George / 748-8191 / 25 RV and 10 tent sites / Located near Elevenmile and Spinney Mountain Reservoirs

RESTAURANTS

Perkins, 5190 North Academy Boulevard / 528-5993 / Open 24 hours / $

The Briarhurst Manor, 404 Manitou Avenue, Manitou Springs 80829 / 685-1864 / Open 5:30PM–9PM for dinner and cocktails / $$-$$$

Grandmother's Kitchen, 212 Highway 24, Woodland Park / 687-3118 / Open 6:00AM for breakfast

Mountain Shadows Restaurant, 2223 Colorado Avenue / 633-2122

FLY SHOPS AND GUIDES

Peak Fly Shop, 5666 North Academy Boulevard, 80918 / 260-1415 / Owner: Brad Tomlinson / Full-service fly shop, guide services recommended, instruction in all aspects of fly fishing, free seminars / Up-to-date stream conditions

Anglers Covey, 917 West Colorado Avenue / 471-2984 / Owner: Kurt Brekke / Full-service fly shop and guide service / Flyfishing and tying classes / Experts on the South Platte

Broadmoor Sporting Classics, P.O. Box 1439, 80901 / 577-5832 / Lead Attendant: Kim Altum / Orvis endorsed fly shop / Guide service

Colorado Springs Angler, 3609-19B Austin Bluffs Pkwy / 531-5413 / Owner: Len Gay / Full-service flyfishing store, fly tying and fishing classes / Guide service

Pikes Peak Angler, 119 North Tejon / 636-3348 / Located in Blick's Sporting Goods, downtown / Manager: Ed Harris / Complete flyfishing store and guide service / Flyfishing, fly tying classes

Roth Angling, 144-4 Crystal Park Road, Manitou Springs 80829 / 685-0316 / Owner: Mark Roth / Custom fly shop, custom flies, rods, and art work / Call ahead of time

Colorado Fishing Adventures, 6421 Pulpit Rock Drive, 80918 / 598-5787 / Owner: Gary Willhart / Guide service for the South Platte and Southwest Colorado

Flies and Lies, 8570 South Highway 67, Deckers 80135 / 303-647-2237 / Owner: Dick Johnson / Right on the South Platte River at Deckers / Fly shop, equipment, up-to-date fishing information

General Fishing Tackle, 3201 North El Paso / 634-3348

SPORTING GOODS

Great Outdoors Sporting Goods, 520 West Midland Avenue, Woodland Park / 687-0401

Sports Hut, 719 Dale, Fountain / 382-7646

Tackle Shack, 430 West Fillmore / 635-1359

Tricos, 535 Lionstone Drive / 574-5480

All American Sports, 3690 North Academy Boulevard / 574-4400

Blick's Sporting Goods, 119 North Tejon / 636-3348

Gart's Sports, 106 North Tejon / 473-3143

Gart's Sports, 1409 North Academy Boulevard / 574-1400

Gart's Sports, 7730 North Academy Boulevard / 532-1020

Grand West Outfitters , 3250 North Academy Boulevard / 596-3031

Mountain Chalet, 226 North Tejon / 633-0732

HOSPITALS

Penrose Hospital, 2215 North Cascade Avenue / 776-5000

Memorial Hospital, 1400 East Boulder / 365-5000

AIRPORTS

Colorado Springs Airport, 7770 Drennan Road / 550-1900 / United: 800-241-6522 / American: 800-433-7300 / Delta: 800-221-1212 / Western Pacific: 800-722-5775

Ellicott Airport, 1757 Log Road, Ellicott / 683-2701 / Private planes

AUTO RENTAL

Advantage Rent-A-Car, 1645 North Newport Road / Colorado Springs Airport / 574-1144

Avis Rent-A-Car, 7770 Drennan Road / Colorado Springs Airport / 596-2751

Thrifty Car Rentals, 380-9800 / www.thrifty.com

AUTO SERVICE

AA Auto Repair, 602 West Colorado Avenue / 471-2067

Darrell's Automotive, 570 East Chester Avenue, Woodland Park / 687-3313

Mobile Car Repair, 338-1777

Locksmith
Action Locksmith Services, 339-8400, 1-888-235-4545
Colorado State Safe and Lock Co., 3013 North Hancock Avenue / 471-0096
Slim Jim's Auto Locksmiths, 598-5940

For More Information
Colorado Springs Chamber
  of Commerce
2 North Cascade
Colorado Springs,CO 80903
635-1551

Woodland Park Chamber
  of Commerce
210 East Midland Avenue
Woodland Park, CO 80863
687-9885

Manitou Springs Chamber of Commerce
354 Manitou Avenue
Manitou Springs, CO 80829
685-5089

Fort Collins
Elevation – 4,984 • Population – 87,758 • Area Code – 970

Accomodations
Comfort Inn, 1638 East Mulberry / 484-2444 / 25 rooms / $$$
Mulberry Inn, 4333 East Mulberry / 493-9000 / 121 rooms / Dogs allowed for a fee / $$$
Inn at Fort Collins, 2612 South College Avenue / 226-2600 / 60 rooms / Dogs allowed / $$
Holiday Inn, 425 West Prospect Road / 482-2626 / 253 rooms / Dogs allowed / $$$
Trout Lodge, 1078 Ramona Drive, Red Feather Lakes / 881-2964

Bed and Breakfast
Gypsy Terrace B and B, 4167 Poudre Canyon Highway, Bellvue / 224-9389 / Located in the beautiful Poudre Canyon / $$$
Scorched Tree B and B, 31601 Poudre Canyon Highway, Rustic / 881-2817 / Innkeeper: Brenda Way / Also in the Poudre Canyon / $$$

Camping
Beaver Meadows Resort Ranch, Red Feathers Lakes / 881-2450
Columbine Lodge, 9940 Poudre Canyon Highway, Bellvue / 484-3013

Restaurants
The Breakfast Club, 121 West Monroe Drive / 223-7193 / Open 6AM for breakfast / $
Charco Broiler, 1716 East Mulberry / 482-1472 / Opens Monday–Saturday 6AM, Sunday 11AM / Cocktails / $-$$
Silver Grill Cafe, 218 Walnut / 484-4656 / Open 6AM–2PM / $
Hickory House South, 6013 South College Avenue / 226-5070 / Open Monday–Saturday 6:30AM–10PM, Sunday 7:30AM / Cocktails / $-$$

Perkins Restaurant, 310 South College Avenue / 484-5981 / Open 24 hours

Canino's Italian Restaurant, 613 South College Avenue / 493-7205

FLY SHOPS AND GUIDES

Rocky Mountain Fly Shop, 124 East Monroe Drive / 223-7735 / Owner: Steve Solano / Full-service fly shop, guiding, equipment rentals, tying classes, flyfishing classes / North Park lakes, local information

St. Peters Fly Shop, 202 Remington Street / 498-8968 / Owner: Frank Praznik / Full-service fly shop, guiding, equipment rentals, tying seminars, flyfishing classes / Guided float trips on the North Platte and Yampa Rivers provided by Elkhorn Outfitters

Rocky Mountain Adventures, 1117 North Highway 287 / 493-4005 / Owner: Bill Peisner / Flyfishing guide service / Float trips on the Cache la Poudre and North Platte River in North Park / Two private ranches in North Park with trophy trout lakes and private sections of river to fish / Rentals available

Elkhorn Outfitters Fishing Adventures, 484-6272 / Owner: Brian Shipley

Rocky Ridge Sporting and Conservation Club, 633 Gait Circle / 221-4868 / Manager: Mike Moreng / Private sporting club offering lake fishing for trophy Kamloops rainbows and walleye / Call to book reservations and a guide

SPORTING GOODS

Alkire's Sporting Goods, 1211 9th Street, Greeley / 352-9501

Betty's Bait and Tackle, 429 West Wilcox Lane / 484-7459

Don's Pro Shop, 3121 Old Highway 287, LaPorte / 493-0534

Dusty Bait and Tackle, 2020 North College Avenue / 495-9880

First Stop Sporting Goods, 1006 North College Avenue / 493-3525

Fort Collins Outdoor World, 1611 South College Avenue / 221-5166

Gart Sports, 215 East Foothills Parkway / 226-4913

Gart Sport Superstore, 425 South College Avenue / 482-5307

Jax Surplus, 1200 North College Avenue / 221-0544

Outback Sports, 328 South Link Lane / 484-6582

Vern's Place, 4120 West CR 54G, LaPorte / 482-5511

HOSPITALS

Poudre Valley Hospital, 1024 Lemay Avenue / 495-7000

AIRPORTS

Denver International Airport, 342-2000, 342-0400 / United: 800-241-6522 / Delta: 800-221-1212 / American: 800-433-7300 / TWA: 800-221-2000

Ft. Collins/Loveland Airport, 4824 Earhart Road, Loveland / 667-2574 / United Express: 800-241-6522

Fort Collins Downtown Airport, 2200 Airway Avenue / 484-4186 / Private planes

AUTO RENTAL

Advantage Rent-A-Car, 2539 South College Avenue / 224-2211

Avis Rent-A-Car, 344 East Foothills Parkway / 229-9115, 800-831-2847

Dollar Rent-A-Car, 7704 South College Avenue / 226-6855

Enterprise Rent-A-Car, 2100 South College Avenue / 224-2592, 800-325-8007
Price King Rent-A-Car, 203 Mulberry / 490-2000

AUTO SERVICE
King's Auto Service, 203 West Mulberry / 490-2000
Poudre Valley Automotive, 3020 East Mulberry / 221-2054 / Towing, repairs
Import Car Service and Repair, 1943 East Lincoln Avenue / 221-4700

LOCKSMITH
Pop-A-Lock, 484-0025
Dave's Locksmithing, 208 South Mason / 221-5397, 482-6050

FOR MORE INFORMATION
Chamber of Commerce
225 South Meldrum
Fort Collins, CO 80522
482-3746

Cañon City
Elevation – 5,332 • Population – 12,687 • Area Code–719

ACCOMMODATIONS
Best Western Royal Gorge Motel, 1925 Fremont Drive / 275-3377 / 67 rooms /
  Dogs allowed / $$$
Cañon Inn, Highway 50 at Dozier / 275-8676 / 277 rooms / Dogs allowed / $$$
Day's Inn, 217 North Raynolds / 269-1100 / 36 rooms / $$$
Parkview Motel, 231 Royal Gorge Boulevard / 275-0624 / 33 rooms / Dogs allowed /
  $$$
Pioneer Motel, 201 Main Street / 269-1745 / Hosts: Neal and Barbara Hargrave /
  20 rooms / $$$
Super 8 Motel, 209 North 19th Street / 275-8687 / 50 rooms / $$$

BED AND BREAKFAST
Deweese Lodge / 1226 Elm Avenue / 269-1881

CAMPING
Arkansas River KOA, 21435 Highway 50 (Cotopaxi) / 275-9308 / 49 RV sites and 29
  tent sites

RESTAURANTS
Chile Wagon Restaurant, 0807 Cyanide Avenue / 275-4885 / Open 5PM–10PM for
  dinner and cocktails / $
Harvest Inn, 1925 Fremont Drive / 275-1299 / Open 5:30AM–10PM / Cocktails / $
K-Bob's Steak House, 3103 East Highway 50 / 275-0215
Ortega's Restaurant, 2301 East Main Street / 275-9437 / Open 11AM–9PM /
  Cocktails / $
Waffle Wagon, 315 Royal Gorge Boulevard / 269-3428 / Open 6AM for breakfast;
  good start for a long day on the Arkansas River / $

Fly Shops and Sporting Goods

Royal Gorge Anglers, 1210 Royal Gorge Boulevard / 269-3474 / Owner: Bill Edrington / Website: www.royalgorgeanglers/com / Email: rganglers@fly-shop.com / Specializing in guide trips to the Arkansas and South Platte drainages / Full service fly shop

Bubba's Sporting Goods, 723 Main Street / 275-4626

Capricorn Sports, 275-4351

Jimmy's Sport Shop, 311 Main Street / 275-3685

Hospitals

St. Thomas More Health Systems, 1338 Phay Avenue / 269-2000

Airports

Fremont County Airport, 60298 Highway 50, Florence / 784-3816 / Private planes

Colorado Springs Airport, 7770 Drennan Road / 550-1900 / United: 800-241-6522 / American: 800-433-7300 / Delta: 800-221-1212 / Western Pacific: 800-722-5775

Pueblo Municipal, 948-4423 / United Express: 800-241-6522

Auto Rental

Enterprise Rent-A-Car, 910 Main Street / 269-8000

Auto Service

Cañon City Tire and Service, 1504 Royal Gorge Boulevard / 275-1624

Jim's Tire and Alignment Service, 1005 South 9th Street / 275-1576

Ron's Pit Stop, 1328 Royal Gorge Boulevard / 269-1431

Zerby Automotive, 718 South 8th Street / 275-2523

Locksmith

Middick's Locksmith Shop, 1327 Royal Gorge Boulevard / 275-7787

Visitor Information

Greater Cañon City Chamber of Commerce
P.O. Bin 749
Cañon City, CO 81215-0749
1-800-876-7922

Salida

Elevation–7,036 • Population–4,737 • Area Code–719

Accommodations

Comfort Inn, 315 East Rainbow Boulevard / 539-5000 / 44 rooms / $$$

Holiday Inn Express, 7400 West US Highway 50 / 539-8500 / 66 rooms / $$$

Mountain Motel, 1425 East Rainbow Boulevard / 539-4420 / 8 rooms / $$

Redwood Lodge, 7310 US Highway 50 / 539-2528 / 25 rooms / $$$

Bed and Breakfast

Tudor Rose, 6720 Paradise Road / 1-800-379-0889 / $$$

River Run Inn, 8495 Cr. 160 / 719-539-3818, 1-800-385-6925 / Innkeeper: Virginia Nemmers / ¼ mile off Arkansas River, land butts up to BLM land / $$$

CAMPING
Cutty's Camping Resort, 3428 CR 6 (Coaldale) / 942-4222
Heart of the Rockies Campground, 16105 West Highway 50 / 539-4051 / 45 RV sites and 22 tent sites
Pleasant Valley Campground of Howard, 0018 CR. 47 / 942-3484 / 57 RV and 10 tent sites
Sugar Bush General Store and Campground, 9229 Highway 50 / 942-3363 / 13 RV sites and 18 tent sites

RESTAURANTS
Country Bounty, 413 West US Highway 50 / 719-539-3546 / Open 6:30AM-9PM / $
Il Vicino Pizzeria and Brewpub, 136 East 2nd Street / 539-5219 / Open 11:30AM– 11PM / Good pizza and local brew / $
Patio Pancake Palace, 640 East Rainbow Boulevard / 539-9905 / Open 6AM for breakfast / $
Windmill Restaurant, 720 East US Highway 50 / 719-539-3594 / Open 11AM–10PM / Cocktails / $

FLY SHOPS AND SPORTING GOODS
Arkansas River Fly Shop, 7500 US Highway 50 / 539-3474 / Owners Rod and Connie Patch are very helpful with flyfishing information for the Arkansas River / All the goodies and guided trips also available
Browner's Guide Service, 228 North F Street / 539-4506, 1-800-288-0675 / Chris and Matt Brown offer a full-service fly shop and guide service for the Arkansas River and the surrounding high country
Triple J Trout Ranch / 539-3094
Homestead Sports Center, 11238 West Highway 50, Poncha Springs / 539-7507
Salida Sporting Goods, 511 East Highway 50 / 539-6221
American Outdoor Sports, 645 East Rainbow Boulevard / 530-0725
G and G Sporting Goods, East Highway 50 / 539-4303
Good Brothers Inc., 116 South F Street / 539-7777
Headwaters Outdoor Equipment, 228 North F Street / 539-4506

HOSPITALS
Regional Medical Center, 448 East 1st Street / 539-6661 / 24-hour emergency room

AIRPORTS
Salida / Harriet Alexander Field, 9255 County Road 140 / 539-3720 / Private planes
Colorado Springs Airport, 7770 Drennan Road / 550-1900 / United: 800-241-6522 / American: 800-433-7300 / Delta: 800-221-1212 / Western Pacific: 800-722-5775
Pueblo Municipal, 948-4423 / United Express: 800-241-6522
Salida Travel Inc., 203 G Street / 539-2567

AUTO RENTAL
Salida Motors, 943 East Highway 50 / 539-6633

Auto Service
A-1 Auto Service, 445 West Rainbow Boulevard / 539-7251
Brad's Automotive Repair, 249 F Street / 539-3419
Monarch Road Service, 22455 West Highway 50 / 539-4065

Locksmith
Gunnison Security Inc., 1-800-641-6118
Walt's Lock and Key, 1220 I Street / 539-6432

For More Information
Chamber of Commerce
406 West Rainbow Boulevard
Salida, CO 81201
539-2068

Buena Vista
Elevation: 7,954 Population: 1,752 • Area Code: 719

Accommodations
Cottonwood Chalets, 15981 County Road 306 / 395-8036
Piñon Court Motel, 227 US Highway 24 North / 395-2433 / 11 rooms / Dogs
allowed / $$
Topaz Lodge, Main and Highway 24 / 395-2427 / 18 rooms / Dogs allowed for a
fee / $$$

Bed and Breakfast
Vista Inn, 733 US Highway 24 North / 395-8009 / 41 rooms / Dogs allowed / $$$

Camping
Brown's Campground, 11430 County Road 197 / 395-8301 / 44 RV sites and 16
tent sites
Buena Vista KOA, 27700 County Road 303 / 395-8318 / 66 RV sites and 32 tent sites
Crazy Horse Camping Resort, 33975 Highway 24 / 395-2323 / 89 RV sites and 50
tent sites
Mt. Princeton RV Park, 30380 County Road 383 / 395-6206

Restaurants
Buffalo Bar and Grill, 710 North Highway 24 / 395-6472
El Duran Mexican Restaurant, 301 East Main / 395-2120 / 24 hours / Cocktails /
$-$$
High Country Coffees and Cafe, 713 South Highway 24 / 395-2634 / Open 7AM–
9PM / $
Kit and Sandy's Restaurant, 304 South Highway 24 / 395-6940

Sporting Goods
Between the Lines, 17920-YS Highway 285, Nathrop / 539-2067
Good Brothers Inc., 320 Charles Street / 395-9348

Hi-Rocky Gift and Sport Store, 111 Cottonwood Avenue / 395-2258
The Trailhead, 707 Highway 24 North / 395-8001

AIRPORTS
Buena Vista Municipal Airport, 27960 County Road 319 / 395-2496 / Private planes
Colorado Springs Airport, 7770 Drennan Road / 550-1900 / United: 800-241-6522 / American: 800-433-7300 / Delta: 800-221-1212 / Western Pacific: 800-722-5775
Pueblo Municipal, 948-4423 / United Express: 800-241-6522
Peak Experience Travel Inc., 322 North Railroad / 395-8677

AUTO RENTAL
Crazy Horse Jeep Rentals, 33975 North Highway 24 / 395-2323

AUTO SERVICE
Buena Vista Texaco, 101 Highway 24 South / 395-6711
Foreman Sales and Service, 222 South Highway 24 / 395-2902
Smitty's Garage, 395-8030

LOCKSMITH
Barney's Locksmith Service, 29600 County Road 353 / 395-6656

FOR MORE INFORMATION
Chamber of Commerce
343 US Highway 24 South
Buena Vista, CO 81211
395-6612

Leadville

Elevation – 10,152 • Population – 2,629 • Area Code – 719

ACCOMMODATIONS
Longhorn Motel, 1515 North Poplar Street / 486-3155 / 12 rooms / Dogs allowed / $$
Mountain Peaks Motel, #1 Harrison Avenue / 486-3178 / 12 rooms / Dogs allowed for a fee / $$
Pan Ark Lodge, 5827 Highway 24 / 486-1063, 800-443-1063
Timberline Motel, 216 Harrison Avenue / 486-1876, 800-352-1876 / 15 rooms / $$$

BED AND BREAKFAST
Peri and Ed's Mountain Hideaway, 201 West 8th Street / 486-0716, 800-933-3715 / Innkeepers: Peri and Ed Solder
Mt. Elbert Lodge, PO Box 40 Twin Lakes, 81251 / 486-0594, 800-381-4433

CAMPING
Sugar Loafin' Campground, 486-1031 / 73 RV sites and 22 tent sites

RESTAURANTS

Buckeye Creek Restaurant, 4 miles north on Highway 91 / 486-2276 / Open 4PM–9PM / $$$

Columbine Cafe, 612 Harrison Avenue / 486-3599 / Open 6:30AM–9PM / Breakfast all day / $

High Country Restaurant, 115 Harrison Avenue / 486-3992 / Open 11AM–10PM / $

Leadville Diner, 115 West 4th Street / 486-3812 / Open 6:30AM / $

SPORTING GOODS

Bill's Sport Shop Inc., 225 Harrison Avenue / 486-0739

Buckhorn Sporting Goods, 616 Harrison Avenue / 486-3111

Otto's Hardware and General Mercantile, 1902 Poplar / 486-2220

HOSPITALS

St. Vincent General Hospital, 825 West 4th and Washington / 486-0230

AIRPORTS

Leadville Airport, Highway 24 and CR. 23 / 486-2627 / Private planes

Colorado Springs Airport, 7770 Drennan Road / 550-1900 / United / 800-241-6522 / American: 800-433-7300 / Delta: 800-221-1212 / Western Pacific: 800-722-5775

Pueblo Municipal, 948-4423 / United Express: 800-241-6522

AUTO SERVICE

Bart's Auto Repair Center, 201 Harrison Avenue 486-0188, 486-1277 / Towing available

North Poplar Standard, 2400 Poplar Street / 486-2716 / Tire repair

LOCKSMITH

Lockworks of Leadville, 107 East 5th / 486-3390, 486-4990

FOR MORE INFORMATION

Greater Leadville Area Chamber of Commerce
809 Harrison Avenue
Leadville, CO 80461
486-3900, 1-800-933-3901

Pueblo

Elevation – 4,695 • Population: 98,640 • Area Code – 719

ACCOMMODATIONS

Hampton Inn, 4703 North Freeway / 544-4700 / 112 rooms / Dogs allowed for a fee / $$$

Ramada Inn, 2001 North Hudson / 542-3750 / 180 rooms / Dogs allowed / $$$

Super 8 Motel, 1100 West Highway 50 / 545-4104 / 60 rooms / Dogs allowed / $$$

RESTAURANTS

Ianne's Whiskey Ridge, 4333 Thatcher Avenue / 564-8551 / Open 4PM–10PM / Cocktails / Highly recommended /$$

Jorge's Sombrero Restaurant and Lounge, 1319 East Evans Avenue / 564-6486 / Open 11AM–9PM / Cocktails / $

The Pantry Restaurant, 107-1/2 East Abriendo Avenue / 543-8072 / Open 6AM for breakfast / $

Two and Nine Bar, 2912 North Elizabeth / 544-5507 / Open evenings for sandwiches and drinks / $

FLY SHOPS AND SPORTING GOODS
Sports Hut, 332 South McCulloch Boulevard / 547-2848
T and M Sporting Goods, 2023 Lakeview Avenue / 564-0790

HOSPITALS
Proactive Medical Care Center, 431 Quincy / 583-2273

AIRPORTS
Colorado Springs Airport, 7770 Drennan Road / 550-1900 / United: 800-241-6522 / American: 800-433-7300 / Delta: 800-221-1212 / Western Pacific: 800-722-5775
Pueblo Municipal, 948-4423 / United Express: 800-241-6522

AUTO RENTAL
Avis Rent-A-Car, 948-9665
Budget Rent-A-Car / 948-3363

AUTO SERVICE
Scottie's, 615 South Main / 545-7557
Car Doctor, 2205 East 4th / 542-0457 / Mobile service and towing

FOR MORE INFORMATION
Pueblo Chamber of Commerce
302 North Santa Fe Avenue
Pueblo, CO 81003
542-1704

Estes Park
Elevation–7,522 • Population–3,184 • Area Code–970

ACCOMMODATIONS
Comfort Inn, 1450 Big Thompson Avenue / 586-2358 / 75 rooms / $$$
Holiday Inn, 101 South St. Vrain Avenue / 586-2332 / 150 rooms / $$$

BED AND BREAKFAST
Black Dog Inn, 650 South St. Vrain Avenue / 586-0374 / 4 rooms / $$$
Riversong B and B, Estes Park / 586-4666 / Innkeepers: Gary and Sue Mansfield / $$$
Antlers Pointe Log Cabins, 1515 Fish Hatchery Road / 586-8881 / $$$

CAMPING

Blue Arrow Campground, 1665 Spur Highway 66 / 586-5342 / 170 RV sites and 24 tent sites

Estes Park Campground, 3420 Tunnel Road / 586-4188 / 12 RV sites and 65 tent sites

Rocky Mountain National Park, General Information: 586-1206 / Park Headquarters: 586-1242

RESTAURANTS

Bob and Tony's Pizza, 124 West Elkhorn Avenue / 586-2044

Ed's Cantina and Grill, 362 East Elkhorn Avenue / 586-2919

Philly Billy's, 401 East Elkhorn Avenue / 586-0383

The Dunraven Inn, 2470 Highway 66 / 586-6409

FLY SHOPS AND SPORTING GOODS

Estes Angler, 338 West Riverside Drive / 586-2110, 800-586-2110 / Owner: Dale Darling / Full-service fly shop and guide service / Specialist for Rocky Mountain National Park / Rentals available

St. Vrain Angler, 418 Main Street Longmont, / 651-6061 / Owner: Dale Darling / Full-service fly shop, guide service, private lakes, flyfishing instruction, rentals

Colorado Wilderness Sports, 358 East Elkhorn Avenue / 586-6548

Rocky Mountain Adventures Inc., 1360 Big Thompson Avenue / 586-6191

Coast to Coast/Ben Franklin Stores, 461 East Wonderview Avenue / 586-3496

Outdoor World, 156 East Elkhorn Avenue / 586-2114

Scot's Sporting Goods, 870 Moraine Avenue / 586-2877

HOSPITALS

Estes Park Medical Center, 555 Prospect Avenue / 586-2317

AIRPORTS

Denver International Airport, 342-2000, 342-0400 / United: 800-241-6522 / Delta: 800-221-1212 / American: 800-433-7300 / TWA: 800-221-2000

AUTO RENTAL

Dollar Rent-A-Car, 1211 Woodstock Drive / 586-3319

AUTO SERVICE

Advanced Auto, 931 Juniper Lane / 586-6572

Alpine Automotive, 508 Pine River Lane / 586-6506

Gorman's Highway 7 Garage, 245 Highway 7 Bus Rt. / 303-747-0401

LOCKSMITH

The Village Locksmith, 343 South St. Vrain / 586-2780, 800-988-5614

FOR MORE INFORMATION

Chamber of Commerce
500 Big Thompson Avenue
Estes Park, CO 80517
586-4431

Loveland

Elevation – 4,982 • Population – 37,352 • Area Code – 970

ACCOMMODATIONS
Dreamland Motel, 617 East Eisenhower Boulevard / 667-2748
River Court Lodge, 1044 Big Thompson Canyon Road / 667-3587
Best Western, 5542 East Highway 34 / 667-7810, 800-528-1234 / www.bestwestern.com
King's Court, 928 North Lincoln Avenue / 667-4035

BED AND BREAKFAST
The Lovelander, 217 West 4th Street / 669-0798
Sylvan Dale Guest Ranch, 2939 North County Road 31D / 667-3915 / Host: Suzan Jessup / $$$

CAMPING
Fireside RV Park and Cabins, 6850 West Highway 34 / 667-2903
Riverview RV Park and Campground, 7806 West Highway 34 / 667-9910 / 133 RV sites and 30 tent sites

RESTAURANTS
Summit Restaurant, 3208 East Eisenhower Boulevard / 669-6648 / Open 10AM–10:30PM / Steaks and drinks / $$
Mi Tierra Restaurant, 198 East 29th Street / 663-1209 / Open 11AM–10PM / Mexican food and cocktails / $
Johnny James Restaurant, 1140 Lincoln Avenue / 622-8300 / Open 11AM–10PM / American food and cocktails / $$
Egg and I, 2525 Lincoln Avenue / 635-0050 / Open Monday–Saturday 6AM / $
Perkins, 2222 East Eisenhower Boulevard / 663-1944 / Open 6AM–12AM / $

FLY SHOPS AND SPORTING GOODS
Bob's Fly Tying Specialties, 406 South Lincoln Avenue / 667-1107 / Owner: Bob Paul / Web page: www.inetmkt.com/bobs / email: bob@streamside.com / Full-service fly shop / Expert tying instruction by Julie Ray / Greg Sheets coaches individuals in rod building / Hospitality
Butte House Fly Shop, 4412 West Eisenhower Boulevard / 667-9772 / Owner: Aaron Rutledge / Full-service fly shop / Classes and clinics for all phases of the sport
Brown's Corner Sporting Goods, 1310 East Eisenhower Boulevard / 663-4913
Bennett's Tackle, 121 Bunyan Avenue, Berthoud 80513 / 303-532-2213

HOSPITALS
McKee Medical Center, 2000 Boise Avenue / 669-4640

AIRPORTS

Fort Collins/Loveland Municipal Airport , 4900 Earhart Road / 962-2850 / United Express: 800-241-6522

Denver International Airport, 342-2000, 342-0400 / United: 800-241-6522 / Delta: 800-221-1212 / American: 800-433-7300 / TWA: 800-221-2000

AUTO RENTAL

Enterprise Rent-A-Car, 3210 Garfield Avenue / 669-7119

AUTO SERVICE

Anything Automotive, 400 East Garfield Avenue / 667-8797

Stan's Auto Service Inc., 1019 South Lincoln Avenue / 667-6852 / 24-hour towing

LOCKSMITH

Dave's Lock and Safe, 2316 North Lincoln Avenue / 669-8910

FOR MORE INFORMATION

Loveland Chamber of Commerce
5400 Stone Creek Circle #200
Loveland, CO 80538
667-6311

Roosevelt National Forest
970-498-2770

Boulder

Elevation – 5,363 • Population – 83,312 • Area Code – 303

ACCOMMODATIONS

Golden Buff Motor Lodge, 1725 28th Street / 442-7450 / 112 rooms / $$$

Holiday Inn, 800 28th Street / 443-3322 / 165 rooms / Dogs allowed / $$$

Homewood Suites, 4950 Baseline Road / 499-9922 / 112 rooms / Dogs allowed for a fee / $$$

RESTAURANTS

Tom's Tavern, 1047 Pearl Street / 442-9363 / Open 11AM-12PM for casual dinner and drinks / $

The Sink, 1165 13th Street / 444-7465 / Open 11AM–10PM / Great pizza and wide variety of beer / $-$$

La Peep Restaurant, 2525 Arapahoe Avenue / 444-5119 / Open 6:30AM for breakfast / $

JJ McCabe's Sports Bar, 945 Walnut Avenue / 449-4130 / Sandwiches and drinks

FLY SHOPS AND SPORTING GOODS

Front Range Anglers, 629-B South Broadway, 80303 / 494-1375 / Owners: Brad Befus and Ron Young / Full service, classes, guide service / Monday–Saturday 9:30AM–6PM, Sunday 10AM–5PM

Boulder Outdoor Center, 2510 47th / 444-8420, 1-800-364-9376

Bucking Brown Trout Company, 26 East 1st Street, Nederland 80466 / 258-3225 / email: buckingb@earthnet.net / Owner: Jonathan Beggs / Full service fly shop, guide service, instruction; guide trips on private water and Indian Peaks Wilderness Area

Kinsley and Company / 1155 13th Street / 442-6204, 800-442-7420 / Owners: Court Dixon, Ed Capson, and Do Phan / Orvis endorsed guide service and fly shop

McGuckin Hardware, 2525 Arapahoe Avenue / 443-1822

Mountain Sports, 821 Pearl Street / 443-6770

Rocky Mountain Outfitters, 1738 Pearl / 444-9080

Southcreek Ltd., 415 Main Street, Lyons 80540 / 303-823-6402 / Owner: Michael D. Clark / Selection of flies for the St. Vrain Creek tied by A.K. Best / Builder of fine bamboo rods

HOSPITALS

Boulder Community Hospital, 1100 Balsam Avenue / 440-2273

AIRPORTS

Denver International Airport, 342-2000, 342-0400 / United: 800-241-6522 / Delta: 800-221-1212 / American: 800-433-7300 / TWA: 800-221-2000

AUTO RENTAL

Avis Rent-A-Car, 4800 Baseline Road Suite D 109A / 499-1136

Enterprise Rent-A-Car, 5472 Arapahoe Road / 449-9466

AUTO SERVICE

The Four Wheeler, 6519 Arapahoe Avenue / 443-8488

M and D Automotive, 4919 Broadway / 447-2425

FOR MORE INFORMATION

Boulder Chamber of Commerce
2440 Pearl Street
Boulder, CO 80302
442-1044

South Park

When the center of conversation is flyfishing in South Park, wind will be the heated part of the discussion. South Park sits in the middle of the Rampart and Sawatch Ranges, right where a wind tunnel is formed. Wind blows just about every day in the park. Now, I'm not a meteorologist, but I figure it has to have something to do with the lack of things getting in the way. This part of the state is out in the wide open spaces.

South Park is a very popular destination for the fly angler, and for good reason: the upper South Platte River has long been known for larger than average trout. The state record rainbow of 18 pounds once lived here. Rainbows and browns in the 10-pound class still live here and are caught on occasion. Of these waters, the tailwater below Spinney Mountain Reservoir is the most famous and fruitful.

I have divided the South Platte River into two sections, one included here with South Park and the other in the Front Range section. The river definitely has two totally different demeanors. The upper Platte is a meandering, wide-open meadow stream, while the water below Cheesman Reservoir is a tumbling, gradient river enclosed by canyon walls. Accesses to the river between these areas are so far apart that it only seems natural to talk about them as two different rivers.

An awesome string of reservoirs goes along with the excellent stream fishing, starting with Antero, followed by Spinney Mountain, and finally Elevenmile Reservoir. All have the potential to reward the angler with a wall hanger. Please take photos, get a fiberglass mount, and give someone else a chance at that wonderful feeling. It is a great thing when the same fish can grace several walls.

Tarryall Reservoir and Tarryall Creek are also worth taking a look at while in South Park. Trout will not be as big, especially in the creek, but a little peace and quiet can be found there while the crowds are hammering at the more popular water on the South Platte.

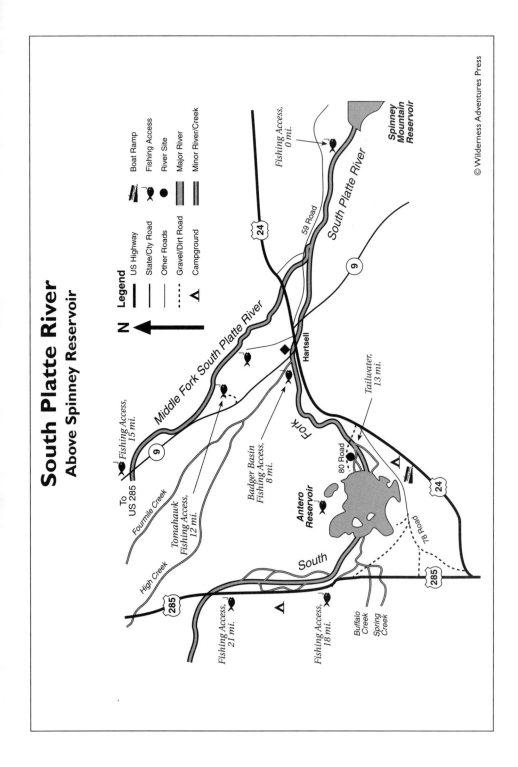

South Platte River
Above Spinney Reservoir

Legend

US Highway	
State/Cty Road	
Other Roads	
Gravel/Dirt Road	
Campground	△
Boat Ramp	
Fishing Access	
River Site	
Major River	
Minor River/Creek	

N

Spinney Mountain Reservoir

South Platte River

Fishing Access, 0 mi.

59 Road

24

9

Hartsell

Middle Fork South Platte River

Fishing Access, 15 mi.

To US 285

9

Fourmile Creek

Tomahawk Fishing Access, 12 mi.

High Creek

Badger Basin Fishing Access, 8 mi.

Fork

Antero Reservoir

80 Road

Tailwater, 13 mi.

24

78 Road

285

South

285

Fishing Access, 21 mi.

Fishing Access, 18 mi.

Buffalo Creek

Spring Creek

SOUTH PLATTE RIVER

Above Spinney Mountain Reservoir

The waters above Spinney Mountain include the entire upper river to the head-waters. US 24 is the major go-between from Colorado Springs to South Park. To access the river right above Spinney, from US 24 turn left (south) on CR 23. A sign on US 24 will prompt the turn. Three miles brings you to a tee in the road. Turn right on CR 592 towards Spinney Mountain Reservoir. Continue past Spinney to the first parking lot on the left. A State Parks pass is required. A daily pass can be purchased at the parking area.

The river is a 10- to 15-minute walk south of the parking area. This section of river is closed during the winter. It is open to fishing by mid-April, just in time for the spring runs of rainbows and Snake River cutthroats from Spinney.

This is a great time to spot big fish in the clear, low water. Spawning activity is at its peak, and hooking several trout over 20 inches is a distinct possibility. The closer you get to the lake, the more fish you are apt to see. Red midge patterns, pheasant tail nymphs, and buckskins from sizes 16 to 20 will hook your share of trout. However, as much as I hate to say it, San Juan worms and egg patterns take the most fish.

Black or purple woolly buggers and small bucktail streamers dropped into the deeper pools and undercuts can prove very exciting.

Runoff will put a halt to things mid- to late May. Time to head over to the lake and look for a Callibaetis hatch.

The river up to Badger Basin, eight miles west of Spinney on US 24, is fishable starting early July. Caddis will be the predominant hatch, and the resident brown trout like to feed on the emerging and adult stages. A low-riding olive CDC caddis or LaFontaine sparkle caddis work well for this smooth surfaced stream. Expect to catch browns between 10–14 inches and a few holdover rainbows and cutthroats up to 18 inches.

Attractor and hopper patterns entice trout to the surface when caddis activity has slowed. Rio Grande King trudes, Royal Wulffs, Letort crickets and hoppers, and a foam Madam-X are large, juicy morsels.

The fall is always a favorite time of the year in South Park. The area above Antero Reservoir along the South Fork is a great spot to check out at this time. Take US 24 west to the intersection with US 285. Turn right (north) on 285. Accesses to the river are on the right hand side of the road. Brown and brook trout are eager participants. Once Antero has recovered from the work on the dam and the new stocking has taken hold, this will be a good piece of river to check out.

The Middle Fork, paralleling Colorado 9 north of Hartsel, is host to the Tomahawk State Wildlife Area. Two well-marked accesses from Colorado 9 lead you to the lower and upper end of the area.

The lower end, a braided, oftentimes very small stream, is loaded with undercut banks and is home to browns in the 20-inch range. Most of these trout are holdovers

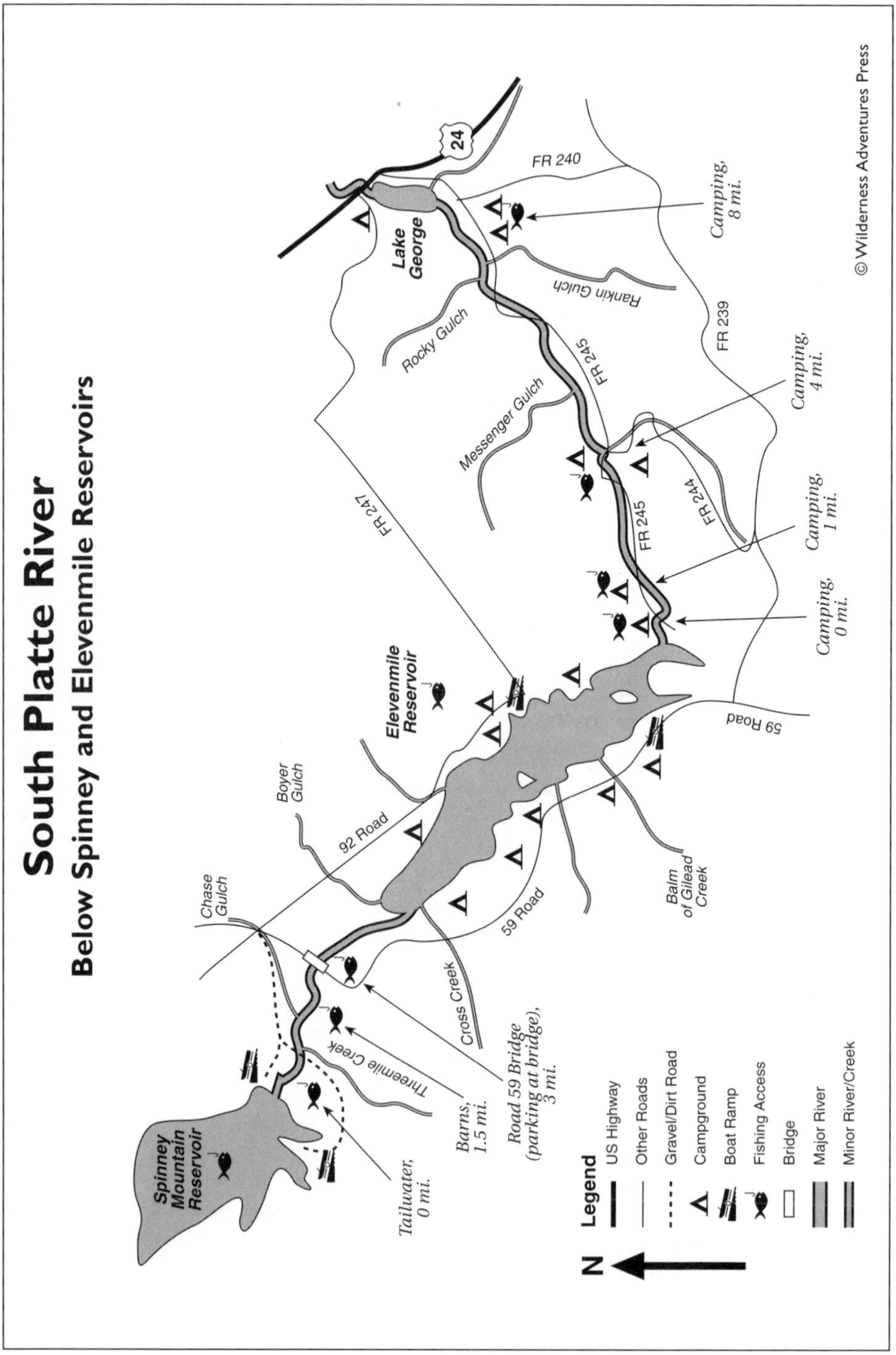

South Platte River
Below Spinney and Elevenmile Reservoirs

© Wilderness Adventures Press

FR 240

Camping, 8 mi.

Lake George

Rankin Gulch

Rocky Gulch

FR 239

Messenger Gulch

FR 245

Camping, 4 mi.

Camping, 1 mi.

FR 244

FR 245

Camping, 0 mi.

FR 247

Elevenmile Reservoir

59 Road

Boyer Gulch

92 Road

59 Road

Chase Gulch

Balm of Gilead Creek

Cross Creek

Threemile Creek

Barns, 1.5 mi.

Road 59 Bridge (parking at bridge), 3 mi.

Spinney Mountain Reservoir

Tailwater, 0 mi.

Legend

US Highway	
Other Roads	
Gravel/Dirt Road	
Campground	
Boat Ramp	
Fishing Access	
Bridge	
Major River	
Minor River/Creek	

N

*Eric Neufeld
landing a nice
South Platte rainbow
below Spinney
Mountain Reservoir.*

from a fall run that have taken up residence. They are there, but getting to these crafty old brutes during the fall of the year is tough, to say the least. The growth along the stream is not designed for a stealthy approach. Early morning streamer fishing is your best chance. Muddler Minnows and woolly buggers sucked back under the cut banks is one of your options. Landing one of these guys will take every bit of skill, and then some.

It shouldn't be easy all the time!

The upper end of Tomahawk opens into a single channel up to 15 feet wide, retaining a few undercuts with plenty of 10- to 12-inch browns. Big browns come up

*Darrel Sickmon with a huge rainbow he nailed
in the South Platte below Spinney Reservoir.*

here to spawn in the fall but do not hang around long. I've spooked browns here in late September that would go 25 to 28 inches. Emphasis is on spooked.

Nymph fishing here is fairly straightforward. However, the deeper pools and spots near the cutbanks should draw your undivided attention. Buckskins, Prince nymphs, pheasant tails, and San Juan worms should take a couple of the smaller, eager browns.

Below Spinney Mountain Reservoir

The South Platte River below Spinney Mountain Reservoir is one of the state's most regularly fished streams. It is referred to as Spinney Mile, Spinney, and the Dream Stream. It's one of the few great stretches of river in the state for big trout. You can fish here every month of the year, and most people do. Wind is a factor 90 percent of the time.

Its popularity has had detrimental effects on the river over the last five years. In the fall of 1994, I heard the river hadn't any fish left, so I made a trip to South Park for an inspection. Sure enough, I couldn't spook a fish, let alone find one to catch. Some say pressure and the trampling of the stream bottom moved the trout back into Elevenmile Reservoir. Bank erosion from cattle feeding along the stream was another theory. And still another laid the blame on whirling disease.

Word got around, and the river saw few fishermen the next year. Trout Unlimited and others made stream habitat improvements and planted willows along the bank. Evidently, these efforts worked; the quality of the stream returned, and trout took up residency once again. With the diversity and quantity of food available in this tailwater, it's easy to see why they reestablished so quickly.

US 24 from Colorado Springs is the main road to and from Spinney Mile. As you drop down the west side of Wilkerson Pass on US 24, look for a sign directing you to Spinney Mountain and Elevenmile Reservoirs. Turn left (south) on CR 23 and follow it to the tee in the road. Turn left (east) on CR 592. Take the next right, CR 59, to the parking areas.

You can also cross the dam at Spinney Mountain Reservoir and get to the water right below the dam. Turn right on CR 592 instead of left. Take the next left into Spinney Mountain. A State Parks permit is required at this entrance.

For the most part, this flat meadow stream is fished with small flies. Midges, small mayfly nymphs, and emerger patterns of both are a must. February is the month to start finding good midge activity, but May and June are when the best hatches arrive. There are several types of midges that hatch here: tiny (a size 24 is sometimes too big), big (a size 16), and just about everything in between.

A woolly bugger in the water during any period of time when insects aren't out is good for a fish or two.

Short line nymphing with or without an indicator is standard practice in this water. In my opinion, a dual-fly setup also gives the angler an extra edge. Along with the small midge pattern, an orange or 19½ scud in sizes 14 to 16 is a good second fly. Rods in the 4- and 5-weight range up to 9 feet long are favorites here. Twelve-foot leaders tapered to 6X or 7X are the norm.

There are lots of scuds in this river, mostly olive in color. They seem to change shades from lighter shades in spring, when the stream bottom hasn't yet recovered from the winter, to darker shades of olive and gray when the stream bottom becomes a rich green color.

The key to success here is a quiet approach while moving upstream, trying not to spook these trout. As Roger Hill says in his book, *Fly Fishing the South Platte River*, "All trout have a blind spot in their rearview mirror." They become very tolerant of human presence, but catching them after they have been disturbed is difficult.

Spotting a trout and casting to that fish is very popular in this water. A sharp eye, peering into the riffles and the slack water behind the few rocks that exist here, should spot a holding trout. Rainbows, browns, and Snake River cutthroat measured in the several pounds range call this stream home. However, the average trout will be 16 to 18 inches. The big fish are usually spawners from Elevenmile Reservoir in the spring and fall.

One of the best hatches to attend at Spinney Mile is the PMD in mid June. It is best to start the day nymphing a size 16 or 18 biot PMD nymph or a pheasant tail. Emerging nymphs will be popping the surface by 10:00 AM, and the hatch will last until around 1:00 PM. The trout love these bugs, and the surface will be boiling in no

*Author displays a long rainbow taken on the South Platte
below Spinney Reservoir. (Photo by Gus Ridlen)*

time. The corner pools, with their emerging insects, seem to be a favorite spot for fish to move into. A floating nymph or a light olive CDC mayfly emerger will work throughout the hatch. A #14 or #16 PMD comparadun is a good pattern when you start seeing the duns disappear in a swirl, usually towards the end of the hatch. This hatch peters out in early July.

A caddis hatch occurs at the same time as the PMDs and can create confusion detecting which bug the trout are feeding on. The trout rising in the riffles are normally feeding on this small tan caddis. A size 16 to 18 light elk hair or CDC caddis will hook the trout in this faster water.

Mark your calendar with an X on the 15th of July to remind you of the trico hatch below Spinney. This is the most sought-after hatch on this stretch of water. Clouds of white-winged mayflies fill the morning skies of July and August. At about 9:00 AM, the trico spinner will hit the water, and all hell breaks loose. Every trout in the river is up and feeding on this minute table fair. In fact, I've seen trout get to the surface and take four to six spinners at a time. They rhythmically slide back and move slightly side-to-side as they pick off the helpless spent wings.

Fly size is critical in this situation. Once, I drifted my #24 black spinner right through the middle of this multiple rise situation without even a glance from the trout. Cast after cast without a look. I stuck my seine into the water and picked up a net full of the naturals. I laid my #24 next to them, and it looked like a gorilla. I had nothing that small, and still don't, so I went to 3X and a bugger. This is when I really started to hate tricos!

About noon the water is silent. You wouldn't know there were 20 to 25 fish rising inside good casting range just a half hour earlier. Take a break. Have some lunch and a beer to calm your nerves.

At about 3:00 PM, start hitting the banks with terrestrials. Hoppers, beetles, and ants have been swept into the water, and an occasional nose can be seen lifting through the surface. A #10 Rio Grande King trude is my favorite.

October is time for the big brown trout and kokanee salmon to enter the river from Elevenmile Reservoir. Woolly buggers early in the morning and late in the day can hook a number of rainbows and brown trout. Nymph fishing the deep pockets and corner pools during the day from the dam down to the old red barns is the best water to find the trout. Browns near 10 pounds are caught every year here in the fall. Olive scuds, San Juan worms, and small midge patterns should be used.

This water gets a lot of pressure from guides and individuals alike. I've encountered several problems with folks fishing here. Anglers can get a bad case of the "creeps" when someone else is catching fish. They seem to creep a little closer, and a little closer, until they are in your back pocket trying to fish the same water as you. Everybody can have a good time if common courtesies are followed.

Below Elevenmile Reservoir

Referred to as Elevenmile Canyon, this is one of the best early season fisheries, especially if you would like to start the year dry-fly fishing. From US 24 at the town of Lake George, turn left (south) on FR 245. A sign on US 24 will indicate the direction to Elevenmile Canyon. A pass is required before entering the canyon, although the area is not affiliated with the State Parks.

By mid-February, midges are hatching during the warm part of the day, and trout will rise to them for a couple of hours. Warm may not be the best word to use in this case; it's cold in Colorado in February at 5,000 feet, let alone at 8,000 feet.

Gus, my longtime fishing partner, shares, "A Griffith's gnat may take a few fish, but eventually a thinly dubbed or thread-bodied adult midge pattern will need to be used. I caught browns and rainbows to 14 inches on an early brown stone dry fly in a size 20. It was the closest thing to a dry midge in my box. It worked until the sun drifted off the water and the trout stopped rising."

Definitely look for the deeper slow pools. This is where the trout will be holed-up for the winter.

As the water starts to warm in mid-April, Baetis are hatching. I don't want to call them blue-winged olives because of their darker color. One of the mayflies that hatch at this time has a very dark gray abdomen with blackish segmentation lines and rate at least a size 18. Another is a smaller size 20 with a medium gray body; a blue dun describes it best.

A happy Chris Clothier below Spinney on the South Platte. (Photo by Gus Ridlen)

Look for trout, up to 14 inches, rising in the slick water. Pools and eddies are the areas where most trout will be feeding on emergers and duns.

Dick Rock, a guide for The Peak Fly Shop in Colorado Springs, suggests, "An RS-2 emerger is one of the best patterns for the Baetis hatch. Carry sizes 16 through 22 with a dark muskrat body." He adds, "It can be used along with a nymph or paired up with a dry fly to cover any stage of the hatch."

Pheasant tail and beadhead pheasant tail nymphs will cover the subsurface flies. Blue duns, parachute Adams, and slate thorax duns are productive dry flies.

Look for a small golden stonefly hatch late April and into May. Nymphing is the best bet while these insects are migrating. Light hare's ears, golden stone nymphs, and Prince nymphs in size 14 through 16 regularly pick up trout at the tail end of riffles.

The upper third of the canyon, above the bridge at Springer Gulch, is flies and lures only and can be the best place in the river in the spring. Large rainbows that have been sulking in the deep pools all winter are in the flats dusting off their reds. Twenty-inch rainbows inhabit the canyon, and this is the time to get to know a couple of them.

Another great thing about Elevenmile Canyon is its secluded location. When everyone in South Park is getting blown away, you can find shelter from the fierce winds. As a bonus, you'll get a chance at a trophy rainbow.

Rock informs, "Runoff in the canyon is not usually a big deal." Water releases from the dam rarely go over 400 cfs. He adds, "In fact, 250 cfs is a normal high water flow."

Flows can fluctuate. On one hand, you have the guys up above making room in Elevenmile Reservoir for runoff, and on the other you have the Denver Water Board meeting demands of the city. The transfer of water on the South Platte River is truly an amazing thing.

By late May, water temperatures climb into the 50s, and the free-living caddis start to emerge. Sporadic hatches continue throughout the summer. Late afternoons and evenings are the best times to catch rising fish on elk hair caddis.

A light olive pale morning dun shows up by mid-June and will hatch sporadically throughout the summer. Overcast days may spurn the hatch along, but there is no set pattern for this hatch. Expect to see the hatch by 10:00 AM. With a little luck, a #16 PMD comparadun will net you a couple trout.

Flows fall back into the 150 cfs range by mid-July and are about as close to perfect as you can get.

Summer is a great opportunity to use attractor dry flies as searching patterns. Smaller trout will take small H & L variants, Royal Wulffs, and hoppers from the surface. However, if you are looking for a bigger than average trout, nymphing is the answer. "The bigger fish in the canyon eat nymphs most of the time." Rock says, "Expect to find the bigger browns holding in the deep pocket water and occasionally at the head of riffles. Large rainbows wait silently in the deep pools, and you just about have to set the fly in their mouth to catch them."

Rock passes on a few conservation ideas. "The canyon is not patrolled on a regular basis by the Division of Wildlife, which has developed a problem. Poaching! The lower half of the canyon is a put-and-take fishery with smaller trout. The upper canyon is regulated but not enforced like it should be. People are coming up with bait and killing the better fish. I could have told you, just a couple of years ago, the average fish would have been 14 to 16 inches. Now the average has to be under 14 inches. This fishery has the capability of sustaining good populations of large trout if everyone does their part to protect it."

Stream Facts: South Platte River

Seasons
* Fishing is open all year.

Special Regulations
* From the confluence of the Middle Fork and the South Fork of the South Platte to Spinney Mountain Reservoir (Gold Medal Water): Artificial flies and lures only. All trout between 12 and 20 inches must be released immediately. Bag and possession limit for trout is 2 fish, of which no more than 1 can be greater than 20 inches.
* From the outlet of Spinney Mountain Reservoir downstream to Elevenmile Reservoir (Gold Medal Water): Artificial flies and lures only. All fish must be released immediately.
* From below Elevenmile Dam downstream to the bridge at Springer Gulch (Elevenmile Canyon): Artificial flies and lures only. Bag and possession limit for trout is 2 fish, 16 inches or longer.

Trout
* Rainbow trout; some over 20 inches.
* Browns: fall spawn runs can bring 6- to 10-pounders out of the lakes.
* Brook trout: above Spinney Mountain Reservoir.
* Snake River cutthroat: above and below Spinney Mountain Reservoir.

River Miles
Above Spinney Mountain Reservoir:
* Fishing access—0
* Badger Basin fishing access—8
* Antero tailwater—13
* DOW fishing access—18
* Tomahawk State Wildlife fishing access (Middle Fork)—12

Below Spinney Mountain Reservoir:
* Tailwater—0
* Barns—1.5
* Road 59 Bridge—3

Below Elevenmile Reservoir:
* Camping—0
* Cove Campground—1
* Springer Gulch Campground—4
* Riverside Campground—8

River Characteristics
* Mostly tailwater fisheries. Dams include Antero, Spinney Mountain, and Elevenmile. Winding meadow stream. Bring protection from the wind.

River Flows
* Winter, 50–150 cfs
* Spring, 100–300 cfs
* Runoff, 500 cfs and up
* Fall, 50–200 cfs

Maps
* *Colorado Atlas & Gazetteer*, pages 48, 49, 60, 61
* Pike National Forest

SOUTH PLATTE RIVER (BELOW SPINNEY) MAJOR HATCHES

Insect	A	M	J	J	A	S	O	N	Time	Flies
Midge								█	M/A/E	Olive Biot Midge #16–#26; Brown Biot Midge #16–#26; Candy Kane #16–#26; Black Beauty #18–#26; Brassie #16–#26; Blood Midge #16–#26; AK's Midge Larva #16–#24; Feather Duster Midge #18–#20; Disco Midge #18–#26; Black Beauty Pupa #18–#26; CDC Biot Suspender Midge #18–#26; Griffith's Gnat #16–#24; Palomino Midge #18–#24; Green Machine #20–#24; Fore & Aft #16–#22
Tricos					█				M	Parachute Adams #20–#24; Trico Spinner #18–#26; Double Trico Spinner #18; Thorax Dun #16–#22; Poor's Witch #18–#22
PMD			█						M/A	Biot PMD Nymph #16; Pheasant Tail Nymph #16–#22; Lt. Cahill Comparadun #12–#18; Sparkle Dun #14–#18; Parachute PMD #14–#18; Dark Hare's Ear #14–#18; Light Olive Comparadun
Caddis				█					M/A	Olive Caddis Nymph #10–#20; Breadcrust #10–#18; Buckskin #16–#20; LaFontaine's Sparkle Caddis Pupa #10–#20; Elk Hair Caddis #10–#22; CDC Caddis #14–#20; Lawson's Caddis Emerger #14–#18; Spent Partridge Caddis #14–#18
Blue-winged Olives	█						█		M	Olive Biot Nymph #18–#22; RS-2 #16–#24; Pheasant Tail Nymph #16–#20; Olive Quill Emerger #18–#24; AK's Olive Quill #16–#22; Parachute Adams #12–#22; Olive Comparadun #16–#20; Gray Spinner #18–#24; Slate Thorax Dun #16–#22; CDC Baetis Dun #16–#22

HATCH TIME CODE: M = morning; A = afternoon; E = evening; D = dark; SF = spinner fall; / = continuation through periods

SOUTH PLATTE RIVER (BELOW SPINNEY) MAJOR HATCHES (CONT.)

Insect	A	M	J	J	A	S	O	N	Time	Flies
Golden Stone Flies			▮						M	Gold-winged Prince Nymph #12–#14; Kaufmann's Golden Stonefly #12–#14; Foam Yellow Sally #14–#18; Light Hare's Ear Nymph
Scuds			▮	▮	▮	▮	▮	▮		Olive-gray Scud #12–#16; Orange Scud #10–#16; 19½ Scud #12–#18; Tan Scud #12–#16; Flashback Scud #12–#16
Terrestrials			▮	▮	▮	▮			A	Rio Grande King Trude #8–#16; Royal Wulff #10–#16; Humpy #10–#16; Foam Madam X #8–#12; Renegade #10–#16; Black Ant #14–#20; Gartside Hopper #8–#10; Henry's Fork Hopper #8–#12
Streamers					▮	▮	▮	▮	M/E	Black Woolly Bugger #2–#10; Brown Woolly Bugger #4–#10; Purple Woolly Bugger #4–#10; Spruce Fly #4–#10; Dark Spruce Fly #4–#10 ; Black-Nosed Dace #6–#8

HATCH TIME CODE: M = morning; A = afternoon; E = evening; D = dark; SF = spinner fall; / = continuation through periods

SOUTH PLATTE RIVER (ELEVENMILE CANYON) MAJOR HATCHES

Insect	A	M	J	J	A	S	O	N	Time	Flies
Midge									M/A/E	Olive Biot Midge #16–#24; Brown Biot Midge #16–#24; Black Beauty #18–#24; Brassie #16–#24; Miracle Nymph #16–#20; AK's Midge Larva #16–#22; Black Beauty Pupa #18–#24; CDC Biot Suspender Midge #18–#24; Griffith's Gnat #16–#22; Palomino Midge #18–#22
Blue-winged Olives									M/A	Olive Biot Nymph #18–#22; RS-2 #16–#24; Pheasant Tail Nymph #16–#20; Beadhead Pheasant Tail Nymph #16–#22; Flashback Pheasant Tail Nymph #16–#20; Dark Gray Quill Emerger #18–#24; Parachute Adams #12–#22; Gray Comparadun #16–#20; Gray Spinner #18–#24; Slate Thorax Dun #16–#22; CDC Baetis Dun #16–#22; Barr Emerger #16–#22
Caddis									A/E	Olive Caddis Nymph #10–#20; Buckskin #16–#20; LaFontaine's Sparkle Caddis Pupa #10–#20; Elk Hair Caddis #10–#22; CDC Caddis #14–#20; Balloon Caddis #12–#16; Lawson's Caddis Emerger #14–#18; Spent Partridge Caddis #14–#18
Golden Stone									M/A	Sandy's Gold #10; Gold-winged Prince Nymph #12–#14; Foam Yellow Sally #12–#18

HATCH TIME CODE: M = morning; A = afternoon; E = evening; D = dark; SF = spinner fall; / = continuation through periods

SOUTH PLATTE RIVER (ELEVENMILE CANYON) MAJOR HATCHES (CONT.)

Insect	A	M	J	J	A	S	O	N	Time	Flies
Pale Morning Dun			▓	▓	▓				M	Biot PMD Nymph #16; Pheasant Tail Nymph #16–#22; Beadhead Pheasant Tail Nymph #14–#20; Lt. Cahill Comparadun #12–#18; Sparkle Dun #14–#18; Parachute PMD #14–#18; Dark Hare's Ear #14–#18; Light Olive Comparadun #14–#18
Streamers	▓	▓	▓	▓	▓	▓	▓		M/E	Black Woolly Bugger #2–#10; Platte River Special #4–#10; Spruce Fly #4–#10; Dark Spruce Fly #4–#10
Attractors			▓	▓	▓	▓			A/E	Rio Grande King Trude #8–#16; Royal Wulff #10–#16; Foam Madam X #8–#12; Renegade #10–#16; Black Ant #14–#20; Gartside Hopper #8–#12; Henry's Fork Hopper #8–#12

HATCH TIME CODE: M = morning; A = afternoon; E = evening; D = dark; SF = spinner fall; / = continuation through periods

ANTERO RESERVOIR

Antero Reservoir is the first of several reservoirs along the South Platte drainage. Located on US 24 west of the town of Hartsel, its source is the South Fork of the South Platte below the Sawatch Mountain Range to the west.

In 1996, Antero was slowly drained to allow the Denver Water Department to work on the dam outlet. As the water level dropped, fishermen took advantage of the opportunity to take home trout from this dying pond before they all succumbed. Exposed vegetation brought with it the horrific smell of hydrogen sulfide. It was not a pretty sight, watching the slow death of such a well-enjoyed body of water.

However, a bad story always has its good side. It was estimated that over 90 percent of the fish in this reservoir were suckers. Bald eagles gorged themselves on the exposed fare. In the spring of 1997, the Division of Wildlife worked through the muck, shocking and netting any fish that may have survived. They also administered a dose of rotenone to kill any remaining fish (hopefully just suckers). This should provide the reservoir with a fresh start.

The outlook is good for the chance of a quick recovery. The mountain range to the west has had over 100 percent of normal snowpack in recent years, so filling the reservoir might only take a few months once reclamation efforts are finished. Greg Gerlich, a biologist with the Division of Wildlife, predicts, "When a sufficient water level is achieved to prevent the chance of winter kill, we will kick-start the reservoir with catchable-sized rainbows, followed by brown and cutthroat fingerlings." With the absence of the suckers, living space and food will be plentiful. In this nutrient-rich, high-plains reservoir, trout should grow fast and gain a considerable amount of weight in a short period of time. Look for this to be an outstanding fishery by late 1998, with a full season of bent rods in 1999.

Lake Facts: Antero Reservoir

Seasons
• From ice-out to ice-on

Special Regulations
• Boating prohibited from 9:00 PM to 4:00 AM

Trout
• Rainbows
• Browns
• Brook trout
• Snake River cutthroat

Lake Size
• 2000 acres

Lake Character
• Shallow lake
• Nutrient-rich high plains reservoir

Antero Reservoir

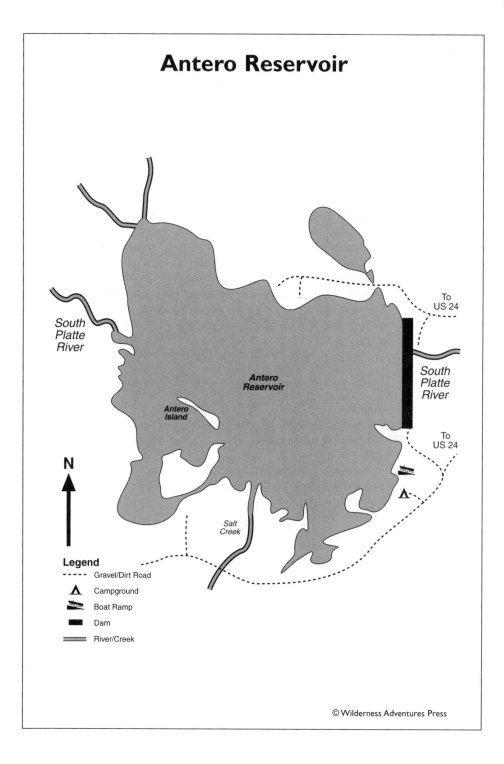

To
US 24

South
Platte
River

South
Platte
River

*Antero
Reservoir*

To
US 24

*Antero
Island*

N

*Salt
Creek*

Legend
- - - - - Gravel/Dirt Road
Campground
Boat Ramp
Dam
River/Creek

© Wilderness Adventures Press

SPINNEY MOUNTAIN RESERVOIR

When the announcement of Spinney Mountain Reservoir's opening hits the papers, usually in mid-April, chaos hits. Fishermen from all over the state pour forth for a first crack at trophy trout. Cars, trucks, boats, and trailers line up in the dark, waiting for the gate to open a half-hour before the sun rises.

And for good reason. Spinney Mountain's Gold Medal Water rating is well deserved. Rainbows, browns, and Snake River cutthroats can tip the scales at 5 pounds on a regular basis. A scale with double-digit capability may be needed for the angler lucky enough to land these big trout. Bag and possession limit is one trout over 20 inches.

Boats, flotillas of belly boats, and shore fishermen assault the lake with total abandon. The boats like to work the deeper channels, float tubers work the bays, and people line up wherever there's room, especially along the dam. Pods of rainbows, well over 20 inches, cruise up and down the dam, feeding at will.

Fly fishermen along the dam present orange scuds, Prince nymphs, and soft hackle midges in sizes 12 to 16 under a strike indicator. It's like a chain reaction when someone hooks up. A few minutes later, someone else down the dam hooks a cruiser, then another a little farther down. About an hour and a half later it happens again. A black or purple woolly bugger put out in front of one of these fish can provide great visual action.

Float tubing (or any of the new floating crafts) is the best method of getting around the lake, but be sure that your legs are in good shape. A tug of war with the wind is imminent. Depending on wind direction, you can pick and choose your game plan; parking and boat ramps are available on both the north and south sides of the lake, and both sides of the lake have excellent vegetation and structure for trout to linger in. A quick note: you don't have to get too far from shore to hook a trophy.

US 24 is the main road to and from Spinney Mountain Reservoir. As you drop down the west side of Wilkerson Pass on US 24, look for a sign directing you to Spinney Mountain and Elevenmile Reservoirs. Turn left (south) on CR 23 and follow it to the tee in the road. Turn right on CR 592. Take the next left into Spinney Mountain. A State Parks permit is required.

Scuds are a main food source and are available year round, as are leeches and crawfish. With just these three entrees, the trout can grow to large proportions. However, amongst the weed beds live several other insects. Midges, mayflies, and damselflies also feed the fish and afford the fly angler many other opportunities.

May and June contribute the best mayfly and midge hatches of the year. The midges show up first and give the fly angler the first chance at rising trout. The lake midges can be pretty large. They rate at least a size 16, sometimes up to a size 12. Midges inhabit just about all areas of Spinney Mountain, which can be good and bad. The good news is that anywhere you find a hatch, there's a good chance you'll find trout to feed on them, so it may not make a lot of difference where you choose to fish.

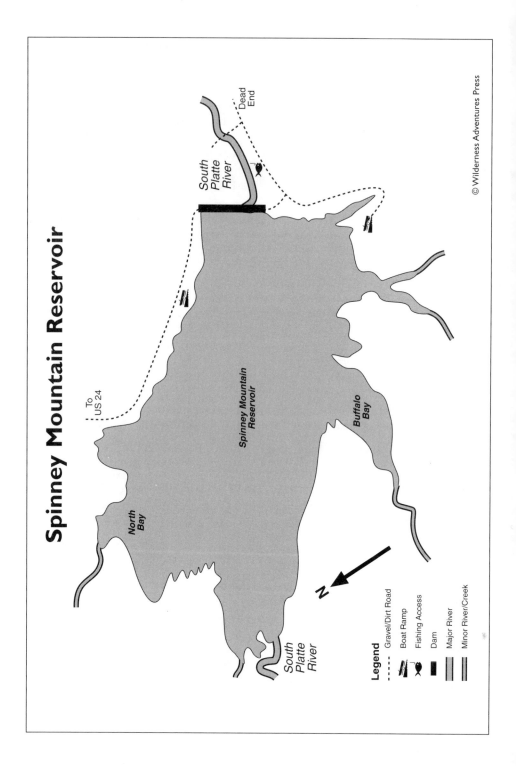

Spinney Mountain Reservoir

To US 24

South Platte River

Dead End

South Platte River

North Bay

Spinney Mountain Reservoir

Buffalo Bay

N

© Wilderness Adventures Press

Legend

- Gravel/Dirt Road
- Boat Ramp
- Fishing Access
- Dam
- Major River
- Minor River/Creek

The bad news is that some water is easier to fish than others; the deeper the water, the more difficult it is to make a good presentation.

These early midges are bottom dwellers, often gray in color as they emerge from the silt. A thin, gray soft hackle midge attached to a 12-foot leader, inching its way to the surface, is a good initial setup. An indicator can afford you the luxury of controlling the depth of the fly very easily. Start with the fly as close to the bottom as possible, using small split shot 18 to 24 inches from the fly. Give the rod tip a slight bump, which moves the fly upwards. Not too much; a couple inches of movement is all you want. Let the fly settle again and repeat the upward action. A strike can happen as the fly is settling back to the bottom, so be prepared. This method takes a lot of patience, but there are a lot of midges eaten by trout before you ever know a hatch is taking place.

As the pupae near the surface, trout will move to the surface with them. Slight disturbances, often called bulges, are the telltale sign that insects are close to the surface. You can use the same presentation technique as before, but this time use less weight, letting the fly ascend and hang in the top foot of water. A slow, finger-over-finger retrieve is an effective way to imitate the movement of these midges. Randall Kaufmann and Ron Cordes make mention of the way trout feed on midges in their book, *Lake Fishing with a Fly*: "Most strikes will occur near the bottom or close to the top, seldom in between."

Callibaetis is the next important hatch, often intermingling with the midge hatches. I've seen good hatches and had productive days fishing these mayflies, but nothing like the stories, by reliable sources, about how dense this hatch can be. Barry Reynolds told me, "The top of the water is a blanket of speckled mayfly wings. There were so many bugs on the water, my Adams would totally disappear."

Reynolds says, "It's quite a phenomenon to see, but impossible to fish successfully. I tried an old trick you taught me. I tied on a number 10 Rio Grande King trude. I was able to see the fly, barely, and did have a 16-incher take the damn thing!"

These mayfly nymphs prefer shallow water and weed beds near the shore. These mottled brownish and olive nymphs are about a size 14 or 16. Reynolds has taught me a trick or two as well when it comes to fishing Spinney, such as using the #14 ginger hare's ear nymph. I had tied a few dozen of this fly for the Trout Fisher, our home fly shop in Denver, but had never fished it. Reynolds bought a few of them. To make a long story short, he kicked ass with it, inching it through the top 6 to 12 inches of water. Once the story got out, I ended up tying more of them than I would have liked.

I can only guess the trout take this fly as a *Callibaetis* nymph. And take it they do, to the point that it becomes nothing but a shredded piece of fuzz and crystal flash, and then they take it again. Fished with a floating line and only the weight that is added to the hook shank before tying the fly, this imitation is deadly. A slow, 4-inch retrieve with a couple second pause between strips has proven itself time and again. Varying the depth by counting the fly down is the only change you need to make to this presentation.

Back to the adults. A size 14 to 16 Adams, gray comparadun, or thorax dun are good imitations when the trout are keyed into the duns. Late morning is the primary

While most anglers focus on the South Platte River, Spinney Mountain Reservoir also offers top trouting. Here, Matt Mask displays a typical cutthroat.

time to expect this stage of the hatch. However, the bigger rainbows and cutthroats like the egg laying, or spinner, stage much better. A rusty spinner, with its wings spread out on top of the water, will entice the better trout into coming to the surface.

Spinney Mountain is also a prime northern pike fishery. By the first of June, pike are in the shallow bays and on the prowl. The north bay is a wide shallow expanse and is prime water for pike. Water warms in this bay more quickly than most, and by 12:00 noon action will be picking up. Wading is the preferred method of getting to the pike.

Bunny flies are the fly of choice for northern pike. Black is by far the best color, while sizes 1/0 to 3/0 are big enough to give any northern a sore jaw. It is visible in any type of water. White is also a good color, but it is best used in clear water. Yellow and chartreuse should be used in water mucked up from windy conditions, something you will see often at Spinney. Clouser minnows, Lefty's deceivers, and woolly buggers are other flies to add to the pike fly box.

Seven- to 9-weight rods are needed to handle these flies. On the end of a 9-foot leader, they feel like a lame duck instead of just a strip of rabbit hair. A leader for casting pike flies is designed differently than a basic tapered trout leader; try a 9-foot piece of level 0x monofilament from the fly line with an 18-inch piece of nylon coated

High mountain scenery at Spinney Mountain Reservoir.

steel wire tippet. The connection is made with an Albright Special knot. The fly line should be a special bass bug taper or a pike/muskie line. They are designed like a shooting head. It makes a long distance cast with a large, air-resistant fly much easier. Both Cortland and Scientific Angler make a line for this use.

Northerns are built for speed with their broad flat tail. They will exhibit that speed when first hooked, so a reel with a good disk drag is essential. My personal preference is a Ross G-4 or a SW-III that will handle any battle these guys may put up. There are other excellent reels for this application; make sure you use one that's well built.

Barry Reynolds, along with John Berryman (authors of *Pike on a Fly*), suggests, "I like to start the day with a slow retrieve, no more than 4- to 6-inch strips. As the water warms, I'll make adjustments. Faster intervals between longer strips. Another important technique I use is changing the direction of the fly. Moving the fly up or to either side will often provoke a strike."

Wade to a depth you are comfortable with and start making systematic casts in all directions; this is referred to as fan casting. This is a very effective way to cover a lot of water in a short period of time. Oftentimes you may see a wake moving toward your fly soon after it hits the water. Hang on; more than likely you'll get hit. Other times, a pike may follow your fly all the way in to your feet, then take it and scare the hell out of you. Either way, this is exciting fishing.

Camping is not allowed in the Spinney Mountain State Wildlife area. However, Elevenmile Reservoir, just downstream, has 300 campsites.

Lake Facts: Spinney Mountain Reservoir

Seasons
- Lake is closed during the winter. Normally opens after ice off, generally in mid-April.

Special regulations
- State Parks Pass required.
- Artificial flies and lures only.
- Bag and possession limit for trout is 1 fish, 20 inches or longer.
- Fishing allowed ½ hour after sunrise to ½ hour after sunset.
- Bag and possession limit for northern pike is 10 fish, no more than 1 greater than 34 inches.

Trout
- Rainbows over 24 inches inhabit this rich impoundment.
- Snake River Cutthroat; the biggest I have heard of was 13 pounds.
- Browns are present in fewer numbers, but are healthy brutes.

Other species
- Northern Pike
- Kokanee salmon

Lake size
- 2520 acres

Lake character
- The water depth goes to about 55 feet at the dam, but averages 10 to 20 feet in the bays and inlet areas. Weed beds thrive in all the bays and flats. Tremendous amounts of food cause trout to call these weed beds home. This very diverse food source grows trout to trophy class. Spring is a great time to fish here, as the trout are on the move and very active.

Maps
- Fish-n-Map Company, 303-421-5994

SPINNEY MOUNTAIN RESERVOIR MAJOR HATCHES

Insect	A	M	J	J	A	S	O	N	Time	Flies
Midge									M/A/E	Olive Biot Midge #12–#18; Brown Biot Midge #12–#18; Blood Midge #12–#18; Feather Duster Midge #14–#20; Black Beauty Pupa #12–#18; CDC Biot Suspender Midge #12–#18; Griffith's Gnat #12–#20; Palomino Midge #12–#20; Gray Soft Hackle #12–#18
Scuds									M/A/E	Olive Scud #12–#16; Orange Scud #10–#16; 19½ Scud #12–#18; Tan Scud #12–#16; Flashback Scud #12–#16
Crawfish									M/A/E	Prince Nymph #8–#10; Halfback #4–#10; Beadhead Prince Nymph #8–#10; Kaufmann's Brown Stonefly #4–#8; Steve's BRO Bug #6–#10; Whitlock's Crawfish #4–#10; Kaufmann's Crawfish #4–#8
Callibaetis									M/A	Olive Biot Nymph #14–#16; Ginger Hare's Ear #14–#16; RS-2 #14–#16; Pheasant Tail Nymph #12–#16; Beadhead Pheasant Tail Nymph #14–#16; Flashback Pheasant Tail Nymph #14–#16; Olive Quill Emerger #16–#18; Parachute Adams #12–#16; Gray Comparadun #12–#16; Rusty Spinner #12–#16
Damselflies									M/A	Swimming Damsel #8–#12; Flashback Damsel #8–#12; Paradamsel #8–#12; Crystal-winged Damsel #8–#12; Stalcup's Adult Damselfly #8–#12
Streamers									M/E	Black Woolly Bugger #2–#10; Brown Woolly Bugger #4–#10; Purple Woolly Bugger #4–#10; Platte River Special #4–#10; Spruce Fly #4–#10; Dark Spruce Fly #4–#10; Black-nosed Dace #6–#8

HATCH TIME CODE: M = morning; A = afternoon; E = evening; D = dark; SF = spinner fall; / = continuation through periods

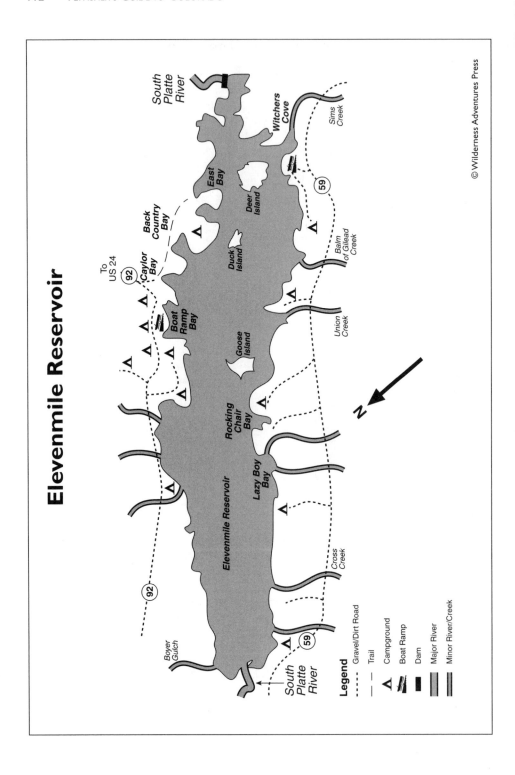

ELEVENMILE RESERVOIR

Like Spinney Mountain, US 24 is the main road to and from Elevenmile Reservoir. As you drop down the west side of Wilkerson Pass on US 24, look for the sign directing you to Spinney Mountain and Elevenmile Reservoirs. Turn left (south) on CR 23 and follow it to the tee in the road. Turn left on CR 592 (turning right takes you to Spinney Mountain). Continue on this road to the reservoir. A State Parks permit is required.

Another option, and a quicker route, is to take FR 247 south from US 24 at the west side of Lake George. This is a much more scenic drive.

Elevenmile is known for its big trout and northern pike. However, it is primarily a bait fishing lake and carries an 8-fish bag and possession limit. For some reason, the majority of dignified flyfishermen shy away from these unrestricted waters; after all, Spinney is just a few minutes away. However, a few sites and events are definitely worthy of investigation.

There is an awesome event that occurs at Elevenmile Reservoir in June. I know you'll think I'm crazy, but I wouldn't mention this if it wasn't so damn much fun.

Jim Neiberger and I were fishing a PMD hatch below Spinney Mountain on the South Platte several years ago when one of those South Park squalls came through, raining and hailing us off the river. For about an hour we watched as the river got wiped out by streamside flooding. It was only 2:00 in the afternoon, the weather was clearing, and we didn't want to head home just yet. Neiberger suggested we go to the inlet area of Elevenmile, as he wanted to check something out.

We parked on the southwest end of the lake at the first fishing access, jumped out, and headed to the water. What I saw next was definitely a first for me. Carp, big carp well over 10 pounds, were coming clean out of the water and tail walking like a tarpon trying to throw a Chico's cockroach, hitting the water with a resounding belly flop.

Neiberger told me to load up a #6 halfback nymph with 3X tippet, "It's a close imitation of a crawfish. This lake is loaded with them." I couldn't believe it, and my hands were shaking. I got it tied on, finally, and waded out. These huge fish were jumping everywhere, some so close I could touch them with my rod tip.

Jim caught one of about 7 or 8 pounds. This fish battled for all he was worth. Ten to fifteen minutes later, he had this gnarly looking thing at his feet. Totally unbelievable.

Hey, this is bait water; what do you expect from an exalted couple of hackers?

June also presents the best window for the fly angler to hook a 20-pound northern pike. After the pike have spawned, they like to hang out in the warm shallow bays looking for an easy meal, sometimes in less than a foot of water.

Look for water temperatures in the high fifties to mid-sixties while on your hunt for the big fish. Testing the water with a thermometer, instead of a blind cast, can save a lot of time in determining where to fish. Shallows warm at different rates during the day, depending on sun and wind direction. The shallows on the northwest side of the lake and the bays on the south side should be checked out by 11:00 AM. Continue your search until early evening.

Cover is another important element to successful pike fishing. This predator likes to lie in wait and attack from thick vegetation or submerged structure. Cast near

Big flies for pike on Elevenmile Reservoir.

these areas with a black bunny fly or a deer-hair popper for some possible "dry fly" action. Vary your retrieve from slow to fast, short to long, and everything in between. There is no set way to do things that will work every time.

Barry Reynolds observes, "One of the most frustrating things about pike is the follow. They come in behind your fly and follow it, sometimes all the way to your feet." He adds, "This can happen cast after cast. I try to take it away from them, just like a bait fish may try to escape the jaws of death. A fast, foot-long retrieve in front of the pike or taking your rod tip to the side and pulling the fly into the pike's side view can produce a quick lunging strike."

Generally speaking, a slower retrieve is best when the water is in the 50s; i.e., earlier in the day. Pick up the pace and length of your retrieve as the water warms towards midafternoon.

Once the water temperature is near 70 degrees, generally occurring in late July and August, the pike will head for deeper, cooler water; unfortunately, this is somewhat out of the fly angler's range. However, the fish still like to visit the shallow water in the early mornings and late evenings for breakfast and dinner.

There is some normalcy for the flyfisher who wants to catch trout. This lake has all the goodies, including scuds, leeches, damsels and crawfish. Rainbows, browns, and Snake River cutthroat are well fed here and can grow to be "slabs". A favorite area for trout is in Witchers Cove, located in the southeast corner of the reservoir. Good structure, including sharp dropoffs and submerged rocks, provides excellent habitat.

A very good damselfly hatch occurs in July. The best fishing for this hatch is on the south side of the lake. The bays here have good vegetation growth and the damsels thrive in this environment.

There are 300 campsites available, and several fishing accesses surround the lake. Boat ramps are at the North Shore Campground and Witchers Cove.

Lake Facts: Elevenmile Reservoir

Seasons
- For flyfishing, from ice-out to ice-on.

Special Regulations
- State Parks pass required.
- Bag and possession limit for trout is 8 fish, no more than 2 longer than 16 inches.
- Bag and possession limit for Northern Pike is 10 fish, no more than 1 greater than 34 inches.

Trout
- Rainbow over 20 inches are common.
- Browns are large. Spawners can be found in the inlet area in the fall.
- Snake River cutthroat.

Other Species
- Northern Pike
- Carp
- Kokanee salmon

Lake Size
- 3300 acres

Lake Character
- A long lake, with bays and inlet areas on both the north and south sides of the lake. Good structural fishing, lots of outcroppings and stream channels. Good lake for float tubing, but wind can hamper mobility.

Maps
- Fish-n-Map Company, 303-421-5994

ELEVENMILE RESERVOIR MAJOR HATCHES

Insect	A	M	J	J	A	S	O	N	Time	Flies
Midge									M/A/E	Olive Biot Midge #12–#18; Brown Biot Midge #12–#18; Blood Midge #12–#18; Feather Duster Midge #14–#20; Black Beauty Pupa #12–#18; CDC Biot Suspender Midge #12–#18; Griffith's Gnat #12–#20; Palomino Midge #12–#20
Crawfish									M/A/E/D	Prince Nymph #8–#10; Halfback #4–#10; Beadhead Prince Nymph #8–#10; Kaufmann's Brown Stonefly #4–#8; Steve's BRO Bug #6–#10; Whitlock's Crawfish #4–#10; Kaufmann's Crawfish #4–#8
Damselflies									M/A	Swimming Damsel #8–#12; Flashback Damsel #8–#12; Paradamsel #8–#12; Crystal-winged Damsel #8–#12; Stalcup's Adult Damselfly #8–#12
Callibaetis									M/A	Olive Biot Nymph #14–#16; RS-2 #14–#16; Pheasant Tail Nymph #12–#16; Beadhead Pheasant Tail Nymph #14–#16; Flashback Pheasant Tail Nymph #14–#16; Olive Quill Emerger #16–#18; Parachute Adams #12–#16; Gray Comparadun #12–#16; Rusty Spinner #12–#16
Scuds									M/A/E/D	Olive Scud #12–#16; Orange Scud #10–#16; 19½ Scud #12–#18; Tan Scud #12–#16; Flashback Scud #12–#16
Streamers									M/E/D	Black Woolly Bugger #2–#10; Brown Woolly Bugger #4–#10; Purple Woolly Bugger #4–#10; Platte River Special #4–#10; Spruce Fly #4–#10; Dark Spruce Fly #4–#10; Black-nosed Dace #6–#8

HATCH TIME CODE: M = morning; A = afternoon; E = evening; D = dark; SF = spinner fall; / = continuation through periods

TARRYALL CREEK

Tarryall Creek is a tributary of the South Platte and enters the river about nine miles below Elevenmile Canyon. From US 24, just west of Lake George, turn right (north) on CR 77. Your first sighting of Tarryall Creek will be about 7 miles north.

Tarryall is not very popular with flyfishers due to the quality water along the South Platte in South Park. In addition, private water hampers access along most of the stream. In fact, accesses have changed so much lately, a 2-mile stretch of the creek above Tarryall Reservoir is the only sure place you can fish.

This small stream has primarily brown trout for sport, while rainbows come in a close second. Searching patterns such as golden stones, Prince nymphs, hare's ears, halfbacks, and San Juan worms should find a willing taker. There is some good pocket water above the reservoir, and you should concentrate your efforts in these areas. Expect to catch trout up to 12–14 inches. Some of the larger fish in the reservoir do migrate into this water to spawn in the spring and fall.

A state lease about a half-mile above the lake on the Eagle Rock Ranch is a good piece of water. Part of the creek runs through the landowner's back yard in clear view of the house; he does not mind passage through this area but would appreciate you not fishing this short stretch.

National forest access is at the confluence with the South Platte. Take FR 210 east from CR 77. A 2-mile trail at the end of this road leads to the confluence.

Tarryall Creek

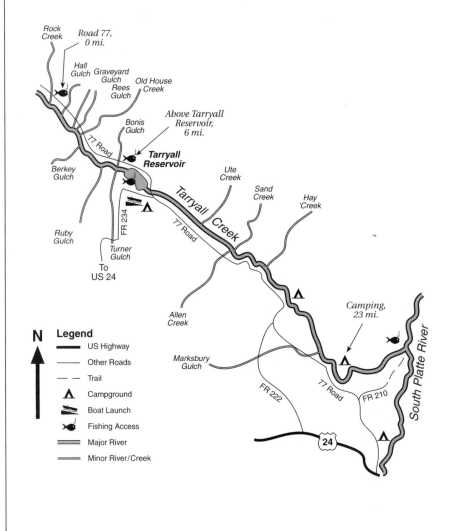

Rock Creek

Road 77, 0 mi.

Hall Gulch

Graveyard Gulch

Rees Gulch

Old House Creek

Bonis Gulch

Above Tarryall Reservoir, 6 mi.

Tarryall Reservoir

Berkey Gulch

Ute Creek

Sand Creek

Hay 'Creek

77 Road

Ruby Gulch

FR 234

77 Road

Turner Gulch

To US 24

Tarryall Creek

Allen Creek

Camping, 23 mi.

Marksbury Gulch

South Platte River

Legend

N

▬▬▬	US Highway
———	Other Roads
– – –	Trail
▲	Campground
🛶	Boat Launch
🐟	Fishing Access
▬▬▬	Major River
═══	Minor River/Creek

FR 222

77 Road

FR 210

24

© Wilderness Adventures Press

TARRYALL RESERVOIR

Located at the northern boundary of South Park, Tarryall can be found north of US 24 on CR 77. From US 24, just west of Lake George, turn right (north) on CR 77; the reservoir is found just over 20 miles on this road.

Tarryall Reservoir will ice off about May 1, and good trout fishing will start right away. Fishing from shore on the east side of the lake is possible since there are no trees or brush to get in the way and there is good structure for trout in search of an easy meal. Midge emergers and snail patterns under a strike indicator can hook a cruising trout. Snails often can be seen floating on the surface throughout the year.

As the shallows start to warm in June, northern pike can be found holding in 4 to 8 feet of water in the north end of the lake. Wading is possible, but this end of the lake is pretty soft from the silt; float tubes are best for fishing on Tarryall. A 7- to 9-weight rod is best for casting the heavy, air-resistant pike flies. Bunny flies, Clouser minnows, and Lefty deceivers are proven patterns for Mr. Esox. Slow, patient retrieves early in the day work best. By afternoon, the water warms, and the pike fishing improves. A faster, more erratic retrieve can entice quick, aggressive strikes.

The vegetation comes alive with insect activity by mid-June. Speckled mayflies will hatch in the morning along with midges. This is the best dry fly fishing opportunity of the year. Adams and parachute Adams in sizes 14 to 16 work well for the mayflies. Griffith's gnats and olive palomino midges in sizes 14 to 18 will cover fish rising to midges. A two fly setup covering both species is also a good idea unless it is very obvious which insect they are feeding on.

Damsel hatches follow in July and August. Nymphs start their migration in the late morning. Hoards of damsel nymphs swim towards shore and trout continue to feed on them throughout the afternoon. An olive marabou damsel nymph moving out of the weed beds towards shore is the best presentation to imitate the damsel movement.

Leeches, scuds, and small fish are year round food sources. Imitations of them should be fished whenever there's no obvious feeding activity.

Camping and a boat ramp are available on the southwest corner of the lake.

Lake Facts: Tarryall Reservoir

Seasons
- For flyfishing, from ice-out to ice-on

Trout
- Rainbow trout
- Brown trout

Other Species
- Northern Pike

Lake Size
- 180 acres

Lake Character
- Located at 8,860 feet, this lake has good structure and excellent vegetation growth, providing shelter and a good food source for the fish species here. The north end of the lake, the inlet area, is very shallow, but the weed beds start to develop at about 8 feet and can be a good ambush area for the predatory northerns to hang out. Trout move in and out of the belly section of the lake where weed growth is best.

Boat Ramp
- Southwest corner of the lake

Maps
- Fish-n-Map Company, 303-421-5994
- Pike National Forest

TARRYALL RESERVOIR MAJOR HATCHES

Insect	A	M	J	J	A	S	O	N	Time	Flies
Midge		▓						▓	M/A/E	Olive Biot Midge #12–#18; Brown Biot Midge #12–#18; Blood Midge #12–#18; Feather Duster Midge #14–#20; Black Beauty Pupa #12–#18; CDC Biot Suspender Midge #12–#18; Griffith's Gnat #12–#20; Palomino Midge #12–#20
Snails and Scuds		▓						▓	M/A/E	Olive Scud #12–#16; Orange Scud #10–#16; 19½ Scud #12–#18; Tan Scud #12–#16; Flashback Scud #12–#16; Marty's Gray Snail #12–#14; Peacock Snail #12–#14
Damselflies					▓				M/A	Marabou Damsel Nymph #8–#12; Swimming Damsel #8–#12; Flashback Damsel #8–#12; Paradamsel #8–#12; Crystal-winged Damsel #8–#12; Stalcup's Adult Damselfly #8–#12
Callibaetis				▓					M/A	Olive Biot Nymph #14–#16; Ginger Hare's Ear #14–#16; RS-2 #14–#16; Pheasant Tail Nymph #12–#16; Beadhead Pheasant Tail Nymph #14–#16; Flashback Pheasant Tail Nymph #14–#16; Olive Quill Emerger #16–#18; Parachute Adams #12–#16; Gray Comparadun #12–#16; Rusty Spinner #12–#16
Streamers		▓						▓	M/A/E	Black Woolly Bugger #2–#10; Brown Woolly Bugger #4–#10; Spruce Fly #4–#10; Dark Spruce Fly #4–#10; Black-nosed Dace #6–#8

HATCH TIME CODE: M = morning; A = afternoon; E = evening; D = dark; SF = spinner fall; / = continuation through periods

SOUTH PARK HUB CITY
Fairplay

Population – 387 • Elevation – 9,953 • Area Code – 719

ACCOMMODATIONS
Bristlecone Pine Motel, 801 Main Street / 836-3278 / 12 units / Dogs allowed / $$
Fairplay Hotel and Restaurant, 500 Main Street / 836-2565 / 25 units / Dogs allowed / $$$
Western Inn Motel and RV Park, 490 West Highway 285 / 836-2026

BED AND BREAKFAST
Hand Hotel B and B, 531 Front Street / 836-3595 / Innkeeper: Coral Schayler / $$

CAMPING
Chaparral Park and General Store, 19015 CR 59 / 836-0308 / Located at Spinney Mountain Reservoir / 37 acres / 13 electric hook ups, over 50 primitive sites / Groceries and tackle

RESTAURANTS
Brown Burro Cafe, 706 Main Street / 836-2804 / Breakfast: 6AM–9PM / $
J Bar J Restaurant and Lounge, 410 South Highway 285 / 836-9971 / 7AM–10PM / Cocktails / $
The Mustard Seed, 21980½ South Highway 285 / 836-2883 / 6:30AM–8:30PM / Cocktails / $

SPORTING GOODS
Fairplay Country Store, 401 Main Street / 836-2903

HOSPITALS
Timberline Clinic, 980 Main Street / 836-3455

AIRPORTS
See Denver airports information

AUTO SERVICE
Fairplay Towing and Repair, 410 Highway 285 / 836-2966
South Park Auto, 22077 Highway 285 / 836-2748

FOR MORE INFORMATION
South Park Chamber of Commerce
620 Main Street
Fairplay, CO 80440
836-3410

South Central Colorado

 The Rio Grande and Conejos River are usually included with and considered southwest Colorado streams. However, unlike the other major rivers of southwest Colorado, these drainages are actually on the east side of the Continental Divide. In addition, prime rivers and streams in the southwest are numerous, and finding information is easier when they are separated from the Rio Grande and the Conejos.

The Rio Grande is a big, sprawling western river that offers many opportunities to the fly angler. A fast gradient stream, it offers lots of pocket water, many long riffles and deep runs, and much of the upper river produces good-sized trout, both browns and rainbows. The lower river, between South Fork and Del Norte, is slower and wider and has earned a designation as Gold Medal Water.

The Conejos drainage is fairly secluded for its proximity to major population centers and does not get the pressure of the more famous trout rivers in the state.

As you drive south out of Alamosa, you would never guess a great trout stream is just an hour away. Even as Colorado 17 directs you west and your creative imagination is dreaming of a trout stream, the views don't give much reassurance. Then, out of nowhere, the Conejos parallels the road, and your dream comes true. The Conejos is one of the prettiest rivers in Colorado, and it offers several miles of public access.

The Conejos River, its tributaries, and high mountain lakes in the region provide all types of flyfishing opportunity. Good insect hatches and superb dry flyfishing are their main offerings.

For the more athletically inclined flyfisher, small streams, miles of foot trails, and several high mountain lakes near the river's headwaters are tempting.

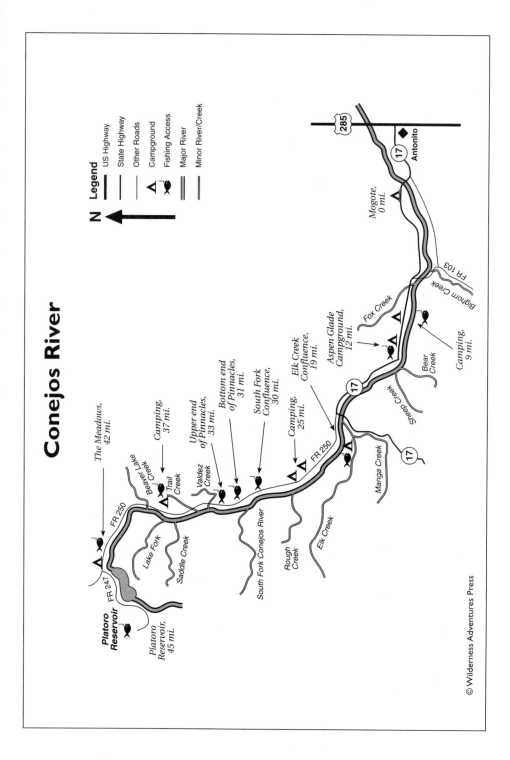

Conejos River

Legend
N
— US Highway
— State Highway
— Other Roads
▲ Campground
⚲ Fishing Access
— Major River
— Minor River/Creek

The Meadows, 42 mi.

Camping, 37 mi.

Beaver Lake
Beaver Creek
Trail Creek
FR 250

Upper end of Pinnacles, 33 mi.

Valdez Creek

Bottom end of Pinnacles, 31 mi.

South Fork Confluence, 30 mi.

Camping, 25 mi.

FR 250

Elk Creek Confluence, 19 mi.

Aspen Glade Campground, 12 mi.

17

Fox Creek

Camping, 9 mi.

Bear Creek

Sheep Creek

Manga Creek

17

Elk Creek

Rough Creek

South Fork Conejos River

Saddle Creek

Lake Fork

FR 250

Platoro Reservoir
FR 247

Platoro Reservoir, 45 mi.

Mogote, 0 mi.

FR 103

Bighorn Creek

285

17

Antonito

© Wilderness Adventures Press

CONEJOS RIVER

The Conejos River, "Conejos" meaning "rabbits" in Spanish, is one of the real sleepers when it comes to flyfishing opportunities in this state.

What few people realize is this: the Conejos and its tributaries provide seclusion from the crowded, more popular rivers in the state while offering unpressured fish in wild surroundings. That's a tough combination to find anywhere in the West today.

The main river is technically a tailwater below Platoro Reservoir. However, Randy Keys, who along with his wife Naomi run Cottonwood Meadows Fly Shop, says, "In my opinion the Conejos fishes much more like a freestone river than a tailwater."

An 8-mile stretch of water from Platoro to Lake Fork Campground is very good public water. Flowing through a meadow, the river has deep pools and riffles. However, low water flows during the winter induce heavy winter kills of trout, so the river maintains basically a put-and-take status. Most of its trout average 10 to 12 inches.

Below the campground, the river plunges into a canyon called the Pinnacles. This is definitely a trip for the more adventurous fly angler. A considerable walk, deep pools and tough currents await you if you choose to fish that section. This is flies and lures only water, with a 2 fish over 16-inch limit.

In the canyon, a flyfisher always holds an opportunity to take a 20-inch brown. There are some nice fish holding in its depths.

Below the Pinnacles, the river offers a mix of private and public water extending downstream to a point where Colorado 17 passes the river. Below that intersection, at Menkhaven, there is a flyfishing-only stretch that offers a beautiful mix of water for 4 miles. Public access to the river can also be found at the Aspen Glade and Mogote Campgrounds.

There are some excellent early season opportunities on the Conejos, although flows generally begin picking up by April 1. The river will fish well until mid-May, when the water rises and turns off-color.

Prior to and during runoff, nymphs offer anglers their best chances for success. You are not going to see much surface activity during that time. Beadhead pheasant-tail nymphs in sizes 14 to 18 are local favorites. Midges and a few mayflies come off, but the browns and rainbows are not eager to come to the surface this early in the year. Instead, they'll sulk near the bottom and pick off those unfortunate nymphs.

"I like fishing high water after runoff has peaked and the water level is starting to decline," Keys says. "The last week in June is usually when this happens. The fish are pretty active at this time and have basically had little or no pressure for five or six months. A size 8 or 10 beadhead pattern, fished along the edges, is effective.

"The best approach to nymph fishing on the Conejos is to cast directly upstream and let the flies drift back to you."

The Conejos' first big hatch is that of the large stoneflies, which are often called salmonflies by the river's dedicated anglers. You can look for salmonflies in conjunction with elevated flows in May and June. This hatch moves upstream at a rather rapid rate and is short-lived. A good place to look for the hatch is the flyfishing-only water near Menkhaven.

The Conejos River offers a variety of habitat, and its riffles may be the best holding water during summer. Here, Shannon Skelton works a nice riffle with nymphs.

In high snowpack years, the hatch peaks while the water is very high. Wading and fishing is tough, but moving big brown or black stonefly nymphs through the pocket water near the bank and the edge of riffles provides good action.

Nymphs in sizes 4 or 6 imitate the migrating salmonflies. Low water years can provide an awesome opportunity to fish this hatch because the lower flows give the angler better access to the trout. Usually by mid-July the hatch is on its downslide.

Strong caddis hatches usually begin around July 1, and that marks the beginning of the best dry flyfishing of the year.

First to appear on the menu is a large, spotted caddis. Rainbows and browns up to 16 inches share the river equally and feed aggressively throughout the day on those large caddis.

A size 10 or 12 elk hair or Goddard caddis is the best imitation for the adult, while a LaFontaine sparkle caddis is the best emergent pattern. A nymph dropper drifted under a dry fly is also another good setup.

To fish a dropper, attach a piece of tippet about 18 inches long to the hook bend of the dry fly and add a hare's ear, green caddis, or pheasant tail in either beadhead or regular style to imitate any nymphs or emergers that are drifting along under the surface.

"I like to use glass bead patterns to add a little color and translucency to the fly, Keys says. "Again, I like to use an upstream cast and drift."

Micro caddis hatch the remainder of the summer, extending into mid-September. As with most caddis hatches, concentrate your efforts at the tail end of riffles, at slack water opportunities along the bank, and behind midstream boulders. High-floating caddis patterns from sizes 14 through 18 should cover any rising situation when caddis are involved.

Other hatches during the peak of the fishing season include several large mayflies.

Brown drakes start hatching in mid-June and last through early July. They look a lot like a green drake but are darker in color. This hatch can be heavy at times and can fill the evening sky with thousands of insects. Brown paradrakes and standard brown drake patterns should be at least a size 12 to imitate this mayfly. Explosive dry fly action awaits the evening angler.

Red quills are on the water from late June to mid-July. An AK's Western red quill can move several fish. When fishing that hatch, cast to a rising fish, and only to that fish; this is always the best approach for a successful day.

To confuse matters, there can be multiple hatches at this time of year. Fortunately, a well presented fly is usually more important than a precise imitation. If need be, take the time to identify a specific insect that a trout is rising to and match it. Focus on the size of the fly first, then the silhouette, and finally concern yourself with color. This plan works more often than not.

Pale morning duns are the next mayfly to emerge, and you'll start to see them in mid- to late July. I have found trout all over the state particularly fond of this bug.

Floating nymphs and emerging patterns work well during the early stages of this hatch, which occurs about 10:00 AM. Nymphs will emerge from the riffles and converge into feeding lanes as they drift downstream. Watch pockets along the banks and the slicks behind the bigger rocks for rising trout. A size 16 pheasant-tail nymph is one of the best imitations for the PMD nymph. A light olive emerger pattern, light comparadun, or parachute dun in sizes 14 through 18 should cover any surface action you encounter.

Terrestrials become important in August and early September. Hoppers, ants, and beetles become food sources during the midday hours. Stimulators, Royal Wulffs, and humpies of all colors ranging from size 12 to 16 are good attractor flies. Peacock beetles #16, black ants #18, and size 10 hoppers are more specific imitations of the terrestrials themselves.

In the fall, the Conejos lights up in a sea of crimson and gold, making it one of the prettiest trout streams in the state. Fall colors mark the beginning of the blue-winged olive hatch, and that can really turn the trout on. Then, as the snow flies and water temperature cools, flyfishers are faced with the proposition of midge fishing the rest of the winter.

There is camping, primitive and improved, all along the river. Campsites can fill up quickly on weekends in July and August, so plan ahead or try to arrive a day early. Lodging and RV sites are located in the town of Mogote.

Shannon Skelton nymphing a prime run on the Conejos River.

To reach the Conejos from Interstate 25 at Walsenburg, take US 160 to Alamosa. From Alamosa, go south just under 30 miles on US 285 to Antonito. Turn west on Colorado 17 to the town of Mogote. Cottonwood Meadows Fly Shop is located here and can provide you with up-to-date fishing information, flow rates, and lodging.

Just past Menkhaven you must take FR 250 to reach the upper river. Three Forks, about 4 miles above Platoro Reservoir is where the North Fork, Middle Fork, and the Rio Azul meet to form the Conejos River. From the southern end of Platoro Reservoir, a trailhead leads you back into the headwaters.

Tributaries of the Conejos

Elk Creek

Elk Creek is a major tributary of the Conejos and is well worth a visit when you are flyfishing in southcentral Colorado.

There is access to the creek at Elk Creek Campground, located adjacent to Colorado 17 just past the intersection with FR 250. This part of the stream is stocked with rainbows and receives a fair amount of pressure. Another access is about a mile past the campground entrance road at the La Manga trailhead. These accesses are good for a quick stop to check out the stream.

You could spend your time more wisely by walking up the Elk Creek trail. This trail follows the stream for 12 miles and can be moderately difficult to navigate. The first part of the stream you will encounter is fast pocket water as it flows through a tight canyon. The trail is above the stream and the walk into and out of this canyon can test your endurance. The fishing can be difficult, without much room to work. The tight quarters require a rod of 8 feet or less and leaders of 7.5 feet.

Golden stones inhabit this tumbling stretch of water, and just about any large nymph, such as Prince nymphs and halfbacks, will hook rainbows, browns, and brook trout in the 10- to 12-inch range. However, dropping a big dry fly on the water can provide exciting takes.

Any obstruction in the stream may provide a resting spot for trout, and every piece of slack water should be tested with a quick presentation.

High-floating attractor flies like size 12 Royal Wulffs, humpies, a Madam X, and bivisibles look like a big meal and produce quick and aggressive rises.

Continuing upstream a couple miles will bring you to the first of three meadow sections. Tactics must change as you start fishing the slower, more technical water. A quiet approach and keeping your silhouette off the water are critical.

Pale morning duns hatch in the meadow section during July and early August. This hatch will test all your casting and presentation skills on this slow, clear water. Light olive comparaduns or thorax style flies in sizes 14 to 16 give the trout a nice low-riding presentation.

The second meadow is over 6 miles from Elk Creek campground, and an overnight trip is usually needed to explore any farther upstream. The trout in the second meadow have seen fewer people. This means they are larger and not as skittish. That, of course, means you should try to cast a fly there if you can.

Lake Fork

Lake Fork is accessed by a trail south of Lake Fork Campground at the intersection with FR 105. The trail follows the stream for several miles and provides solitude and great dry flyfishing for the angler willing to get off the beaten path.

Lake Fork is a tumbling little stream full of pockets and clear pools. For the small stream connoisseur, it's a treat to fish here.

Fallen timber and undercuts provide excellent trout habitat. Rio Grande cutthroat abound, and they are protected by catch and release regulations.

Those fish are eager to pounce on caddis or stonefly imitations, especially when those bugs are present on the water.

In my mind, you should go to Lake Fork with the intention of strictly catching trout on a dry fly. Any number of flies will do; elk hair caddis, stimulators, Royal Wulffs, renegades, and an Adams in sizes 12 to 16 are all effective.

Stream Facts: Conejos River

Seasons
- Open all year

Special Regulations
- On Bear Creek Subdivision, H.E.B.O. Corporation properties, and the Douglas properties from Aspen Glade campground upstream approximately 4 miles to Menkhaven, public use prohibited except for flyfishing with artificial flies only. Bag and possession limit for trout is 2 fish, 16 inches or longer.
- From Saddle Creek Bridge downstream to and including the Hamilton property at the confluence of the Conejos river and the South Fork of the Conejos River; all waters on the Hamilton property subject to these regulations: Artificial flies and lures only. Bag and possession limit for trout is 2 fish, 16 inches or longer.
- From the Menkhaven Ranch downstream to Aspen Glade Campground: Wild Trout Water. Bag and possession limit for trout is 2 fish, 16 inches or longer.
- Lake Fork of the Conejos River regulated as Wild Trout Water, artificial flies and lures only. Cutthroat must be released immediately.

Trout
- Rainbows: average fish is in the 12- to 16-inch range.
- Browns share the river 50/50 with rainbows.
- Rio Grande cutthroat are available, yet protected, in the upper reaches and tributaries.
- Brook trout are also available above Platoro Reservoir and in high lakes.

River Miles
- Mogote—0
- Glade Campground—12
- Elk Creek confluence—19
- Spectacle Lake Campground Fishing Access—27
- South Fork confluence—30
- Trailhead for the South Fork, bottom of Pinnacles—31
- Top of Pinnacles—33
- The Meadows—42
- Platoro Reservoir—45

River characteristics
- The Conejos has just about every type of water a river could possibly have. Small stream conditions above Platoro can be reached via foot trail. Below Platoro is a wide meadow stream with deep pools, undercut banks, and riffles. The canyon water of the Pinnacles is deep, fast, pocket water, and it offers the best opportunity to catch some of the biggest trout in the river. Below the canyon is a varying stream with a mix of pocket water, deeper runs, corner pools, and riffles.

River Flows
- Winter, a meager 7 cfs is not uncommon
- Spring, April through mid May, 50 cfs
- Runoff, June, 300–500 cfs
- Summer, July and August, 200–300 cfs
- Fall, September and October, 50–100 cfs

Maps
- *Colorado Atlas & Gazetteer*, pages 89 & 90
- Rio Grande National Forest

CONEJOS RIVER MAJOR HATCHES

Insect	A	M	J	J	A	S	O	N	Time	Flies
Midge									M/A/E	Olive Biot Midge #16–#24; Brown Biot Midge #16–#24; Black Beauty #16–#24; Brassie #16–#24; Blood Midge #16–#24; Miracle Nymph #16–#20; AK's Midge Larva #16–#22; Black Beauty Pupa #18–#24; CDC Biot Suspender Midge #18–#24; Griffith's Gnat #16–#22; Palomino Midge #18–#22
Caddis									A/E	Olive Caddis Nymph #10–#20; Breadcrust #10–#18; Beadhead Breadcrust #10–#18; Buckskin #16–#20; LaFontaine's Sparkle Caddis Pupa #10–#20; Elk Hair Caddis #10–#22; Goddard Caddis #10–#16; CDC Caddis #14–#20; Macramé Caddis #12–#16; Balloon Caddis #12–#16; Lawson's Caddis Emerger #14–#18
Stonefly									M/A	Sandy's Gold #6–#10; Gold-winged Prince Nymph #8–#10; Kaufmann's Golden Stonefly #6–#12; Stimulator #8–#12; Foam Yellow Sally #12–#18; Halfback #4–#10; Prince Nymph #8–#16; Beadhead Prince Nymph #8–#16; Kaufmann's Brown Stonefly #4–#8; Sofa Pillow #6–#8; Stimulator #8–#12; Bitch Creek Nymph #10
Brown Drake									A/E	Brown Drake Emerger #10–#12; Parachute Green Drake #10–#12; Brown Drake #10–#12; Adams #10–#12; Dark Hare's Ear #10–#12

HATCH TIME CODE: M = morning; A = afternoon; E = evening; D = dark; SF = spinner fall; / = continuation through periods.

CONEJOS RIVER MAJOR HATCHES (CONT.)

Insect	A	M	J	J	A	S	O	N	Time	Flies
Pale Morning Dun				█					M/A	Biot PMD Nymph #16; Pheasant Tail Nymph #16–#22; Beadhead Pheasant Tail Nymph #14–#20; Lt. Cahill Comparadun #12–#18; Sparkle Dun #14–#18; Parachute PMD #14–#18; Dark Hare's Ear #14–#18; Olive Comparadun #14–#16
Red Quill				█					M/A	AK's Red Quill #14–#18; Rusty Spinner #12–#20
Terrestrial					█	█			A/E	Rio Grande King Trude #8–#16; Royal Wulff #10–#16; Humpy #10–#16; Foam Madam X #8–#12; Renegade #10–#16; Black Ant #14–#20; Gartside Hopper #8–#10; Henry's Fork Hopper #8–#12; Peacock Beetle #12–#18
Blue-winged Olive					█		█		M/A	Olive Biot Nymph #18–#22; RS-2 #16–#24; Pheasant Tail Nymph #16–#20; Beadhead Pheasant Tail Nymph #16–#22; Flashback Pheasant Tail Nymph #16–#20; Olive Quill Emerger #18–#24; AK's Olive Quill #16–#22; Parachute Adams #12–#22; Olive Comparadun #16–#20; Gray Spinner #18–#24; Slate Thorax Dun #16–#22
Streamers					█			█	M/E	Black Woolly Bugger #2–#10; Brown Woolly Bugger #4–#10; Platte River Special #4–#10; Spruce Fly #4–#10; Dark Spruce Fly #4–#10; Black-nosed Dace #6–#8; Muddler Minnow #4–#10

HATCH TIME CODE: M = morning; A = afternoon; E = evening; D = dark; SF = spinner fall; / = continuation through periods.

Platoro Reservoir

Platoro Reservoir was built in 1947 for irrigation needs in the lower valley. It has a good population of stocked rainbows and kokanee salmon. Browns pushing a few pounds can be caught on occasion. This lake is easy to access from FR 250 as you follow the Conejos River upstream. The lake rests at 10,000 feet and is late opening for any flyfishing. Mid-June through early July is the best time to attempt a trip to this lake.

High Mountain Lakes Near the Conejos River

There are several walk-in and backpacking opportunities in the Conejos River area for the adventurous angler. One thing is certain: the farther you get off the beaten path, the more trout you are sure to find.

All the lakes in the area fish about the same, and they are located in the 10,000- to 11,000-foot range. Access and fishing opportunity is limited to the warmer summer months.

All of the lakes hold populations of trout, mostly rainbows, brookies, Rio Grande cutthroat, and a brown trout or two.

Expect to see midge, mayfly, damselfly, and caddis activity throughout the short summer warm spell. Scuds can be found in most of these lakes. Don't forget woolly buggers—I haven't found many trout in a lake that won't feast on this leech pattern sometime during the day—or night, as far as that is concerned.

There are accesses to three lakes west of the Lake Fork Campground on FR 105. Big Lake, Bear Lake, and Tobacco Lake have some of the best potential for larger trout.

The forest roads in the area are definitely made for four-wheel drive vehicles. Be prepared for difficult travel, as the roads are slick from melting snow and rain showers much of the summer. The foot trails can be strenuous due to the radical elevation changes.

Big Lake

Big Lake is populated by Rio Grande cutthroat and brown trout. The lake is managed as catch and release to maintain the cutthroats.

Not an easy lake to get to, anglers must follow a trailhead south of the Lake Fork Campground for 5 miles over plenty of downed timber, uphill all the way.

Another option is to take FR 105, a four-wheel drive road, west from FR 250. Nearly 6 miles up FR 105, FR 100 takes off to the right. Follow FR 100 to a trailhead leading to Big Lake. A shorter walk, but a 1,000-foot change in elevation in a mile, makes the trip back to the fishing car a tough one. Take care.

Mid- to late summer is the best time to take on this challenge. Callibaetis and caddis can provide good surface action at that time.

Bear Lake

About a mile up FR 105 from FR 250 is the trailhead for Bear Lake. This laborious, 3-mile climb takes you nearly 2,000 feet uphill to the lake. Not easy! Your reward for the hike, however, is an opportunity to catch large brook, rainbow, and brown trout to 20 inches. You'll also find good surface fishing with Griffith's gnats, a parachute Adams, and gray comparaduns in sizes 14 to 18. Orange and olive scud patterns in sizes 12 to 16, fished early in the morning and late in the evening, are your best bets for hooking large fish. Streamers such as woolly buggers and bright colored bucktails also take a few of the more aggressive trout.

Tobacco Lake

This glacial lake sits at the base of Conejos Peak, 11,000 feet above sea level. Tobacco Lake is the highest of the three in this area and has cutthroat trout up to 18 inches. When trout get this big in a high mountain lake you can count on scuds being part of their diet, so pack a few along with you.

The trailhead is located about 10 miles up FR 105 from FR 250. FR 105 can be pretty rough this far from the main road. The lake is more than a mile from the trailhead with about 800 feet of elevation change.

Other South Central Lake Opportunities

Smith Reservoir

Smith reservoir is located about 4 miles south of Blanca. From US 160, turn south on CR 12 and follow the road to the Smith Reservoir State Wildlife Area.

Smith is best known as a bait fishing lake for weekend campers. Lawn chairs, forked sticks holding up a pole loaded with power bait, and Coleman coolers full of icy cold beer are the most common shoreline decor, so you better decide if you can handle that situation before heading to Smith.

All of the parking areas and the boat ramp are on the west and south sides of the lake. This is where the majority of people hang out. If you can get by all of the elitist and webbed-feet jokes long enough to get in the water, a quick kick over to the east side of the lake can provide a quality flyfishing experience. The west side of the lake has a rocky bottom that holds good fish. It's worth a quick drift up and down with a woolly bugger before you wave good bye to the gang on the bank.

I wouldn't have brought this lake to your attention if it hadn't been for the fish. The rainbow trout in this lake average a surprising 16 to 18 inches and are fat from a seafood diet of scuds and snails.

John Brandstatter, an employee for the state wildlife programs and frequent visitor to the area, explains, "The vegetation growth on the east side of the lake keeps most of the bait fisherman away, but is prime water for a flyfisherman."

Inside the weed beds is an incredible biomass of food. Scuds and snails are prolific, with the scuds reaching an inch or better in length, almost big enough for human consumption. Sizes 8 through 12 olive, tan, and orange scud patterns work well throughout the year.

Damselflies, mayflies, and midges hatch with regularity, with the damselfly hatch in late May being the most important to the fly angler. Large numbers of those insects migrate though the vegetation heading for shore. Normally the hatch starts during late morning, and the nymphs will be swimming fairly close to the surface.

Smith Reservoir

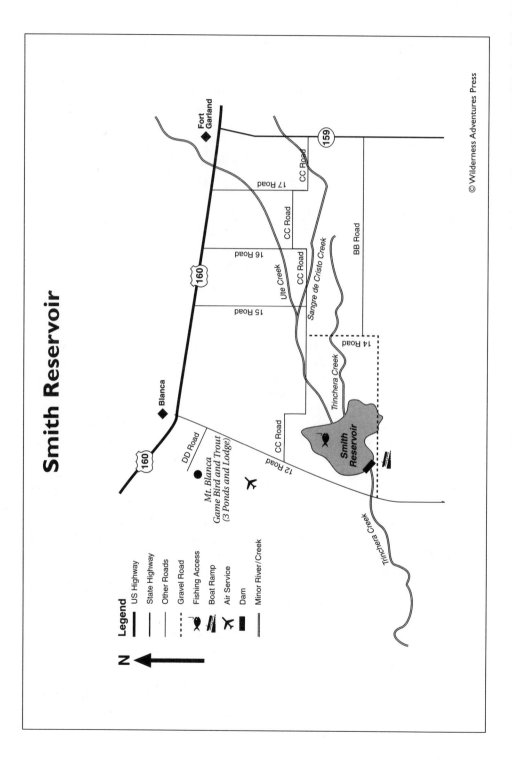

© Wilderness Adventures Press

They use their big gills, what some people would call tails, to aid in the propelling force as they wiggle their bodies much like a small fish. Imitating this movement with your fly should be thought out not only with the retrieve, but with the fly design as well. A swimming damsel nymph with a marabou tail about half the length of the body helps imitate the side to side movement of the natural. Sizes 10 to 14 should be good for the overall length of the nymph.

Your retrieve should be very consistent and 4 inches in length. Very little, if any, split shot should be used because the nymphs are traveling so close to the surface.

Here's a nifty little trick that works well when trying to imitate the swimming action of a damsel nymph: when your leader comes off the reel or when you pull a new one out of the bag, leave the butt section curled and straighten only the front half. After you make the cast, let the fly settle a few seconds, then make a strip. This tightens up the leader. When you pause, the leader will try to coil back up, making an erratic up and down, side to side movement. You will be surprised how long that darn leader will stay curled. It will take quite a few heavy fish and long fights to lose this effect.

Prior to the hatches in May, any combination of a scud and halfback, peacock snail and damsel nymph, or a straight-up woolly bugger can be effective stripped, inched, or jigged in and around the weed beds. By late June, the weed beds can be unmanageable. It's time to hit the streams again and leave Smith Reservoir until next year.

Mt. Blanca Game Bird and Trout

A resort located about 3.5 miles south of US 160, Mount Blanca provides trophy trout fishing in three private ponds. For those of you who also like to bird hunt, package deals can be put together to provide excellent hunting for pheasant, chukar, and quail. Beautiful accommodations and a reasonably priced restaurant provide a relaxing atmosphere. Contact Ray Lukondi or Bill Binnian at 719-379-3825 or 379-3681 for more information.

Bob Hufman is the flyfishing guide for Mt. Blanca and the person in charge of taking care of the ponds. It's a job made easy by a couple of important factors: the ponds are aerated during winter to prevent winter kill, and they are fed by natural warm springs—a perfect environment for trophy rainbows and brown trout.

Many trout over 20 inches are caught every year. Fishing is catch and release only, and angling pressure is dispersed evenly over the three ponds so the trout are not being hooked on a regular basis. This is good for the visiting angler. The trout are not leader shy, so 5X can be used for most dry flyfishing and 4X is used for nymphing. Standard 8- or 9-foot rods handling a 5- or 6-weight line are ideal for these 10-acre ponds. Make sure a float tube is on your list of things to bring.

There are several species of trout here. Donaldson trout are stocked at about 8 inches and are now topping out at 14 inches. They are very strong fighters and jump like trout possessed. Rainbows and cuttbows have a strong hold in the lakes and average 16 to 20 inches, with a few well over 20 and pushing 10 pounds. Again, these trout are stocked in the 4- to 8-inch range and grow at a pace the lakes allow, which is very quickly. Browns are well established and average 2 to 3 pounds. Hooking a 6- to 7-pounder is not uncommon. Late September and October are the best times to pursue a trophy brown. And, last but not least, one of the lakes has a good brook trout population. Don't be surprised if you latch onto a 3- to 4-pound brookie!

Prime flyfishing starts in April. Good hatches of cream-colored midges draw these trout to the surface during the warmer afternoons. A size 18 cream midge sitting on the top will do the trick. Later in the month and into May a black midge shows up, and a black beauty midge emerger, size 18, is the productive pattern.

Hufman said, "We had a huge gray mayfly hatch the first week of May in 1997. This was the first time we've seen this insect, but the trout seemed to know it very well. They didn't hesitate to sip in every one they saw. I think it shows the overall health of our ponds."

Callibaetis follow shortly after, as do damselflies. When I questioned the early time frame for these hatches, Hufman answered, "Natural springs that feed the lakes warm the temperature of the water nearly 5 degrees higher than any other water nearby. So hatches always seem to be two, maybe three weeks earlier than normal."

The Callibaetis are easily matched with a size 12, 14 or 16 parachute Adams in the late morning. A rusty spinner is used for the egg laying stage as the mayfly dies in the surface film.

A swimming damsel nymph with the distinctive bead eyes is one of Hufman's favorite flies for the damsel hatch. "I like the heavier eyes so I don't have to cast the dreaded split shot," he said. "Working the fly toward the shore in a slow rhythmical motion draws the most strikes. Sizes 8 through 12 in light olive, tan, and brown will cover most situations. Any adult damsel pattern will take fish from the surface late in the afternoon as the damsels are hovering over the water."

Hufman thinks the main food sources are the flathead minnows, leeches, and suckers that live here. The regular black and a spotted brown leech can be found throughout the lakes.

"A sink tip line should be packed right next to the American Express card—don't leave home without it," Hufmann said. "I usually try to get my clients to fish streamers at least one time during the day."

Black and brown woolly buggers, muddler minnows, and black zonkers are all effective. Other nymph patterns to add to your box for a trip to Mt. Blanca are beadhead hare's ears, Prince nymphs, zug bugs and Carey specials. Dry flies to add are an orange stimulator, Rio Grande King trude, and a renegade.

I encourage you to give Mt. Blanca a try—you shouldn't be disappointed. Its opportunities really typify the south central part of the state. Friendly folks, great weather, and excellent fishing.

Sanchez Reservoir

To reach Sanchez Reservoir from US 160 in Fort Garland, take Colorado 159 south about 15 miles to San Luis. Take a left (southeast) on CR P.6, 3 miles to CR 21. Turn right (south) on CR 21 and continue for 5 miles to the entrance of Sanchez Reservoir State Wildlife Area.

Sanchez is a prime northern pike fishery with most of its fish averaging 25 inches. John Brandstatter, a frequent flyfisherman at Sanchez said, "It's not

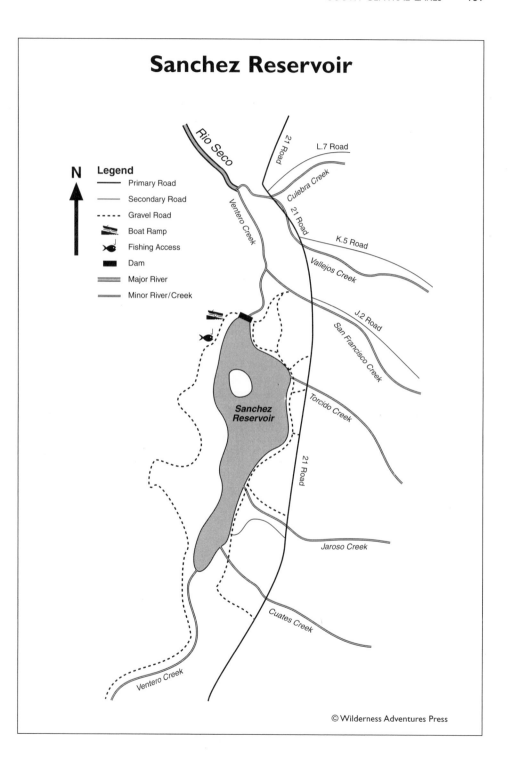

Sanchez Reservoir

Legend
— Primary Road
— Secondary Road
- - - Gravel Road
Boat Ramp
Fishing Access
Dam
Major River
Minor River/Creek

N

Rio Seco

21 Road

L.7 Road

Culebra Creek

Ventero Creek

21 Road

K.5 Road

Vallejos Creek

J.2 Road

San Francisco Creek

Torcido Creek

Sanchez
Reservoir

21 Road

Jaroso Creek

Cuates Creek

Ventero Creek

© Wilderness Adventures Press

They may not be as pretty as trout, but large carp can provide one heck of a battle on a light fly rod. John Brandstatter hoists a 16-pounder for the camera.

uncommon to catch 25 to 50 pike in a day here. Unlike most pike lakes, a bunny fly is not the best pattern here; it seems to be too big. A Lefty's deceiver, tied on a size 2 to size 1/0 hook is ideal. Colors to use should imitate the large numbers of perch that live here. Green bucktail on top, with a mixture of yellow, orange, and white for the sides of the fly works very well. Whenever I kill a pike, I check its stomach contents, and they have always been eating perch."

A 6-weight is plenty of rod for Sanchez, due to the smaller flies. A standard 9-foot leader with a steel tippet or heavy mono will land these fish. Brandstatter also takes a brown trout or two while fishing for the pike.

"There are not many trout in the lake because of the high summer temperatures, but a lunker brown trout may take your perch fly," he said. "A 5- to 8-pounder will put up one hell of a fight."

Carp are also a possibility here, although one that Brandstatter is a little reluctant to tell about. "I believe the biggest common carp in the state live in Sanchez," he said. "They probably average 15 pounds."

Carp are very skittish and spook easily. Sight fishing is the most fun, and you should be able to find them working any shallow water within casting range. Presentation of the fly is critical. Casting the fly far enough in front of the cruising carp, so water disturbance is held to a minimum, is a proven plan. When the carp moves into the vicinity of your imitation, give the fly a short strip, no longer than 4 inches. Pause and repeat the process. Bright shrimp patterns, damselfly nymphs, small halfbacks, and Carey specials work well for just about any carp.

Starting May 1, fishing becomes good for pike and carp, and it lasts through summer.

RIO GRANDE

Sometimes referred to as the Little Madison, the Rio Grande is among the best big western rivers in Colorado. The giant stonefly hatch here, also known as the salmonfly, is one of the most consistent hatches in the state. Big bugs and big water is the name of the game.

From below Rio Grande Reservoir to the town of Del Norte, the Rio Grande has some of the greatest water a trout stream could offer. In fact, the water from South Fork to Del Norte is Gold Medal Water, Colorado's highest rating for trout water. Very good mayfly hatches also occur in this stretch from mid-June through July, which is a great time to float the river.

In 1984, the Division of Wildlife stocked the river with a wild strain of rainbow trout from the Colorado River basin. Due to new regulations to help their survival, the rainbows took hold and are now doing quite nicely, although whirling disease is present and may reduce rainbow populations in the future. For that reason, all rainbows caught must be released back into the stream immediately. The Rio Grande's trout average 14 to 18 inches—quite good for a freestone river in Colorado.

To reach the upper river, from US 160 at South Fork take Colorado 149 northwest toward Creede. Stay on the road for about 35 miles to FR 520. Turn left (west) on FR 520 to the Rio Grande Reservoir. Starting below the reservoir, the river can be accessed by a short walk from the road. Thirty Mile and River Hill campgrounds are below the dam and also provide fishing access.

The Rio Grande, from the dam extending downstream about 8 miles, is located in the Weminuche Wilderness Area and is open to fishing.

In that section, the river is braided in places, creating several channels through this relatively flat stretch of water. It rates about 25 feet wide and can be covered with an easy cast. Willows line the bank along this water, so watch your backcast.

Late June and early July are the best times to reach this water. Depending on snowpack, the river may be high and difficult to wade at that time, but the salmonfly hatch has moved its way up here from the lower river and is well worth the struggle to reach.

When fishing salmonflies in that section, nymphing in the deep channels with halfbacks, Kaufmann's stones, and Bitch Creek nymphs proves productive for large, smart browns and rainbows. These fish see a lot of flies during the peak of the season, so well presented, drag-free drifts are required. Nine- to 10-foot rods with leaders up to 12 feet help with short line nymphing tactics. Make sure to get the fly down on the bottom. Several split shot may be needed to do so.

Green Drake and pale morning dun hatches can be excellent in July and early August. The water is much easier to wade by now, and searching out rising trout is great fun, a highly relaxing way to spend a day.

A size 10 or 12 parachute Adams is a favorite fly used by many locals. Standard green drake patterns also hook their share of fish. If the trout are onto PMDs, a size 14 to size 16 parachute Adams or a light olive PMD will do well.

Rio Grande
Rio Grande Reservoir to Wagon Wheel Gap

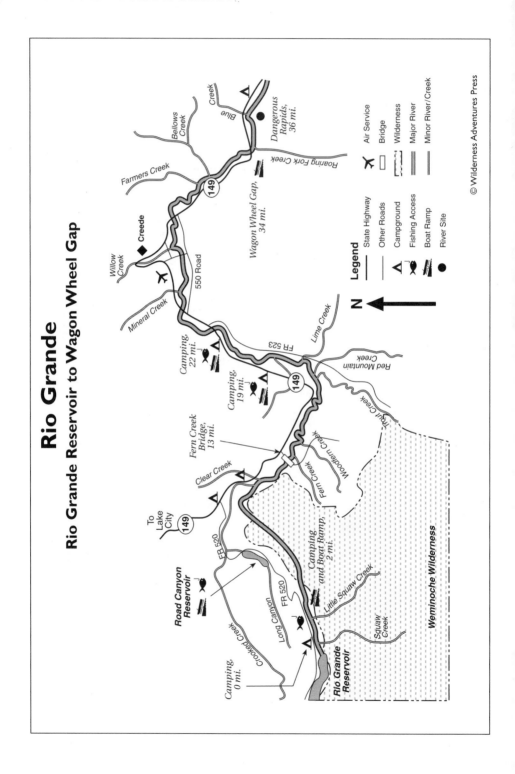

Legend

N

State Highway
Other Roads
Campground
Fishing Access
Boat Ramp
River Site

Air Service
Bridge
Wilderness
Major River
Minor River/Creek

© Wilderness Adventures Press

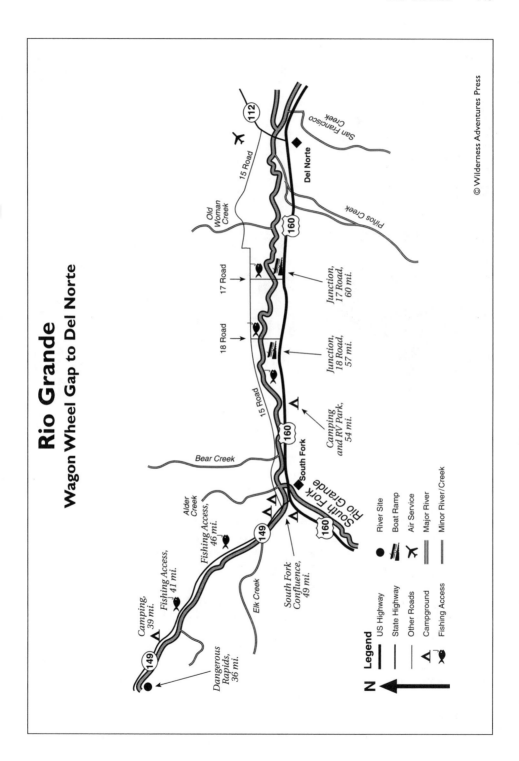

Rio Grande
Wagon Wheel Gap to Del Norte

Legend

N

US Highway	River Site
State Highway	Boat Ramp
Other Roads	Air Service
Campground	Major River
Fishing Access	Minor River/Creek

© Wilderness Adventures Press

The Rio Grande cuts through some of Colorado's most colorful country.

About 5 miles below the dam, the river pinches into the Box Canyon, also known as Six Mile Canyon. This rugged canyon is inaccessible during high water, and even damn hard to get to when the water is down. A 2-mile hike downstream from River Hill Campground is a bushwhacking adventure just to reach the canyon. Plan your day well; you will have to walk back out. Alternatively, pack your camping gear and spend the night. I haven't talked to any flyfisher who has tried to float the canyon (I may not have talked to enough fishermen), even though there is a boat ramp at River Hill. Most leave this for the more experienced rafters; many class three and some class four rapids are located in that stretch. However, these hidden pieces of water must offer good fishing if for no other reason than their remoteness.

Ed Wagner, owner of the Rod & Reel Fly Shop in Creede, suggests, "August and September are the best months to walk into the canyon. Flows are low and stable. Once you get to the river, there should be ample shoreline to follow, making the fishing much easier than during the high flow months of June and July.

"(Fortunately) the control of flows is very good. There will always be fluctuation during runoff, but changes are usually gradual. Good planning downstream in the agricultural business has a lot to do with the consistency of flow rates. It's a blessing for all flyfishermen. The Rio Grande is one of the first rivers in the state that is fishable after runoff. We see a lot of people from the northern part of the state in July during high snowpack years."

Below the canyon, the river flows through private land for a few miles. The next fishing accesses and boat ramps as we go downstream are at the Rio Grande and Marshall Park campgrounds, which rest 9 miles and 6 miles west of Creede, respectively. About 2 miles of open water above and below Rio Grande and a mile of water at Marshall Park are available.

A good mix of water types prove to be good habitat for the predominant brown trout, and the stonefly hatch gets them going by July 1.

Rod Wintz, an experienced guide with 34 years of fishing the Rio Grande under his belt, said, "I like to start floating this stretch right after peak flows. The river is receding, and the water near the banks is clear normally by June 15 during years with average snowfall, give or take a week or two when conditions vary."

Flows usually peak at about 2,000 cfs and average 1,200 to 1,600 cfs through July.

Wintz and his wife Marilyn manage Wason Ranch, which is located 2 miles southeast of Creede on Colorado 149. The ranch has 4 miles of private river, a pond, and lodging. It's an excellent place to test the waters if you like that type of experience.

"The stonefly hatch is one of the best periods of time to fish the Rio Grande," Wintz said. "Floating the river gives you outstanding access to the river that most people will never see. I have my clients cast a size 6 sofa pillow or orange jughead near the bank and under the willows. Browns and rainbows up to 18 inches come up and slam these big flies!"

When the adult stones are not on the water, it's a sure bet that trout taking refuge along the banks from the heavy currents will feed on the nymph stage of the insect. Halfbacks, Bitch Creek nymphs, and woolly buggers with enough weight to make them sink quickly will draw the fish out of hiding for these big mouthfuls.

"For a full day float I like to put in at Seven Mile Bridge and take out at Wagon Wheel Gap, which is located at Marshall Park Campground," Wintz said. The river averages a nice 50 feet wide through this area with class one and two rapids.

Wintz says this is 99 percent private water, and Colorado law says you can not get out of the boat or anchor without permission from the landowner, so permission is needed to fish.

Another good float is from South Fork to the Hannah Lane take out, which takes about 6 hours.

Gary Willmart, another outstanding guide on the Rio Grande and owner of Colorado Fishing Adventures, said, "A couple years ago, on July 3, I floated this stretch with John Randolph, the editor of *Fly Fisherman* magazine. The stones were hatching, as were the green drakes. It was totally incredible. We caught a lot of fish on stimulators and big dry flies."

To enjoy good days like that, keeping the boat in a position to cast under the willows along the bank is essential.

"You have to be ready for anything on this stretch of water," Willmart said, "especially at this time of year. This is when the river is alive and insect activity is peaking."

*Fall is a great time to work the Rio Grande. Here, the author
displays a brown trout. (Photo by Gus Ridlen)*

The Rio Grande also has good caddis, pale morning dun, and red quill hatches. If the trout switch over to one of these insects, you may have to change patterns. As I said earlier, large flies work best. In fact, it seems like you can always use a fly one size bigger than the natural. Carry sizes 10 to 14 Troth's elk hair caddis, sizes 12 to 16 PMDs, and size 12 red quills. A big rusty spinner is also a good evening fly, and don't forget the size 12 parachute Adams.

By mid-August, when flows reach 500 cfs, opportunities to float the river with driftboats are usually about over. Wade-fishing at that point is the way to go. Rafting is still an option since they do not push as much water.

Fall is also a great time to fish the Rio Grande, when fishing pressure is at a minimum and the trout are still rising. In a day, you can easily catch 10 to 15 fish that range from 10 to 14 inches.

Above Rio Grande Reservoir

The river above Rio Grande Reservoir is accessible from FR 520 at the west end of the reservoir. At Lost Trail Campground, the road requires a four-wheel drive but leads to several miles of fishing in the upper Rio Grande. A mountain bike can also be used.

By either route, you'll find the best fishing beginning about 2 miles in. In that section, the river rates about 8 to 15 feet wide and is lined by thick brush. Climb in, work either up or downstream, and cast from the middle.

Light, short rods favor these tight quarters. Leaders, no longer than 7 to 9 feet, tapered to 4X or 5X, are ideal.

July and August are the best months to attempt this outing. Brown, rainbow, and cutthroat trout will rise to any high-floating attractor pattern. Royal Wulffs, Rio Grande King trudes, renegades, and humpies in any size you may be toting around will grab their attention.

This is truly a beautiful piece of Colorado, so bring along a camera.

South Fork Rio Grande

To reach the South Fork Rio Grande from South Fork, take US 160 south toward Wolf Creek Pass. The river parallels the highway to the intersection with FR 410. Then it follows FR 410 to Big Meadows Reservoir.

The river just above South Fork is private until you get to a fisherman parking area and campground called Highway Springs, about 2.5 miles from town.

Park Creek Campground is the next access, another 3 miles upstream. From the intersection at US 160 and FR 410, the river is open to the reservoir.

The South Fork of the Rio Grande is a major tributary to the main stem of the Rio Grande. The confluence is in the town of South Fork; hence the town's name.

Tremendous amounts of snow fall every winter in the San Juan Mountains to the west. This rugged basin drains water from the ominous Wolf Creek Pass area to the northeast.

The upper river can be accessed from a trailhead at Big Meadows Reservoir. The water here is enclosed with thick brush and willows. It's tough fishing this small free-stone; wading in the middle of the stream is about the only effective way to fish it. However, small rainbows and brook trout rise freely to big, high-floating attractor patterns. Stiff hackled Wulffs and caddis imitations work fine.

Below Big Meadows, the river plunges quickly though a narrow canyon, with sections of fishable pocket water. This is where the better fish will hold. Browns are more numerous than rainbows and brook trout. The browns average 8 to 12 inches, with a few pushing 15 inches.

The river widens around the campgrounds and has mostly smaller, stocked trout. Shorter rods, up to 8 feet in a 4- or 5-weight, should be used to help control your line in the canopied sections of water. Casting from one knee helps keep the line lower on your backcast and may save you time retrieving flies from the overhanging limbs. Don't forget the trusty roll cast in those particularly tough spots.

While fishing the South Fork, take care while wading—the stream bottom is slick with rounded rocks. Felt soles are a must.

The best time to stretch your legs in this productive stream is after runoff, usually in early July. Golden stones and caddis can hatch with regularity by mid-July. Stimulators in sizes 10 and 14 elk hair caddis should be cast into and around any

South Fork Rio Grande

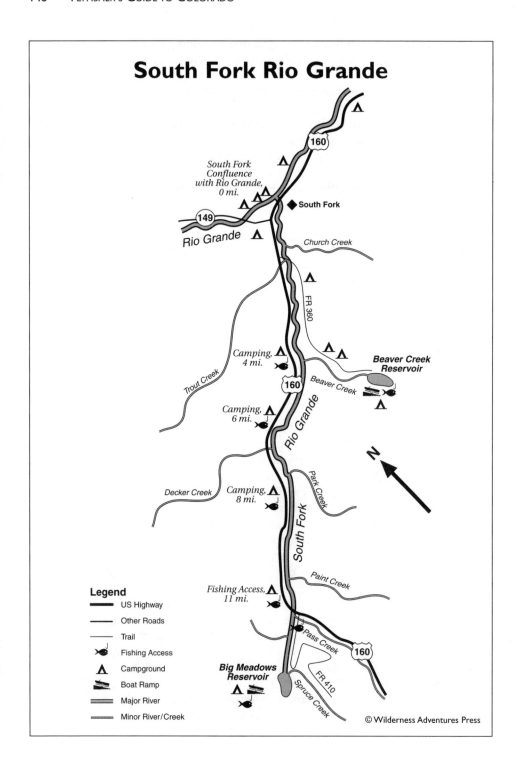

© Wilderness Adventures Press

obstruction. Trout will use any refuge from the fast water and feed on anything that looks like food. Late afternoons and evenings are the best hours to spend on the stream when looking for consistent risers.

Green drakes hatch in late July and can draw the attention of every fish in this stream, especially in the afternoon just after lunch. Again, high-floating, heavy-hackled green drake patterns, like the Wulff pattern Jack Dennis ties, should be used in this fast choppy water. Gink 'em up good and be ready as soon as the fly touches the water. Takes often occur within seconds of it hitting the surface.

Pale evening duns are active from late July through the first week of August. A light tan, size 14 mayfly pattern is a good representation of this insect. A gray fox variant, light cahill, or tan parachute are adequate imitations.

As the PMDs tail off, try terrestrials—they can slay trout during the dog days of August. In fact, a big hopper, plopped against the bank, is almost irresistible to the eager trout.

Stream Facts: Rio Grande

Seasons
- Open all year

Special Regulations
- From upper boundary of Rio Grande campground downstream to upper boundary of Marshall Park campground and from Willow Creek to Goose Creek: Artificial flies and lures only. Rainbow trout must be released immediately. Bag and possession limit for brown trout is 2 fish, 12 inches or shorter.
- From Collier Bridge downstream to west fence of Masonic Park and from Highway 149 bridge at South Fork downstream to the Rio Grande Canal diversion structure (the latter section is considered Gold Medal Water): Artificial flies and lures only. Rainbow trout must be released immediately. Bag and possession limit for brown trout is 2 fish, 16 inches or longer.
- From the west fence of Masonic Park to Farmers' Union Canal near Del Norte: Wild Trout Water.

Trout
- Browns, the predominant species, average 12–14 inches. Some may push 18 inches in the upper reaches.
- Rainbows average 12–16 inches.
- Rio Grande cutthroats: a few in the upper river.

River Miles
- Thirtymile Campground—0
- Camping and Boat Ramp—2
- Fern Creek Bridge—13
- Camping—19
- Rio Grande Campground—22
- Wagon Wheel Gap—34
- Dangerous Rapids—36
- Camping—39
- Palisade Campground—41
- Collier State Wildlife Area—46
- South Fork—49
- Camping & RV Park—54
- CR 18—57
- CR 17—60

River Characteristics
- The Rio Grande is a classic, big Western river. Wide riffles and pocket water that hold a great population of stoneflies, referred to by the natives in the area as "Willow Flies." Definitely a river that can be floated during high water months. June and July floats are most popular from South Fork to Del Norte.

River Flows
- Winter, 200–300 cfs
- Spring, 400–700 cfs
- Runoff, mid-May–June, 1,000–2,200 cfs
- Summer, 500–800 cfs
- Fall, 300–350 cfs

Maps
- *Colorado Atlas & Gazetteer*, pages 77, 78, 79
- Rio Grande National Forest

RIO GRANDE MAJOR HATCHES

Insect	A	M	J	J	A	S	O	N	Time	Flies
Midge	█	█	█	█	█	█	█	█	M/A/E	Olive Biot Midge #16; Brown Biot Midge #16; Black Beauty #16; Brassie #16; Crane Fly Nymph #6–#10; Griffith's Gnat #1
Caddis		█	█	█					A/E	Olive Caddis Nymph #10–#14; Breadcrust #10–#14; Beadhead Breadcrust #10–#14; Buckskin #14–#16; LaFontaine's Sparkle Caddis Pupa #10–#14; Elk Hair Caddis #10–#14; Goddard Caddis #10–#14; Macramé Caddis #12–#16; Balloon Caddis #12–#16; Lawson's Caddis Emerger #12–#16; Spent Partridge Caddis #12–#16
Stoneflies			█						A/E	Sandy's Gold #6–#10; Gold-winged Prince Nymph #8–#10; Kaufmann's Golden Stonefly #6–#12; Stimulator #8–#12; Foam Yellow Sally #12–#18; Halfback #4–#10; Prince Nymph #8–#10; Beadhead Prince Nymph #8–#10; Kaufmann's Brown Stonefly #4–#8; Sofa Pillow #6–#8; Stimulator #8–#12; Bitch Creek Nymph #10
Green Drake			█	█					M/A	Green Drake Emerger #10–#12; Lawson's Parachute Green Drake #10–#12; Green Drake #10–#12; Adams #10–#12; Olive Hare's Ear #10–#12
Red Quill				█					M/A	AK's Red Quill #10–#16; Rusty Spinner #1

HATCH TIME CODE: M = morning; A = afternoon; E = evening; D = dark; SF = spinner fall; / = continuation through periods.

RIO GRANDE MAJOR HATCHES (CONT.)

Insect	A	M	J	J	A	S	O	N	Time	Flies
Blue-winged Olives	▮	▮					▮	▮	M/A	Olive Biot Nymph #14–#18; RS-2 #14–#16; Pheasant Tail Nymph #12–#16; Beadhead Pheasant Tail Nymph #12–#16; Flashback Pheasant Tail Nymph #12–#16; Parachute Adams #10–#16; Slate Thorax Dun #12–#16
Pale Morning Dun			▮	▮					M/A	Biot PMD Nymph #12–#16; Pheasant Tail Nymph #12–#16; Beadhead Pheasant Tail Nymph #12–#16; Lt. Cahill Comparadun #12–#16; Sparkle Dun #12–#18; Parachute PMD #12–#16; Dark Hare's Ear #12–#16; Olive Comparadun #14–#18
Terrestrials				▮	▮	▮	▮		A/E	Rio Grande King Trude #8–#16; Rio Grande King #10–#16; Royal Wulff #10–#16; Humpy #10–#16; Foam Madam X #8–#12; Renegade #10–#16; Black Ant #14; Cinnamon Ant #14; Gartside Hopper #8–#10; Henry's Fork Hopper #8–#12
Streamers	▮	▮				▮	▮		M/E	Black Woolly Bugger #2–#10; Brown Woolly Bugger #4–#10; Platte River Special #4–#10; Spruce Fly #4–#10; Dark Spruce Fly #4–#10; Black-nosed Dace #6–#8; Muddler Minnow #4–#10; Matuka Muddler #4–#10

HATCH TIME CODE: M = morning; A = afternoon; E = evening; D = dark; SF = spinner fall; / = continuation through periods.

SOUTH CENTRAL HUB CITIES
Creede
Population–362 • Elevation–8,852 • Area Code–719

ACCOMMODATIONS
Wason Ranch Company, Box 220 / 658-2413 / Hosts: Rod and Marilyn Wintz / Two bedroom cabins and three bedroom cottages on the Rio Grande / No pets, kennel available in Creede / Highly recommended / $$-$$$

Snowshoe Motel, Highway 149 in town / 658-2315 / Owners: Mark and Julia Viergutz / 14 rooms, 2 kitchenettes / Small dogs allowed / $$$

Creede Hotel, Box 284 / 658-2608 / Hosts: Rich and Kathy Ormsby / Restaurant and 7 rooms / Open 7AM–10:30AM for breakfast / 4PM–9PM for dinner / $$$

4UR Ranch, 1238 FR 605 / 658-2202 / Managers: Rock and Christen Swenson / Private fishing on the Rio Grande River and Goose Creek / Reservations needed well in advance / Package deals / $$$

BED AND BREAKFAST
The Old Firehouse, Main Street / 658-0212 / Innkeeper: Katherine Brennand / $$$

RESTAURANTS
Creede Hotel Dining Room, 658-2608 / Hosts: Rich and Kathy Ormsby / Open 7AM for breakfast, 4AM–9PM for dinner

Mucker's Bucket Saloon, Highway 149 / 658-9997 / Hosts: Chuck and Kathy Lehman / Open 7AM–9PM daily / 8AM on Sunday / Bar open until 2AM / $

Old Miner's Inn, Highway 149 / 658-2767 / Open 11AM–9PM / Cocktails / $-$$

FLY SHOPS AND SPORTING GOODS
Rod and Reel Fly Shop, 101 Creede Avenue / 658-2955 / Owner: Ed Wagner / Full-service fly shop, in business for 12 years / Orvis and Sage / Guided wade fishing on the Rio Grande / Fishing and tying classes

The Ramble House, 116 Creede Avenue / 658-2482 / email: rambhse@rmi.net / Owners: Shane and Suzan Birdsey / Full-service fly shop and gift store / Large selection of flies for local water

Wason Ranch Company, Box 220 / 658-2413 / Owners: Rod & Marilyn Wintz / Guided float trips on the Rio Grande / With 34 years of experience in the area, Rod can show you places the average flyfisherman may never see / 4 miles private water on Rio Grande and a small stocked lake / Log cabins available

San Juan Sports, 658-2359

HOSPITALS
Los Piños Health Center, 1280 Grande Avenue, Del Norte / 657-3342 / Del Norte is 40 miles southwest of Creede on Highway 160

AIRPORTS
Alamosa San Luis Valley Regional Airport, 2500 State Avenue / 589-6444 / United Express: 800-241-6522

Mineral County Airport, Creede / 658-9962 / Private planes

FOR MORE INFORMATION
Creede-Mineral County Chamber of Commerce
Creede Avenue
Creede, CO 81130
658-2374

South Fork

Population–100 • Elevation–8,180 • Area Code–719

ACCOMMODATIONS
Foothills Lodge, 0035 Silverthread Lane / 873-5969 / $$
Aspen Ridge Cabins and RV, 710 Highway 149 / 873-5921 / 7 cabins / Dogs allowed / $$
Rainbow Lodge, 30359 Highway 160 / 873-5571 / Dogs allowed13 rooms–$$, 16 cabins–$$$
South Fork Lodge, 0364 Highway 149 / 873-5303 / 12 cabins / Dogs allowed for a fee / $$
Ute Bluff Lodge and Motel, 27680 Highway 160 / 873-5595 / Dogs allowed / 22 rooms–$$, 8 cabins–$$$

CAMPING
Goodnight's Lonesome Dove RV and Cabins, southwest of South Fork on Highway 160 / 873-1072

RESTAURANTS
Arrowhead Inn, 31119 Highway 160 / 873-0104 / Breakfast and lunch, open 7AM / Cocktails / $
Brown's Sandwich Shop, 29411 Highway 160 / 873-5582 / Open 8AM–9PM / $
The Hungry Logger, 0047 Highway 149 / 873-5504 / Hosts: Vicki and James Kehr / Open 6AM–9PM / Cocktails / $
Rock A Way Inn, 30333 W Highway 160 / 873-5581 / Hosts: Lew and Donna Sailee / Opens 8AM

FLY SHOPS AND SPORTING GOODS
Rainbow Sporting Goods and Grocery, 30306 Highway 160 / 873-5545
The Powder Connection Ski and Gift Shop, 31101 Highway 160 / 873-5644

HOSPITALS
Rio Grande Hospital, 1280 Grande Avenue, Del Norte / 657-2510 / 16 miles east of South Fork on Highway 160

AIRPORTS
Alamosa San Luis Valley Regional Airport, 2500 State Avenue / 589-6444 / United Express: 800-241-6522
Leach Airport, 2159 County Rd. 53, Center / 754-3966 / 30 miles northeast of South Fork on Highway 112 / Private planes

AUTO SERVICE
Walker's Automotive Repair, 29803 Highway 160 / 873-5923

FOR MORE INFORMATION
South Fork Chamber of Commerce
0254 Highway 149
South Fork, CO 81154
873-5512

Del Norte
Population – 1,674 • Elevation – 7,874 • Area Code – 970

ACCOMMODATIONS
Del Norte Motel, 1050 Grande Avenue, 657-3581, 800-372-2331 / 15 units / Dogs allowed / $$

El Rancho Motel, 1160 Grande Avenue / 657-3332 / 16 units / Small dogs allowed / $$

RESTAURANTS
Berwick's Coffee Shop, 13319 Highway 160 / 657-3512 / Open 7AM–9PM / $

La Fuente Supper Club and Restaurant, 540 Grande Avenue / 657-0629 / Open 7AM–9PM / Cocktails / $

Tin Cup Cafe, 216 Oak Street / 657-3832 / Open 11–8PM / $

SPORTING GOODS
Jaho True Value Hardware, 616 Grande Avenue / 657-3666

HOSPITALS
San Luis Valley Regional Medical Center, 106 Blanca Avenue / 589-2511

AIRPORTS
Alamosa San Luis Valley Regional Airport, 2500 State Avenue / 589-6444 / United Express / 800-241-6522

AUTO RENTAL
L & M Auto Rentals, Municipal Airport / 589-4651

AUTO SERVICE
Max's Repair Shop, 810 4th Street / 657-3959

FOR MORE INFORMATION
Del Norte Chamber of Commerce
PO Box 148
Del Norte, CO 81132
657-2845

Alamosa

Population – 7,579 • Elevation – 7,544 • Area Code:719

ACCOMMODATIONS

Alamosa Lamplighter Motel, 425 Main / 589-6636 / $$$

Alamosa Super 8 Motel, 2505 Main Street / 589-6447

Best Western Motel, 1919 Main / 589-2567 / 120 units / Dogs allowed for a fee / $$$

Holiday Inn, 333 Santa Fe Avenue / 589-4412

Sky-Vue Motel, 250 Broadway Avenue / 589-4945 800-805-9164 / 20 units / Dogs allowed / $$

Mt. Blanca Game Bird and Trout, PO Box 236, Blanca, 81123 / 379-3825 $$-$$$ Lodging and restaurant / Guided fishing for large rainbows and brown on three private ponds / Package deals available

BED AND BREAKFAST

Cottonwood Inn and Gallery B and B, 123 San Juan Avenue / 589-3882 / Innkeeper: Julie Mordecai / $$$

CAMPING

KOA Campground, Highway 160 East / 589-9757 / 38 RV sites and 14 tent sites / Showers, store

Navajo Trail Campground, 7665 West Highway 160 / 589-9460 / 46 RV sites and 6 tent sites

RESTAURANTS

Bauer's Campus Pancake House and Restaurant, 435 Poncho Avenue / 589-4202 Open 5AM / $

El Charro Cafe, 421 6th Street / 589-2262 / Open 11AM–9:30PM / $

Oscar's Cafe, 710 Main / 589-9230 / Open 11AM–8PM / Cocktails / $

True Grits Steakhouse, 100 Santa Fe Avenue / 589-9954 / Good steaks / Open until 9PM / Cocktails / $$

SPORTING GOODS

Alamosa Sporting Goods, 1114 Main / 589-3006

Kristi Mountain Sports, Villa Mall / West Highway 160 / 589-9759

Spencer Sporting Goods, 616 Main / 589-4361

HOSPITALS

San Luis Valley Regional Medical Center, 106 Blanca Avenue / 589-2511

AIRPORTS

Alamosa San Luis Valley Regional Airport, 2500 State Avenue / 589-6444 / United Express: 800-241-6522

AUTO RENTAL

L & M Auto Rentals, Municipal Airport / 589-4651

Auto Service
Art's Auto and Tire Service, 1280 Main / 589-3243
Automotive Concepts LLC., 6778 S. Highway 17 / 589-1749
Clark Auto Service, 8533 Tremont Avenue / 589-4485

For More Information
Chamber of Commerce
Cole Park
Alamosa, CO 81101
589-3681

Antonito

Population – 875 • Elevation – 7,888 • Area Code – 719

Accommodations
Narrow Gauge Railroad Inn Motel, Highway 285 and Highway 17 / 376-5441 / 33 units / Dogs allowed / $$
Park Motel, 376-5582 / 12 units / Dogs allowed / $$
Cottonwood Meadows Fly Shop, 34591 Highway 17 / 376-5660 / Hosts: Randy and Naomi Keys / Four cabins next to the shop, one cabin 10 miles up Highway 17 along the river / Dogs allowed / $$-$$$

Bed and Breakfast
Conejos River Quest Ranch, 25390 Highway 17 / 376-2464 / $$$

Camping
Conejos River Campground, 26714 Highway 17 / 376-5943 / 58 RV and tent sites
Josey's Mogote Meadow, 34127 Highway 17 / 376-5774 / Hosts: Bob and Anne Josey / Full hook-ups, tent sites, showers, nightly campfire, Sunday pancake breakfast
Ponderosa Campground, 19600 Highway 17 / 376-5857 / 35 RV sites and 3 tent sites
Rocky Mountain Lodge, 7700 Forest Service Road / 376-5597

Restaurants
Dutch Mill Cafe, 401 Main / 376-2373 / Tasty Breakfast burrito / Open 6AM–9PM / $
Red Bear Restaurant and Lounge, 0044 Forest Service Road 250 / 376-5964 / Open 10AM–9PM / Cocktails / $-$$

Fly Shops and Sporting Goods
Cottonwood Meadows Fly Shop, 34591 Highway 17 / 376-5660 / Owners: Randy and Naomi Keys / Full-service fly shop and guide service / Specializing in walk and wade trips on the Conejos River, local small streams, and mountain lakes / Lessons, lodging available

HOSPITALS
Guadalupe Health Center, Dahlia and 10th Streets / 376-5426
San Luis Valley Regional Medical Center, 106 Blanca Avenue, Alamosa / 30 miles
north of Antonito / 589-2511

AIRPORTS
Alamosa San Luis Valley Regional Airport, 2500 State Avenue / 589-6444 / 30
miles north of Antonito / United Express: 800-241-6522

AUTO RENTAL
L & M Auto Rentals, Municipal Airport, Alamosa / 589-4651

AUTO SERVICE
Curtis Motor Co., 527 Main / 376-5915
Antonito Auto Repair, 217 Main / 376-5394

Southwest Colorado

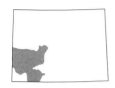

Southwest Colorado has long been known as a flyfishing destination, but until I started delving into the area, I didn't realize how much it really offered.

Three major drainages are covered in this section: the San Juan, the Animas, and the Gunnison, and they contain some of the finest trout streams and some of the best flyfishing opportunities for large trout in the world. The avid fly angler could while away two lifetimes on these rivers and never feel that he covered all of them adequately.

Of the three drainages, the Gunnison is by far the largest and most diverse. It is made up of some of the best trout water in the state. The Taylor River, one of the main tributaries of the Gunnison, has some of the state's largest rainbow trout. In May 1997, a rainbow 34 inches long and estimated at 22 pounds was caught and released below Taylor Park Reservoir. There are many fish over 10 pounds swimming in its depths.

The Lake Fork of the Gunnison, a major tributary of the Gunnison which flows into Blue Mesa Reservoir, can provide days of flyfishing opportunities. Streams located nearby, like Henson Creek, Cebolla Creek, and Big Blue Creek, help make up more than 250 miles of fishable water near the hub town of Lake City.

As if those waters didn't offer enough opportunity, the Uncompahgre River below Ridgeway Reservoir is another of the state's finest. It offers perfect large trout habitat, with fishing conditions rivaling that of an amusement park when lots of anglers hit the water.

The Gunnison Basin is also home to the world famous Black Canyon of the Gunnison. This is an outstanding section of river to fish, and its scenic beauty and remoteness will amaze you. Definitely worth an 'X' or two on your calendar of events.

The San Juan drainage is located in one of the most spectacular areas of the state. As you top Wolf Creek Pass in the San Juans you will see Colorado at its finest. From Pagosa Springs, the fly angler is presented with several fishing opportunities within 50 miles of town. Most of the main river is on private property; however, by taking to the backroads with a backpack and a good pair of hiking boots, you can find virtually untouched streams holding wild, beautiful trout.

The Animas and Dolores drainages are in the southwestern-most part of the state and are excellent fisheries. In fact, as of May 1997, a section of the Animas River was the state's latest recipient of the Gold Medal Water distinction.

The Dolores has had its ups and downs over the last few years, but changes are being made to help stabilize flows and bring this tailwater back to a top-notch fishery. This is a difficult fishery to get the hang of. Smart trout, good insect hatches, and low, clear water makes for a challenging experience.

Wherever you choose to wet a line in the southwest, I'm positive it will be a rewarding adventure. The San Juan National Forest is a gorgeous area to visit with abundant trout streams and high mountain lakes. Enjoy!

Animas River

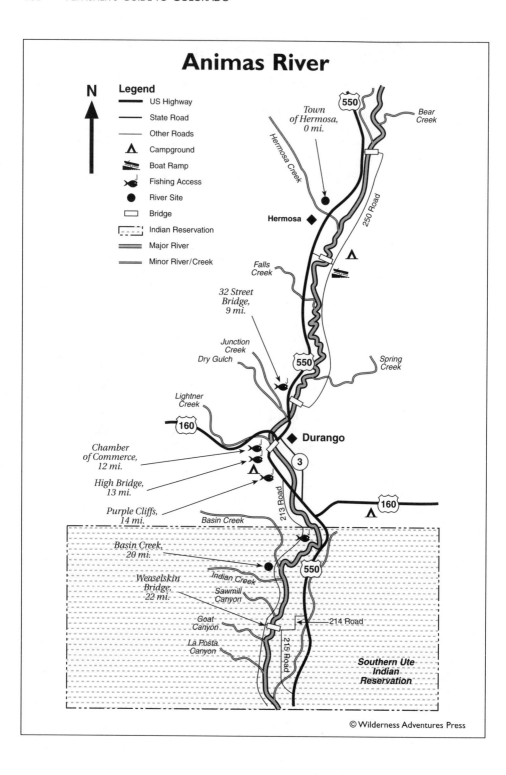

Legend

▬▬▬	US Highway
───	State Road
───	Other Roads
▲	Campground
⛴	Boat Ramp
✦	Fishing Access
●	River Site
▭	Bridge
⸤⸣	Indian Reservation
▬▬	Major River
▬▬	Minor River/Creek

N

Town of Hermosa, 0 mi.

550

Bear Creek

Hermosa Creek

250 Road

Hermosa ◆

Falls Creek

32 Street Bridge, 9 mi.

Junction Creek
Dry Gulch

550

Spring Creek

Lightner Creek

160

Durango ◆

3

Chamber of Commerce, 12 mi.

High Bridge, 13 mi.

Purple Cliffs, 14 mi.

213 Road

160

Basin Creek

Basin Creek, 20 mi.

Weaselskin Bridge, 22 mi.

Indian Creek

550

Sawmill Canyon

214 Road

Goat Canyon

215 Road

La Posta Canyon

Southern Ute Indian Reservation

© Wilderness Adventures Press

ANIMAS RIVER

For those flyfishers who like to wage their battles with trout on large rivers, the Animas offers a classic staging ground. Its wide flows, complete with long riffles, deep runs, and extended flats, offer trout and trout fishers plenty of prime habitat to probe. And, fortunately, access to the river is quite good.

The Animas flows south from the San Juan Mountains north of Silverton through Durango to the San Juan River in New Mexico. Most access sites are in or near the town of Durango. Durango is a major hub city where flyfishers can find all the amenities they need. The town is located at the intersection of US 160 and US 550.

The main access to the river is in Durango. It extends from the confluence of Lightner Creek, near the intersection of US 160 and US 550, downstream to an area called the Purple Cliffs.

This stretch of water carries the state's newest Gold Medal Water designation and can only be fished with flies and artificial lures.

Another interesting option when fishing the Animas is to take the Durango and Silverton Narrow Gauge Railroad into the Animas Canyon north of Durango. Unless you want to ride this slow moving train a few hours before getting a chance to fish, it is recommended to drive to Rockwood before climbing aboard. Rockwood is about 16 miles north of Durango on US 550.

Once there, ride the train for about 12 miles to the Animas' confluence with Cascade Creek. Just ask the conductor to drop you off and find out when the train will be coming back through. Usually you can fish until late in the afternoon before your ride comes by. If you want to spend more time on the water, pack some gear in and spend the night in the wilderness. Reservations can be made by calling 970-247-2733

The Animas is a big river for the state of Colorado. It is better than 100 feet wide as it flows through Durango, and it's filled with large boulders that provide excellent habitat for better than average trout. This freestone stream has the classic make-up: riffles, broken with deep pockets that level out into great runs that hold trout year-round, are abundant. If you like big water, this is one of the best destinations in the state.

However, wading can be difficult, and crossing the river is almost impossible. For that reason, you may want to fish this river early in the season, before elevated flows. At that time you can encounter some very good midge and blue-winged olive hatches.

If you do choose to chase the early hatches, expect to find trout in the 10- to 16-inch range smacking your favorite patterns.

A palomino midge in sizes 16 through 22, with a spot of floatant on the emerging wing, is one of my favorite suspender patterns. Griffith's gnats are also effective when the trout are sipping on the surface. Effective subsurface nymph patterns include olive biot midges, black beauties, and brassies.

April is when flyfishers can expect to see Baetis on the water and their presence, as it does everywhere, will draw fish to the surface.

The best Baetis hatches occur when the weather is wet and cool. Slow water pockets are the areas to watch for rising trout. Look for the major emergence of the hatch to happen around lunchtime. For that reason, I never leave the river for lunch in the spring. I have experienced some of the best dry-fly fishing while fighting off those gnawing hunger pains. Toss a food bar in the vest to tide you over, but please don't leave the river—you'll disappoint yourself.

A parachute Adams, AK's olive quill, and CDC duns in sizes 16 through 20 are good choices for the adult BWO imitation. When possible, a downstream drift into the feeding lane of a trout is always the best approach. If you can't drop a fly into a trout's path from downstream, try an upstream reach or hook cast. Always be prepared to go under with pheasant tails, RS-2s, and olive biot nymphs if you can't take fish up top.

Spring fishing presents no particular problem when it comes to rod choice. Any rod that is comfortable and can turn over a 10- or 12-foot leader is fine.

While dry-fly fishing can be excellent, sometimes the bugs just don't come off in masses and a day can be spent nymph fishing. Rods of 9 feet or longer serve the nymph fisher best.

During summer, when the river is much higher and mobility is limited, rods of 9.5 or 10 feet provide better mending and line control.

The water starts to clear after runoff, depending on the nuances of runoff, usually by the first week in July. At that time, the river will come alive with caddis.

Doug Buck, who manages Durango Fly Goods, touts, "The caddis hatch here can rate as good as the hatch on the Arkansas. Large numbers of caddis will cloud the evening sky as they fly back upstream for their mating and egg laying rituals."

Fishing during the peak of the hatch can provide awesome fishing, but don't fret if you miss the heavy fireworks; caddis will hatch throughout summer, offering excellent dry fly opportunities each evening. High floating caddis patterns such as the Troth elk hair, Goddard, and parachute hare's ear caddis, ranging from sizes 12 to 18, should do in any situation. Breadcrusts, olive hare's ears and LaFontaine's deep sparkle pupa in gray and tan coloration work well for nymphing the tail of riffles.

While the Animas River insect populations provide the classic flyfishing options, don't rule out throwing the big nasty stuff here. According to Buck, minnows draw their fare share of strikes from large brown trout. "Sculpins are a very important food source in the Animas," he said. "Imitations can be fished all year, especially in late summer and fall. Zonkers, muddler minnows, and olive woolly buggers can draw vicious strikes from the bigger browns in the river. Most takes happen as you pull the fly around the back side of rocks. Make sure to keep the fly as near to bottom as possible."

Some large browns migrate upstream from the lower river to spawn in late September and October. They can be found on the shallow gravel bars near the banks in the Gold Medal section of the river.

Blue-winged olives will be back on the water from mid-September through early November. Hatches are sporadic, but if you do catch one the trout will rise at the chance to chow down on this delicacy just one more time before the long winter puts them down for good.

High stick nymphing on the Animas River.

Again, late morning and early afternoon are good times to be on the water if you are looking to catch the entire hatch (and why shouldn't you be?).

When fishing the Animas, you'll want to stay in Durango. There is plenty of lodging available, but try to make reservations in advance—I have had to go west about 30 miles to Mancos to get a room on occasion when I failed to make advance reservations.

Camping is available at the KOAs in town and in the national forest surrounding the area.

TRIBUTARIES TO THE ANIMAS RIVER

Hermosa Creek

To reach Hermosa Creek from Durango, go north 10 miles on US 550 to the town of Hermosa. Turn west on FR 576, which follows the stream to the Hermosa Creek trailhead. The stream is easily accessed from this trail, which spans 15 miles before it meets with the East Fork of Hermosa Creek.

This stream is an excellent option for a flyfisher who likes to combine trout with a backpack or mountain bike adventure.

Where you hike or ride along the trail, expect Hermosa Creek to offer small stream conditions, including stretches of steep canyons with pocket water, plunge pools and trout, both rainbows and brookies, that rate about 8 to 12 inches long.

Like small stream fish anywhere you find them, Hermosa Creek's trout will take any well-presented attractor pattern, especially when it is drifted through the slack water pockets.

Royal Wulffs, an H & L variant, and Rio Grande king trudes in sizes 12 to 16 will hook these feisty trout in the 10-inch class. A cuttbow of 14 to 16 inches may be found in the pools of this creek, but they are not the norm.

The trip either by foot or bike presents many challenges. Steep terrain and rocky trails are the norm. Get in shape for this excursion or you'll pay severely in sweat… and maybe some blood and tears.

However, Hermosa Creek can be very rewarding, and with any flyfishing trip where you are off the beaten path, it can provide solitude from the maddening crowds.

The East Fork of Hermosa Creek can be accessed from FR 578, which is about 25 miles north of Durango on US 550. The East Fork is a Colorado River cutthroat recovery area and regulated as catch and release. FR 578 parallels the stream to Sig Creek Campground where camping is available for the overnighters.

This small meadow stream requires a more tactful approach. In fact, it is difficult to manage a full day without spooking a few of these wary trout. The open conditions demand a careful advance to the stream. Tippets should drop into the 6X and 7X range, with small parachute Adams and Griffith's gnats being required to draw strikes.

Florida River

The Florida River is a small tributary to the Animas River, and it is easily reached from Durango, which makes it a perfect day trip away from the Animas River if you are looking for a change of pace.

To reach the Florida from Durango, take CR 240, also known as Florida Road, northeast about 14 miles to CR 243. Follow CR 243 north to the upper end of Lemon Reservoir and its junction with FR 597. Another 2 miles north on CR 243 you'll find the Transfer Park Campground.

The river parallels the gravel road here, and easy access can be found. However, the river above Transfer Park Campground runs through a rugged canyon and is difficult to access. Bushwhacking is the only way in. It's a good bet that you will not see any other anglers if you choose to battle the brush. Splendid views and tight stream conditions are found once you are in the canyon, and that alone makes a trip here worth the effort.

Another area worth checking out is located below City Reservoir, which can be reached via Endlich Mesa Trail. Take FR 597, a rough four-wheel drive road, east to where the road ends. Endlich Mesa Trail starts here and heads northeast 6 miles to City Reservoir.

The stream below the reservoir flows through a wide, open meadow known as Lowe Park. The stream takes stealth and patience to fish successfully. The wild trout here range between 8 and 12 inches and are quite spooky in open surroundings. A leader up to 10 feet, tapered to 6X, should be used to make delicate presentations with small mayfly patterns.

Animas River near Purple Cliffs.

Good mayfly hatches do occur up here, and a parachute Adams works well for most situations. Carry sizes 16 through 20. AK's olive quill, rusty spinners, and tan comparaduns also work well for the slow moving stream.

Caddis hatches may keep an angler busy in the summer evenings. Tan CDC caddis, LaFontaine's sparkle pupa, and small trude patterns in sizes 14 through 18 should cover the gambit of opportunities presented here.

The hike up to Lowe Park is a tough 6 miles and ends at an elevation just over 10,500 feet. Do not attempt this hike until mid- to late June, with mid-July offering the best opportunity to travel the backcountry. A backpack trip of at least a couple days is necessary to enjoy the surroundings without being in too big of a rush. Pack smart. Rain gear, a water filter, and warm clothes for the cool evenings are a must. Hip boots would be nice for wading through the stream, but not a necessity. Definitely, this is a trip for the person who wants a true wilderness experience.

Stream Facts: Animas River

Seasons
- Open all year

Special regulations
- From Lightner Creek to the Purple Cliffs: Artificial flies and lures. Possession limit is 2 trout, 16 inches or longer.

Trout
- Browns are the dominant species, and they average 10 to 16 inches in the quality water. They run smaller in the upper river.
- Rainbows average 10 to 14 inches.
- Brook trout are present in the upper stretches.

River Miles
- Town of Hermosa (FA up Hermosa Creek)—0
- 32nd Street Bridge—9
- Chamber of Commerce—12
- High Bridge (Road 213)—13
- Purple Cliffs—14
- Basin Creek—20
- Weaselskin Bridge—22

River Characteristics
- The Animas is a freestone its full length from the time it starts in the San Juan Mountains to its confluence with the San Juan River in New Mexico. It's a big, heavy river most of the time, and it offers excellent pocket water fishing. Long riffles and runs make up most of the central part of the river with a good population of caddis and mayflies.

River Flows
- Winter and spring, 250–700 cfs
- Runoff, can exceed 2,000 cfs
- Summer and fall, 350–1,000 cfs

Maps
- *Colorado Atlas & Gazetteer*, page 86
- San Juan National Forest

ANIMAS RIVER MAJOR HATCHES

Insect	A	M	J	J	A	S	O	N	Time	Flies
Caddis				▌	▌	▌			A/E	Olive Caddis Nymph #10–#20; Breadcrust #10–#18; Beadhead Breadcrust #10–#18; Buckskin #16–#20; LaFontaine's Sparkle Caddis Pupa #10–#20; Elk Hair Caddis #10–#22; Goddard Caddis #10–#16; Serendipity #16–#24; Balloon Caddis #12–#16; Lawson's Caddis Emerger #14–#18; Spent Partridge Caddis #14–#18
Pale Morning Dun				▌	▌				M/A	Biot PMD Nymph #16; Pheasant Tail Nymph #16–#22; Beadhead Pheasant Tail Nymph #14–#20; Lt. Cahill Comparadun #12–#18; AK's Red Quill #14–#18; Rusty Spinner #12–#20; Sparkle Dun #14–#18; Parachute PMD #14–#18; Dark Hare's Ear #14–#18
Blue-winged Olive		▌	▌			▌	▌		M/A	Olive Biot Nymph #14–#20; RS-2 #16–#20; Pheasant Tail Nymph #14–#20; Beadhead Pheasant Tail Nymph #12–#20; Flashback Pheasant Tail Nymph #16–#20; Olive Quill Emerger #16–#20; AK's Olive Quill #16–#22; Parachute Adams #12–#22; Gray Spinner #18–#24; Slate Thorax Dun #16–#22
Midge		▌	▌			▌	▌		M/A/E	Olive Biot Midge #16–#20; Black Beauty #16–#20; Brassie #16–#20; Crane Fly Nymph #6–#10; Black Beauty Pupa #18–#20; Griffith's Gnat #16–#22; Palomino Midge #18–#22

HATCH TIME CODE: M = morning; A = afternoon; E = evening; D = dark; SF = spinner fall; / = continuation through periods.

ANIMAS RIVER MAJOR HATCHES (CONT.)

Insect	A	M	J	J	A	S	O	N	Time	Flies
Streamers/Sculpins							████		M/E	Black Woolly Bugger #2–#10; Brown Woolly Bugger #4–#10; Platte River Special #4–#10; Spruce Fly #4–#10; Dark Spruce Fly #4–#10; Black-nosed Dace #6–#8; Muddler Minnow #4–#10; Matuka Sculpin #4–#10; Matuka Muddler #4–#10; Whitlock's Hair Sculpin #4–#6; Steve's BRO Bug #6–#10; Zonkers #6–#10
Terrestrials					████				A/E	Rio Grande King Trude #8–#16; Royal Wulff #10–#16; Humpy #10–#16; Foam Madam X #8–#12; Renegade #10–#16; Black Ant #14–#20; Cinnamon Ant #14–#20; Peacock Beetle #12–#18; Gartside Hopper #8–#10; Henry's Fork Hopper #8–#12
Golden Stonefly			████						A/E	Sandy's Gold #6–#10; Gold-winged Prince Nymph #8–#10; Kaufmann's Golden Stonefly #6–#12; Stimulator #8–#12; Foam Yellow Sally #12–#18; Prince Nymph #8–#16; Beadhead Prince Nymph #8–#16

HATCH TIME CODE: M = morning; A = afternoon; E = evening; D = dark; SF = spinner fall; / = continuation through periods.

COCHETOPA CREEK

Cochetopa Creek may not rank as one of the big Colorado flyfishing destinations, but it offers some decent trout in a nice setting, and there is ample access.

Those facts alone should perk your interest. Throw in the opportunity to catch wild trout on light rods and plenty of good insect hatches, and you should see why Cochetopa garners some attention and merits a section in this book.

The creek is best fished during summer, which unofficially begins here in July after runoff. A section of the creek that flows through the Coleman lease is the most popular area for the flyfisher.

In that section, the stream zigzags back and forth through a lovely flat meadow. It creates interesting water types as it cuts under the banks and slows into the numerous bend pools—some are much deeper than you would think. Shallow riffles connect the pools.

Dry-fly fishing is the norm here, and brown and rainbow trout, ranging from 8 to 12 inches, rise freely.

Paul Seipel, an avid Cochetopa fisher, suggests, "This is a great piece of water for a smaller rod. Seven- to 8-foot, 2- and 3-weights are ideal. If you have a cane rod, this would a perfect place to get it wet."

Given the nature of the stream as it meanders out in the wide open, stealth is the first order of business. Approach the water with a low profile, on your hands and knees more often than not. Or cast from a considerable distance while wading in the middle of the stream. Preferably, try a downstream cast and drift.

"The stream is usually gin-clear during the mid- and late summer months," Seipel said. "Leaders at least 10 feet in length, tapered to 6X, are needed to fool these trout on a regular basis."

Although hatches do occur here, they are very sporadic and cannot be counted on. Caddis are seen around the stream, and when they are present, trout will key on them. Keeping the size of the patterns small is the key to consistent success. Size 16 to 22 CDC caddis, elk hair caddis, and partridge caddis are standard for these clear conditions.

Mayfly patterns are also a very good choice on Cochetopa. A parachute Adams, olive comparaduns, and rusty spinners, again in sizes 16 to 22, consistently take trout as they drift over the corner pools.

Meadow streams are always known for good terrestrial populations, and Cochetopa Creek is no exception. The wild resident trout see a number of terrestrials in August and September, so small hoppers and crickets are good fly choices, especially on windy days when a sudden gust of wind may blow bugs into the water.

The Letort series of hoppers and crickets from sizes 12 to 16 are nice clean patterns for this creek. Ants and beetles are favorites in September, probably due to their smaller size. Black ants and peacock beetles in sizes 18 to 20 should grace a corner of your fly box for this section of stream.

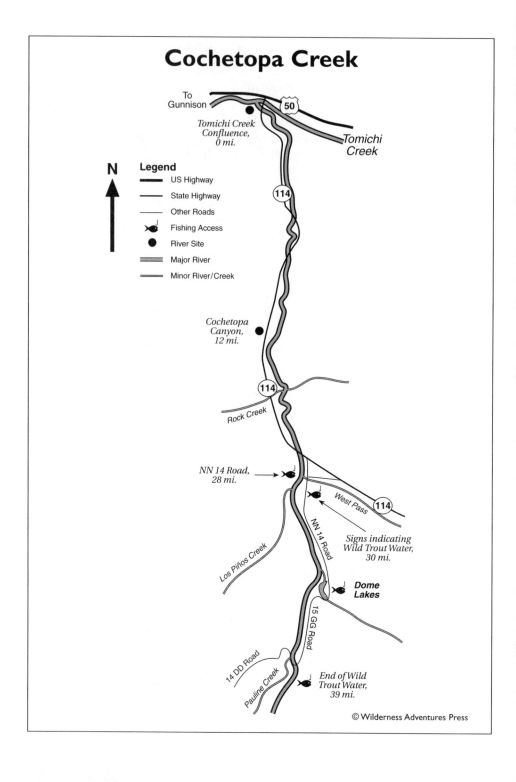

Cochetopa Creek

To Gunnison

Tomichi Creek Confluence, 0 mi.

Tomichi Creek

N

Legend

━━━ US Highway
─── State Highway
─── Other Roads
✕🐟 Fishing Access
● River Site
▓▓▓ Major River
▒▒▒ Minor River/Creek

Cochetopa Canyon, 12 mi.

Rock Creek

NN 14 Road, 28 mi.

West Pass

Signs indicating Wild Trout Water, 30 mi.

Los Piños Creek

NN 14 Road

Dome Lakes

15 GG Road

14 DD Road

Pauline Creek

End of Wild Trout Water, 39 mi.

© Wilderness Adventures Press

Cochetopa Creek

The national forest in the upper reaches of this basin provides days of small stream fishing for all species of trout. Streams flowing into the Cochetopa worth looking into are Chavez Creek and Stewart Creek. Los Piños Creek and its tributaries can also be a fun getaway. Expect small brook and cutthroat trout under 10 inches when fishing those small waters. Also expect tight casting conditions; you will fetch your fly from overhanging brush when fishing this stream.

Due to that cover, these small streams are not for everyone. But for the person willing to hone new skills in flyfishing, and who doesn't mind losing a few flies, Cochetopa and the other streams will not disappoint.

To reach Cochetopa Creek from Gunnison, take US 50 east about 8 miles to its intersection with Colorado 114. Take Colorado 114 south to FR NN-14. Follow FR NN-14, also known as Old Agency Road, toward Dome Lakes State Wildlife Area. At the intersection with FR KK-14, the creek is on the Coleman Easement. You'll find the signs indicating Division of Wildlife Wild Trout Water. Starting from this point, the easement contains about 5 miles of Cochetopa Creek (going upstream). This easement also has 2 miles of Los Piños Creek and a half-mile of Archuleta Creek. Continuing south on FR NN-14 just past Dome Lakes, turn right on FR 15-GG and continue south, paralleling Cochetopa, until you reach a trailhead into the Gunnison National Forest. There, a foot trail follows public water.

Stream Facts: Cochetopa Creek

Seasons
• Open all year

Special Regulations
• In the Cochetopa State Wildlife Area: Artificial flies and lures only. All trout must be returned to the water immediately.

Trout
• Browns averaging 8–14 inches
• Rainbows
• Brookies
• Cutthroats

River Miles
• Confluence with Tomichi Creek—0
• Cochetopa Canyon—12
• Road NN 14—28
• Signs indicating Wild Trout water—30
• End of Wild Trout Water—39 FA

River Characteristics
• Meadow stream in the upper reaches mixed with pocket water. Lots of pools, good dry-fly fishing.

River Flows
• Unregulated freestone. Unfishable during runoff months of May and June. Best fished in July and on through the fall.

Maps
• *Colorado Atlas & Gazetteer*, page 68
• Gunnison National Forest

COCHETOPA CREEK MAJOR HATCHES

Insect	A	M	J	J	A	S	O	N	Time	Flies
Caddis			█	█	█				A/E	Olive Caddis Nymph #16–#20; Buckskin #16–#20; LaFontaine's Sparkle Caddis Pupa #16–#20; Elk Hair Caddis #16–#22; CDC Caddis #16–#20; Lawson's Caddis Emerger #16–#20; Spent Partridge Caddis #16–#20
Blue-winged Olive				█	█	█			M/A	Olive Biot Nymph #18–#22; RS-2 #16–#24; Pheasant Tail Nymph #16–#20; Beadhead Pheasant Tail Nymph #16–#22; Olive Quill Emerger #18–#24; AK's Olive Quill #16–#22; Parachute Adams #12–#22; Olive Comparadun #16–#20; Gray Spinner #18–#24
Pale Morning Dun				█					M/A	Biot PMD Nymph #16; Pheasant Tail Nymph #16–#22; Beadhead Pheasant Tail Nymph #14–#20; Lt. Cahill Comparadun #12–#18; Sparkle Dun #14–#18; Parachute PMD #14–#18; Dark Hare's Ear #14–#18
Terrestrials					█	█			A/E	Rio Grande King Trude #12–#16; Royal Wulff #12–#16; Humpy #12–#16; Renegade #12–#18; Black Ant #16–#20; Cinnamon Ant #16–#20; Peacock Beetle #16–#20; Black Beetle #16–#20; Gartside Hopper #12–#16; Henry's Fork Hopper #12–#16
Midge				█	█	█	█		M/A/E	Olive Biot Midge #16–#24; Brown Biot Midge #16–#24; Black Beauty #18–#24; Brassie #16–#24; Black Beauty Pupa #18–#24; CDC Biot Suspender Midge #18–#24; Griffith's Gnat #16–#22; Palomino Midge #18–#22

HATCH TIME CODE: M = morning; A = afternoon; E = evening; D = dark; SF = spinner fall; / = continuation through periods.

GUNNISON RIVER

The Gunnison River headwaters begin at the little town of Almont, where the Taylor and East rivers merge. At that point, the Gunnison is already a considerable river; it is estimated that the Gunnison drains nearly 4,000 square miles of Colorado's high country before it empties into the Colorado River near Grand Junction.

For flyfishers, the Gunnison is one of the most desirable rivers in Colorado. With its various sections and large trout, it offers numerous diversions.

The river can be divided into two distinct sections: the upper and lower river. The upper section runs from the headwaters downstream to Blue Mesa Reservoir. That section rates about 20 miles long. The lower section starts below Blue Mesa Reservoir at East Portal. Below East Portal, it charges through the highly beautiful and extremely rugged Black Canyon before its confluence with the North Fork of the Gunnison.

The Upper Gunnison

Spring flyfishing on the Gunnison can be excellent, but you better enjoy fishing nymphs; most of the action will be had subsurface because the cool water temperatures and lack of any significant insect activity keeps the trout near bottom.

However, these trout will eat stonefly nymphs if they are presented along the edge of slow water at the tailout of a run. The pockets in front and behind boulders also provide excellent holding water for opportunistic feeders.

Favorite spring nymph patterns include Prince nymphs, halfbacks, and 20-inchers in sizes 6 through 12. Make sure you carry a few of each in your fly box.

A recently developed pattern called Theo's gold-bead stone is coming on as a major producer here. You can buy those patterns at High Mountain Drifters in Gunnison.

A leader set up to carry two nymphs is standard when fishing the Gunnison. Any of the above flies, paired up with a size 14 beadhead hare's ear, beadhead pheasant tail, or a size 16 buckskin is a good choice. Glo-bugs can also be very productive in the spring.

Depending on ambient temperatures and the rate of snowmelt, mid-May is when the river becomes high and off-color. At that time everyone is waiting for high water to recede. When it does, generally in mid- to late June, willow flies migrate to shore, and fishing really perks.

Nymphing can be very productive with large stonefly patterns fished in the pockets near the bank prior to the hatch. But wading can be difficult when the water is high, so wear neoprene waders with a wading belt, and try a pair of studded, felt-soled wading boots.

By July, the upper river clears, and excellent dry fly action begins. Size 4 sofa pillows, stimulators, and adult Bird's stones represent the large stoneflies, and trout are fairly eager to inhale those patterns.

When fishing those huge dries, you'll want to toss them along the bank where willows are hanging over the water. Explosive rises can be expected.

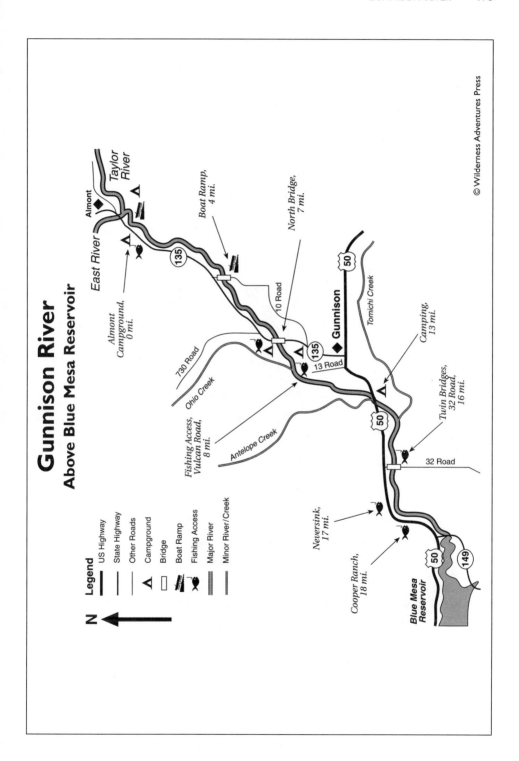

Gunnison River
Above Blue Mesa Reservoir

N

© Wilderness Adventures Press

Legend
— US Highway
— State Highway
— Other Roads
△ Campground
▢ Bridge
⛵ Boat Ramp
🐟 Fishing Access
═ Major River
═ Minor River/Creek

Taylor River

East River

Almont

Almont Campground, 0 mi.

Boat Ramp, 4 mi.

North Bridge, 7 mi.

135

10 Road

730 Road

Ohio Creek

Fishing Access, Vulcan Road, 8 mi.

Antelope Creek

135

13 Road

Gunnison

50

Tomichi Creek

Camping, 13 mi.

Twin Bridges, 32 Road, 16 mi.

50

32 Road

Neversink, 17 mi.

Cooper Ranch, 18 mi.

50

149

Blue Mesa Reservoir

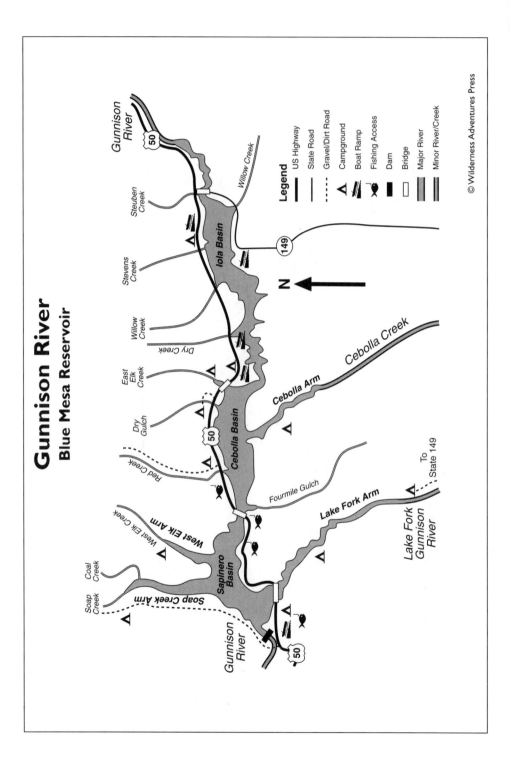

Gunnison River
Blue Mesa Reservoir

© Wilderness Adventures Press

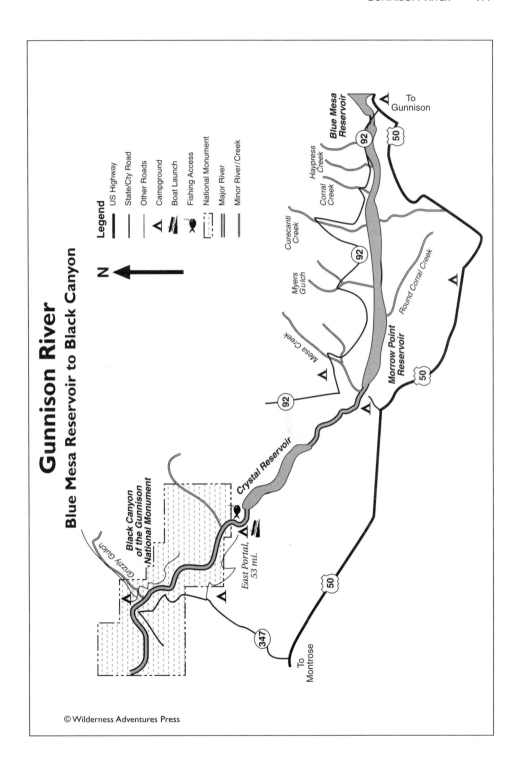

Gunnison River
Blue Mesa Reservoir to Black Canyon

N

Legend

▬▬	US Highway
───	State/Cty Road
───	Other Roads
▲	Campground
🎣	Boat Launch
🐟	Fishing Access
⌐¦⌐	National Monument
	Major River
	Minor River/Creek

Black Canyon
of the Gunnison
National Monument

Grizzly Gulch

Crystal Reservoir

East Portal,
53 mi.

Morrow Point
Reservoir

Mesa Creek

Myers
Gulch

Curecanti
Creek

Corral
Creek

Haypress
Creek

Blue Mesa
Reservoir

Round Corral Creek

92

92

92

50

50

50

347

To
Montrose

To
Gunnison

© Wilderness Adventures Press

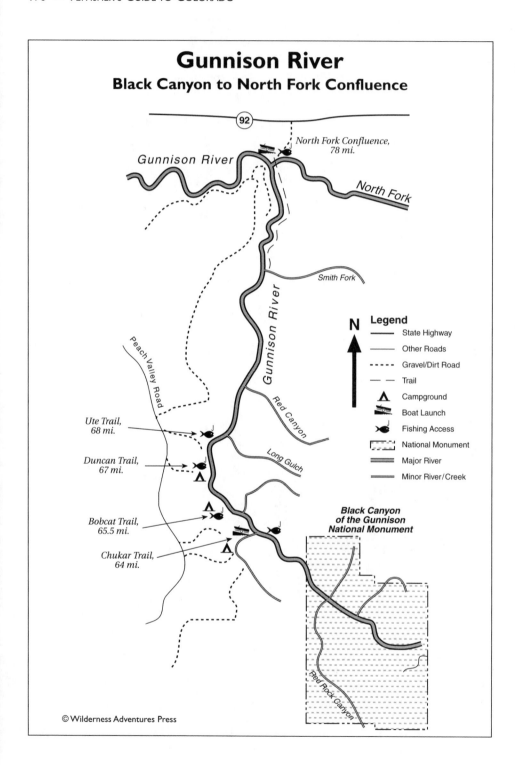

Gunnison River
Black Canyon to North Fork Confluence

92

North Fork Confluence,
78 mi.

Gunnison River

North Fork

Smith Fork

Gunnison River

N

Legend

State Highway
Other Roads
Gravel/Dirt Road
Trail
Campground
Boat Launch
Fishing Access
National Monument
Major River
Minor River/Creek

Peach Valley Road

Red Canyon

Ute Trail,
68 mi.

Duncan Trail,
67 mi.

Long Gulch

**Black Canyon
of the Gunnison
National Monument**

Bobcat Trail,
65.5 mi.

Chukar Trail,
64 mi.

Red Rock Canyon

© Wilderness Adventures Press

Around July 4, green drakes emerge on the river, and they can provide fantastic action. Mike Wilson, owner of High Mountain Drifters in Gunnison, said of the green drake, "Good hatches start about the Fourth of July and last 10 to 14 days. The water is in near perfect condition, and trout will rise consistently to these large mayflies from midafternoon on into the evening."

Lawson's paradrake, a green drake Wulff, and AK's hair wing green drakes in sizes 10 or 12 will bring fish to the surface. A green drake emerger drifting under one of those big dries will take its share of trout, too.

When fishing a green drake dry, followed by the emerger, make a normal cast, mend as needed and pay close attention. If the dry fly goes under, a trout may have taken the emerger, so set the hook.

Look for blue-winged olives, pale morning duns and red quills hatching in late July. They rate about a size 16 or 18. To match those bugs, you'll want to stock up on standard mayfly imitations. "A parachute Adams has by far been the best producer in recent years," Wilson said. "I carry sizes 10 through 18, and I never leave home without them."

Of course, caddis hatches should not be overlooked on the Gunnison. They can be found on the water most of the summer. Evenings are the best time to concentrate your efforts with an adult caddis pattern. Sizes ranging from 12 through 18 will cover the variety of species that may be encountered. Try some in gray coloration. You may want to try a tan caddis during fall.

Wilson adds, "The upper Gunnison River has had a little help from its friends since the onslaught of whirling disease. A group called the Gunnison Country Trout Partnership has taken donations from local residents and businesses to purchase rainbow trout (whirling disease free) to replace the losses occurring in the last four or five years. Everyone would rather have wild trout, but at this point in time, we have no other options."

There are a couple of fall events worth noting. First, kokanee salmon run up the river from Blue Mesa Reservoir starting in mid-August, and they continue their spawning efforts through early October. The pools will be full of resting salmon. "The salmon are not interested in eating; however, they will strike at a bright streamer, like a Micky Finn, out of habit or because they are irritated with it," Wilson said. "Nymph fishing can be productive, too, but a perfectly dead drifted nymph is required to hook them."

At the Neversink and Cooper Ranch picnic areas, just above Blue Mesa Reservoir, fishing in October for big browns migrating out of the reservoir can be incredible.

Moving a woolly bugger from the bottom of the runs up into the shallows is an excellent tactic. The morning and evenings are the best times to latch onto a brown over 20 inches and pushing 5 to 6 pounds. Big stonefly nymphs and glo-bugs dead drifted during the middle of the day may also do the trick.

To access the upper river during any of the hatches, you may want to put in a boat or raft at the Almont Campground where 2 miles of public access begins. There is a boat ramp located there, and it is the place to begin a 4-mile, half-day float to the

Dave Pinkerton with a dandy rainbow from the lower Gunnison Gorge. (Photo by Jim Neiberger)

bridge at CR 10 or a 7-mile, full-day float downstream to the Colorado 135 bridge. Either drift has lots of trout and a good variety of water available.

The best time to float the river extends between late June and August with a drift boat. A cataraft, inflatable raft, or water otter will extend your floating season by about a month.

This Class II water is easily maneuvered by the average oarsman. Much of the river below Almont is private, so stay in the boat to prevent any question about trespassing.

The Lower Gunnison

The Black Canyon of the Gunnison is one of the most impressive places a fly-fisher can ever visit; it cuts through massive canyon walls, offers big roiling water, lots of large trout, and wildlife galore.

As you float through this stretch of river, if that is what you choose to do (and you should try it), you will see why this section, which is included in the Black Canyon National Monument, should receive a Wild and Scenic designation.

Unbelievable views from the rim of the canyon will amaze you. The semi-arid country in which the gorge is cut has never been developed. Campgrounds, a ranger station, and a few improved trails along the top of the canyon are all the man-made scars you will find.

Maintaining this area as one of the few remaining wilderness canyons in the western states is a good idea. Aside from the hefty browns and rainbows inhabiting the river, the canyon is home to river otters, beaver, and muskrat. Desert sheep have been introduced, and mule deer are abundant on the side hills. Golden eagles can be seen soaring in the sky above, while prairie falcons and great horned owls nest in the vertical cliffs of the gorge. Overall, you would be hard pressed to find a better flyfishing experience.

To reach the Black Canyon from Montrose, take US 50 east to Colorado 347. Colorado 347 takes you north into the National Monument and follows the south rim of the canyon. Fishing access can be found at East Portal by taking the East Portal Road. The East Portal is below a narrow impoundment called Crystal Reservoir. This area can be fished downstream along the bank. There is a boat ramp for serious rafters who wish to float the National Monument section. There is no fisherman that I have talked to who floats this section. Several portages and Class IV and V rapids keep anglers out. Some brave anglers take their float tube to the dam and work the big flat water below it. Rainbows and browns ranging from 14 to 22 inches are caught regularly. Streamer fishing is the best producer here. Woolly buggers, black nosed dace, and marabou muddlers are a few favorite patterns. Black is always a good color, but yellow and white marabou is worth a try on the muddlers. Subsurface offerings such as halfbacks, Carey specials, and Prince nymphs can also be dead drifted behind the tube.

A float trip through the lower end of the canyon will astound you. Outfitting permits are limited for the canyon, and there are only a few guides who can float here.

The gorge can be floated by any experienced oarsman who signs in at the bottom of Chukar Trail. Most of the river from Chukar Trail downstream to the take-out at the confluence with the North Fork of the Gunnison is rated at Class I and II. However, 17 Class III rapids, like the upper and lower Pucker, the Squeeze, and Jumping Jack Splash, will test the best boaters in this 14-mile float.

Chukar Trail can be reached from the town of Olathe by taking US 50 south 1 mile to Falcon Road. Turn east on Falcon Road and continue for about 4 miles to the intersection with Peach Valley Road. Take Peach Valley Road about 2 miles to Chukar Road and turn right. The road will take you within a mile of the river. Your raft will have to be carried to the water from the parking area. Acquiring the help of a horse or mule might be a good idea. Leroy Jagodinski at the Gunnison River Pleasure Park should be able to help you with this situation and supply a shuttle service. Reach him at 970-872-2525.

A word of caution: if either Peach Valley or Chukar Roads are wet, they are likely impassable. Weather is unpredictable, so I would recommend a backup plan just in case.

Care has been taken with the regulations here to help maintain a minimum impact on the canyon. This section of river is considered a Wilderness Study Area (WSA). Registration is mandatory; register at the Chukar boat put-in.

If you are hiking down into the canyon, register at the Duncan, Bobcat, or Ute trailheads. You must select a campsite at the time of registration. Camp only in designated campsites. Boaters may spend a maximum of 3 nights in the WSA and can only stay one night in any campsite. Open wood fires are prohibited within the WSA. Cooking is with stoves or firepans with charcoal. Portable toilets are mandatory for overnight boaters. What goes in must come out. Walk-in groups are encouraged to pack out human waste or camp at the Chukar Trail or the Ute Park where toilets are available. Boaters should wear U.S. Coast Guard approved whitewater life jackets. Rafts must carry a repair kit, extra oar, a spare life jacket, and an adequate first aid kit.

As you can see, this is not a simple overnight fishing trip. Hours of planning are involved, and safety precautions must be taken. However, a float through the Gunnison Gorge should rate as a trip of a lifetime. My recommendation is to hire a guide and save the time for tying yourself some big stonefly patterns.

The Black Canyon trip that everyone raves about is when the big salmonflies emerge sometime in June. If you want to catch that hatch, wait until the water temperature rates about 50 degrees. That's easier said than done—it's not like you can just go down to the river and check the temperature before you plan a trip. If you do hit it just right, dry-fly fishing with size 4 salmonflies can be awesome.

Sofa pillows, orange stimulators, and a McSalmon are patterns used for this incredible surface activity.

Flows through the Black Canyon are controlled by dam releases, so you are always vulnerable to varying flows in May and June. But even high flows shouldn't spoil your float or your fishing.

Tom Graddock, a guide with Telluride Outside, says, "The river can fish very well with high flows. Water clarity is more important to a successful day of fishing than the level of the water."

There are varying water types through the canyon, including deep pools, riffles and runs. However, those slack water pockets and eddies along the bank are prime water to plop the huge salmonflies. It doesn't happen often, but a 3-day float during this hatch may reward you with 3 days of never having to use split shot. More realistically, though, you may pass through the hatch for 1 day of your float as it moves upstream. When the surface action subsides, you'll have to go underneath.

If you do hit the salmonflies just right, expect the 2-inch long adults to be present in the afternoons, mating and plopping on the water with a splash.

The trout are very opportunistic when it comes to feeding on this meaty insect. In fact, they become so keyed into the disturbance these big flies make on the water that you may not need a lot of hatching activity to raise fish.

There are some real lunkers living in this canyon. The deep pools, excellent food sources, and the controlled amounts of water are conducive to growing better than average trout. The Gunnison River is considered Gold Medal Water from just above Chukar Trail to the confluence with the North Fork of the Gunnison.

Sherman Hebein from the Division of Wildlife said, "At last count, rainbows still account for about 90 pounds per acre while browns are doing a bit better at 115

Andrew Tashie with a rainbow from the Gunnison River Gorge in Black Canyon of the Gunnison National Monument. (Photo by Jason White)

pounds per acre. However, the rainbows, having lost about 3 age classes due to whirling disease, average 16 inches or better."

Browns average about 14 inches with numerous fish in the 18- to 20-inch range available. Browns are always susceptible to a well-presented streamer no matter when you fish the river. Starting out in the morning, with a woolly bugger scooting along the bottom of the deep pools, can be productive. Expect heavy strikes; this is when some of the bigger fish are taken. A black marabou muddler is a good choice at the end of day when the shadows are long.

Big flies, big fish, lots of split shot, and windy conditions require a pretty healthy stick. Nine- to 10-foot, 6- and 7-weight rods are recommended. Long leaders of 10 to 12 feet are used for line control and nymphing this deep water.

Other important Black Canyon hatches are caddis, which are present throughout summer, PMDs in late June and July, and the little yellow stonefly, which also occurs in June and July.

Caddis seem to be around 90 percent of the time during summer. They emerge from every section of the river, especially the faster, more aerated water. A good selection of gray and dark olive elk-hair caddis, ranging in size from 14 to 16, should always be carried. A LaFontaine sparkle pupa is also a good producer. Size 12 tan caddis can be found in late July and August. Dry-fly fishing with caddis is usually best in the evenings.

Pale morning duns and green drake patterns are important hatches in June and July in the lower canyon. The PMDs emerge in the mornings and can be on the water for a couple hours starting about 9 AM. A light olive parachute in size 16 will match the hatch nicely.

On the other hand, green drakes hatch in the afternoons and evenings. Big, bushy western green drakes work well to match those flies. The Gunnison's trout like big flies floating on the surface.

The little yellow stonefly hatch is another one you'll want to match. It can be very productive on the Gunnison, due to the number of flies on the water and the willingness of trout to eat them.

A size 14 or 16 yellow-bodied caddis pattern works for this hatch, but a fly called the yellow sally is a local favorite. It is best fished in the slack water along the bank. These insects spend much of their day in the cover of streamside vegetation where a gust of wind can send them on a little float trip of their own.

Flows in late summer provide clear water conditions, and it's a great time to work terrestrial patterns. Hoppers are especially important.

Stefan Cobb and Kimberly Moore own Inland Drifters in Carbondale. They prefer to float an 8-mile stretch of the river between the North Fork confluence and Delta during summer. "This is a great section of river to catch rainbows up to 6 pounds on a hopper pattern," Cobb said. "Annie's yellow foam hopper is one of the best producers for us. It's big and floats like a cork."

To float that Delta stretch, put in at the confluence of the North Fork and take out at the Colorado 65 Bridge, about 3 miles east of Delta. Signs warning boaters not to proceed past this point are indication for the take out.

I wade fished the water just above the confluence with the North Fork several years ago in early October. I got 1 trout on a bucktail streamer and then met a couple backpackers who said they did well with a royal Wulff. I had seen no indication of surface activity, but tied one on anyway. The fly wasn't on the water more than a second when it disappeared in a splashy rise. A 12-inch rainbow came to net quickly. Needless to say, I totally enjoyed myself for the next few hours.

The Gunnison from its head to the water below the Black Canyon is as diverse a river as we have in the state. It would take a lifetime to explore and really get to know this river. For most of us, we will only sample the river in bits, but when the river is on, that is enough to make most flyfishers happy.

Getting to the Gunnison

To reach the upper Gunnison, travel 160 miles west on US 50 from I-25 in Pueblo. The lower Gunnison may be easily reached from I-70 at Grand Junction. Take US 50 south for about 40 miles to Delta. Take Colorado 92 east 10 miles to the Gunnison River Pleasure Park at the confluence with the North Fork. This is the take out for floats that have come down the canyon or access to the lower canyon by foot trail. To reach the top of the canyon, continue to Montrose from Delta, another 20 miles, then head east on US 50 another 10 miles to CR 347 to reach the top of the canyon. There is fishing access at East Portal.

A Word on Whirling Disease

All stretches of the Gunnison River have been hit with whirling disease, and rainbow populations are reduced significantly. However, the rainbows in the river at this time are going to be above average in size. Without a carefully engineered stocking program, rainbows could be nonexistent in the future.

Sherman Hebein, a fisheries biologist with the Division of Wildlife in Montrose, has found three to four age classes of rainbows missing in the Gunnison. He said, "We are working on this problem from several fronts. One major area we are gathering information on relates to the life cycle of the deadly spore itself. If we can find a point in time when the spore is less active, we may find a window for a successful stocking. We plan to use the Colorado River strain rainbow for this stocking program. To help reduce the chances of spreading the whirling disease spore from one location to another, clean all mud and aquatic plants from your waders and gear. Wash your boat and trailer at a car wash or use a diluted mix of water and chlorine bleach to rinse the boat. If you do kill a fish for food, the entrails should be considered solid waste. Use a trash dumpster. Do not throw them back into the water or use a garbage disposal."

Tomichi Creek

Tomichi Creek flows into the Gunnison River just west of Gunnison. Unfortunately, this creek is all private.

Dan Hall in Lake City leases about 3 miles of the stream, 8 miles east of Gunnison near the town of Parlin. Contact Hall at 970-944-2281.

A typical meadow stream flowing through hay fields, Tomichi has nice undercut banks as it weaves its way along these lowlands. The stream is about 20 feet wide with pools reaching 6 feet deep.

Great caddis hatches occur throughout summer with the best fishing starting in July. Browns averaging 14-18 inches will rise to a low-riding size 16 CDC caddis or a LaFontaine sparkle caddis. Thin tippets and downstream drifts are required to consistently hook these wary browns.

Pale morning duns and blue-winged olives hatch regularly and provide excellent opportunities for the skillful angler to match the hatch. Morning hours are the best times to catch these mayfly hatches. This wide-open stream should be approached from a low profile position with little false casting.

Stream Facts: Gunnison River

Seasons
- Open all year

Special Regulations
- From the confluence with the East and Taylor Rivers downstream to the bridge crossing Gunnison CR 10: Artificial flies and lures only. Rainbow trout must be released immediately. Bag and possession limit for brown trout is 2 fish, 16 inches or longer.
- From East and Taylor Rivers downstream to Blue Mesa Reservoir at US 50 and Colorado 149, including all canals and tributaries: Taking kokanee salmon is prohibited from September 1 to October 31.
- From Colorado 135 bridge, 1.5 miles north of Gunnison, downstream to US 50 bridge: Artificial flies and lures only. Rainbow trout must be released immediately. Bag and possession limit for brown trout is 2 fish, 16 inches or longer.
- Fishing prohibited from Blue Mesa Dam downstream 225 yards.
- Fishing is prohibited from Morrow Point Dam downstream 130 yards.
- Fishing prohibited from Crystal Dam downstream 200 yards.
- From the upstream boundary of the Black Canyon of the Gunnison National Monument to the North Fork of the Gunnison River: Gold Medal Water, artificial flies and lures only. Rainbow trout must be released immediately. Brown trout between 12 and 16 inches must be released immediately. Bag and possession limit for brown trout is 4 fish, 12 inches or less or 3 fish less than 12 inches and 1 fish over 16 inches.

Trout
- Browns are the dominant species, and they average 10 to 15 inches.
- Rainbows average slightly bigger than browns, but there are fewer of them.
- Kokanee salmon are spread through the upper river in August and September.

River Miles
- Almont Campground—0
- Boat ramp—4
- North Bridge—7
- Fishing access, Vulcan Road—8
- Camping (Gunnison KOA)—13
- Twin Bridges, CR 32—16
- Neversink—17
- Cooper Ranch—18
- East Portal—53
- Chukar Trail—64
- Bobcat Trail—65.5
- Duncan Trail—67
- Ute Trail—68
- North Fork Confluence—78

River Characteristics
- The upper river is freestone in nature with many large tributaries flowing into it. Care must be taken when wading this deep current. Mostly deep runs and riffles hold fish. Below Blue Mesa Reservoir is the Black Canyon of the Gunnison. Big pocket water and deep pools. A float trip through this canyon is a trip of a lifetime.

River Flows

Above Gunnison:
- Winter and spring, 250–800 cfs
- Runoff 1,500–3,500 cfs
- Summer and fall, 500–800 cfs

Black Canyon and below:
- Winter and spring, 300–1,500 cfs
- Runoff, up to 7,000 cfs
- Summer and fall, 700–1,500 cfs

Boat Ramps

- Almont Campground
- Boat ramp off bridge over CR 10
- North Bridge
- East Portal
- Chukar Trail
- North Fork Confluence

Maps

- *Colorado Atlas & Gazetteer,* pages 56, 57, 58, 67, 68
- Gunnison National Forest

GUNNISON RIVER MAJOR HATCHES

Insect	A	M	J	J	A	S	O	N	Time	Flies
Stonefly/Salmonfly			■						M/A/E	Twenty Incher #4–#12; Halfback #4–#10; Prince Nymph #8–#16; Beadhead Prince Nymph #8–#16; Kaufmann's Brown Stonefly #4–#8; Sandy's Gold #6–#10; Gold-winged Prince Nymph #8–#10; Theo's Gold Bead Stone #6–#10; Kaufmann's Golden Stonefly #6–#12; Sofa Pillow #4–#8; Stimulator #4–#12; MacSalmon #4–#8; Bird's Stonefly #4–#8; Bitch Creek Nymph #10
Little Yellow Stonefly			■		■				M/A/E	Foam Yellow Sally #16–#20; Stimulator #14–#18; Prince Nymph #14–#18; Gold-winged Prince Nymph #14–#18; Beadhead Prince Nymph #14–#18
Green Drake					■				A/E	Green Drake #10–#12; Green Drake Wulff #10–#12; Adams #10–#12; Olive Hare's Ear #10–#12
Caddis		■	■		■	■			A/E	Olive Caddis Nymph #10–#16; Breadcrust #10–#18; Beadhead Breadcrust #10–#18; Buckskin #14–#18; LaFontaine's Sparkle Caddis Pupa #10–#16; Elk Hair Caddis #10–#16; Goddard Caddis #10–#16; CDC Caddis #14–#20; Macramé Caddis #12–#16; Balloon Caddis #12–#16; Lawson's Caddis Emerger #14–#18; Spent Partridge Caddis #14–#18
Pale Morning Dun					■				M/A	Biot PMD Nymph #16; Pheasant Tail Nymph #14–#16; Beadhead Pheasant Tail Nymph #14–#16; Lt. Cahill Comparadun #12–#18; Sparkle Dun #14–#18; Parachute PMD #14–#18; Dark Hare's Ear #14–#18

HATCH TIME CODE: M = morning; A = afternoon; E = evening; D = dark; SF = spinner fall; / = continuation through periods.

GUNNISON RIVER MAJOR HATCHES (CONT.)

Insect	A	M	J	J	A	S	O	N	Time	Flies
Blue-winged Olive							■		M/A	Olive Biot Nymph #14–#18; RS-2 #14–#18; Pheasant Tail Nymph #12–#16; Beadhead Pheasant Tail Nymph #12–#16; Flashback Pheasant Tail Nymph #12–#16; AK's Olive Quill #14–#18; Parachute Adams #12–#18; Olive Comparadun #14–#18; Gray Spinner #14–#16; Slate Thorax Dun #14–#18; Air-flo Cut Wing Dun #14–#18
Terrestrials					■				A/E	Rio Grande King Trude #8–#16; Royal Wulff #10–#16; Humpy #10–#16; Foam Madam X #8–#12; Renegade #10–#16; Black Ant #14–#20; Cinnamon Ant #14–#20; Annie's Yellow Foam Hopper #6–#10; Gartside Hopper #8–#10; Henry's Fork Hopper #8–#12
Midge							■	■	M/A/E	Olive Biot Midge #16; Brown Biot Midge #16; Black Beauty #14–#18; Brassie #14–#18; Feather Duster Midge #14–#18; Crane Fly Nymph #6–#10; Griffith's Gnat #16
Streamers								■	M/A/E	Black Woolly Bugger #2–#10; Brown Woolly Bugger #4–#10; Platte River Special #4–#10; Spruce Fly #4–#10; Dark Spruce Fly #4–#10; Black-nosed Dace #6–#8; Mick Finn #4–#10; Muddler Minnow #4–#10; Marabou Muddler #4–#10; Matuka Sculpin #4–#10; Matuka Muddler #4–#10; Steve's BRO Bug #6–#10
Red Quill					■				M/E	AK's Western Red Quill #14–#18; Rusty Spinner #12–#20

HATCH TIME CODE: M = morning; A = afternoon; E = evening; D = dark; SF = spinner fall; / = continuation through periods.

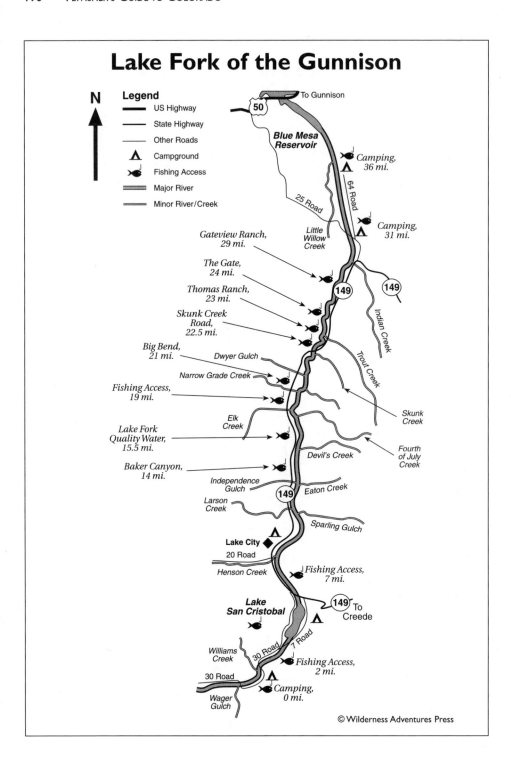

Lake Fork of the Gunnison

N

Legend
▬ US Highway
— State Highway
— Other Roads
⛺ Campground
🎣 Fishing Access
▬ Major River
▬ Minor River/Creek

To Gunnison

50

Blue Mesa Reservoir

Camping, 36 mi.

64 Road

Camping, 31 mi.

25 Road

Little Willow Creek

Gateview Ranch, 29 mi.

149

149

The Gate, 24 mi.

Thomas Ranch, 23 mi.

Indian Creek

Skunk Creek Road, 22.5 mi.

Trout Creek

Big Bend, 21 mi.

Dwyer Gulch

Narrow Grade Creek

Fishing Access, 19 mi.

Skunk Creek

Elk Creek

Lake Fork Quality Water, 15.5 mi.

Fourth of July Creek

Devil's Creek

Baker Canyon, 14 mi.

Independence Gulch

Eaton Creek

149

Larson Creek

Sparling Gulch

Lake City ◆

20 Road

Henson Creek

Fishing Access, 7 mi.

149 To Creede

Lake San Cristobal

🎣

Williams Creek

30 Road

7 Road

Fishing Access, 2 mi.

30 Road

Camping, 0 mi.

Wager Gulch

© Wilderness Adventures Press

LAKE FORK OF THE GUNNISON

The area within a 50-mile radius around Lake City is blessed with over 250 miles of public fishing access to some of Colorado's finest trout streams.

One of the most important drainages is the Lake Fork. It heads below the Continental Divide near Handies Peak and flows northeast along CR 30 to Lake San Cristobal. From Lake San Cristobal, the Lake Fork parallels Colorado 149 to Gateview. There are several well-marked accesses along Colorado 149 where anglers can get at the river.

Lake Fork continues north along CR 64 to Blue Mesa Reservoir. The water from Red Bridge Campground to Gateview Campground is open fishing.

Lake City is centrally located along the Lake Fork and can be reached from US 50 near Gunnison via Colorado 149. The river above Lake San Cristobal is reached by taking CR 30 south from Lake City.

The stream above the lake is small, and accesses are at Williams Creek and Mill Creek Campgrounds. More water opens up in Gunnison National Forest above the campgrounds. Private property is well marked.

July through September is the best time to fish Lake Fork and the surrounding streams. The small stream conditions on the upper river, including mostly small plunge pools and pocket water, provide excellent dry-fly fishing opportunities.

Caddis imitations and attractor patterns work nicely for the stream's aggressive trout. Browns and brookies up to 12 inches, mixed with a few rainbows, are the common catch. And during the caddis hatch, they rise freely to an elk hair caddis, royal Wulff, or a trude.

The Lake Fork below San Cristobal picks up considerable pace and size and is not an easy river for beginners to fish; its bottom is slick and the currents are tricky, so care should be taken while wading.

If you can navigate its flows, you'll find good pocket water, nice deep runs, and insect-rich riffles. The river is not particularly hard to read; however, maneuvering into position to make a good presentation is where the difficulty lies. A fast 9-foot rod carrying a 5-weight line is recommended for most conditions.

Dan Hall, owner of Dan's Fly Shop in Lake City, said, "Our big hatch of the year on the Lake Fork is the golden stonefly. It happens in late June and early July. However, it is tough to fish since this coincides with high water. Even though the water is high, this is your first chance at some good dry-fly fishing. When the adults are on the water, a size 8 orange stimulator or Sofa Pillow match them well. The best tactic is to stay on or near the banks and hit quiet pockets on the edges."

A good section of water to hit during the hatch is along CR 64 between Red Bridge Campground and the arm of Blue Mesa Reservoir. This section consists of quick riffles dumping into deep pools. That combination defines perfect stonefly water, and some say the hatch here rivals any in the state.

Lyndon Lampert, a guide and employee with Dan's Fly Shop, said, "Nymphing is the most consistent means of taking fish while the stoneflies are on the move. Good nymphs to use include a golden stone or a Bitch Creek nymph in size 8. These big nymphs also work well early in the year before runoff."

Don't be too disappointed if you miss the stonefly hatch; after runoff the river comes alive with insect activity. "Bugs on the Lake Fork include abundant species of caddis, green and gray drakes, and fairly consistent hatches of BWOs and PMDs," Lampert said. "July is the best month for dry-fly fishing. Unless the hatch is heavy, Lake Fork trout are generally not super selective. General caddis and mayfly patterns work well."

Tan and gray elk hair caddis ranging from size 12 to 18 should cover most situations. The river's current is fast and the riffles can be rough, so well-hackled, high floating patterns are recommended. Expect browns and rainbows ranging from 10 to 16 inches when you do hook a fish.

For the mayfly hatches, a basic parachute Adams, Quill Gordon, and a blue-winged olive will suffice.

While dry flies will cover most situations, you may have to go under the surface at times to hook trout. According to Lampert, there are quite a few patterns that work well when bounced along the bottom rocks.

"Dry-fly fishing is somewhat sporadic toward the end of the summer, so be prepared with nymphal patterns such as pheasant tails, olive caddis nymphs, and beadhead Prince nymphs."

As fall comes rolling over the mountains in late August and September, terrestrial fishing can be outstanding. A favorite setup in the fall on Lake Fork is a large yellow hopper pattern, size 12 to size 18, with a size 16 beadhead hare's ear dropper following it. Add about 2 feet of 5X tippet to the bend of the hopper's hook and tie on the hare's ear. Work the tail end of the riffles and the back side of midstream rocks. Trout like to hang in the more oxygenated water during the warmer months. This dual fly setup covers surface and subsurface opportunities.

The lower river in Sapinero Canyon is a great place to pull out your streamer box in late September and October. Big browns move up out of Blue Mesa Reservoir and into the upper Lake Fork for their fall ritual.

Woolly buggers and bucktail streamers grab strong takes from browns in the 18- to 20-inch range. Don't be surprised if a fish in the 5- to 6-pound range snaps an ill-prepared tippet.

LAKE FORK TRIBUTARIES

Henson Creek

Henson Creek is an excellent late season stream, with August and September the best times to throw a line here.

A PMD hatch in September is best imitated by a size 16 light Cahill. The late PMD hatch is odd because the water is cold, but expect trout to rise eagerly to your offerings. Due to its free-rising fish, Henson Creek is an excellent choice if you're looking for a place to take beginning anglers.

To reach Henson Creek, follow CR 20 toward Capital City. The creek parallels the road, and accesses can be found all the way up.

Cebolla Creek

Cebolla Creek is not a tributary of the Lake Fork, but it flows into Blue Mesa Reservoir just one drainage to the east.

It is a good stream for beginners and intermediates, and access is plentiful. It usually clears from runoff in early to mid-June, which is slightly sooner than other streams in the area.

To reach the creek, take Colorado 149 south out of Lake City about 8 miles to FR 788. Turn left (north) on FR 788. Your first sight of Cebolla Creek will be at the 4-mile mark. Another mile down the road you will find Hidden Valley Campground. There are 8 miles of open water in the national forest. The next access is at the Cebolla State Wildlife Area. There are 1.5 miles of accessible water here. Another 5 miles downstream is Cebolla Campground, and about a mile of water is available here.

Cebolla Creek has an excellent aquatic food base with strong hatches of all aquatic insects. Expect small stream conditions with very good dry-fly fishing. A 7- to 8-foot rod casting a 3- or 4-weight line works perfectly here.

Big Blue Creek

To reach Big Blue Creek, take Colorado 149 north from Lake City about 11 miles to CR 868, also known as Alpine Road. Turn left (west) and travel about 8 miles to Alpine Campground. The creek flows in from the south and is a beginner's paradise. Lots of small brook trout make things easy.

Lake San Cristobal

Lake San Cristobal is just south of Lake City off of Colorado 149. There is some good midge fishing in the evenings for rainbows. Fish rise to Griffith's gnats, palomino midges, and small parachute Adams, especially in the inlet and outlet areas.

Stream Facts: Lake Fork of the Gunnison

Seasons
- Open all year

Special Regulations
- From the inlet of Lake San Cristobal upstream to the first bridge crossing: Artificial flies only.
- From High Bridge Gulch downstream 1.2 miles to BLM boundary: Artificial flies only. Bag and possession limit for trout is 2 fish over 16 inches.

Trout
- Rainbows average 12 to 14 inches, with a few larger fish.
- Browns are also present.

River Miles
- Camping (Mill Creek Campground) — 0
- Fishing access — 2
- Fishing access — 7
- Baker Canyon — 14
- Lake Fork Quality Water — 15.5
- Fishing Access — 19
- Big Bend — 21
- Skunk Creek Road — 22.5
- Thomas Ranch — 23
- The Gate — 24
- Gateview Ranch — 29
- Camping (Red Bridge Campground) — 31
- Camping (Gateview Campground) — 36

River Characteristics
- The Lake Fork is a medium-sized river by Colorado standards, definitely western in personality. Pocket water and long riffles make up the majority of the river. Stoneflies are the important insects in this freestone river with very good hatches in late June. Good dry fly fishing and adequate accesses provide the fly angler with abundant opportunities.

River Flows
- Winter and spring, 100–300 cfs
- Runoff, 600–1,500 cfs
- Summer and fall, 200–700 cfs
- Best wading opportunities arrive at 250 cfs.

Maps
- *Colorado Atlas & Gazetteer,* page 67
- Uncompahgre National Forest

LAKE FORK GUNNISON RIVER MAJOR HATCHES

Insect	A	M	J	J	A	S	O	N	Time	Flies
Golden Stonefly				X					A/E	Sandy's Gold #6–#10; Gold-winged Prince Nymph #8–#10; Kaufmann's Golden Stonefly #6–#12; Foam Yellow Sally #12–#18; Halfback #4–#10; Prince Nymph #8–#16; Beadhead Prince Nymph #8–#16; Kaufmann's Brown Stonefly #4–#8; Sofa Pillow #6–#8; Orange Stimulator #8–#12; Bitch Creek Nymph #10
Caddis		X			X	X			M/A/E	Olive Caddis Nymph #10–#20; Breadcrust #10–#18; Beadhead Breadcrust #10–#18; Buckskin #16–#20; LaFontaine's Sparkle Caddis Pupa #10–#20; Elk Hair Caddis #10–#20; Goddard Caddis #10–#16; Macramé Caddis #12–#16; Lawson's Caddis Emerger #14–#18; Spent Partridge Caddis #14–#18
Green and Gray Drakes				X					A/E	Green Drake Emerger #10–#14; Lawson's Parachute Green Drake #10–#14; Green Drake #10–#14; Adams #10–#14; Olive Hare's Ear #10–#12; Quill Gordon #10–#14
Pale Morning Dun					X				M/A	Biot PMD Nymph #16; Pheasant Tail Nymph #16; Beadhead Pheasant Tail Nymph #14–#18; Lt. Cahill Comparadun #12–#18; Sparkle Dun #14–#18; Parachute PMD #14–#18; Dark Hare's Ear #14–#18

HATCH TIME CODE: M = morning; A = afternoon; E = evening; D = dark; SF = spinner fall; / = continuation through periods.

LAKE FORK GUNNISON RIVER MAJOR HATCHES (CONT.)

Insect	A	M	J	J	A	S	O	N	Time	Flies
Blue-winged Olive							▓		M/A	Olive Biot Nymph #14-#18; RS-2 #14-#18; Pheasant Tail Nymph #16-#20; Beadhead Pheasant Tail Nymph #16-#20; Flashback Pheasant Tail Nymph #16-#20; Olive Quill Emerger #14-#18; AK's Olive Quill #14-#20; Parachute Adams #12-#20; Olive Comparadun #14-#20; Gray Spinner #14-#20
Terrestrials				▓	▓	▓			A/E	Rio Grande King Trude #8-#16; Royal Wulff #10-#16; Humpy #10-#16; Foam Madam X #8-#12; Renegade #10-#16; Black Ant #14-#20; Cinnamon Ant #14-#20; Gartside Hopper #8-#10; Henry's Fork Hopper #8-#12
Streamers								▓	M/E	Black Woolly Bugger #2-#10; Brown Woolly Bugger #4-#10; Platte River Special #4-#10; Spruce Fly #4-#10; Muddler Minnow #4-#10; Matuka Sculpin #4-#10
Midge		▓	▓	▓	▓	▓	▓	▓	M/A/E	Olive Biot Midge #16-#20; Brown Biot Midge #16-#20; Black Beauty #18-#20; Brassie #16-#20; Miracle Nymph #16-#20; Black Beauty Pupa #18-#20; CDC Biot Suspender Midge #18-#20; Griffith's Gnat #16-#20; Palomino Midge #18-#20

HATCH TIME CODE: M = morning; A = afternoon; E = evening; D = dark; SF = spinner fall; / = continuation through periods.

TAYLOR RIVER

The Taylor River flows through Taylor Park, forming Taylor Park Reservoir; a tremendous tailwater occurs below the dam. The river below the reservoir is the area of most interest; however, the river above the reservoir can be very good for small trout ranging from 8 to 12 inches.

To reach the river from Gunnison, take Colorado 135 north 11 miles to Almont. Turn right onto FR 742 and follow the river all the way to Taylor Park Reservoir. Several fishing accesses and campgrounds for public use are located along FR 742.

If you are coming from the east, take US 24 to Buena Vista and take FR 587, also known as Cottonwood Pass Road, west about 30 miles to Taylor Park. This gravel road is closed during the winter, so the alternate route would be US 50 west out of Salida to Gunnison.

A short section of water below the dam, designated as catch and release, flies and artificial lures only, has become one of the most popular rivers in the state. And for good reason. A rainbow trout 34 inches long, weighing an estimated 22 pounds, was landed and released here May of 1997. Many trout over 10 pounds are hooked here year round. The reason is due to the *Mysis* shrimp drifting into the river from Taylor Park Reservoir.

"Hooked" is a much better term than "caught." These fat rainbows, when hooked, react like wild beasts and put up some of the best battles any angler could experience. They jump, they surge, they shake their heads, and they have learned how to cut your leader on the jagged rocks in the river. I know it has happened to me, and I have talked to several anglers who will tell you the same thing. They go straight for the rocks and try to drag your leader around the sharp corners, effectively setting themselves free.

To make things a bit more difficult, special considerations must be made when it comes to equipment. A rod with backbone and a sensitive tip is needed to handle these trout. The sensitive tip helps play the trout on the light tippets required to get the trout to take your fly. The backbone is needed to put the heat on every opportunity the hefty 'bows give you. Four- and 5-weights are normally used, but there are times when you wish you could drag out a 10-weight.

That's not all: these trout have become wise to split shot. Trout can easily be seen in this section of river, and fishing to individual fish is the norm. I can't think of anything more fun than spotting a trout and fishing to that fish. It can also be very frustrating. Believe it or not, as your nymphs drift toward one of these trout and it sees the split shot, it slides out of the way then returns to its original position after the nymph has passed.

Reports of slightly better strike ratios come from anglers using the fluorocarbon tippet materials. Long leaders tapered to 6X are needed to present the small nymphs used here. Midge patterns down to size 22, *Mysis* shrimp from sizes 18 to 14, and pheasant tails up to a size 16 are common fare. Light tippets are needed to let these small nymphs drift as naturally as possible.

Taylor River

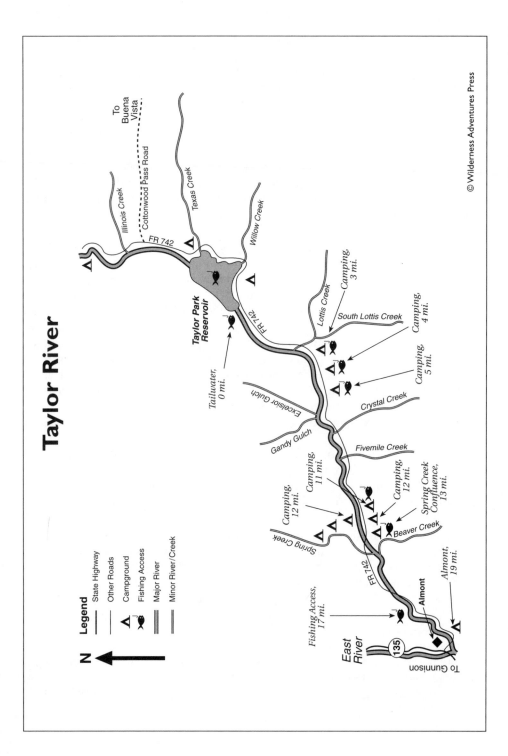

© Wilderness Adventures Press

For those of you who fare well in the cold, you can fish the river though the winter. Weather must always be a consideration or those who travel long distances. Snow can make many of the mountain passes treacherous and difficult to cross. Also, the river bank may have as much as 2 or 3 feet of snow along it, making it difficult getting up and down the river.

No matter when you fish here, *Mysis* shrimp will more than likely be in the water. This white shrimp is the primary food source for the trout that call this river home; surely they are responsible for the phenomenal size of these trout. April and May are good months to use a *Mysis* pattern. The reservoir above has just turned over and has released a lot of shrimp into the river. Someone is always coming up with a new *Mysis* pattern, so check with the local shops in Gunnison, Almont, and Crested Butte for the hot fly. I like Craig Burton's version in a size 18.

A major downfall with the river below the dam is the number of people who flock here in an attempt to put their name on a trophy. Crowds can be unbelievable. Trying to fish during the middle of the week doesn't help much.

Midges will be hatching with regularity in the spring. I have found a midge pattern to be a good second fly to use with a shrimp. Olive biot midges, black beauties, and a white midge called a candy cane are good choices.

The green drake hatch in late July and August rates as the best on the river. The hatch is sparse in the upper river close to the dam, but the big fish belly up and eat as many of them as they can. As you fish closer to Almont, the hatch is much thicker and more consistent. However, the size of the trout goes down considerably. Wild browns and stocked rainbows range from 10 to 14 inches in the lower river.

The green drake patterns you choose for the river below the dam should be more realistic in nature. A more traditional pattern with hen tip wings and fewer turns of hackle in a size 12 makes for a better pattern here. Lawson's paradrake is also a good producer. The water is not as rough or as fast as the lower river, so sparser flies float just fine. Green drake Wulffs and olive humpies work well for the lower river.

Another fine hatch on the upper river is the pale morning dun emergence. This mayfly has a pink abdomen and ginger colored wings and legs. It rates about a size 18 and comes off in late July. I've seen rainbows well over 20 inches find a feeding lane near the bank and literally take every dun that comes within sight. You can surprise them with a pink, quill-bodied dun attached to a 12-foot leader tapered to 6X. A sharp hook cast or a downstream drift is needed to allow the fly to come into their view first with the fly line well out of sight. This is a great hatch and should be checked out.

Caddis hatches are very important on the lower river throughout the summer. They can hatch early in the afternoon and continue for a few hours. LaFontaine's sparkle pupa works very well as the trout are rising at the tail end of the long riffles in the lower river. Campgrounds and pulloffs along the road provide miles of access on the river. After a lull in action during the late afternoon, the evening fishing with a #14 olive elk hair caddis can be outstanding.

The Taylor River may have the largest trout in the state.
Here's Gus with a slab. (Photo by Deb Ridlen)

As with the upper Gunnison and the East rivers, kokanee salmon will migrate into the lower sections of the Taylor in late August and September. Find the deepest holes, and you should find the salmon resting for their next surge upstream. Standard nymphs can catch the salmon. Prince nymphs and soft hackle hare's ears hook their fair share. They have one thing on their mind: propagating the species. The salmon are not feeding at this time; however, they do take a well-presented fly.

Taylor Park

Taylor Park Reservoir has a good population of northern pike, brown trout, and lake trout. Northerns are best fished in late June and July when they are still moving in and out of the shallow water near the bank. The inlet area on the north side of the lake is best for chasing pike with a fly rod.

Fall fishing for brown trout in the inlet of the lake and the Taylor River above the lake is good in September and October. A woolly bugger is the fly of choice.

Other fishing opportunities in the park worth checking out are Texas Creek, Spring Creek, Spring Creek Reservoir, and Willow Creek. They offer more of a wilderness setting and fewer people.

Stream Facts: Taylor River

Seasons
- Fishing is open all year long.

Special Regulations
- No access or fishing from Taylor Dam downstream 325 yards.
- From 325 yards below Taylor Dam downstream to the upper boundary of Cockrell private property (approximately .4 miles): Artificial flies and lures only, all fish must be released immediately.

Trout
- Rainbows. A rainbow of about 17 pounds was shocked in the water right below the dam a couple of years ago. The state record was caught and released in May of 1997, estimated at 22 pounds.
- Browns average 14 to 18 inches, a few over 20 inches.
- Kokanee salmon are in the river in the fall.

River Miles
- Tailwater—0 • Camping (One Mile)—12
- Camping (Lottis Creek)—3   • Camping (North Bank)—12
- Camping (Cold Springs)—4   • Spring Creek Confluence—13
- Camping (Lodge—5 • Fishing Access—17
- Camping (Rosy Lane)—11   • Almont—19

River Characteristics
- The river below Taylor Reservoir is a classic tailwater fishery. One major difference is the fact that these trout are fed *Mysis* shrimp. They grow big, strong and smart. This stretch of river gets a lot of pressure. Along with a tremendous amount of midges, a hatch of green drakes in late July and early August will rival any in the state. As you get closer to Almont, the river is pocket water mixed with deep runs.

River Flows
- Winter and spring, 150–350 cfs
- Runoff, releases are controlled below the dam. In May and June flows can range from 700–1500 cfs
- Summer and fall, 250–500 cfs

Maps
- *Colorado Atlas & Gazetteer*, pages 58, 59
- Gunnison National Forest

TAYLOR RIVER MAJOR HATCHES

Insect	A	M	J	J	A	S	O	N	Time	Flies
Mysis Shrimp	▮							▮	M/A/E	Burton's Mysis Shrimp #14–#18; Dorsey's Mysis Shrimp #14–#18
Green Drake				▮					A/E	Green Drake Emerger #10–#12; Lawson's Parachute Green Drake #10–#12; AK's Hair-winged Green Drake #10–#12; Colorado Western Green Drake #10–#12; Adams #10–#12; Olive Hare's Ear #10–#12
Pale Morning Dun					▮				M/A	Biot PMD Nymph #16; Pheasant Tail Nymph #16–#22; Beadhead Pheasant Tail Nymph #14–#20; Lt. Cahill Comparadun #12–#18; Sparkle Dun #14–#18; Parachute PMD #14–#18; Dark Hare's Ear #14–#18; AK's Pink Quill PMD #14–#18; Pink Comparadun #14–#18
Blue-winged Olive	▮					▮			M/A	Olive Biot Nymph #18–#22; RS-2 #16–#24; Pheasant Tail Nymph #16–#22; Beadhead Pheasant Tail Nymph #16–#22; Flashback Pheasant Tail Nymph #16–#22; Olive Quill Emerger #18–#24; AK's Olive Quill #16–#22; Parachute Adams #16–#22; Olive Comparadun #16–#20; Gray Spinner #18–#24; CDC Baetis Dun #16–#22; Barr Emerger #16–#22; Air-flo Cut-wing Dun #16–#22
Midge	▮							▮	M/A/E	Olive Biot Midge #16–#24; Black Biot Midge #16–#24; Candy Kane #16–#24; Black Beauty #18–#24; Brassie #16–#24; Blood Midge #16–#24; Miracle Nymph #16–#20; AK's Midge Larva #16–#22; Feather Duster Midge #18–#20; Disco Midge #18–#24; Crane Fly Nymph #6–#10; Black Beauty Pupa #18–#24; CDC Biot Suspender Midge #18–#24; Griffith's Gnat #16–#22; Palomino Midge #18–#22

HATCH TIME CODE: M = morning; A = afternoon; E = evening; D = dark; SF = spinner fall; / = continuation through periods.

TAYLOR RIVER MAJOR HATCHES (CONT.)

Insect	A	M	J	J	A	S	O	N	Time	Flies
Golden Stonefly			■	■					M/A/E	Sandy's Gold #6–#10; Gold-winged Prince Nymph #8–#10; Kaufmann's Golden Stonefly #6–#12; Stimulator #8–#12; Foam Yellow Sally #12–#18; Prince Nymph #8–#16; Beadhead Prince Nymph #8–#16
Terrestrials				■	■	■			A/E	Rio Grande King Trude #8–#16; Royal Wulff #10–#16; Humpy #10–#16; Renegade #10–#16; Black Ant #14–#20; Cinnamon Ant #14–#20; Henry's Fork Hopper #8–#12
Streamers		■						■	M/E	Black Woolly Bugger #2–#10; Spruce Fly #4–#10; Black-nosed Dace #6–#8; Muddler Minnow #6–#10
Red Quill					■					AK's Red Quill #14–#18; Rusty Spinner #12–#20
Caddis					■	■			M/A/E	Olive Caddis Nymph #10–#20; Breadcrust #10–#18; Beadhead Breadcrust #10–#18; Buckskin #16–#20; LaFontaine's Sparkle Caddis Pupa #10–#20; Elk Hair Caddis #10–#22; Goddard Caddis #10–#16; CDC Caddis #14–#20; St. Vrain Caddis #14–#16; Macramé Caddis #12–#16; Balloon Caddis #12–#16; Lawson's Caddis Emerger #14–#18; Spent Partridge Caddis #14–#18

HATCH TIME CODE: M = morning; A = afternoon; E = evening; D = dark; SF = spinner fall; / = continuation through periods.

East River

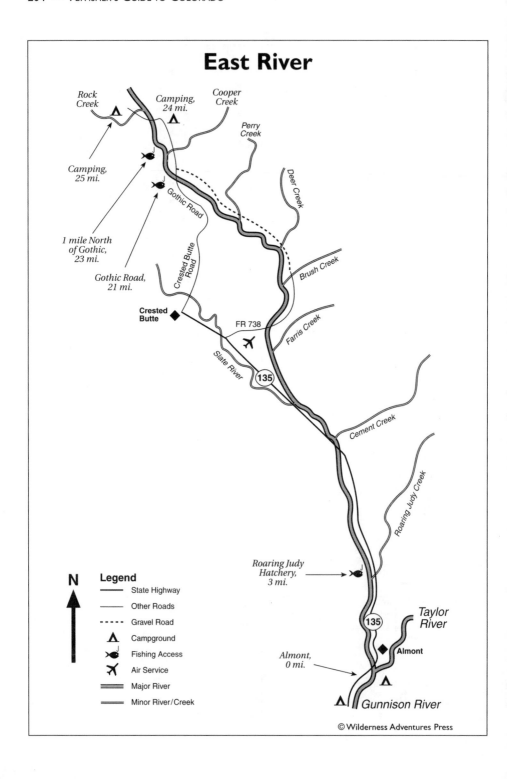

Rock Creek

Camping, 24 mi.

Cooper Creek

Perry Creek

Deer Creek

Camping, 25 mi.

Gothic Road

1 mile North of Gothic, 23 mi.

Crested Butte Road

Gothic Road, 21 mi.

Brush Creek

Crested Butte

FR 738

Farris Creek

Slate River

135

Cement Creek

Roaring Judy Creek

Roaring Judy Hatchery, 3 mi.

Taylor River

135

Almont

Almont, 0 mi.

Gunnison River

Legend

N

—— State Highway

—— Other Roads

---- Gravel Road

▲ Campground

🐟 Fishing Access

✈ Air Service

━━ Major River

── Minor River/Creek

© Wilderness Adventures Press

EAST RIVER

From Gunnison, take Colorado 135 north 11 miles to Almont. This is where the East and Taylor rivers merge to form the Gunnison River. The East River parallels Colorado 135 to the north and passes through the Almont Triangle State Wildlife Area, an area also referred to as the Roaring Judy Fish Hatchery. This is the first and only public fishing access to the river until you get into the national forest above Crested Butte, another 20 miles upstream. This section is also designated Wild Trout Water and is flyfishing only. The state record brown trout was caught in the Roaring Judy Ponds in 1988. It was 36 inches long and weighed 30.5 pounds; that's one big trout! The ponds are very popular during high water in May and June.

The river flowing through this section is comprised of long riffles with several bends, creating excellent feeding lanes. Around the corner of the bends, the water deepens and the surface turns slick, making for good dry fly presentations. These conditions produce good brown and rainbow trout averaging 10 to 15 inches. Unfortunately, it's a short piece of water, and crowding can be a problem.

Rod Cesario, owner of Dragonfly Anglers in Crested Butte, says, "Our best hatch of the year is the green drake in late July and early August. The river is in near perfect condition. Running clear with good flows." He notices, "This hatch is no different from other green drake hatches I've seen before. When this mayfly is on the water, every trout in the river takes notice. The hatch starts in the afternoon and continues through the evening, often until after dark." All standard green drake patterns work here; make sure to carry an emerging green drake or a size 12 olive soft hackle.

Caddis are also very active during the summer months after runoff. Expect the best rising activity to be in the evenings. Low riding CDC caddis or Lawson's spent caddis in sizes 14 to 18 work well. Olive and tan are good color choices.

Other mayflies include pale morning duns, red quills, and blue-winged olives. The PMDs hatch about the same time of the month as the green drakes. However, some trout will choose the smaller mayfly, so be prepared for a complex hatch situation. One thing in your favor: the small mayflies hatch in the morning and the drakes in the afternoon, but be aware that they do intermingle.

A rusty spinner is a secret weapon in all the streams of the upper Gunnison basin. It is a good early morning and late evening pattern, although I have used it during the slow times in the afternoon as an attractor pattern and have done amazingly well. I love watching the lazy, sipping rise to a spinner pattern.

Olives in sizes 14 to 20 are needed from mid-August to October. Parachute Adams, comparaduns, and AK's olive quill are good imitations. All types of pheasant tail nymphs, including beadheads and flashbacks, should be used for nymphing situations.

Late summer is a great time to fish attractor patterns. A favorite technique of Cesario's goes as follows: "An effective and enjoyable approach for late summer dry fly fishing is to start with a size 12 Royal Wulff or a Rio Grande King trude tied to a 9-foot 5X leader. Add a 12 to 16 inch piece of 5X tippet to the bend of the hook. Tie on a beadhead pheasant tail, Prince, or hare's ear." As for which water to watch, Cesario

Jason White with an East River brown. (Photo by Andrew Tashie)

says, "I look for shallow riffles, maybe 2 to 3 feet deep, and work the pair of flies over every square inch. This technique produces regularly for me."

About the middle of August, kokanee salmon can be found in the river. A run comes up the Gunnison River from Blue Mesa Reservoir and disperses up the East and Taylor rivers. Simple, old, run-of-the-mill nymphs can catch the salmon. Prince nymphs and soft hackle hare's ears hook their fair share. The salmon are not feeding at this time; they have more important business to attend to. However, whether it's instinct or irritation, they do take a fly. Most of the salmon look like clones. While they only average 14 to 16 inches, they can put up quite a tussle. Bright-colored buck-tail streamers and woolly buggers are worth a try.

The upper river in the Gunnison National Forest above Crested Butte is a smaller stream with good accesses along FR 317 and at the Avery and Gothic Campgrounds. Cesario says of it, "This truly is a beautiful stream, with excellent trout habitat. It meanders slowly through meadow sections, with undercut banks forming deep pools holding rainbows, browns, cutthroat, and brookies."

Within this good pocket water, expect the trout to be in the 8- to 10-inch range. Nymph fishing the pools and pockets can be very productive in the mornings while waiting for better dry-fly fishing in the afternoon and evening.

Stream Facts: East River

Seasons
- Fishing is open all year.

Special Regulations
- From the upstream property boundary at Roaring Judy Fish Hatchery downstream to the Taylor River: Artificial Flies and lures only. Bag and possession limit is 8 trout. Taking Kokanee salmon is prohibited.
- From the bridge at the Roaring Judy Fish Hatchery downstream 1 mile: Wild Trout Water.

Trout
- Browns average 10 to 15 inches. An occasional fish may go 16 to 18 inches.
- Rainbows are found in both the upper and lower river.
- Cutthroat are found in the upper river.
- Brook trout are also found in the upper river.

River Miles
- Almont—0
- Roaring Judy hatchery—3
- Gothic Road—21
- 1 mile north of Gothic—23
- Camping (Avery)—24
- Camping (Gothic)—25

River Characteristics
- The East is a free flowing stream though some of the best country Colorado has to offer. Unfortunately, the river has limited access. The water above Almont is a good sized river with a mix of fast riffles. It winds its way back and forth, creating good corner pools. The upper river is a small stream with a mix of meadow stretches and pocket water.

River Flows
- Winter and spring, 75–400 cfs
- Runoff, 1500–2500 cfs
- Summer and fall, 200–500 cfs

Map
- *Colorado Atlas & Gazetteer*, page 58
- Gunnison National Forest

EAST RIVER MAJOR HATCHES

Insect	A	M	J	J	A	S	O	N	Time	Flies
Green Drake				▋					A/E	Green Drake Emerger #10–#12; Lawson's Parachute Green Drake #10–#12; Green Drake #10–#12; Adams #10–#12; Olive Hare's Ear #10–#12
Pale Morning Dun					▋				M/A	Biot PMD Nymph #16; Pheasant Tail Nymph #16; Beadhead Pheasant Tail Nymph #14–#18; Lt. Cahill Comparadun #14–#18; Sparkle Dun #14–#18; Parachute PMD #14–#18; Dark Hare's Ear #18–#18
Blue-winged Olive				▋		▋			M/A	Olive Biot Nymph #14–#20; RS-2 #14–#20; Pheasant Tail Nymph #14–#20; Beadhead Pheasant Tail Nymph #14–#20; Flashback Pheasant Tail Nymph #14–#20; AK's Olive Quill #14–#20; Parachute Adams #12–#20; Olive Comparadun #14–#20; CDC Baetis Dun #14–#20
Caddis			▋			▋			A/E	Olive Caddis Nymph #10–#20; Breadcrust #10–#18; Beadhead Breadcrust #10–#18; Buckskin #16–#20; LaFontaine's Sparkle Caddis Pupa #10–#20; Elk Hair Caddis #10–#22; Goddard Caddis #10–#16; CDC Caddis #14–#20; Balloon Caddis #12–#16; Lawson's Caddis Emerger #14–#18; Spent Partridge Caddis #14–#18
Stonefly		▋			▋				M/A/E	Sandy's Gold #6–#10; Gold-winged Prince Nymph #8–#10; Kaufmann's Golden Stonefly #6–#12; Foam Yellow Sally #12–#18; Halfback #4–#10; Prince Nymph #8–#16; Beadhead Prince Nymph #8–#16; Kaufmann's Brown Stonefly #4–#8; Sofa Pillow #6–#8; Stimulator #8–#12; Bitch Creek Nymph #10

HATCH TIME CODE: M = morning; A = afternoon; E = evening; D = dark; SF = spinner fall; / = continuation through periods.

EAST RIVER MAJOR HATCHES (CONT.)

Insect	A	M	J	J	A	S	O	N	Time	Flies
Terrestrials				■	■	■			A/E	Rio Grande King Trude #8–#16; Royal Wulff #10–#16; Humpy #10–#16; Foam Madam X #8–#12; Renegade #10–#16; Black Ant #14–#20; Cinnamon Ant #14–#20; Gartside Hopper #8–#10; Henry's Fork Hopper #8–#12
Streamers							■	■	M/E	Black Woolly Bugger #2–#10; Brown Woolly Bugger #4–#10; Spruce Fly #4–#10; Dark Spruce Fly #4–#10; Black-nosed Dace #6–#8; Muddler Minnow #4–#10
Red Quill				■	■				A/E	AK's Red Quill #14–#18; Rusty Spinner #12–#20
Midge		■					■	■	M/A/E	Olive Biot Midge #16–#20; Brown Biot Midge #16–#20; Black Beauty #16–#20; Brassie #16–#20; Miracle Nymph #16–#20; Black Beauty Pupa #16–#20; CDC Biot Suspender Midge #16–#20; Griffith's Gnat #14–#18

HATCH TIME CODE: M = morning; A = afternoon; E = evening; D = dark; SF = spinner fall; / = continuation through periods.

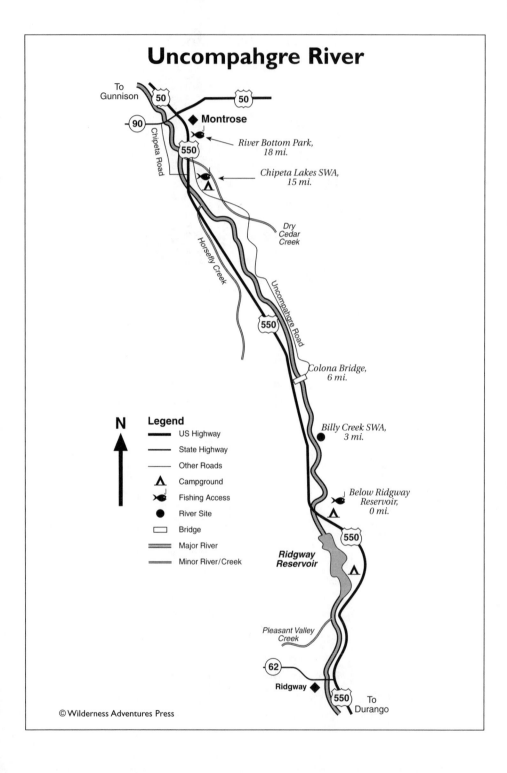

Uncompahgre River

To Gunnison

50

50

90

◆ Montrose

550

← River Bottom Park,
18 mi.

Chipeta Road

← Chipeta Lakes SWA,
15 mi.

Horsefly Creek

Dry
Cedar
Creek

Uncompahgre Road

550

Colona Bridge,
6 mi.

N

Legend
— US Highway
— State Highway
— Other Roads
▲ Campground
🐟 Fishing Access
● River Site
▭ Bridge
═ Major River
═ Minor River/Creek

Billy Creek SWA,
3 mi. ●

Below Ridgway
Reservoir,
0 mi.

▲

550

**Ridgway
Reservoir**

▲

Pleasant Valley
Creek

62

Ridgway ◆

550

To
Durango

© Wilderness Adventures Press

UNCOMPAHGRE RIVER

The Uncompahgre River parallels US 550 from the town of Ouray to Delta, where it flows into the Gunnison River. The river above Ridgway is mostly private and not worth the effort to find the few national forest accesses. In recent years, the river has gotten a name for itself from the water below Ridgway Reservoir where Cow Creek flows into the river, an area also known as Pa-Co-Chu-Puk.

From I-70 at Grand Junction, take US 550 south 60 miles to Montrose. The river below Ridgway Reservoir is another 30 miles south of Montrose. If you happen to be in the south part of the state, from Durango, take US 550 about 70 miles north to the river.

This tailwater went through a major redesign in 1992. The State Parks constructed a recreational area with a campground and asked the Division of Wildlife to determine if the river could sustain a population of trout. After monitoring the stream habitat and stocking the river, the conclusion was made that no habitat existed. The river was too swift and could not sustain a reasonable number of trout.

With the concerted efforts of the Division of Wildlife, State Parks & Recreation, and the Bureau of Reclamation, $200,000 was raised for stream habitat improvements to 2 miles of river below the dam. With simple calculations, that's $100,000 a mile just for a home for trout. Truckloads of large boulders were strategically placed in the stream to form weirs and pools, all-important living quarters trout need to sustain life.

It's now like fishing in a well-groomed park. Sidewalks follow the river, the pools follow one after the other loaded with hefty willing trout, and a gazebo is nearby to have lunch under. This area could be called the Disneyland of flyfishing. Locals call it Puk Park or "Jurassic Park", due to the big trout that inhabit the water. Granted, most of these rainbow trout are big brood fish from hatcheries around the state, but, nonetheless, they are heavy fish averaging 18 to 22 inches in length. "Today the river sustains 1,034 pounds of rainbows per surface acre," says Sherman Hebein, a biologist for the Division of Wildlife in Montrose.

Not only have the improvements helped sustain a trout population, but the insects have started to reestablish themselves in the river. Bob Burk, owner of Cimarron Creek Fly Shop in Montrose, noticed, "We had our first PMD hatch last July. It was good hatch, lasting a couple of weeks with more bugs than would be expected. The best part about it was watching 20-inch rainbows sip the number 16 duns off the surface."

Hooking these trout is not always as easy as it sounds. Jim Neiberger, a good friend and fishing partner, fishes the Uncompahgre quite often. He told me, "We fished the river in December last year. It was one of those bright, warm days when you think it's going to be fun to stay warm and catch some trout. Well, we stayed warm but struggled for a few fish. The next day, it was snowing when we got to the river. By the end of the day, 6 inches of snow were on the ground, but we caught over 50 fish apiece." He adds, "I've experienced this situation several times throughout the

Winter fishing is beautiful and productive on the Uncompahgre. Just make sure you wear thick neoprene waders and some long underwear. (Photo by Jim Neiberger)

year. The trout seem to be dormant under a bright sun and on the move during cloudy conditions."

Hatches are few and far between at this point in time, so nymph fishing is the most consistent way to hook these trout. A black midge pattern from sizes 18 to 22 seems to be the most reliable fly during the winter and spring. Black beauty, black palomino, and black biot midges are good choices. Paired with a miracle nymph or a buckskin in the same size range, you'll have a good tandem setup. I always hate to mention it, and I wouldn't if I didn't fish them myself, but a light pink egg pattern is a great spring fly.

With the stream insect population improving, we hope to see more mayflies and more diverse hatches in the future.

A 10- to 12-foot leader, tapered to 5X or 6X, should be used to get as good a drift as possible. Strike indicators can be used with ease in these slow moving pools, adding to the overall pampering you receive here. Wading is easy until flow rates are in the 400 cfs range, usually occurring in late May and June.

Four- and 5-weight rods are good choices for this smallish stream. There is very little trouble along the banks of the stream, so lengths up to 9 feet are recommended for the majority of your fishing here.

Caddis are the predominant insect in the Uncompahgre, and the first wave begins emerging in May. You may take a few fish on a size 16 elk hair caddis in the afternoons; however, concentrating your efforts on nymph fishing is still the best plan. Breadcrust and hare's ear patterns work well along the bottom of the man-made pools. The cased caddis continue to hatch for about 2 weeks. High flows make the river difficult to fish by the end of the month.

When flows are high, bigger nymphs and more split shot will still take these trout. When hooked in this high water, be prepared for a good fight and expect the reel to get a work out. It's time for beadhead Prince nymphs, halfbacks, and LaFontaine sparkle caddis in sizes 8 to 12. Egg patterns may take a couple fish, but if used as a second fly with one of the patterns mentioned, it works as an attractor, and the trout will take one of the darker flies.

A new fly that has been working during the summer months is called a killer caddis. It has green or yellow glass beads for a body, a dubbed thorax, and some soft hackle to imitate the appendages. Sizes 12 to 16 should be carried.

By September, the midges are the best patterns again. Burk mentioned, "We haven't seen BWOs yet, but we are hopeful."

Downstream, closer to Montrose, there are a few accesses, but they don't handle the number of anglers that Pa-Co-Stick-A-Pig does. The number and size of fish are also reduced. Billy Creek State Wildlife Area has a short stretch of public water; you may find good fish in this section since it is only 3 miles downstream from the main arena. Chipeta Lakes State Wildlife Area also has a small stretch of open water, and camping is available here. In town, open water can be found at River Bottom Park. The water is faster, more difficult to fish, and does not hold as many trout.

Stream Facts: Uncompahgre River

Seasons
• Open all year

Special Regulations
• From Ridgway Dam downstream to the fence just below the USGS gauging station: Fishing prohibited, except where posted.
• From USGS gauging station below Ridgway Dam downstream to Crow Creek: Artificial flies and lures only; all fish must be released immediately.

Trout
• Rainbows. Large brood rainbows are stocked regularly; 20- to 24-inchers are common.
• Browns average 12 to 16 inches with a few pushing 20 inches. Only a few cutthroat are found.

River Miles
• Below Ridgway Reservoir—0
• Billy Creek State Wildlife—3
• Colona Bridge—6
• Chipeta Lakes SWA—15
• River Bottom Park—18

River Characteristics
• "A small stream with a big stream attitude!" is the best way to describe the Uncompahgre. The area below Ridgway Reservoir, through habitat improvements, has one pool after another. It holds some of the biggest fish in the state. Through the town of Montrose you will find more riffle and run situations.

River Flows
• Winter and spring, 100–200 cfs
• Runoff, releases are controlled by the dam but do reach 400–600 cfs
• Fall, 100–300 cfs

Maps
• *Colorado Atlas & Gazetteer*, page 66
• Uncompahgre National Forest

UNCOMPAHGRE RIVER MAJOR HATCHES

Insect	A	M	J	J	A	S	O	N	Time	Flies
Caddis							▓		A/E	Olive Caddis Nymph #10–#20; Breadcrust #10–#18; Beadhead Breadcrust #10–#18; Buckskin #16–#20; LaFontaine's Sparkle Caddis Pupa #10–#20; Killer Caddis #14–#16; Elk Hair Caddis #10–#22; CDC Caddis #14–#20; Balloon Caddis #12–#16; Lawson's Caddis Emerger #14–#18; Spent Partridge Caddis #14–#18
Midge			▓						M/A/E	Olive Biot Midge #16–#22; Brown Biot Midge #16–#22; Black Biot Midge #16–#22; Black Beauty #18–#22; Brassie #16–#22; Blood Midge #16–#22; AK's Midge Larva #16–#22; Disco Midge #18–#22; Black Beauty Pupa #18–#24; CDC Biot Suspender Midge #18–#24; Griffith's Gnat #16–#22; Palomino Midge #18–#22
Pale Morning Dun				▓					M/A	Biot PMD Nymph #16; Pheasant Tail Nymph #16–#22; Beadhead Pheasant Tail Nymph #14–#20; Lt. Cahill Comparadun #12–#18; Sparkle Dun #14–#18; Parachute PMD #14–#18; Dark Hare's Ear #14–#18
Terrestrials					▓				A/E	Rio Grande King Trude #8–#16; Royal Wulff #10–#16; Humpy #10–#16; Foam Madam X #8–#12; Renegade #10–#16; Black Ant #14–#20; Cinnamon Ant #14–#20; Gartside Hopper #8–#10; Henry's Fork Hopper #8–#12
Stonefly						▓			A/E	Gold-winged Prince Nymph #8–#10; Halfback #8–#10; Prince Nymph #8–#16; Beadhead Prince Nymph #8–#16

HATCH TIME CODE: M = morning; A = afternoon; E = evening; D = dark; SF = spinner fall; / = continuation through periods.

DOLORES RIVER

The Lower Dolores

Located in the rolling hills of southwest Colorado, just 20 miles from the Utah border, the Dolores River drainage supplies water for agricultural needs first, and fly-fishing needs second. That fact is extremely unfortunate for flyfishers; the Dolores is only a fragment of the fishery it could be with proper management.

In 1983, the first season after McPhee Dam was finished, the Colorado Division of Wildlife saw the potential for a good tailwater fishery. They stocked over 25,000 brown, rainbow, and Snake River cutthroat trout into the water and immediately classified the river below the dam as catch and release, flies and lures only water.

The trout flourished in their new surroundings, and by 1986 the river turned into a fantastic fishery. The trout grew fast, and it was not long before word spread and the river saw its fair share of angling pressure. A success story?

In 1987, a below average moisture year caused flows to drop well below 100 cfs. The impact was instantaneous. Fishing under the new conditions was not as productive. In the early 1990s, the problems got worse. In fact, stream flows dropped to a paltry 20 cfs at times, and about 50 percent of the river's trout population perished.

There is some hope that a flow level, appropriate to keep trout alive, will be maintained in the future. Cross your fingers with the rest of us.

As bleak as the situation may sound, the Dolores remains a productive, fertile river. It has an outstanding insect base that can produce large trout under prime conditions. However, don't plan on fishing to naive trout; the Dolores River below McPhee Reservoir is one of the most technical fisheries in the state. Bring your best flies, casts, and attitude when you fish here—you'll need them all.

Spring can be one of the best times to chase those difficult trout. Consistent midge hatches keep trout well fed. The browns, rainbows, and cuttbows average 12 to 18 inches, and they congregate in the deeper water near the dam in March. They will move into shallow, smooth water to feed on those minute midges, and that gives the flyfisher an opportunity to throw precise patterns to those fish. However, whether fishing with a nymph, emerger, or dry fly, precise placement of the fly is critical. When trout are feeding in shallow water, let's say less than a foot deep, their peripheral vision is lessened. That means a flyfisher must place the fly right over a trout's snout, without lining a fish, to draw a strike. Due to the wariness of these trout, a 3- to 5-trout day is considered above average. That challenge is fun for me, but a beginner or intermediate angler may disagree.

Baetis and small brown stoneflies hatch in April, and they present a similar scenario. The little stonefly can be imitated with size 16 or 18 Rio Grande or royal trudes.

For the Baetis mayflies, you'll need to cover three stages of the hatch. The nymph, the emerger, and the adult are all important stages and you must determine which stage the fish are keying on to be really successful. Not easy.

Pheasant-tail nymphs, olive biot nymphs, WD-40s, and RS-2s in sizes 16 to 22 should match emerging insects. Precisely tied olive quills with a CDC wing, Stalcup's Baetis, and olive comparaduns are proven patterns up top. Any new trick fly or upscale pattern is worth a try.

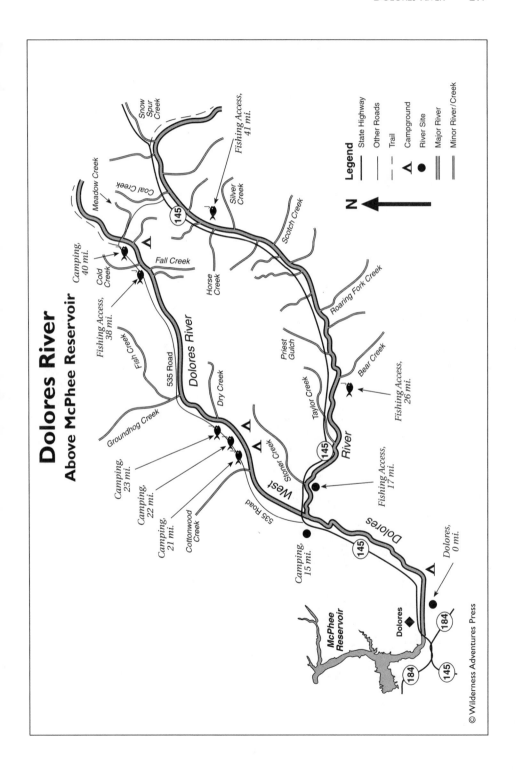

Dolores River
Above McPhee Reservoir

© Wilderness Adventures Press

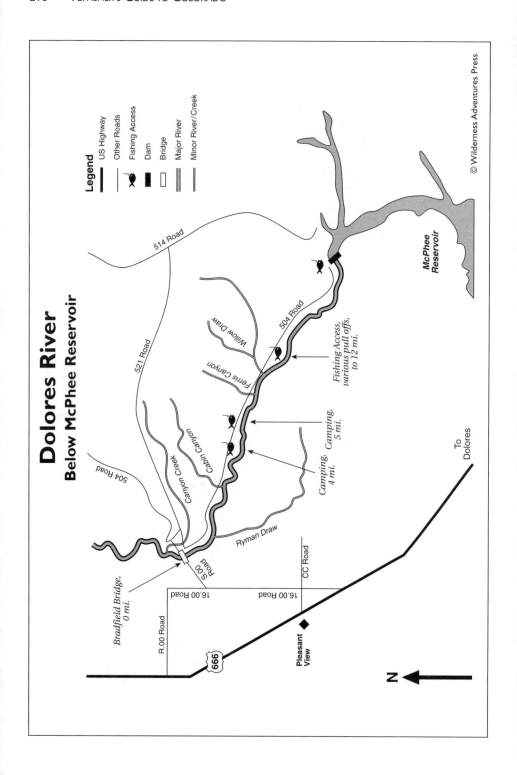

Dolores River
Below McPhee Reservoir

Legend

US Highway
Other Roads
Fishing Access
Dam
Bridge
Major River
Minor River/Creek

© Wilderness Adventures Press

514 Road

521 Road

504 Road

Willow Draw

Ferris Canyon

Canyon Creek

Cabin Canyon

504 Road

Ryman Draw

504 Road

McPhee Reservoir

Fishing Access, various pull offs, to 12 mi.

Camping, 5 mi.

Camping, 4 mi.

Bradfield Bridge, 0 mi.

R.00 Road

S.00 Road

16.00 Road

16.00 Road

CC Road

666

Pleasant View

To Dolores

N

No matter if you're on the Dolores or any other river in the state, fly selection and solid knots are crucial. Here, an angler tests the merit of both before stepping into the river.

After runoff is another prime time to fish the Dolores. "Caddis hatches and higher water make the trout almost stupid," said Frank Smethurst, who guides for Telluride Outside. "The trout are more evenly dispersed throughout the upper river, so locating trout is easier, and a dead drifted size 16 Goddard caddis is taken readily. This is the time when you may hook up with a 20-inch fish.

"The little yellow stonefly also raises a little action on the surface at that time. Standard yellow Sallies and foam yellow Sallies in sizes 14 to 18 should do the trick."

Pale morning dun mayflies hatch in July and August, and they provide excellent surface action. There is definitely something about this mayfly that drives trout wild. A light olive comparadun or a light colored parachute Adams in a size 16 should work for visibly rising trout. Be prepared to go with a floating nymph or emerger if your dry flies are refused. Watch the rise forms for an idea of what fly the trout may be feeding on. If there are no visible mayflies in the area of a riser, and the only part of the trout you see is its back, the floating nymph is a good choice. When you see a freshly emerged dun disappear under a rise, the adult patterns will work.

One food source that is often overlooked is the crawfish. Big trout eat them. A size 6 halfback, wriggling through the pools, imitates the crawfish pretty well. This pattern works exceptionally well in the fall.

August was always known as hopper month when the Dolores was in its prime. Huge trout, often over 20 inches, would rise to hoppers regularly. The trout still rise to hoppers, but it would be an act of God to raise a trout that big these days.

Predictable hatches of blue-winged olives offer flyfishers one last go at this fishery before the end of the year. Size 24 BWO patterns are often needed to match this tiny mayfly. During fall look for low flows and difficult fishing. If you're looking for a guided trip, contact Frank Smethurst at PO Box 801, Telluride, CO 81435, (970)-728-4369.

If you do fish the Dolores, before you put your waders on, please consider a few ideas that were presented to me by Smethurst. He said, "Be courteous of other anglers already on the river. The stream is small and tough enough to fish as it is without fighting other anglers. There are 12 miles of stream to fish, so you don't need to crowd somebody. There are parking spots every half mile or so, and if someone is parked in one, go to the next."

Anglers are more tolerant of each other the closer to the dam you move. Still, maintain a distance and don't crowd.

The Dolores can be reached from Durango via US 160 about 30 miles west to Mancos. Take Colorado 184 north about 20 miles to Colorado 145. Turn left onto Colorado 145 and continue about a mile to the intersection with Colorado 184. Turn right and stay on Colorado 184 for about 8 miles to US 666. Take US 666 north 9 miles to Pleasant View and turn right on FR 505. About a mile east of US 666 take a left and follow signs to the river. When you reach Bradfield Bridge turn right on FR 504, which parallels the river to the dam.

The Upper Dolores

To reach this stretch of water from Dolores, take Colorado 145 northeast toward Lizard Head Pass. The river parallels the highway, which is considered a Colorado Scenic Byway, until it veers south to its head near Bolam Pass in Tin Cup Basin. Public access can be found near Rico and along the road inside the national forest boundaries.

This is a small stream in its upper reaches, with a mix of brown, rainbow and brook trout in the 8- to 12-inch range. This water does receive its share of pressure during summer, due to its proximity to the road. Attractor dry flies are productive here. Royal Wulffs, humpies, and trudes are good producers.

The West Dolores meets the main river about 15 miles east of Dolores at the intersection of Colorado 145 and FR 535. To reach the west fork, take FR 535 north. It parallels the stream and provides several campground options. Most of the West Dolores is located on national forest. Some small sections of private property need to be avoided.

The West Dolores is a bumpy little freestone with a wide variety of water types. It provides a bit more solitude than the main fork. Lots of small rainbow, brown, cutthroat, and brook trout inhabit this stream. There are meadow stretches, nice corner pools and excellent pocket water to hone your fishing and casting skills.

Stream Facts: Dolores River

Seasons
• Open all year

Special Regulations
• From McPhee Reservoir to Bradfield Bridge (about 11 miles): Artificial flies and lures only. All trout must be released immediately.

Trout
• Browns average 14 to 18 inches below McPhee. They average 8 to 12 inches in the upper river.
• Rainbows average 14 to 18 inches below McPhee. Expect them in the 10 to 12 inch range on the upper river.
• Cutthroat range from 8 to 12 inches in the upper river.
• A few brook trout are available in the upper stretches.

River Miles
Below McPhee:
• Bradfield Bridge 0
• Camping (Cabin Canyon Campground) 4
• Camping (Ferris Canyon Campground) 5
• Fishing Access, Various pulloffs, 12

Above McPhee:
• Dolores—0
• Camping (Forks)—15
• Emerson Campground (West Fork)—21
• Mavreeso Campground (West Fork)—22
• West Dolores Campground (West Fork)—23
• Fishing Access (West Fork)—38
• Borro Bridge Campground (West Fork)—40
• Fishing Access—26
• Fishing Access—41

River Characteristics
• Typical tailwater below McPhee Reservoir. There is some pocket water but mostly pools, runs, and riffles. Not many bends to change the current flows. Very technical fishing to wary trout. The upper river is a smallish freestone stream with several national forest accesses.

River Flows
• Winter and spring, 25–75 cfs
• Runoff, 800–1200 cfs
• Summer, 75–150 cfs
• Fall, 100–500 cfs

Maps
• *Colorado Atlas & Gazetteer,* pages 74, 75, 85
• San Juan National Forest

DOLORES RIVER MAJOR HATCHES

Insect	A	M	J	J	A	S	O	N	Time	Flies
Midge	■	■	■	■	■	■	■	■	M/A/E	Olive Biot Midge Pupa #16–#24; Brown Biot Midge Pupa #16–#24; Black Beauty #18–#24; Brassie #16–#24; Blood Midge #16–#24; AK's Midge Larva #16–#22; Disco Midge #18–#24; Black Beauty Pupa #18–#24; CDC Biot Suspender Midge #18–#24; Griffith's Gnat #16–#22; Palomino Midge #18–#22; Red Hot #18–#24; Tan Midge Pupa #8–#24
Blue-winged Olive	■					■			M/A	Olive Biot Nymph #18–#22; RS-2 #16–#24; Pheasant Tail Nymph #16–#20; Beadhead Pheasant Tail Nymph #16–#22; Flashback Pheasant Tail Nymph #16–#20; Olive Quill Emerger #18–#24; AK's Olive Quill #16–#22; Stalcup's Baetis #16–#22; Parachute Adams #12–#22; Olive Comparadun #16–#20; Gray Spinner #18–#24; CDC Baetis Dun #16–#22; Air-flo Cut-wing Dun #16–#22
Pale Morning Dun					■				M/A	Biot PMD Nymph #16; Pheasant Tail Nymph #16–#22; Beadhead Pheasant Tail Nymph #14–#20; Lt. Cahill Comparadun #12–#18; AK's Red Quill #14–#18; Rusty Spinner #12–#20; Sparkle Dun #14–#18; Parachute PMD #14–#18; Dark Hare's Ear #14–#18
Terrestrials						■			A/E	Rio Grande King Trude #12–#16; Royal Wulff #14–#18; Humpy #14–#18; H & L Variant #14–#18; Foam Madam X #8–#12; Renegade #10–#16; Black Ant #14–#20; Cinnamon Ant #14–#20; Black Beetle #14–#18; Gartside Hopper #8–#10; Henry's Fork Hopper #8–#12; Dave's Hopper #8–#12

HATCH TIME CODE: M = morning; A = afternoon; E = evening; D = dark; SF = spinner fall; / = continuation through periods.

DOLORES RIVER MAJOR HATCHES (CONT.)

Insect	A	M	J	J	A	S	O	N	Time	Flies
Early Brown Stonefly	▮								M	Rio Grande King Trude #18; Prince Nymph #14–#18; Beadhead Prince Nymph #14–#18; Dark Elk Hair Caddis #18–#20
Crawfish		▮	▮	▮	▮	▮	▮		M/A/E	Black Woolly Bugger #2–#10; Brown Woolly Bugger #4–#10; Muddler Minnow #4–#10; Halfback #4–#10; Kaufmann's Crawfish #4–#8
Caddis						▮			A/E	Olive Caddis Nymph #10–#20; Breadcrust #10–#18; Buckskin #16–#20; LaFontaine's Sparkle Caddis Pupa #10–#20; Elk Hair Caddis #10–#22; CDC Caddis #14–#20; Macramé Caddis #12–#16; Balloon Caddis #12–#16; Lawson's Caddis Emerger #14–#18; Spent Partridge Caddis #14–#18
Little Yellow Stonefly					▮				M/A	Gold-winged Prince Nymph #18; Yellow Stimulator #14–#18; Foam Yellow Sally #14–#18; Beadhead Prince Nymph #14–#18; Prince Nymph #14–#18

HATCH TIME CODE: M = morning; A = afternoon; E = evening; D = dark; SF = spinner fall; / = continuation through periods.

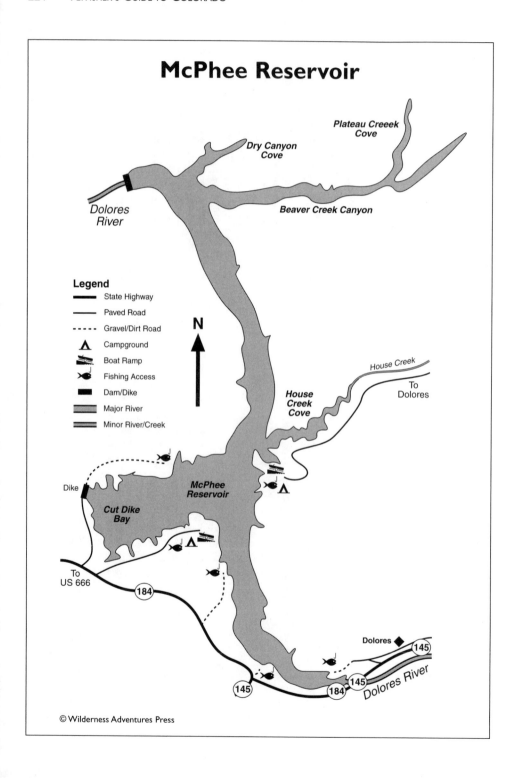

McPhee Reservoir

McPhee is a strangely shaped reservoir with long narrow bays. Despite its appearance, the reservoir, which spans about 4,300 acres and measures up to 250 feet deep, provides some good fishing.

The inlet area gradually drops to about 50 feet with several irregularities that prove good structure for a float tube fisher to cover. However, much of the lake drops very quickly from the shore, sometimes in excess of 100 feet in less than a couple thousand feet from shore. That type of drop is almost impossible to fish, even with high-density sink-tip lines. Due to those difficulties and the fact that smallmouth bass are one of the main species of fish in the lake, flyfishing here hasn't really caught on.

Smallmouth bass (smallies) prefer colder, clearer water than their counterpart, the largemouth bass. They also prefer rocky structure to vegetation for cover, making McPhee the perfect hangout for these fish. Smallies also love crawfish, and McPhee has plenty of them. Smallmouths are very efficient predators and will chow on all sorts of table fare: minnows, aquatic nymphs, and terrestrials, to name a few. But with their love of crawfish, reddish brown woolly buggers and Whitlock's crawfish are probably the best patterns for McPhee. Typical trout flies, both dry and wet, are good choices for smallies, too, as are Clouser's minnows.

Another advantage for the fly angler in pursuit of smallmouths is the fact that these bass seldom move into depths of more than 25 feet—well within the fishable range of a sinking fly line. Even when they do move to deeper water, the dinner bell brings them back into shallower water for food.

Therefore, concentrate your efforts in the early and late part of the day around rock structures in 10 feet of water. Slow retrieves imitate the crawfish and aquatic insects, while faster retrieves are best for imitating baitfish. Cloudy days usually bring the best smallmouth action. You can start fishing McPhee as early as April and continue through November, although May and June may be the best months for all species. For those who like a new experience and the chance to hook a gorgeous fish other than a trout, McPhee is definitely worth checking out.

To reach the reservoir from Durango, take US 160 west to Mancos. Turn right (north) on Colorado 184 and follow for 20 miles to the intersection with Colorado 145. Turn right on Colorado 145 to the town of Dolores to access the inlet area or jog left on Colorado 145, then back to the right on Colorado 184 to accesses on the south end of the lake.

There are a few fishing accesses on the southern part of the reservoir, including the inlet area on the southern tip of the lake. You can also access at the Big Bend access on the inlet bay, and McPhee Recreation Complex, which has a campground, boat ramp, drinking water, and facilities. The west side of the lake can be reached via CR 31 north from Dolores to CR 526. Continue north on CR 526 to the intersection with CR 528. Turn left and continue west to the reservoir. House Creek Recreation Area also has a campground, boat ramp, drinking water, and facilities. Much of the reservoir is inaccessible except by motorboat, so flyfishing is really limited to the improved access sites if you are in a float tube.

San Miguel River

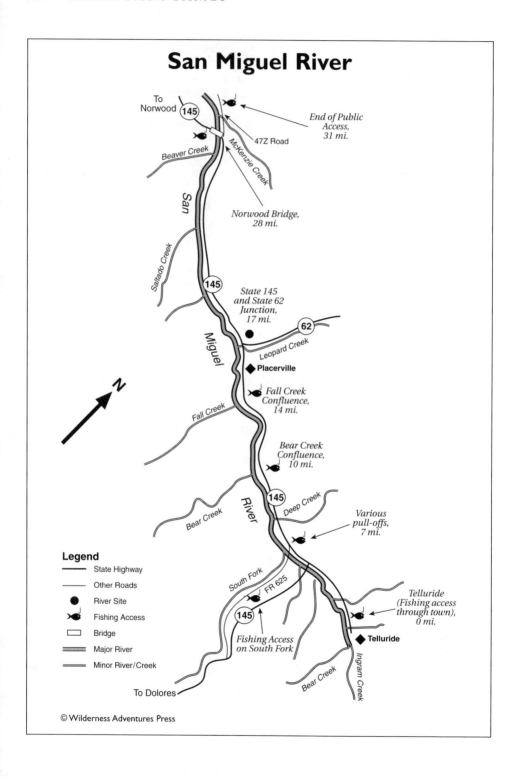

To Norwood (145)

47Z Road

Beaver Creek

McKenzie Creek

End of Public Access, 31 mi.

San

Norwood Bridge, 28 mi.

Saltado Creek

(145)

State 145 and State 62 Junction, 17 mi.

(62)

Leopard Creek

Miguel

Placerville

Fall Creek Confluence, 14 mi.

Fall Creek

Bear Creek Confluence, 10 mi.

N

River

(145)

Deep Creek

Various pull-offs, 7 mi.

Bear Creek

Legend

— State Highway

— Other Roads

● River Site

🐟 Fishing Access

▭ Bridge

═ Major River

Minor River/Creek

South Fork

FR 625

Telluride (Fishing access through town), 0 mi.

(145)

Fishing Access on South Fork

◆ Telluride

Ingram Creek

To Dolores

Bear Creek

© Wilderness Adventures Press

SAN MIGUEL RIVER

The San Miguel River is one of the few remaining freestone streams in Colorado without a dam impounding its waters. Its gradient fall starts above the town of Telluride where Bridal Veil Creek and Ingram Creek come together. Bear Creek enters the San Miguel at the east end of Telluride, making for a good-sized stream as it heads west on its way to the Dolores River.

The San Miguel has not been immune to the years of mining in the southwest part of the state; however, the stream is getting healthier every year.

Frank Smethurst, a resident of Telluride and flyfishing guide for Telluride Outside, says, "I've fished the San Miguel for a long time, and over the last 5 to 10 years I've seen great improvements in bug life. The middle portion of the river has better hatches of caddis and mayflies than I've ever seen!"

To reach the river from Durango, go north about 75 miles on US 550 to Ridgway. Take Colorado 62 west about 25 miles to the intersection with Colorado 145. The river now parallels Colorado 145, and you can turn left (south) and continue another 15 miles to Telluride, or turn north and find accesses to the stream along the highway to the Norwood Bridge. From there, you can take CR 47-Z north about 3 miles to the end of public access at the Cascabel Club.

From Grand Junction take US 50 about 60 miles to Montrose. Go south on US 550 just over 25 miles to Ridgway and follow the previous directions.

Access is well marked along Colorado 145, with pulloffs every couple miles. Please respect private property. Open water can also be found inside the city limits of Telluride.

The San Miguel can be fished as early as February and March during a warm weather stretch. The pools up and down the river hold trout throughout the winter months; however, the local flyfishermen are more apt to take advantage of these times than the traveling angler, as getting over the mountain passes to this area in winter is unpredictable due to weather.

Since the lure of big trout does not plague this river, it flows in peace during the winter and spring months. A lonesome fisherman may encounter hatches of early brown and black stones. Baetis may also be seen. With the river at low flows, an occasional trout may rise along the edge or at the tail end of the deeper pools. A Rio Grande trude in size 16 is a good imitation for the stones, while a parachute Adams is always a good choice for the mayflies.

There could be snow along the river in the early spring, so care should be taken. Avoid walking on ice shelves near the bank. A good dunking in the frigid water is generally not enjoyable, nor are the injuries you could sustain.

Rods from 8 to 9 feet, casting a 4- or 5-weight line, are ideal for the San Miguel. Leaders of 9 to 10 feet in length tapered to 4X should work for most situations.

Most trout will be taken on standard subsurface flies such as Prince nymphs, dark hare's ears, and beadhead pheasant tails. Sizes 14 to 18 will move fish for the persistent angler.

San Miguel River.

All hell breaks loose as runoff hits the Miguel. This freestone runs heavy from early May through mid-June, depending on snow pack. Above-average snowfall may delay the fishery an additional two weeks. After a good scouring, the river is fishable by the first week in July.

Smethurst describes the river, "The San Miguel is a user friendly river. It can be fished successfully by the novice or enjoyed by the most experienced of anglers. Its ease of access and aggressive trout provides great training ground for the beginner. With its fast difficult currents, the more athletic wader can find challenging pocket water holding trout seldom caught."

Golden stones can be seen on the water late in the runoff, but this is very sporadic at best. While the river is still off-color or running high, big golden stonefly nymph patterns move fish from their protective lies.

Caddis and PMD activity is much more reliable. Brownish colored caddis, rating a size 16, hatch in July up and down the river. Brown and rainbow trout averaging 10 to 14 inches can be seen rising to adult caddis from noon, continuing on into the evening. Brown Goddard and dark elk hair caddis draw these aggressive feeders to the surface. Soft hackle hare's ears, olive caddis, and breadcrust nymphs are good subsurface flies while the trout are not rising.

"The current is so quick in this stream that the trout have very little time to decide whether to take a fly or let it go by. A dry fly drifting over any likely looking water along the bank or behind a rock can produce an explosive strike," Smethurst suggests. "Rainbows are always looking for nymphs as they swing around the rocks. Again, when they catch a glimpse of anything resembling food, more often than not, they take it."

Pale morning duns are becoming more abundant in the water between Placerville downstream to Norwood Bridge. The mid-morning hatch can draw every trout in the river into feeding lanes, waiting for emergers and adults to come into view. Concentrate your efforts on structure where the speed of the water is broken. They need the shelter from the energy-draining currents. These are the only areas in the river trout will hold. When hooked, these trout fight better, pound for pound, than any trout I have ever caught. They use the fast currents to test equipment to its max.

Even though the river does not have special regulations, more and more people are realizing the importance of releasing trout so they can be caught again. After taking a trout from these wild currents, I'm sure the thought of watching it swim away will cross your mind. Let your conscience be your guide.

Well-hackled flies, such as a standard light Cahill, gray fox variant and ginger quills in sizes 12 to 16, will do for these undiscriminating trout. Tan RS-2s and light olive floating nymphs work well in the surface film. Pheasant tails and dark hare's ears copy the nymphs.

The fall is a great time to hook the better browns in the river on streamers. Woolly buggers and spruce fly streamers produce energetic strikes along the bottom or near the tail end of the pools.

You need a straightforward approach on the San Miguel to catch fish, nothing fancy. The rough water can be fished by just getting the fly in the water and moving it through the structure. More important than the outstanding fishing to be had, the river receives very little pressure. Solitude can be found in great proportions. Respect other's privacy as you approach the river.

Smethurst suggests, "When you see a car parked on the side of the road, go on to the next pulloff; there are plenty. When everyone uses this simple plan, its not uncommon for an angler to have as much as a half mile or more of river to him or her self."

You can contact Frank Smethurst at PO Box 801, Telluride, CO 81435, or call 9 70-728-4369.

South Fork of the San Miguel River.

San Miguel Tributaries

The South Fork of the San Miguel flows into the main stem of the river west of Telluride about 5 miles. From Colorado 145, take FR 625 south to follow the stream.

Another 4 miles west on Colorado 145, find Big Bear Creek. Take CR 60M south as it parallels the stream.

Fall Creek's confluence with the San Miguel is about 4 miles downstream from Big Bear Creek. It follows CR 57P south to Woods Lake State Wildlife Area.

These streams flow through the national forest, with small stretches of private property mixed in. They are all small streams capable of holding only small trout. Rainbows, browns, and brookies ranging from 6 to 10 inches are common. Beautiful scenery with more of a wilderness experience awaits the angler who likes more seclusion.

Stream Facts: San Miguel River

Seasons
• Open all year

Trout
• Browns are the predominant species, averaging 10 to 14 inches. Trout over 18 inches are caught occasionally.
• Rainbows, strong fighting fish, average between 10 and 14 inches.
• Brookies
• Cutthroat

River Miles
• Telluride—0   • Colorado 145 and 162 Intersection—17
• South Fork Confluence—7   • Norwood Bridge—28
• Bear Creek Confluence—10   • CR 47Z—31
• Fall Creek Confluence—14

River Characteristics
• A small river in nature, filled with a lot of opportunities for the flyfisher. A true mountain stream flowing through the heart of western Colorado. One of the few remaining freestones in Colorado without a dam obstructing its flow. Good pocket water fishing, along with deep runs and bug infested riffles.

River Flows
• Winter and spring, 100–350 cfs
• Runoff, May and June, 600–850 cfs
• Summer and fall, 250–400 cfs

Maps
• *Colorado Atlas & Gazetteer*, pages 65, 66, 76
• Uncompahgre National Forest

SAN MIGUEL RIVER MAJOR HATCHES

Insect	A	M	J	J	A	S	O	N	Time	Flies
Caddis				▓	▓				A/E	Olive Caddis Nymph #10–#20; Breadcrust #10–#18; Beadhead Breadcrust #10–#18; Buckskin #16–#20; LaFontaine's Sparkle Caddis Pupa #10–#20; Soft Hackle Hare's Ear #12–#16; Elk Hair Caddis #10–#22; Goddard Caddis #10–#16; CDC Caddis #14–#20; Balloon Caddis #12–#16; Lawson's Caddis Emerger #14–#18; Spent Partridge Caddis #14–#18
Pale Morning Dun				▓	▓				M/A	Biot PMD Nymph #16; Pheasant Tail Nymph #16–#22; Beadhead Pheasant Tail Nymph #14–#20; Lt. Cahill #12–#18; Gray Fox Variant #12–#16; Olive Floating Nymph #12–#16; Sparkle Dun #14–#18; Parachute PMD #14–#18; Dark Hare's Ear #14–#18
Blue-winged Olive		▓			▓	▓			M/A	Olive Biot Nymph #18–#22; RS-2 #16–#24; Pheasant Tail Nymph #16–#20; Beadhead Pheasant Tail Nymph #16–#20; Flashback Pheasant Tail Nymph #16–#20; Olive Quill Emerger #18–#24; AK's Olive Quill #16–#22; Parachute Adams #12–#22; Olive Comparadun #16–#20; Gray Spinner #18–#24; Air-flo Cut-wing Dun #16–#22

HATCH TIME CODE: M = morning; A = afternoon; E = evening; D = dark; SF = spinner fall; / = continuation through periods.

SAN MIGUEL RIVER MAJOR HATCHES (CONT.)

Insect	A	M	J	J	A	S	O	N	Time	Flies
Terrestrials				▓	▓				A/E	Rio Grande King Trude #8–#16; Royal Wulff #10–#16; Humpy #10–#16; Foam Madam X #8–#12; Renegade #10–#16; Black Ant #14–#20; Cinnamon Ant #14–#20; Peacock Beetle #14–#18; Gartside Hopper #8–#10; Henry's Fork Hopper #8–#12
Golden Stonefly			▓	▓					A/E	Sandy's Gold #6–#10; Gold-winged Prince Nymph #8–#10; Kaufmann's Golden Stonefly #6–#12; Stimulator #8–#16; Foam Yellow Sally #12–#18; Prince Nymph #8–#16; Beadhead Prince Nymph #8–#16; Bitch Creek Nymph #10
Streamers	▓						▓	▓	M/E	Black Woolly Bugger #2–#10; Brown Woolly Bugger #4–#10; Spruce Fly #4–#10; Black-nosed Dace #6–#8; Muddler Minnow #4–#10; Matuka Sculpin #4–#10

HATCH TIME CODE: M = morning; A = afternoon; E = evening; D = dark; SF = spinner fall; / = continuation through periods.

Los Piños River

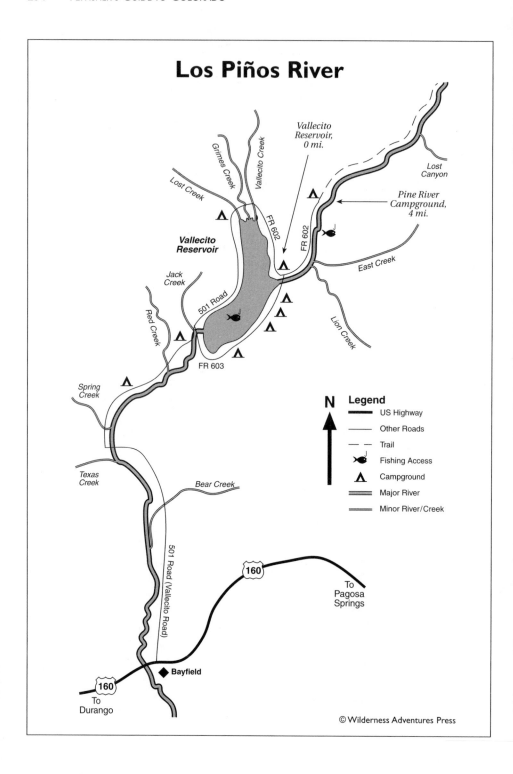

Grimes Creek

Vallecito Creek

Lost Creek

Vallecito Reservoir, 0 mi.

Lost Canyon

Pine River Campground, 4 mi.

FR 602

FR 602

East Creek

Vallecito Reservoir

Jack Creek

501 Road

Red Creek

Lion Creek

FR 603

Spring Creek

Texas Creek

Bear Creek

501 Road (Vallecito Road)

160

To Pagosa Springs

◆ Bayfield

160

To Durango

N

Legend
- US Highway
- Other Roads
- Trail
- Fishing Access
- ▲ Campground
- Major River
- Minor River/Creek

© Wilderness Adventures Press

Los Piños River

The Los Piños, as is the case in much of Colorado, most of the river runs through private land, and the prime 6 miles of river just above Vallecito Reservoir are no exception.

Public access to the river begins at Pine River Campground on the east side of Vallecito Reservoir, but the road ends there, and you have to hit the trail on foot. If you choose to do that, follow trail 523 as it heads northeast from the campground and parallels the river for at least another 25 miles to the Continental Divide in the Weminuche Wilderness Area. A horseback or backpacking trip upstream is the only access. Putting out the effort to make this trip can be very rewarding.

The lower half of the trail has a slight gradient and is a moderately easy hike. The upper part of the trail has a few meadow stretches but climbs faster as it nears the Continental Divide. As soon as you enter the wilderness area, just over a 3-mile walk, the river basically runs through a broad valley with easy access to the stream. Easy wading, wide-open casting, and lots of small trout make it a great place to stop.

Trout in the Los Piños are not picky; an attractor dry fly is all you need to hook aggressive brook and brown trout.

Just above its confluence with Lake Creek, the Los Piños tumbles through a steep canyon. It's very difficult to access, and, once there, the pocket water fishing can be challenging. But there are some very good trout residing in that water, and the eager angler should be able to hook up with some trout reaching 16 inches or more.

Above the canyon, the river opens up into another meadow section known as Willow Park, where it meanders through turn after turn of riffles and deep undercuts. It's easy to wade, even in old tennis shoes. When standing in the stream, you are about 10 miles from the trailhead, so you likely will have the area to yourself while cooling your feet.

The wild trout here are easily taken on any dry fly. Caddis and terrestrials are abundant, but mayfly hatches are sparse.

Elk hair caddis, ranging from size 14 to 18, will cover evening situations. Olive comparaduns and parachute Adams also in similar sizes are good mayfly imitations. A mixed box of ants, beetles and hoppers should also be carried.

For those of you with legs made of steel, the river continues up the mountain and becomes much smaller. Other venues along the way are Flint Creek, about 2 miles above Willow Park, and Flint Lakes, up another 6 miles along Trail 527. Granite and Divide Lakes are about 14 miles from the trailhead. All the lakes will have hatches of Callibaetis, damsels, and midges, with wild trout ranging from 10 to 16 inches. Once there, it's a long walk back to the car, but the fishing can be great.

From Pagosa Springs, take US 160 west just over 40 miles to Bayfield. Bayfield is also 17 miles east of Durango on US 160. Take CR 501, also known as Vallecito Road, north to Vallecito Reservoir. At the north end of the reservoir, take FR 602 around the top of the lake to the Los Piños River. Veer east, following the river through private land to the Pine River Campground. A well-marked and well-used trailhead follows the river into the San Juan National Forest. The first 3 miles of the river and trail above the campground are on private property. Stay on the trail until you reach the national forest boundary.

Jerry and Nancy Freeman, owners of Anasazi Anglers in Durango, guide on private water on the Los Piños River below Vallecito Reservoir. Contact them at 607 Sunnyside Drive, Durango 81301, or call 970-385-4665. Their email address is angler@rmii.com.

Lake Creek and Emerald Lake

There are several destinations in the Los Piños basin besides the river itself, and Lake Creek and Emerald Lake are a couple worth checking out.

To reach them, take Trail 523, from the Pine Campground, up 6 miles to Trail 528. Go left (directly north) on Trail 528, which parallels Lake Creek, another 4 miles to reach Emerald Lakes. The steep hike ascends 1,500 feet in those 4 miles. The trail continues on above the lakes and provides more access to Lake Creek.

The 4 miles of Lake Creek, from its confluence with the Los Piños to Emerald Lakes, are a rugged stream, with mostly pocket water. Brown, rainbow, brook, and cutthroat trout averaging 8 to 12 inches are commonly caught here. Toss the big dry fly stuff at them. Hit every piece of slack water behind the rocks and along the banks with royal Wulffs, humpies, and trude patterns.

Emerald Lake sits at 10,000 feet, but, surprisingly, there is a very good population of cuttbows in the lake. In fact, this strain of trout is used for stocking other high mountain lakes in Colorado.

Those hybrids range from 12 to 18 inches, with a few pushing a couple pounds. The Division of Wildlife calls the lake Wild Trout Water, so the water is governed by artificial flies and lures only regulations and a 2 fish under 14 inches bag limit.

Emerald is a very fertile lake that has a good insect base. Hatches of caddis and Callibaetis mayflies occur during the summer months. Damselflies are also important, as are small terrestrials, such as ants and beetles.

Tan caddis range up to size 10, with a natural Goddard caddis being a good imitation. A standard elk hair caddis will also take these hungry trout during the afternoon and evening hours.

For the Callibaetis, try a size 14 Adams. Callibaetis hatches commonly occur in the morning. Do not discount presenting a nymph during this hatch. A ginger hare's ear or Kaufmann's timberline emerger dropped under the dry can be very effective, especially when you are sight casting to rising trout.

A rusty spinner is an outstanding high mountain lake pattern when the mating insects are on the water.

Damselflies provide excellent fishing, both in the nymphal and adult stages. An olive marabou damsel nymph in size 8 through 12, stripped slowly toward shore in the late morning, is a good pattern. Switching to an adult pattern in the afternoon should keep you in sync with the hatch.

Don't forget about midges. The evening sky can be filled with them. Small biot emergers, Griffith's gnats, and palomino midges should work for any surface activity. Keep the pattern size between 16 and 22.

It's a tough go of it getting to the lakes, but the overall beauty and the wonderful fishing may encourage you to mark a calendar for another excursion into the Los Piños watershed.

Stream Facts: Los Piños River

Seasons
- Open all year. Access difficult until late June and early July.

Special Regulations
- From headwaters to Weminuche Wilderness boundary: Artificial flies and lures only. Bag and possession limit is 2 trout.

Trout
- Rainbows, browns, brookies and cutthroats to 14 inches.

River Miles
- Vallecito Reservoir (private water) — 0
- Pine River Campground (Trailhead 523) — 4
- Lake Creek Confluence (Trailhead 528) — 10
- Willow Park — 14
- Flint Creek Confluence (Trailhead 527) — 16
- Granite Lake — 20

River Characteristics
- Small stream conditions above Vallecito. A trail follows the river giving access to those who hike or ride horses. Expect typical pocket water with lots of structure and several meadow sections.

River Flows
- Above Vallecito Reservoir, the flows are that of a normal small freestone. Unfishable in late May and June.

Maps
- *Colorado Atlas & Gazetteer,* pages 77, 87
- San Juan National Forest

LOS PIÑOS RIVER MAJOR HATCHES

Insect	A	M	J	J	A	S	O	N	Time	Flies
Stonefly				▓					M/A	Sandy's Gold #6–#10; Gold-winged Prince Nymph #8–#10; Kaufmann's Golden Stonefly #6–#12; Stimulator #8–#12; Foam Yellow Sally #12–#18; Halfback #4–#10; Prince Nymph #8–#16; Beadhead Prince Nymph #8–#16; Sofa Pillow #6–#8; Bitch Creek Nymph #10
Caddis			▓	▓	▓	▓			A/E	Olive Caddis Nymph #10–#20; Breadcrust #10–#18; Beadhead Breadcrust #10–#18; Buckskin #16–#20; LaFontaine's Sparkle Caddis Pupa #10–#20; Elk Hair Caddis #10–#22; Goddard Caddis #10–#16
Mayflies			▓	▓	▓	▓			M/A	Olive Biot Nymph #12–#18; RS-2 #14–#18; Pheasant Tail Nymph #12–#18; Beadhead Pheasant Tail Nymph #12–#18; AK's Olive Quill #12–#16; Parachute Adams #12–#20; Green Drake Emerger #10–#12; Lawson's Parachute Green Drake #10–#12; Green Drake #10–#12; AK's Red Quill #14–#18; Rusty Spinner #12–#20; Lt. Cahill Comparadun #12–#18; Sparkle Dun #14–#18; Parachute PMD #14–#18
Terrestrials				▓	▓	▓			A/E	Rio Grande King Trude #8–#16; Royal Wulff #10–#16; Humpy #10–#16; Foam Madam X #8–#12; Renegade #10–#16; Black Ant #14–#20; Peacock Beetle #12–#16; Gartside Hopper #8–#10; Joe's Hopper #8–#12
Midge			▓	▓	▓	▓	▓		A/E	Olive Biot Midge #12–#18; Brown Biot Midge #12–#18; Blood Midge #12–#18; Feather Duster Midge #14–#20; Black Beauty Pupa #12–#18; CDC Biot Suspender Midge #12–#18; Griffith's Gnat #12–#20; Palomino Midge #12–#20

HATCH TIME CODE: M = morning; A = afternoon; E = evening; D = dark; SF = spinner fall; / = continuation through periods.

VALLECITO RESERVOIR

Located 15 miles north of the town of Bayfield on CR 501, Vallecito Reservoir is a popular destination for all anglers. However, most fly anglers have not yet taken advantage of the opportunities held here. Most flyfishers come to the area to fish the Los Piños River and Vallecito Creek above the reservoir. The lake is quite imposing to the flyfisherman, due to its overall size and number of bigger boats cruising for its large fish.

From Durango, take US 160 east to Bayfield. Turn north on CR 501 and follow the signs to the reservoir.

Float tubing seems to be the best means of transportation for the flyfisherman, but catarafts are becoming more and more popular. Whatever means you choose to fish from is personal preference; however, the location you choose to fish is critical. The north and east sides of the lake, where the two main inlet areas come in to the reservoir, are good starting points. The north end of lake has three creek channels gradually sloping to 50 feet. Submerged lumber in the area provides excellent cover for both the trout and pike. Nearing the area where the Los Piños River enters the lake, some 500 feet from the east bank, the lake drops to depths of 35 to 40 feet, providing sharp structure that fish love to hold and feed along. The southeast side of the reservoir probably has some of the best overall structure in the lake. Several small creeks enter the lake, forming small channels that are always good to check out. There are several humps about a half-mile from the east bank coming up to within 10 feet of the surface. These undulations are a main attraction for trolling fishermen; a float tube may be a bit small to compete. Furthermore, the southeast end has two boat ramps and four campgrounds, making it a very popular area.

Vallecito has a very diverse food base that grows very respectable trout and northern pike. Scuds, damsels, leeches, and midges are present, with mayflies and crawfish adding to the fare.

Trout are best fished by moving a woolly bugger in and out of the underwater cover (namely, the stumps in the north end of the reservoir) or by following a shelf near the bank at a certain depth.

"At what depth?" you may ask. A good question, but not always easy to answer. Starting from an area close to the bank with a floating line and a 12-foot leader, you can work water down 8 to 10 feet pretty efficiently. Beyond that, a sinktip or fullsinking line is needed. Systematically cover an area using different amounts of split shot or sinking line, trolling speed, and retrieval action until you find one that works. No one said it would be easy, but covering small areas one at a time makes the process a little easier and less trying on the patience.

At the edge of or over the top of submerged vegetation are also prime waters to cover extensively. This is an area to switch to nymphal patterns. Olive scuds, damsel nymphs, and light colored hare's ear nymphs ranging from size 10 to 16 are productive.

May and June are prime months for insect hatches. Midges, Callibaetis, and damsels will all be active and trout actively feed on them. Typically, standard trout rods up to 10 feet in a 5- or 6-weight are ideal for casting from a float tube.

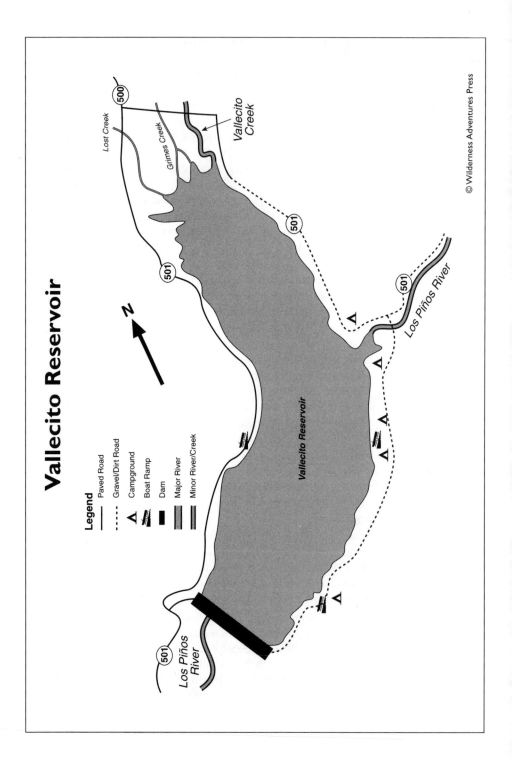

Vallecito Reservoir

Legend

Paved Road
Gravel/Dirt Road
Campground
Boat Ramp
Dam
Major River
Minor River/Creek

Lost Creek

Grimes Creek

Vallecito Creek

Vallecito Reservoir

Los Piños River

Los Piños River

© Wilderness Adventures Press

When going after the northern pike, rods in an 8 to 10 weight are needed to cast the big heavy flies. A fly line with a dramatic weight forward design should be used to aid in casting the heavy flies. There are special bass bug taper or a pike/muskie lines on the market made especially for this type of fishing. It makes a distant cast with a large air resistant fly much easier. Both Cortland and Scientific Angler make a line for this use.

June presents the best window for the fly angler to hook a 20-plus pound northern pike. After the pike have spawned, they like to hang out in the warm shallow water of the north end of the reservoir looking for an easy meal. Look for water temperatures in the high 50s to mid-60s while on your hunt for the big fish. Testing the water with a thermometer, instead of a blind cast, can save a lot of time in determining where to fish. Shallows warm at different rates during the day, depending on sun and wind direction. The shallows on the northeast side of the lake and the small inlet areas on the south side should be checked out by 11:00 a.m. Continue your search until early evening.

Cover is another important element to successful pike fishing. This predator likes to lay in wait and attack from thick vegetation or submerged structure. The stumps in the north end of the lake provide such an area. Cast near these areas with a black bunny fly, woolly bugger, or a deer hair popper for some possible surface action. Vary your retrieve from slow to fast, short to long, and everything in between. There is no set way to do things that will work every time.

Barry Reynolds, author of *Pike on a Fly*, observes, "One of the most frustrating things about pike is the follow. They come in behind your fly and follow it, sometimes all the way to your feet. This can happen cast after cast. I try to take it away from them, just like a bait fish may try to escape the jaws of death. A fast, foot long retrieve in front of the pike or taking your rod tip to the side and pulling the fly into the pike's side view can produce a quick lunging strike."

Generally speaking, earlier in the day, when the water is in the fifties, a slower retrieve is best. Pick up the pace and length of your retrieve as the water warms in the middle of the afternoon. Try to cover a lot of water in a short period of time.

Once the water temperature is near 70 degrees, generally occurring in late July and August, the pike will head for deeper, cooler water. Forget the pike in the hot afternoons. However, they still like to visit the shallow water in the early mornings and late evenings for breakfast and dinner.

There are five campgrounds on the east side of the reservoir and one north of the reservoir on CR 500. All the amenities of home, including stores, restaurants, and even a church, can be found on the west side of the lake. Lodges and cabins are also available. Call the Vallecito Chamber of Commerce at 970-884-9782 or write to P.O. Box 804, Bayfield, CO 81122 for more information.

Lake Facts: Vallecito Reservoir

Seasons
- Ice-out to ice-on for the fly angler

Trout
- Browns: Vallecito has always had a good population of good sized browns. Trout over 20 inches are caught regularly.
- Rainbows average 12 to 18 inches.

Other Species
- Northern Pike: Vallecito held the state record of 30 pounds and an ounce for years. Still a good population of big pike.
- Kokanee salmon

Lake Size
- 2700 acres; 110 feet deep at the dam.

Lake Character
- One of the only lakes I have ever seen with two main inlet streams. Vallecito Creek and Los Piños River come in the north end and east side of the lake, respectively. With two main channels and several small depressions from smaller streambeds in the bottom of the lake, trout and northern pike have lots of structure to feel safe in. The southeast side of the lake has the best overall structure, but this is also where most of the campgrounds are, so weekends may be crowded.

Maps
- Fish-n-Map Company, 303-421-5994
- San Juan National Forest

PIEDRA RIVER

Much of the Piedra is inaccessible by road, making for a more wilderness experience. In fact, the Piedra offers a great backpack opportunity—a good excuse to spend a little time with Mother Nature.

However, a few sections of the upper river can be reached by gravel roads in the San Juan National Forest, lessening the need for a backpack.

To reach the area from Pagosa Springs, go west 2 miles on US 160 to FR 631, also known as Piedra Road, and turn right (north). Stay on FR 631, which is a gravel road, for about 17 miles to FR 636. Turn right on FR 636, and soon you will parallel the stream inside the national forest boundaries. The road comes to a dead end about 4 miles up, and a foot trail follows the upper section of the Middle Fork of the Piedra. Forest Road 637 turns off of FR 636, about 2 miles from the intersection with FR 631, and heads to the East Fork of the Piedra. This fork is difficult to reach, so if you visit, plan on hiking up and down the stream once you get to it. A four-wheel drive is recommended, especially if the road is wet. This will be a great wilderness excursion if you go, so plan a couple days fishing.

Another section that is important to backpacking flyfishers is the north-central part of the river as it flows southwest along Trail 596. Trail 596 can be reached from either the upper or lower end of the river. The trailhead begins at the bridge over the Piedra River on FR 631 and heads southwest following the river. This bridge is about 15 miles from US 160 out of Pagosa Springs. The lower end of the trail can be reached from FR 622, also known as First Fork Road. Go 20 miles west of Pagosa Springs on Highway 160 to First Fork Road. Turn right (north) and continue north about 12 miles to the end of the gravel road at Piedra Bridge. Trail 596 heads northeast following the river 12 miles to FR 631.

Wherever you choose to fish on the Piedra, try to hit the stream after mid-June. Trails in the area should be open by that time, and the river should be relatively clear.

As described, the Middle Fork is the easiest section to reach. This wonderful little freestone river is very good stonefly water, so bring patterns accordingly. Big golden stoneflies and the lesser yellow stone are active by mid- to late June, and they provide good surface activity through July.

Normally, fishing is productive with stonefly nymphs at the tail end of the long riffles. Gold-winged Prince nymphs and Kaufmann's golden stones are simple patterns to use here. Remember, the stones are migrating toward shore, and they hatch into an adult while resting on willow branches or rocks. With that in mind, the slower edges near the bank are excellent areas to drift the subsurface patterns.

However, why fish nymphs if you can fish a dry fly? Yellow stimulators in sizes 14 and 16 cover the small yellow stones, while larger golden stones can be imitated with a high floating Bird's stone in sizes 6 through 10. The best approach is to fish from the middle of the stream, casting into any slack water pocket along the banks. Expect wild rainbow and brown trout ranging from 8 to 12 inches to come out of nowhere and clobber your fly.

Piedra River

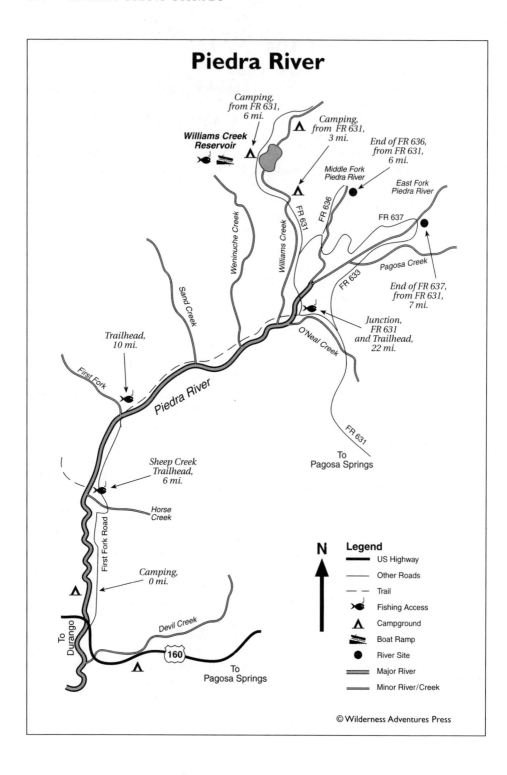

Camping,
from FR 631,
6 mi.

Camping,
from FR 631,
3 mi.

**Williams Creek
Reservoir**

End of FR 636,
from FR 631,
6 mi.

Middle Fork
Piedra River

East Fork
Piedra River

FR 637

Weminuche Creek

Williams Creek

FR 631

FR 636

Pagosa Creek

End of FR 637,
from FR 631,
7 mi.

Sand Creek

FR 633

Junction,
FR 631
and Trailhead,
22 mi.

Trailhead,
10 mi.

O'Neal Creek

First Fork

Piedra River

FR 631

To
Pagosa Springs

Sheep Creek
Trailhead,
6 mi.

Horse
Creek

First Fork Road

Camping,
0 mi.

Devil Creek

To
Durango

160

To
Pagosa Springs

N

Legend

▬▬	US Highway
—	Other Roads
– –	Trail
🐟	Fishing Access
▲	Campground
🚤	Boat Ramp
●	River Site
▬▬	Major River
▬▬	Minor River/Creek

© Wilderness Adventures Press

Green drakes and PMDs may be seen on the river from mid-July through August. Any well-hackled green drake pattern works for this hatch. If you know green drakes have been hatching on the river prior to your arrival but you do not see a hatch, toss the green drake patterns anyway. The trout become keyed on the big mayfly and will take a well-presented pattern out of instinct, even when the real thing fails to make an appearance. When the smaller PMDs are on the water, a light olive parachute pattern works well.

Caddis are also abundant, and elk hair caddis in sizes 12 to 16 will cover any situation. Gray and tan colored patterns are best.

The East Fork Piedra is much more difficult to reach and fish. There is no distinct trail along the stream, so be prepared to do a little bushwhacking if you choose to fish this stretch.

The stream is also much tighter than the Middle Fork, which makes wading and casting more difficult. The fish run smaller here, as well. Brookies and cutthroats range between 8 and 10 inches on average. Other than those deterrents, expect the same insects and hatch times. On the bright side, this is the closest to an untouched wilderness as you can find in the state. It's beautiful.

The long, 12-mile section of river starting at FR 631 along Trail 596 offers an exciting trip off the beaten path into some very diverse water. You can jump on the trail and fish downstream for a couple miles, turn around and fish back up to the trailhead, trying to remember where you may have jerked a royal Wulff out of the mouth of a nice brown.

This makes for a good day of fishing, but most anglers like to pack in and spend a night or two. There are several flat areas along the river to camp. This is flies and lures only water with a 2 fish possession limit. Rattlesnakes should be a concern.

A good mix of water types on this stretch will keep you thinking and changing your strategy often. This is good stonefly water, too, with the big salmonflies also coming off in abundance. Riffles, runs, and pools make up most of the upper half of this section, and the big bugs love that combination.

The lower half of this stretch tumbles through a canyon known as the Second Box Canyon. Fishing is difficult, and wading along the vertical walls is ass-busting work.

That physical pain can be rewarded by the stonefly hatch if you hit the water by mid-June. Remember, though, that during high water years the river will remain unfishable until July. If you do find good water conditions, try a size 6 halfback underneath and go with a size 4 improved sofa pillow on the surface.

Expect to see many of the same mayfly and caddis species as you would on the Middle Fork. A good mix of patterns such as a parachute Adams, light Cahill, elk hair caddis, and one of my favorite dry flies, the renegade, should be carried.

Anytime during August can offer excellent terrestrial fishing, primarily with grasshoppers. Afternoons are the best time to hit the water with these imitations. Gartside hoppers, Joe's hoppers, and Letort hoppers in size 8 can bring up the best of trout.

Other angling options while you are in the area include Williams Creek and Williams Creek Reservoir. Williams Creek is a major tributary to the Piedra. It parallels FR 631 north to Williams Creek Reservoir and is easily accessed from the road. However, an infrequently fished stretch of the stream is at the confluence with the Piedra. Follow Trail 596 downstream 1 mile from FR 631 to find the creek. Fish up into this faster, heavier gradient stream. Slap big attractor dry flies on the surface, and you are sure to draw strikes.

Williams Creek Reservoir offers good shore flyfishing for rainbows and brookies in the evenings. Try a parachute Adams, Griffith's gnat or a renegade in sizes ranging from 14 to 18. Camping is available just below the reservoir.

Be reminded that this is truly one of the most beautiful wilderness pieces of Colorado. We need your cooperation in maintaining this beauty. Please use good judgment while afoot in this country. Tread lightly, pack out what you pack in, and leave a few smarter trout for the next angler.

Stream Facts: Piedra River

Season
• Open all year. Access is tough until midsummer.

Special Regulations
• From the Piedra River bridge on FR 631 downstream to 1.5 miles from US 160: Artificial flies and lures only. Bag and possession limit is 2 trout.

Trout
• Wild rainbows to 14 inches. Browns, brookies and cutthroats also present.

River Miles
• Camping (Lower Piedra Campground) — 0
• Sheep Creek Trailhead — 6
• Trailhead — 10
• Intersection with FR 631 — 22
• End of FR 637 from FR 631 — 7
• End of FR 636 from FR 631 — 6
• Camping (Bridge Campground on Williams Creek) — 3
• Camping from FR 631 (Williams Creek Campground) — 6

River Characteristics
• From the bridge at FR 631 downstream, the Piedra River is a meadow section followed by a deep canyon. Mostly pocket water and deep pools. Above the bridge is a slower gradient, but small stream conditions remain. Pocket water, plunge pools, and lots of structure.

River Flows
• It is a typical small freestone stream. High water through June makes it unfishable. Low, clear flows through the fall.

Maps
• *Colorado Atlas & Gazetteer*, pages 87, 88
• San Juan National Forest

PIEDRA RIVER MAJOR HATCHES

Insect	A	M	J	J	A	S	O	N	Time	Flies
Stonefly			▓	▓					A/E	Gold-winged Prince Nymph #8–#10; Kaufmann's Golden Stonefly #6–#12; Stimulator #6–#12; Foam Yellow Sally #12–#18; Halfback #4–#10; Prince Nymph #8–#16; Beadhead Prince Nymph #8–#16; Kaufmann's Brown Stonefly #4–#8; Sofa Pillow #6–#8; Bitch Creek Nymph #10
Green Drake				▓	▓				A/E	Green Drake Emerger #10–#12; Lawson's Parachute Green Drake #10–#12; Green Drake #10–#12; Adams #10–#12; Olive Hare's Ear #10–#12
Pale Morning Dun					▓				M/A	Biot PMD Nymph #16; Pheasant Tail Nymph #16–#22; Beadhead Pheasant Tail Nymph #14–#20; Lt. Cahill Comparadun #12–#18; Sparkle Dun #14–#18; Parachute PMD #14–#18; Dark Hare's Ear #14–#18; AK's Red Quill #14–#18; Rusty Spinner #12–#20
Terrestrial				▓	▓	▓			A/E	Rio Grande King Trude #8–#16; Royal Wulff #10–#16; Humpy #10–#16; Foam Madam X #8–#12; Renegade #10–#16; Black Ant #14–#20; Peacock Beetle #12–#16; Gartside Hopper #8–#10; Henry's Fork Hopper #8–#12
Caddis			▓	▓	▓	▓			A/E	Olive Caddis Nymph #10–#20; Breadcrust #10–#18; Beadhead Breadcrust #10–#18; Buckskin #16–#20; LaFontaine's Sparkle Caddis Pupa #10–#20; Elk Hair Caddis #10–#22; Goddard Caddis #10–#16; CDC Caddis #14–#20; Lawson's Caddis Emerger #14–#18; Spent Partridge Caddis #14–#18

HATCH TIME CODE: M = morning; A = afternoon; E = evening; D = dark; SF = spinner fall; / = continuation through periods.

SAN JUAN RIVER

The main river begins as the West Fork and the East Fork come together about 8 miles north of Pagosa Springs on US 160. The San Juan River is private until you reach Pagosa Springs. There is a mile of river open to fishing in town, downstream of the Apache Street bridge. However, much of the East and West Forks are on national forest and can be good small stream flyfishing.

The West Fork

The West Fork is accessible from just below Wolf Creek Pass on the west side. About 8 miles down from the pass, turn onto FR 648 to reach the West Fork Campground. The stream below the campground paralleling the highway is private.

To fish the West Fork, you must be willing to hike or ride a horse a few miles to reach good water. From the campground, Rainbow Trail follows the river into the national forest. Take notice of the mile of private property just above the campground; it is well marked. Please stay on the trail.

The trail is above the stream for the first few miles, and access to the water can be a struggle. This free falling stream is tough for the experienced caster, let alone a beginner. From the confluence with Beaver Creek, there are several small meadows upstream which provide your first real chance to fish the West Fork.

Rainbow, brown, cutthroat, and brook trout up to 12 inches call this stream home. However, the average will be just under 10 inches. With a lack of angling pressure and a short feeding season, these greedy trout will eat anything that floats by. Stoneflies and caddis inhabit the stream and provide the best fare. High floating elk hair caddis and stimulators in sizes 10 to 14 are good choices for this rough pocket water. There is also a small green drake mayfly hatching in July, so be prepared with a size 12 green drake. Again, use lots of hackle to keep the fly riding high.

Not many people would think a 3-mile hike to a stream with 10-inch trout is worth the effort, but this is one of the most picturesque hikes in Colorado. This is a trip for those who like solitude and enjoy lugging an extra 5 pounds of camera and film around with them.

The East Fork

I stumbled upon the East Fork about 12 years ago, late one October night on my way back to Denver after a few days fishing the San Juan River below Navaho Reservoir. The lines on the road started to waver a bit, so I decided to stop for the night. I turned down a gravel road indicating a campground nearby. I found the campground, had a beer, and unrolled the sleeping bag. The night was accompanied by that relaxing babble of water tumbling over rocks which led to a good night's sleep in the back of the truck.

The sun was up in no time, and I needed to hit the road for home. I boiled up water for a cup of coffee and a bowl of oatmeal. The stream was at the end of the campsite, so I stumbled down the trail, coffee in hand, to check it out. I've always had a weakness for small streams, and this one turned out to be no different.

San Juan River

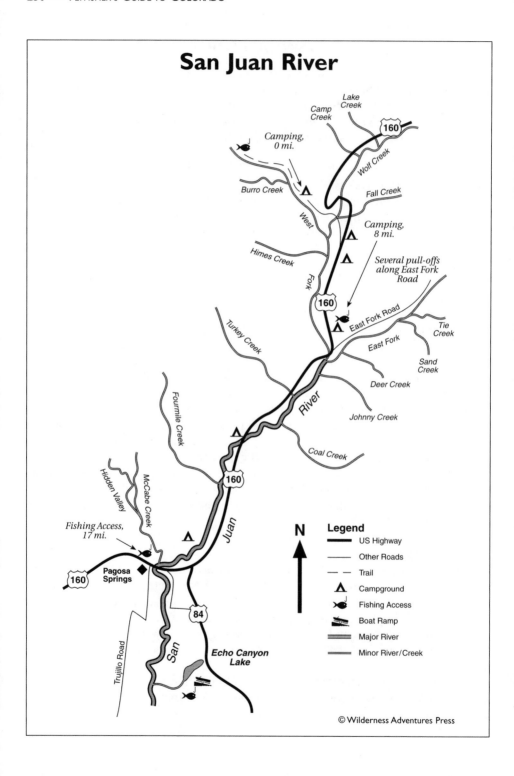

Lake Creek

Camp Creek

160

Camping, 0 mi.

Wolf Creek

Burro Creek

Fall Creek

West

Camping, 8 mi.

Himes Creek

Several pull-offs along East Fork Road

Fork

160

East Fork Road

Tie Creek

Turkey Creek

East Fork

Sand Creek

River

Deer Creek

Fourmile Creek

Johnny Creek

Coal Creek

160

McCabe Creek

Hidden Valley

Juan

N

Fishing Access, 17 mi.

160

Pagosa Springs

84

Trujillo Road

San

Echo Canyon Lake

Legend

▬▬▬	US Highway
──	Other Roads
─ ─	Trail
▲	Campground
🐟	Fishing Access
🛥	Boat Ramp
▬▬▬	Major River
▬▬▬	Minor River/Creek

© Wilderness Adventures Press

I drove upstream about a mile just to look, and ended up loading my new 3-weight for a little action on this gorgeous little freestone. A "little action" is an understatement; rainbows and browns, a couple pushing 14 inches, hammered a size 10 golden stone nymph until noon. Then a trout rose at the tail end of a plunge pool. Three casts with a size 16 parachute Adams was all it took. Needless to say, I was a bit late getting home.

Backtracking my steps, I found out I had turned up the East Fork Road, also known as FR 667. This intersection is about 10 miles northeast of Pagosa Springs on US 160. I had spent the night in the East Fork Campground.

FR 667 parallels the stream for 5 miles to a section of private land. The private land is well marked. This first 5 miles of stream is easily accessed from the road. However, it is a narrow road, and you should park only on the wide pull-off areas. The road and stream continue on through the private land for about 4 miles and reenters the national forest. The road forks and turns rough. A four-wheel drive is recommended to follow either FR 667 up the East Fork or FR 684 up Quartz Creek. It's a good ride with a mountain bike for those who prefer two-wheeled travel. The streams are much smaller but more secluded.

Unfortunately, others have found this stream since I first discovered it. Pressure on the lower 5 miles has made the fishing somewhat more difficult. The trout are still there, but several good drifts through a run are required to move a trout to your fly. A careful approach to the stream is a must.

All variations of stone fly nymphs, including Prince nymphs, golden stones, and halfbacks, pull their share of trout from this stream from spring to fall.

After the first of July, caddis will be the more predominant insect. Hatches should occur in the afternoon and into the evening. Simple imitations will do the trick. Elk hair caddis, Rio Grande trudes, and stimulators in size 12–16 are fine.

There is a fine meadow stretch of water about 3 miles up from East Fork Campground. Terrestrials can prove to be the best approach for this section in August.

It's amazing how good the fishing can be when you jump off the beaten path. Sometimes you need to explore to find a true honey hole. As I pass from one destination to the next, I still return to the East Fork once in a while for an evening of dry-fly fishing.

San Juan in Pagosa Springs

Through the town of Pagosa Springs, most of the water is public, and fishing can be quite good. The river is a good-sized stream, dressed with several improvements.

Gary Willmart, owner of Colorado Fishing Adventures and an experienced guide in the area, says, "A few years ago, the town of Pagosa Springs applied for and received one of the largest grants ever given for stream habitat improvements. The river had large amounts of rocks distributed in it to create pools for the trout, making for some nice holes.

"Special regulations have been placed on this section of river. A daily bag limit of 2 trout has helped tremendously. We have caught browns up to 20 inches right here in town," Willmart adds.

A quiet summer evening on the East Fork of the San Juan.

The river may be fished in late April and early May, but runoff puts a quick halt to that. As with most Colorado rivers, stonefly hatches occur during runoff and make them pretty much unfishable. The best time to be fishing in town is July through September. Caddis hatches will keep an angler busy most of the summer, while a few PMDs pop up in late July. Blue-winged olives are active in September and October.

With good populations of stoneflies, caddis, and mayflies in the San Juan, expect all typical patterns to work here, especially beadhead patterns. Beadhead Prince nymphs, green caddis and pheasant tails are common flies used in this well structured water.

A basic 4- or 5-weight rod of 9 feet does fine on the San Juan. Leaders up to 12 feet in length may be needed to effectively nymph fish the deep pools here in town. A 9- to 10-footer will do for dry-fly fishing.

Willmart suggests, "Terrestrials will be on the water most of the summer. I especially like a Dave's hopper in the afternoons of August."

Unfortunately, the river below town is private or flows through Southern Ute Indian Reservation, making opportunities limited to this small section in town. However, Colorado Fishing Adventures and Backcountry Angler have leases on some of the private water and can guide you if interested. Contact Gary Willmart at 1-888-540-3474 or Gregg Jorgensen at 970-264-4202.

There are more and more fish over 18 inches caught in town each year, with a couple measuring over 20 inches. With the limited amount of water, this is a great half-day venture while traveling the southwest part of the state.

Stream Facts: San Juan River

Seasons
- Open all year

Special Regulations
- From US 160 and US 84 downstream through Pagosa Springs to the intersection of Apache Street with the river: Bag and possession limit for trout is 2 fish for all anglers, including youths under the age of 16.

Trout
- Browns are the predominant species, averaging 10 to 14 inches
- Rainbows
- Cutthroats, in the upper reaches of both forks
- Brook trout, also in the upper forks

River Miles
- West Fork Campground—0
- East Fork Campground—8
- Fishing access—17

River Characteristics
- The west fork is accessed by foot trail. Small stream conditions with pocket water and small meadow sections. FR 667 follows the east fork, also a good small stream. The two forks meet to form the San Juan proper. It becomes a bigger stream, with only one section as it flows through Pagosa Springs accessible to public fishing. A typical freestone river with pocket water, riffle, and pool structure.

River Flows
- Winter and spring, 50–200 cfs
- Runoff, from mid-May through June, 300–700 cfs
- Fall and summer, 200 cfs dropping to under 100 cfs

Maps
- *Colorado Atlas & Gazetteer*, page 88
- San Juan National Forest

SAN JUAN RIVER MAJOR HATCHES

Insect	A	M	J	J	A	S	O	N	Time	Flies
Caddis		▮			▮				A/E	Olive Caddis Nymph #10–#20; Breadcrust #10–#18; Beadhead Breadcrust #10–#18; Buckskin #16–#20; LaFontaine's Sparkle Caddis Pupa #10–#20; Elk Hair Caddis #10–#18; Goddard Caddis #10–#16; CDC Caddis #14–#20; Macramé Caddis #12–#16; Balloon Caddis #12–#16; Lawson's Caddis Emerger #14–#18; Spent Partridge Caddis #14–#18
Golden Stonefly			▮						A/E	Sandy's Gold #6–#10; Gold-winged Prince Nymph #8–#10; Kaufmann's Golden Stonefly #6–#12; Stimulator #8–#12; Foam Yellow Sally #12–#18; Halfback #6–#10; Prince Nymph #8–#16; Beadhead Prince Nymph #8–#16; Sofa Pillow #6–#8
Green Drake				▮					A/E	Green Drake Emerger #10–#12; Lawson's Parachute Green Drake #10–#12; Green Drake #10–#12; Adams #10–#12; Olive Hare's Ear #10–#12
Pale Morning Dun				▮					M/A	Biot PMD Nymph #16; Pheasant Tail Nymph #16; Beadhead Pheasant Tail Nymph #14–#18; Lt. Cahill Comparadun #12–#18; Sparkle Dun #14–#18; Parachute PMD #14–#18; Dark Hare's Ear #14–#18

HATCH TIME CODE: M = morning; A = afternoon; E = evening; D = dark; SF = spinner fall; / = continuation through periods.

SAN JUAN RIVER MAJOR HATCHES (CONT.)

Insect	A	M	J	J	A	S	O	N	Time	Flies
Blue-winged Olive			█	█	█				M/A	Olive Biot Nymph #16–#20; RS-2 #16–#20; Pheasant Tail Nymph #16–#20; Beadhead Pheasant Tail Nymph #16–#20; Flashback Pheasant Tail Nymph #16–#20; Olive Quill Emerger #16–#20; AK's Olive Quill #14–#20; Parachute Adams #12–#20; Olive Comparadun #14–#18; Gray Spinner #14–#20; Slate Thorax Dun #16–#20; CDC Baetis Dun #16–#20; Air-flo Cut-wing Dun #16–#20
Streamers		█				█			M/E	Black Woolly Bugger #2–#10; Spruce Fly #4–#10; Dark Spruce Fly #4–#10; Black-nosed Dace #6–#8; Muddler Minnow #4–#10
Terrestrials			█	█			█		A/E	Rio Grande King Trude #8–#16; Royal Wulff #10–#16; Humpy #10–#16; Foam Madam X #8–#12; Renegade #10–#16; Black Ant #14–#20; Cinnamon Ant #14–#20; Gartside Hopper #8–#10; Henry's Fork Hopper #8–#12
Midge		█				█	█	█	M/A/E	Olive Biot Midge #16–#20; Brown Biot Midge #16–#20; Black Beauty #16–#20; Brassie #16–#20; Black Beauty Pupa #16–#20; CDC Biot Suspender Midge #16–#20; Griffith's Gnat #16–#20; Palomino Midge #16–#20

HATCH TIME CODE: M = morning; A = afternoon; E = evening; D = dark; SF = spinner fall; / = continuation through periods.

SOUTHWEST HUB CITIES
Pagosa Springs
Population – 1,207 • Elevation – 7,079 • Area Code – 970

ACCOMMODATIONS

Oak Ridge Best Western, 158 Hot Springs Boulevard / 264-4173 / 80 units / Permission required for dogs / $$$

First Inn, 260 East Highway 160 / 264-4161 800-903-4162 / 33 units / Permission required for dogs / $$-$$$

The Spa Motel, P.O. Box 37 / Downtown Pagosa Springs / 264-5910, 800-832-5523 / 18 units / Permission required for dogs / $$-$$$

Spring Inn, P.O. Box 1799 / Downtown Pagosa Springs / 264-4168 800-225-0934 / Manager: Stan Zuege, an avid flyfisherman / 23 units / Permission required for dogs / $$$

BED AND BREAKFAST

Davidson's Country Inn, 2763 East Highway 160 / 264-5863 / 7 units / Permission required for dogs / $$$

Be Our Guest, 19 Swiss Valley Drive / 264-6814, 800-484-2275 / 6 units / Permission required for dogs / $$-$$$

CAMPING

Elk Meadows Campground, P.O. Box 238 / 5 miles northeast of Pagosa on Highway 160 / 264-5482 / 50 sites, RV and tent / Dogs welcome / $

Pagosa Riverside Campground, P.O. Box 268 East of Pagosa on Highway 160 / 264-5874 / 86 units, RV and tent / Dogs welcome / $

RESTAURANTS

Amore's House of Pasta, 121 Pagosa Street / 264-2822 / 11AM–9PM / $$

Branding Iron Bar-B-Que, 3 miles east on Highway 160 / 264-4268 / 11AM–8PM / $$

Rolling Pin Bakery and Cafe, 214 Highway 160 / 264-2255 / Breakfast and lunch / Highly recommended for breakfast / 7AM / $

The Sports Page Bar and Grill, 249 North Navajo Trail Drive / 731-3745 / Brunch and dinner / 10AM–10PM

FLY SHOPS/GUIDES

Back Country Angler, 350 Pagosa Street / 264-4202 / Owner: Gregg Jorgensen / Full-service fly shop / Float and wade guide service on the San Juan, Rio Grande, and Piedra Rivers

Colorado Fishing Adventures, 264-4168 / Guide service for Fairfield Resort, 731-4141 / Guide service for Ski and Bow Rack, 264-2370 / Owner: Gary Willmart / 1-888-540-3474

Let It Fly, 1501 West Hwy 160, #2 / 264-3189; Fax 264-3190 / Owner: Mark Miller / Guide service, classes / Full service fly shop

Ski and Bow Rack Inc., East end of Pagosa Springs / 264-2370 / Owner: Larry Fisher / Fly shop and flyfishing gear / Local flies and information / Classes and guiding done by Colorado Fishing Adventures

Lake Capote, 17 miles west of Pagosa on Highway 160 / 731-5256 / Private fishing / Open from May to Labor Day / RV and tent sites / $

Pagosa Clay and Trout Ranch / 731-9830

SPORTING GOODS

Pagosa Sports, 432 Pagosa Street / 264-5811

Pagosa Springs Hardware, 543 San Juan Street / 264-4353

Ponderosa True Value Home Center, Highway 160 and Piedra Road / 731-4111

HOSPITALS

Mary Fisher Medical Center, 95 South Pagosa Boulevard / 731-3700

Pagosa Family Medical Center, 75 South Pagosa Boulevard / 731-4131

AIRPORTS

See Durango airport information

AUTO RENTAL

Budget Rent-A-Car / 731-4477

Bob Sellers Auto Rentals, East, 597 Navajo Trail Drive / 731-3694

AUTO SERVICE

Eddie's Repair, 140 South 10th / 264-5760

JR Towing, 2357 West Highway 160 / 731-4792

LOCKSMITH

Jim's Lock and Key, 227 Hermosa Street / 264-2747, mobile 946-0807 / 24-hour service

FOR MORE INFORMATION

Pagosa Springs Chamber of Commerce
P.O. Box 787
Pagosa Springs, CO 81147
264-2360 / 800-252-2204

Durango

Population – 12,430 • Elevation – 6,512 • Area Code – 970

ACCOMMODATIONS

Durango Inn Best Western, 21382 Highway 160 / 247-3251, 800-547-9090 /
72 rooms / $$$

Brookside Motel, 2331 Main Avenue / 259-0150

Comfort Inn, 2930 Main Avenue / 259-5373

Siesta Motel, 3475 Main Avenue / 247-0741 / 22 rooms / Dogs allowed / $$$

Country West Motel, 40700 Highway 160, Mancos / 533-7073 / 12 rooms / Dogs
allowed / $$-$$$

BED AND BREAKFAST

Gable House B and B, 805 East 5th Avenue / 247-4982 / Ask for Heather / $$$

River House B and B, 495 Animas View Drive / 247-4775 / Innkeepers: Kate and
Crystal / $$$

CAMPING

Alpen Rose RV Park, 27847 Highway 550 / 247-5540 / 100 RV sites and 6 tent sites

Durango KOA North-Ponderosa, 13391 CR 250 / 247-4499 / 140 RV sites and 50
tent sites

RESTAURANTS

Dalton Ranch Bar and Grill, 589 CR 252 / 247-1414 / Open 7AM–8:30PM /
Cocktails / $

Durango Diner, 957 Main Avenue / 247-9889

The Silver Saddle, 3416 Main / 382-2702

The Red Snapper, 144 East 9th / 259-3417 / Open 5PM–10PM for dinner and drinks /
$$

Village Inn, 2850 NorthMain Avenue / 259-1351 / Open 6AM–10PM / $

FLY SHOPS AND GUIDES

Durango Fly Goods, 139 East 5th Street / 259-0999 / Manager: Doug Buck / Full-
service fly shop and guide service / Orvis endorsed / Animas River and local
small streams and high lakes / Instruction

Duranglers Flies and Supplies, 801-B Main Avenue / 385-4081 / Owners: Tom
Knopick and John Flick / Full-service fly shop and guide service

Anasazi Anglers Inc., 607 Sunnyside Drive / 385-4665 / email: angler@rmii.com /
Owners: Jerry and Nancy Freeman / In business 8 years / Guide service on the
Animas River and private water on the Pine River below Vallecito Reservoir /
Fly fishing clinics for women and couples

Don Oliver Fishing Guide, 15 Oak Valley Drive / 382-0364 / Owner: Don Oliver /
Guide service on most water around Durango and the Dolores River below
McPhee Reservoir

Outfitter Sporting Goods, 341 Railroad Avenue / 970-882-7740 / Owner: Joe Ghere / Large selection of flies / Recommends guides for the area

River Drifters Fly Shop and West Fork Outfitters, P.O. Box 300, Dolores 81323 / 970-882-7959, 888-882-8001 / Owner: Eugene Story / Guiding on Dolores River / Orvis fly shop

SPORTING GOODS

Animas Sporting Goods, 1444 Main Avenue / 247-3898

Clayton's Goods for the Woods, Durango Mall / 247-5725

Backcountry Experience, 780 Main Avenue / 247-5830

Gardenswartz Sporting Goods, 863 Main Avenue / 247-2660

HOSPITALS

Mercy Medical Center, 375 East Park Avenue / 247-4311

AIRPORTS

Durango-La Plata County Airport, 1000 Airport Road, Durango / 247-8143 / American West: 800-235-9292 / Mesa: 800-637-2247 / United Express: 800-241-6522

AUTO RENTAL

Avis Rent-A-Car, 1000 Airport Rd / 247-9761

Bob Sellers Auto Rentals, 20541 Highway 160 / 247-1212

Dollar Rent-A-Car, 1300 CR 309 / 259-3012

AUTO SERVICE

Alpine Auto Doctors, 121 West 32nd Street / 259-0760

Durango Car Care Center, 601 East College Drive / 247-3989

McKnight's Towing Service, 50 Animas View Drive / 247-4447

LOCKSMITH

Bob's Lock and Key, 1455 East 2nd Avenue / 385-4870

FOR MORE INFORMATION

Chamber Resort Association
111 South Camino del Rio / P.O. Box 2587
Durango, CO 81301
247-0312 / 800-463-8726

Durango and Silverthorne Narrow Gauge Railroad
479 Main Avenue
247-2733

Telluride

Population – 1,309 • Elevation – 8,745 • Area Code – 970

ACCOMMODATIONS

Victorian Inn, 401 West Pacific Street / 728-6601 / 28 rooms / $$$
Oak Street Inn, 134 NorthOak Street / 728-3383 / 24 rooms / $$$
New Sheridan Hotel, 231 West Colorado Avenue / 728-4351 / 26 rooms / $$$
The Ice House Hotel, 310 South Fir Street / 728-6300 / 42 rooms / $$$

BED AND BREAKFAST

Alpine Inn B and B, 440 West Colorado Avenue / 728-6282 / $$$
Johnstone Inn B and B, 403 West Colorado Avenue / 728-3316 / Innkeeper: Bill
  Schiffbauer / $$$

RESTAURANTS

McCrady's, 115 West Colorado Avenue / 728-4943
The Blue Jay, 22332 Highway 145 / 728-0830 / Open 8AM–9PM / Cocktails / $-$$
Sofio's Restaurant, 110 East Colorado Avenue / 728-4882 / Open 8AM–10PM /
  Cocktails / $
Maggies, 217 East Colorado Avenue / 728-3334 / Breakfast 6:30AM–4PM / $
Baked in Telluride, 127 South Fir Street / 728-4775 / Open 5:30AM–10PM / Rolls
  and coffee, light breakfast / $

FLY SHOPS AND SPORTING GOODS

Telluride Anglers, 121 West Colorado, P.O. Box 3554 / 728-0773 / Owner: Tod
  Herrick / Full-service fly shop
Telluride Sports, 150 West Colorado / 728-4477 800-828-7547
Telluride Outside, 1982 West Highway 145 / P.O. Box 685 / 728-3895, 800-831-6230 /
  Guide service for the San Miguel and Gunnison Rivers
The Telluride Mountaineer, 219 East Colorado / 728-6736
Paragon Ski and Sport, 213 West Colorado / 728-4525
Boarding House, 320 West Colorado / 728-0882
Freewheelin', 101 East Colorado / 728-4734
Screamin' Doggies, 750 West Pacific / 728-6970

HOSPITALS

Telluride Medical Center, 728-3848

AIRPORTS

Telluride Airport, 728-4868 / United Express: 800-241-6522

AUTO RENTAL

Budget Rent-A-Car, 728-4642, 1-800-527-0700
Dollar Rent-a-Car, 728-0884, 1-800-800-4000
Telluride Outside 4x4 Rentals, 728-3895, 1-800-831-6230

AUTO SERVICE
Organic Mechanic, 728-0654
Telluride Towing, 729-0095
The Towman AAA, 675 West Colorado Avenue / 728-4114

LOCKSMITH
Telluride Locksmith, 651 West Pacific Avenue / 728-5625

FOR MORE INFORMATION
Telluride Visitor Services
666 West Colorado / P.O. Box 653
Telluride, CO 81435
1-800-525-3455

Gunnison
Population – 4,636 • Elevation – 7,703 • Area Code 970

ACCOMMODATIONS
Days Inn, 701 West Highway 50 / 641-0608 / 44 rooms / Dogs allowed for a fee / $$$
Island Acres Motel, 38339 West Highway 50 / 641-1442 / 20 rooms / $$
Tomichi Village Inn, East Highway 50 / 641-1131 / 51 rooms / Dogs allowed / $$$
Wildwood Motel, 1312 West Tomichi Avenue / 641-1663 / 18 rooms / $$

BED AND BREAKFAST
Mary Lawrence Inn, 601 North Taylor Street / 641-3343

CAMPING
Gunnison KOA Campground, 1 mile SW of Gunnison / 641-1358
Mesa Campground, 4 miles W on Highway 50 / 641-3186 / 100 RV sites and 16 tent sites
Tall Texan RV and Campground, 2450 Highway 135 N of Gunnison / 641-2927 / 110 RV sites and 25 tent sites

RESTAURANTS
Cattlemen Inn, 301 West Tomichi Avenue / 641-1061 / Open 6:30AM–11AM and 5PM–11PM / Two restaurants, great steaks, bar and lounge, and lodging / $-$$
Garlic Mike's, 1 mile N of Walmart on Highway 135 / 641-2493 / Open 5PM–9:30PM for dinner / Cocktails / $$
The Sidewalk Cafe, 113 West Tomichi Avenue / 641-4130

FLY SHOPS AND SPORTING GOODS
High Mountain Drifters, 115 South Wisconsin / 641-4243 or 800-793-4243 / Owner: Mike Wilson / Full-service fly shop and fly fishing guides / Specializing in the Gunnison River Basin, including private leases on the upper Gunnison, East, Taylor, and Lake Fork Rivers / The best mile of water on the upper Gunnison as well as the area below the public access located below the dam on the Taylor for walk/wade trips / Float the Gunnison and overnight trips to the high country / Male and female guides
Adventure Experiences, Inc., #2 Illinois, CR 742, Almont / 641-4708, 641-0507 / Owner: Tim Kempfe / Full guiding service for the Taylor Park area, including Taylor River, Taylor Park Reservoir / With a remote Base Camp at 10,000 feet, situated in the middle of countless beaver ponds, spring creeks, and high mountain streams / Private cabins with kitchen and bath / With a package deal, all meals are included
Three Rivers Fly Shop, Willowfly Anglers / P.O. Box 339, Almont / 641-1303 / Owner: Tom Evenson / Full-service fly shop and guide service for the Gunnison, Taylor, and East Rivers
Tenderfoot Rafting and Outdoor Adventures, 300 East Tomichi Avenue / 641-2200

Gene Taylor's Sporting Goods, 201 West Tomichi Avenue / 641-1845
Traders Rendezvous, 516 West Tomichi Avenue / 641-5077

HOSPITALS
Gunnison Valley Hospital, 214 East Denver Avenue / 641-1456

AIRPORTS
Gunnison County Airport, 711 West Rio Grande Avenue / 641-2304 / Private planes
Also see Durango airports information

AUTO RENTAL
Avis Rent-A-Car, 641-0263
Budget Rent-A-Car, 641-4403

AUTO SERVICE
Gunnison Auto Works, 115 South 12th / 641-3602
H and H Towing and Auto Repair, 901 West New York Avenue / 641-2628
Precision Alignment and Auto Repair, 510 West Highway 50 / 641-4040

LOCKSMITH
Rule Security Service, 306 North12th / 641-3940

FOR MORE INFORMATION
Gunnison County Chamber of Commerce
500 East Tomichi Avenue / P.O. Box 36
Gunnison, CO 81230
641-1501 / 800-274-7580

Montrose

Population – 8,854 • Elevation – 5,794 • Area Code – 970

ACCOMMODATIONS

Cimarron Inn and Motel, 82401 Highway 50 / 249-6222 / 9 rooms / $$
Comfort Inn of Montrose, 2100 East Main Street / 240-8000 / 51 rooms / $$$
The Traveler's Hotel, 502 South 1st Street / 249-3472 / 16 rooms / $$
Trapper Motel, 1225 East Main Street / 249-3426 / Check before bringing dog along / $$$

BED AND BREAKFAST

The Inn at Arrowhead, 21401 Alpine Plateau Road, Cimarron / 249-5634, 249-3034 / Innkeeper: Mari Rootf / $$$
Uncompahgre Lodge B and B, 21049 Uncompahgre Rd / 240-4000 / Innkeeper: Barbra Helm / $$$

CAMPING

Black Canyon RV Park and Campground, 84348 Highway 550, Cimarron / 249-1147
The Hanging Tree RV Park, 17250 Highway 550 / 249-9966
Montrose KOA, 200 Cedar Avenue / 249-9177

RESTAURANTS

Backwoods Inn, 103 Rose Lane / 249-1961 / Open 4:30PM–10PM for dinner and cocktails / $$
Casa De Mehas, 710 North Townsend / 249-9305 / Open 6:30AM–11PM / Cocktails / $
Pauline's Steakhouse, 1140 NorthTownsend Avenue / 249-3921 / Open 6AM–7:30PM / $
Starvin Arvin's, 1320 Highway 550 / 249-7787 / Open 6AM–10PM / Hardy breakfast at a good price / $

FLY SHOPS AND SPORTING GOODS

Cimarron Creek, 317 East Main Street / 249-0408 / Owner: Bob Burk / Full-service fly shop / Clinics for all phases of fly fishing / Recommends guides for the Gunnison River
Gunnison River Expeditions, 19500 Highway 550 / 249-4441
Montrose Sporting Goods, 245 West Main Street / 249-9292

HOSPITALS

Montrose Memorial Hospital, 800 South 3rd Street / 249-2211

AIRPORTS

Montrose Regional Airport, 2100 Airport Rd / 249-3203 / American West: 800-235-9292 / Mesa: 800-637-2247 / United Express: 800-241-6522

AUTO RENTAL
Budget Rent-A-Car of Montrose, 2100 Airport Rd / 249-6083
Dollar Rent-A-Car, 1520 NorthTownsend Avenue / 249-3770
Thrifty Car Rentals, 2210 Lindustrial Drive / 249-8741

AUTO SERVICE
The Auto Center, 2500 NorthTownsend Avenue 249-6430 / Towing
Craig's Auto Repair, 4410 NorthTownsend Avenue 249-1107
Lionel's Auto Repair, 2171 East Main Street / 249-6070

LOCKSMITH
American Locksmithing, 67542 Sunshine Road / 249-0134

FOR MORE INFORMATION
Montrose Chamber of Commerce
1519 East Main Street
Montrose, CO 81401
249-5000

Division of Wildlife
2300 Townsend Avenue
249-3431

Delta

Population – 3,78 • Elevation – 4,961 • Area Code – 970

ACCOMMODATIONS

Comfort Inn Hotel, 180 Gunnison River Drive / 874-1000 / 47 rooms / $$$
El-D-Rado Motel, 702 Main Street / 874-4493 / 13 rooms / Dogs allowed / $$
Southgate Inn, 2124 Main Street / 874-9726 / 37 rooms / Dogs allowed for a fee,
please call in advance as certain rooms are set aside for pets / $$-$$$

CAMPING

Flying A Motel and Campground, 676 Highway 50 North/ 874-9659 / 33 RV sites /
6 tent sites

RESTAURANTS

C and J Cafe, 311 Main Street / 874-5261 / Open 6AM–8PM / $
Delta Fireside Inn, 820 Highway 92 / 874-4413 / Open 4PM–10PM for dinner and
cocktails / Steaks and seafood / $-$$

FLY SHOP AND GUIDES

Gunnison River Pleasure Park, Highway 92 at the confluence of the North Fork of
the Gunnison with the Gunnison / 907 2810 Lane, Lazear 81420 / 872-2525 /
Owner: Leroy Jagodinski / Full-service fly shop, restaurant, bar, and cabins /
Guide service, raft rentals, shuttle service for the Gunnison River / 12 years
experience

SPORTING GOODS

The Sports Network, 252 Main Street / 874-7811

HOSPITALS

Delta County Memorial Hospital, 100 Stafford Lane / 874-7681

AIRPORTS

See Grand Junction (40 miles north) airports information

AUTO RENTAL

Budget Rent-A-Car, 2828 Walker Field Drive / 244-9155
National Car Rental, Walker Field / 243-6626
Sears Rent-A-Car, 2828 Walker Field Drive / 244-9157

AUTO SERVICE

Affordable Auto Repair, 1801 Highway 50 / 874-5302
Bob's Auto Repair, 308 Meeker Street / 874-9573
Phillip's Automotive Plaza, 900 Main Street / 874-4407

FOR MORE INFORMATION

Delta Area Chamber of Commerce
301 Main Street
Delta, CO 81416
874-8616

Grand Junction
Population–29,03 • Elevation–4,586 • Area Code–970

ACCOMMODATIONS
Comfort Inn, 750 Horizon Drive / 245-3335 / 230 rooms / $$$
Days Inn, 733 Horizon Drive / 245-7200 / 108 rooms / Dogs allowed for a fee / $$$
Timbers Motel, 1810 North Avenue / 245-7275 / 28 rooms / $$
Travelers Inn, 704 Horizon Drive / 245-3080 / 125 rooms / $$

BED AND BREAKFAST
The Cider House B and B, 1126 Grand Avenue / 242-9087 / Innkeeper:
Helen Mills / $$

CAMPING
KOA Campground of Grand Junction, 3238 East I-70 Business Loop / 434-6644 /
134 sites / Showers, groceries, and game room
Rose Park RV Campground, 2910 North Avenue / 243-1292 / 25 RV sites

RESTAURANTS
Bob and Jan's Prime Rib and Lobster House, 2500 North Avenue / 243-6213 /
Open 11AM–10PM for lunch and dinner / Great food / $-$$
The Crystal Cafe and Bake Shop, 314 Main Street / 242-8843
Village Inn, 1910 North Avenue / 243-5467 / Open 24 hours / $

FLY SHOPS AND SPORTING GOODS
Western Anglers, 2454 Highway 6 and 50 #103 / 244-8658 / Owner: Jerry Schaeffer /
Full-service fly shop / Recommends local guides
B & H Sports, 599 Northgate Drive / 245-6605
Gene Taylor's Sporting Goods, 445 West Gunnison Avenue / 242-8165

HOSPITALS
Community Hospital, 2021 North12th Street / 242-0920
St. Mary's Hospital, 2635 North7th Street / 244-2273

AIRPORTS
Walker Field Airport, 2828 Walker Field Drive, Grand Junction / 244-9100 / About
40 miles north of Delta / United Express: 800-241-6522 / Continental: 243-8424 /
Sky West: 242-5365, 800-453-9417 / Delta: 800-221-1212 / American West
Express: 800-235-9292

AUTO RENTAL
Budget Rent-A-Car, 2828 Walker Field Drive / 244-9155
National Car Rental, Walker Field / 243-6626
Sears Rent-A-Car, 2828 Walker Field Drive / 244-9157

AUTO SERVICE
Advanced Automotive, 2493 West Mesa Ct / 242-0580
Bear Automotive Service Inc., 1315 Pitkin Avenue / 245-2585
Ken's Auto Repair, 1801 I-70 Business Loop #C-2 / 241-6062

LOCKSMITH
Simmon's Lock and Key Inc., 322 South 2nd Street / 242-5562

FOR MORE INFORMATION
Grand Junction Chamber of Commerce
360 Grand Avenue
Grand Junction, CO 81501
242-3214

Division of Wildlife
711 Independent Avenue
Grand Junction, CO 81505
248-7175

Crested Butte

Population – 878 • Elevation – 8,885 • Area Code – 970

ACCOMMODATIONS
Cristiana Guesthaus, 621 Maroon Avenue / 349-5326 / 21 rooms / $$$
Elk Mountain Lodge, 129 Gothic Avenue / 349-7533 / 20 rooms / $$$
Inn at Crested Butte, 510 White Rock Avenue / 349-1225 / 17 rooms / $$$
Manor Lodge, 650 Gothic Rd / 349-5365 / 58 rooms / $$

BED AND BREAKFAST
Gothic Inn B and B, 18 Gothic Avenue / 349-7215
Last Resort B and B, 213 3rd Street / 349-0445 / Innkeeper: Rita / $$$

RESTAURANTS
Avalanche Bar and Grill, P.O. Box 5104 / 349-7195 / Open 8AM–9PM / Cocktails / $
Bakery Cafe, 302 Elk Avenue / 349-7280 / Open 7AM for breakfast / $
Powerhouse Bar and Grill, 130 Elk Avenue / 349-5494 / Open 5PM for dinner and
   drinks, over 50 different margaritas / Mesquite grill / $$
The Slogar, 517 2nd Street / 349-5765
Soupcon, 127 Elk Avenue / 349-5448 / Open 6PM–8PM for dinner and cocktails /
   Great food / $$$

FLY SHOPS AND SPORTING GOODS
Dragonfly Anglers, 307 Elk Avenue, P.O. Box 1116 / 349-1228 / Owner: Rod Cesario /
   Full-service guiding / Walk/Wade trips around Crested Butte / Float trips on the
   Gunnison River / Also fishing on a private ranch in Gunnison County
Alpine Outside, 315 6th Street / 349-5011
Troutfitter Sports, 114 Elk Avenue, P.O. Box 2779 / 349-1323
The Alpineer, 419 6th Street / 349-6286
The Colorado Boarder, 32 Crested Mountain Lane / 349-9828
Critter Mountain Wear, 318 Elk Avenue / 349-0450
Efflin Sports, 10 Crested Butte Way / 349-6121
Gene Taylor's Sports, 19 Emmons Rd / 349-5386

HOSPITALS
Crested Butte Medical Clinic, 349-6651

AIRPORTS
See Montrose and Gunnison airports information

AUTO RENTAL
Avis Rent-A-Car, 641-0263
Budget Rent-A-Car, 641-4403

AUTO SERVICE

Alpine Express Auto Repair, Riverland Industrial Park / 349-6138
Crested Butte Auto Repair, 301 Belleview Avenue / 349-5251

LOCKSMITH

High Valley Locksmith Service, 228 White Rock Road / 349-7400

FOR MORE INFORMATION

Crested Butte Chamber of Commerce
7 Emmons Road
349-6438

Crested Butte Central Reservations
800-782-6037

Lake City

Population – 350 • Elevation – 8,671 • Area Code – 970

ACCOMMODATIONS

Alpine Village, P.O. Box 86 / 944-2266 / Hosts: Curtis and Fray Coates / 11 rooms /
Dogs allowed / $$

Matterhorn Motel, P.O. Box 603 / 944 2210 / Hosts: Richard and Linda Walker /
12 rooms and 2 cabins / Dogs allowed / $$

Silver Spur Motel, P.O. Box 126, 944-2231 / Hosts John and Venice Benvenuto /
14 rooms / $$

The Texas Resort, P.O. Box 156 / 944- 2246 / Hosts: Steve and Gayle Meredith /
16 rooms / $$$

BED AND BREAKFAST

Cinnamon Inn, P.O. Box 533 / 944-2641 / Hosts: Mel and Gwen Faber / $$$
Old Carson Inn B and B, Box 144 / 944-2511 / Hosts: Don and Judy Berry / $$$

CAMPING

Castle Lakes Campground Resort, Box 909 / 944-2622 / Hosts: Dick and Mary Lee
Cooper / 36 RV sites and 12 tent sites

Chick's Trailer and RV Park, Box 627 / 944-2287 / Hosts: David and Jacque
Terhune

Henson Creek RV Park, Box 612 / 944-2394 Hosts: The Morrow Family / 33 RV sites

River Fork Camper and Trailer Park, Box 514 / 944-2389, 944-9519 / Hosts: Mike,
Janet, and Bjorn Doody

Woodlake Park, Box 400 / 944-2283, 817-536-4079 (winter) / Hosts: Latellya Smith /
13 RV and tent sites

RESTAURANTS

The Happy Camper Sports Grill, Gunnison and 3rd / 944-2494 / Open 5PM for
sandwiches and drinks / $-$$

Lake City Cafe, Downtown Lake City / 944-2733 / Hosts: Jim and Kent Milski /
Open 7AM for breakfast / $

Mountain Harvest Restaurant, Highway 149 North944-2332 / Open 11AM–9PM /
Great chicken-fried steak / $

M and T's Smokey Deli, 944-2538

FLY SHOPS AND SPORTING GOODS

Dan's Fly Shop, P.O. Box 220 / 944-2281 / Owner: Dan Hall / Website:
xmission.com/~gastown/flyfishing / Email: lampert@gunnison.com / Full-
service, custom rods and flies / Lake Fork Angling Services guides on the Lake
Fork of the Gunnison, Gunnison River, Henson Creek, and Cebolla Creek / All
levels of fishing classes for the fly angler / Exceptionally beautiful trips

The General Store, Box 143 Highway 149 / 944-2513 / John and Karen Roose

The Sportsman, Box 340 Highway 149 / 944-2526 / Lynn Hudgeons

The Tackle Box, 144South Gunnison Avenue / 944-2306
Timberline Craftsman, 944-2334 / Betty Houston
Town Square Mini-Mart and Tackle Shop, 944-2236
Back Country Navigator, 944-6277

HOSPITALS
Lake City Area Medical Center, 944-2331

AIRPORTS
See Montrose and Gunnison airports information; Montrose is about 100 miles northwest, and Gunnison is about 50 miles north.

AUTO RENTAL
Rocky Mountain Jeep Rental, 944-2262
Lake City Auto and Conoco, 944-2311

AUTO SERVICE
Lake City Auto and Conoco, 944-2311
Sportsman's Texaco Station and Garage, 944-2525

FOR MORE INFORMATION
Lake City Chamber of Commerce
Box 430
Lake City, Co 81235
970-944-2527 / 800-569-1874

Road Conditions / 641-8008, ext.990

Search and Rescue / 944-2291

Central Colorado

Here we are in the heart of Colorado, and at the center of attention is the state's lifeblood—the Colorado River.

The Colorado is a river of many faces, and it tantalizes flyfishers throughout. At its headwaters in Rocky Mountain National Park, it's a small brook trout stream. Further downstream, where it picks up water from the West Slope, it is a meandering river full of brawny brown and rainbow trout.

The Middle Park area, which flows through a ranching valley between Granby and Kremmling, is the best section for flyfishers, and access there is easy: Highway 40 parallels the river and it's only a 2-hour drive from Denver. Just don't expect heavy doses of solitude while fishing that stream because the area is more than a little popular.

Despite its tasty attributes, the Colorado is not the only seductive water in the region. In fact, its tributaries, including the Fraser River, Troublesome Creek, Muddy Creek, Blue River, Eagle River, Roaring Fork River, the Fryingpan River (a tributary of the Roaring Fork), and several other smaller streams are all viable trout waters that offer seasonal delights for the avid angler.

COLORADO RIVER

The Colorado River, which is called the "Raddy" by the gang I hang out with, is among the top trout streams in Colorado.

Unfortunately, in recent years the river has been diagnosed with a nasty affliction: whirling disease. Rainbow populations have dropped due to the disease, but a good number of large, well-conditioned rainbows remain, and they are supplemented by a healthy population of aggressive brown trout.

The river begins in Rocky Mountain National Park then heads west on its trek across western Colorado (see the section on Rocky Mountain National Park in the Front Range chapter for more information on this portion of the river). Through its run, the river can be divided into three distinct water types. At Granby, the Fraser River confluence, the Colorado is an average size, meandering river that flows mostly through ranchland. One exception is a short stretch called Byers Canyon, located just west of Hot Sulphur Springs. The river parallels US 40 on its way to Kremmling. This entire area is referred to as Middle Park.

At Kremmling and the Blue River confluence, the river picks up speed and size and races into Gore Canyon. At the bottom of the canyon, anglers can launch a boat or raft and float to many take-outs on its way to Dotsero.

Just west of Dotsero, the Colorado dives into the ominous Glenwood Canyon. Although the canyon is a whitewater rafter's dream come true, flyfishers avoid the spot like the plague. However, a quick stop at the Grizzly Creek Rest Area in the middle of the canyon can be rewarding.

At Glenwood Springs the Colorado is wide and deep, especially where the Roaring Fork River adds to its flows. Below the Roaring Fork confluence, the Colorado sweeps through a wide valley on its way to the state line.

The following lists the Colorado's various sections with detailed information on hatches, timing and tactics.

Granby to Kremmling

To reach this section of the Colorado from I-70 westbound out of Denver, take US 40 over Berthoud Pass to Granby. The Colorado River parallels US 40 as it turns west toward Hot Sulphur Springs. A small impoundment called Windy Gap Reservoir collects water from the Fraser and Colorado rivers for transport to the east slope through a system called the Colorado-Big Thompson Project. The Division of Wildlife has named the region from Windy Gap to the Troublesome Creek confluence a Gold Medal Water.

Pteronarcys, also know as the salmonfly, is abundant in this stretch, but it usually hatches during peak runoff; this considerably lessens a flyfisher's opportunity to hit the motherlode. Still, there are many anglers who "hunt" for this hatch. And hunt is a good word choice, because the hatch is elusive. The big insects can be highly evident one day and gone the next. For those who luck out and hit the hatch, they act like they've been touched by God. That is why people continue to chase the hatch today, despite slim odds of success.

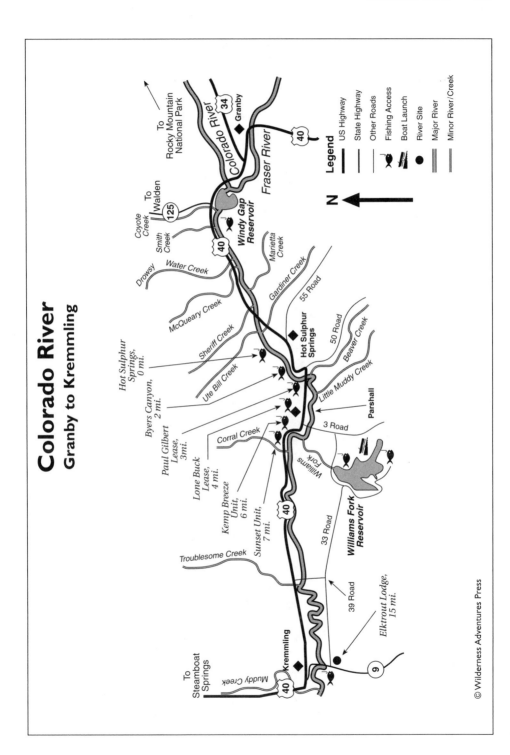

Colorado River
Granby to Kremmling

© Wilderness Adventures Press

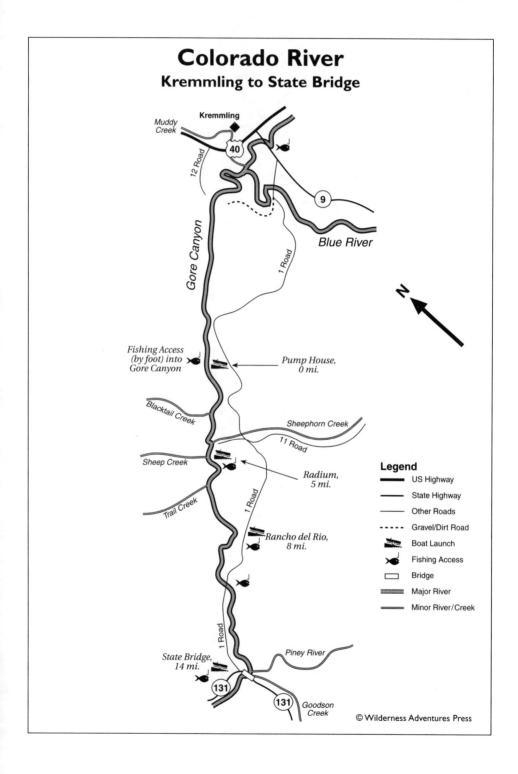

Colorado River
Kremmling to State Bridge

Kremmling

Muddy Creek

12 Road

40

9

Blue River

Gore Canyon

1 Road

N

Fishing Access (by foot) into Gore Canyon

Pump House, 0 mi.

Blacktail Creek

Sheephorn Creek

11 Road

Sheep Creek

Radium, 5 mi.

Trail Creek

1 Road

Rancho del Rio, 8 mi.

Legend

▬▬▬	US Highway
▬▬▬	State Highway
———	Other Roads
- - - -	Gravel/Dirt Road
🚤	Boat Launch
🐟	Fishing Access
▭	Bridge
▓▓▓	Major River
▓▓▓	Minor River/Creek

State Bridge, 14 mi.

Piney River

131

131

Goodson Creek

© Wilderness Adventures Press

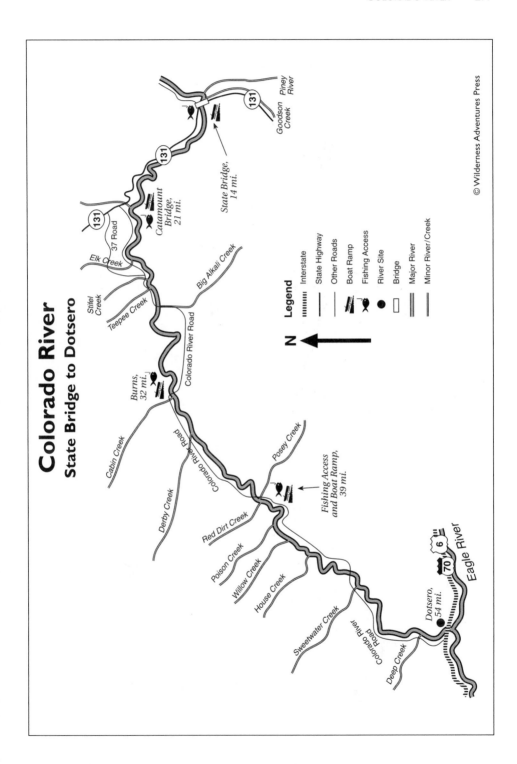

Colorado River
State Bridge to Dotsero

© Wilderness Adventures Press

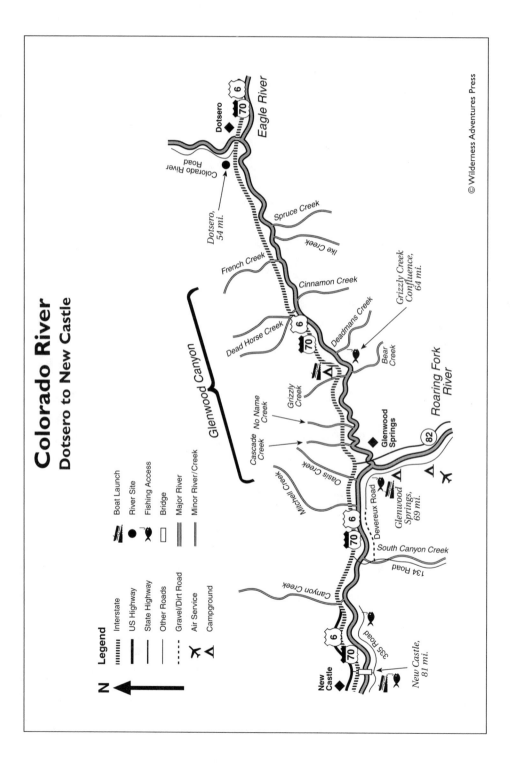

Colorado River
Dotsero to New Castle

Legend

N

Interstate	
US Highway	
State Highway	
Other Roads	
Gravel/Dirt Road	
Air Service	
Campground	

Boat Launch	
River Site	
Fishing Access	
Bridge	
Major River	
Minor River/Creek	

© Wilderness Adventures Press

If you decide to chase this hatch, look for salmonflies to begin their migration to the banks in April and May. When they move to shallow water, trout will pick off nymphs as they bounce along the bottom rocks. Drifting size 4 and 6 halfbacks and brown Kaufmann stones can be effective.

Normally stoneflies crawl from the water and break out of their carapaces sometime in late May. In early June the adults are readily visible along the river, their huge orange and black 2-inch long bodies standing out in the air like some creature straight out of an alien movie.

If you are lucky enough to catch the hatch at this stage, and do try to catch it, dry-fly fishing with a size 4, 6X long, sofa pillow, orange stimulator, or a Bird's stone will draw strikes. If you don't catch adults out and about, turn over a few rocks near shore and you are sure to find nymphs. Trout will be keyed in on those, so it pays to drag a large stonefly nymph or a bugger along the bottom rocks, just a few feet out from shore.

You can access the salmonfly hatch at Hot Sulphur Springs, Byers Canyon, and Sunset BLM unit access sites.

Pete McNeill, owner of Riverside Anglers in Hot Sulphur Springs, said, "This is a tough time to fish the river due to the heavy water. However, I think it is my favorite time to fish the Colorado. Most people will not fight the high water, but I would rather fight the high water, not the crowds. Most of the bugs will be in the willows near the bank and the trout, finding refuge from strong currents, will be laying in wait for a big kerplunk. Long casts are needed to reach these lies and the more noise you can make with the fly hitting the water, the better."

Rick Typher, owner of Denver Angler and an advocate for the Colorado's salmonfly hatch, adds, "High water in Byers Canyon is a blast! No crowds, no waders, big tippets, big flies, and big fish. Just doesn't get any better than that."

When fishing the Colorado stonefly hatch, Typher suggested that flyfishers bring a mix of size 2 through 8 stoneflies, heavy tippet in the 2X, 1X and 0X range and (dry fly purists cringe in unison) lots of split shot.

Don't fret if you miss the Colorado's big salmonfly hatch. The Raddy also has golden stones in great numbers, and they hatch in late June. A yellow or olive stimulator, size 8, is best for the adult imitation. Again, nymphs will always produce. Sandy's gold, gold Prince nymphs, and Kaufmann golden stonefly patterns in sizes 6 through 10 are effective.

"I like to fish the stimulator all summer, but I go down a size every 10 days or so until I'm fishing a size 18 in August," McNeill said.

If the stonefly hatches aren't your game, try some smaller patterns, like scuds. I found a very good population of scuds in the Kemp-Breeze unit west of Parshall. Large olive scuds from a half-inch to three-quarters of an inch long are a prime food source during high water.

Caddis will be present throughout summer, after runoff. Good hatches emerge through the long riffles in this section, and you can bet that the trout will be chowing heavy. Standard elk hair caddis, CDC caddis, and balloon caddis in sizes 12 through 18 should cover any situation. Look for the best caddis action during late afternoon and early evening.

The Colorado River and a wayward moose at Hot Sulphur Springs.

The Colorado's earliest major mayfly hatch is the pale morning dun, which generally arrives the second week of June. The dainty pinkish-colored duns rate a size 16, although they could rate a size 14 at times.

Comparaduns work well for the slower water along the banks and at the tail end of runs, but a standard hackled pattern works better for trout rising in the faster choppy water because it rides high and is more visible. You may find risers in many kinds of water during the PMD hatch as trout disperse into various feeding lanes. Keep a sharp eye on any likely looking seam or eddy along the bank.

When fishing the PMD hatch, keep an eye out for red quills; quills often intermingle with PMDs during the first couple weeks of July, and trout may key specifically on a particular species. If you are not drawing strikes with a PMD pattern, switch to red quill imitations, like a size 18 AK's western red quill. A rusty spinner is also a killer fly at the end of the day when the egg-layers come back to the water.

Blue quills emerge in late July and August along with another small insect called the Trico. Look for heaviest emergences from mid-September through October.

Blue quills and blue-winged olives hatch sporadically on the Colorado, but they can produce excellent dry-fly fishing. While the spring olive hatch is not as good on the Colorado as it is on some other area streams, you will encounter good numbers of the bugs in late summer and fall. Look for blue quills from late July through August and expect the larger blue-winged olives in September and October. Expect

On its long journey through the state, the Colorado River offers every water type and lots of scenery. Here, the river cuts between steep walls in Byers Canyon.

the heaviest emergence of blue-wings during the second week of September, usually after noon.

When you flyfish Colorado, no matter what stream you choose to ply, you should always have a fly box put together with a selection of BWO patterns from size 16 to 24. Carry it, keep it stocked; you will use them.

Hoppers, ants, and beetles can be an important addition to the fly selection repertoire in August and September. The valley is a prime breeding ground for terrestrials, and, believe me, the trout like to eat them. Several kinds of hoppers and ants

Glenwood Canyon,
Colorado River.

are always crawling in the willows along the bank, making them very susceptible to a good dunking and eventually a diet supplement for a brown trout.

During late summer and early fall, expect a Trico hatch, but don't count on a bliz-zard spinnerfall. Instead, you'll find the Tricos spotty at best, especially in the Kemp-Breeze unit. However, as the river slows and develops a silt bottom near the Elktrout Lodge at Kremmling, Trico hatches can be outstanding.

Throughout this section, no matter which hatch you choose to chase, expect to catch some nice fish, especially browns—they are more abundant than rainbows, with the average fish ranging between 12 and 14 inches. Larger fish exist; browns to 18 inches are caught regularly. The big rainbows that haven't been taken by whirling disease range from 4 to 6 years old and they measure 14 to 18 inches. A few of the big old dogs, the real brutes in the 5- to 6-pound range, are sometimes encountered.

Elktrout Lodge

Located 2 miles east of Kremmling on CR 33, Elktrout Lodge provides fly anglers with opportunities to fish 5 miles of private water on the Colorado River and more than 2 miles of the Blue River. Add 4 miles of Troublesome Creek and 15 springfed ponds, and you literally can book yourself into flyfishing heaven.

Elktrout is Orvis endorsed and offers 3- to 6-day packages including lodging, meals, and as much fishing as you can get in. Just 22 guests are allowed at the lodge at one time, so there is ample elbow room on the water.

Marty Cecil, manager of the lodge, said, "(The best time for) catching numbers of large trout is mid-May to early June on the ponds. Ice has just come off and (the trout are) hungry. For excellent mayfly hatches, green drakes on the Blue (River) in July or Tricos on the Colorado in September can be awesome."

The ponds have a variety of trout in them, including Kamloops rainbows, Donaldsons (a rainbow/steelhead cross), browns, cutthroat, and brook trout. All of the ponds enjoy excellent Callibaetis, Caenis, and PMD hatches in June and July. Caddis show up in July and August. Scuds, snails, and damsels are also important food sources in these rich ponds. Float tubes are provided, and they give an angler the ability to sight fish to huge trout, a wholly religious experience. Rods in the 9- to 10-foot range that throw 4- to 6-weight line are good choices.

The rivers on the property are excellent after runoff, when major hatches come off. In addition to green drakes and Tricos, other important hatches include stoneflies, caddis, red quills, PMDs, and Baetis. Terrestrial fishing in August can be outstanding throughout this wide meadow stream. All fishing is done with barbless hooks, and all trout caught are released.

A small fly shop at the lodge can provide you with a few items, like flies and tippet material. Contact the lodge at 970-724-3343 or fax: 970-724-9063, or write to Elktrout Lodge, PO Box 614, Kremmling, CO 80459. Web page: www.elktrout.com

Kremmling to Dotsero

As it travels southwest from Kremmling, the Raddy picks up considerable flow from Troublesome Creek, Muddy Creek and the Blue River and becomes a wide river not easily waded.

Access is limited due to a lack of roads and an abundance of private property. There is a small access on the south side of the Colorado at the Colorado 9 bridge. Fishing is allowed on the east side of the bridge only. You can put in a raft here, but the only place to take out is 11 miles downstream at Pump House, below Gore Canyon. Gore Canyon has class IV and V rapids, and I do not recommend that stretch to float.

To reach the bottom of the canyon, head south out of Kremmling on Colorado 9 for roughly 5 miles to CR 1. Turn right (west) on CR 1 and travel about 11 miles over a gravel road to Inspiration Point. Take another gravel road 2 miles along the river downstream to Pump House. Because this section has big water, pack a large rod. Six-weight rods are minimum, 7-and 8-weights are best.

Below Gore Canyon, fishing perks up during the last week of June or the first week in July, depending on runoff. During that time, the water is still high, but clearing. That high water can throw a wade fisher off balance, and slick rocks do nothing but encourage a dunking. Care should be taken at all times while wading. Chest waders are recommended if you plan to get in the water. However, much of your casting can be done from the bank. Wade fishing is much easier during fall.

When fishing the big, deep water you'll encounter here, come prepared with big flies and larger sizes of split shot. Halfbacks, girdle bugs, and woolly buggers in sizes 2 through 8 need to get deep quickly and stay there for any chance to take larger than average trout. Big browns and rainbows, some well over 20 inches, lurk in the deep pools. When hooked, they will test your terminal tackle and angling ability to the limit. Because of the size of fish, heavy tippets can be used. A 3X rating is about right.

A trail leading up the canyon on the south side of the river provides a few miles of fishing and camping. The Pump House is one of the prime put-ins, starting July 1, for float fishermen. It has two launch sites, a parking area, 12 campsites, picnic areas, and drinking water. A good half-day float trip would be from the Pump House to Radium, which is about 4 miles of river.

For the full-day adventure, take out at Rancho Del Rio. That float covers 6 miles of river and has a few Class II and III rapids. An experienced oarsman should have no trouble negotiating this stretch, but beginners should use caution. Rancho Del Rio has a boat ramp, parking, a few grocers, and a shuttle service.

During summer, you may find some stoneflies, caddis, and several mayflies in that stretch below the Pump House. From a boat, throw big dry flies or streamers. They work exceptionally well. Stimulators in sizes 8 through 12, trailed by a size 16 caddis pupa, are a favorite dual fly setup. A Rio Grande king trude is also a good choice when trailed with a caddis pupa dropper. The bigger fly brings a fish up to the top where it may spy the pupa and eat it.

When drifting the river, oarsmen should keep a flyfisher within a short cast of the bank, because you'll want to flip a fly under the overhanging brush and into shadowy areas.

Dave Bishop, of Gorsuch Outfitters in Vail, says, "The best thing about the Colorado River is the dry-fly fishing and the beautiful scenery. (You don't have to throw nymphs)."

Bishop, who guides on the river, continued, "The Colorado has improved tremendously in the last three years due to Wolford Reservoir (which backs up Muddy Creek). The water coming in the Colorado River from Muddy Creek is now clear. Also, a paper plant was closed in Kremmling, and that has added to the improvements."

Glenwood Canyon,
Colorado RIver.

Bob Nock, a guide at Eagle River Anglers, said, "We take stream samples regularly, and we have seen the insect population skyrocket. There are more caddis and stoneflies. We picked up a rock last summer that had five different species of mayflies, ranging from size 20 to size 14. These are big-time improvements."

While insect populations are clearly improving, this section of the Colorado is still best fished by lobbing heavy streamers to the bank. Let them land and then make a couple quick strips. Swinging a streamer around rocks, letting the imitation settle into the dead area behind, is also a good approach. The main thing to remember when fishing from a boat is this: try to achieve long drifts. Your fly has to be on top of or in the water to catch fish.

From Rancho Del Rio, a 4-mile float will get you to State Bridge. State Bridge is the next major take-out and put-in. Facilities include parking, cabins and showers. State Bridge is located 15 miles north of I-70 on Colorado 131 from the Wolcott exit. Wade fishing is available upstream from the bridge and can be quite good. Follow CR 1, also known as Trough Road, upstream to several accesses.

Below State Bridge, the river takes on the meandering nature of a broad, valley stream. Long, deep runs and slow pools make up the majority of the river downstream to Dotsero. Everybody I have talked to suggests fishing this stretch of water during late summer and fall. At that time, the water is low and clear, the brown trout are aggressive, and it's a great chance to see the river at its best: fall color in the scrub oak, cedar, and sagebrush hills.

Effective fall dry flies for this section include hoppers, caddis, and humpies. Woolly buggers are the choice for subsurface dredging.

Catamount Bridge is the next major take out and covers about 14 miles of river from State Bridge. Floating that stretch could make for a long day, so many floaters plan an overnight trip through here. Primitive camping can be found along the river in several places.

Catamount can also be reached by car. Take CR 301 7 miles west of Colorado 131 at the town of McCoy. CR 301 provides several walk-in and wading accesses to the river by following it downstream.

Five miles downstream from Catamount Bridge is Burns. A small grocery store, gas station, rental cabins, and a post office make up this little burg. A class III rapid, Rodeo Rapid, is right below Burns, so be careful. This one is tricky as it tumbles over some big boulders. You might want to scout before maneuvering through it.

Pinball Point is the next boat ramp, 4 miles downstream from Burns. Alamo Creek is next, another 4 miles down. Cottonwood Island is about 8 miles from Alamo and has boat access also. A take out at Dotsero, another 8 miles downstream, finishes this section. The Eagle River joins the Colorado River about a quarter mile from this take out.

Dotsero to New Castle

Looking at the Dotsero to New Castle stretch of the Colorado, I would never have thought to stop there in a million years to catch trout—sizable trout at that!

It just doesn't look like prime trout water. However, looks can be deceiving. In fact, you can find good fishing right at the Grizzly Creek rest area in the middle of Glenwood Canyon off I-70.

Big tumbling waves, huge rocks, and water the color of milky tea actually does hold a number of rainbow and brown trout, as you, too, will find out if you fish there. Grizzly Creek, which flows into this section, is also a favorite creek for mountain whitefish to spawn in during fall.

Forget your waders and grab a pair of hiking boots to navigate the rocks along the bank. To fish the Colorado in the Canyon, get your longest fly rod, hopefully a 5- or 6-weight, and get ready to do some deep short-line nymphing. A Prince nymph in size 6 to 12 and a size 14 buckskin is a killer pair of flies to move through this heavy pocket water. Trout grub that combination like a child munching sweet tarts.

The Colorado from the bottom of Glenwood Canyon to New Castle has a great caddis hatch in late April. This is where the first caddis hatches are seen before they head up the Roaring Fork. To reach the Canyon, take exit 116 off I-70 in Glenwood Springs. At the confluence with the Roaring Fork, the Two Rivers Park has access to fishing and a boat ramp for those who wish to float down to New Castle.

Nymphing is the best method of taking trout here. Breadcrusts, LaFontaine's green caddis pupa, and buckskins will work. Wading is limited in the heavy current, but, lucky for us, feeding trout should be in the shallow edges, so getting to the trout is usually not a problem. However, the river is so big that finding these pods of feeding trout may be difficult. Occasionally you may find trout feeding on the surface, and a simple size 16 elk hair caddis, presented over a consistent riser, should net a strike.

The bridge at New Castle, about 12 miles west of Glenwood Springs on I-70, is a good access to the river. Late afternoons and evenings are the best times to test this water. Caddis are coming back to the river to lay eggs, and trout here can be very receptive to any dry caddis pattern. A CDC caddis works well in the slower water on the north side of the river.

Soon after the caddis hatch, the river is unfishable due to runoff. Not until fall does that section return to fishable form. Come back with streamers and egg patterns as the fish fatten up for winter, and you can rock them.

Stream Facts: Colorado River

Seasons
• Open all year

Special Regulations
• From the lower end of Byers Canyon, about 3 miles west of Hot Sulphur Springs, to Troublesome Creek, which is 5 miles east of Kremmling: Artificial flies and lures. All trout must be returned to the water immediately.
• From the confluence with Troublesome Creek downstream to the confluence with Rifle Creek: Bag and possession limit is 2 fish.

Trout
• Rainbow; the Colorado is famous for its large fish. Whirling disease has diminished the overall population. Still a few lunkers left, however.
• Browns have a good population averaging 12 to 14 inches. Browns to 18 inches are common.
• Cutthroat are in the upper reaches.
• Brook trout are also in the upper reaches.

River Miles
From Hot Sulphur Springs to Kremmling:
• Hot Sulphur Springs—0
• Byers Canyon—2
• Paul Gilbert lease—3
• Lone Buck lease—4

• Kemp Breeze Unit—6
• Sunset Unit—7
• Elktrout Lodge—15

From Pump House to New Castle:
• Pump House—0
• Radium—5
• Rancho Del Rio—8
• State Bridge—14
• Catamount Bridge—21
• Burns—32

• Fishing access—39
• Dotsero—54
• Grizzly Creek Confluence—64
• Glenwood Springs (Roaring Fork Confluence)—69
• New Castle—81

River Characteristics
• The Colorado is a large meadow stream as it flows west of Granby except for the short stretch that curls through Byers Canyon; long riffles and deep runs best characterizes this stretch of water. The water always seems a little stained, and heavy flows can make wading difficult. West of Kremmling, the river drops into Gore Canyon and becomes floatable at the bottom of the canyon. It's a much bigger river here, with fewer riffles and more deep runs. Below Glenwood Canyon, the river is fishable for trout to about New Castle. Deep water with large rocks, well defined holding water.

River Flows
Near Parshall:
- Spring, 300–600 cfs
- Runoff, starting early May, 2000–3500 cfs
- Summer, 500–1000 cfs
- Fall, 350–500 cfs

Near Glenwood Springs:
- Spring, 1500–2000 cfs
- Runoff, 10,000–13,000 cfs
- Summer, 3000–5000 cfs
- Fall, 2000–3000 cfs

Boat Ramps
From Pump House to New Castle:
- Pump House—0
- Radium—5
- Rancho Del Rio—8
- State Bridge—14
- Catamount Bridge—21
- Burns—32
- Pinball Point—36
- Alamo Creek—40
- Cottonwood Island—48
- Dotsero—54
- Grizzly Creek—64
- Glenwood Springs—69
- New Castle—81

Maps
- *Colorado Atlas & Gazetteer*, pages 28, 27, 37, 36, 35
- Arapaho National Forest

COLORADO RIVER MAJOR HATCHES

Insect	A	M	J	J	A	S	O	N	Time	Flies
Midge									M/A/E	Olive Biot Midge #16–#24; Brown Biot Midge #16–#24; Black Beauty #18–#24; Brassie #16–#24; Blood Midge #16–#24; Miracle Nymph #16–#20; AK's Midge Larva #16–#22; Disco Midge #18–#24; Crane Fly Nymph #6–#10; Black Beauty Pupa #18–#24; CDC Biot Suspender Midge #18–#24; Griffith's Gnat #16–#22; Palomino Midge #18–#22; Serendipity #16–#24
Baetis									M/A	Olive Biot Nymph #18–#22; RS-2 #16–#24; Pheasant Tail Nymph #16–#20; Beadhead Pheasant Tail Nymph #16–#22; Flashback Pheasant Tail Nymph #16–#20; Olive Quill Emerger #18–#24; AK's Olive Quill #16–#22; Parachute Adams #16–#22; Olive Comparadun #16–#20; Gray Spinner #18–#24; Slate Thorax Dun #16–#22; CDC Baetis Dun #16–#22; Air-flo Cut-wing Dun #16–#22
Caddis									A/E	Olive Caddis Nymph #10–#20; Breadcrust #10–#18; Beadhead Breadcrust #10–#18; Buckskin #16–#20; LaFontaine's Sparkle Caddis Pupa #10–#20; Elk Hair Caddis #10–#22; Goddard Caddis #10–#16; CDC Caddis #14–#20; Macramé Caddis #12–#16; Balloon Caddis #12–#16; Lawson's Caddis Emerger #14–#18; Spent Partridge Caddis #14–#18
Stonefly									M/A	Halfback #4–#20; 20-Incher #4–#10; Prince Nymph #8–#16; Beadhead Prince Nymph #8–#16; Kaufmann's Brown Stonefly #4–#8; Sofa Pillow #4–#8; Stimulator #4–#12; Bird's Stone #4–#8; Yuk Bug, Brown #4–#8

HATCH TIME CODE: M = morning; A = afternoon; E = evening; D = dark; SF = spinner fall; / = continuation through periods.

COLORADO RIVER MAJOR HATCHES (CONT.)

Insect	A	M	J	J	A	S	O	N	Time	Flies
Trico				█	█		█		M	Parachute Adams #20–#24; Trico Spinner #18–#26; Double Trico Spinner #18; Thorax Dun #16–#22; Poor's Witch #18–#22
Pale Morning Dun			█	█					M/A	Biot PMD Nymph #16; Pheasant Tail Nymph #16–#22; Beadhead Pheasant Tail Nymph #14–#20; Lt. Cahill Comparadun #12–#18; Sparkle Dun #14–#18; Parachute PMD #14–#18; Dark Hare's Ear #14–#18
Red Quill					█				A/E	AK's Red Quill #14–#18; Rusty Spinner #12–#20
Terrestrials					█	█			A/E	Rio Grande King Trude #8–#16; Royal Wulff #10–#16; Humpy #10–#16; Foam Madam X #8–#12; Renegade #10–#16; Black Ant #14–#20; Cinnamon Ant #14–#20; Gartside Hopper #8–#10; Henry's Fork Hopper #8–#12
Streamers				█			█		M/E	Black Woolly Bugger #2–#10; Brown Woolly Bugger #4–#10; Platte River Special #4–#10; Spruce Fly #4–#10; Dark Spruce Fly #4–#10; Black-nosed Dace #6–#8; Muddler Minnow #4–#10; Matuka Sculpin #4–#10; Matuka Muddler #4–#10; Whitlock's Hair Sculpin #4–#6; Steve's BRO Bug #6–#10
Scuds			█				█		M/E	Olive Scud #12–#16; Orange Scud #10–#16; 19½ Scud #12–#18; Tan Scud #12–#16; Flashback Scud #12–#16
Golden Stonefly			█			█			A/E	Sandy's Gold #6–#10; Gold-winged Prince Nymph #8–#10; Kaufmann's Golden Stonefly #6–#12; Orange Stimulator #8–#18; Foam Yellow Sally #12–#18; Yellow Stimulator #8–#18

HATCH TIME CODE: M = morning; A = afternoon; E = evening; D = dark; SF = spinner fall; / = continuation through periods.

FRASER RIVER

The Fraser River headwaters begin just below the Continental Divide at Berthoud Pass. On the way to its confluence with the Colorado River, the Fraser passes through several towns — including Fraser, Tabernash, and Granby — and much of the stream flows through the Arapahoe National Forest. That means most of the stream is open to public fishing.

One of the main access sites is at Robbers Roost Campground, located about 6 miles south of Winter Park. At Robbers Roost, the stream is small and holds diminutive brook trout and browns. Typically, there are not any major hatches in the headwaters area, so the most effective way to fish is with nymphs or large attractor dry fly patterns. Work the pockets and seams with a hare's ear, Prince nymph, or golden stone, and you are sure to hook lots of fish. Those big attractor dries come into play during summer when they are the prime meal ticket.

For this section of water, you may want to take a short rod, 7 or 8 feet, because the brush can make casting difficult. However, if you want seclusion, this is the place to be, and difficult casts are just an afterthought.

There is also a prime access north of Tabernash where a state lease and a mile of river on BLM land offers open fishing. However, unless you hang glide or know how to parachute, access to these prime stretches is limited. Walking a mile of railroad tracks, owned by the railroad, is the only way to the state lease. The BLM land is located even farther downstream and probably never gets fished.

If you do make the trek and find yourself wading this water, make sure you do it in late July. In my opinion, July is the prime time to fish this stretch. Green drakes should be present and they offer excellent dry fly and nymphing action. Caddis and PMDs should also bring rising brown, rainbow, and brook trout, up to 16 inches long, to the surface. All of the standard nymph, emerger and adult dry fly patterns for those species will work wonders.

In July, expect flows in the 200 to 400 cfs range to make wading somewhat difficult in the deeper portions. Working the banks away from the strong midstream currents offers the best holding water for these spooky trout.

For information on current stream conditions and timely fly patterns, see Jim Nelson at Nelson Fly & Tackle in Tabernash, or call 970-726-8558.

Stream Facts: Fraser River

Seasons
- Open all year

Special Regulations
- From Meadow Creek downstream to the Colorado River: Bag and possession limit is 2 trout.

Trout
- Brown average 10 to 14 inches.
- Rainbows: smaller in the headwaters, up to 12 inches in the lower river.
- Brook trout: smaller in the headwaters, up to 12 inches in the lower river.

River Characteristics
- A small stream as it flows down US 40 through the middle of the valley. Some accesses in the national forest. Most of the better water flows through private land. Stretches of meadow stream with tight conditions. The state lease near Tabernash flows through a canyon with pockets and deep runs.

River Flows
- March, 50–100 cfs
- Runoff in April and May drives the flows to 600–1,000 cfs
- By July, the river is fishable through the summer and fall

Maps
- *Colorado Atlas & Gazetteer*, pages 28, 38, 39
- Arapahoe National Forest

FRASER RIVER MAJOR HATCHES

Insect	A	M	J	J	A	S	O	N	Time	Flies
Midge			▮	▮	▮	▮	▮	▮	M/A/E	Olive Biot Midge #16–#24; Brown Biot Midge #16–#24; Black Beauty #18–#24; Brassie #16–#24; Blood Midge #16–#24; Crane Fly Nymph #6–#10; Black Beauty Pupa #18–#24; CDC Biot Suspender Midge #18–#24; Griffith's Gnat #16–#22; Palomino Midge #18–#22
Caddis			▮	▮	▮				A/E	Olive Caddis Nymph #10–#20; Breadcrust #10–#18; Beadhead Breadcrust #10–#18; Buckskin #16–#20; LaFontaine's Sparkle Caddis Pupa #10–#20; Elk Hair Caddis #10–#22; Goddard Caddis #10–#16; CDC Caddis #14–#20; Macramé Caddis #12–#16; Balloon Caddis #12–#16; Lawson's Caddis Emerger #14–#18; Spent Partridge Caddis #14–#18
Green Drake			▮	▮					M/A	Green Drake Emerger #10–#12; Lawson's Parachute Green Drake #10–#12; Green Drake #10–#12; Adams #10–#12; Olive Hare's Ear #10–#12
Baetis		▮				▮	▮		M/A	Olive Biot Nymph #18–#22; RS-2 #16–#24; Pheasant Tail Nymph #16–#20; Beadhead Pheasant Tail Nymph #16–#22; Flashback Pheasant Tail Nymph #16–#20; Olive Quill Emerger #18–#24; AK's Olive Quill #16–#22; Parachute Adams #14–#22; Olive Comparadun #16–#20; Gray Spinner #18–#24; Slate Thorax Dun #16–#22; CDC Baetis Dun #16–#22; Air-flo Cut-wing Dun #16–#22

HATCH TIME CODE: M = morning; A = afternoon; E = evening; D = dark; SF = spinner fall; / = continuation through periods.

FRASER RIVER MAJOR HATCHES (CONT.)

Insect	A	M	J	J	A	S	O	N	Time	Flies
Pale Morning Dun				X					M/A	Biot PMD Nymph #16; Pheasant Tail Nymph #16–#22; Beadhead Pheasant Tail Nymph #14–#20; Lt. Cahill Comparadun #12–#18; Sparkle Dun #14–#18; Parachute PMD #14–#18; Dark Hare's Ear #14–#18; Light Olive Comparadun #14–#18
Stonefly			X						M/A	Halfback #4–#10; Prince Nymph #8–#16; Beadhead Prince Nymph #8–#16; Kaufmann's Brown Stonefly #4–#8; Sofa Pillow #6–#8; Stimulator #8–#12
Terrestrials				X	X	X			A/E	Rio Grande King Trude #8–#16; Royal Wulff #10–#16; Humpy #10–#16; Foam Madam X #8–#12; Renegade #10–#16; Black Ant #14–#20; Cinnamon Ant #14–#20; Gartside Hopper #8–#10; Henry's Fork Hopper #8–#12
Golden Stonefly			X	X	X				A/E	Sandy's Gold #6–#10; Gold-winged Prince Nymph #8–#10; Kaufmann's Golden Stonefly #6–#12; Stimulator #8–#12; Foam Yellow Sally #12–#18

HATCH TIME CODE: M = morning; A = afternoon; E = evening; D = dark; SF = spinner fall; / = continuation through periods.

WILLIAMS FORK RIVER

The Williams Fork, a nifty tailwater that measures just 2 miles long, sparks the interest of anglers every spring because it offers large, migrating rainbows that move out of the Colorado River.

During spring, flyfishers may find a foot of snow on the ground, but that is little deterrent for those suffering from the pull of large trout, not to mention serious bouts with cabin fever.

Despite the cold weather, don't expect to be alone when you fish the Williams Fork; since the river was opened to public fishing a few years ago, angling pressure in March has been heavy—with good reason.

Rainbows over 20 inches and some extending to 5 pounds or more are caught and released here every year. Resident brown trout, averaging 12 to 16 inches, are also abundant in this artificial flies and lures only water.

The Williams Fork is assembled with nice pocket water, some glorious riffles, and many deep runs—classic mountain trout water.

Nymphing is the most productive way to fish this water, although you can take some fish up top during good hatches.

"I do 90 percent of my fishing in March and April with three nymphs—a size 20 pheasant tail, a number 16 breadcrust, and a size 18 buckskin," said Pat Dorsey of Master Angler Guide Service. "I mess around with beadhead versions and they seem to be equally effective."

Anyone who has fished with Dorsey knows he is a fish magnet. He finds and hooks trout in almost any situation. By following his advice you might, too.

"Line and fly control are key!" he said. "I keep as much fly line off the water as I can to eliminate drag. (That tactic is often called high-sticking or short-lining). A strike indicator, along with adjusting the amount of split shot, helps control fly depth."

When fishing in that manner, one mistake you don't want to make is to move a fly right at the point of presentation.

"A mistake I see a lot of folks make is inadvertently moving their flies while they are making a presentation," Dorsey said. "Moving the rod tip up and down during a drift creates an unnatural movement of the imitation and results in fewer strikes."

To avoid that undesirable outcome, hold your flyrod steady for a good presentation. Speaking of rods, a 9-foot, 5-weight is ideal for this water. Leaders up to 10 or 12 feet help scoot the fly around the pockets and allow deep drifts.

Large trout in this section like to hold along the banks, and they can be found in surprisingly shallow water at the edges of the riffles and runs. Due to their presence in shallow water, stealth plays a major role in your success or lack of it when fishing the Williams Fork.

When fishing, watch your step and your shadow, and approach these areas with care. One sudden move or flash will send your trophy off to the hinterland.

Baetis mayflies hatch sporadically by mid-April on the Williams Fork; however, dry-fly fishing is held to a minimum. Duns and emergers can be seen on the

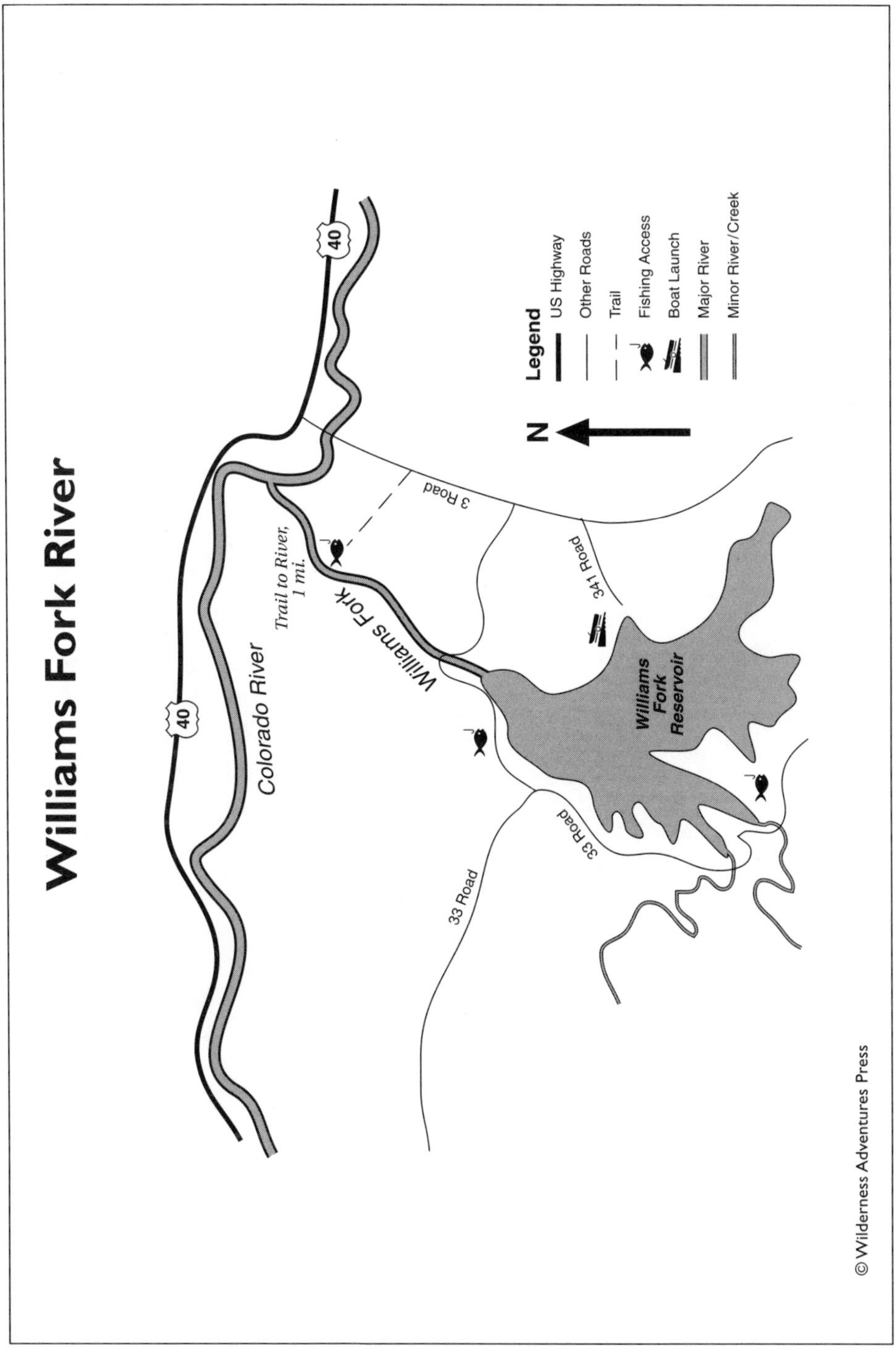
Williams Fork River
40
Colorado River
40
Trail to River,
1 mi.
Williams Fork
3 Road
341 Road
Williams Fork Reservoir
33 Road
33 Road
N
Legend
US Highway
Other Roads
Trail
Fishing Access
Boat Launch
Major River
Minor River/Creek
© Wilderness Adventures Press

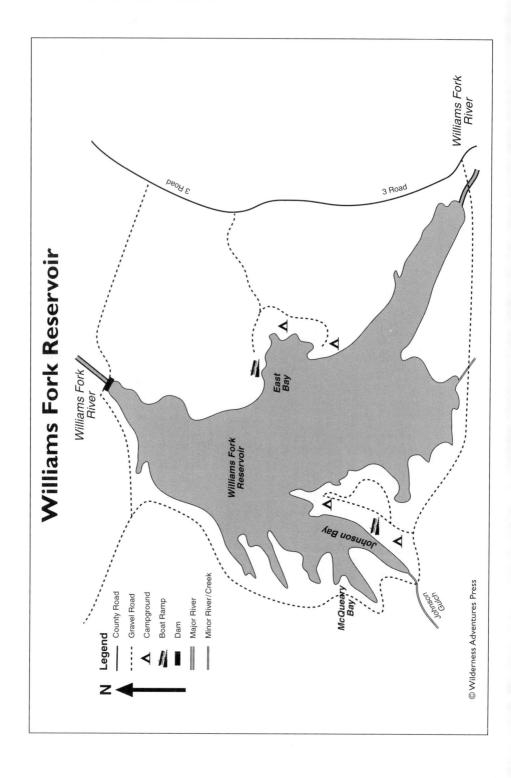

Williams Fork Reservoir

N

Legend
County Road
Gravel Road
Campground
Boat Ramp
Dam
Major River
Minor River/Creek

Williams Fork River

3 Road

Williams Fork River

East Bay

Williams Fork River

Williams Fork Reservoir

Johnson Bay

McQueary Bay

Johnson Gulch

© Wilderness Adventures Press

Bob Teague playing a rainbow in a prime Williams Fork run.
(Photo by Pat Dorsey)

surface, but rising fish are few and far between. Don't fret if you encounter that situation. Nymphing with small mayfly and midge patterns along the current seams and at the tailouts of deeper runs are the best producers. A small gray caddis may be seen on the surface in late April, but you should stick with subsurface imitations. They produce best.

As the snow melts and runoff begins, the stream may turn off-color quickly. It is best to let the stream rest until runoff is over. Depending on snowpack and dam releases, the river should be fishable by late June, definitely by the first week of July.

Abundant caddis hatches at that time turn resident brown trout into gluttons. You should carry elk hair caddis in olives and tans, sizes 14 through 18. LaFontaine's sparkle caddis and beadhead caddis nymphs should cover the hatch.

Pale morning duns and red quills may be encountered through summer. Standard, light olive PMD patterns and a western red quill in sizes 14 to 20 will draw strikes. Don't forget a size 16 rusty spinner; it's a great late day fly on almost any river in the state, including the Williams Fork.

While it fishes very well throughout summer, the Williams Fork is not without its problems. I hate to leave a bad taste in your mouth after giving this river such high regards, but the future of its rainbows is totally dependent on the speed at which the Colorado River recovers from whirling disease, if it truly does recover. Wish them luck.

Barry Reynolds and a huge pike caught at Williams Fork Reservoir.

The Williams Fork is located south of Parshall off US 40. Take CR 3 off of US 40 and follow it about a mile to the parking area where a mile walk along a well-marked trail leads you to the river.

Williams Fork Reservoir

To reach Williams Fork Reservoir from US 40 at Parshall, take CR 3 south 3miles to the reservoir. Williams Fork Reservoir has rainbow, brown, and lake trout, along with kokanee salmon and northern pike. That variety makes it a great, entertaining fishery.

Northern pike are the gamefish most fly anglers chase here, and the action really perks in June. As water temperatures rise into the upper 50-degree range and the pike come off the spawn, their feeding activity is at its peak. Northerns over 20 pounds are hooked every year, and bigger fish are lost. Hard-core, in-the-know flyfishers feel that Williams Fork could produce the next state-record pike. The current record weighs just an ounce over 30 pounds. This opportunity alone accounts for most of the interest in fishing here. Unofficially at this time, a pike of nearly 31 pounds was taken in 1997.

During June, look for pike on the west side of the lake. Make sure to scout out several fingers and two main bays, Johnson and McQueary, where the water warms quickest. Follow CR 3 to the inlet of the reservoir and take the gravel road west to reach this area of the lake. The shoreline dips in and out, causing several shallow points which offer prime holding water for pike. Wading the shallows and covering as much water as possible is the game plan most flyfishermen follow.

Eight to 10-weight rods are most effective for pike, not only to cast the big bunny-fur bugs, but also to handle the windy conditions that are persistent during the early season.

Because pike have very sharp teeth, a common setup includes a 9-foot section of level OX monofilament running from the fly line. Onto that, tie an 18-inch piece of nylon coated steel wire tippet. Connect the leader to the fly line and the tippet to the leader with an Albright knot.

When fishing pike, you should use a special bass bug taper or a pike/muskie line. They are designed as an exaggerated weight forward, making a long-distance cast with a large air-resistant fly much easier. Believe me, purchase one of these lines and use it, and you will likely avoid any painful stiffness in your casting arm.

Suckers are the main forage for pike, especially after the spawn when they move into the shallows. Bunny bugs will draw strikes when the fish are in close, and black seems to be the best color by far because it is visible in any water. White is also a good choice, but it is best used in clear water. Yellow and chartreuse are used in water that is mucked up from windy conditions. Clouser minnows, Lefty's deceivers, and woolly buggers are other flies to add to your pike fly box.

Northerns are built for speed, and you'll certainly notice that attribute when you first hook one. They seem especially irritable when they feel the sting of that hook. When you consider the overall average size of these fish, a reel with a good disk drag is at once recognized as essential equipment.

When fishing Williams Fork Reservoir, I like to start the day trout fishing, waiting for the water to warm. A midge hatches in June that rates about size 12, and it draws the attention of cruising trout, especially in the bays. If midges are not present, nymphs such as hare's ears, damsels, and zug bugs are good choices to strip slowly in a searching pattern.

As the water warms, usually around noon, start your search for pike. Wade to a comfortable depth and start making systematic casts in all directions; this is referred to as fan casting. Don't forget to cast back toward shore; you never know where those pike will cruise. Work any structure especially well; pike like even the slightest bit of cover. Takes can be quick and explosive, and any slack line lying on the water will go flying through the guides in a flash. This is usually when the battle with a big fish is won or lost, so keep control of your line and don't let it rest next to your legs in a nasty rat-nest. Also, don't let it get wrapped around your leg. Not only could you lose the fish of a fly rodding lifetime, but I don't think a line racing up your leg at 40 miles an hour would feel too good when it met a dead end, if you know what I mean.

There are several retrieves that work for aggressive northerns. A steady 4- to 6-inch stripping action with a short pause between will get their attention, but often this is not enough to induce a strike. If you witness a follow, then a refusal, tactics need to become aggressive. The steady retrieve with a quick, escaping action is a good approach.

Gene Blyth under summer sun on the Williams Fork. (Photo by Pat Dorsey)

Barry Reynolds, known around Colorado as Mr. Esox, suggests another tactic.

"When the takes are few and far between, I like to throw a curve at them," he said. "As I am making the retrieve, I will stop, make a rolling mend to one side or the other and make a couple of quick strips. The fly will dart to the side, giving any pike following the fly a new angle to look at. This evasive action of the fly will often produce a strike."

Quality pike fishing lasts until early August or until the water temperature jumps over 60 degrees and pushes fish into deep water. During late summer when the water is warm, early morning may be the best time to hit the shallows with the big streamers.

If you are going to stay overnight at the reservoir, camping and boat ramps are available on both the east and west sides of the lake.

Stream Facts: Williams Fork River

Seasons
- Open all year

Special Regulations
- From Williams Fork Dam downstream to the Colorado River: Artificial flies and lures only. All fish must be released to the water immediately.

Trout
- Rainbows, 12–16 inches with bigger fish in the spring and fall.
- Browns, predominant species, average 12–16 inches.

River Miles
- A little over 2 miles long. Access is a pretty good hike from parking area to river.

River Characteristics
- A short tailwater, just a little over 2 miles in length. Large migratory trout from the Colorado River pull up into the river in the spring and fall. Fast riffles, deep runs, and willow lined banks present the most experienced angler with many challenges.

River Flows
- Spring, 100–250 cfs
- Runoff, about mid-May through June, 500–1,000 cfs
- Summer, 250–400 cfs
- Fall, 100–250 cfs

Maps
- *Colorado Atlas & Gazetteer*, page 27
- Arapahoe National Forest

WILLIAMS FORK RIVER MAJOR HATCHES

Insect	A	M	J	J	A	S	O	N	Time	Flies
Midge		▓				▓			M/A/E	Olive Biot Midge #16–#24; Brown Biot Midge #16–#24; Black Beauty #18–#24; Brassie #16–#24; Blood Midge #16–#24; Disco Midge #18–#24; Black Beauty Pupa #18–#24; CDC Biot Suspender Midge #18–#24; Griffith's Gnat #16–#22; Palomino Midge #18–#22
Caddis		▓			▓				A/E	Olive Caddis Nymph #10–#20; Breadcrust #10–#18; Beadhead Breadcrust #10–#18; Buckskin #16–#20; LaFontaine's Sparkle Caddis Pupa #10–#20; Elk Hair Caddis #10–#22; Goddard Caddis #10–#16; CDC Caddis #14–#20; Macramé Caddis #12–#16; Balloon Caddis #12–#16; Lawson's Caddis Emerger #14–#18; Spent Partridge Caddis #14–#18
Baetis		▓				▓			M/A	Olive Biot Nymph #18–#22; RS-2 #16–#24; Pheasant Tail Nymph #16–#20; Beadhead Pheasant Tail Nymph #16–#22; Flashback Pheasant Tail Nymph #16–#20; Olive Quill Emerger #18–#24; AK's Olive Quill #16–#22; Parachute Adams #12–#22; Olive Comparadun #16–#20; Gray Spinner #18–#24; Slate Thorax Dun #16–#22; CDC Baetis Dun #16–#22; Barr Emerger #16–#22; Air-flo Cut-wing Dun #16–#22
Pale Morning Dun				▓	▓				M/A	Biot PMD Nymph #16; Pheasant Tail Nymph #16–#22; Beadhead Pheasant Tail Nymph #14–#20; Lt. Cahill Comparadun #12–#18; Sparkle Dun #14–#18; Parachute PMD #14–#18; Dark Hare's Ear #14–#18
Terrestrials				▓	▓				A/E	Rio Grande King Trude #8–#16; Royal Wulff #10–#16; Humpy #10–#16; Foam Madam X #8–#12; Renegade #10–#16; Black Ant #14–#20; Cinnamon Ant #14–#20; Gartside Hopper #8–#10; Henry's Fork Hopper #8–#12

HATCH TIME CODE: M = morning; A = afternoon; E = evening; D = dark; SF = spinner fall; / = continuation through periods.

WILLIAMS FORK RIVER MAJOR HATCHES (CONT.)

Insect	A	M	J	J	A	S	O	N	Time	Flies
Streamers		X						X	M/E	Black Woolly Bugger #2–#10; Platte River Special #4–#10; Spruce Fly #4–#10; Black-nosed Dace #6–#8; Muddler Minnow #4–#10; Matuka Muddler #4–#10
Green Drake					X				A/E	Green Drake Emerger #10–#12; Lawson's Parachute Green Drake #10–#12; Green Drake #10–#12; Adams #10–#12; Olive Hare's Ear #10–#12
Red Quill					X	X			A/E	AK's Red Quill #14–#18; Rusty Spinner #12–#20
Trico				X	X	X	X		M	Parachute Adams #20–#24; Trico Spinner #18–#26; Double Trico Spinner #18; Thorax Dun #16–#22; Poor's Witch #18–#22
Scuds	X	X	X	X	X	X	X	X	M/E	Olive Scud #12–#16; Orange Scud #10–#16; 19½ Scud #12–#18; Tan Scud #12–#16; Flashback Scud #12–#16
Golden Stonefly			X	X					A/E	Sandy's Gold #6–#10; Gold-winged Prince Nymph #8–#10; Kaufmann's Golden Stonefly #6–#12; Stimulator #8–#12; Foam Yellow Sally #12–#18
Stonefly						X	X		M/A	Halfback #4–#10; Prince Nymph #8–#16; Beadhead Prince Nymph #8–#16; Kaufmann's Brown Stonefly #4–#8; Sofa Pillow #6–#8; Stimulator #8–#12; Bitch Creek Nymph #10

HATCH TIME CODE: M = morning; A = afternoon; E = evening; D = dark; SF = spinner fall; / = continuation through periods.

Wolford Mountain Reservoir

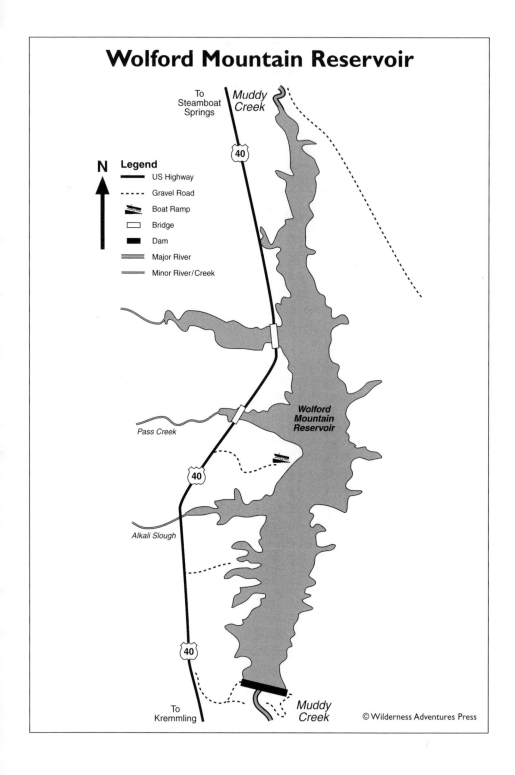

To
Steamboat
Springs

*Muddy
Creek*

40

N

Legend
— US Highway
---- Gravel Road
Boat Ramp
Bridge
Dam
Major River
Minor River/Creek

Pass Creek

*Wolford
Mountain
Reservoir*

40

Alkali Slough

40

To
Kremmling

*Muddy
Creek*

© Wilderness Adventures Press

MUDDY CREEK

The addition of Wolford Mountain Reservoir has turned Muddy Creek into a beautiful tailwater that has the potential to become a great trout fishery.

The cool, clear water below the reservoir is home to 10- to 12-inch stocked rainbows and brown trout at this time. The stream has some good riffles, slow corner pools, and a few dreadfully silted areas. With minimum stream habitat improvements, this tailwater should host a thriving population of trout.

Flows are expected to be sufficient enough to maintain the trout's needs; however, there are no set regulations at this point, which is a dangerous proposition when tailwaters are concerned. I personally can't wait for a chance to check out Muddy Creek in the 4-mile section below the reservoir.

Access is available just below the Wolford Mountain Dam via a short hike down a bluff to the stream. About a mile of water is fishable until private property blocks the way. A BLM road called the Skyline Drive, 3 miles north of Kremmling, leads to the stream below that private water. The river is open to fishing downstream from Kremmling before it dumps into the Colorado River.

Wolford Mountain Reservoir

Wolford Mountain Reservoir is a recent addition to Colorado's excellent stillwater options. It is an artificial impoundment, opened on Memorial Day, 1996, which should take some pressure off of the popular Middle Park and North Park waters.

Prior to its opening, the Colorado River Water Conservation District, which operates the reservoir, stocked the lake with 46,000 fingerling cuttbow and rainbow trout. The Division of Wildlife has kicked in with 250,000 kokanee salmon and 100,000 Snake River cutthroats. Fishing, to say the least, has been developing nicely.

Rainbows in the 14- to 18-inch range are available at Wolford, which rates about 1,480 acres. The reservoir is located 5 miles north of Kremmling off US 40. Muddy Creek fills the reservoir from the north as it meanders down the valley from Rabbit Ears Pass. Wolford is a fee area, and a day use permit is required. Camping can be reserved by calling 1-800-416-6992. Forty-eight RV sites with hook-ups are available. There is a boat ramp on the west side of the lake near the main campground.

The southern end of the reservoir has several bays and looks to be the best area to concentrate your float tubing efforts. The lake has not established a record of insect hatches yet, but they are sure to come. Damselflies, dragonflies, caddis, and maybe even some Callibaetis are expected.

Standard lake techniques, like fishing the edges of dropoffs and developing weedbeds, should take trout. Woolly buggers, damsel nymphs, and even streamers that imitate the smaller stocked trout could be the ticket to enticing larger trout.

Blue River

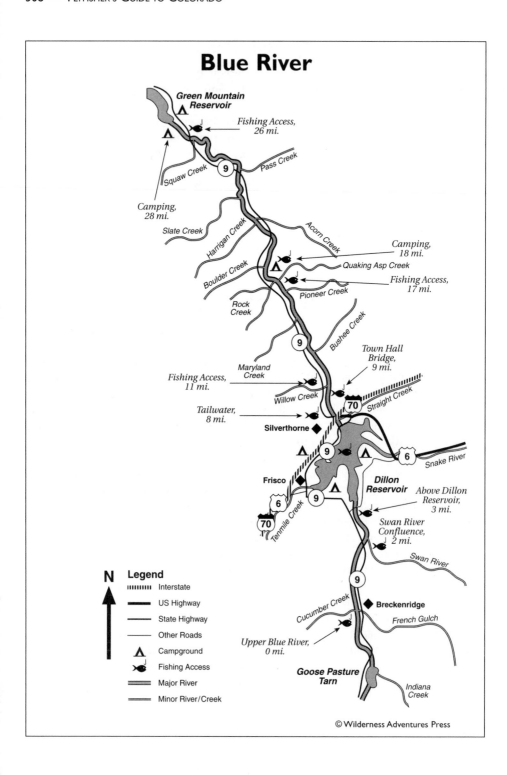

Green Mountain
Reservoir

Fishing Access,
26 mi.

Pass Creek

Camping,
28 mi.

Squaw Creek

Slate Creek

Harrigan Creek

Acorn Creek

Camping,
18 mi.

Quaking Asp Creek

Boulder Creek

Pioneer Creek

Fishing Access,
17 mi.

Rock
Creek

Bushee Creek

Town Hall
Bridge,
9 mi.

Fishing Access,
11 mi.

Maryland
Creek

Willow Creek

Straight Creek

Tailwater,
8 mi.

Silverthorne

Snake River

Frisco

Dillon
Reservoir

Above Dillon
Reservoir,
3 mi.

Tenmile Creek

Swan River
Confluence,
2 mi.

Swan River

Breckenridge

Cucumber Creek

French Gulch

Upper Blue River,
0 mi.

Goose Pasture
Tarn

Indiana
Creek

N Legend

⋯⋯⋯	Interstate
▬▬	US Highway
──	State Highway
──	Other Roads
Λ	Campground
🐟	Fishing Access
▬▬▬	Major River
──	Minor River/Creek

© Wilderness Adventures Press

BLUE RIVER

For Denver area flyfishers, the Blue River, which rests just an hour-and-a-half west of the city off I-70, is an excellent after-work and short weekend option. However, due to its location, it can suffer from crowding.

Despite its location and a good population of trout, not many people consider the Blue their favorite river. However, for those who know the Blue, "Big trout," "Broken tippet" and "the one that came off," are all phrases that are commonly heard as those anglers head home from the river.

It hasn't always been that way; improvements on the Blue over the last four or five years have benefited the fishery. New catch and release regulations to strengthen the population of larger fish and the fact that the rainbows, browns, and brookies in this river have bellied up to a diet of seafood—a white shrimp called *Mysis*—have played a big part in these improvements.

The Blue below Dillon Reservoir is not a typical Colorado tailwater. In fact, fishing the Blue below Dillon is a somewhat urban experience—it flows through Silverthorne, and those fast food joints, gas stations, and factory outlet stores make a strange setting for a blue ribbon trout stream.

But the Blue truly deserves its title—rainbows over 5 pounds are regularly caught and many 10-pounders are lost, right under Interstate 70. Due to its scenery, some holes have been thoughtfully named. Local guides often call the area "Asbestos Alley" to describe the smell of hot brake pads from 18-wheelers as they slow themselves coming down the pass from Eisenhower Tunnel. Behind 7-11 there is a nice hole called "The Big Gulp" that holds a trout or two. This is the only river in Colorado that I know of where people carrying Samsonite luggage, loaded with new blue jeans from the outlet stores, stop and cheer when you hook a fish in "Spectator Hole".

The Blue sets itself apart from other tailwaters because of the prehistoric freshwater *Mysis* shrimp. The *Mysis* is available to trout most of the year because they live in Dillon Reservoir and filter downstream. The best *Mysis* "hatch" begins in spring when warm water at the bottom of the lake pushes toward the surface, causing the lake to turn over. In turn, this churns up the *Mysis* in the lake, and they are pulled through the dam. *Mysis* shrimp patterns are most effective in the first 2 miles below Dillon Reservoir. The shrimp do not seem to drift much farther downstream than that—they may all get eaten by those huge trout.

While *Mysis* shrimp are an anomaly in Colorado, they are also found in the Fryingpan and Taylor Rivers. Those rivers, undoubtedly, could have the largest trout in Colorado swimming at the bottom of their crystalline pools. The Blue River does not deviate from these examples: the average rainbow in the Blue's catch and release water is 16 inches, with trout over 5 pounds being caught on a regular basis. Big boys in the 10-pound class can be caught on *Mysis*, too. Blue River brown trout average 14 inches, while a sneaky brook trout or two might reach 18 inches.

Hatches are sparse along the Blue's first mile below the dam, so nymphing tactics generally work best here.

Why would anyone want to stand in a half-frozen stream? These guys are braving the weather for a shot at 10-pound rainbows! Dig out your 5mm neoprenes and some wool gloves.

Crosby Beane, of Breckenridge Outfitters, suggested a few ideas that make great sense when nymphing.

"Maintaining your leader in a straight line from the tip of the rod all the way to the fly is essential," Beane said. "(You have to) stay in control of your flies. This is vital to detecting a strike the instant a fish takes. A high stick with a large yarn indicator, precise split shot placement, and continuous mending will help you present your drifting flies drag free. If you do not feel the flies ticking the bottom once in a while, change the indicator depth, or adjust the amount of split shot."

With a sharp, attentive eye, watch for a hesitation or irregularity in the drift of the indicator; this is your signal to strike a fish. A common mistake is the tendency to get lazy and not make these adjustments. On the Blue, laziness will send some anglers home wondering why all those other folks caught fish when they couldn't draw a strike. When a hesitation of the indicator occurs, your strike should be no more than a quick raising of the rod tip to tighten the leader, effectively taking the slack out of the line. When the surge of one of these fish bends your rod, hang on!

If catching very large visible trout sparks your interest (and why shouldn't it?), you can do so on the Blue. One of the best methods for fishing this stretch of water is to sight fish when the flows are between 100 and 300 cfs. By moving slowly along the bank, peering into the water at the tail end of riffles or seams at the edge of a run, you should spot fish. Making a perfect drift, using the right fly, and wearing a good pair of

Eric Neufeld hoists a monster rainbow that he took on a frigid winter day. (Photo by Jim Auman)

polarized glasses can make your big fish dreams come true. Burton's *Mysis* or Dorsey's *Mysis* shrimp patterns teamed with a black beauty midge is a great combination. When fishing that setup, watch for a trout to give you an indication that it ate your fly.

Eric Neufeld, a great friend and a fine angler, refers to this as "Looking for the Wink." Often, Neufeld said, a trout will open its mouth to reveal pearly white gums, flash to one side, or move from its position entirely. If you see such movement, set up and see if anyone is home. Biot midges, brassies, and hare's ear nymphs, tied in sizes 18 to 24 and in gray, olive, and black coloration are other flies to consider.

The most effective midge pattern is the black beauty, tied by Pat Dorsey who runs Master Angler in Parker. The black beauty is tied with a black thread body with fine copper wire ribbed through it and a head of fine black dubbing.

Flows on the Blue River range from 100 cfs to 200 cfs during the winter months, which makes it a river that is fishable all year long.

As the weather starts to warm the area in early April through mid-May, look for sporadic blue-winged olive hatches. At that time, standing below the Town Hall bridge and casting into tricky currents with a size 18 or 20 olive quill emerger will often raise a trout. Presentations to these fish, which have undoubtedly seen many fakes, must be perfectly free of drag with a tippet that is invisible, meaning 6X or 7X.

Flows below the dam usually kick up in late May and June to accommodate snowmelt from the surrounding peaks, which dramatically backdrop this wonderful fragment of Colorado. During runoff, flows fluctuate from 500 cfs to 1,500 cfs, depending on the snowpack. However, the river remains fishable with nymphs even at 1,000 cfs, although wading can be difficult and is not recommended for the inexperienced.

During the winter and early spring season, neoprene waders and felt-soled boots are a necessity for a comfortable day fishing the Blue. A 9-foot rod is important since most of your time will be spent nymph fishing. Four or 5-weights are sufficient for most conditions.

As runoff tapers, dry-fly fishing in the 2-mile section below the dam hits its peak. Hatches of green drakes are expected by mid-July, with PMDs and red quills coming off right behind. Fishing access and parking between Dillon Reservoir and Green Mountain Reservoir is plentiful. However, below Green Mountain Reservoir, the river is almost all private. Elktrout Lodge in Kremmling can book trips on this stretch of the river.

Hatch duration for the green drakes is typically two to three weeks. A size 12 olive hare's ear for the green drake nymph is very effective. Adult green drake patterns in late July are a must, and the trout love to eat Lawson's paradrakes and hair-winged Wulffs. A fly tied by locals called the "crippler" can be deadly in the early stages of the drake hatch, too.

Red quills and PMDs may be present, too; quills last about two weeks and PMDs extend about five weeks.

Caddis activity gets going in mid-June and extends to mid-August. Caddis patterns should include the breadcrust, LaFontaine's sparkle pupa, and soft hackle hare's ears. Elk hair caddis, low riding partridge caddis, and CDC caddis are excellent choices for surface risers. Blue River caddis range from size 12 to 18.

Another bug, the yellow sally, a small adult stonefly, can bring fish to the surface in July and August. You should definitely harbor a couple small yellow stimulators or humpies in your fly box to match them.

As noted earlier, these insect hatches and the chance for dry-fly fishing are much better the farther downstream from Dillon Reservoir that you go. The size of trout goes down the lower you go, but fishing is still very respectable. Rainbows average about 12 inches, while eager browns can be caught in the 10-inch range.

September and October bring with them the fall olive hatch, and, more than likely, the last chance for trout on a dry fly until April. Popular dry flies to match Baetis should include AK's olive quill, a parachute Adams or two, sparkle duns, and olive comparaduns, all in small sizes, like size 16 through 20. Subsurface mayfly patterns should consist of pheasant tail nymphs, beadhead pheasant tails, and RS-2 emergers in sizes 16 through 24.

The river's resident brown trout and kokanee salmon (from Green Mountain Reservoir) spawn during fall, and they can be taken with nymphs and streamers.

Above Dillon Reservoir, extending upstream to Breckenridge, the Blue is a very good small stream fishery. In the early years when mining was at full strength, this section of river was dredged up to 30 feet deep to find the precious ores that lay beneath its streambed. The stream was rebuilt with a classic riffle, run, and pool environment,

Jim Neiberger defines "hard core" as late night winter bouts with huge Blue River rainbows. It may not be comfortable, but it is rewarding. (Photo by Mark Moe)

and a good population of trout set up camp. A note: This stretch is closed to fishing from October 1 to January 1 to protect spawning brown trout from Dillon Reservoir.

When any river enjoys a location so close to home and grows such large fish it becomes a "hot spot." Expect to see a lot of anglers investigating the Blue on weekends. If you can, take to the river on a weekday. If you must visit on a weekend, many of those anglers may be carrying a rock over their shoulder, since it may be the only one left to stand on. Be courteous and use good stream etiquette.

Tributaries of the Blue River

Other good streams in the area include Tenmile Creek and the Snake River, which flow into Dillon Reservoir from the west and east, respectively. Most of the fish in those streams run 10 to 14 inches, until fall brings an influx of large brown and brook trout out of Dillon Reservoir and into these smaller tributaries to spawn. Rock Creek and Indiana Creek are small brook trout streams. Swan River, which is a Colorado River cutthroat recovery area, is located just east of Breckenridge.

Local Lakes

Opportunities to hike, drive, or ride a mountain bike into alpine lakes are plentiful in the area. About 20 miles west of Silverthorne, off I-70, Black Lakes #1 and #2 can provide a quick stop for a couple hours of enjoyment. Easily accessible, these lakes are stocked and can be fished from shore. Lakes in the Tenmile Range west of Breckenridge, such as Rainbow, Mohawk, and Blue lakes, are very good diversions. The Cataract Lakes west of Green Mountain Reservoir are also excellent brook trout lakes.

Stream Facts: Blue River

Seasons
- Open all year. From October 1 to January 1, the water above Dillon Reservoir is protected for the brown trout to spawn without interference.

Special Regulations
- From north inlet at CR 3 (3 miles north of Breckenridge) downstream to its confluence with the Colorado River: Artificial flies and lures.
- Above Dillon Reservoir: 2 trout, 16 inches or longer.
- Below Dillon Reservoir, downstream to the north city limits of Silverthorne: All fish must be returned to the water immediately.
- From the north city limits of Silverthorne to its confluence with the Colorado River: Possession limit of 2 trout, 16 inches or longer.
- Methods and possession limits do not pertain to Dillon Reservoir or Green Mountain Reservoir.

Trout
- Rainbows up to and over 10 pounds below Dillon Reservoir
- Browns to 20 inches below Dillon Reservoir.
- Snake River cutthroat
- Brook trout

Other Species
- Kokanee salmon

River Miles
- Swan River Confluence—2
- Tailwater—8
- Town Hall Bridge (Silverthorne)—9
- Fishing access—11
- Fishing access—17
- Camping—18
- Fishing access—26
- Camping—28

River Characteristics•
- Small stream above Dillon Reservoir. Easily accessible, some spawning runs of browns in the fall. Below Dillon Reservoir, the river offers classic tailwater fishing. Slick bottom and cold water. *Mysis* shrimp right below the dam for a couple miles produces BIG FISH. Some midge hatches and BWO's come off in that section, but better hatches are seen downstream. Mostly private water below Green Mountain Reservoir.

River Flows
- Winter and spring, 100–200 cfs
- Runoff can be buffered by Dillon Reservoir, but flows can reach 1,000–1,500 cfs
- Summer and fall, 150–400 cfs

Maps
- *Colorado Atlas & Gazetteer*, page 38
- Arapaho National Forest

BLUE RIVER MAJOR HATCHES

Insect	A	M	J	J	A	S	O	N	Time	Flies
Midge	▓	▓	▓	▓	▓	▓	▓	▓	M/A/E	Olive Biot Midge #16–#24; Black Biot Midge #16–#24; Gray Biot Midge #16–#24; Candy Kane #16–#24; Black Beauty #18–#24; Brassie #16–#24; Blood Midge #16–#24; Miracle Nymph #16–#20; AK's Midge Larva #16–#22; Disco Midge #18–#24; Black Beauty Pupa #18–#24; CDC Biot Suspender Midge #18–#24; Griffith's Gnat #16–#22; Palomino Midge #18–#22; Serendipity #16–#24
Mysis	▓	▓	▓	▓	▓	▓	▓	▓	M/A/E	Burton's Mysis Shrimp #14–#18; White Flashback Scud #14–#16; Dorsey's Mysis Shrimp #14–#18
Caddis					▓	▓			A/E	Olive Caddis Nymph #10–#20; Breadcrust #10–#18; Beadhead Breadcrust #10–#18; Buckskin #16–#20; LaFontaine's Sparkle Caddis Pupa #10–#20; Elk Hair Caddis #10–#22; Goddard Caddis #10–#16; CDC Caddis #14–#20; Macramé Caddis #12–#16; Balloon Caddis #12–#16; Lawson's Caddis Emerger #14–#18; Spent Partridge Caddis #14–#18
Green Drake			▓	▓					M/A	Green Drake Emerger #10–#12; Lawson's Parachute Green Drake #10–#12; Green Drake #10–#12; Adams #10–#12; Olive Hare's Ear #10–#12; Crippler #10–#12
Baetis	▓						▓		M/A	Olive Biot Nymph #18–#22; RS-2 #16–#24; Pheasant Tail Nymph #16–#20; Beadhead Pheasant Tail Nymph #16–#22; Flashback Pheasant Tail Nymph #16–#20; Olive Quill Emerger #18–#24; AK's Olive Quill #16–#22; Parachute Adams #14–#22; Olive Comparadun #16–#20; Gray Spinner #18–#24; Slate Thorax Dun #16–#22; CDC Baetis Dun #16–#22; Air-flo Cutwing Dun #16–#22

HATCH TIME CODE: M = morning; A = afternoon; E = evening; D = dark; SF = spinner fall; / = continuation through periods.

BLUE RIVER MAJOR HATCHES (CONT.)

Insect	A	M	J	J	A	S	O	N	Time	Flies
Pale Morning Dun					▇				M/A	Biot PMD Nymph #16; Pheasant Tail Nymph #16–#22; Beadhead Pheasant Tail Nymph #14–#20; Lt. Cahill Comparadun #12–#18; Sparkle Dun #14–#18; Parachute PMD #14–#18; Dark Hare's Ear #14–#18; Light Olive Comparadun #14–#18
Terrestrials				▇	▇				A/E	Rio Grande King Trude #8–#16; Royal Wulff #10–#16; Humpy #10–#16; Foam Madam X #8–#12; Renegade #10–#16; Black Ant #14–#20; Cinnamon Ant #14–#20; Gartside Hopper #8–#10; Henry's Fork Hopper #8–#12
Streamers	▇	▇	▇	▇		▇	▇		M/E	Black Woolly Bugger #2–#10; Platte River Special #4–#10; Spruce Fly #4–#10; Muddler Minnow #4–#10; Matuka Muddler #4–#10
Red Quill				▇					A/E	AK's Red Quill #14–#18; Rusty Spinner #12–#20
Golden Stonefly			▇						A/E	Sandy's Gold #6–#10; Gold-winged Prince Nymph #8–#10; Kaufmann's Golden Stonefly #6–#12; Stimulator #8–#12; Prince Nymph #8–#16; Beadhead Prince Nymph #8–#16

HATCH TIME CODE: M = morning; A = afternoon; E = evening; D = dark; SF = spinner fall; / = continuation through periods.

EAGLE RIVER

I started fishing the Eagle River back when I was a spinfisherman, drifting a single salmon egg through the prime runs. The fishing was excellent, but the more time I spent on the river, the more I realized what I was missing out on—those great caddis, mayfly, and stonefly hatches.

As the fly rod became my chosen weapon, the Eagle turned into a great piece of training water. Mixed with several types of water and a variety of insects, my skills sharpened quickly as I learned how to read fly water.

The Eagle River, named by the Ute Indians who said it has as many tributaries as there are feathers in an eagle's tail, begins where the East and South forks come together below Tennessee Pass on US 24 south of Minturn.

Much of the upper river runs through private property, and access is difficult if not impossible. At its confluence with Gore Creek, also known as Dowd's Junction, the Eagle follows the interstate west where it runs through more private land and a couple of fancy golf courses. However, 3 miles west of Edwards you can access the Squaw Creek public lease. This is prime pocket water with a flies and lures only, 2 fish over 16 inches regulation on it.

About 4 miles west of Edwards, I-70 passes over the river and US 6. You can park off of US 6 just west of the bridge and access the river. This is a good stretch of water with a little over a mile of public fishing up and downstream.

This is an excellent area to fish during spring, starting around April Fools' Day, because two channels flow around an island to form a deep pool. In April, flows are low and the water is clear but frigid. The only real food source for the trout is the midge, and they eat piles of them at that time.

I find that a gray biot midge, size 20, is very effective in that section. In fact, any small gray or black nymph, such as a gray may nymph, RS-2, or black beauty midge, will take fish. A 10- or 12-foot leader, tapered to 6X, is a must. A strike indicator will help in the deep, slow water. Patience is a virtue on this section. You need to work the water systematically, covering every possible holding spot until you find the right depth and speed. Move your indicator up or down the leader and adjust your split shot to achieve the proper drift. The "chuck and take your chances" method rarely works when the water is cold, so keep those large flies packed away in the proper fly box.

Downstream from that section, flyfishers will bump into another section of private property. But you'll encounter a well-marked pull off, a mile east of Wolcott, where a quarter mile of access is available. There, you'll find a nice riffle that tumbles into a pool and thins back into shallow pockets. My favorite time to fish this spot is during late summer when terrestrials draw solid takes.

One August afternoon, my friend Gus and I were across the stream from each other with several trout rising between us. We both stopped to tie on new flies since we didn't have so much as a look with the Royal Wulff and parachute Adams we were using. I was knotting on my fly when I asked Gus, "What's it going to be?"

"An ant," he replied.

Eagle River

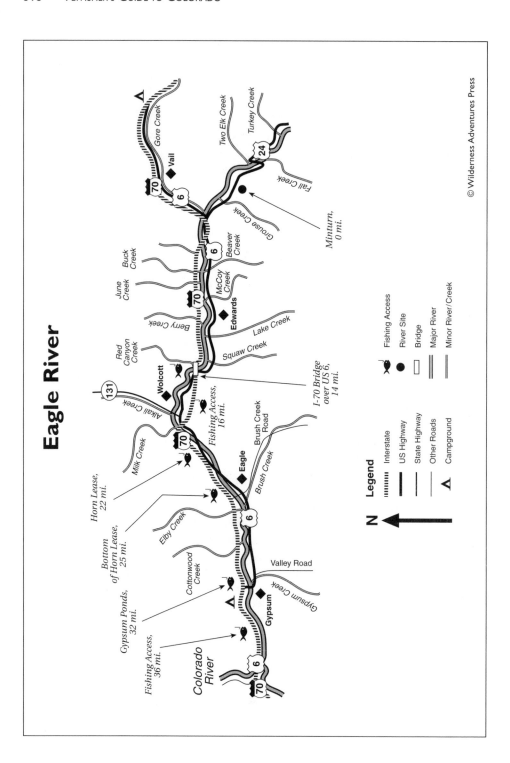

© Wilderness Adventures Press

Legend

N

| Interstate |
| US Highway |
| State Highway |
| Other Roads |
| Campground |

- Fishing Access
- River Site
- Bridge
- Major River
- Minor River/Creek

As on most streams, nymphs work well on the Eagle. Here, a flyfisher probes a prime run with a two-fly setup under a strike indicator.

Coincidentally, that was the fly I was tying on. Amazing how great minds think alike!

In no time Gus hooked and lost a trout. I hooked a 12-inch rainbow. Then Gus hooked and lost three more fish due to a broken hook. Ants, as we discovered, are great late summer imitations on the Eagle, along with royal humpies, coachman trudes, and elk hair caddis.

A little over a mile west of Wolcott, off US 6, the Horn Lease provides 6 miles of fishing access that stretch downstream within a mile of Eagle. Sharp red cliffs backdrop the lower half of this stretch, and access is on the road side of the river only. The far side is private.

After runoff, which usually extends from the third week in June through the first week in July, the Eagle's water is high but clearing. Care must be taken while wading the stream because the bottom rocks are slick. Fishing at that time of the year can be phenomenal, due to an excellent caddis hatch that rivals any in the state. Besides caddis, a small pink PMD, maybe a size 18 or 20, hatches. It's as if the fly just wants to make things difficult for flyfishers. I wish I could tell you the secret of consistently hooking trout while both of these bugs are hatching, but it's often a case of the trout keying on one insect or the other. You have to change patterns until you find the right fly.

When the caddis hatch, a two-fly setup works well. A size 16 olive LaFontaine sparkle emerger with a size 18 olive caddis nymph tagging along in the surface film grabs the eager trout's attention. When fishing that rig, I like to move around and look for rising fish. There are many pockets formed by rocks and seams along the bank, so you must pay close attention to the water. If you spot a fish, often a downstream drift works best.

If PMDs are hatching, you'll always find a few trout rising to them. However, aside from a Trico hatch I've fished on the Platte, this is by far some of the toughest fishing I've found. Nice rainbows and browns, up to 16 inches, will be rising to the duns, but I've tried numerous dry flies and even a variety of emergers and met with only limited success. However, believe it or not, an orange asher trimmed up with a pair of nippers has taken a 17-inch rainbow and an 18-inch brown when they were visibly feeding on duns. I can't explain why they eat that fly in that situation.

Green drakes hatch in late July, and they can provide relief from those damn quills. Just don't be fooled by the green drake emergence. You may only see a few of them on the water, but the trout notice anything that even closely resembles them. Trout will rise to a size 12 Lawson's paradrake or a dark hair-winged Wulff without hesitation.

During fall, you may want to direct your attention to the Gypsum state wildlife area and some open BLM land west of Gypsum. That area fishes especially well during fall. You can find the area just above the Eagle's confluence with the Colorado, and many large brown trout move out of the big river and into the Eagle during September, October, and November.

Egg patterns, preferably cream-colored glow bug yarns with a touch of Oregon cheese mixed with it, are deadly in this stretch. Look for the browns to hold in shallow runs during early morning before they move into deeper corner pools during the day.

Small midge patterns, pheasant tails, and caddis nymphs may take a fish or two during the day in deep water. And don't forget woolly buggers and sculpins; they can bring jarring strikes when swung across the current late in the day.

There are several prime floats on the river, but the two most popular drifts are probably Edwards to Wolcott for a half-day and Edwards to Eagle for the full day.

Late June through July, when flows are still high but clear, is the best time for floating those stretches. While you can float the river in any boat, Bob Nock of Eagle River Anglers in Eagle prefers a cataraft.

"We use a 16-foot cataraft (because) drift boats can take a beating down this narrow channel with inexperienced oarsmen behind the wheel. And make sure to take out at the visitor's center in Eagle. Rodeo Falls is just on the other side of town, and it can be a boat breaker."

During a float, dry-fly fishing will be the game and a dual dry fly set up is a killer here. Dave Bishop, of Gorsuch Outfitters in Vail, said, "A size 10 western coachman trude with a size 16 ginger or olive LaFontaine sparkle pupa trailing behind is a standard setup. (To fish it) attach an 18-inch tippet to the bend of the trude, then tie on

When fall-run brown trout head into the Eagle River, flyfishers can hook fish on large patterns such as woolly buggers and zonkers.

the caddis. The trude usually hooks a couple of fish, but its chief function is to serve as a strike indicator for the caddis."

You'll want to cast those patterns to every slick and seam that comes along, especially along the bank. The high water of June and July usually has trout pushed out of the middle of the stream into the easier, slower water near the bank.

Another good float on the Eagle extends from the Eagle County Fairgrounds, on the west side of Eagle, to Gypsum or to the BLM campground west of Gypsum, depending on how far you want to float. This is a much slower float because the river levels a bit and meanders from corner to corner. A good population of brown and rainbows, averaging 12 to 16 inches, inhabit this water. Expect a good battle from some very strong trout.

While the Eagle River generally fishes well throughout, I've seen it go through several cycles during the years I have fished it, apparently due to prior mining activities.

Just as I started to flyfish 12 years ago, rainbows started to show up. Good hatches of several types of insects, including a population of stoneflies, were sweeping the river. A year later all the trout were bigger than I had ever seen: rainbows averaged 14 inches with several close to 18 inches; browns were pushing the 16-inch range. Then, as if the light switch was turned off, fewer and smaller fish, mostly browns, were the norm. Apparently the mines filled with water, and seepage of the nasty metals trickled back into the stream. But things seem to be on the rebound.

"New ownership of the mine has done an incredible clean up job, and zinc and magnesium levels have dropped considerably," said Bishop. "The rainbows are returning to areas where we have not seen them in years. There are also more browns closer to the mine than ever."

Today, the Eagle is in fine shape and continues to get better, so it's definitely worth a look when you are in central Colorado.

Gore Creek

Located just 100 miles west of Denver, Gore Creek flows through the resort town of Vail and offers excellent flyfishing options for such a highly visited area.

Gore Creek is not large, but the section from Red Sandstone Creek to its confluence with the Eagle River is listed as Gold Medal Water.

The first access to the stream is at the East Vail exit off of I-70. The stream runs south of the interstate and can be fished upstream into the national forest and downstream to the golf course.

An open, meadow stream, with willows lining the banks, Gore Creek provides good dry-fly fishing for small browns and brookies. After runoff and all the way through fall is the best time to test your casting skills here. Eight-foot, 3- or 4-weight rods are excellent choices for this creek and its small fish.

The second access to Gore Creek is at its confluence with the Eagle River. To reach that spot, take I-70 to the intersection with US 24, a place known as Dowd's Junction. There is parking and a pedestrian bridge over the Eagle. The Gore can be fished on the north side of the stream for about 2 miles. Make sure you stay on the north side where the bike path and railroad tracks indicate public access. This is the Gold Medal Water and holds bigger trout; rainbows, browns, and cutthroats up to 16 inches call this water home.

No matter what stretch you choose to fish, look for caddis and a good green drake hatch after runoff. Caddis should be present in the afternoons and trout will pluck them off the surface along the cut banks. Any of the standard high-floating caddis patterns in sizes 12 through 16 should draw strikes.

When you fish the caddis hatch, try to put off that run into Vail until after dark—dry-fly fishing can be a blast at dusk. If you do stay late, you'll likely see flights of

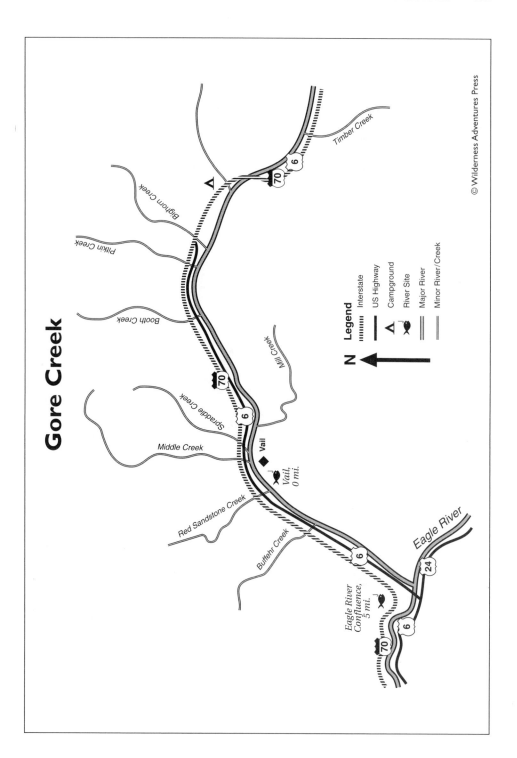

Gore Creek

Timber Creek

Bighorn Creek

Pitkin Creek

Booth Creek

Mill Creek

Straddle Creek

Middle Creek

Vail

Vail,
0 mi.

Red Sandstone Creek

Buffehr Creek

Eagle River

Eagle River
Confluence,
5 mi.

Legend

N

Interstate

US Highway

Campground

River Site

Major River

Minor River/Creek

*Greg Garcia and
a nice Eagle River
rainbow.*

caddis moving upstream, preparing to lay eggs. The caddis flies' presence will be felt on the water through August and maybe even a few days into September. Come prepared with a fly box loaded with caddis patterns.

The green drake is a much sparser hatch, but it grabs the attention of every fish in the river. Late mornings in late July are the best time to catch drakes on the water. Dark green humpies and western green drake patterns in sizes 10 through 12 will draw strikes.

Red quills and PMDs fill the void during summer, and Baetis show up in the fall.

With its variety of hatches, proximity to Vail, and its eager trout, Gore Creek is worthy of your visit. It is not a stream that garners a lot of pressure, and the late summer evenings can be a kick. Give it a try.

Stream Facts: Eagle River

Seasons
- Open all year

Special Regulations
- From Gore Creek downstream to the Colorado River: Bag and possession limit is 2 trout.
- Squaw Creek lease: Flies and lures only. Bag and possession limit is 2 trout over 16 inches.

Trout
- Rainbows, Browns, cutthroat; brookies in the upper stretches.

River Miles
- Minturn—0
- Avon—7
- Squaw Creek lease—11
- I- 70 bridge at US—6 14
- Fishing access— 16
- Horn Lease—22
- Bottom of Horn Lease—25
- Gypsum Ponds—32
- Fishing access—36

River Characteristics
- The Eagle River is a freestone river its full length, from the time it starts just below the Continental Divide in the White River National Forest to its confluence with the Colorado River at Dotsero. A wonderfully diverse river, the Eagle offers pockets, runs, and riffles that can keep you busy for days. A slick bottom makes wading tricky. Runoff can be big. River fishes best in early spring and right after runoff.

River Flows
- Spring, 150–500 cfs
- Runoff, 1,000–2,900 cfs
- Summer, July, 700–1,500 cfs
- Fall, 200–400 cfs

Maps
- *Colorado Atlas & Gazetteer*, pages 47, 37, 36
- White River National Forest

EAGLE RIVER MAJOR HATCHES

Insect	A	M	J	J	A	S	O	N	Time	Flies
Midge									M/A/E	Olive Biot Midge #16-#24; Gray Biot Midge #16-#24; Black Beauty #18-#24; Brassie #16-#24; Blood Midge #16-#24; Miracle Nymph #16-#20; AK's Midge Larva #16-#22; Black Beauty Pupa #18-#24; CDC Biot Suspender Midge #18-#24; Chartreuse Serendipity #16-#20; Griffith's Gnat #16-#22; Palomino Midge #18-#22
Baetis									M/A	Olive Biot Nymph #18-#22; RS-2 #16-#24; Pheasant Tail Nymph #16-#20; Beadhead Pheasant Tail Nymph #16-#22; Flashback Pheasant Tail Nymph #16-#20; Olive Quill Emerger #18-#24; AK's Olive Quill #16-#22; Parachute Adams #16-#22; Olive Comparadun #16-#20; Gray Spinner #18-#24; CDC Baetis Dun #16-#22; Air-flo Cut-wing Dun #16-#22; Poor's Witch #18-#22
Green Drake									A	Green Drake Emerger #10-#12; Lawson's Parachute Green Drake #10-#12; Green Drake #10-#12; Adams #10-#12; Olive Hare's Ear #10-#12
Red Quill									M/A	AK's Red Quill #14-#20; Rusty Spinner #12-#20
Pale Morning Dun									M/A	Biot PMD Nymph #16; Pheasant Tail Nymph #16-#22; Beadhead Pheasant Tail Nymph #14-#20; Lt. Cahill Comparadun #12-#18; Sparkle Dun #14-#18; Parachute PMD #14-#18; Dark Hare's Ear #14-#18; Light Olive Comparadun #16-#20

HATCH TIME CODE: M = morning; A = afternoon; E = evening; D = dark; SF = spinner fall; / = continuation through periods.

EAGLE RIVER MAJOR HATCHES (CONT.)

Insect	A	M	J	J	A	S	O	N	Time	Flies
Caddis			█	█	█	█			A/E	Olive Caddis Nymph #10–#20; Breadcrust #10–#18; Beadhead Breadcrust #10–#18; Buckskin #16–#20; LaFontaine's Sparkle Caddis Pupa #10–#20; Elk Hair Caddis #10–#22; Goddard Caddis #10–#16; CDC Caddis #14–#20; Macramé Caddis #12–#16; Balloon Caddis #12–#16; Lawson's Caddis Emerger #14–#18; Spent Partridge Caddis #14–#18
Terrestrials				█	█				A/E	Rio Grande King Trude #8–#16; Royal Wulff #10–#16; Royal Humpy #10–#16; Foam Madam X #8–#12; Renegade #10–#16; Black Ant #14–#20; Cinnamon Ant #14–#20; Gartside Hopper #8–#10; Henry's Fork Hopper #8–#12
Stonefly			█						M/A	Halfback #4–#10; Prince Nymph #8–#16; Beadhead Prince Nymph #8–#16; Kaufmann's Brown Stonefly #4–#8; Stimulator #8–#12
Streamers	█	█	█	█	█	█	█		M/E	Black Woolly Bugger #2–#10; Platte River Special #4–#10; Spruce Fly #4–#10; Dark Spruce Fly #4–#10; Black-nosed Dace #6–#8; Muddler Minnow #4–#10; Matuka Sculpin #4–#10; Matuka Muddler #4–#10; Whitlock's Hair Sculpin #4–#6; Steve's BRO Bug #6–#10
Golden Stonefly				█	█				A/E	Sandy's Gold #6–#10; Gold-winged Prince Nymph #8–#10; Kaufmann's Golden Stonefly #6–#12; Stimulator #8–#12; Foam Yellow Sally #12–#18

HATCH TIME CODE: M = morning; A = afternoon; E = evening; D = dark; SF = spinner fall; / = continuation through periods.

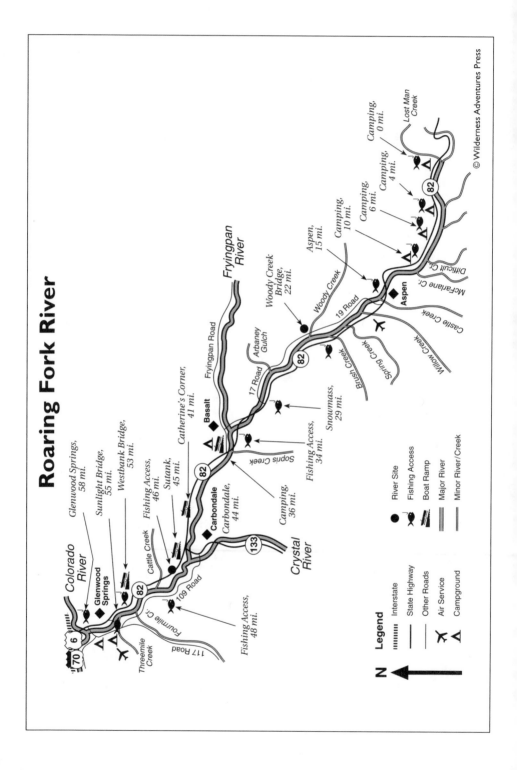

Roaring Fork River

Colorado River

Glenwood Springs, 58 mi.

Sunlight Bridge, 55 mi.

Westbank Bridge, 53 mi.

Glenwood Springs

Cattle Creek

Fishing Access, 46 mi.

Sutank, 45 mi.

Catherine's Corner, 41 mi.

Threemile Creek

Fourmile Cr.

117 Road

Fishing Access, 48 mi.

109 Road

133

Crystal River

Carbondale

Carbondale, 44 mi.

Camping, 36 mi.

Sopris Creek

Fishing Access, 34 mi.

Basalt

Fryingpan Road

17 Road

Arbaney Gulch

Fryingpan River

Snowmass, 29 mi.

Brush Creek

Spring Creek

Willow Creek

Woody Creek Bridge, 22 mi.

Woody Creek

19 Road

Aspen, 15 mi.

Aspen

Castle Creek

McFarlane Cr.

Difficult Cr.

Camping, 10 mi.

Camping, 6 mi.

Camping, 4 mi.

Camping, 0 mi.

Lost Man Creek

82

© Wilderness Adventures Press

Legend

N

Interstate	River Site
State Highway	Fishing Access
Other Roads	Boat Ramp
Air Service	Major River
Campground	Minor River/Creek

ROARING FORK RIVER

The Ute Indians called the lower Roaring Fork Valley their home, and at one time the whole lower valley was designated as the Northern Ute Indian Reservation. They called the Roaring Fork River "Thunder River," which referred to the thunderous sound the river can make.

To understand the true nature of this river, realize that in its 70-mile descent to the Colorado River, the Roaring Fork drops more in elevation than the Mississippi River does over its full length.

Glenwood Springs was one of the oldest known gathering places for the Ute Indians. They named it Yampah, meaning "big medicine," and felt that bathing in the hot springs there made them better hunters. However, as with most Indians, they were moved from their beautiful homeland when settlers took over.

After the Meeker Massacre, Colorow, the last Chieftain, and his people were moved to another reservation in Utah. Colorow preferred the Glenwood Springs area and visited from time to time. The settler ladies soon learned that he had a profound fondness for their biscuits and honey. It was said that he weighed 300 pounds at death.

Captain Richard Sopris was the first white man in recorded history to use the hot springs. In 1860, he and his survey party camped and rested there. Mount Sopris, located south of Glenwood Springs, carries the captain's name.

Over the years, many wealthy and important visitors from all over the world, including Teddy Roosevelt, visited the springs. Roosevelt was instrumental in forming the White River National Forest, the first of many national forests.

For flyfishing purposes, the Roaring Fork is a true freestone stream from its headwaters, beginning just below Independence Pass, to its confluence with the Colorado River at Glenwood Springs. It parallels Colorado 82 from start to finish, and several accesses along the river offer easy approaches.

The headwaters above Aspen flow through White River National Forest. Several pulloffs and four campgrounds provide access to this tumbling small stream. Private property shows up a few miles southeast of Aspen. However, a half-mile piece of water, known as the North Star access, is located 2 miles upstream from Aspen and is well marked.

Good-sized brook trout, along with a few rainbows, are fair game for the fly angler. Fishing is definitely best after mid-June, and continues through summer and fall. However, once the snow flies, Colorado 82, also known as the Independence Pass Road, is closed.

As with most small streams, big dry flies draw quick takes as they pass over any slow-water pocket along the bank or the tail-end of a plunge pool.

Below Aspen, the north side of the river is open from the Rio Grande Trailhead downstream to the upper Woody Creek Bridge, just over 5 miles of water. This is Wild Trout Water, catch and release, flies only.

At lower Woody Creek Bridge, an access is located on the south side of the river and public access extends upstream for 2 miles. That section is designated as flies and lures only, with a 2 fish over 16 inches limit.

Old Snowmass Bridge, about 5 miles downstream from lower Woody Creek Bridge, provides access to a mile of open water down to Lazy Glen Trailer Park.

The town of Basalt is 5 miles downstream from Snowmass, and 3 miles of river access is available there. Fishing is allowed on the north side of the river from the upper bypass bridge downstream to the lower bypass bridge.

In this section, the Roaring Fork becomes wider and flows with much less gradient. Riffles form, along with more distinct pockets, providing good holding water. Solid caddis and mayfly populations produce excellent hatches in this stretch, so there is good dry fly fishing through the season.

Caddis generally emerge in May, just before runoff, and continue to hatch sporadically through summer. The best mayfly hatches occur after runoff. Pale morning duns and green drakes provide superb fishing, and a mix of rainbows and browns, ranging between 10 and 16 inches, are generally eager to inhale standard patterns. Mountain whitefish are present, too, and they are often hooked when fishing with nymphs.

During my inaugural year of flyfishing, one of my first trips was to the Roaring Fork at Snowmass Bridge.

It was early November, and I was inexperienced in the ways of deep, moving water. Wearing hip boots, I fell victim to the slick bottom rocks. Three times! Unprepared, without dry clothes, I gave up on fishing and decided that a trip to the laundry in Aspen—to dry clothes—was in order.

As shown by my wading debacle, the Fork is deceptively strong in that stretch. I'm not the first and I won't be the last to take a bone-chilling dip among the greasy stones of the Fork. However, you can make things easier on yourself by donning high-back chest waders and good, felt-soled boots. You may even consider studded felt for this river.

No matter where you choose to fish the Fork, probably the ideal rod choice is a 9-foot, 6-weight. A 9-foot, 5-weight will work well, too, being large enough to throw large, weighted nymphs when needed. A 9-foot, 4-weight can be awfully nice to throw when the fish are rising to dry flies.

The most popular section of the Roaring Fork stretches from Basalt down to the Colorado River; this section is fishable all year. Although the river remains open through winter, slush can be a deterrent in the morning hours. Around noon, even on some of the coldest days, you can get in a few hours of decent fishing as the slush dissipates. Mountain whitefish are often encountered during winter, so be prepared to hook a few and don't be afraid to put some in the smoker. They are quite good table fare, and they put up a good battle trying to free themselves from the hook.

Midges are the main source of food during winter. Good hatches start in February and continue through April. When fishing midges, I always fish a size 20 dark biot midge with a zug bug or a Prince nymph as a trailer. A miracle nymph, palomino midge, golden stone, or a buckskin are also good early season choices.

Baetis mayflies hatch as early as March in the lower river and move up to Basalt by mid-April. Baetis will begin to pop through the surface around noon each day, and they continue their emergence for an hour or so. Nymphing the deeper pools and the

The Roaring Fork is an intimate stream that holds nice populations of rainbow and brown trout. Chris Clothier took this fish from a mid-depth run in front of him.

edges of runs with black pheasant tail or olive biot nymphs, sizes 16 through 20, can be very effective from midmorning until noon. If trout start to rise, expect to see them along the banks in the slow, shallow eddies.

Bruce Stolbach at Alpine Angling in Basalt says, "The Roaring Fork is an edge fishing river, meaning most of your presentations should be kept within a couple yards of the bank."

Emerger patterns stuck in the surface film near those banks should produce well. As the olive hatch lingers, trout could focus on duns. A parachute Adams, blue quill, and blue-winged olive in sizes 16 through 20 are common patterns used for the adult, dun stage of this hatch. If you receive refusals on nymph or emerger patterns, quickly switch to a dun representation.

Late April is the start of the Mother's Day caddis hatch. As with all hatches on the Fork, the caddis start in Glenwood Springs and move upstream at a steady pace. They reach Aspen by the second week in May, but at that time it's a good chance the river will be blown out.

I like to fish that hatch during the last week in April at Glenwood Springs. There are several in-town access points, including the airport access that offers about a quarter mile of public fishing on the south bank. To reach that access, take CR 117 to the airport and fish at the south end of the runway. The Glenwood Park access, also on CR 117, is located upstream from Threemile Creek, a half-mile downstream on the south side of the river. Sunlight Bridge offers almost a mile of river access on the south side and a quarter-mile on north side.

The lower end of town, extending to the Roaring Fork's confluence with the Colorado River, is a great stop in the evening when caddis return to the water to lay eggs. The female caddis are bloated with dark green, almost peacock colored, egg-filled abdomens, and the trout love to drill them at that time. Hey, who could pass up on an easy bit of caviar?

When those caddis are laying eggs, look for rises in the slack water side of braided seams. Also probe where large boulders break the current; outstanding feeding lanes form there.

While the trout certainly feed hard when those caddis return to the river, fishing can be difficult; spotting your fly in the dim light is not easy, and fly selection can be perplexing. A low-riding, spent caddis pattern, like a Lawson's size 16 , gives the best silhouette and is a good choice in the evening.

The Roaring Fork's most popular hatch by far is the green drake emergence that comes off in early July. For six weeks, those huge mayflies march upstream until they bump into the dam at Ruedi Reservoir on the Fryingpan River. At that point, they taper off. Stolbach notes, "The green drake hatch is definitely a late afternoon (emergence). It continues to get better the later it gets in the day. Often, night falls before you know it, and you end up fishing by sound, setting up on any noise that even remotely indicates a fish may have risen to your fly. Our guides refer to it as the night strike." He adds, "We do specialized trips for this hatch. We start our floats at 3 or 3:30 PM in Carbondale and fish down to the Westbank Bridge by the time it gets dark."

The Sopris RV Park has an improved boat ramp for put-ins at Carbondale. From there it's an excellent half-day, 8-mile float down to Westbank Bridge. Considered the easiest section of the river to float, a moderately experienced oarsman should be able to handle this piece of water.

During July and August, a small yellow stonefly, called a yellow sally, is important to the fly angler. They can be seen on the water at the same time as the green drakes. A dual fly set-up shown to me several years ago by a guide who floated us down the Madison River in Montana also works well here. Tie a size 12 green drake to the end of a 10-foot, 4X leader. Add an 18-inch section of 5X tippet to the bend of the green drake and tie on a size 16 yellow sally. A big dry fly, trailed by a small dry, covers both insects and gives any particular trout a look at both options.

Banging the banks with terrestrials during the heat of August and September can be effective as we burn a little time waiting for the fall BWO hatch, but overall fishing is a little slow during the hot months.

October can prove to be outstanding for the minute blue-wings. Overcast days offer the best conditions for heavy hatches, while the bright days support sporadic hatches. The same blue-winged olive patterns used in the spring work in the fall.

The Roaring Fork offers excellent opportunities for large rainbow and brown trout. Here, the author battles a scrappy trout. (Photo by Jim Neiberger)

Stolbach told me, "The biggest trout of the year are caught in October and November in the lower river. The big browns are on the prowl for sculpins and they feed late in the day and through the night. Staying out a little later than usual and fishing the deep pools could be rewarded with a trophy."

Browns over 20 inches are caught on Matuka sculpins, muddler minnows, and woolly buggers. Don't be surprised if a rainbow of several pounds hammers one of those big flies, too.

Overall, the Roaring Fork Valley is a sportsman's paradise. Besides fishing, the area offers excellent hunting. If you are going to stay in town, book reservations ahead of time, especially during fall when the hunters show up in hordes.

Stream Facts: Roaring Fork River

Seasons
- Open all year

Special Regulations
- From McFarlane Creek downstream to upper Woody Creek Bridge: Artificial flies only. All fish must be released immediately
- From upper Woody Creek Bridge to the Colorado River: Artificial flies and lures only. Bag and possession limit for trout is 2 fish, 16 inches or longer.
- From Holum Lake downstream to Wood Creek Bridge: Wild Trout Water.
- From Crystal River downstream to the Colorado River: Gold Medal Water.

Fish
- Rainbows, Browns, Whitefish

River Miles
- Lost Man Campground—0
- Lincoln Gulch Campground—4
- Weller Campground—6
- Difficult Campground—10
- North Star Fishing Access, Aspen—15
- Fishing Access (Rio Grande Trail)—17
- Upper Woody Creek Bridge—22
- Lower Woody Creek Bridge—24
- Old Snowmass Bridge—29
- Fishing access—34
- Camping (Basalt KOA)—36
- Hook's Bridge—37
- Catherine's Corner—41
- Carbondale—44
- Sutank (Confluence with the Crystal River)—45
- Fishing access—46
- Aspen Glen access—48
- Westbank Bridge—53
- Sunlight Bridge—55
- Glenwood Springs—58

River Characteristics
- A freestone its full length. The stretch above upper Woody Creek Bridge near Aspen is Wild Trout Water, relying on natural reproduction. Rainbows average a pound in this area. Downstream, the river gains momentum as the Fryingpan River, Crystal River, and many small streams join with the Fork. This Gold Medal Stretch is best known for its brown trout, with many in the 2- to 4-pound class. A trophy can be caught here, though they are few and far between.

River Flows
- Winter and spring, 400–500 cfs
- Runoff, 3,000–6,000 cfs
- Summer, late July 1,200–1,500 cfs
- Fall, 600–800 cfs

Boat Ramps
- Upper bypass Bridge—34
- Below Basalt—35
- Hook's Bridge—37
- Sopris RV Park—44
- Westbank Bridge—53
- Glenwood Springs, Two Rivers Park—58

Maps
- *Colorado Atlas & Gazetteer*, pages 35, 45, 46, 47
- White River National Forest
- Rivers Publishing, Inc., Box 2146, Basalt, CO 81621 / 970-963-1084

ROARING FORK RIVER MAJOR HATCHES

Insect	A	M	J	J	A	S	O	N	Time	Flies
Midge						▮	▮		M/A/E	Olive Biot Midge #16–#24; Brown Biot Midge #16–#24; Black Beauty #18–#24; Brassie #16–#24; Blood Midge #16–#24; Miracle Nymph #16–#20; AK's Midge Larva #16–#22; Crane Fly Nymph #6–#10; Black Beauty Pupa #18–#24; CDC Biot Suspender Midge #18–#24; Griffith's Gnat #16–#22; Palomino Midge #18–#22; Serendipity #16–#24
Baetis							▮		M/A	Olive Biot Nymph #16–#20; RS-2 #16–#20; Pheasant Tail Nymph #16–#20; Beadhead Pheasant Tail Nymph #16–#20; Flashback Pheasant Tail Nymph #16–#20; Olive Quill Emerger #18–#22; AK's Olive Quill #16–#20; Blue Quill #16–#20; Blue Dun #16–#20; Parachute Adams #14–#22; Olive Comparadun #16–#20; Gray Spinner #18–#24; CDC Baetis Dun #16–#22; Air-flo Cut-wing Dun #16–#22
Green Drake			▮		▮				A/E	Green Drake Emerger #10–#12; Lawson's Parachute Green Drake #10–#12; Green Drake #10–#12; Adams #10–#12; Olive Hare's Ear #10–#12
Caddis		▮				▮			A/E	Olive Caddis Nymph #10–#20; Breadcrust #10–#18; Beadhead Breadcrust #10–#18; Buckskin #16–#20; LaFontaine's Sparkle Caddis Pupa #10–#20; Elk Hair Caddis #10–#22; Goddard Caddis #10–#16; CDC Caddis #14–#20; St. Vrain Caddis #14–#16; Macramé Caddis #12–#16; Balloon Caddis #12–#16; Lawson's Caddis Emerger #14–#18; Spent Partridge Caddis #14–#18
Red Quill					▮				A/E	AK's Red Quill #14–#18; Rusty Spinner #12–#20

HATCH TIME CODE: M = morning; A = afternoon; E = evening; D = dark; SF = spinner fall; / = continuation through periods.

ROARING FORK RIVER MAJOR HATCHES (CONT.)

Insect	A	M	J	J	A	S	O	N	Time	Flies
Pale Morning Dun			▓	▓	▓	▓			M/A	Biot PMD Nymph #16; Pheasant Tail Nymph #16–#22; Beadhead Pheasant Tail Nymph #14–#20; Lt. Cahill Comparadun #12–#18; Sparkle Dun #14–#18; Parachute PMD #14–#18; Dark Hare's Ear #14–#18
Terrestrials				▓	▓	▓			A/E	Rio Grande King Trude #8–#16; Royal Wulff #10–#16; Humpy #10–#16; Foam Madam X #8–#12; Renegade #10–#16; Black Ant #14–#20; Cinnamon Ant #14–#20; Gartside Hopper #8–#10; Henry's Fork Hopper #8–#12
Stonefly		▓	▓						M/A	Halfback #4–#10; Prince Nymph #8–#16; Beadhead Prince Nymph #8–#16; Kaufmann's Brown Stonefly #4–#8; Sofa Pillow #6–#8; Stimulator #8–#12; Bitch Creek Nymph #10
Streamers							▓	▓	M/E	Black Woolly Bugger #2–#10; Brown Woolly Bugger #4–#10; Platte River Special #4–#10; Spruce Fly #4–#10; Dark Spruce Fly #4–#10; Muddler Minnow #4–#10; Matuka Sculpin #4–#10; Matuka Muddler #4–#10; Whitlock's Hair Sculpin #4–#6; Steve's BRO Bug #6–#10
Golden Stonefly				▓	▓				A/E	Sandy's Gold #6–#10; Gold-winged Prince Nymph #8–#10; Kaufmann's Golden Stonefly #6–#12; Stimulator #8–#12; Foam Yellow Sally #12–#18

HATCH TIME CODE: M = morning; A = afternoon; E = evening; D = dark; SF = spinner fall; / = continuation through periods.

FRYINGPAN RIVER

Everybody knows where the Fryingpan River is, or so it seems. The river is talked about, written about, and fished more than any other stream in Colorado. This fame is well deserved; it is one of the West's, if not the world's, greatest trout streams. Trout live there in abundance, and insect hatches are heavy and predictable. Trout feed on those bugs like there's no tomorrow.

It hasn't always been that way. In fact, when Ruedi Dam was built in 1968, many people thought the river had offered its last quality fishing. Instead, the Fryingpan turned into a great tailwater fishery offering a good chance for flyfishers to take large trout.

While the Fryingpan is certainly a worthy destination for Colorado flyfishers, it receives pressure to the point that I say "forget it" most of the time. For example, Jim Neiberger, a close friend and fishing partner, called after a trip to the Pan during his Christmas break and told me, "I've never seen this many people fishing the river this time of year. I counted 52 anglers in the mile of water below Ruedi!"

Compared to the eastern waters, that may not sound like a lot of people, but out West, that's a pile of anglers. Only you can judge whether the river is too overrun for your own liking.

Despite those crowds, Neiberger and I find good reason to show up at the Pan a couple times a year—the river's monstrous rainbows that live in its tasty runs below Ruedi Reservoir are the big attraction. And the rainbows aren't the only option: this Gold Medal stream hosts brown, cutthroat, and brook trout all running to large size. In fact, a brook trout was caught and released there in 1996 weighing just shy of 8 pounds! On any given day, a flyfisher might catch all species. On one particularly great September day, A.K. Best took the grand slam, a rainbow, brown, brook and cutt—all on dry flies!

The Fryingpan is fishable all year, and the main diet and the main reason why those trout grow so large is due to the *Mysis* shrimp.

Mysis were originally planted in Ruedi Reservoir to bolster trout forage in that stillwater. The shrimp did little to benefit those trout, but they drifted into the river below the reservoir and drastically improved the size of trout and the fishing potential of the Pan. Today, *Mysis* shrimp are the preferred food item for the river's fish, and a number of effective patterns will draw strikes. The Burton's Mysis and Dorsey's *Mysis* are a couple of the best imitations. Anglers should carry those patterns in sizes 14 through 18, with the smaller patterns generally working best.

A plunge pool below the dam, known as the Toilet Bowl, is full of *Mysis*-eating trout that push 10 pounds and often grow larger. Anglers can fish *Mysis* patterns year-round in that water, especially after heavy water releases from the dam when millions of the tiny shrimp wash downstream.

Due to heavy pressure on the Fryingpan's trout, special tactics are required to catch fish consistently. Shannon Skelton, a.k.a. Little Haus, a fishing partner and business associate of mine, is one of the more successful fishermen on that water.

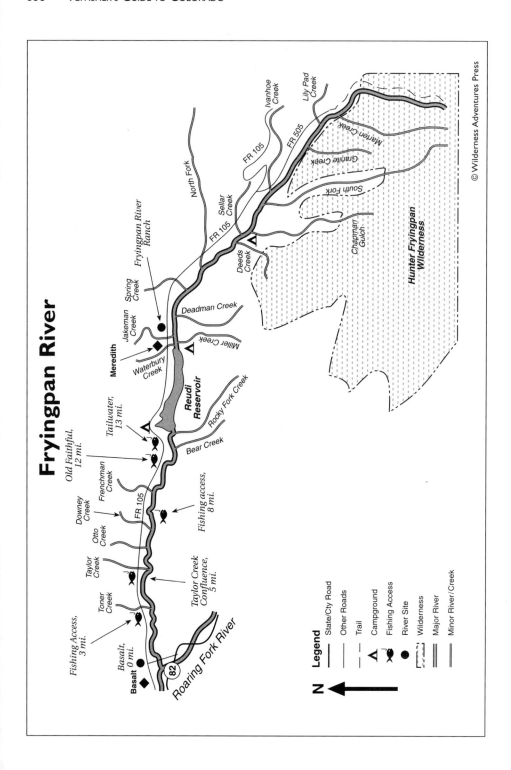

Fryingpan River

© Wilderness Adventures Press

Legend

	State/City Road
	Other Roads
	Trail
▲	Campground
🐟	Fishing Access
●	River Site
	Wilderness
	Major River
	Minor River/Creek

"When you fish the Pan, you need to do things differently," Skelton said. "Most flyfishermen get in a groove, and they use the same techniques everywhere they fish. It may work every place else you fish, but you will lag behind a bit on the Fryingpan. The first change I made on the Pan that made a significant difference was when I pulled the strike indicator off (my line). I've seen enough evidence to convince me that the trout in the upper Pan are indicator shy."

The best time of the year to visit the Fryingpan is during late winter and early spring, from February through April. At that time the water is low and clear, and spotting unsuspecting trout is easy. Skelton likes the inside of a seam when searching for feeding trout at that time.

"When the river makes even the slightest turn, it creates a slow seam on the inside bank as the faster current heads for the far bank," he said. "Trout love these spots and it makes for great sightfishing!" The Bend Pool, a half-mile below the dam, is a prime example of this scenario. "When drifting your fly to a particular trout, it is best to pay close attention to the fish rather than your leader. When a fish winks at you, set the hook."

"Winking," as Skelton calls it, refers to when a trout opens its mouth, changes position, or flashes its side at you. If you see any of those distinct movements, or anything else that appears odd, it probably means the fish just ate your fly. Set the hook, pronto.

When fishing the river in March and April, you'll encounter lots of midges and blue-winged olives. When you encounter those bugs, you may also see some rising fish, but the most productive way to fish that hatch is with nymphs and larvae. However, Skelton insists that leader and tippet selection are nearly as crucial as fly selection during that time.

"I take a 10-foot leader tapered to 5X and cut a foot and a half of the tippet off," he said. "Then I add 18 inches of 6X fluorocarbon tippet. Then I tie on a size 18 buckskin and add another piece of 6X tippet, 12 inches long, to the eye of the buckskin. My second fly is what I call a candy cane. It is a white fly with red ribbing, size 22."

Other patterns that you need to carry in the spring are black biot midges, olive biot mayfly nymphs, AK's midge larva, and dun softhackles for imitating the emerging midges. Carry those patterns in sizes 18 through 24.

In April, when the olive mayflies are hatching, AK's olive quill, an airflo dun, and a gray spinner are good choices.

Pale morning duns offer the next significant hatch, and they arrive just after runoff in June. PMDs are cute, distinctive mayflies that have a pink abdomen and ginger legs and wings. Check in at Fryingpan Anglers in Basalt for a quill-bodied fly tied by A.K. Best that best imitates that insect.

A good midmorning hatch that can produce an excellent rise, the PMD emergence starts near Basalt and moves upstream quickly. The Strawberry Rock access, 3 miles upstream from Basalt, is a good place to catch this hatch a few days after it starts. As the hatch gets closer to the dam, a section that locals call the Old Faithful Pullout can experience a heavy emergence. After the initial burst, expect to see sporadic, yet productive, PMD activity through summer.

Spotting a back like the one on this rising trout in the Fryingpan River could give an angler a heart attack. (Photo by Jim Neiberger)

After the PMDs, you have to look out because the grand hatch of summer, the one that draws anglers to the river in droves and eager trout to the surface like idiotic, starving lunatics, takes place. *E. Grandis*, a huge, olive-colored mayfly that is best known as the green drake, is a fly that any healthy, cold-blooded trout can't resist. And they don't. This is one insect that brings the biggest fish in the river to the surface where they feed with abandon.

The lower river may see the hatch as early as July 4, but most often the hatch arrives during the second week of the month. It takes about two weeks for the hatch to progress to the upper reaches of the river, and fishing is great wherever they emerge.

The green drake nymph is dark olive and measures about three-quarters of an inch long. It prefers slow, deep runs and can migrate into eddies before hatching. A size 12 dark olive hare's ear drifted along the bottom near the edge of a run will take fish. Something to note: green drakes are not the most graceful of emerging insects. Typically, it requires several attempts to make it to the surface, and once there the insect struggles for minutes to unfold its wings and get airborne. This bumbling activity is well suited to the feeding nature of trout. As those nymphs struggle, rainbows, browns and brookies will focus on emergers and nymphs as they near the surface. You may see their backs and fins breaking the surface; when you do, try a size

10 olive soft hackle and fish it with a rising motion at the end of your drift. Your inclination will be to fish a dry fly, but stick with the softhackle early in the emergence.

When you see duns coasting on the surface and trout eating them, it's time to tie on your favorite green drake adult pattern. A size 10 cripple works wonders during the middle and latter stages of the hatch.

Art Rowell with Fryingpan Anglers in Basalt notes, "We carry over a dozen different green drake dry fly patterns, but the most productive is AK's hair-winged drake.

"This hatch can go well after dark and there is no sense in quitting when the action is still good. Especially on a moonlit night, a #10, white-winged H & L variant or a Royal Wulff can still be seen on the water, and the trout take them readily," adds Rowell.

If you are an early riser, a trip to the river between 6:00 and 7:00 AM will see the drakes coming back to the water to lay eggs. Big spinners will be all over the surface of the river. A grayish, olive biot bodied spinner with fan wings in a size 10 is a great imitation of the actual fly.

This is all well and good, but you must remember these trout see a lot of flies and lots of felt-soled boots walking through their territory, so expect the fishing to remain on the difficult side. Patience, and picking your trout is your key to success. Presenting your fly at the same rhythm the trout is feeding in will help you take trout during this hatch.

Another exciting event on the Fryingpan is the caddis hatch, which is part of the Mother's Day hatch from the Roaring Fork River below. The #16 to #18 peacock colored caddis makes its way to the middle sections of the Pan by mid- to late May.

The caddis continue throughout the summer and can provide outstanding dry flyfishing. During the hot months, caddis can be seen in the evenings fluttering and skating across the top of the water.

Rowell suggests, "This activity brings the trout to the surface with hard, slashing rises. When you see highly-visible, splashy rises, you can bet they are taking caddis adults." He adds, "We like to use a parachute caddis, a fly that floats well and is easy to see. It also skitters on the surface easily when the trout are really chasing the caddis."

In late August and September, the Pumpkin Caddis hatch. This large, orange-bodied caddis rates about a size 12 and can produce explosive action. When the trout are feeding on this very active caddis, there is no need to set the hook; they usually set the hook themselves. Again, evenings are the best time to experience this activity.

While midsummer, with its green drake emergence, offers the most appealing attributes, fall is absolutely the most gorgeous time to visit the Fryingpan due to fall colors.

In fact, by the second week in September, the Fryingpan Canyon is in full color. Anglers should expect to encounter Baetis dancing the mayfly jig, hovering over the river, driving trout nuts. Fortunately, at that time, the river runs about 100 to 200 cfs, which is ideal for wading.

On the typical fall afternoon, you will find yourself fishing size 20 Baetis dry flies to rising trout. The hatch is predictable, and the trout feed willingly with winter just

Shannon Skelton and a beautifully colored, 20-inch Fryingpan rainbow. (Photo by Terry Francis)

a month or two away. Because of the consistency at that time of year, you'll find company on the river. Try visiting on a Tuesday or Wednesday, rather than a weekend, and you will be rewarded with a pleasant experience.

If you want to ensure a lack of competition, contact Fryingpan River Ranch. It has private water on the upper river, and they also access high mountain lakes above Ruedi Reservoir. Contact Jim and Paula Rea at 970-927-3570 or 800-352-0980 for information on lodging and fishing packages.

For those of you who do not know how to reach the Fryingpan, start at Glenwood Springs, 160 miles west of Denver. From Glenwood Springs, head south on Colorado 82 to Basalt, where the Fryingpan converges with the Roaring Fork. From there, take FR 105, also known as Fryingpan Road, east to Ruedi Reservoir. The river parallels the road for 14 miles. Public accesses and private sections are easily distinguished. The Aspen Airport is located 18 miles southeast of Basalt, for those who want to travel by air.

Stream Facts: Fryingpan River

Seasons
- Open all year. The river below Ruedi Reservoir is accessible through winter, courtesy of road maintenance. The river above Ruedi is hit-or-miss because of weather.

Special Regulations
- From Ruedi Reservoir downstream to the Roaring Fork River is Gold Medal Water with an artificial flies and lures only restriction. All trout, except browns, must be released immediately. Bag and possession limit for brown trout is 2 fish, less than 14 inches.

Trout
- Rainbows below Ruedi Reservoir reach double digit weight.
- Browns
- Cutthroat
- Brook trout. A fish was landed and released in 1996 that could have been a state record brookie .

River Miles
- Basalt—0
- Fishing access—8
- Strawberry Rock Access—3
- Old Faithful—12
- Taylor Creek Confluence—5
- Tailwater—13

River Characteristics
- The upper Fryingpan is a smallish stream. Below Ruedi Reservoir is your typical tailwater fishery, with an exceptional amount of bug life surviving. Located in a narrow deep canyon 13 miles long, it is about the only place known to man where a grand slam (rainbow, brown, cutthroat, and brook trout in the 20-inch class) can be caught in one day.

River Flows
- Winter, 100–200 cfs
- Spring, 200–400 cfs
- Runoff, 500–800 cfs
- Summer and fall, 100–300 cfs

Maps
- *Colorado Atlas & Gazetteer,* page 46
- White River National Forest / 970-945-2521
- Rivers Publishing, Inc., Box 2146, Basalt, CO 81621 / 970-963-1084

FRYINGPAN RIVER MAJOR HATCHES

Insect	A	M	J	J	A	S	O	N	Time	Flies
Midge									M/A/E	Olive Biot Midge #16–#24; Black Biot Midge #16–#24; Candy Cane #16–#24; Black Beauty #18–#24; Brassie #16–#24; Blood Midge #16–#24; Miracle Nymph #16–#20; AK's Midge Larva #16–#22; Feather Duster Midge #18–#20; Disco Midge #18–#24; Crane Fly Nymph #6–#10; Black Beauty Pupa #18–#24; CDC Biot Suspender Midge #18–#24; Griffith's Gnat #22–#22; Palomino Midge #18–#22
Baetis									M/A	Olive Biot Nymph #18–#22; RS-2 #16–#24; Pheasant Tail Nymph #16–#22; Beadhead Pheasant Tail Nymph #16–#22; Flashback Pheasant Tail Nymph #16–#22; Olive Quill emerger #18–#24; AK's Olive Quill #16–#22; Parachute Adams #16–#22; Olive Comparadun #16–#20; Gray Spinner #18–#24; CDC Baetis Dun #16–#22; Barr Emerger #16–#22; Air-flo Cut-wing Dun #16–#22
Green Drake									M/A	Green Drake Emerger #10–#12; Lawson's Parachute Green Drake #10–#12; AK's Hair-winged Green Drake #10–#12; Adams #10–#12; Olive Hare's Ear #10–#12
Red Quill									A/E	AK's Red Quill #14–#18; Rusty Spinner #12–#20
Mysis									M/A/E	Burton's Mysis Shrimp #14–#18
Caddis									A/E	Olive Caddis Nymph #10–#20; Breadcrust #10–#18; Beadhead Breadcrust #10–#18; Buckskin #16–#20; LaFontaine's Sparkle Caddis Pupa #10–#20; Elk Hair Caddis #10–#22; Goddard Caddis #10–#16; CDC Caddis #14–#20; St. Vrain Caddis #14–#16; Macramé Caddis #12–#16; Balloon Caddis #12–#16; Lawson's Caddis Emerger #14–#18; Spent Partridge Caddis #14–#18

HATCH TIME CODE: M = morning; A = afternoon; E = evening; D = dark; SF = spinner fall; / = continuation through periods.

FRYINGPAN RIVER MAJOR HATCHES (CONT.)

Insect	A	M	J	J	A	S	O	N	Time	Flies
Pale Morning Dun		▮	▮	▮					M/A	Biot PMD Nymph #16; Pheasant Tail Nymph #16–#22; Beadhead Pheasant Tail Nymph #14–#20; Lt. Cahill Comparadun #12–#18; Sparkle Dun #14–#18; Parachute PMD #14–#18; Dark Hare's Ear #14–#18; AK's Pink Quill #14–#18; Pink Comparadun #14–#18
Crane Fly					▮				M/A	Tan or Olive Crane Fly Larvae #6–#12; Rubber Band Nymph #8–#14; Spent-wing Crane Fly #14–#18
Golden Stonefly			▮	▮					M/A	Sandy's Gold #6–#10; Gold-winged Prince Nymph #8–#10; Kaufmann's Golden Stonefly #6–#12; Stimulator #8–#12; Foam Yellow Sally #12–#18; Prince Nymph #8–#16; Beadhead Prince Nymph #8–#16
Streamers		▮						▮	M/E	Black Woolly Bugger #2–#10; Spruce Fly #4–#10; Black-nosed Dace #6–#8
Terrestrials				▮	▮	▮			A/E	Rio Grande King Tde #8–#16; Royal Wulff #10–#16; Humpy #10–#16; Renegade #10–#16; Black Ant #14–#20; Cinnamon Ant #14–#20; Henry's Fork Hopper #8–#12
Trico					▮	▮			M	Parachute Adams #24–#20; Trico Spinner #26–#18; Double Trico Spinner #18; Thorax Dun #22–#16; Poor's Witch #22–#18
Pseudocloens						▮	▮		A/E	Olive Biot Nymph #20–#24; RS-2 #20–#24; Olive Quill Emerger #20–#24; AK's Olive Quill #22; Olive CDC Comparadun #20–#24; Gray Spinner #22–#24; Slate Thorax Dun #22–#24
Scuds								▮	M/E	Olive Scud #12–#16; Orange Scud #10–#16; 19½ Scud #12–#18; Tan Scud #12–#16; Flashback Scud #12–#16

HATCH TIME CODE: M = morning; A = afternoon; E = evening; D = dark; SF = spinner fall; / = continuation through periods.

Crystal River

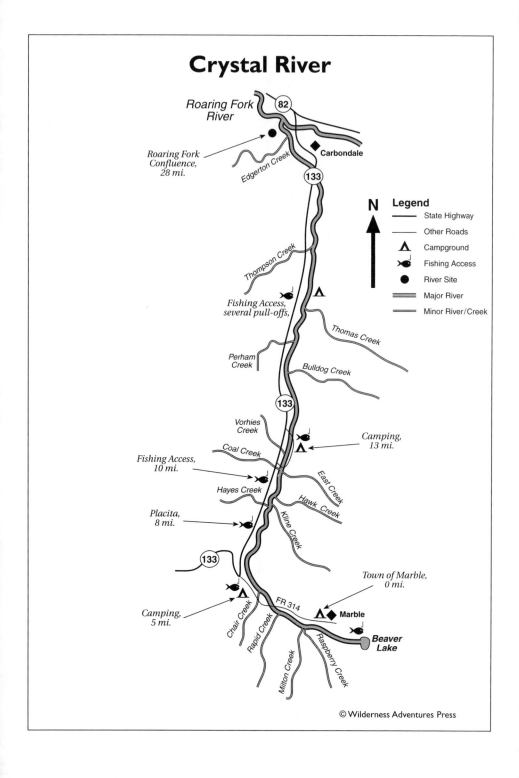

Roaring Fork River

82

Roaring Fork Confluence, 28 mi.

Carbondale

Edgerton Creek

133

N

Legend

—— State Highway
— Other Roads
▲ Campground
✖ Fishing Access
● River Site
▬ Major River
▬ Minor River/Creek

Thompson Creek

Fishing Access, several pull-offs,

Thomas Creek

Perham Creek

Bulldog Creek

133

Vorhies Creek

Coal Creek

Camping, 13 mi.

Fishing Access, 10 mi.

Hayes Creek

East Creek

Hawk Creek

Placita, 8 mi.

Kline Creek

133

Town of Marble, 0 mi.

Camping, 5 mi.

Chair Creek

FR 314

Marble

Rapid Creek

Milton Creek

Raspberry Creek

Beaver Lake

© Wilderness Adventures Press

CRYSTAL RIVER

The Crystal River, a major tributary of the Roaring Fork, is a small freestone stream in its upper stretches with numerous pockets and plunge pools and plenty of eager, if not large, trout.

It is best fished after runoff in July and August, when flyfishers will encounter caddis flies and small yellow stoneflies. At that time, small caddis patterns and even the large attractors, like royal Wulffs and humpies, will draw strikes.

During late summer, wading the river is easy, so you can work down the middle of the Crystal, casting dry flies to the banks and unsuspecting trout. Pop your flies to the banks, but don't forget to cover the slicks behind and in front of midstream rocks. One suggestion is to take the time to walk a short distance from the campgrounds to find water that does not get fished very often. Your extra legwork will pay dividends.

While most Crystal River trout run 9 to 12 inches—an even mix of browns, rainbows, and brook trout—don't be surprised if someone tells you they caught a fish in the 3- to 5-pound range. You may even hook a fish of those desirable proportions yourself.

The Division of Wildlife drops a few brood fish in the stream from time to time. Though they may have their fins rubbed raw by hatchery raceways and their snouts may be scuffed a bit, they are a challenge to land in the little Crystal.

While it definitely offers some decent fishing opportunities, the Crystal is sometimes overlooked by anglers due to its lack of access. However, sections of the Crystal that flow through the White River National Forest provide rewarding experiences. If nothing else, the drive is beautiful and shows off Colorado at its scenic best.

The Crystal is located south of Carbondale, just off Colorado 133. In fact, the river parallels the highway to its intersection with FR 314. FR 314 parallels the river to the town of Marble; however, the river twists through private land until it reaches the Redstone Campground, 15 miles south of Carbondale.

There are several pulloffs and two campgrounds, Redstone and Bogan Flats, that provide national forest fishing access. There is also an access to the Crystal in Marble at Beaver Lake.

While it will likely never draw the attention of the big-name Colorado rivers, the Crystal offers a nice, small stream option in beautiful country. A day trip to this river can be rewarding.

*Crystal River
at Redstone
Campground.*

Stream Facts: Crystal River

River Miles
- Marble—0
- Camping—5
- Campground at Placita—8
- Fishing access—10
- Camping—13
- Roaring Fork Confluence—28

Central Hub Cities
Kremmling
Population – 1,244 • Elevation – 7,364 • Area Code – 970

ACCOMMODATIONS

Elktrout Lodge, 1853 CR 33 / P.O. Box 614 / 724-3343 Managers: Colleen Paine and Marty Cecil / Orvis endorsed / 8 rooms in the lodge, 3 cabins Located on the Colorado River / Guided packages for private water on the Colorado and Blue Rivers / Private ponds / $$$

Bob's Western Motel, 110 West Park Avenue / 724-3266 / 39 units / Dogs allowed / $$

Hotel Eastin, 105 South 2nd Street 724-3261 / 27 units / $

Modern Hotel, 214 Park Center Avenue / 724-9341

BED AND BREAKFAST

Mountain Breeze B and B, 724-3861 / Hosts: Cindy and Lindsay Nicholson / $$$

CAMPING

Kremmling RV Park, CR 22 and Highway 40 / 724-9593 / 20 full hook ups, showers, tent sites

Alpine RV Park, 115 West Central Avenue / 724-9655 / 18 full hook ups

Pump House Campground, 12 miles west of Kremmling on CR 1 (Trough Road.) / Unimproved, 12 sites

RESTAURANTS

Lone Moose Restaurant and Lounge, 115 West Park Avenue / 724-9987

Quarter Circle Saloon, 106 West Park Avenue / 724-9601 / Open 11AM–2AM / Cocktails / $-$$

The Wagon, 276 Central Avenue / 724-9219

FLY SHOPS/GUIDES AND SPORTING GOODS

Elktrout Lodge, 1853 CR 33 P.O. Box 614 / 724-3343 / Web page: www.elktrout.com / Managers: Colleen Paine and Marty Cecil / Orvis endorsed / Located on the Colorado River / Guided packages for private water on the Colorado and Blue Rivers / Private ponds / Small fly shop

Chuck McGuire Fly Fishing, P.O. Box 1244 / 724-3811 / Owner: Chuck McGuire / Guided fly fishing

Fishin' Hole Sporting Goods, Highway 40 / 724-9407

Motion Sports, 208 Eagle Avenue / 724-9067

Sportsman Quick Stop, 200 Park Center Avenue / 724-9523

HOSPITALS

Kremmling Memorial Hospital, 214 South 4th Street / 724-3442

AIRPORTS

Kremmling Airport, 450 Airport Road / 724-9428 / Private airplanes
Also see Denver airports information

AUTO RENTAL

Avis Rent-A-Car, Denver International Airport / 342-5500, 800-831-2847
Enterprise Rent-A-Car, Denver International Airport / 342-7350, 800-325-8007
Thrifty Car Rental, Denver International Airport / 342-9400, 800-367-2277

AUTO SERVICE

Cunningham Automotive, 103 North Pine Avenue / 724-3660
Fettig Auto Repair, 1105 Eagle Avenue / 724-9536
West Grand Automotive, 912 East Park Avenue / 724-9410

FOR MORE INFORMATION

Kremmling Chamber of Commerce
P.O. Box 471
Kremmling, CO 80459
724-3472
email: krcoc@rkymtnhi.com

Granby

Population – 966 • Elevation – 7,935 • Area Code – 970

ACCOMMODATIONS

Blue Spruce Motel, 170 East Agate / 887-3300 / 14 units / Dogs allowed / $$-$$$
Frontier Motel, 232 West Agate / 887-2544 / 23 units / $$-$$$
Homestead Motel, 851 West Agate / 887-3665 / 10 units / Dogs allowed / $$$

RESTAURANTS

Chuckwagon Restaurant and Lounge, 903 West Agate Avenue / 887-9900 / Open 6AM–9PM daily / Breakfast / Cocktails / $
Longbranch Restaurant, 185 East Agate Avenue / 887-2209 / Open 11AM–9:30PM / Cocktails / $$
Silver Spur Saloon and Steak House, 15 East Agate Avenue / 887-9556 / Open 11AM–9PM / Cocktails / $$

FLY SHOPS / GUIDES AND SPORTING GOODS

Nelson Fly and Tackle, 72149 Highway 40 P.O. Box 336, Tabernash 80478 / 726-8558 / Owner: Jim Nelson / Full-service fly shop / Quality, friendly service / Recommends guides for the area
Devil's Thumb Ranch Resort, P.O. Box 750, Tabernash 80478 / 800-933-4339 / Web site: rkymtnhi.com/devthumb / Owner: Barry Gordon / Manager of flyfishing: Jason Cross / Private water and guide service
Fletcher's Sporting Goods, 217 West Agate Avenue / 887-3747 / Owners: Jim and Georgia Kauffman / Licenses and fishing supplies

HOSPITALS

Granby Medical Center, 480 East Agate Avenue / 887-2117

AIRPORTS

Granby-Grand County Airport, 725-3347 / Private airplanes
Also see Denver airports information

AUTO RENTAL

Avis Rent-A-Car, Denver International Airport / 342-5500, 800-831-2847
Enterprise Rent-A-Car, Denver International Airport / 342-7350, 800-325-8007
Thrifty Car Rental, Denver International Airport / 342-9400, 800-367-2277

AUTO SERVICE

D J Towing and Automotive, 62429 Highway 40 / 887-9414
Steve's Towing and Repair, 622 East Garnet Avenue / 887-3661

LOCKSMITH

Independent Key and Locksmith, 925 East Grant Avenue / 887-3040, cell 531-1467

FOR MORE INFORMATION

Granby Chamber of Commerce
81 West Jasper Avenue
Granby, CO 80446
887-2311

Hot Sulphur Springs

Population – 347 • Elevation – 7,670 • Area Code – 970

ACCOMMODATIONS

Ute Trail Motel, 120 East Highway 40 / 725-0123, 800-506-0099 / Hosts: Spaulding and Sarah Goetze / Continental breakfast / Pets allowed / $-$$

Canyon Motel, Highway 40 West / 725-3395 / Dogs allowed / $-$$

K C Cabins, 417 Byers Avenue / 725-3329 / $-$$

Riverside Hotel, 509 Grand Avenue / 725-3589 / $-$$

BED AND BREAKFAST

Stagecoach Country Inn, 412 Nevada / 725-3910 / Innkeepers: Lou and Kathy Bridges / $$$

CAMPING

Pioneer Park, 725-3933

RESTAURANTS

County Seat Cafe, 517 Byers Avenue / 725-3309 / Open 6:30AM, 7days a week / $

M-Bar-Eleven, 419 Grand Avenue / 725-9984

FLY SHOPS AND GUIDES

Riverside Angler, located in the Ute Trail and Riverside Motels / 725-0025 / Owners: Pete McNeill and Dave Ziegler / Full-service flyshop and guide service

Dave Parri's Outfitting, P.O. Box 254 / 725-3531 / Owner: Dave Parri

HOSPITALS

Granby Medical Center, 480 East Agate Avenue, Granby (9 miles east) / 887-2117

AIRPORTS

Kremmling Airport, 450 Airport Road / 724-9428 / Private airplanes

Granby-Grand County Airport, 725-3347 / Private airplanes

Also see Denver airports information

AUTO RENTAL

Avis Rent-A-Car, Denver International Airport / 342-5500, 800-831-2847

Enterprise Rent-A-Car, Denver International Airport / 342-7350, 800-325-8007

Thrifty Car Rental, Denver International Airport / 342-9400, 800-367-2277

AUTO SERVICE

D J Towing and Automotive, 62429 Highway 40, Granby / 887-9414

Steve's Towing and Repair, 622 East Garnet Avenue, Granby / 887-3661

LOCKSMITH

Independent Key and Locksmith, 925 East Grant, Granby / 887-3040, cell 531-1467

FOR MORE INFORMATION

Granby Chamber of Commerce
81 West Jasper Avenue
Granby, CO 80446
887-2311

Silverthorne

Population – 1,768 • Elevation – 8,790• Area Code – 970

ACCOMMODATIONS

Hampton Inn, 560 Silverthorne Lane / 468-6200 / 160 units / $$$

First Interstate Inn, 357 Blue River Pkwy / 468-5170 / 36 units / Dogs allowed for a fee / $$-$$$

Super 8 Motel, 808 Little Beaver Trail, Dillon 80435 / 468-8888, 800-800-8000 / 60 units / $$$

Best Western, 1202 North Summit Boulevard, Frisco 80443 / 668-5094 / 127 units / Dogs allowed / $$$

Holiday Inn, 1129 North Summit Boulevard, Frisco 80443 / 668-5000, 800-782-7669 / 200 units / $$$

BED AND BREAKFAST

Creekside Inn, 51 West Main Street, Frisco 80443 / 668-5607, 800-668-7320 / Innkeeper: Arlene Houley / 7 rooms / $$$

CAMPING

Blue River Campground, Only camping area between Dillon and Green Mountain Reservoirs / 24 sites / Contact the U.S. Forest Service at 970-468-5400

Tiger Run RV Resort, 0085 Tiger Run Road / 453-9690

RESTAURANTS

Sunshine Cafe, Summit Plaza Shopping Center / 468-6663 / Open 7AM–9:30 / Cocktails / $-$$

Ge Jo's Italian Restaurant, 409 Main Street, Frisco 80443 / 668-3308 / Open 5PM–9PM / Cocktails / $$-$$$

Ristorante al Lago, 240 Lake Dillon Drive, Dillon 80435 / 468-6111

Dragon Chinese Restaurant, 290 Summit Place / 468-2509 / Open for dinner and drinks / $$

Siverheels Southwest Grill, 81 Buffalo Drive / 468-2926

Village Inn, 531 Silverthorne Lane / 468-1331 / Open 24 hours / Breakfast / $

FLY SHOPS/GUIDES AND SPORTING GOODS

Arapahoe Anglers, 191 Blue River Pkwy / P.O. Box 2540 / 970-262-2878, 888-876-8818 / email: aanglers@csn.net / Web-site: www.fishcolorado.com / Owner: Greg Ward / Full-service flyshop and guide service / Blue River, Colorado River, local streams, and high mountain lakes / Experienced guides

Summit Guides, Keystone Village, P.O. Box 2489 / 970-468-8945 / Owner: Dale Fields / Full-service fly shop / Float and wade trips on the Blue, Colorado, and Eagle Rivers / Rentals and classes

Gold Medal Fly Shop, 1130 Blue River Pkwy / P.O. Box 1399 / 468-8961 / Owner: Jerry McLean / Full-service fly shop and guide service / Blue and Colorado Rivers / Rentals and classes

Antler's, 908 North Summit Boulevard, Frisco 80443 / 668-3152
Eddie Bear's Sporting Good Store, 591 Blue River Pkwy / 468-9320
Wilderness Sports, 266 Summit Plaza / 468-5687

HOSPITALS
Summit Medical Center, Highway 9 at School Road, Frisco 80443 / 668-3300

AIRPORTS
Eagle County Regional Airport, 1193 Cooley Mesa Road, Gypsum 81637 /
    524-9490 / United: 800-241-6522
Also see Denver airports information

AUTO RENTAL
Enterprise Rent-A-Car, 1202 North Summit Boulevard / 668-1727, 800-325-8007

AUTO SERVICE
Action Auto, 273 Warren Avenue / 468-8294
Frisco Tire and Service, 208 3rd Avenue, Frisco / 668-3007

LOCKSMITH
A.M. Locksmiths Inc., 220 Main Street, Suite F, Frisco / 668-0740 / 24-hour service
Summit Towing, 461 Adams Avenue / 468-6061

FOR MORE INFORMATION
Summit County Chamber of Commerce
011 South Summit Boulevard
Silverthorne, CO 80498
668-5800

Breckenridge

Population – 1,285 • Elevation – 9,603 • Area Code – 970

ACCOMMODATIONS

Lodge at Breckenridge, 112 Overlook Drive / 453-9300 / 45 units / $$$
Breckenridge Mountain Lodge, 600 South Ridge / 453-2333 / 70 units / $$$
Little Mountain Lodge, 98 Sunbeam Drive / 453-1969 / 12 units / $$$
Breckenridge Wayside Inn, 165 Tiger Road / 453-5540, 800-927-7669 / 37 units /
  Dogs allowed / $$

RESTAURANTS

Adams Street Grill, 10 West Adams Avenue / 453-4700
Blue River Bistro, 305 North Main Street 453-6974 / Open 11AM–9PM / Cocktails / $$
Village Pub, Bell Tower Mall / 453-0369 / Open 11AM–9PM / Cocktails / $
Horseshoe II, 115 South Main / 453-7463

FLY SHOPS AND SPORTING GOODS

Breckenridge Outfitters, 100 North Main Suite 206 / 453-4135 / Owners: Ian Davis
  and Crosby Beane / Website: www.breck.net/breckout / Email: breckout@col-
  orado.net / Full-service fly shop / Orvis endorsed / Guide service, wade fishing
  on the Blue, Colorado, and South Platte Rivers / Private ponds / Rentals
Mountain Angler, 311 South Main, Box 467 / 453-4665 / Owner: Jackson Streit /
  Guide service, float and wade trips, Blue, Colorado, and Eagle Rivers / Rentals
  and classes

HOSPITALS

Summit Medical Center, Highway 9 at School Road, Frisco / 668-3300

AIRPORTS

Eagle County Regional Airport, 1193 Cooley Mesa Road, Gypsum 81637 /
  524-9490 / United: 800-241-6522
Also see Denver airport information

AUTO RENTAL

Enterprise Rent-A-Car, 555 South Columbine Drive / 547-9060

AUTO SERVICE

High Country Towing and Repair, 0295 CR 980 / 453-0388
Ron's Service Inc., 156 Summit County Road 450 / 453-2103

LOCKSMITH

Breckenridge Lock and Key Inc., 111 South Main / 453-4452

FOR MORE INFORMATION

Breckenridge Resort Chamber
309 North Main
Breckenridge, CO 80424
453-6018

Aspen

Population – 5,049 • Elevation – 7,908 • Area Code – 970

ACCOMMODATIONS

Aspen Club Lodge, 709 East Durant Avenue / 925-6760 / 90 units / Dogs allowed / $$$

Grand Aspen Hotel, 515 South Galena / 925-1150

Little Nell Hotel, 675 East Durant Avenue / 920-4600, 1-800-525-6200 / 92 units / Dogs allowed / $$$

BED AND BREAKFAST

Starry Pines B and B, 2262 Snowmass Creek Road / 927-4202 / Innkeeper: Shelley Burg / $$$

RESTAURANTS

Little Annie's Eating House, 517 E. Hyman Avenue / 925-1098 / Open 11AM–10PM / Bar opens at 2PM / $

Cantina, 411 East Main / 925-3663 / Open 11AM–10PM / Cocktails / $

The Steak Pit, Hopkins and Monarch / 925-3459 / Open for dinner and drinks from 6–10 PM / $$

FLY SHOPS AND SPORTING GOODS

Elkstream Outfitters Inc., 6400 Highway 82 / 928-8380, 800-287-9656 / Fax: 945-5455 / Owner: Jon van Ingen / Guiding on the Roaring Fork, Frying Pan, Crystal, Eagle and Colorado Rivers / Pick up and accommodations available

Aspen Outfitting Company, 315 East Dean Avenue / 925-3406 / Owner: John Hollinger / Guide service for the Roaring Fork valley

Aspen Sports, 303 East Durant Avenue / 925-6332 / Owner: Eric Wallace / Guide service and sporting goods

Aspen Trout Guides Inc., 614 East Durant Avenue / 920-1050, 925-7875 / Owner: Scott Nichols / Guide service for the Roaring Fork valley

Oxbow Outfitters Co., 623 East Durant Avenue / 925-1505, 800-421-1505 / Owner: Mike Chmura / Guide service for the Roaring Fork valley

Western Sports, 555 East Durant / 963-0696 / Owner: Robert Woods / Open June - September / Fly shop, sporting goods, and guide service

The Outfitters, Snowmass Village Mall / 923-5959

Stajduhar Ranches Inc., 923-3008

HOSPITALS

Aspen Valley Hospital, 0401 Castle Creek Road / 925-1120

AIRPORTS

Pitkin County Airport, 69 East Airport Road, Aspen 81611 / 920-5380 / Aspen Mountain Air: 800-432-1359 / United Express: 800-241-6522

Eagle County Regional Airport, 1193 Cooley Mesa Road, Gypsum 81637 / 524-9490 / United: 800-241-6522

Also see Denver airports information

AUTO RENTAL
Roaring Fork Transit Agency, 420 East Durant / 925-8484
Avis Rent-A-Car, 0233 East Airport Road / 925-2355, 1-800-831-2847
Thrifty Rent-A-Car, 0233 East Airport Road / 920-2305, 1-800-367-2277

AUTO SERVICE
Auto Tech, 627 Rio Grande Place, 920-3055
Palazzi Towing, 925-3549
Red Canyon Towing, 7420 Highway 82 / 945-7177, 1-800-308-1240

LOCKSMITH
Day and Night Locksmith Service, Aspen / 920-9669
The Village Locksmith, Snowmass Center / 923-2351

FOR MORE INFORMATION
Aspen Chamber Resort Association
425 Rio Grande Place
Aspen, CO 81611
925-5656

Aspen Ranger District
806 West Hallam
Aspen, CO 81611
925-3445

Basalt

Population – 1,128 • Elevation – 6,624 • Area Code – 970

ACCOMMODATIONS
Aspenalt Lodge (Best Western), 160 Highway 82 / 927-3191 / 35 units / $$$
Aspenwood Lodge, 220 Midland Avenue / 927-4747 / 26 units / Dogs allowed for a
fee / $$$

RESTAURANTS
Bistro Basalt, 202 Midland Avenue / 927-2682 / Open 11AM–10PM / Cocktails / $$
Stubbies Sports Bar and Eatery, 0123 Emma Road / 927-0501 / Open 11AM–2AM /
Cocktails / $$
The Rotisserie, 130 Highway 82 / 927-4773

FLYSHOPS AND GUIDES
Fryingpan Anglers, 123 Emma Road, Suite 100 / 927-3441 / email: anglers@rof.net /
Web page: www.expo.flyshop.com/frypan / Owner: Roy Palm / Full-service fly
shop, largest selection of flies in the state / Excellent guide service for the
Fryingpan, Roaring Fork, and Colorado Rivers
Taylor Creek Fly Shop Inc., City Market Shopping Center / 927-4374 / Owner: Bill
Fitzsimmons

AIRPORTS
See Aspen and Denver airports information

AUTO SERVICE
Basalt Auto Inc., 190 Fiou Lane / 927-2886

FOR MORE INFORMATION
Basalt Chamber of Commerce
Basalt, CO 81621
927-4031

Carbondale

Population – 3,004 • Elevation – 6,181 • Area Code – 970

ACCOMMODATIONS

Country Inn, 920 Cowen Drive / 963-8880 / 42 units / $$$
Days Inn, Highway 82 and Highway 133 / 963-9111 / 69 units / $$$
Thunder River Lodge Inc., 0179 Highway 133 / 963-2543 / 10 units / Dogs allowed /
$$

BED AND BREAKFAST

Mt. Sopris Inn, 0165 Mt. Sopris Ranch Road, Box 126 / 1-800-437-8675

RESTAURANTS

Blue Creek Grill, 68 El Jebel Road, El Jebel / 963-3946 / Open for dinner and
drinks from 5–9PM / $$
The Relay Station, 14913 Highway 82 / 963-1334 / $$
Peppino's Pizza, 524 Main / 963-2993 / Open 11AM-9PM / $$

FLY SHOPS AND GUIDES

Alpine Angling and Adventure Travel, 981 Cowen / 963-9245 / Website:
www.rfanglers.com / Owners: Bruce Stolbach, Tony Fotopulos, Louis Thomp-
son, and Jeff Dysart / Full-service fly shop and guide service for the Roaring
Fork valley / Specializing in the Roaring Fork, Fryingpan, and lower Colorado
Rivers / Ten years of experience
Inland Drifters, 0928 Highway 133 / 963-7438 / Web page: www.inlanddrifters.com
/ Owners: Stefan Cobb and Kimberly Moore / Guided float trips on the Roaring
Fork, Crystal, Colorado, Gunnison, and North Fork of the Gunnison
Western Sports, 400 East Valley Road / 963-3030 / email: wsport@rof.net / Web
page: www.wsports.com / Owner: Robert Woods / Fly shop, sporting goods,
and guide service / Float and wade trips
Troutfitters of Aspen, 0038 Stagecoach Circle / 963-0696 / Owner: Gary Hubbel /
Guide service
AAA Float Anglers, 0848 Roaring Fork Road 106 / 963-3354
Capital Peak Outfitters, 0554 Valley Road / 963-0211
Horizon River Adventures Inc., 963-4660

AIRPORT

See Aspen and Denver airports information

AUTO SERVICE

Jed's Automotive, 0762 Highway 133 / 963-8402

LOCKSMITH

Valley Lock and Key, 579 Main Carbondale / 963-1235

FOR MORE INFORMATION

Carbondale Chamber of Commerce
0590 Highway 133
Carbondale, CO 81623
963-1890

Sopris Ranger District
Box 309 / 620 Main
Carbondale, CO 81623
963-2266

Glenwood Springs
Population – 7,266 • Elevation – 5,746 • Area Code – 970

ACCOMMODATIONS
Best Western Antlers, 171 West 6th Street / 945-8535, 800-626-0609 / 100 units / $$$
Cedar Lodge Motel, 2102 Grand Avenue / 945-6579, 800-854-3761 / 50 units / $$$
Hotel Colorado, 526 Pine Street / 945-6511, 800-544-3998 / 128 units / Dogs allowed / $$$
Terra Vista Motel, 52089 Highway 6 and 24 / 945-6475
Homestead Inn, 52039 Highway 6 and 24 / 945-8817, 800-456-6685 / Hosts: Margaret and Waclaw Topor / 35 units / Dogs allowed / $$$

RESTAURANTS
Andre's Restaurant and Pizzeria, 51753 Highway 6 / 945-5367
Dos Hombres, 51783 Highway 6 and 24 / 928-0490 / Open 11AM–10PM / Cocktails / $
19th Street Diner, 1908 Grand Avenue / 945-9133 / Awesome French toast / Open 6AM / $
Riviera Supper Club, 702 Grand Avenue / 945-7692 / Open for dinner and drinks from 5–10PM / $$
Smoking Willies, 101 West Highway 6 / 945-2479 / Open 11AM–10PM / Cocktails / $
Village Inn, 102 West 6th / 945-9275 / 24 hours / $

FLY SHOPS AND SPORTING GOODS
Roaring Fork Anglers, 2114 Grand Avenue / 945-0180 / Owners: Tony Fotopulos, Bruch Stolbach, Louis Thomopson, and Jeff Dysart / Website: www.rfanglers.com / Full-service fly shop and guide service / Float the Roaring Fork River with Roaring Fork Anglers' expert guides / Established 1980
Elkstream Outfitters Inc., 6400 Highway 82 / 928-8380, 800-287-9656 / fax: 945-5455 / Owner: Jon van Ingen / Guiding on the Roaring Fork, Frying Pan, Crystal, Eagle and Colorado Rivers / Pick up and accommodations available
Army and Factory Surplus, 945-7796
Colorado Canoe and Kayak, 928-9949
K-Mart, 945-2357
Payless/Center Drugs, 945-7401
Relay Sports, 715 Grand Avenue / 928-0936
Summit Canyon Mountaineering, 945-6994
Timberline Sporting Goods, 101 East 3rd, Rifle 81650 / 1-800-625-4868

HOSPITALS
Valley View Hospital, 945-6535
State Patrol Emergency, 945-6198

AIRPORTS
Glenwood Aviation, 1172 Airport Center Road / 945-2385

AUTO RENTAL
Enterprise Rent-A-Car, 124 West 6th Street / 945-8360
Glenwood Springs Ford Rentals, 55 Storm King Road / 945-2317
Silver Wheels Rent-A-Car, 2518 South Glen Avenue / 945-7107

AUTO SERVICE
Al's Towing and Recovery, 925-2265, 927-4105
Automotive Services, 3710 Highway 82 / 945-1217
Jason's Auto Repair, 1539 County Road 130 / 945-2745
Taylor's Auto and RV Center, 51101 Highway 6 and 24 / 945-1500

LOCKSMITH
All Valley Lock-Out, 927-4357
Gene's Lock and Key, 805 Colorado Avenue / 945-6307
Glenwood Lock and Key, 945-7561

FOR MORE INFORMATION
Chamber Resort Association
945-6589, 800-221-0098

White River National Forest
945-2521

Eagle

Population – 1,580 • Elevation – 6,600 • Area Code – 970

ACCOMMODATIONS

Best Western Eagle Lodge, 200 Loren Lane / 328-6316 / 50 units / Dogs allowed / $$$

Eagle Villas, 0405 Nogel Road / 328-0104

Holiday Inn Express, 0075 Pond Road / 328-8088, 328-8077

Inn at Riverwalk, 0022 Main Street, Edwards 81632 / 926-0606 / 60 units / Dogs allowed for a fee / $$$

BED AND BREAKFAST

Wolcott Inn, 27190 Highway 6, Wolcott 81655 / 926-5463 / Innkeeper: Jan Joufaul / 6 rooms / $$

RESTAURANTS

Brenner's Family Restaurant, 706 Castle Drive / 328-7388 / Open 8AM–9PM / Cocktails / $

Fortune's Pizza and Subs, 221 Broadway / 328-7339

Jackie's Olde West Restaurant and Saloon, 101 Loren Lane / 328-7277 / Open 6AM–10PM / Cocktails / $

The Tortilla Company, 0032-E Eagle Park Drive / 328-5667

The Valley Restaurant, 10663 Highway 6, Gypsum 81637 / 524-7350

FLY SHOPS AND SPORTING GOODS

Eagle River Anglers, 101½ Loren Lane / 328-2323 / Owner: Bob Nock / Fly shop and guide service / Float and wade trips on the Eagle, Colorado and Roaring Fork Rivers / Horse and pack trips into the Flat Tops Wilderness area / Shuttle service

Monarch River Guides, 4199 Trough Road, Bond 80423 / 653-4210

Eagle Pharmacy, 301 Broadway / 328-6875

The Sports Recycler, 34510-A6 Highway 6, Edwards 81632 / 926-3867

HOSPITALS

Vail Valley Medical Center, 181 West Meadow Drive, Vail 81657

AIRPORTS

Eagle County Regional Airport, 1193 Cooley Mesa Road, Gypsum 81637 / 524-9490 / United: 800-241-6522

Also see Denver airports information

AUTO RENTAL

Avis Rent-A-Car, 524-7571

Dollar Rent-A-Car, 524-7334

Eagle Rent-A-Car, 524-7098

Thrifty Rent-A-Car, 524-8003

Auto Service

American Eagle Tire and Automotive Center, 0725 Chamber Avenue / 328-7133
Viking Garage Inc., 0064 Eagle Park East Drive / 328-2374
RBJ Automotive Inc., 11126 Highway 6, Gypsum 81637 / 524-288

Locksmith

Alpine Locksmith, Edwards / 926-8000
Lightning Services, 307 1st, Gypsum 81637 / 524-9377

For More Information

Eagle Valley Chamber of Commerce
0100 Fairgrounds Road
Eagle, CO 81631
328-5220

Vail

Population – 3,659 • Elevation – 8,150 • Area Code – 970

Accommodations
Black Bear Inn, 2405 Elliott Ranch Road / 476-1304 / $$$
Christiania, 356 Hanson Ranch Road / 476-5641 / 22 units / $$$
Lodge At Vail, 174 Gore Creek Drive / 476-5011 / 150 units / $$$
Vail Village Inn, 100 East Meadow Drive / 476-5622/ 125 units / $$$

Restaurants
Sweet Basil, 193 Gore Creek Drive / 476-0125 / Opens 6AM for breakfast / $
Tyrolean Restaurant and Lounge, 400 East Meadow Drive / 476-2204 / 6AM–10PM /
  Cocktails / $$-$$$
Up The Creek Bar and Grill, 223 Gore Creek Drive / 476-8141 / Open
  11:30AM–9PM / Cocktails / $$
Wild Flower, In the Lodge At Vail / 476-8111 / Open 6AM–10PM / Cocktails / $$-$$$

Fly Shops and Sporting Goods
Gorsuch Outfitters, 263 East Gore Creek Drive / 476-2294 / email: flyfish@vail.net /
  Owners: Dave and John Bishop / Full-service fly shop and guided flyfishing /
  Eagle River, Colorado River, Roaring Fork River / Check out their website:
  www.vail.net/gorsuch-outfitters
Fly Fishing Outfitters Inc., Box 2861 / 476-3474, 800-595-8090 / email: fish@vail.net /
  Owner: Bill Perry / Located on the Eagle River / Eight year veterans in the Eagle
  Valley / float and wade guide trips / Colorado River, Blue River, Roaring Fork River,
  Gore Creek / Private lakes
Gore Creek Fly Fisherman Inc., 183 East Gore Creek Drive / 476-3296, 800-369-
  3044 / Owner: Christine Lokay / Flyshop and guide service
Vail Rod and Gun Club, Box 1848 / 476-3639

Hospitals
Vail Valley Medical Center, 181 West Meadow Drive / 476-2451

Airports
Eagle County Regional Airport, 1193 Cooley Mesa Road, Gypsum 81637 /
  524-9490 / United: 800-241-6522
Wings of Eagle Travel and Tour Co., 328-6000
Also see Denver airports information

Auto Rental
Frontier Car Rental, 0024 Allen Circle, Edwards / 926-5308
Thrifty Car Rental, 241 South Frontage Road West / 476-8718

AUTO SERVICE
See the town of Eagle

LOCKSMITH
See the town of Eagle

FOR MORE INFORMATION
Vail Valley Tourism and Convention Bureau
100 East Meadow Drive
Vail, CO 81657
476-5677

Northwest Colorado

As my Trooper crept over Rabbit Ears Pass, my thoughts were not on an opportunity to fish private water on the Yampa River, but, instead, on trying to stay between the white lines. Or should I say, "What lines?"

The only lines I could see were tire tracks carved into the snow from a car in front of me. The early spring snow was falling hard and fast, and it had obliterated the road. Four inches had fallen and it didn't look like it would stop anytime soon. There were several of us staying within sight of each other's taillights, plowing our way toward Steamboat Springs.

I had the feeling that they were not going fishing. Fresh powder under a pair of waxed skis was a more likely scenario for them. Mt. Werner's excellent slopes have always been a favorite for downhill skiers, and the surrounding area has trails for cross country skiing, snowshoeing and snowmobiling.

However, for me, the area means one thing—flyfishing—and there is plenty of that pursuit to be had.

The northwest corner of Colorado is primarily a section of high plains dropping off the west side of the Continental Divide. The Yampa River is the main drainage carrying water out of this fun-filled part of the state, and it is very diverse. Its headwaters begin in the Flat Tops Wilderness Area as the Bear River. When this smallish stream reaches the town of Yampa, the Bear merges with Chimney Creek to form the Yampa. From its meager beginnings, where little brook trout dwell, the Yampa becomes a large meandering river containing northern pike and smallmouth bass.

Stagecoach Reservoir is the first of two impoundments along the Yampa drainage. Below Stagecoach, extending for about 6 miles is a great tailwater fishery before it falls into Lake Catamount. Believe it or not, some of the best trout fishing on the Yampa is actually right in the town of Steamboat Springs.

North of Steamboat Springs are two outstanding trout fisheries, Steamboat Lake and Pearl Lake. Steamboat Lake has a good population of rainbows and Snake River cutthroat in trophy proportions. Pearl Lake holds one of the state's best grayling populations, and that unique fish can offer some splendid days on the water with a fly rod. The Elk River parallels County Road 129 on the way up to the lakes.

Another important flyfishing area is the White River. The White is located farther west and south near the town of Meeker, and it offers outstanding flyfishing opportunities for trout. East of Meeker is Trappers Lake, a popular stillwater that rests at 9,500 feet and harbors the Colorado River strain of cutthroat.

Overall, northwest Colorado has an abundance of flyfishing opportunities. Covered here are the major attractions. Rest assured, there are smaller waters that lend themselves nicely to an adventurous angler who's not afraid to hike. Check in with a local fly shop for more details.

YAMPA RIVER

With its variety of water types and sizable fish, the Yampa River is the first choice among northwest Colorado flyfishers. At its headwaters, the Yampa is a small, quaint stream. That changes at the town of Yampa and Stagecoach Reservoir. Below the reservoir, the Yampa becomes an average-sized tailwater. At Steamboat Springs, the Yampa's stream conditions improve as it becomes a meandering river perfectly suited to fishing from a drift boat.

The Yampa's fish species are as diverse as the river itself. Small brook trout and cutthroats are available in the upper river, fat rainbows and browns below Stagecoach Reservoir, and pike and smallmouth bass on to the west.

Getting to the river early in the year is key to a productive trip. Early can be as soon as late February. The snowfall can be heavy in this area, but warm weather can come sooner than most would expect. Meltoff, as I will refer to it, is not exactly runoff. Meltoff refers to the melting of low-lying valley snow. That act turns the river murky, and the fishing turns off as though someone hit the light switch. The severity of meltoff can change from year to year, depending on when the warm weather hits and for how long it remains.

Midges hatch through the spring months, and the trout do feed on them. You'll see little black dots all over the patches of snow and, by looking close, you'll recognize those dots as black midges. You likely will not see rising fish during that time— it's still too cold out—but the fish will willingly eat larvae and pupae patterns that are drifted slowly along the bottom.

The favorite pattern of Steve Henderson, a guide and fly shop manager for Bucking Rainbow Outfitters in Steamboat Springs, is a blood worm. "I call it a mini annelid," Henderson said, "and I like to tie that pattern on a size 16 or 18 scud hook. I wrap a fluorescent orange thread base with clear larva lace wrapped over the top. It is a simple pattern to tie."

Mark Campbell, along with his wife Lisa, own Bucking Rainbow Outfitters. Campbell, a faithful Yampa flyfisher, is a promoter of the blood midge, too. But, he warns, you can't rely on one fly on the Yampa—when you think you've mastered the river, the trout will change their tune and focus on another offering. "You can't let yourself be fooled by the success of one day's fishing," Campbell said. "Just when you think you've found the perfect fly, go fish the next day! On Monday they'll be on the blood midge, Tuesday, black is the color, Wednesday, a beadhead latex midge is the fly with fish written all over it."

If the weather is favorable, the river is not murky, and you choose the right fly, you can have some fantastic days on the Yampa in March. I found some good action at that time with the experts, Henderson and Campbell.

In fact, one late March day they offered to take me out on a section of the river after it had rained and snowed the previous evening. That is an offer I can rarely turn down, so off we went to a stretch below Stagecoach Reservoir.

Yampa River
Yampa to Steamboat Springs

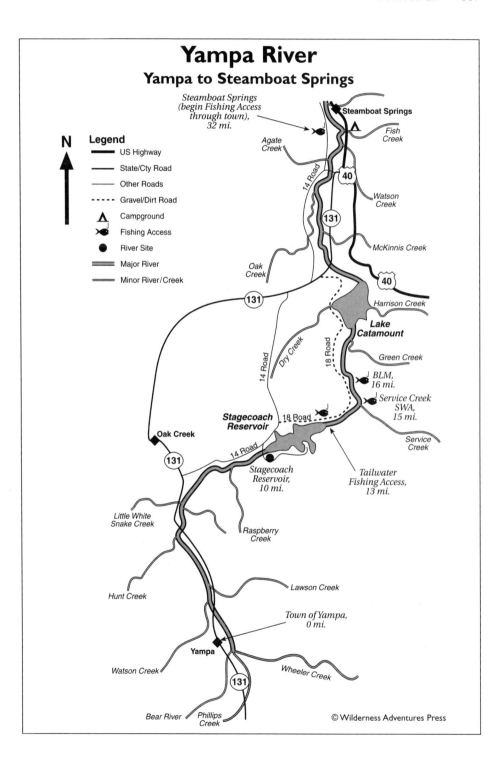

Steamboat Springs
(begin Fishing Access
through town),
32 mi.

Steamboat Springs

Fish
Creek

Agate
Creek

N

Legend

━━━ US Highway

──── State/Cty Road

──── Other Roads

- - - - Gravel/Dirt Road

Λ Campground

Fishing Access

River Site

Major River

Minor River/Creek

14 Road

40

131

Watson
Creek

McKinnis Creek

Oak
Creek

40

Harrison Creek

131

*Lake
Catamount*

Dry Creek

18 Road

14 Road

Green Creek

BLM,
16 mi.

Service Creek
SWA,
15 mi.

*Stagecoach
Reservoir*

18 Road

Service
Creek

◆ **Oak Creek**

14 Road

131

Stagecoach
Reservoir,
10 mi.

*Tailwater
Fishing Access,
13 mi.*

Little White
Snake Creek

Raspberry
Creek

Hunt Creek

Lawson Creek

Town of Yampa,
0 mi.

◆ **Yampa**

Watson Creek

Wheeler Creek

131

Bear River Phillips
Creek

© Wilderness Adventures Press

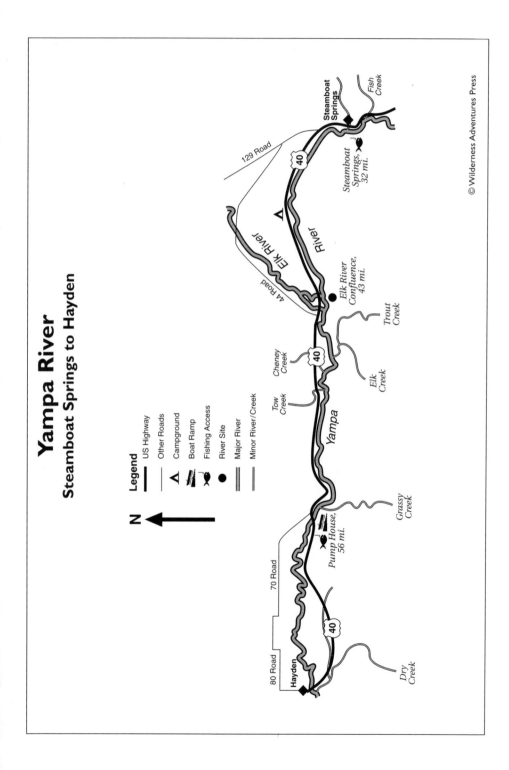

Yampa River
Steamboat Springs to Hayden

Legend

— US Highway
— Other Roads
△ Campground
 Boat Ramp
 Fishing Access
● River Site
 Major River
 Minor River/Creek

N

Steamboat Springs

Fish Creek

Steamboat Springs, 32 mi.

129 Road

40

Elk River

River

44 Road

Elk River Confluence, 43 mi.

Trout Creek

Cheney Creek

40

Elk Creek

Tow Creek

Yampa

Grassy Creek

Pump House, 56 mi.

70 Road

40

80 Road

Hayden

Dry Creek

© Wilderness Adventures Press

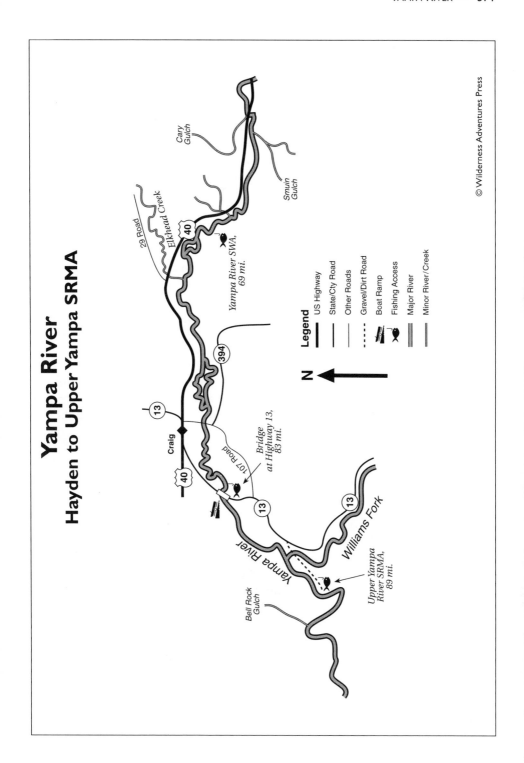

Yampa River
Hayden to Upper Yampa SRMA

N

Cary Gulch

Smuin Gulch

29 Road

Elkhead Creek

40

Yampa River SWA, 69 mi.

394

13

Craig

40

107 Road

Bridge at Highway 13, 83 mi.

13

Williams Fork

13

Yampa River

Bell Rock Gulch

Upper Yampa River SRMA, 89 mi.

Legend

US Highway
State/Cty Road
Other Roads
Gravel/Dirt Road
Boat Ramp
Fishing Access
Major River
Minor River/Creek

© Wilderness Adventures Press

Really, that section was our only option because the river was running off-color through town. Soon, we backed snowmobiles off the trailer. I'll have to admit, this was the first time I'd gone flyfishing on a snowmobile—a unique experience in itself.

After an entertaining ride, we high-stepped it down to the river through snow that measured a foot or more deep. We walked upstream to a point where Henderson told me, "There is a nice shelf below this run and it's deep enough to hold fish."

He pointed out a seam on the inside of the run and suggested starting my drift there. After a dozen good drifts, I could tell I was nowhere near the bottom. I added a split shot and was still not on the turf. So I added even more shot. Finally, I was ticking my Prince nymph and buckskin along the rocks where they needed to be. I swept the entire run, changed position a time or two and changed the drift a tad. Wham! Good take, no hook up. I cast again and allowed the fly to run the same course. Often fish won't take after being missed once, but this fish must have been really hungry because he sucked in the Prince like nothing was wrong. And then he took off downstream, showing his wide tail as he cleared the water. Even in 43-degree water, these trout are scrappy, and they throw their weight around aggressively. In a few moments, I had the 18-inch rainbow a few yards away from my feet, splashing in the shallows. When he glanced up, he spit the hook back where it came from. That was all right; during the cold fishing season, I'd rather not get my hands wet.

You don't have to risk cold fingers to fish the Yampa effectively. In fact, drifting the Yampa below Steamboat Springs in late June through July offers a great opportunity to take a northern pike on a fly. During that time, the river is swollen and forms big slow eddies and sloughs along its banks, which create excellent habitat for northerns. Anchoring down a boat and methodically fanning big black bunny flies through that holding water is the best way to hook those fish.

Structure is of great importance when hunting pike, so you'll want to look for a logjam or some conveniently placed pile of junk in those eddies. When you spot water like that, get your fly as close to that structure as possible and hang on tight—pike strikes can be explosive.

Barry Reynolds, author of *Pike on a Fly*, shared a unique experience he had on the Yampa River. "We came across some old vehicles along the edge of the river that a landowner used to shore the bank," he said. "I made a cast near the back end of a '57 Chevy and a 37-inch northern came out of the trunk and hammered my fly!"

To catch pike like that, Reynolds uses some specific tactics, including varying the action on his flies. "I like to start the day with a slow retrieve, no more than 4- to 6-inch strips," he said. "As the water warms, I'll make adjustments. Faster intervals between longer strips. Another important technique I use is changing the direction of the fly. Moving the fly up or to either side will often provoke a strike."

The same can be said when fishing for smallmouth bass, which are available in the river and should not be overlooked. "They are scattered throughout the river

Netting a rainbow during winter on the Yampa River.

below Steamboat, more predominately downstream towards Hayden and Craig," Reynolds said. "They take the bunny fly, and they will be just about anywhere a trout would be."

Fishery biologists from the Division of Wildlife encourage anglers to harvest all northern pike from the Yampa Valley. There is an overabundance of the species, and they need to be thinned to help maintain a good balance among the trout and small-mouth bass population. Too many pike leads to fewer large trout and no small trout. When all the large trout are gone, nothing but hungry, skinny pike will remain. Take what you can; they are really a good fish to eat.

Seven- to 9-weight rods are needed to handle pike and bass flies. On the end of a 9-foot trout leader a large fly feels like a wet sock and makes for difficult casts. However, pike leaders are designed differently and they allow for long casts with those heavy flies. My favorite pike leader is a 9-foot piece of level OX monofilament attached to the fly line. To that, I attach the same leader Barry Reynolds uses, an 18-inch section of nylon-coated steel wire tippet. Connect those sections with an Albright Special knot.

Anglers should consider the fly line when fishing for bass and pike, too. The fly line should be a special bass bug taper or a pike/muskie line. They are designed like a shooting head, and they make long casts with a large air resistant fly much easier. Both Cortland and Scientific Angler make a line for this use.

When hooked, pike exhibit an awesome burst of speed, so a reel with a good disk drag is essential.

Bunny flies seem to be the fly of choice for northern pike. Black is by far the best color, and sizes 1/0 to 3/0 are big enough to give any northern a sore jaw. That fly is visible in any type of water, including the murky waters that you can encounter on the Yampa during high flows. White is also a good color, but it is best used in clear water. Yellow and chartreuse can be used in water that is mucked up from windy conditions. Clouser minnows, Lefty's deceivers, and woolly buggers are other flies to add to the fly box.

By mid-July, the river clears up, and some excellent aquatic insect hatches begin. At that time, expect to see pale morning duns and caddis hatching through the town of Steamboat Springs. A few late golden stoneflies may also be seen flying around.

"The river flowing through town is one of the best opportunities in the state to catch a grand slam," Henderson said. "Rainbows and browns average 14 to 18 inches, while the Snake River cutts are a bit smaller. Brookies are in here, but there are just a few of them."

Late afternoons and evenings are the best times to find trout feeding on the surface. Standard elk hair caddis patterns in sizes 14 through 18, olive, tan or gray, cover the variety of insects encountered.

During the caddis hatch, pockets along the bank and places where brush overhangs the river are excellent spots to cast a fly into. If there are no takers, try a smaller fly or go to a lower riding pattern, such as a spent partridge caddis or a LaFontaine sparkle caddis.

If the trout do not feel like eating your dry fly, switch to nymphs. Pheasant tails, hare's ears, and beadhead caddis nymphs, ranging from size 12 to 18, are standard go-to's. If you've covered good water where trout just had to be and you didn't receive a strike on your dry, go back to the deeper runs and pinch on a few split shot. A golden stonefly nymph is a good choice as a second fly.

August is definitely the best month for all kinds of dry flyfishing on the Yampa. Hopper activity is at its peak, the caddis are still fluttering, and the little golden stone is present, too.

Hustling to the river early in the morning with a rusty spinner or a parachute PMD can be productive. Focus on quiet water along the banks, as the trout probably have taken to their resting spots as soon as the sun hits the water. By midmorning, you may want to go get a late breakfast or early lunch and take a siesta. That's not required, but fishing will slow down for trout in the afternoon. Tossing pike flies on a couple of sloughs across from the Comfort Inn at the east end of Steamboat will keep you on the water during the slow trout hours.

All stretches of the river will come alive as the sun drops in the western sky. Have some fun! Search for risers and kick any attractor pattern out in front of them. Royal Wulffs, irresistibles, orange humpies, and yellow stimulators, all in size 12, draw strikes.

Yampa River below Stagecoach Reservoir.

If you want to go with a hopper, try a size 10. The sunsets in this part of the country are outstanding, especially with the sound of slurping fish within casting range.

"September is the month most of us here look forward to," Campbell said. "The Baetis come off and every trout in the river takes notice!" He adds, "The best olive patterns for the Yampa in September should have a darker body than most imitations. In fact, they are almost brown and they can be matched with a size 18. Parachute and standard winged patterns should have a spot reserved in your fly box."

Henderson showed me a BWO olive dressed from a material called Aire-Flow for the wings. "It's called the Aire-Flow, cut-winged dun," he said. "This parachute-hackled fly sits low in the water and must give a great presentation because it has worked very well for us on the Yampa. This hatch can literally be as good as any BWO hatch in the state. In fact, it's as good as any I've seen on the Green River (in Utah below Flaming Gorge Dam). That's not always good for the fisherman, though. There are so many sailboats on the water that yours will surely go unnoticed a large percentage of the time. If you just can't resist the temptation, be on the water by 11 AM."

In late September, brown trout are making their prespawn move and can be seen holding in much shallower water than they are normally found. The main challenge at that time is not to spook those fish.

If all those trout options aren't enough, head to Craig and Juniper Hot Springs – that is where the greatest concentration of smallmouth bass hang out. Stories of 4-pounders coming out of the river there are common.

The Yampa Valley is one of the most diverse and beautiful flyfishing destinations in Colorado. Hope your schedule permits a few days here, soon.

Elk River

The Elk is a main tributary to the Yampa River, and it carries the water from Mt. Zirkel Wilderness Area to the main river.

The Elk parallels CR 129 north of Steamboat Springs, then enters ranch lands in the Elk River Valley, about 19 miles north of Steamboat Springs off CR 129. Turning right (east) on FR 400 will lead you to the headwaters of the upper Elk. Trailheads and four-wheel drive roads begin at the Seedhouse Campground where the North Fork and the Middle Fork of the Elk merge.

I wish I could tell you the Elk is open to the public around every corner, but just the opposite is the case. As I drove along the river and explored the water as it flowed under bridges and along CR 129, I found some outstanding runs, long riffles, and corner pools all just beyond the signs indicating "No Trespassing". Most of the water is private from the confluence with the Yampa to just above the little town of Glen Eden on FR 400 where Routt National Forest begins. Check with local guide services in Steamboat Springs for a chance to access the Elk as it meanders through the lower stretches of the river, or take your chances pounding on doors.

One exception is at the Christina State Wildlife Area, located about 5 miles north of the intersection of US 40 on CR 129. A short section of the river is available to fish at the Elk's confluence with Mad Creek.

After runoff, which is generally over by July 4, caddis hatches offer prime fishing on the lower Elk. Expect to catch browns and rainbows up to 14 inches on elk hair caddis. Whitefish will be caught if you go with a nymph.

For the adventurer, a trail leading up Mad Creek can provide a full day of enjoyment while fishing tumbling pocket water for browns and rainbows in the 8- to 12-inch range. Mid- to late July is the best time to attempt this hike. The water will be down and clear, making it a great time for dry-fly fishing. Caddis and stoneflies make up the majority of the food sources in this little stream. However, any well-presented attractor pattern drifted along the pockets near the bank or behind midstream rocks will move these eager fish to your fly.

Elk hair caddis, yellow stimulators, renegades, royal Wulffs, and orange humpies, up to a size 12, will draw strikes when attached to your 5X tippet. A rod no longer than 8 feet that casts a 3- or 4-weight line is your best option. A 7½-foot leader is plenty long for these sometimes very tight quarters. If you must nymph fish (that's something I don't do when I have an opportunity to throw dry flies), golden stone nymphs, hare's ears, and beadhead caddis nymphs will do.

From Hinman Campground on FR 400 the river opens up into national forest land. The river is smaller up there with a good mix of water types. Pocket water is the norm, but long, deep runs can be found, and they are productive, too.

Browns, rainbows, and a few brook trout can be caught in the 8- to 12-inch range. Stories of 20-inch trout have surfaced from this part of the river. Some locals believe

Elk River

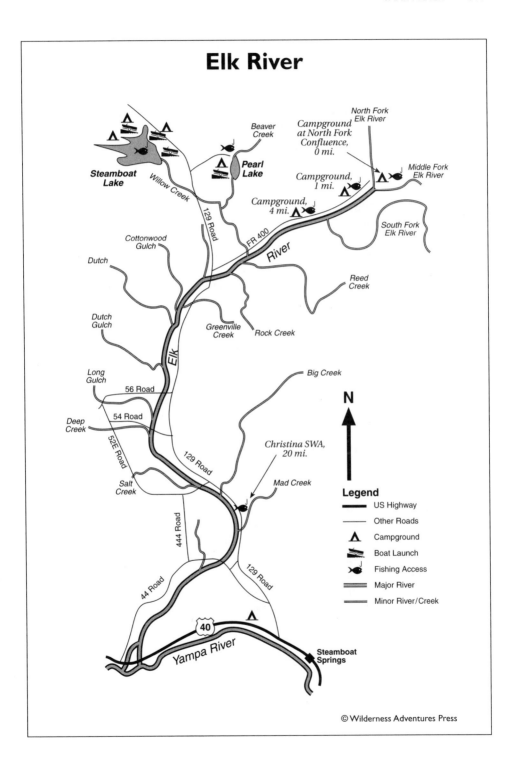

North Fork
Elk River

Beaver
Creek

Campground
at North Fork
Confluence,
0 mi.

Pearl
Lake

Campground,
1 mi.

Middle Fork
Elk River

Steamboat
Lake

Willow Creek

Campground,
4 mi.

South Fork
Elk River

129 Road

FR 400

River

Cottonwood
Gulch

Dutch

Reed
Creek

Dutch
Gulch

Greenville
Creek

Rock Creek

Elk

Long
Gulch

Big Creek

56 Road

N

54 Road

Deep
Creek

52E Road

Christina SWA,
20 mi.

129 Road

Salt
Creek

Mad Creek

444 Road

129 Road

44 Road

Legend

	US Highway
	Other Roads
Λ	Campground
	Boat Launch
	Fishing Access
	Major River
	Minor River/Creek

40

Yampa River

Steamboat
Springs

© Wilderness Adventures Press

fish from private clubs in the area have gotten into the drainage. Don't plan a trip here expecting such huge trout, but it wouldn't be earth-shaking to catch a big one.

Wading in this stretch of the Elk is pretty straightforward. Rock hopping, crossing the stream, and crawling under brush to get into casting position are all part of the game. Runoff is usually heaviest from mid-May extending to mid-June, and you should consider fishing elsewhere at that time.

After runoff, expect to see caddis, stoneflies, and a few mayflies showing themselves. Trout will be looking for caddis in the surface film during their afternoon and evening snack times. A high-floating, size 14 olive caddis with a light colored elk hair wing for good visibility should draw aggressive strikes. Stimulators, small hopper patterns, and orange humpies are other attractors that are favored here. Nymph fishing can be effective during most of the year with golden stones, beadhead hare's ears, Prince nymphs, and breadcrusts.

Another option a fly angler has is a four-wheel drive road heading north from Seedhouse Campground along the North Fork. This road is acceptable for travel by mid- to late summer, depending on rain. The higher you go, the smaller the stream becomes, and you'll see fewer people.

Bear River

The Bear River is actually considered the headwaters for the Yampa and is located west of the town of Yampa on CR 7. The first 9 miles of stream west of Yampa are private. From there you enter Routt National Forest, and all the water up to and including Stillwater Reservoir is open to fishing. The first good access is directly below Yamcola Reservoir. Small stream conditions and trout to about 10 inches should be expected.

The next reservoir upstream from Yamcola is Upper Stillwater Reservoir (Yampa Reservoir). Camping and fishing is available there. Above this body of water is a great stretch of stream where small brook trout and a few cutthroats can be caught on dries during the summer months.

Stillwater Reservoir marks the end of the road—for vehicles, that is. Trailheads leading in all directions start here. Most take you into the Flat Tops Wilderness area. High mountain lakes abound in this very striking area. Backpacking into this area in August may provide one of those unforgettable experiences. Wildflowers are in full bloom, and the area teams with trout.

A pack rod, a box of flies with a good mix of dries and nymphs, and a spool of 5X tippet should keep you in business for a day or two excursion into the high country.

Stream Facts: Yampa River

Seasons
- Fishing is open all year.

Special Regulations
- From Elk River to Stagecoach Dam: Bag and possession limit for trout is 2 fish. From Walton Creek 3.5 miles downstream to the 5th Street bridge in Steamboat Springs: Artificial flies and lures only. From Catamount Lake inlet to Stagecoach Dam: Artificial flies and lures only. The whole Yampa Valley: Bag and possession limit on all warmwater species including northern pike is unlimited, due to the need to protect Colorado squawfish, the humpback chub, and razorback sucker.

Fish
- Rainbows to 20 inches below Stagecoach Reservoir and in town
- Browns
- Snake River cutthroat
- Brook trout
- Northern pike, up to 40 inches
- Smallmouth bass, a few 4-pounders

River Miles
- Yampa—0
- Stagecoach Reservoir—10
- Steamboat Springs—32
- Confluence with Elk River—43
- Pump House—56
- Yampa River SWA—69
- Bridge at Colorado 13—83
- Juniper Hot Springs—126

River Characteristics
- The Yampa River starts as a small stream at the town of Yampa. The Bear River and Chimney creek meet here to form the Yampa. From Yampa it flows though a sagebrush-filled valley to Stagecoach Reservoir. The tailwater fishery below Stagecoach is a fine stretch of water. The river picks up speed into the town of Steamboat Springs. As it heads west out of Steamboat Springs, the river starts to widen. It becomes a fairly slow meandering river with an added adventure for the flyfisherman.

River Flows
- Winter flows from 75–200 cfs
- Spring flows from 150–500 cfs
- Runoff from mid May through June can rip at 2500–3000 cfs
- Summer and fall flows from 1,000 down to 200 cfs

Boat Ramps
- Pump House, mile 56; first public boat ramp
- Yampa River SWA, mile 69
- Bridge at Highway 13, mile 83

Maps
- *Colorado Atlas & Gazetteer*, pages 25 and 26
- Routt National Forest

YAMPA RIVER MAJOR HATCHES

Insect	A	M	J	J	A	S	O	N	Time	Flies
Midge		▮	▮	▮	▮	▮	▮	▮	M/E	Olive Biot Midge #16–#24; Brown Biot Midge #16–#24; Black Beauty #18–#24; Brassie #16–#24; Blood Midge #16–#24; Disco Midge #18–#24; Crane Fly Nymph #6–#10; CDC Biot Suspender Midge #18–#24; Chartreuse Serendipity #16–#20; Griffith's Gnat #16–#22; Palomino Midge #18–#22
Baetis		▮	▮		▮	▮			M	RS-2 #16–#24; Pheasant Tail Nymph #16–#20; Beadhead Pheasant Tail Nymph #16–#22; Flashback Pheasant Tail Nymph #16–#20; Olive Quill Emerger #18–#224; Parachute Adams #12–#22; Olive Comparadun #16–#20; Gray Spinner #18–#24; Slate Thorax Dun #16–#22; CDC Baetis Dun #16–#22; Barr Emerger #16–#22; Air-Flow Cut-wing Dun #16–#22
Caddis			▮	▮					M/A/E	Olive Caddis Nymph #10–#20; Breadcrust #10–#18; Buckskin #16–#20; LaFontaine's Sparkle Caddis Pupa #10–#20; Elk Hair Caddis #10–#22; CDC Caddis #14–#20; Macramé Caddis #12–#16; Balloon Caddis #12–#16; Lawson's Caddis Emerger #14–#18; Spent Partridge Caddis #14–#18
Stonefly			▮						A	Sandy's Gold #6–#10 Gold-winged Prince Nymph #8–#10; Kaufmann's Golden Stonefly #6–#12; Stimulator #8–#12; Foam Yellow Sally #12–#18; Halfback #4–#10; Prince Nymph #8–#16; Beadhead Prince Nymph #8–#16; Kaufmann's Brown Stonefly #4–#8; Stimulator #8–#12

HATCH TIME CODE: M = morning; A = afternoon; E = evening; D = dark; SF = spinner fall; / = continuation through periods.

YAMPA RIVER MAJOR HATCHES (CONT.)

Insect	A	M	J	J	A	S	O	N	Time	Flies
Streamers		▓	▓	▓	▓	▓	▓	▓	M/E	Black Woolly Bugger #2–#10; Brown Woolly Bugger #4–#10; Spruce Fly #4–#10; Dark Spruce Fly #4–#10; Muddler Minnow #4–#10; Matuka Sculpin #4–#10; Matuka Muddler #4–#10; Whitlock's Hair Sculpin #4–#6; Steve's BRO Bug #6–#10
Terrestrials				▓	▓				A	Rio Grande King Trude #8–#16; Royal Wulff #10–#16; Humpy #10–#16; Foam Madam X #8–#12; Renegade #10–#16; Black Ant #14–#20; Cinnamon Ant #14–#20; Henry's Fork Hopper #8–#12
Red Quill			▓	▓					E	AK's Red Quill #14–#18; Rusty Spinner #12–#20
Pale Morning Dun			▓	▓	▓				M	Biot PMD Nymph #16; Pheasant Tail Nymph #16–#22; Beadhead Pheasant Tail Nymph #14–#20; Lt. Cahill Comparadun #12–#18; Sparkle Dun #14–#18; Parachute PMD #14–#18

HATCH TIME CODE: M = morning; A = afternoon; E = evening; D = dark; SF = spinner fall; / = continuation through periods.

Pearl Lake

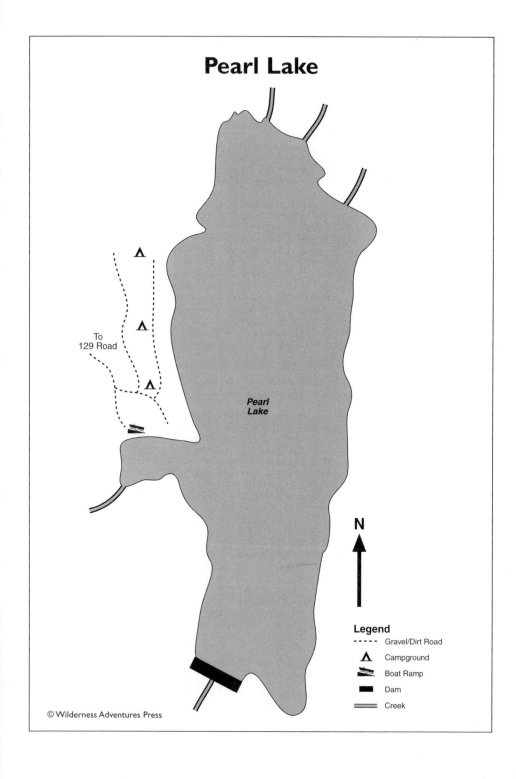

To
129 Road

*Pearl
Lake*

N

Legend
- - - - - Gravel/Dirt Road
Λ   Campground
   Boat Ramp
■   Dam
══   Creek

© Wilderness Adventures Press

Pearl Lake

Find the closet you stored all your flyfishing gear in last winter, get it out, clean your line, and check your waders for leaks. It's time to put your equipment back to work on Pearl Lake, one of the first lakes to lose its ice after another harsh Rocky Mountain winter.

When this lake opens up, generally between mid-April and early May, you can find some fantastic fishing for Colorado cutthroat trout and grayling.

Pearl Lake offers the flyfisher a unique opportunity to catch trophy sized Colorado River cutthroats. They were transplanted from Trappers Lake west and south of the lake. Special possession regulations of 2 fish over 18 inches and fishing by flies and lures have nurtured this fishery to an outstanding level.

Pearl Lake's trout, especially the large trout, feed heavily on crawfish scuds and flathead minnows. They also forage on a plethora of damselflies and Callibaetis mayflies.

You wouldn't be here if you weren't after a trophy cutthroat, so be prepared to put in some time and concentrate your efforts with a crawfish pattern. The north end of the lake, where stream inlets are located, can provide one of the best opportunities for a big trout. From the north end of the campground on the west side of the lake, kick due east to the other side. Attach a size 6 brown woolly bugger with a pair of heavy eyes to the end of a sink-tip or full-sink line. A very short leader, 3 or 4 feet, is used when fishing in that manner. The shorter leader helps keep the fly at the level of the sinking line. With the sinking line, try to keep your fly at or near the 15- to 20-foot range. If you fish the bottom, try to crawl your pattern along—do not strip it in quickly.

The bottom of the north end of the lake has submerged brush and other structure along the stream channels, which makes excellent trout habitat. However, it also provides an easy place to lose flies. Be prepared to lose a few flies and miss a few strikes. But when you do get a heavy strike, there will be no doubt. Put heat on the fish quickly so the trout cannot break you off in the brush. Bringing one of these beautiful trout to net is an experience long remembered.

Another fish you'll encounter at Pearl Lake is the grayling. The Colorado state record is just over a pound, and there are some specimens in Pearl that approach that weight.

Unknowingly, local angler and guide Steve Henderson has caught and released a few that would have gone close to 2 pounds, easy. "Even though I know what the record is now," Henderson said, "I'll still release 'em." Good for him.

Grayling are usually found in deeper water, literally inaccessible to the fly angler. However, during spring, grayling move to shallow water and feed on crawfish. When the fish are feeding shallow, Henderson uses a unique set-up. "Use a floating line with a 9-foot leader tapered to 5X," he said, "I tie on a size 10 or 12 scramsel. This is basically a brown, beadhead damsel pattern, but it looks enough like a small crawfish to grab attention. I then attach a strike indicator about 2½ feet away from the fly. The reason for the strike indicator is to control the depth of the fly and help detect the very subtle strikes. Move the fly with a 2- or 3-inch tug, followed by a 5- to 10-second rest."

By July, when the weather warms, caddis and damsel activity arrive with it. At that time, weed beds have developed in the small bay on the west side of the lake and along the northwest bank in the shallow water. Aquatic insects breed in those weeds, and trout are attracted to those areas like a magnet. These areas are the best places to focus on for a chance at a caddis emergence. The damselflies will also find their way to shore from these areas.

With a nice campground and a boat ramp, this is a great place to spend a few days and fish, enjoy the outdoors, and relax.

The turnoff to Pearl is located about 23 miles north of Steamboat Springs on CR 129. Turn right (east) at the sign for Pearl Lake onto CR 209. Stay in touch with Bucking Rainbow Outfitter in Steamboat Springs (970-879-4693) for ice-off information.

Lake Facts: Pearl Lake

Seasons
- Ice-off occurs about mid-May. Lake is usually frozen by late November or December.

Special Regulations
- Artificial flies and lures only. Bag and possession limit is 2 fish over 18 inches.

Fish
- Colorado River Cutthroat: 14-inch average, while a trout over 18 inches is common.
- Grayling—could be a state record here.

Lake Size
- 190 acres, 75–80 feet deep at the south end near the dam.

Boat Ramps
- One ramp on the west side of the lake.

Camping
- 39 campsites; picnic sites available.

Lake Character
- The elevation here is 5,080 feet. The large Colorado River cutthroats make this a special place. Lots of submerged brush on the north end of this narrow lake. It's 80 feet deep at the dam. The overall structure of the lake is a basic bowl, with the shoreline falling into deep water quickly.

Maps
Fish-n-Map Company, 303-421-5994

PEARL LAKE MAJOR HATCHES

Insect	A	M	J	J	A	S	O	N	Time	Flies
Crawfish/Fathead Minnows/Streamers								▓	M/A/E	Black Woolly Bugger #2–#10; Brown Woolly Bugger #4–#10; Spruce Fly #4–#10; Dark Spruce Fly #4–#10; Black-nosed Dace #6–#8; Muddler Minnow #4–#10; Matuka Sculpin #4–#10; Steve's BRO Bug #6–#10; Whitlock's Crawfish #4–#10; Kaufmann's Crawfish #4–#8
Scuds								▓	M/A/E	Olive Scud #12–#16; Orange Scud #10–#16; 19½ Scud #12–#18; Tan Scud #12–#16; Flashback Scud #12–#16
Midge								▓	M/A/E	Olive Biot Midge #14–#18; Brassie #14–#18; Blood Midge #16–#24; Miracle Nymph #14–#18; AK's Midge Larva #16–#22; Black Beauty Pupa #18–#20; CDC Biot Suspender Midge #14–#18; Griffith's Gnat #16–#18; Palomino Midge #16–#18; Serendipity #16–#18
Damselflies			▓						M/A	Swimming Damsel #8–#12; Flashback Damsel #8–#12; Beadhead Damsel #10–#12
Caddis					▓				M/A/E	Olive Caddis Nymph #10–#20; Buckskin #16–#20; LaFontaine's Sparkle Caddis Pupa #10–#20; Elk Hair Caddis #10–#22; CDC Caddis #14–#20; Macramé Caddis #12–#16; Lawson's Caddis Emerger #14–#18; Spent Partridge Caddis #14–#18
Callibaetis					▓				M/A	Olive Biot Nymph #14–#18; Pheasant Tail Nymph #14–#18; Beadhead Pheasant Tail Nymph #14–#18; AK's Red Quill #16; Parachute Adams #12–#16; Gray Comparadun #16; Rusty Spinner #14–#18; Slate Thorax Dun #16

HATCH TIME CODE: M = morning; A = afternoon; E = evening; D = dark; SF = spinner fall; / = continuation through periods.

Steamboat Lake and Pearl Lake

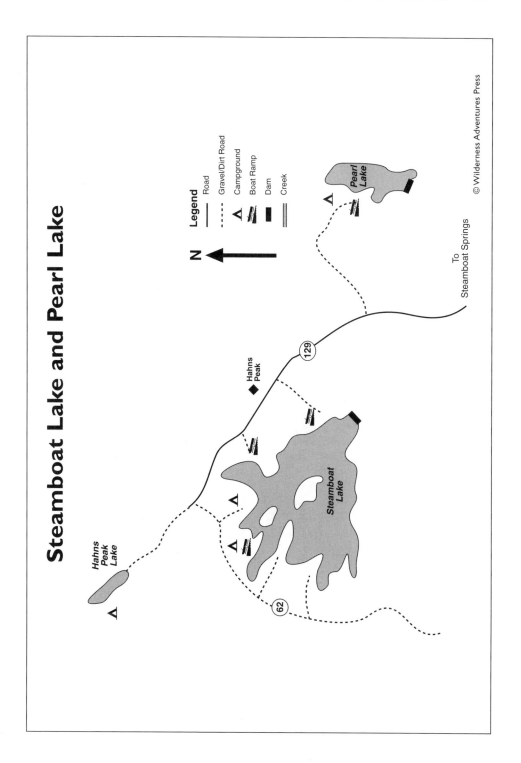

Legend

— Road
---- Gravel/Dirt Road
△ Campground
Boat Ramp
■ Dam
Creek

N

Hahns Peak Lake

Hahns Peak

Steamboat Lake

129

62

Pearl Lake

To Steamboat Springs

© Wilderness Adventures Press

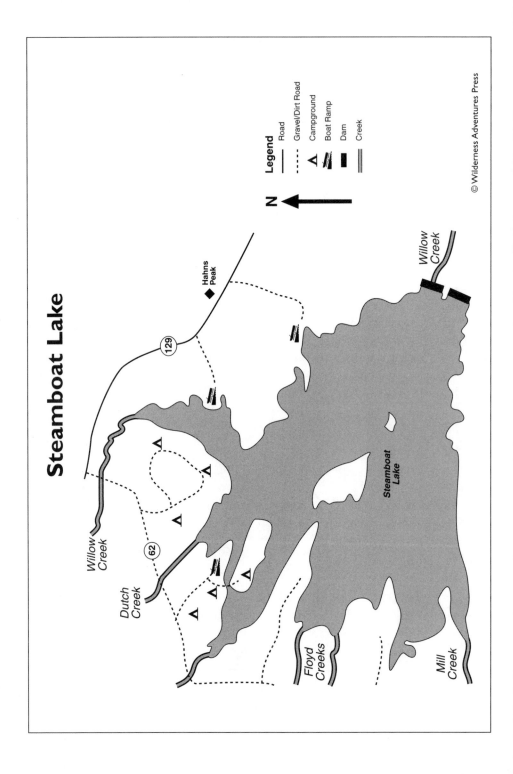

STEAMBOAT LAKE

Steamboat Lake, a 1,060-acre stillwater located just north of Steamboat Springs, offers a superb rainbow fishery, with lesser numbers of cutthroat trout. As of 1996, it was the state's latest recipient of Gold Medal Water designation.

The west side of the lake has several stream inlets, and I would say it's the best place to start your flyfishing effort. And ice-off is the time to try it. At that time, trout are looking for a good meal after the long winter freeze, and they will recklessly feed.

The only downfall to fishing after ice-out is the weather; you can bump into any kind, ranging from 70-degree days to pummeling snow, so be prepared. Rain gear and layered clothing are important. Ear muffs and gloves are not a bad idea, either. Do not forget the sunscreen.

Steve Henderson, of Bucking Rainbow Outfitters, said, "Crawfish are the main source of nourishment in Steamboat Lake. Float tubing while dragging a sink tip line (and a crayfish pattern) behind you is one of the best methods of flyfishing this lake."

Mill Creek enters the lake at the far southwest corner, and it is also a great place to find fish during spring. The inlet forms a narrow bay with a channel up to 20 feet deep. Kick slowly through the north part of the main channel with a Whitlock's crawfish moving along the bottom. Test different depths and different presentations until you have a taker. A taker may consist of a beautiful rainbow trout in the 20-inch range, and that fish may weigh 4 pounds or more. Don't blame the trout for their bulbous dimensions—you would also be big and wide if you were eating nothing but lobster tails all your life.

Working your fly parallel to structure while maintaining a certain depth is a well known and proven technique. You may want to kick a few hundred yards along a shoreline, trying to keep a fly at 7 to 10 feet. If you don't draw strikes, turn around, move out to deeper water, and keep your fly at 10 to 15 feet.

Directly east from the end of Mill Creek Bay, about 300 to 400 yards, is a large hump on the bottom of the lake. The top of the hump is about 5 feet under the surface. The north side of the hump drops very quickly to 40 feet, and the whole area is a magnet for trout. Again, floating west to east and vice versa, covering this shelf in the 5- to 20-foot depth, is the best tactic. Fishing a weighted woolly bugger is also a good bet. "Woolly buggers are major favorites among lake fishermen," Henderson said. "Brown and olive are good colors to imitate crawfish. Sizes 2 through 10 should cover the gambit." He added, "Tying lead eyes on helps get the fly down quicker. Another thing lead eyes do is aid in varying your presentation. Jigging the fly up and down as you troll along gives the fly extra animation and movement, hopefully enticing a strike."

There are hatches of midges in the spring at Steamboat, but they do not generally present any dry fly opportunities. If fish are boiling, they are probably taking ascending midges as they struggle towards the surface to hatch. A floating line with a 9- to 12-foot leader tapered to 5X or 6X is the setup for this situation. Midges usually hatch from a certain area, and the trout will cruise over this spot time and time again.

Fish rising to damsels on Steamboat Lake.

Let the trout do the work. Remain in one spot or kick slowly around—sooner or later a trout will cross your path.

Be aware that wind will somewhat hinder these plans; just try to stay within casting range without disturbing the area. Hook-ups with these trout on this size tippet will test your skills to the limit.

I always use a dual fly setup when fishing Steamboat. A #14 to #18 CDC biot midge works well to imitate the pupating insects. Add a beadhead gray hackle peacock or dark soft hackle hare's ear to complete the tandem.

If you see a trout disturb the surface and decipher which direction it is going, deliver a cast out in front of the fish. Once your flies are in the water, resist the temptation to move them too much and, more importantly, too fast.

As the days get long and the water gets warmer during summer, fishing Steamboat Lake becomes an early morning and a late evening game. Opportunities may arise to fish sporadic mayfly hatches and damselfly migrations during the day, but overall the action is slow. Thank your stars if you catch a trout on one of those patterns, but don't count on doing that.

To reach Steamboat Lake, travel north from Steamboat Springs on CR 129 for 26 miles. That route will plant you on the front porch of the Steamboat Lake State Park office. The park requires a state parks pass to enter and fish. A daily or yearly pass can be purchased there. Park telephone numbers are 970-879-3922 or 866-3437.

Turn left (south) on Road 62, the main entrance, to find area campgrounds. There are 183 campsites available between two campgrounds, Dutch Hill and Sunrise Vista, which are located on the north side of the lake. Following this gravel road around to the west side of the lake provides other fishing accesses and parking areas at Rainbow Point and Meadow Point.

From CR 129, south of the main entrance and near Hahns Peak Village, another gravel road takes you to Sage Flats. A boat ramp and facilities are available. About a quarter of a mile north of Hahns Village on 129, parking and another boat ramp are available at Placer Point.

Lake Facts: Steamboat Lake

Seasons
- Ice-off occurs about mid-May. Flyfishing until it's too cold to fish. Lake is usually frozen by late November and December.

Special Regulations
- Gold Medal Water

Trout
- Rainbows are predominant; 16-inch average, while a trout over 20 is common.
- Snake River cutthroat: 16–18 inch cutts are the norm.
- Browns, very few. Don't count on hooking a brown here.

Lake Size
- 1060 acres
- 75–80 feet deep at the southeast corner near the dam

Boat Ramps
- Sage Flats, southeast side of lake
- Placer Cove, northeast side of lake
- Dutch Hill Campground, northwest side of lake

Camping
- Sunrise Vista Campground
- Dutch Hill Campground
- Tables and fire grills available, 183 campsites between the two

Lake Character
- The elevation here is 8,025 feet making it an ideal habitat for the wily trout. There are a number of small streams entering Steamboat Lake. Each one of them forms a bay with a stream channel down the middle. Lots of depth changes throughout the bottom of the lake, making for excellent structural fishing.

Maps
- Fish-n-Map Company, 303-421-5994

STEAMBOAT LAKE MAJOR HATCHES

Insect	A	M	J	J	A	S	O	N	Time	Flies
Crawfish/Streamers			▓	▓	▓	▓	▓		M/A/E	Black Woolly Bugger #2–#10; Brown Woolly Bugger #4–#10; Spruce Fly #4–#10; Dark Spruce Fly #4–#10; Black-nosed Dace #6–#8; Muddler Minnow #4–#10; Matuka Muddler #4–#10; Steve's BRO Bug #6–#10; Whitlock's Crawfish #4–#10; Kaufmann's Crawfish #4–#8
Damselflies				▓					A	Swimming Damsel #8–#12; Flashback Damsel #8–#12; Beadhead Damsel #10–#12
Midge			▓	▓	▓	▓	▓		M/A/E	Olive Biot Midge #16–#24; Brown Biot Midge #16–#24; Black Beauty #18–#24; Brassie #16–#24; Blood Midge #16–#24; Miracle Nymph #16–#20; AK's Midge Larva #16–#22; Black Beauty Pupa #18–#24; CDC Biot Suspender Midge #18–#24; Griffith's Gnat #16–#22; Palomino Midge #18–#22
Scuds			▓	▓	▓	▓	▓		M/E	Olive Scud #12–#16; Orange Scud #10–#16; 19½ Scud #12–#18; Tan Scud #12–#16; Flashback Scud #12–#16

HATCH TIME CODE: M = morning; A = afternoon; E = evening; D = dark; SF = spinner fall; / = continuation through periods.

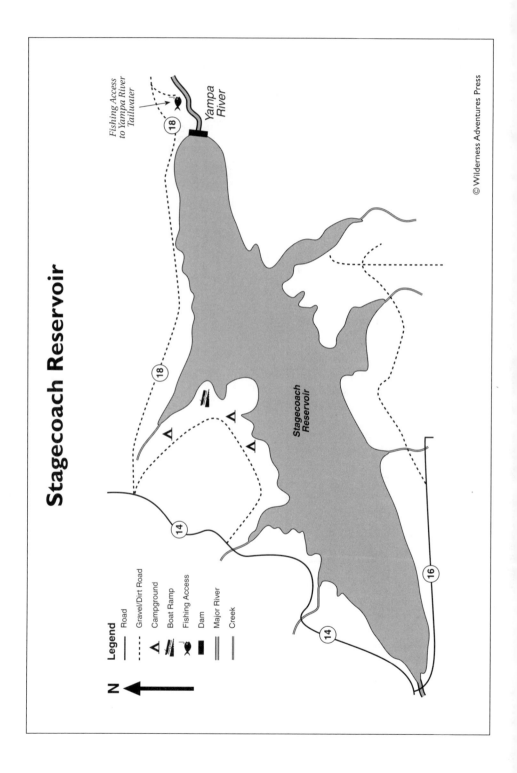

Stagecoach Reservoir

Stagecoach State Recreation Area is located south of Steamboat Springs on CR 14. Take US 40 south out of town to the Colorado 131 intersection. Turn right (west) on CR 18 to CR 14. Turn left on CR 14 and follow signs to the reservoir. A State Parks pass is required before entering. Daily and yearly park passes are available at the entrance.

This reservoir is a nonregulated lake, so expect to be fishing with lots of bait fishermen. With an 8-fish limit, trout populations can fluctuate. Coolers carry out several trout each year. Northern pike also take their toll on the smaller stocked trout, although the fertile waters of Stagecoach do grow trout quite rapidly.

Flyfishing at Stagecoach begins in mid- to late April, depending on how quickly ice clears from the lake. Trout will be cruising the bays formed by the feeder streams on both the north and south side of the lake. Road 16 will take you around to the south side of the lake to a couple of very important stream inlet areas. Selecting the best water is the key to a successful day of hooking hefty rainbows and cutthroats up to 5 pounds. Trout will average 14 inches; however, you should hook a couple in the 18-inch range with black or brown woolly buggers. While fishing a bugger, you may expect to catch a northern pike or two.

The bays around the campground on the north side of the lake do get fished hard, so moving to alternate areas is the best idea for float tubing. The Yampa River enters the west end of the lake and is only 20 to 30 feet deep along the river channel. Most of this end of the lake averages about 10 feet deep. The inlet provides several options to concentrate your efforts. The water will warm sooner in the shallow water, drawing fish to the area to feed. Kicking parallel to the northern shoreline, working your leech pattern slowly along the bottom in 10 to 15 feet, is productive. This half of the inlet is best because of the inherent structure. Submerged brush in addition to the presence of the river channel provides the best opportunities to show your fly to the most trout.

A 9- to 10-foot, 6- or 7-weight rod, equipped with a 10-foot sink tip and short leader, is a good starting setup for the inlet area. An extra spool with a floating line and 12-foot leader will give you access to trout that may be feeding on emerging midges in this end of the lake.

The bays on the south side of the lake provide outstanding feeding spots during May and June. Weed beds are developing nicely, and scud, damselfly, and mayfly activity is moving trout in from the depths.

Olive scuds twitched around these beds in sizes 12 to 16 and tied on a long, shanked hook imitate the swimming shrimp best. Stripping scuds early in the morning and late in the evenings prove to be the best times.

Sporadic hatches of Callibaetis start to show by late May. Start looking for the hatch late morning. Parachute Adams or a gray comparadun presented in front of a riser can produce a quick take. Spinner falls in the late afternoon should not be missed. A #14 rusty spinner is always a good choice for this situation.

Stagecoach Reservoir

Mid- to late June is the time for the major damselfly hatches. Light olive swimming damsel nymphs stripped towards the bank best imitates the damsels seeking land and attempting to crawl out of their nymphal shucks.

These bays have excellent break lines for trout to move from one depth to another with quick access to the deep water in the middle of the lake. Small slots between the two bays are also good places to work with buggers and big nymphs.

Stagecoach Reservoir is becoming a premier location for northern pike. Apparently planted here by a pike lover, they have done very well, and anyone interested in pike on a fly will not be disappointed. Mid-May usually marks the post spawn for Northerns. Lurking in the warmer water of the shallows, pike are looking for an easy meal to prey upon. Black bunny bugs seem to be a favorite of pike all around the state, and Stagecoach is no exception. Yellow and chartreuse are other colors you should carry, depending on the clarity of the water. The bright colors work best when windy conditions have turned the water to a murky, churned-up mess.

Seven- to 9-weight rods are needed to handle these flies. They feel like a wet sock on the end of a 9-foot leader. A leader for casting pike flies is designed differently than a basic tapered trout leader. A 9-foot piece of level 0x monofilament from the fly line with an 18-inch piece of nylon-coated steel wire tippet, connected with an Albright Special knot, is the going thing.

The fly line should be a special bass bug taper or a pike/muskie line. They are designed like a shooting head. It makes a long-distance cast with a large air resistant fly much easier.

A reel with a good disk drag is essential. A Ross G-4 or a SW-III or IV will handle any blazing runs these guys may put up.

The early part of the day should be spent wading shallow water, moving the bunny bug very slowly. If you have pike following your fly but not taking it, a smaller fly like a Clouser minnow or Lefty deceiver may turn the tide. As the water warms, the pike will definitely become more aggressive, and tactics should change. Faster moving flies provoke pike to attack. Changing directions as if the fly were trying to get away also may close the deal.

Improved camping facilities are available. Boat rentals, dump stations, and picnic areas are also located at the main campground on the north side of the reservoir.

Lake Facts: Stagecoach Reservoir

Seasons
- Ice-off occurs about mid-May. Flyfishing until it's too cold to fish. Lake is usually frozen by December.

Special Regulations
- Standard regulations apply

Fish
- Rainbow trout; 16-inch trout are common, with fish running up to 5 pounds.
- Snake River cutthroat trout; 14-inch average, while a trout over 18 inches is common.
- Northern Pike

Lake Size
- 780 acres
- 100 feet deep at the east end near the dam

Boat Ramps
- One ramp on the north side of the lake
- A future ramp on the southeast side

Camping
- 100 campsites; picnic sites available

Lake Character
- The elevation here is 7,200 feet. The rainbows and Snake River cutthroats make up the trout available. Northern pike have a growing population in the lake. Lots of submerged brush on the west end of this lake. Several bays with submerged brush.

Maps
- Fish-n-Map Company, 303-421-5994

WHITE RIVER

The White River is nestled off the main highways and byways of northwestern Colorado, which makes it an excellent destination for those who want to get away from people.

The river flows out of Trapper's Lake, then cuts through Meeker, which rests just north of I-70, 40 miles from the Rifle exit on Colorado 13. From Craig, turn off US 40 and travel south on Colorado 13 for about 50 miles to the river. The drive in either direction has the look of the high plains, which it is. Fragrant sage, sharply cut stream drainages, ranchland, and mule deer—lots of mule deer—are seen through the window. This part of the state, just west of the Flat Tops Wilderness Area, is best known for its hunting. Elk and deer are abundant, and by all means, if you love to hunt, you should try to pursue them here. However, I feel sorry for those who only hunt and do not take the opportunity to cast a fly in the White River, surrounding streams, and high mountain lakes. They are missing out on the most underfished areas of the state.

What happens to a river that does not get the fishing pressure of well-known and pounded streams? In my experience, it grows peacefully, naturally, and unimpeded. That's the White River for you; it's a clear, smallish stream filled with modest, eager cutthroats at its headwaters above Trapper's Lake. The river changes pace along the way, just like Mother Nature intended. It gains strength as it is fed by several small streams. Pocket water in that stretch holds rainbows and browns averaging 10 to 14 inches. From there, the river tumbles down into ranchland, soaking alfalfa fields and watering cattle. The river meanders through the ranchland, creating long riffles, deep runs and nice corner pools. And, best of all, bigger fish!

Your first chance to fish the river is right in the town of Meeker at City Park. In that stretch, the river is in great shape by April, when midge activity reigns and trout actively feed on those tiny morsels.

Blue-winged olives start popping out by mid-April, which drives the trout to the surface to feed. At that time, river flows range from 300 to 400 cfs, which is perfect, and it's not uncommon to see 12- to 16-inch rainbows and browns feeding on those small olive mayflies. Otto Shults, a Meeker native and serious White River flyfisher, says that the hatch begins around 10:30 am and extends past noon. Most of the olives rate a size 18.

To match those bugs, a parachute Adams, olive comparadun or a slate wing thorax dun is a good choice. A pheasant tail nymph, quill emerger or an olive biot nymph will cover the subsurface meal ticket. Hook sizes should range from size 16 through size 20.

While you could encounter large trout anywhere on the White, Shults likes the catch and release Nelson Prather stretch, where he landed a 6-pound rainbow in April 1997. Shults knows some people will question the merit of his catch because the White is not a tailwater, but he insists large fish are there because whirling disease has not affected the river. And Prather's fish wasn't the only big one living in that stretch—a 10-pound German brown was taken right in town in 1995.

White River

N

Legend
— State/Cty Road
— Other Roads
△ Campground
✕ Fishing Access
░ Wilderness
▬ Major River
— Minor River/Creek

Meeker Pasture SWA, 1 mi.

Nelson Prather Access, 4 mi.

Little Beaver Creek

Wakara, 5 mi.

Meeker

Meeker, City Park, 0 mi.

4 Road

8 Road

White

Road 4 Upper Access to Wakara, 6.5 mi.

Sleepy Cat Ponds, 14.5 mi.

Road 17, 20 mi.

Buford Store

Cattle Creek

Big Beaver Creek

Lake Avery

North Elk Creek

Miller Creek

River

South Fork White River

Bridge at Road 10, 18 mi.

Cherry Creek

Forbes Creek

Crooks Creek

Fawn Creek Confluence, 26 mi.

Fawn Creek

8 Road

Lost Creek Confluence, 30 mi.

Lost Creek

National Forest Campground, 32 mi.

Long Park Creek

Missouri Creek

Snell Creek Confluence, 36 mi.

North Fork White River

Snell Creek

8 Road

Ripple Creek

Skinny Fish Creek

Hime's Peak Campground, 43 mi.

Trapper's Lake

Trapper's Lake, 47 mi.

Marvine Creek

Mirror Creek

Paradise Creek

Big Fish Creek

Flat Tops Wilderness (open to fishing)

© Wilderness Adventures Press

The absolute best time to see the White in action is the second week in May. An incredible caddis hatch occurs in town and moves its way upstream until runoff takes over the controls.

To reach an excellent stretch of river where caddis activity is always good in May, follow Road 8 to the Lost Creek Ranger Station. This is where the pavement ends and the maintained dirt road starts. It's also an area where Trout Unlimited, with the help of the Division of Wildlife and the Forest Service, has completed thousands of dollars in stream improvements.

"Caddis are the main diet for the trout in the White River," Shults said. "When they start to hatch, the trout get keyed in and feed heavily. Stonefly nymphs are the secondary food source and they are starting to crawl around this time of year. Their hatch occurs during the apex of runoff, so fishing to them is near impossible."

When caddis come off, they will be in full swing by 11 am, and their presence on the water can last all day. Prior to the hatch, nymphing with a size 14 soft hackle hare's ear, which imitates pupating caddis, or with a size 10 Prince nymph, which imitates stoneflies, can start the day on a positive note. The tailout of pockets and the top end of a run are excellent holding areas and should be covered adequately with a nymph.

When the surface starts to boil, a dry fly is in order. Olive elk hair caddis, dark-gray bodied CDC caddis, or Lawson's caddis emergers, ranging from size 14 to 18, should make for a few good fly selections. Spotting the rising fish and presenting the fly with a downstream drift is very effective.

While that early season caddis hatch can be a blast, don't overlook the caddis action after runoff. Evening fishing during summer can be a joy. Those caddis will be mixed in with a plethora of mayflies, including pale morning duns and green drakes, which hatch sporadically in July through early August. Midmornings are usually the best time to catch one of these hatches, but you may find an emergence or spinner-fall in the evening, too.

While the caddis and mayflies are certainly the glory flies, Shults says you should not overlook terrestrials in the late summer and early September. "There is a black beetle with orange markings that feeds on the rabbit brush along the river in September," he said. "Rabbit brush pollinates after the first frost and drives these black beetles wild."

One little mishap, and "plop"! into the water the beetles fall. Slurp! The beetle disappears. Since there is no fall Baetis hatch on the White, beetles fill the void and offer the last chance of the season to catch fish on the surface. However, just because you can't take a fish on the surface does not mean you should pack your bags and head home. Nymph fishing is productive throughout fall and winter. Stay with the caddis nymph and stonefly combination. With that combo, don't be surprised to hook a few whitefish. Whities spawn during fall and they are eager to scarf nymphs.

Overall, the White River offers up a host of opportunities for the fly angler. Pass up on a few days of fall hunting and visit this river. Just make sure to pack a few beetle patterns in your vest, and don't be too surprised if a nice size fish drills your offering.

Author casting to the pocket water on the White River.

Several side roads and campgrounds along small tributaries of the White offer seclusion and selective wild trout. On this stream you have a realistic chance for a large brown that has run up from a private ranch below town. If a hotel is the only place to live while on the road, Meeker has that small town feel and super friendly people. Good Luck!

Stream Facts: White River

Seasons
- Fishing is open all year

Special Regulations
- Trout Unlimited Access at Nelson Prather: Catch and release; all fish must be returned to the water immediately.

Fish
- Rainbows, browns, cutthroat, and brook trout in the upper reaches
- Mountain whitefish

River Miles
- Meeker City Park—0 • Road 17—20
- Nelson Prather Access—1 • Fawn Creek Confluence—26
- Meeker Pasture SWA—4 • Lost Creek Confluence—30
- Wakara—5 • National Forest Campground—32
- Road 4 upper access to Wakara—6.6 • Snell Creek Confluence—36
- Sleepy Cat Ponds—14.5 • Hime's Peak Campground—43
- Bridge at Road 10—18 • Trappers Lake—47

River Characteristics
- The North Fork of the White River starts at Trappers Lake as a small stream flowing to the west towards Buford. Just west of Buford, the South Fork converges with the North Fork to form the White River. The White River is a freestone river filled with long riffles, runs, and corner pools up to the town of Meeker. This is the most important part of the river for the flyfisherman.

River Flows
- Spring 300–500 cfs
- Runoff 1,000–2,000 cfs
- Summer 500–800 cfs
- Fall 300–500 cfs

Maps
- *Colorado Atlas & Gazetteer*, pages 24,25,34,35
- Routt National Forest
- White River National Forest

WHITE RIVER MAJOR HATCHES

Insect	A	M	J	J	A	S	O	N	Time	Flies
Caddis		█	█	█	█	█			M/E	Olive Caddis Nymph #10–#20; Breadcrust #10–#18; Beadhead Breadcrust #10–#18; Buckskin #16–#20; LaFontaine's Sparkle Caddis Pupa #10–#20; Elk Hair Caddis #10–#22; CDC Caddis #14–#20; Macramé Caddis #12–#16; Lawson's Caddis Emerger #14–#18; Spent Partridge Caddis #14–#18
Stonefly			█	█					M/A/E	Sandy's Gold #6–#10; Gold-winged Prince Nymph #8–#10; Kaufmann's Golden Stonefly #6–#12; Stimulator #8–#12; Halfback #4–#10; Prince Nymph #8–#16; Beadhead Prince Nymph #8–#16; Kaufmann's Brown Stonefly #4–#8; Stimulator #8–#12
Baetis		█	█						M	Olive Biot Nymph #18–#22; RS-2 #16–#24; Pheasant Tail Nymph #16–#20; Beadhead Pheasant Tail Nymph #16–#22; Olive Quill Emerger #18–#24; AK's Olive Quill #16–#22; Parachute Adams #12–#22; Olive Comparadun #16–#20; Slate Thorax Dun #16–#22
Midge		█	█	█	█	█	█		M/A/E	Olive Biot Midge #16–#24; Brown Biot Midge #16–#24; Black Beauty #18–#24; Brassie #16–#24; Miracle Nymph #16–#20; Black Beauty Pupa #18–#24; CDC Biot Suspender Midge #18–#24; Griffith's Gnat #16–#22; Palomino Midge #18–#22

HATCH TIME CODE: M = morning; A = afternoon; E = evening; D = dark; SF = spinner fall; / = continuation through periods.

WHITE RIVER MAJOR HATCHES (CONT.)

Insect	A	M	J	J	A	S	O	N	Time	Flies
Beetles/Terrestrials							▓		A/E	Rio Grande King Trude #8–#16; Royal Wulff #10–#16; Humpy #10–#16; Renegade #10–#16; Black Ant #14–#20; Gartside Hopper #8–#10; Black Beetle #16
Pale Morning Dun					▓				M	Biot PMD Nymph #16; Pheasant Tail Nymph #16–#22; Beadhead Pheasant Tail Nymph #14–#20; Lt. Cahill Comparadun #12–#18; Sparkle Dun #14–#18; Parachute PMD #14–#18; Dark Hare's Ear #14–#18
Green Drake			▓						A	Green Drake Emerger #10–#12; Lawson's Parachute Green Drake #10–#12; Green Drake #10–#12; Adams #10–#12; Olive Hare's Ear #10–#12
Red Quill			▓						A/E	AK's Red Quill #14–#18; Rusty Spinner #12–#20
Streamers	▓							▓	M/E	Black Woolly Bugger #2–#10; Spruce Fly #4–#10; Dark Spruce Fly #4–#10; Black-nosed Dace #6–#8; Muddler Minnow #4–#10; Matuka Sculpin #4–#10

HATCH TIME CODE: M = morning; A = afternoon; E = evening; D = dark; SF = spinner fall; / = continuation through periods.

TRAPPERS LAKE

Although some fly anglers dismiss stillwaters and lakes as boring, Trappers Lake, which is located in the gorgeous Flat Tops Wilderness, is far from that.

If the lake didn't even hold fish, it would be worth a visit. It rests in the White River National Forest, and the scenery is striking. Flyfishers will be happy to learn that it also offers some outstanding fishing for native Colorado River cutthroat trout.

Trappers Lake is located at the end of Road 8, east of Meeker about 50 miles. And what a great place to end a road. Just don't count on seeing the end of the road until after spring thaw. Usually, the lake itself thaws by mid-May, and that is perhaps the best time to pursue its trout. If you do choose to fish the lake at that time of the year, be aware that the water is very cold. You'll need to bundle up to avoid hypothermia, especially if you fish from a float tube, which happens to be the most effective method on this water. A fair amount of fish can also be caught from shore. The cuts are hungry and love a well-presented woolly bugger no matter if it's thrown at them from a floattube or the shore. In May, after a long, hungry winter, the fly just needs to be in the water and moving, and it will draw strikes.

Test retrieval rates—slow short strips, long fast strips—and anything in between. Cutthroat up to 16 inches should be tussling with you most of the day. If the trout are not cooperating, they might be resting low down in the water column; let the fly go deeper before you start the retrieve. This is as easy as it gets.

According to Otto Shults, a local flyfisher, a special fly, one that some flyfishers might look down upon, works wonders here. "It's actually a little leadheaded jig, maybe a 1/16th ounce, with a chartreuse body and a black marabou tail," Shults said. "(When fishing that fly), make the cast, let it fall a bit, then get that tail moving. The bright-colored body must have something to do with its effectiveness."

Midges take over as the important food source for the rest of the year. Evenings on the lake can be phenomenal, with trout rising to emerging and adult midges just about everywhere a trout can rise. Griffith's gnats, parachute Adams, and small CDC biot midges should catch the attention of an unsuspecting cutthroat. A damselfly or two can be seen during the summer months, but damsel patterns seem to go unnoticed.

If you bring the family to this lake, you should have a good time. There is plenty of room for the kids to play. Five campgrounds are available at the lake. "Bring the kids up to Trappers," Shults said. "This is one of the best answers for the problems youths are having today. Outdoor activity, especially fishing, is great for the body, mind, and soul."

While Trappers is the big draw in the area, there are numerous smaller lakes that also provide good fishing. However, you will have to use your own feet to reach them. Trails going into the Flat Tops are numerous for the backpacker, but some of the country can be tough to negotiate. Get some detailed topographic maps before you head out.

Northwest Hub Cities
Steamboat Springs
Population – 8,100 • Elevation – 6,695 • Area Code – 970

ACCOMMODATIONS

Holiday Inn, 3190 South Lincoln Avenue / 879-2250 / 83 units / Dogs allowed / $$$

Rabbit Ears Motel, 201 Lincoln Avenue / 879-1150 / 66 units / Dogs allowed / Continental breakfast / $$$

Comfort Inn, 1055 Walton Creek Road / 879-6669/ 52 units / Dogs allowed / $$$

Alpiner Lodge, 424 Lincoln Avenue / 879-1430 / 33 units / Dogs allowed for a fee / $$$

BED AND BREAKFAST

Country Inn at Steamboat Lake, 61276 RCR 129 / 879-3906, 800-934-STAY / Innkeeper: Tom Berry / $$$

Steamboat B and B, 442 Pine / 879-5724 / Innkeeper: Gordon Hattersly / $$$

Caroline's B and B, 838 Merritt / 870-1696, 800-856-4029

Clermont Country Inn, 917 Lincoln Avenue / 879-3083

CAMPING

Ski Town KOA Campground, 2 miles West on Highway 40 / 879-0273 / RV and tent camping on Yampa River / Store, showers, pool

Fish Creek Campground, 15 tent sites and 30 RV

RESTAURANTS

Village Inn, 3190 South Lincoln Avenue / 879-3224 / 24 hours / $

Spring City Diner, Highway 40 / 879-8099 / Open 7AM – 9PM / Cocktails / $$

Dos Amigos, 1910 Mt. Werner Road / 879-4270 / Mexican food / Cocktails / $

The Butcher Shop, 1940 Ski Time Square Drive / 879-2484

The Shack, 740 Lincoln Avenue / 879-9975 / Great breakfast / Open 6AM – 2PM / $

FLY SHOPS / GUIDES AND SPORTING GOODS

Bucking Rainbow Outfitters, 402 Lincoln Avenue P.O. Box 775616 / 879-4693 / Owners: Mark and Lisa Campbell / Orvis authorized fly shop / Guide service, specializing in float trips on the Yampa and North Platte Rivers / Private waters / General store and deli (a great sourdough turkey sandwich)

Buggywhip's, P.O. Box 770477 / 879-8033, 800-759-0343 / Jim Blackburn guides on the Yampa, Colorado, North Platte, Eagle, Blue, Elk, and Arkansas Rivers

Guided Fly Fishing, P.O. Box 880632 / 879-7238 / Larry Mann is owner and guide / Private river access; local rivers and lakes; Colorado, Blue, and Eagle Rivers

Steamboat Fishing Company Inc., P.O. Box 776250, 635 Lincoln Avenue / 879-6552 / Owner: Duncan Draper / Fully guided trips on private, local, and high mountain rivers and lakes

Straightline, P.O. Box 4887, 744 Lincoln Avenue / 879-7568, 800-354-5463 / Owners: Bruce, Brett, and Robert Lee / Float and wade trips on the Colorado and Yampa Rivers / Local, private, and high mountain excursions
Back Door Sport Ltd., 811 Yampa / 879-6249
Good Time Sports, 730 Lincoln Avenue / 879-7818
Inside Edge Sports, 1835 Central Park Plaza / 879-1250
Lahaina Ski and Sport, Gondola Square / 879-2323
Shop and Hop Food Store, 35775 East US Highway 40 / 879-2489
Sportstalker, 2305 Mt. Werner Circle / 879-0371
Colorado River Guides, P.O. Box 711, Oak Creek 80467 / 736-2406, 800- 938-7238
Spiro's Trading Post, 107 Main, Oak Creek 80467 / 736-2443

HOSPITALS
Routt Memorial Hospital, 80 Park Avenue / 879-1322

AIRPORTS
Steamboat Springs Airport, 3 miles north of town on Elk River Road / 879-9042 / Private planes
Yampa Valley Airport, 276-3669 / American Airlines: 800-433-7300 / Delta: 800-221-1212 / United Express: 800-241-6522 / Continental Express: 800-523-3273
Steamboat Reservations and Travel Inc., 879-3202

AUTO RENTAL
Advantage Rent-A-Car, 879-5737
Avis Rent-A-Car, 879-3785
Economy Rentals, 879-1179

AUTO SERVICE
Stambaugh Motors Inc., 879-8886
Repair Dynamics Inc., 879-3232

LOCKSMITH
Rip Van Winkle Locksmith Service, Sundance Plaza, 879-3211
Grama's, 40488 Downhill Drive / 879-1178

FOR MORE INFORMATION
Steamboat Springs Chamber Resort Association
1255 South Lincoln Avenue
Steamboat Springs, CO 80477
879-0882
www.steamboat-chamber.com

Meeker

Population – 2,098 • Elevation – 6,249 • Area Code – 970

ACCOMMODATIONS

Rustic Lodge and Saloon, 878-3136 / 6 units / Dogs allowed if well mannered / $$
Valley Motel, 723 Market Street / 878-3656 / 21 units / Dogs allowed / $$
White River Inn, 219 East Market Street / 878-5031 / Owners: L.D. and Jewell
   Grove; mention you are flyfishing / 21 units / $$

CAMPING

Rim Rock Campground, 73179 Highway 64 / 878-4486
Rocky Mountain Recreation Co., 878-4078
National Forest, Himes Peak, Marvine, North & South Fork Campgrounds / 878-4039

RESTAURANTS

Clark's Big Burger, 858 West Market / 878-3240 / Open 11AM–10PM / $
Meeker Cafe, 560 Main, 878-5062 / Open 7AM-9pm / Cocktails / $
Whispering Pines Restaurant, 410 East Market / 878-5382 / Open 6AM–9PM / $
Pizza Pro, 975 West Market, 878-4645 / Open 11AM–9PM / $

GUIDES AND SPORTING GOODS

Cherokee Outfitters, P.O. Box 537 / 878-5750
Wyatt's Sport Center, 223 West Market / 878-4428
Rocky Mountain Archery Pro Shop, 654 Main / 878-4300
Lone Tom Outfitting, 12888 RBC 8 / 878-5122
Marvine Outfitters, P.O. Box 130 / 878-4320
Downing's Hardware, 624 Market / 878-4608

HOSPITALS

Pioneers Hospital, 345 Cleveland / 878-5047

AIRPORTS

Meeker Airport, 921 East Market / 878-5045
Yampa Valley Airport, 276-3669 / American Airlines: 800-433-7300 /
   Delta: 800-221-1212 / United Express: 800-241-6522 / Continental
   Express: 800-523-3273

AUTO SERVICE

J Byroad's Auto Service and Repair, 7th and Main / 878-3301
Jack's Automotive Service, 6th and Market / 878-5606
Valley Repair Inc., 431 East Market / 878-3316

LOCKSMITH

Sheriff's Custom Arsenal, 442 Market / 878-3160

FOR MORE INFORMATION

Meeker Chamber of Commerce
710 West Market
Meeker, CO 81641
878-5510

North Park

North Park is best known by flyfishers for its cold water lakes, Delaney Buttes, and Lake John, but it also offers excellent lesser-known moving water options, especially on the North Platte River and its gushing tributaries.

On those rivers, flyfishers can find decent brook trout, rainbows and brown trout. All of the fishing accesses are located within 15 miles of Walden, Colorado, making Walden a perfect place to base your activities. However, that small town is extremely popular during the hunting season, so make your reservations well in advance.

North Platte River

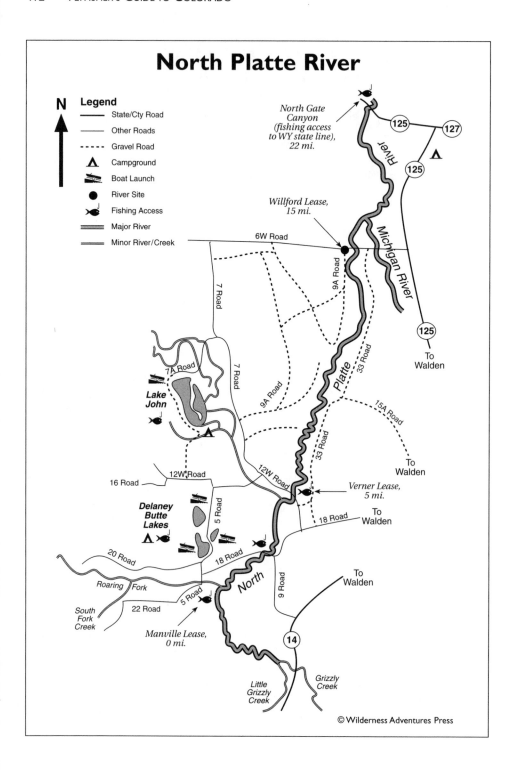

Legend

———	State/Cty Road
———	Other Roads
- - - -	Gravel Road
Λ	Campground
🛶	Boat Launch
●	River Site
🐟	Fishing Access
▨	Major River
▬	Minor River/Creek

North Gate Canyon *(fishing access to WY state line), 22 mi.*

125   127

Λ

125

River

Willford Lease, 15 mi.

6W Road

9A Road

Michigan River

125

To Walden

7 Road

7A Road

7 Road

9A Road

Platte

33 Road

Lake John

15A Road

To Walden

33 Road

12W Road

16 Road

12W Road

Delaney Butte Lakes

5 Road

Verner Lease, 5 mi.

18 Road

To Walden

20 Road

18 Road

North

To Walden

Roaring Fork

9 Road

South Fork Creek

22 Road

5 Road

Manville Lease, 0 mi.

14

Little Grizzly Creek

Grizzly Creek

© Wilderness Adventures Press

NORTH PLATTE RIVER

Best known for its excellent fishing in Wyoming, especially around Gray Reef and the Miracle Mile—which draws anglers from around the world—people should realize that the North Platte River isn't all that bad in Colorado, either.

In fact, don't let the pull of Wyoming lead you away from opportunities in Colorado. The North Platte in North Park—the headwaters of the river—is underfished, so its trout see little pressure when compared to the Wyoming sections; they aren't exactly educated.

The confluence of Grizzly Creek and Little Grizzly Creek mark the start of the North Platte in Colorado, just southwest of Walden. The upper reaches are private, but guest ranches, such as Little Grizzly Creek Ranch, provide access to the beautiful headwaters area. Lots of wild trout and an untouched setting offer great days astream. The first access to the river is on the Brownlee and Verner State Wildlife Areas.

To reach that site from Walden, go west a half-mile on Colorado 14 to CR 12W. Veer right on CR 12 and follow that road 5.3 miles to CR 18. Take CR 18 west for a half mile to Brownlee access. Just down the road is Verner access. Those accesses offer a couple miles of good water to fish. Through that section, the stream is a flat, meandering, meadow-like water that is best fished just after runoff. Prior to runoff, dense snow and low water conditions impede success.

Runoff usually hits quickly in late April and May, but the river drops into marginally fishable shape by mid-May. In fact, late May and early June are the best times for a flyfisher to hit the water. Streamers, like woolly buggers and bright, attention getting bucktails, fished along the bank, are excellent patterns. Large nymphs, like halfbacks, crane fly larvae, and Bitch Creeks, also hook trout. Again, drifting nymphs in the deep water near the banks is your best bet. To fish that deep water effectively, you'll need heavy split shot above your nymph.

Browns are most often encountered on the North Platte, and they will often take the fly within a few yards of the bank. The browns are self-sustaining, and they are managed as a wild trout fishery. Rainbows make up only 25 percent of the trout population. All of the upper North Platte's trout average between 12 and 14 inches, although a few browns over 18 inches are caught each year.

June is perhaps the best time to take a North Platte rainbow or brown on a dry fly. Caddis are by far the most plentiful insect in June, and they often emerge from the riffles during late morning. Watch for splashy rises—if you see that display, tie on an emerger, like an X-caddis, or try an olive elk hair in sizes 12 to 16. Really, the caddis emergence is an event you do not want to miss.

Mark Campbell, of Bucking Rainbow Outfitters in Steamboat Springs, suggests, "An elk hair caddis is the best producer on this river. I catch more fish in two months on a caddis than any other fly during the rest of the year."

Mayflies also make their move in June, and some nice trout can be found feeding on blue-winged olives in the slick water flats, alongside with those caddis, during late morning. Look for trout feeding on mayflies at the tailout of riffles and near the

North Platte River.

bank in soft water. The standard olive patterns, like a size 16 parachute olive, will draw strikes. However, a dead-drifted pheasant-tail nymph and quill emergers should grab a trout's attention if they are not grubbing adults.

A large mayfly known as the western March brown may also be seen sporadically during afternoons. A size 10 or 12 light tan adult mayfly pattern, like a parachute Adams or a cripple, will draw the attention of surface feeders. A note on the March brown: it ascends to the surface rapidly when hatching, so a light brown soft-hackle, lifted from the bottom or swung at the end of a drift, is a very effective imitation. Takes can be especially solid when fishing soft hackles. You might wonder who's fishing for whom when they try to take your rod down with them.

During high water years, runoff can play havoc through July, and fishing may be difficult, to say the least. In July, the river is drawn down by irrigation needs, and water temperatures rise. And with that change, productive afternoon fishing on the upper river ceases. However, each night, just as the sun drops below the Park Range, you might find some fish working. Browns, particularly, may rise for a hopper or some other wayward terrestrial, especially in the meadow sections. During July and August, the only solid all-day option on the North Platte is the 5 miles of Gold Medal Water located upstream from the Wyoming state line.

A beautiful day for flyfishing on the North Platte. (Photo by Cole Bartholomew)

To reach that water, take US 125 north from Walden for 18 miles where you will find FR 896. A sign indicating entrance into Routt National Forest and fishing access sites will prompt you to turn right. Do so, and follow the road to the river in Northgate Canyon.

In Northgate, the best option is to walk downstream. The river is big here, characterized by pocket water fishing for brown and rainbow trout that range between 14 and 16 inches. Late in the day, high-riding caddis dry flies, cast into slack water, will draw rises. The bigger fish require nymph and streamer tactics to be taken. Drifting halfbacks, girdle bugs, and cranefly larvae in and around the rock gardens can produce some large fish. When the nymphs won't work, try a weighted woolly bugger and prepare to slay. Again, casting into the pockets and along the deeper banks is where the better fish will be found.

Stream Facts: North Platte River

Seasons
- Fishing is open all year.

Special Regulations
- From the southern border of Routt National Forest downstream to the Wyoming state line (Northgate Canyon): Gold Medal and Wild Trout Water. Artificial flies and lures only.

Bag and Possession Limit
- Limit is 2 fish on Brownlee and Verner leases, artificial flies and lures only.

Trout
- Browns average 12–16 inches, a few over 18 inches
- Rainbows average 12–14 inches

River Miles
- Manville lease—0
- Verner—5
- Willford lease—15
- North Gate Canyon—22

River Characteristics
- The entire upper river is a slow, meandering meadow stream with several tributaries adding water to the river in a hurry. As the river heads into Wyoming it flows through Northgate Canyon. Northgate offers big tough pocket water, but fishing can be excellent for the hardy, vigorous hiker who knows how to ply deep pocket water with nymphs and streamers.

River Flows
- Spring: upper river, 100–200 cfs
- Spring: Northgate Canyon, 500–700 cfs
- Runoff: 500–2,000 cfs
- Late summer: upper river, below 100 cfs
- Late summer: lower river, 300–600 cfs

Maps
- *Colorado Atlas & Gazetteer*, page 17
- Routt National Forest

NORTH PLATTE RIVER MAJOR HATCHES

Insect	A	M	J	J	A	S	O	N	Time	Flies
Midge	▓	▓	▓	▓	▓	▓	▓	▓	M/A/E	Olive Biot Midge #16–#24; Brown Biot Midge #16–#24; Black Beauty #18–#24; Brassie #16–#24; AK's Midge Larva #16–#22; Crane Fly Nymph #6–#10; Black Beauty Pupa #18–#24; CDC Biot Suspender Midge #18–#24; Griffith's Gnat #16–#22; Palomino Midge #18–#22
Blue-winged Olive			▓						M/A	Olive Biot Nymph #18–#22; RS-2 #16–#24; Pheasant Tail Nymph #16–#20; Beadhead Pheasant Tail Nymph #16–#22; Flashback Pheasant Tail Nymph #16–#20 ; Olive Quill Emerger #18–#24; Parachute Adams #12–#22; Olive Comparadun #16–#20; Gray Spinner #18–#24; CDC Baetis Dun #16–#22
March Brown				▓					A/E	March Brown Comparadun #10–#14; Western March Brown #10–#14; Western March Brown Soft Hackle #10–#14; AK's Red Quill #10–#14; Rusty Spinner #12–#14; Hare's Ear Nymph #10–#14
Caddis				▓	▓	▓			M/A/E	Olive Caddis Nymph #10–#20; Breadcrust #10–#18; Beadhead Breadcrust #10–#18; Buckskin #16–#20; LaFontaine's Sparkle Caddis Pupa #10–#20; Elk Hair Caddis #10–#22; Goddard Caddis #10–#16; CDC Caddis #14–#20; Macramé Caddis #12–#16; Balloon Caddis #12–#16; Lawson's Caddis Emerger #14–#18; Spent Partridge Caddis #14–#18

HATCH TIME CODE: M = morning; A = afternoon; E = evening; D = dark; SF = spinner fall; / = continuation through periods.

NORTH PLATTE RIVER MAJOR HATCHES (CONT.)

Insect	A	M	J	J	A	S	O	N	Time	Flies
Streamers							▮		M/E	Black Woolly Bugger #10–#2; Platte River Special #10–#4; Spruce fly #10–#4; Dark spruce fly #10–#4 ; Black-Nosed dace #8–#6; Muddler Minnow #10–#4; Steve's BRO Bug #10–#6; Girdle bug #10–#6
Terrestrials					▮				A/E	Rio Grande King trude #16–#8; Royal Wulff #16–#10; Humpy #16–#10; Foam Madam X #12–#8; Renegade #16–#10; Black ant #20–#14; Cinnamon ant #20–#14; Gartside Hopper #10–#8; Henry's Fork hopper #12–#8
Stoneflies			▮						M/A	Sandy's Gold #10–#6; Kaufmann's golden stonefly #12–#6; Halfback #10–#4; Prince nymph #16–#8; Bead head Prince nymph #16–#8; Kaufmann's brown stonefly #8–#4; Bitch Creek nymph #10

HATCH TIME CODE: M = morning; A = afternoon; E = evening; D = dark; SF = spinner fall; / = continuation through periods.

MICHIGAN RIVER

The Michigan River is one of the North Platte's major tributaries, and its fishing opportunities mirror those you'll find on the bigger river, except for this: gaining access to the Michigan can be very difficult. Where you can access the river, bankside brush and willows make it very difficult to negotiate.

The Michigan's season begins in early spring, but a flyfisher may find that slogging around in melting snow and mud is not a tremendous experience. However, a brief window of opportunity from mid- to late April may give you a chance to fling woolly buggers and large nymphs as you move from corner pool to corner pool. Walking directly down the middle of the channel or crawling through the brush are your only options for mobility. Thin, hungry trout to 16 inches will pounce on your offerings if the brush doesn't devour you first. In May, as warm days melt snow and runoff from the Medicine Bow Mountains fills the river, angling opportunities cease.

Though it is affected by runoff, the Michigan, like the North Platte, offers good dry fly opportunities in June. Caddis, blue-winged olives, and a few March brown drakes can be seen this time of year.

An elk hair caddis is by far the best pattern to use, due to the fact that caddis numbers are greater than others. Dropping your fly in any off-speed area where a

The author with a nice brown taken from the Michigan River. (Photo by Cole Bartholomew)

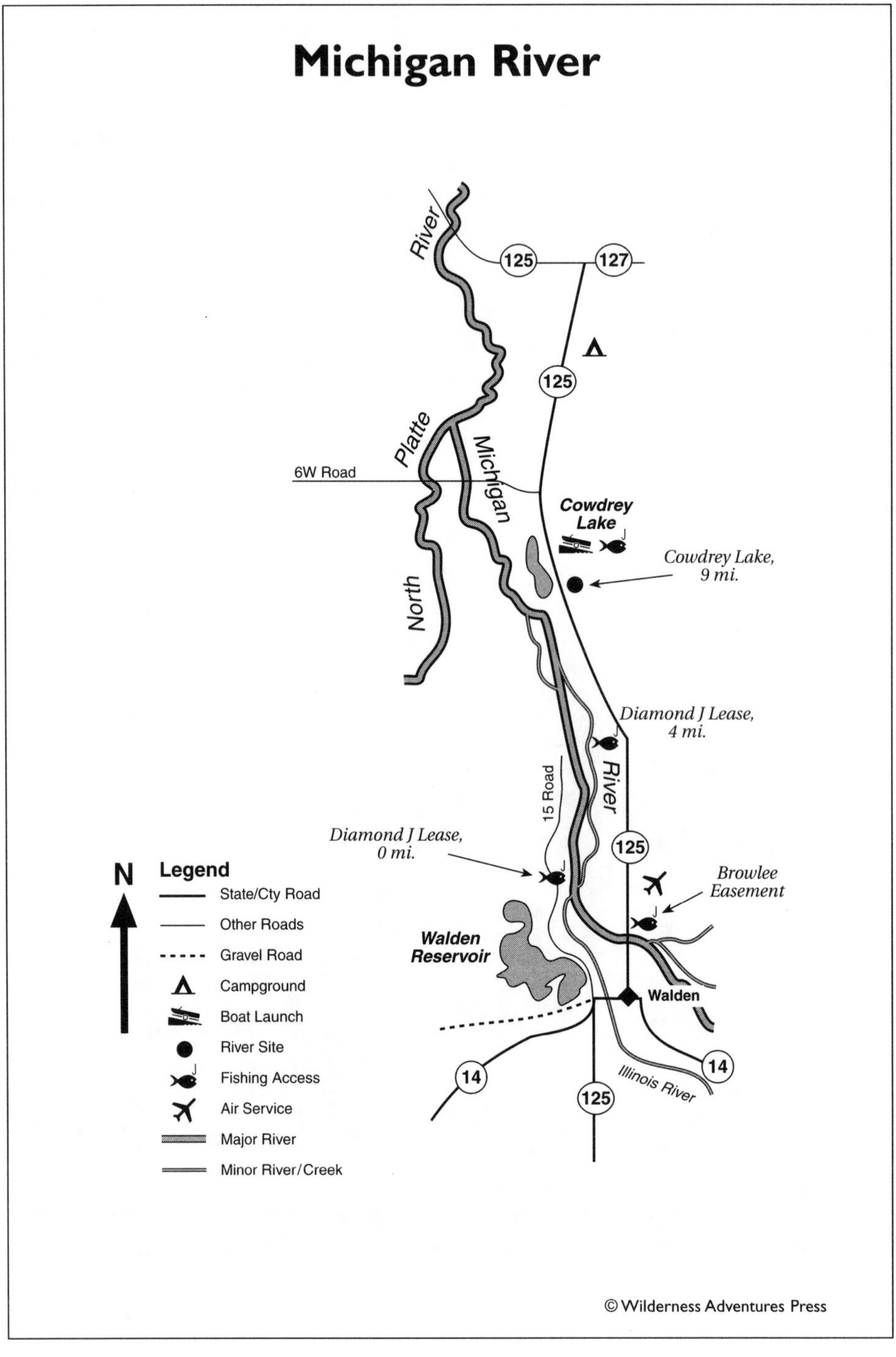

Michigan River

Platte River

North Platte River

Michigan River

6W Road

125
127
125

Cowdrey Lake

Cowdrey Lake, 9 mi.

Diamond J Lease, 4 mi.

15 Road

River

125

Diamond J Lease, 0 mi.

Browlee Easement

Walden Reservoir

Walden

14
125
14

Illinois River

Legend

N

	State/Cty Road
	Other Roads
-----	Gravel Road
⋀	Campground
🚣	Boat Launch
●	River Site
🐟	Fishing Access
✈	Air Service
	Major River
	Minor River/Creek

© Wilderness Adventures Press

backcast is allowed in tight surroundings is worth a try. If the current is heavy, be sure to work the banks religiously. Learning how to roll-cast is a good idea before you head out on the stream.

The Michigan is a good river for terrestrial fishing in July and August, depending on flows. Land-born insects drop to the water from tangles of brush along the banks. Hoppers, Rio Grande kings, and beetles are productive patterns.

Take into account that mosquitoes are also seen in abundance, and they can be a real pest. Repellent is a must when fishing the river, unless you like exiting the water in close resemblance to a well-used pincushion.

If you find the Michigan to your liking and you want to see more of the river, I have heard of some landowners, who, if asked politely, may grant access across their property. Good luck, but I offer no guarantee.

MICHIGAN RIVER MAJOR HATCHES

Insect	A	M	J	J	A	S	O	N	Time	Flies
Midge	■	■	■	■	■	■	■	■	M/A/E	Olive Biot Midge #16–#24; Brown Biot Midge #16–#24; Black Beauty #18–#24; Brassie #16–#24; AK's Midge Larva #16–#22; Crane Fly Nymph #6–#10; Black Beauty Pupa #18–#24; CDC Biot Suspender Midge #18–#24; Griffith's Gnat #16–#22; Palomino Midge #18–#22
Blue-winged Olive	■	■	■				■		M/A	Olive Biot Nymph #18–#22; RS-2 #16–#24; Pheasant Tail Nymph #16–#20; Beadhead Pheasant Tail Nymph #16–#22; Flashback Pheasant Tail Nymph #16–#20; Olive Quill Emerger #18–#24; Parachute Adams #12–#22; Olive Comparadun #16–#20; Gray Spinner #18–#24; CDC Baetis Dun #16–#22
March Brown			■	■					A/E	March Brown Comparadun #10–#14; Western March Brown #10–#14; Western March Brown Soft Hackle #10–#14; AK's Red Quill #10–#14; Rusty Spinner #12–#14; Hare's Ear Nymph #10–#14
Caddis			■	■	■	■			M/A/E	Olive Caddis Nymph #10–#20; Breadcrust #10–#18; Beadhead Breadcrust #10–#18; Buckskin #16–#20; LaFontaine's Sparkle Caddis Pupa #10–#20; Elk Hair Caddis #10–#22; Goddard Caddis #10–#16; CDC Caddis #14–#22; Macramé Caddis #12–#16; Balloon Caddis #12–#16; Lawson's Caddis Emerger #14–#18; Spent Partridge Caddis #14–#18

HATCH TIME CODE: M = morning; A = afternoon; E = evening; D = dark; SF = spinner fall; / = continuation through periods.

MICHIGAN RIVER MAJOR HATCHES (CONT.)

Insect	A	M	J	J	A	S	O	N	Time	Flies
Streamers		█						█	M/A/E	Black Woolly Bugger #2–#10; Platte River Special #4–#10; Spruce Fly #4–#10; Dark Spruce Fly #4–#10; Black-nosed Dace #6–#8; Muddler Minnow #4–#10; Steve's BRO Bug #6–#10; Black Leech #4–#10
Terrestrials						█			A/E	Rio Grande King Trude #8–#16; Royal Wulff #10–#16; Humpy #10–#16; Foam Madam X #8–#12; Renegade #10–#16; Black Ant #14–#20; Cinnamon Ant #14–#20; Gartside Hopper #8–#10; Henry's Fork Hopper #8–#12
Stoneflies			█						M/A	Sandy's Gold #6–#10; Kaufmann's Golden Stonefly #6–#12; Halfback #4–#10; Prince Nymph #8–#16; Beadhead Prince Nymph #8–#16; Kaufmann's Brown Stonefly #4–#8; Bitch Creek Nymph #10

HATCH TIME CODE: M = morning; A = afternoon; E = evening; D = dark; SF = spinner fall; / = continuation through periods.

ROARING FORK RIVER

After a long morning spent kicking in a float tube on the Delaney Butte Lakes, a quick trip down the road to the Roaring Fork River can be an exciting break from the monotony of stillwater fishing.

As with other local waters, the Roaring Fork is best fished in June. The water is still high and off-color, but it is definitely fishable.

The stream has several deep cut banks as it meanders through its meadow sections, and fallen timber, root snags, shallow riffles, and deep pools offer additional prime trout habitat. Streamer fishing is at its best here, and browns up to 18 inches can be pulled from that structure. Black-nosed dace patterns, woolly buggers, and Platte River specials work wonders. Brook trout to 14 inches have surprised me on occasion. When fishing the river, stay back from the bank as much as possible because trout hold in the slack pockets near the bank.

Depending on annual snowpack, the Roaring Fork can measure but a trickle in late August, and any respectable trout will be long gone. Productive fishing will not peak until late September as the water cools.

The Roaring Fork is located on the Manville State Wildlife Area west of Walden and almost directly south of the Delaney Butte Lakes. Take CR 12 west for 5 miles from Walden to CR 18. Continue on CR 18 for 4.5 miles to CR 5. Turn left (south) on CR 5 to the lease.

Roaring Fork River.

LAKE JOHN

This high plains lake, which rests east of the Mt. Zirkel Wilderness Area in central North Park, has always been known for its large trout.

In past years, fish weighing over 10 pounds were often caught. Unfortunately, competition with rough fish stunted growth of those monsters, and the lake was offering only limited opportunities.

Due to its potential, the Colorado Division of Wildlife treated the lake for rough fish several years ago and now the lake again offers trout in the 16- to 20-inch range, although most of those fish are small stockers. Currently, the possession limit is 4 fish, and the lake is mostly utilized by baitchuckers. However, there are some opportunities for flyfishers.

Dan Filler, a local flyfishing guide and Colorado native who has fished Lake John for many years, uses one particular tactic that might turn your head. It sure did mine.

"For the most part, trout here feed on or near the bottom," he said. "I found that a 25-foot leader with varying amounts of split shot works best for me while trying to work the edges of the weed beds. I've never used (a sinking line). The water is so clear that I like the monofilament in the water instead of the fly line. I think it's an advantage."

Lake John's flyfishing opportunities begin when midges hatch, just after ice-out. At that time, a size 12 or a size 14 rusty brown midge larvae pattern—kind of a descendant of the blood midge—is very effective. Adding a sparse soft hackle near the head of the fly may give it a little better movement in the water. When those midges make it to the surface, gray uglies, gray hackle peacocks and Griffith's gnats in the same sizes hook up with these hefty trout. The holdover trout of Lake John average 17 inches, with a few larger specimens thrown in on the side.

Rainbows are the primary species here, with browns following a close second. Snake River cutthroat and a brookie or two round out the opportunities. Snails, as well as black water beetles, are important food sources during spring. Snails are pretty hard to imitate when it comes to flies, but there are a few good patterns out there. It probably doesn't need to be said, but here goes: fish those snail patterns painfully slow—they are not speed demons. Stomach samples often turn up the black beetle, and a size 14 black deer-hair beetle allowed to fall into the vegetation draws powerful takes. In June, submerged weed beds are in full bloom and Callibaetis mayflies hatch in mass. To reach those weed beds, you'll need a float tube. Once in the proximity of weed beds, try a flashback Callibaetis, but don't move your fly too fast. According to Filler, a slow to moderately fast retrieve is best.

"Most lake fishing is done with your fingers," Filler said. "A finger over finger retrieve is by far the best way to imitate the movement of all nymphs, especially Callibaetis. A light hare's ear in a size 16 is one of my favorite patterns."

Floating a rusty spinner in the surface film late in the day can also take good trout. Watch the rise patterns of cruising fish and present the fly out in front of them. If they notice the spent-winged fly without being spooked, a deliberate rise should follow.

Tubers working the weed line on Lake John.

Damselflies are also a very important hatch on Lake John. Late June and July are the best months for damsel migrations, and fishing can be excellent at that time. The southwest end of the lake has a nice submerged ridge about 1,000 feet from the west shore. Excellent vegetation growth provides a great population of damselflies. Swimming damselfly nymphs along this ridge can promote a sore arm and several lost flies in the course of a day—all due to large trout inhaling your offerings.

Outstanding trout growth rates in Lake John can also be attributed to the numerous scuds and dragonflies that inhabit the water. Scud activity is best in the very early mornings and again during the waning minutes of light at the end of the day. Standard scud and dragonfly patterns will work during those times.

While fishing Lake John is mostly a relaxing proposition, weather should always be taken into consideration while fishing any high plains lake. Wind is a common nemesis on this water, and storm cells rapidly pop over the hills from the west. They should be taken very seriously. When you see a storm approaching, get off the lake! I've seen some of the most awesome lightning strikes in my life as these storms top over Mt. Zirkel.

To reach Lake John from Walden, go west out of town on CR 12 for 5 miles. CR 12 turns north and continues another 3 miles to CR 7. Go north on CR 7 to the Lake John entrance. Camping and an RV park are available at the lake.

Lake Facts: Lake John

Seasons
- Flyfishing starts as soon as the ice comes off, usually in late April.

Special Regulations
- Bag and possession limit for trout is 4 fish. Camping prohibited except in established areas.

Trout
- Rainbows average 17 inches
- Browns also grow quickly and are aggressive fighters
- Snake River cutthroat and brook trout also persist

Lake Size
- 565 acres

Lake Character
- A very healthy lake that grows trout quickly. Vegetation growth is tremendous, and fishing from shore is only good during the early spring. Float tubing is the norm. Located at 8,058 feet, the lake has several break lines, allowing trout easy access to deep water. The north end of the lake has the best overall structure and gets the most angling pressure.

Maps
- Fish-n-Map Company, 303-421-5994

LAKE JOHN MAJOR HATCHES

Insect	A	M	J	J	A	S	O	N	Time	Flies
Midge								▓	M/A/E	Olive Biot Midge #12–#18; Brown Biot Midge #12–#18; Black Beauty #12–#18; Blood Midge #12–#18; Feather Duster Midge #14–#18; Black Beauty Pupa #12–#18; CDC Biot Suspender Midge #12–#18; Gray Soft Hackle #12–#18; Griffith's Gnat #14–#18; Palomino Midge #14–#18
Scuds								▓		Olive Scud #12–#16; Orange Scud #10–#16; 19½ Scud #12–#18; Tan Scud #12–#18; Flashback Scud #12–#18; Black Deer Hair Beetle #14
Damselflies					▓				M/A	Swimming Damsel #8–#12; Flashback Damsel #8–#12; Para-damsel #8–#12; Brown Damsel #10–#14; Crystal-winged Damsel #8–#12; Stalcup's Adult Damselfly #8–#12
Callibaetis					▓				M/A	Olive Biot Nymph #14–#16; Ginger Hare's Ear #14–#16; RS-2 #14–#16; Pheasant Tail Nymph #12–#16; Beadhead Pheasant Tail Nymph #14–#16; Flashback Pheasant Tail Nymph #14–#16; Olive Quill Emerger #14–#16; Parachute Adams #12–#16; Gray Comparadun #12–#16; Rusty Spinner #12–#16
Streamers								▓	M/A/E	Black Woolly Bugger #2–#10; Brown Woolly Bugger #4–#10; Spruce Fly #4–#10; Dark Spruce Fly #4–#10; Black-nosed Dace #6–#8; Muddler Minnow #4–#10; Steve's BRO Bug #6–#10

HATCH TIME CODE: M = morning; A = afternoon; E = evening; D = dark; SF = spinner fall; / = continuation through periods.

HOHNHOLZ LAKES

Hohnholz Lakes is designated as a State Wildlife Area, and it contains three lakes within it. Lake #3, which spans about 40 acres, is perhaps the most appealing to fly-fishers, due to its artificial fly and lure restriction and a limited possession limit of 4 trout.

Those regulations deter some trout-bonkers and allow the fishery to thrive. In my mind, Lake #3 is by far the best in quality.

Fishing on Lake #3 is best from mid-May through July for trout that range from 12 to 18 inches. Midge hatches start the action, and those diminutive insects manage to bring fish to the surface. Dark olive or brown biot midge patterns with CDC tied in at the head allows the midge to suspend in the surface film, which imitates the pupating stage of the insect. This is the stage of the hatch that most trout key on when feeding. Sizes 14 through 20 cover any midge that may appear. A tandem fly setup is always an effective option. To fish tandem flies, add an 18-inch section of tippet to the eye or the hook of the first fly, then tie on a Griffith's gnat or a black zing midge to complete the rig.

Midges hatch most of the year, but May is the best time to concentrate on the emergence. Callibaetis, a gray mayfly with speckled wings, generally hatch on Lake #3 by late May or early June. A light olive or ginger hare's ear is a good nymphal pattern to match those Callibaetis. Early-morning hours should be spent slowly twitching the nymph in shallow water. By noon, Adams, gray thorax duns, and quill Gordons are a few patterns that imitate the adult stage. A rusty spinner or a Poor's witch is a good choice when Callibaetis mayfly spinners come back to the water in the evening to lay eggs. Damselfly migrations keep the fly angler busy the rest of the summer.

During the damsel hatch, Rich Pilatzke, a good friend and avid lake fisherman, points out that trout may key on the direction of that swimming insect. So a flyfisher should, too. "Just remember damsels are migrating toward land," he said, "So your fly should move in that direction, too. Olive and brown swimming damselfly nymphs in sizes 10 through 14 should cover fly selection."

Occasionally, trout in Lake #3 will eagerly take adult damsels from the surface, so make sure to carry a #10 blue or light olive Borger braided butt adult pattern just in case you see that type of activity.

All of the Hohnholz Lakes are located 30 miles north of Colorado 14 on CR 103. From Ft. Collins, take Colorado 14 to the upper end of Poudre Canyon and turn right (north) on CR 103, also known as Laramie River Road, just before you get to Chambers Lake. From the Laramie River Campground, follow a dirt road west. Hohnholz Lake #3 is the last lake in the chain.

LARAMIE RIVER

If you want to fish the Laramie River, and you should want to fish the Laramie, you'll want to hit it during an enormous hatch of gray drakes.

That event occurs as the water clears in late June, although it can vary a bit from year to year. If you are on the river when the hatch occurs, make sure you have a half-dozen size 12 quill Gordons tucked into your fly box and another on the end of your line. At dusk and into the night, the sky can literally be filled with large mayflies, especially on cool evenings.

When the cool weather arrives, drakes come out of hiding, and you'll find them dipping their fannies on the water to lay eggs. Brown trout, up to 15 inches long, just go berserk when they catch those bugs in that vulnerable position. In fact, you can find every fish in the river with its nose sticking out of the water slurping in dinner.

Those drakes are not the only big hatch on the Laramie. In fact, you can expect to see dark caddis and red quills on any given June evening, too. Caddis activity during the day can also spark the interest of the Laramie's trout, and that makes for a full day of fishing.

A mile stretch of the Laramie River flows through Hohnholz Lake State Wildlife Area. See previous information on Hohnholz Lakes for directions. Camping is available at the Laramie River Campground. Mosquito repellent is a necessity—they can eat you alive if you don't have protection.

SEYMOUR RESERVOIR

Secluded from North Park proper, Seymour Reservoir provides a quiet getaway from fishing pressure at Delaney Buttes. And you'll find good fishing for smaller yet beautiful trout at Seymour. You'll also find some decent options in the surrounding small streams.

To reach the area, take Colorado 14 south 16 miles from Walden to CR 11. Turn left onto CR 11 and continue another 3 miles to the Seymour Lake State Wildlife area. Following CR 11 south leads you to some high lakes worth taking a look at. Slack-Weiss Reservoir, Flat Lake and Beaver Lake are located just off of FR 700.

DELANEY BUTTE LAKES

The Delaney Butte Lakes are found west of Walden by following Colorado 14 a half mile west out of town to CR 12W. Veer right, and remain on 12W for eight miles to CR 7. Turn right on CR 7 to find the entrance to the lakes.

North Delaney Butte

North Delaney is the best known of three lakes in this chain of waters. You'll find it by continuing past the first two lakes as you enter the area.

North Delaney is managed as a Gold Medal Water fishery, a designation that produces an opportunity for quality flyfishing. The Division of Wildlife collects eggs from

Delaney Butte Lakes

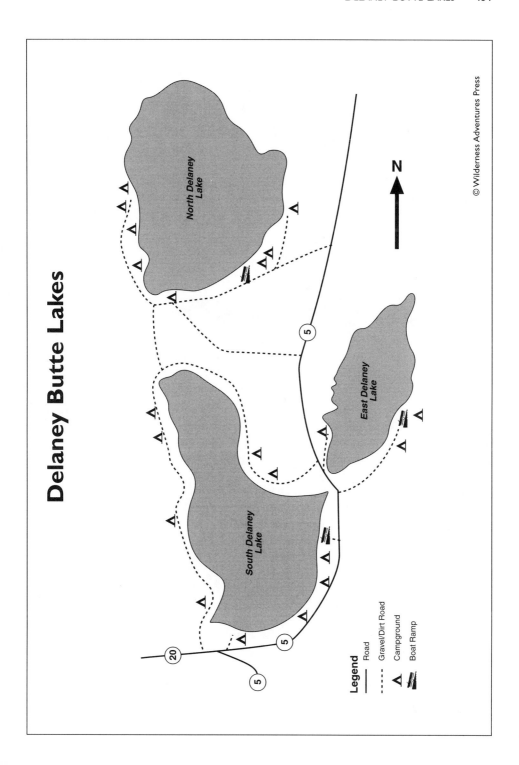

N

© Wilderness Adventures Press

Legend
— Road
‑‑‑ Gravel/Dirt Road
▲ Campground
🚤 Boat Ramp

North Delaney Lake

South Delaney Lake

East Delaney Lake

A large brown waiting to be released at Delaney Butte. (Photo by Jim Neiberger)

brown trout in this lake during fall for hatchery reproduction. In fact, the healthy population of browns in North Delaney supplies trout for most of the state's stocking program. To help protect this valuable fishery, all trout between 14 and 20 inches must be released immediately. The bag limit on non-essential spawners is 2 fish.

While North Delaney can fish well on almost any day, there are a couple of prime times to hang your flippers in North Delaney.

June offers the damselfly hatch, and those insects may last through summer, providing excellent opportunities to take large fish on nymphs. The peak of the hatch arrives around July 4. The nymphs get active late in the morning on their vulnerable trek toward dry land. Brown trout cruise the outer edge of weed beds, picking off the damsel nymphs as they swim out into the open. The best weed beds are on the southeast side of the lake. Position yourself between the weed bed and shore while casting a #12 olive swimming damsel nymph over the top of the bed. Strip your offering back to the tube.

A 9- to 10-foot, 5- or 6-weight rod is great for casting from a float tube. A floating line with a 12-foot leader tapered to 5X is a good setup for this situation. Split shot can be added to adjust the sink rate of the fly.

Around noon, damsels will crawl onto your float tube with you. Campbell, who fishes the lake avidly, exclaims, "This damselfly hatch is totally insane! It's pretty spooky seeing all these bugs swimming by your float tube."

Personally, I find the hatch frustrating. When I first fished the lake, I'd heard this damselfly thing was awesome. I found out I had a lot to learn. I could see the nymphs swimming by, and I saw the occasional flash of a trout feeding, but no luck.

It took 45 minutes to figure out the damsels were moving toward the shore while my fly was landing near the shore and moving back toward me. I got out of the tube and stood on the bank. That was the ticket. Soon enough, an 18-inch brown trout was at my feet waiting to be released.

If you're not a nymph fisher, the damsel hatch can provide some limited options. Late in the evenings, adult imitations, like Stalcup's adult damselfly, will draw fish up top. In fact, it's not uncommon to see trout come out of the water trying to catch a damsel in flight.

Prior to the damselfly hatch, you can find some good action when a large brown caddis emerges. Expect to see the bug in late morning. It drives trout nuts.

Steve Henderson, a guide for Bucking Rainbow Outfitters, said, "The caddis hatch is nothing short of spectacular. A high floating Goddard caddis in sizes 10 to 14 best imitates these motor boating caddis." He adds, "It's not uncommon to see a caddis motoring on the water for over 100 feet before taking flight or disappearing in a thrashing rise."

When insects disappear in those swirls, count on a large trout having made the disturbance. Those large caddis are a quality meal, and the fish that eat them are healthy specimens. Fish over 20 inches are not uncommon.

Caddis can be present in the evenings, too, and North Delaney is an especially good evening fishery. During that time, try a large size 10 to 12 rusty orange caddis and hang on! An orange-colored fly against the orange backdrop of the sunset works very well.

Callibaetis mayflies may hatch at the same time as caddis. It's always fun to watch mayflies hatch, but if there are caddis on the water, stick with caddis patterns. However, when you see mayflies on the water in the evening, go with a rusty spinner or a Poor's witch; these work well when the mayfly spinners move back to the water to lay eggs.

You do not have to wait until summer to catch fish at North Delaney. In fact, in April a large size 12 black midge hatches, and its presence sparks the first significant feeding activity of the year. "A very thin-bodied, black soft hackle scooting through the top foot of water can draw an aggressive take when trout are bulging," said Chuck Prather of Flyfishing Services in Littleton. "A number 12 black gnat or a standard hackled midge pattern works for trout that decide to feed directly off the surface."

In the off times when surface activity is not present, several nymph patterns will take fish. Scuds are a year-round food source, but they are most effective right after ice-off. Olive, orange, and tan patterns, tied on #12 to #16 nymph hooks cover the more popular patterns. Prince nymphs, ginger hare's ears, and cased peeking caddis nymphs are all good searching patterns. Concentrate your efforts around the weed beds in the south part of the lake in 8 to 20 feet of water.

If you prefer fishing streamers, drag a big black woolly bugger slowly along the edges of bottom-hugging vegetation

During the electric season, be prepared for nasty thunderstorms moving over the hills from the west. It is best to get the hell off the lake before a storm gets too close, or you will get wet and possibly pan-fried. A graphite fly rod doubles as an excellent lightening rod. Storms move fast and can be violent.

There is unimproved camping adjacent to the lake. The best sites are located on the west side of the lake.

South and East Delaney Butte Lakes

South Delaney recently changed to a fly and lure only lake, and although a lot of people squawked about it, the fishery has since improved. Although East is the smallest of the three Delaney Butte lakes, flyfishers should not overlook this water.

Even though the lakes are all close together, they fish quite differently and hatches can be localized; you may find bugs hatching and fish feeding on one while nothing happens on another.

The south and east lakes are prime Callibaetis water. Starting in the latter part of May, continuing into July, the big gray mayfly offers a good shot at some large trout.

Fishing the nymphal stage of the mayfly hatch proves very effective. The actual nymph has a distinctive olive wingcase and legs. A fly called a parrot Callibaetis, introduced to me by Rich Pilatzke, is an excellent pattern. It has a few moose body fibers for a tail, and the abdomen is made of light hare's ear and ribbed with fine gold wire. The wingcase is made from the green fibers from a parrot feather; hence the name. The tips of the feather are pulled back for the legs.

Nymphs can be fished either with a sink-tip line or suspended from a strike indicator on a floating line. Concentrate most of your efforts in the north half of both lakes. Vegetation grows dense in the 6- to 15-foot range, and those weedy areas host the most significant Callibaetis populations.

Callibaetis emerge around 10 or 11 am. In late May, when the water is cool, try a size 14 crippled mayfly pattern early in the hatch. Mayflies become trapped in the surface film and are slow getting off the water. The cripple will accurately match those struggling insects.

You will likely find Callibaetis duns and spinners on the water throughout the afternoon and early evening, too, and trout usually rise for them.

As with all the Delaney lakes, a great damsel hatch starts in June and continues into August. Cast a marabou damselfly nymph from shore and then retrieve it. From a tube or boat, work a fly toward and parallel to shore.

In low light conditions —early mornings, late evenings, and overcast days—a large black leech imitation, preferably a woolly bugger, trolled along the weed edges will entice some fish to 18 inches—a large fish in these lakes.

Camping is available in several areas around the lakes.

Lake Facts: North Delaney Butte

Seasons
* For flyfishing, from ice-out to ice-on

Special Regulations
* Artificial flies and lures only. Bag and possession limit for trout is 2 fish. All brown trout between 14 and 20 inches must be released immediately. Boating prohibited if it creates a whitewater wake.
* Gold Metal Water

Trout
* Browns over 20 inches are caught regularly.
* Rainbows: not many in the lake but the ones caught will be hefty.

Lake Size
* 160 acres

Lake Character
* A brown trout fishery at 8,145 feet in elevation. The basic shape and contours of the lake resemble a bowl reaching a depth of 27 feet. Large weed beds form in the summer, providing shelter and an amazing amount of food sources.

Boat Ramp
* South side of the lake

Maps
* *Colorado Atlas & Gazetteer*, page 17
* Fish-n-Map Company, 303-421-5994

Lake Facts: East Delaney Butte

Seasons
* For flyfishing, from ice-out to ice-on

Special Regulations
* Artificial flies and lures only. Bag and possession limit for trout is 2 fish. Boating prohibited if it creates a whitewater wake.

Trout
* Rainbows average 14–16 inches
* Snake River cutthroat

Lake Size
* 80 acres

Lake Character

- Smallish lake sitting at 8,113 feet elevation. A good mix of rainbows and cutthroat trout to 16 inches. The northeast corner of the lake has a sharp drop off to a depth of 24 feet, which makes for great fishing opportunities.

Boat Ramp

- Southeast side of the lake

Maps

- *Colorado Atlas & Gazetteer*, page 17
- Fish-n-Map Company, 303-421-5994

Lake Facts: South Delaney Butte

Seasons

- For flyfishing, from ice-out to ice-on

Special Regulations

- Artificial flies and lures only. Bag and possession limit for trout is 2 fish. Boating prohibited if it creates a whitewater wake.

Trout

- Rainbows over 18 inches are common.
- Snake River cutthroat have a good population and grow well here.

Lake Size

- 170 acres

Lake Character

- The largest of the Delaney Butte chain, it sits at 8,115 feet elevation. The southeast end of the lake has good break lines to hold trout any time of the year. Good weed beds develop in the northeastern side of the lake. The deepest spot in the lake is 21 feet.

Boat Ramp

- East side of the lake

Maps

- *Colorado Atlas & Gazetteer*, page 17
- Fish-n-Map Company, 303-421-5994

DELANEY BUTTE LAKES MAJOR HATCHES

Insect	A	M	J	J	A	S	O	N	Time	Flies
Midge								■	M/A/E	Olive Biot Midge #12–#18; Brown Biot Midge #12–#18; Black Beauty #12–#18; Blood Midge #12–#18; Feather Duster Midge #14–#18; Black Beauty Pupa #12–#18; CDC Biot Suspender Midge #12–#18; Gray Soft Hackle #12–#18; Griffith's Gnat #14–#18; Palomino Midge #14–#18
Damselflies					■				M/A	Swimming Damsel #8–#12; Flashback Damsel #8–#12; Para-damsel #8–#12; Brown Damsel #10–#14; Crystal-winged Damsel #8–#12; Stalcup's Adult Damselfly #8–#12; Marabou Damsel Nymph #8–#12
Caddis				■					A/E	Olive Caddis Nymph #10–#16; Breadcrust #10–#16; LaFontaine's Sparkle Caddis Pupa, Brown #10–#16; Brown Elk Hair Caddis #10–#16; Brown Goddard Caddis #10–#16; Dark Macramé Caddis #10–#16; Lawson's Caddis Emerger, Brown #10–#16; Spent Partridge Caddis #10–#16
Scuds								■	M/A/E	Olive Scud #12–#16; Orange Scud #10–#16; 19½ Scud #12–#18; Tan Scud #12–#16; Flashback Scud #12–#16

HATCH TIME CODE: M = morning; A = afternoon; E = evening; D = dark; SF = spinner fall; / = continuation through periods.

DELANEY BUTTE LAKES MAJOR HATCHES (CONT.)

Insect	A	M	J	J	A	S	O	N	Time	Flies
Streamers	■	■	■	■	■	■	■	■	M/A/E	Black Woolly Bugger #2–#10; Brown Woolly Bugger #4–#10; Spruce Fly #4–#10; Dark Spruce Fly #4–#10; Black-nosed Dace #6–#8; Muddler Minnow #4–#10; Steve's BRO Bug #6–#10
Callibaetis			■	■	■				M/A	Olive Biot Nymph #14–#16; Olive Callibaetis Nymph #14–#18; Ginger Hare's Ear #14–#16; RS-2 #14–#16; Pheasant Tail Nymph #12–#16; Beadhead Pheasant Tail Nymph #14–#16; Flashback Pheasant Tail Nymph #14–#16; Olive Quill Emerger #14–#16; Parachute Adams #12–#16; Gray Comparadun #12–#16; Rusty Spinner #12–#16; Quigley Cripple #14
Blue-winged Olive						■	■		M	Olive Biot Nymph #16–#18; RS-2 #16–#18; Pheasant Tail Nymph #16–#20; Beadhead Pheasant Tail Nymph #16–#20; Flashback Pheasant Tail Nymph #16–#20; Olive Quill Emerger #18–#20; AK's Olive Quill #16–#18; Parachute Adams #12–#20; Olive Comparadun #16–#20; Gray Spinner #18–#20; CDC Baetis Dun #16–#20; Air-flo Cut-wing Dun #16–#20

HATCH TIME CODE: M = morning; A = afternoon; E = evening; D = dark; SF = spinner fall; / = continuation through periods.

North Park Hub City
Walden
Population–890 • Elevation–8,099 • Area Code–970

ACCOMMODATIONS
Little Grizzly Creek Ranch, 777 CR 1 / 723-4209 / web page: www.little-grizzly-creek.com/lgc / email: / Private flyfishing at the guest ranch / $$$
Whistling Elk Ranch, P.O. Box 2, Rand 80473 / 970-723-8311 / Private flyfishing
North Park Motel, 625 Main / 723-4271 / 16 units / $$
Village Inn, 409 Main / 723-4378 / 10 units / Dogs allowed / $$

BED AND BREAKFAST
Winding River B and B, 715 4th Street / 723-4587, 723-4565 / Proprietors: Darleen West and Debbie Holsinger / $$$

CAMPING
North Park KOA Campground, 53337 Highway 14 / 723-4310 / 5 cabins, 29 RV sites, and 5 tent sites / Showers
Richard's RV Park, P.O. Box 410 / 723-4407 / 33 sites at the south end of Lake John

RESTAURANTS
Coffee Pot Inn, 460 Main / 723-4670 / Good breakfast / Open 6AM–10PM / Cocktails / $
Elk Horn Bar and Cafe, 486 Main / 723-9996 / Open 6AM–9PM / Cocktails /$
Paradise Lanes, 680 Main / 723-8616 10AM–9PM Monday–Saturday / Cocktails / $
Teedo's Drive-In, 508 Main / 723-8272

FLY SHOPS AND SPORTING GOODS
Flies Only Tackle Shop, Box 37, Cowdrey 80434, 723-8248 or Box 968, Walden 80480, 723-4741/ Owner: Jay Edwards / Fly shop / Great local information
Corkle's Little Market, 1 mile north of Walden / 723-8211 / Fishing supplies & licenses
Sportsman Supply, 400 Main / 723-4343
Walden Hardware, 467 Main / 723-4655

HOSPITALS
Routt Memorial Hospital, 80 Park Avenue, Steamboat Springs / 879-1322

AIRPORTS
Steamboat Springs Airport, 879-9042
Yampa Valley Airport, 276-3669 / American Airlines: 800-433-7300 / Delta: 800-221-1212 / United Express: 800-241-6522 / Continental Express: 800-523-3273

AUTO SERVICE
Texan's Tune-Up, 197 CR 17A / 723-4608

FOR MORE INFORMATION
North Park Chamber of Commerce
P.O. Box 66 / 491 Main
Walden, CO 80480

Routt National Forest
P.O. Box 158
Walden, CO 80480

Warmwater Flyfishing

This warmwater flyfishing section is a little different than material you might find in other Colorado angling guidebooks. But over the last five years, warmwater flyfishing has become very popular throughout the United States. Fortunately, Colorado offers some of the best options: largemouth bass, tiger muskie, carp, northern pike and even walleye, among other species, are attainable for the flyfisher in Colorado.

I've lived in the Front Range of Colorado all my life, and I grew up a half-mile from a little sand pit that offered yellow perch and bluegills. I'd go down to the pit with my meager assemblage of tackle and spend days on end hooking those panfish. It was great fun.

How quickly we forget things. I've lived in Aurora almost 15 years, without giving warmwater fishing a serious try until the last couple years. I should have done it sooner! The Denver Metro area offers some of the best warmwater action in the state, and there is ample access to most waters. Here is some helpful information that can be applied when you fish any of the area warmwater fisheries.

Food Sources and Imitations

Most of the lakes in the metro area have a wide range of food sources. Crawfish, many different kinds of shad, flathead minnows, frogs, leeches, terrestrials, dragonflies, damselflies, midges, and Callibaetis mayflies are all included on the menu. Popular patterns to imitate those food sources include Whitlock's crayfish, zonker, D's minnow, Clouser's minnow, bunny leech, deer hair poppers, cork panfish popper, and woolly buggers. Insect imitations should include Kaufmann's dragon nymph, marabou damsel nymph, any beadhead pattern, hoppers and beetles, and even dry flies like an Adams, a Wulff, or an irresistible.

Regulations and Bag Limits

Although the current regulations apply through the year 2000, it's always a good idea to check the current regulation status of the water you wish to fish. A regulation booklet is available at most fly shops and sporting goods outlets. Current limits include:

- Largemouth Bass—5
- Smallmouth Bass—5
- Spotted Bass—5
- White Bass—10
- Wiper—10
- Crappie—10
- Bluegill and perch—20
- Walleye and saugeye—5

Barry Reynolds and John Berryman, two warmwater flyfishing enthusiasts, were kind enough to take time out of their busy writing schedules to put together information on some of their favorite warmwater lakes for this book.

The following information has been provided by Berryman and Reynolds and should lead you to some exciting days on Colorado's wonderful warmwater fisheries. Enjoy!

Horsetooth Reservoir

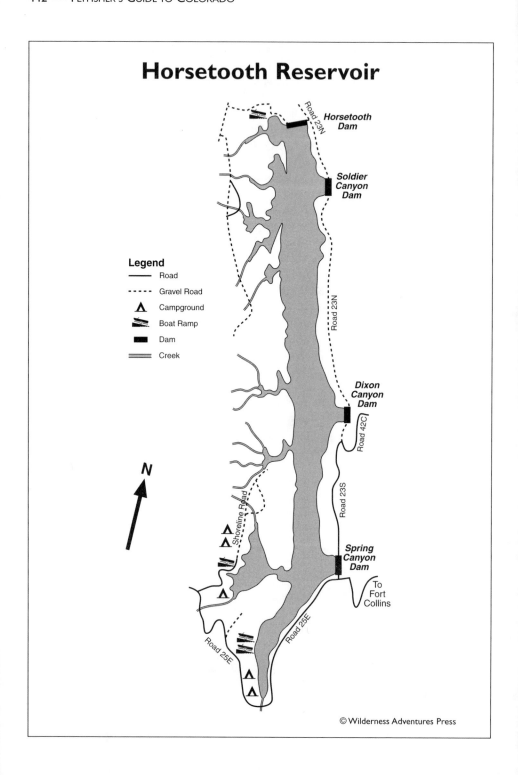

Legend
— Road
- - - Gravel Road
△ Campground
Boat Ramp
■ Dam
Creek

Road 23N

Horsetooth
Dam

Soldier
Canyon
Dam

Road 23N

Dixon
Canyon
Dam

Road 42C

N

Shoreline Road

Road 23S

Spring
Canyon
Dam

To
Fort
Collins

Road 25E

Road 25E

© Wilderness Adventures Press

HORSETOOTH RESERVOIR

Horsetooth Reservoir is located immediately west of Fort Collins, Colorado. The 1,850-acre reservoir is formed by a series of four dams.

Long and thin in shape, Horsetooth averages about a half-mile wide and is about 7 miles long. Because the lake is so close to Fort Collins, it can receive heavy use, particularly on weekends. But thoughtful lake managers have designated most of the coves in the lake as wakeless areas, and an angler can usually find a calm place to fish that is not prey to hordes of waterskiers and jetboaters.

Naturally, for a lake of this size a boat is helpful. During the week, a small boat or canoe will probably do the trick, but during weekends, when the lake becomes crowded with recreational boaters, a larger boat is recommended. If you are restricted to a small boat or even a float tube, hug the shore.

For the float tube fisher, there is some good news; the lake is reasonably accessible by roads and trails. All of the dam areas can be accessed by road, and most of the coves can be accessed either by gravel roads or footpaths/bike trails. A mountain bike and a back-packed belly boat will provide access to much of the lake's most productive fishing areas. The coves are also reasonably sheltered from the wind, again making them attractive to belly boaters and small craft.

The news is less favorable for wading anglers. In most areas of the lake, the bottom slopes off rather quickly. Those who choose to wade will probably be limited to staying within a few feet of shore, or to seeking places on the shore where there is room for a backcast.

Horsetooth Reservoir is best accessed off of I-25. Take exit 265 (Harmony Street), drive through Fort Collins, and follow the signs to the reservoir. A nonboater can gain admission to the lake for $5 a day; boaters pay an additional $5.

There are four boat ramps available, all on the west side of the lake. Two are located at the southern end of the lake (South Bay, a restaurant, is also located there). One is located in Inlet Bay (there is also a marina at Inlet Bay), and the fourth is located at the far north end of the reservoir.

Fee campgrounds, totaling 189 spaces and equipped with tables and fire grates, are also located near the boat ramps. On weekends, these fill up quickly. More adventurous people camp in the coves, some sleeping aboard larger boats, others pitching a tent ashore. These areas can also become a tight squeeze on weekends, and sanitary facilities are not available.

As one would expect of a lake of this size, the food sources are varied. Crayfish, a variety of minnows, young-of-the-year gamefish, and aquatic insects are all available to the rainbow trout, lake trout, crappie, largemouth and smallmouth bass, and walleye that inhabit the lake.

Most flyfishers visit the lake for its bass and rainbow trout, though a few flyfishers report success with walleyes, particularly early in the year, at night or during low light conditions.

For the bass fly rodder, the rip-rap areas along dams and the rocky rubble at the points of the lake's many coves are usually productive. These areas, particularly on the east, or "dam side" of the lake, can be exposed to wind. For this reason, and because bass flies are typically larger than trout flies, 6- or 7-weight rods are helpful, particularly for anglers who do not have access to a boat and who may need to punch a fly out against the wind.

In the mornings and evenings, hair, cork, or foam poppers are often productive. Later in the day, Clouser minnows, larger woolly buggers and rabbit strip minnows are good choices.

Because the shore slopes off quickly in most areas, sink-tip or full-sink lines will help an angler get his offering down to the fish.

The lake's population of stocked rainbows can be found in the inlet areas of coves (making them reasonably accessible to the wading/walking flyrodder), and over rocky or graveled bottoms along the west side of the lake. Some of these graveled areas may be difficult to reach without a boat and almost all of them are exposed to wind and wakes from powerboats. Dry flies are generally more effective in the morning and evening, and such basic patterns as an Adams or a dark and light Cahill work fine.

During the day, and particularly when boating activity is high, large swimming nymphs (dragons, damsels) and streamers (woolly buggers, Clouser minnows, zonkers, etc.) are more productive. Once again, a sink-tip or full-sink line will be helpful, and heavier rods will be appropriate for flyfishers who may have to fight the wind.

Walleyes are found in the corners of the dams on the east side of the lake and over gravel areas on the west side of the lake. On a day-to-day basis, the walleyes will be deeper than the rainbows that inhabit the same areas, and full-sink lines—and patience—are a necessity during daylight hours. At night, or during gloomy days, walleyes can often be somewhat shallower, permitting anglers who are equipped with sink-tip lines to get a crack at them.

Minnow imitations are the way to go for walleyes, and Zonkers, rabbit strip minnows, and, especially, heavily-weighted Clousers are all good choices. A good map of the lake is available from the Fish-n-Map Company. For lake information, call 970- 226-4517.

PUEBLO RESERVOIR

Pueblo Reservoir, a 4,500-acre impoundment, is located a few miles west of Pueblo, Colorado.

The irregularly shaped impoundment, formed by the damming of the Arkansas River, is generally oriented on an east-west axis. The lake is about 9 miles long, and some of the coves (Boggs Creek, Rock Creek) are themselves several miles long.

The lake is accessed by driving west from Pueblo on either US 50 or Colorado 96. US 50 will provide the most immediate access to the north side of the reservoir and to the North Shore Marina, while Colorado 96 will provide the most immediate access to the south side of the reservoir, to the South Shore Marina, and to a fishing access road which is found off of Old Highway 96.

For the shore-bound angler, the Colorado 96 access route is probably the best choice. For the boater, either route will work fine. For the camper, Colorado 96 provides more immediate access to more campsites.

Pueblo Reservoir

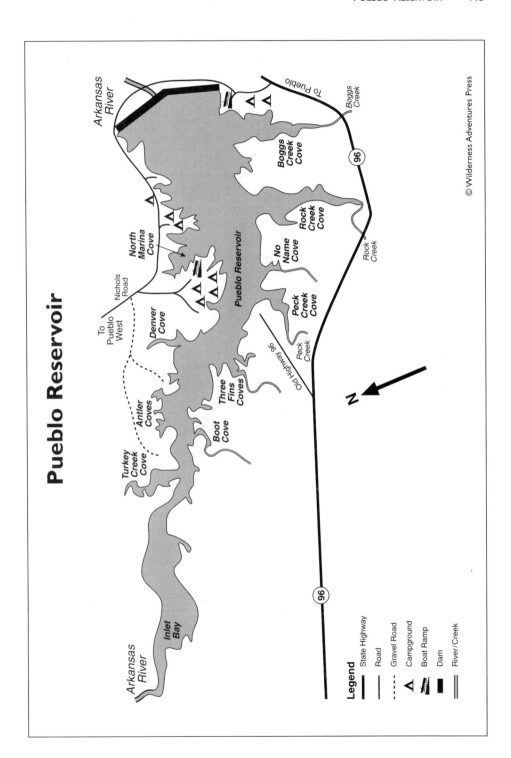

Legend

▬▬	State Highway
—	Road
┈┈	Gravel Road
▲	Campground
▨	Boat Ramp
▮	Dam
▬	River/Creek

In terms of lake character, Pueblo Reservoir has much in common with Horsetooth Reservoir. Like Horsetooth, Pueblo's proximity to a major population center (Colorado Springs/Pueblo) means that the lake can receive heavy pressure, particularly on weekends and holidays. Unfortunately, wakeless areas are harder to find on Pueblo Reservoir, and the fly rodder may have to contend with water skiers, jet skiers, and recreational boaters. Anglers seeking a little solitude need to be on the lake early, or late, in the day. Due to access problems (discussed in more detail below), a boat is even more helpful on Pueblo Reservoir. Unlike Horsetooth, which is comparatively sheltered, Pueblo resides on the prairie. Winds can spring up with very little warning, putting small craft and belly boats in jeopardy. Tent campers will also want to be wary of the wind.

There are 197 campsites clustered in the Northern Plains area of the reservoir, west of the North Shore Marina. Additional campsites are available at Juniper Breaks Campground (northeast of the North Shore Marina) and at Arkansas Campground (adjacent to the South Shore Marina). Like most Colorado prairie campgrounds, trees are few and far between, sites can be dusty in the summer, and awnings or portable sun-rooms can make camping much more pleasant in the dog days of summer. The North Shore and South Shore marinas are well equipped, and rental slips are usually available. However, finding a slip with access to electrical power for battery charging can be a problem.

Unlike Horsetooth, Pueblo is missing the network of roads that makes accessing it reasonably easy. To complicate matters, much of the shoreline consists of very steep bluffs and cliffs. The hiking angler should include rock-scrambling among his skills if he intends to fish the lake from the shore. As mentioned above, a fishing access road, located about .2 miles from the Old Highway 96 turnoff, provides some access to the west end of the reservoir. The terrain here is a little less forbidding, but the ability to scramble will still be required. The north side of the west end of the reservoir can be accessed by taking McCulloch Boulevard south from US 50 to Nichols Road. A little more than .2 miles past a railroad crossing, a dirt road heads roughly west and provides access to the lake.

Generally speaking, for the shore or belly boat angler, the east end of the reservoir is steeper and more difficult to access than the west end. Though a boat is very helpful, because the lake can experience strong winds, anglers, and particularly belly boaters and users of small craft, should keep an eye on the weather at all times. This is particularly true on weekends, when an approaching storm can result in traffic jams at the boat ramps.

The lake provides good habitat for its varied populations of fish, and for the flyrodder, Pueblo is a consistent bass lake.

Casting close to undercut bluffs can produce everything from smallies to crappies to rainbows to walleyes. During the day, the fly rodder will probably be most successful on smallmouths. Mornings and evenings can be good for surface flies, while during the day, streamers such as Clouser's minnow, rabbit-strip flies, and rubberlegged jigs, such as a Calcascieu pigboat, will probably be most productive.

As evening arrives, or during any low light condition, walleyes move into water that is shallow enough to permit reasonably effective flyfishing, providing a sink-tip or full-sink line is used. Once again, minnow imitations, as discussed above, are usually the way to go.

Most of the reservoir's coves are productive, particularly at the points leading into the coves and in areas of submerged brush, often found toward the back of the coves. Generally, the entrance to a cove will consist of steep bluffs, often with significant structure and undercuts. These areas will often hold fish.

As the angler moves back into the coves, the bluffs gradually decrease in size, giving way to areas of submerged brush and rock rubble. These areas can also hold fish, with the caveat that in the height of summer, the water temperatures may become too high for smallies, crappies, rainbows, and walleyes. Generally speaking, the largemouth will be able to remain in the shallows—assuming their food doesn't leave for cooler water.

Pueblo Reservoir is deepest and widest at the dam, and "upstream" (east) of the dam the lake gradually narrows and becomes much shallower. The narrower and shallower portions of the lake warm first in the spring, so if the water temperatures close to the dam are a bit low, motoring upstream is in order.

Pueblo's water level can, and does, fluctuate dramatically from year to year—perhaps over 20 feet at times. Low water conditions can make finding areas of flooded timber and brush quite simple. For this reason, the topographic map available from the Fish-n-Map Company is particularly helpful.

JOHN MARTIN RESERVOIR

Like Pueblo Reservoir, John Martin Reservoir is an impoundment of the Arkansas River. John Martin is east of Pueblo, just south of US 50 between Las Animas and Lamar. The lake is oriented in an east-west direction, and the north side of the reservoir is reasonably accessible by roads and trails. A railroad track parallels the south side of the reservoir quite closely, making access by car or foot to the southern half of the east end of the reservoir very difficult. All of the dam areas can be accessed by road, and most of the coves can be reached either by gravel roads or footpaths/bike trails. Most of the access roads are actually county roads, and referral to Fish-n-Map Company's map of the reservoir will be very helpful.

Because the lake is more distant from large population centers, it usually receives less pressure than Horsetooth or Pueblo reservoirs. Anglers who are able to fish during the week will often have the lake to themselves.

Civilization is found in the nearby towns of Las Animas and Lamar; for those who want a bit of comfort, Las Animas is probably a better choice than Lamar.

Just below the dam, a very nice campground (next to the tiny Lake Hasty) can be found. Unlike most Colorado prairie campgrounds, the Lake Hasty Campground features plenty of shade and grass and is overall one of Colorado's nicer prairie campgrounds. Open camping areas are available on the north side of the lake, just upstream from the dam. This is traditional Colorado tent-on-the-prairie camping.

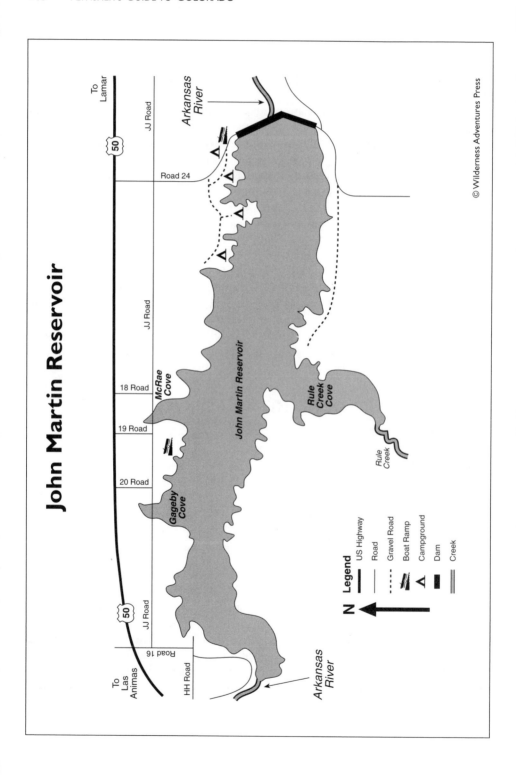

© Wilderness Adventures Press

Trees are few, it can be dusty, and the campsites are very exposed to wind. However, enduring those problems may be well worth your time.

John Martin is home to largemouth and smallmouth bass, perch, walleye, white bass, crappie, bluegill, carp, bullhead, channel catfish, and wipers. For the fly rodder, the species-of-choice are the largemouth bass, smallmouth bass, crappie, wiper, and walleye.

Topographically, John Martin is a gentler impoundment than Pueblo. The rocky bluffs can be present, particularly during low water (like Pueblo Reservoir, John Martin's water level can fluctuate dramatically), but overall they are not as steep or forbidding as those of Pueblo Reservoir. Prior to the damming of the river, these gentler slopes provided a good home to a variety of trees and brush; subsequent to the flooding of the reservoir, the brush became fish habitat, and large portions of the lake are still completely covered with brush.

During low water, the brush is easy to find. During high water, referral to the Fish-n-Map Company's map will help an angler locate areas of submerged brush.

In addition to fishing the brush, the reservoir's points and coves can be productive. Generally speaking, the shallower areas will be home to bass, and the deeper areas, near the entrances, will hold white bass and wipers. Although the impoundment doesn't feature precipitous dropoffs, the shoreline still shelves quite rapidly. Moving a few boat-lengths farther out into the lake can take an angler from bass country to white bass and wiper country.

For John Martin's warmwater species, fly selection is similar to patterns used at Horsetooth and Pueblo reservoirs.

This reservoir fishes especially well for white bass and wipers, both of which are true bass (the wiper is a sterile hybrid between the white bass and the striped bass). Both are schooling fish, aggressive predators, and spring spawners (the sterile wiper exhibits a false spawn). Both offer fine sport to the fly angler.

The significant difference between the two fish is this: a nice white bass weighs perhaps 3 pounds, is fine sport on your trout rod, and the resulting tussle will please you greatly. In contrast, a big wiper may weigh over 20 pounds and it will bend your 8-weight just as far as a 20-pound true striper would. The resulting battle will (or should) be thrilling, if not terrifying.

While many wipers and whites are caught on spinning gear, and often by trolling, the fly rodder has the best odds of tagging a scrappy white or a brutal wiper. Why? Both fish will come into the shallows in the spring to spawn. At this time, they are feeding aggressively, and both fish can make their presence known with splashing and associated fandangos. Because these fish are in shallow water, unweighted streamers (deceivers, unweighted woolly buggers, and zonkers) are probably the first weapon of choice. Baitfish colors (silver, blue, silver/olive, etc.) seem to be preferred. But do not ignore surface flies at this time. Both whites and wipers are, for lack of a better word, pumped-up during the spawn, particularly in the morning and evening.

Whites, because of their smaller size, will respond best to flies that are between 1.5 and 2 inches long. The bigger wipers will take much larger offerings. Three- to 4-inch streamers may be required to get their attention.

Mornings and evenings are also productive, due to the presence of baitfish. In fact, schools of baitfish that hide in deep water or in cover during the day will often take advantage of low light conditions to visit "food factories" in the shallows.

Often, whites and wipers (and for that matter, walleyes, bass, and trout) will follow them in. While most fish are likely to feed quietly, whites and wipers tend to gang up on their prey. Watch for schools of baitfish milling around in confusion, or even leaping from the water. Try to assess where the threat is coming from, and, even if you can't see the predatory whites or wipers, cast in that direction.

Whites and wipers will occasionally succeed in driving a school of suspended, midlake baitfish to the surface. An unmistakable commotion is the result, with doomed baitfish leaping from the water. You'll see larger whites or wipers splashing in pursuit. Overhead, flocks of birds circle, just waiting to snap up cripples. The action at such a site can be fast and furious for a stealthy angler who can plop a baitfish imitation into the center of the fracas.

The well-equipped angler will have two rods ready. The first will contain floating line and an unweighted streamer, or even a popper or diver. This combination works well when the fish are at the surface. Generally, if a strike is going to happen, it happens very quickly. The second rod will contain high-density sink tip, or even fullsink line, and it will be tipped with a weighted baitfish imitation. Zonkers, Clousers, rabbit strip minnows, D's minnows, and large beadhead woolly buggers are all good choices to tie on that line. This setup is kept ready for use when the baitfish eventually scatter or succeed in moving back toward the depths. At such times, commotion on the water will magically, and almost instantly, cease. Often, the combination of a sinking line and weighted fly will enable the angler to tag another fish or two.

When the action wanes, stop what you are doing and just look for fish—they may repeat their previous performance.

NEENOSHE, NEEGRONDA, AND QUEENS RESERVOIRS

Northeast of John Martin Reservoir, north of Lamar, and off US 287 lie three small reservoirs: Neenoshe, Neegronda, and Queens. The three offer excellent action on walleye, perch, crappie, largemouth, channel catfish, white bass, northern pike, bluegill, bullhead and carp.

At 3,700 acres, Neenoshe is the largest, followed by Neegronda at 3,400 acres and Queens at 1,900 acres. All three reservoirs have boat ramps. Improved campsites are available at Neegronda, while open campsites are found at Neenoshe.

Nearby John Martin Reservoir is the big draw, so these impoundments are typically underused, particularly during the week. To fish these waters, you may have to spend the night next to the shore unless you like to drive. From the reservoirs, you're about 25 miles from the nearest motels. Though camping is far from luxurious, the reasonably remote setting of the reservoirs means you are also somewhat less likely to be rudely awakened to the dulcet tones emanating from a boombox the size of a small piano, wafting across the placid waters at two in the morning.

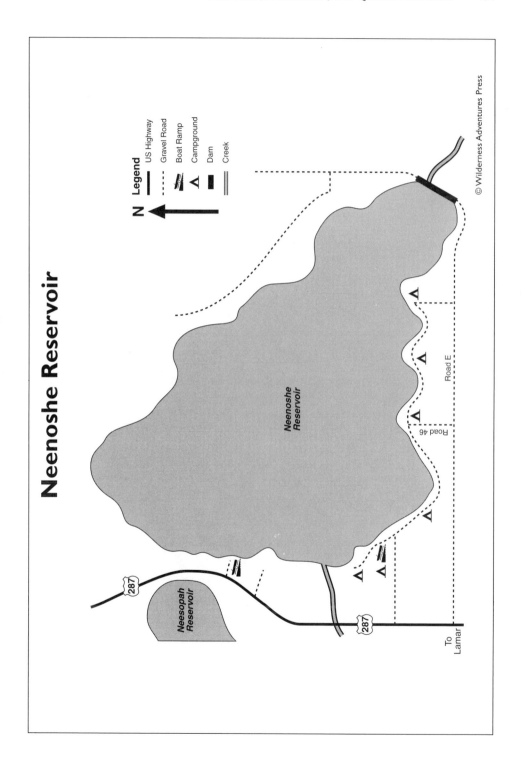

Neegronda Reservoir

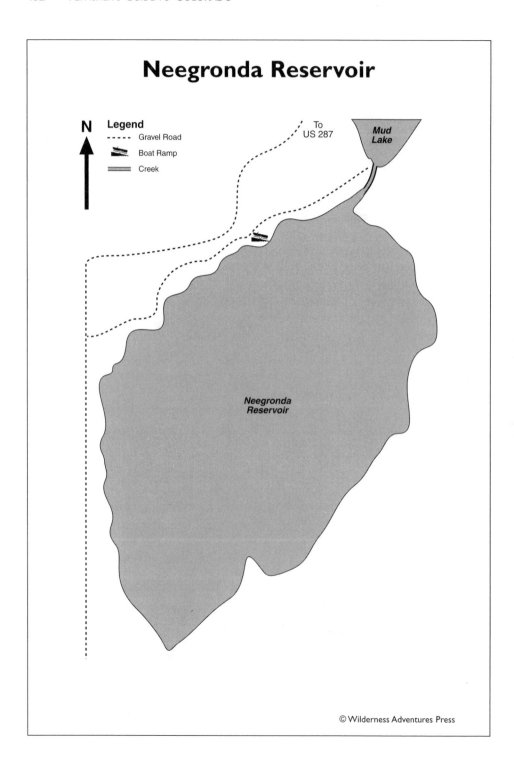

N

Legend
- - - - Gravel Road
Boat Ramp
Creek

To
US 287

Mud
Lake

Neegronda
Reservoir

© Wilderness Adventures Press

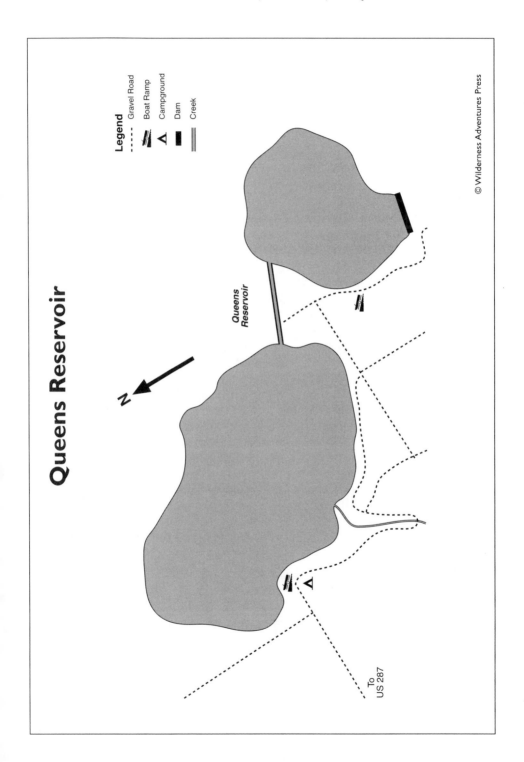

Queens Reservoir

Queens
Reservoir

N

To
US 287

Legend

---- Gravel Road
⚓ Boat Ramp
△ Campground
▬ Dam
═ Creek

Collectively, these reservoirs are great places for belly boats, personal water craft, or canoes and johnboats equipped with small gas or electric motors—provided that the angler keeps an eye on the weather.

These prairie lakes are quite different in character from the reservoirs mentioned previously. Collectively, these reservoirs present the flyfisher with a series of problems, which are tempered by the quality fishing.

Their small size and good shore access mean that they can be fished very efficiently and thoroughly from small craft or belly boats. Unfortunately, there is nothing to stop the wind but a barbed-wire fence. Unwary anglers can get in real trouble, and it can happen very quickly.

The topography is gentle, and large portions of all three impoundments are shallow. In addition, the shorelines are quite smooth, lacking the long, deep coves of the reservoirs discussed previously. The bottom of these reservoirs slopes off gradually, so wading anglers have a good shot at fish. But the wading conditions can be muddy and exhausting.

The deepest portions of Neenoshe are 55 feet deep; large portions of all three impoundments are less than 30 feet deep. Armed with a full-sink line and patience, a fly rodder can cover a great deal of territory but will have to look out for brush.

One of the nicest things about these reservoirs is the lack of large, noisy powerboats and the diversity of species present.

When they fish best, these reservoirs produce all-day action, commencing with shallow, dawn walleyes, northerns, and bass; moving through crappie, perch, bluegills, and even subsurface whites and wipers during the day; ending with more bass, northerns, and walleyes in the evening.

Because of the diversity of fish in these reservoirs, they are good places for your kid to catch his or her first fish, and to do so in a reasonably pristine setting. That diversity also means that whatever you have rattling around in your flybox—from a size 16 Adams to a 3/0 Deceiver—has the opportunity to catch something.

Maps of all three reservoirs are printed on the same map as Pueblo and John Martin Reservoirs by the Fish-n-Map Company. Convenient, eh?

HORSESHOE RESERVOIR AND MARTIN LAKE

Just west of the town of Walsenburg on US 160 in Lathrop State Park, you'll find Horseshoe Reservoir and Martin Lake.

These small lakes are two of the prettiest of the prairie reservoirs. The shorelines have many trees and other greenery, and the "no gas motors" rule on both lakes makes fishing the kind of quiet, contemplative experience that fly-rodders dream of.

Both lakes are suited to canoes, belly boats, johnboats, and the like. The shorelines are very accessible, permitting the less serious anglers the opportunity to baitfish from under the shade of a tree while you go about your "serious" fishing. And your serious fishing is likely to be rewarded.

The lakes feature good populations of fish, some of which will be quite novel to the Colorado angler. In the 170-acre Horseshoe Reservoir, rainbow trout, splake, saugeye, smallmouth, channel catfish, black crappie, cutthroat trout, tiger muskie, and red-eared sunfish can all be found.

On the adjoining 206-acre Martin Lake, anglers can cast to rainbow trout, wiper, channel catfish, blue catfish, and red-eared sunfish. Many anglers regard these two lakes as the most consistent, warm/coolwater fly rod lakes in the state, reporting fish being taken with regularity as long as the lakes are open. Because the lakes are so small, the angler can work likely areas systematically. And, as is the case with the Neenoshe-Neegronda-Queens Reservoir complex, the diversity of species present in Horseshoe and Martin means that just about any fly the angler has in his box has the potential to catch something. Small, trout-sized dries, streamers, and nymphs will work fine on the lakes' populations of trout, sunfish, and crappie. Larger, deeper running streamers like Clousers will do for the lakes' saugeye and splake. Even large bunny-flies, rabbit-strip minnows, D's minnows, and the like will handle subsurface presentations to the bass and tiger muskies found in the lakes. Corks, hair, or foam poppers, divers, and sliders will draw surface strikes.

Topographically, these lakes are quite gentle, and that gently sloping bottom gives fly rodders the ability to cover much of each lake with full-sink or sink-tip lines. Though large parts of these lakes are shallow, wading may be hampered by mud and weeds. A belly boat is probably the best tool for the job. Simple boat ramps are present at each lake, fine for launching canoes and the like. We are unaware of any topographic maps of these lakes.

Though Walsenburg, with modern motels, fast food, and video games, is only about 5 miles away, visitors to Lathrop should strongly consider camping. The campgrounds are some of the nicest prairie campgrounds in the state and feature such welcome amenities as showers and laundromats.

METRO DENVER URBAN LAKES AND RESERVOIRS
by Marty Bartholomew

Traveling in Denver

The metro Denver area consists of Denver proper and several important surrounding cities, including: Aurora to the east; Thornton, Westminster, and Northglenn, to the north; Arvada, Wheatridge, Lakewood, and Golden to the west; and Littleton and Englewood to the south. Traveling the Denver metro area is fairly simple if you familiarize yourself with:

- I-70, which runs east and west.
- I-25, which is the main north-south route.
- Interconnections such as I-225 can be used for traveling the east and southeast.
- I-470 is a quick way to get from the southern-most part of the city to I-70 on the west side of town just before I-70 takes to the foothills.
- US 285 (Hamden Avenue) is another east-west route in the southern part of the city. The westbound lane heads out of town towards Bailey and Fairplay.
- US 6 is also an east-west route. It is for travel in the central part of the city.

• US 36 connects with the northern suburbs from I-25 and on into Boulder. Boulder is about 30 miles northwest of Denver in the beautiful foothills. Warm and cold water fishing are both popular in this area.

Southeast Metro Denver Area

Aurora Reservoir

With the need for more city water storage, Aurora Reservoir was completed and opened to the public in the early 1990s.

Aurora Reservoir is located east of Aurora on Quincy Avenue. From I-225, exit south on Parker Road (Colorado 83) and continue to Quincy Avenue. Turn left (east) on Quincy. Continue eastbound on Quincy about 7 miles. The entrance to the reservoir is 1 mile east of Gun Club Mile Road.

The 820-acre, 100-foot deep lake is home for some heavy duty rainbow and brown trout. Largemouth bass, crappie, yellow perch, wipers, and walleye round out the warmwater species important to the fly angler.

Regular hatches of midges, up to a size 12, damselflies in mid-May though July, and increasing amounts of other food sources keep the fish actively feeding during the most important fishing months.

Boats with electric motors, rowboats, and float tubes are the most popular means of transportation around the lake. With a hard surface trail around the lake, many prefer to ride a bike to get to their favorite spots.

Aurora does offer a daily or a yearly permit that can be purchased at the entrance; the fees are $4 for a daily permit, $25 for the yearly. Trout are limited to 2 in possession. All bass, wipers, and walleye under 15 inches must be returned to the water, while 4 fish over 15 inches may be kept.

Cherry Creek Reservoir

The east entrance to Cherry Creek State Recreational Area is just south of the I-225 and Parker Road (Colorado 83) intersection. Take Parker Road south to Princeton Place and turn west; the park headquarters are just ahead. A State Parks pass is required for vehicles; walk-in trails are abundant at no charge. The west entrance can be found by taking I-225 to the South Yosemite Street exit. Take Yosemite south to Union Avenue and turn left (east) on Union to the west entrance.

Managed by the Colorado Division of Parks and Outdoor Recreation and the Army Corps of Engineers, this park is open 24 hours a day.

This 800-acre bowl of water was built primarily for flood control in the late 1960s. It has managed to become a very popular state park with excellent fishing opportunities. Large walleye, very likely a state record, swim these waters with a variety of other species: wipers, northern pike, tiger muskie, largemouth bass, carp, and stocked rainbow trout are sought by flyfishers. A large population of panfish, such as crappie, yellow perch, bluegill, and green sunfish will keep any respectable angler busy.

The south end of the lake has a regular lumber yard of stumps and logs, providing shelter for a wide variety of species. Largemouth bass up to 4 pounds have been taken in the submerged timber. The water is shallow here, so float tubes work well in this area.

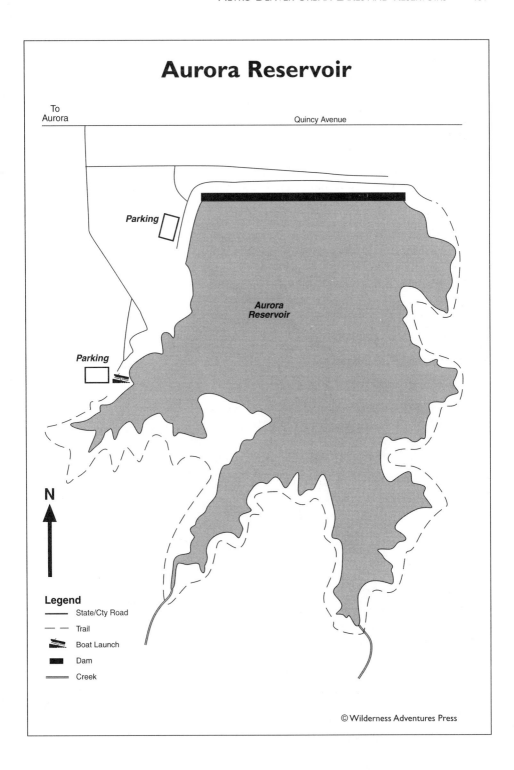

Aurora Reservoir

To
Aurora

Quincy Avenue

Parking

Parking

Aurora
Reservoir

N

Legend
—— State/Cty Road
– – Trail
Boat Launch
Dam
Creek

© Wilderness Adventures Press

Cherry Creek Reservoir

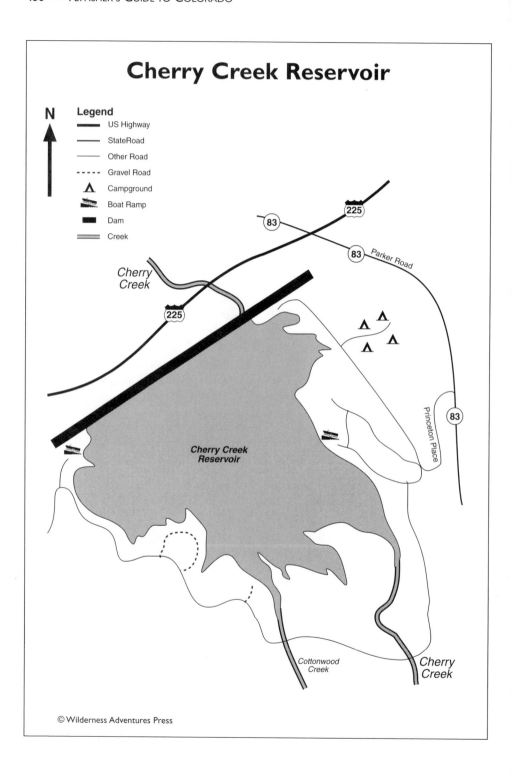

N

Legend
- US Highway
- StateRoad
- Other Road
- Gravel Road
- Campground
- Boat Ramp
- Dam
- Creek

Cherry Creek

225

83

225

83 Parker Road

83

Princeton Place

Cherry Creek
Reservoir

Cottonwood
Creek

Cherry
Creek

© Wilderness Adventures Press

The structure around the west marina is another favorite spot during spring for crappie and smallmouth bass. Small beadhead patterns, damsel nymphs, dragon nymphs, and Whitlock's crayfish jigged along the bottom will entice the spawning panfish.

Southeast of the marina are a series of sandbars that are worth trolling. Sinktip or fullsinking lines are a must for this area. Water depth between the sand bars can reach 25 feet. Clouser's minnows, woolly buggers, and D's minnows trolled behind a belly boat at different depths are proven methods for success.

Another area of Cherry Creek Reservoir that would interest the flyfisher is along the dam. Starting at the tower on the east end of the dam, flaunting small lead or beadhead marabou flies should produce yellow perch. Moving west a few hundred yards through the riprap, another bar, call the Skier Drop, can hold some fish. Rainbows like to hold along the edges of this area. The area from that point extending west to the marina is best known for its walleye. The only advice to pass along for catching these walleye is to fish at night. Clouser's minnows in black, white, blue and white, and chartreuse are the best colors.

Remember, experimenting with depth, flies, and patience is needed to catch walleye.

Quincy Reservoir

If a chance at the state record tiger muskie perks your interest, try Quincy Reservoir; a few have been taken out of this watering hole. This 160-acre reservoir is raw water storage for the City of Aurora, with a water treatment plant located across the street. Quincy is operated as a recreational facility by the Aurora Parks & Recreation Department.

To find Quincy Reservoir, take I-225 to Parker Road (Colorado 83) and exit east. Parker Road veers to the south after the first signal light. From the exit, it is about 2 miles to East Quincy Avenue, where you should turn left (east). The reservoir is 3 miles east of Parker Road on the south side of Quincy. There are two parking lots for anglers.

A handicapped pier is available for those who can't get around as well as they would like, and other handicapped facilities were constructed by a local Trout Unlimited chapter. What might an angler catch off the end of this pier? Glad you asked! Besides tiger muskie, brown and rainbow trout do well here. Artificial habitat structures have been utilized so that largemouth bass and yellow perch also find good cover.

Flyfishing Quincy for trout can be at its best just as the gates open in the spring. Ice is totally off the reservoir before it is opened. Cabin fever can be a chronic problem in late March and early April, so Quincy definitely catches its share of traffic this time of year. Add in good hatches of midges that bring the trout to the surface in feeding frenzies, and you've got a great day ahead of you. Small larval patterns in olives, blacks and reds, fished with a slow upward movement from the bottom, are standard patterns early in the year.

As the fish start to boil just under the surface, emergers and soft-hackled patterns work well. Darrel Sickman, manager at the Trout Fisher in Denver, has used red biot emergers with great success for years. Griffith's gnats, parachute Adams, and standard midge dry flies in sizes 14 to 22 should take care of any surface action.

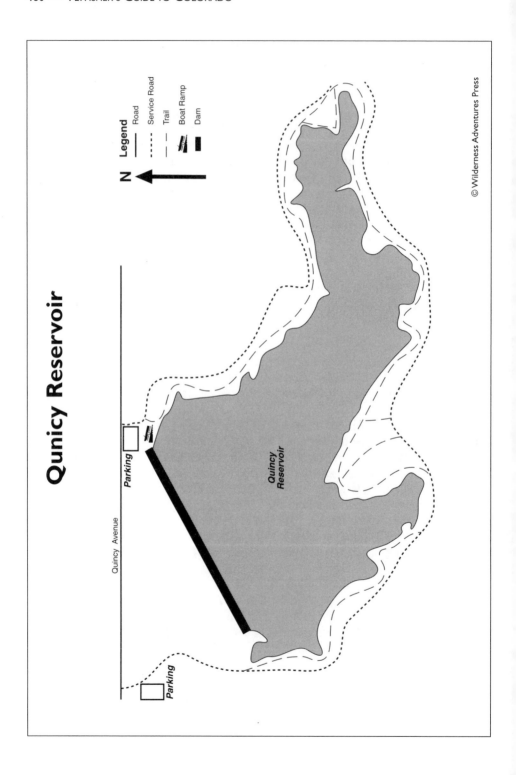

Don't forget to bring some woolly buggers, damsel nymphs, gold ribbed hare's ears, and pheasant tails for nonhatch periods.

May, June, and July bring with them a much more diverse list of food sources, as well as opportunities to catch a full gambit of fish species. Bass will spawn as the water temperature rises to the mid-fifties, making them more aggressive and territorial. Perch look for an easy meal, and the tiger muskies, in turn, are looking for perch. The largemouth bass will take leech and streamer patterns, and yellow perch take a variety of swimming nymphs and small streamers. Tiger muskie are on the prowl for big meals and can surprise you at any time. Large, 2/0 and 3/0 strip minnows and bunny flies, tied in black and purple, work well. D's minnows and Clouser's minnows tied to imitate the local baitfish, such as perch, small bass, and shiners, are favorites. Catching tigers takes a lot of patience.

Callibaetis mayflies start hatching in May, damselflies make their annual migration to the shore, and a few caddis will hatch in the early summer; all can bring on feeding binges.

August and September offer explosive action with terrestrial patterns. Hoppers, ants, and beetles are easy prey for all fish in this reservoir. A foam Madam-X, in a size 10, imitates hoppers. Ant patterns in size 12 and a variety of attractor patterns will also draw strikes.

Anglers shouldn't squawk too loud about the Aurora Parks Permit required to fish here. Rangers are on duty at all times and do check for permits on a regular basis. Yearly and daily passes are available at the ranger hut at the east gate. The number of anglers allowed is limited to 100 at any given time. Other special regulations include:

- Artificial flies and lures only.
- Nonmotorized boats with a permit allowed.
- Tiger muskie under 30 inches must be returned to the water immediately.
- Possession limit on trout is 2 fish, 16 inches or longer.
- All bass under 15 inches must be returned to the water immediately.
- Fishing is prohibited during the winter months.

Southwest Metro Denver Area

Chatfield Ponds

Chatfield Ponds are located on the south end of the Chatfield State Recreation Area. See the following section on Chatfield Reservoir for directions.

The Chatfield ponds, five of them, are loaded with bluegill, crappie, green sunfish, and yellow perch. All can be taken on dry flies. The only crafts allowed on these ponds are belly boats, so the fly angler has a great chance to fish all 140 acres of water in a day without being doused with a speedboat wave.

While kicking around these ponds, both on foot or float tube, watch for cruising largemouth and smallmouth bass. A well presented leech or crawfish pattern will draw strikes. Damselflies are also present throughout summer, and they will take bass, too.

A State Parks pass is required to fish the ponds; however, walk-in access is possible from Colorado 75 at no cost. All bass in possession must be 15 inches or longer.

Chatfield Reservoir

To reach Chatfield Reservoir from I-470, exit south on Wadsworth Boulevard (Colorado 75). Turn left (east) on Deer Creek Canyon Road. This is the north entrance to Chatfield State Recreation Area. The Colorado Division of Parks & Outdoor Recreation manages this facility in conjuction with the Army Corps of Engineers, and a State Parks permit is required. Parking, camping, and picnicking are available throughout the area. A boat ramp is available on the north side of the lake, next to the dam; a boat permit is required to fish here. Boat rentals, handicapped fishing pier, and restrooms are also available.

Brown trout and stocked rainbow trout find a home in the water under this 1,100-acre South Platte River impoundment. In fact, trout can be caught in the river above and below the reservoir. But this isn't the area's only offering: Chatfield has gained a reputation as a smallmouth bass fishery over the last few years. Along with largemouth bass, crappie, carp, green sunfish, walleye, and yellow perch, this reservoir will keep a fly angler on his toes.

All bass in possession must be 15 inches or longer.

South Platte Park Ponds

These ponds are located below Chatfield Reservoir on the north side of I-470. The entrance is west of Santa Fe Drive on west-bound I-470. Originally, these ponds were used as flood protection for the city of Littleton. With flood control now basically out of the picture, these lakes are managed by the City of Littleton and the South Suburban Park & Recreation District as a recreational park.

Fishing and hiking are the primary diversions here. The five ponds total 80 acres, and they offer largemouth bass, bluegill, and yellow perch with a few stocked rainbows around, too.

All bass under 15 inches must be released back into the water immediately. With the special regulations on the bass, an angler has a good shot at a largemouth bass over 2 or 3 pounds.

West Central Metro Denver Area

Bear Creek Reservoir

The entrance to Bear Creek Reservoir is about a mile east of I-470 on Morrison Road. Exit east on Morrison Road (Colorado 8) from I-470, and you can't miss the reservoir. As a recreational project, activities such as hiking, archery, nature and waterfowl study makes this a very diverse facility.

This 205-acre impoundment, completed in 1982, holds largemouth bass, smallmouth bass, bluegill, green sunfish, yellow perch, tiger muskie, and stocked rainbow trout.

From May to September, the lake opens at 6 AM and closes at 10 PM; daily fees are $3, and yearly fees are $25. The visitor will find several picnic areas on the north and the west parts of the park. The Lakewood Department of Community Resources maintains a boat ramp on the north side of the lake and allows motors up to 10 horsepower. Wakes are illegal.

Chatfield Reservoir

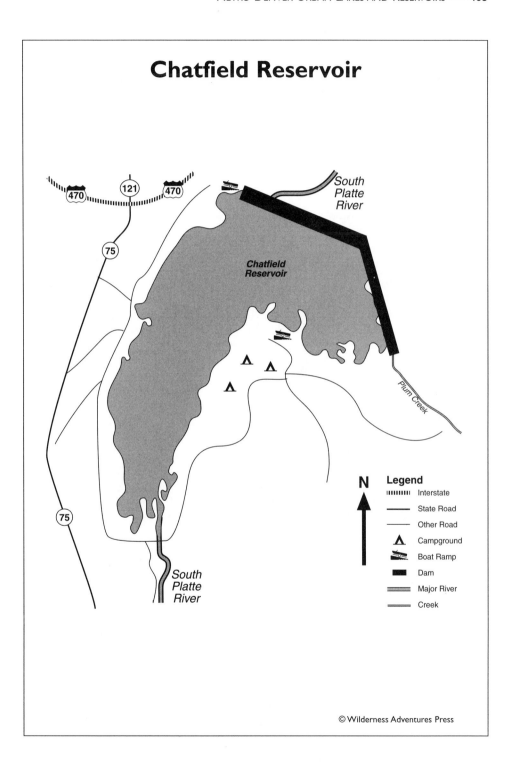

470 121 470

75

South Platte River

Chatfield Reservoir

75

South Platte River

Plum Creek

N

Legend

ꜛꜛꜛꜛꜛ	Interstate
———	State Road
———	Other Road
⛺	Campground
🚤	Boat Ramp
■	Dam
≈≈≈	Major River
≈≈≈	Creek

© Wilderness Adventures Press

Berkeley Lake

The main entrance to Berkeley Lake is on 46th Avenue, between Sheridan Boulevard and Tennyson Street. Another entrance exists on the east side of the lake from Tennyson Street.

Denver Parks and Recreation has the burden of opening this lake to the public at 5 am; it closes at 11 pm. No boats are allowed on this 40-acre lake.

With a good population of fish to be caught here—including largemouth bass, orange-spotted sunfish, crappie, bluegill, green sunfish, and carp—a flyfisher should keep busy. Catchable-sized rainbow trout are also stocked here early in the season.

Crow Hill Lake

From I-70, exit south on Kipling Street. Turn left (east) on 26th Avenue. Parking is on the north side of 26th.

Since wading and float tubing are prohibited here, a hard-surface footpath surrounding this 53-acre lake is the only way to go.

Largemouth bass, bluegill, carp, crappie, yellow perch, and green sunfish are all available. Artificial structures have been utilized in this fairly shallow lake—only 13 feet at its maximum depth—for habitat improvement.

The lake is open from 5 AM to 11 PM during the summer months.

Kendrick Reservoir

One amongst a cluster of ponds in the city of Lakewood, Kendrick Reservoir can be found north of West Jewell Avenue and west of Garrison Street. From US 285 (Hampden Avenue), take Kipling Boulevard north to Jewell. Turn right (east) on Jewell, then left on Garrison. Parking is available on the north side of the lake. Kendrick opens at the break of dawn and is maintained by the Foothills Metropolitan Recreation and Parks District. Boats are prohibited, so all fishing must be from shore.

Kendrick has a wide variety of fish species. The most sought after is, surprisingly, the carp. Carp grow to a healthy size in this shallow lake. A few largemouth bass, lots of bluegill, yellow perch, and other sunfish can be caught.

This 33-acre lake includes a handicapped fishing pier on the southwest shore.

Prospect Park Lakes

The Prospect Park Lakes, including Bass Lake, Prospect Lake, North Prospect Lake, and West Lake, are located south of West 44th Avenue and east of I-70.

All of the lakes have largemouth bass, bluegill, crappie, and green sunfish. The bluegill and bass spawn in late May and June. Damselflies and midges hatch through July, so fishing activity should be concentrated in these months. These are great lakes to dry flyfish for bluegills. These little guys will take just about any dry. Renegades, an Adams, and any dry caddis will do. Long casts are not required.

West Lake, the largest lake at 46 acres, and Bass Lake are south of Clear Creek; fishing on these lakes is by flies and artificial lures only. North Prospect is a 16-acre lake. Prospect, considered the best largemouth bass lake, is only 7 acres but has a depth of 22 feet. Boats are not permitted on Bass Lake. Nonmotorized boats and float tubes are allowed on all other lakes with a Wheatridge Parks permit. You can get a permit at park headquarters. Bass under 15 inches must be released.

Sloans Lake

Want to catch a carp? Try Sloans Lake and its 174 acres of prime carp water. Pack a few Whitlock's swimming nymphs and a stiff 7-weight rod along for a day of casting to these large spooky beasts.

To reach Sloans Lake, exit I-70 south on Sheridan Boulevard. Sloan Lake is located east of Sheridan Boulevard and between West 25th Avenue and West 17th Avenue.

Denver Parks and Recreation Department maintains this recreation area. With a boat ramp, playground, restrooms, and hard-surface trail around the lake, this facility provides a little something for everyone.

Rainbow trout are stocked in the spring for the put-and-take fisherman. Bluegill, crappie, green and orange-spotted sunfish are abundant and fairly easy to catch on a fly. The lake can be crowded at times in the summer months, but with all the shoreline available, access can be found.

Ward Road Pond

Conveniently located at the northeast corner of I-70 and Ward Road, this pond is a great opportunity to catch largemouth bass on a fly rod.

The City of Arvada and Division of Wildlife watch over this 7-acre pond with care and maintain it as a catch and release area. Fishing with artificial flies and lures is the only sport or recreation allowed. Nonmotorized boats and float tubes are allowed to pursue the bass and sunfish cruising this deep little pond.

The damselfly hatch during the summer months keeps the fish busy chasing nymphs as they migrate toward shore. Leech, crawfish, and streamer patterns are all very good fish takers when presented correctly.

Smith Reservoir

Only 44 acres, Smith Reservoir is probably one of the best smallmouth bass fisheries in the Metro area. In fact, this reservoir has staked claim to a couple state record smallies in the past.

Smallmouth prefer clear water and rocky structure (in contrast, largemouth bass like vegetation for cover). Smallies also prefer water temperatures in the high 50s to low 70s to maintain a consistent feeding pattern. Crawfish are a favorite food. However, fly patterns imitating many other food sources—such as leech, shad, and nymphal patterns—will also take a smallie.

Smith Reservoir is administered by the Lakewood Department of Community Resources. The gates open at dawn and close at 10:30 PM. You can find it at the northeast corner of South Kipling Street and Jewell Avenue. To get there, from Hamden Avenue take Kipling Street north to Jewell Avenue. Parking is east of South Moore Court.

North Metro Denver Area

Adams County Fairground Lakes

Two bodies of water, Mann Lake and Public Works Pond, are located on the Adams County Fairgrounds. The fairgrounds are located northeast of the Denver metro area near Henderson. To reach them from I-70, take I-76 north to US 85. Go north on US 85 to 124th Avenue and then turn left (west) on 124th to the Adams County Fairgrounds entrance.

Larger of the two waters, Mann Lake has about 55 surface-acres and a depth in the 20-foot range. The Public Works Pond is 30 acres and also approximately 20 feet deep. Opportunities to catch largemouth bass, bluegill, green sunfish, black crappie, yellow perch, and carp await the warmwater flyangler. Regulations specify that all bass under 15 inches must be released immediately.

The fairgrounds open at 5 am and close at 11 pm. Handicapped access can be found at the pier on Public Works Pond. Boats are prohibited.

Lake Arbor

Lake Arbor is truly an urban lake, and you might see anything while fishing its waters. To reach Arbor from I-25, take US 36 northwest to 80th Avenue. Exit left on 80th to Lamar Street, which is just west of Wadsworth Boulevard. Turn right on Lamar, and you'll see the 37-acre lake on the right hand side of the road.

The City of Arvada and North Jeffco Recreation and Parks are the caretakers of this great facility. They open the gates to the public at dawn. Piers and restrooms for the physically challenged are available, and a playground exists for the pleasure of the little ones. The gates close at 11 PM.

Nonmotorized boats and float tubes are used to entice fish from the 19-foot depths of this lake. The lake also contains artificial structure for fish habitat improvement. Largemouth bass, bluegill, and crappie are all available, along with a heavy carp or two. All bass under 15 inches must be returned to the water.

Barr Lake

Barr Lake, a 1,660-acre impoundment, is located at Barr Lake State Park off of 128th Avenue on Picadilly Road. To reach the lake from I-76, exit onto Bromley Lane going east. Turn right (south) on Picadilly Road; the entrance of the park is about a mile farther.

Barr Lake State Park is a wildlife refuge as well as a water storage facility for irrigation needs. It is operated by the Colorado Division of Parks & Outdoor Recreation. When you fish this water, you'll have the opportunity to view waterfowl, herons, deer, and a bald eagle or two.

When the gates open at 5 am, expect a day of sight casting to better-than-average carp, stripping Clouser's minnows in front of wipers, and taking a perch or a stocked rainbow trout on a dry fly. Tiger muskie, largemouth bass, and smallmouth bass will test the best of fly casters.

Water levels fluctuate often in the summer months, so one day is rarely the same as another. When the water warms, aquatic plants bloom to the point where fishing with a fly becomes very difficult. Ice-off through early summer is the best time to fly-fish Barr Lake.

Free walk-in access is available, with trails in all directions around the lake. A boat ramp is on the east side of lake by the parking area. A State Parks pass or daily permit is needed to park a vehicle. A nature center and picnic area are also available.

Wipers in possession must be 15 inches or longer. Fishing is not allowed from the dam, and motorized boats are not allowed in the refuge area located on the southwest end of the lake.

Ketner Lake

To reach Ketner Lake from I-25, take US 36 northwest to Sheridan Boulevard. Exit left off Sheridan to 88th Avenue. Take a right (west) on 88th and follow it to Wadsworth. Turn right on Wadsworth and follow it to West 100th Avenue. Take a left on to West 100th Avenue; at Country Side Drive, hang a right. Ketner Lake will be on the right side of the road by Kensington Park.

The city of Westminster cares for the 25-acre lake. Largemouth and smallmouth bass, crappie, bluegill, green sunfish, and yellow perch cruise its 30-foot depths. Belly boats can be used when fishing. All bass (largemouth and smallmouth) under 15 inches must be released.

Pomona Lake

Pomona, a little 31-acre lake in Arvada, is home to a number of largemouth bass, yellow perch, crappie, and green sunfish.

Jeffco Recreation and Parks opens the lake from dawn to 11 PM. Boats are not allowed on the water. A well maintained trail around the lake does provide easy wade access.

You can find Pomona Lake in Meadow Glen Park, on Club Crest Drive north of West 80th Avenue. From I-25, take US 36 northwest to 80th. Take a left on 80th and follow it to Club Crest Drive; then take a right to get to Pomona.

Standley Lake

Standley Lake is located in Westminster off 88th Avenue and Kipling Street. To reach Standley from I-25, take US 36 northwest to Sheridan Boulevard. Exit left on Sheridan and take a right (west) on 88th Avenue. At Kipling Street take a right (north). A fee parking area is just off of Kipling.

Standley Lake's 1,210 surface-acres are susceptible to fanatical level fluctuations, due to city demands. The lake's fishing hours are posted, and fishermen can walk in and fish at no charge. Fishing is prohibited on the dam.

Two boat ramps are found on the east side of the lake; however, the city of Westminster requires purchase of a boat permit.

Catchable-sized rainbows are stocked alongside the lake's naturally produced counterparts: largemouth bass, smallmouth bass, wipers, walleye, green sunfish, and carp. Special regulations require release of all wipers under 15 inches.

Boulder Area

Boulder Reservoir

To reach Boulder Reservoir, travel west on US 36 to Boulder. As US 36 turns north and goes through the city of Boulder, it turns into 28th Street. Follow 28th to Colorado 119 (the Longmont Diagonal) and turn right. Head northeast to Jay Road and turn left (west). Immediately turn right (north) onto 51st Street.

Once at Boulder Reservoir—a 540-acre lake reaching about 40 feet deep—back your belly boat into this very diverse fishery that includes rainbow trout (stocked in spring), black crappie, carp, yellow perch, bluegill, largemouth bass, and walleye.

Boulder Parks and Recreation Department opens the lake to fishing at 7 AM and closes it at dusk. Fishing hours from November 1 to the close of waterfowl season are from 10 AM to 2 PM. Motorboats require a city permit, while nonmotorized boats have free access. Entrance with a vehicle requires a permit; walk-ins are free.

Sawhill Ponds

The 16 ponds that make up Sawhill Ponds are very popular. These ponds range in size from one to 10 acres, and they provide excellent fishing for largemouth bass. There are also bluegill, a few crappie, and yellow perch to keep the fly rodder busy.

Boulder Parks and Recreation Department opens the gates at dawn and allows fishing until dusk. While boats are prohibited, float tubes are allowed. All bass under 15 inches must be released immediately. It's artificial flies and lures only, except on ponds 1 and 1-A.

Finding Sawhill Ponds is quite easy. Traveling west on US 36 into Boulder, just as you enter the city limits, turn right (east) on Baseline Road. Follow Baseline east and turn left (north) on North 75th Street. The entrance to the ponds is on the west side of North 75th Street, 5 miles north of Baseline.

Sterns Lake

Tiger muskie were stocked in Sterns Lake several years ago, and they are becoming a favorite gamefish for area fly anglers.

They can be found moving into shallow water as the water temperature reaches 45 to 50 degrees, usually occurring by mid- to late April. Consequently, this is when the tigers become most available to a fly caster, since boats and wading are not allowed. The flies used for tigers resemble big, colorful, wet socks with eyes. D's minnow, the bunny fly, and large Clouser's minnows are among the best producers. All tigers under 30 inches must be released back into the water immediately.

Sterns Lake covers about 24 acres and has a good variety of warmwater species. Don't be surprised if a largemouth bass hammers one of your large flies while you fish for tigers. Crappie and bluegill can also be caught throughout the year.

The lake is located north of Broomfield. To reach this lake, go west on US 36 from Denver. Exit north on South 112th Street (US 287). Three miles north of Broomfield, turn left (west) on Dillon Road, then turn left (south) on South 104th Street. The entrance to the lake is on the east side of South 104th Street.

Teller Lake

Teller Lake is another great warmwater pond located west of the Boulder area. Largemouth bass, bluegill, yellow perch, crappie, and carp are available.

The lake is located about 8 miles northwest of Lafayette. To reach this 28-acre lake, go west on US 36 from Denver. Exit north on South 112th Street (US 287) and drive to Lafayette. On the north end of town, turn left (west) on Baseline Road, and turn right (north) on North 107th Street. Go two miles to Arapahoe Road and turn left (west). The entrance to the lake is 1.5 miles west of North 95th Street. Turn right (north) on the dirt road at the sign for the lake. All bass under 15 inches must be released.

Walden Ponds

Walden Ponds are located just north of the Sawhill Ponds off North 75th Street, just east of Boulder.

To reach Walden Ponds, take US 36 in Boulder and exit east on either Valmont Drive or Arapahoe Road. Then turn left (north) on North 75th Street. The entrance to the ponds is a half mile north of Valmont.

There are five ponds that make up this chain, and each offers good flyfishing. Picnic Pond, which is the northeastern body of water and the smallest of the ponds, is restricted to handicapped and elderly persons. There are no fishing restrictions on that pond.

Cottonwood Marsh, Duck Pond, Island Lake, and Bass Pond make up the remainder of this recreation area. A healthy population of largemouth bass, bluegill, crappie, and carp await a well presented fly. Artificial flies and lures only restrictions apply and all bass caught must be released. Fishing on these ponds is open from dawn to dusk.

Catch and Release

Everyone thinks that the only consideration when catching and releasing trout is getting a fish into the water quickly after you land it. While that certainly plays a huge role in a fish's chance for survival, there are other important factors that contribute to a successful release.

Unfortunately, one of the biggest factors in a fish going back to the stream healthy or belly-up is how long you fight it. You can not fight a fish forever. Instead, you must work hard on a trout by making him play against the flex of your fly rod. That's what a rod is for—make it bend and a fish will tire.

Paul Faust, an excellent guide on the San Juan River in New Mexico and a man familiar with hooking and fighting large trout, showed me how to pressure a fish with the rod low to the water and held to the side of the body. By using his technique, an angler can keep a fish off-balance. For example, if a fish runs hard left, the fisher should hold the rod to the right and vice versa. Pressure from the side will pull the fish sideways to the current, making it work harder and tire faster, which brings a fish to net faster and, of course, heightens the chance of survival.

Once you get a fish in close, try to net it rather than drag it up on the bank or grip it in your hand. Try to touch a fish as little as possible and use forceps to remove the hook. Remember, barbless hooks are much easier to remove than those with barbs. Stick one in your earlobe, and that realization arrives immediately.

Once the hook is removed, slide a fish out of the net and hold it by the tail with one hand. The other hand should rest on the fish's belly, gently supporting its weight. Face a fish into the current and gently move it back and forth. Whether there is another hog-dog rising or not, take the time to make sure a trout has gained its strength and is ready to fight the relentless current again. When it's ready to go, he'll wag his tail and send a plume of water into your face—don't get mad. It's better than a wet kiss.

While it seems that most of us enter the sport with a good catch and release ethic already in place, some flyfishers enter the sport with notions of barbecued trout. If you fall into that category, you will likely learn that there is not much need, let alone good reason, to kill trout. You can buy a trout from the grocery store that will suffice on the table. If you have to eat a trout that you've caught, please take a fish from a lake or reservoir where populations are supplemented by hatchery stocks. On rivers and streams it takes many years to grow a large trout, and those are the fish that need to be protected. If you really want to look cool, release the largest fish you catch with no hesitation.

If that thought makes you shake, realize that the age of killing a fish to prove to everybody that you caught a fish is in the past. At some point you'll realize that it just doesn't matter what everybody thinks. If someone doesn't believe that you caught a fish, I say to hell with him or her.

A situation that still cuts me up is when a spectator watches a fish being released and makes some snide remark like, "What a waste; I would have taken that one home." Or "I would have paid you for that." Some can't see why people would fish if they don't knock every catch on the head and take it home to eat. Those critics forget that the fish they caught last year is still in the freezer with a thick coat of frost encasing its body. To those thoughtless people I say, "What a waste of life, you should have let that one go, boy!"

In today's cluttered world, with an influx of people trying this sport, everyone should see the merit of catch and release. If we all took the largest fish of the day home for dinner, there would not be a stream worth fishing in Colorado, let alone the rest of the West. If you introduce someone to the sport—and I hope you do (we need a good lobby base to fight off the consumptive, trout stream-wrecking industrial interests)—please take the time to explain the merits of catch and release.

Stream Etiquette

The sharpness of the morning air had subsided, the sun was high in the east sky, and my anticipation of a blue-winged olive hatch was typical flyfisher mentality for a late October day in Colorado.

I noticed the first surface disturbance before there were even any bugs on the water. Emergers just had to be making their way to the top, I mused. What better conditions? The hatch was just starting, and I had the river to myself. Shunning strong temptation, I passed up the first rise and headed for a favorite spot to search for duns on the water.

My timing was perfect. When I arrived, mayflies were drifting on the surface and the bank on the far side of a corner pool was alive with feeding rainbows.

I promptly knotted an olive quill dun to the end of my tippet, piled 30 feet of line at my feet, and made my first cast. After a few good downstream drifts without a look, I figured change would serve best, so I tied on a low-riding thorax dun and watched a rainbow take a look.

"On the right track," I thought.

Unfortunately, that's when I noticed another fisherman walking up the far bank toward my rainbows, the only thing that could spook a receptive pod of risers and ruin a perfect day. Sure enough, that bonehead, a smoldering stogie sticking out the side of his mouth, proceeded to walk right up the bank, oblivious of my effort to wave him back. That put a quick, disturbing end to my stalk.

That incident was not the first time another angler thoughtlessly ruined my best efforts. In fact, on that same wonderful stretch of the South Platte River the following year, I was drilling trout on a size 16 pheasant tail nymph, feeling eager to switch over to dry flies when the PMD hatch started in earnest.

When the PMDs came off, they came off sparse, but I was getting enough action on a size 14 PMD to draw the attention of some guys downstream. One idiot actually walked up the bank to me yelling, "What ya usin'?"

I boasted, "A size 14 PMD!"

The man quipped, "They don't take any flies that big on this stream."

I shrugged my shoulders, then proceeded to catch and release a 17-inch rainbow while he picked his jaw off the ground.

A day on the Platte when size 14 PMDs come off is monumental, and I don't mind helping people enjoy the action, but I do despise people who invade my space and spook my fish.

With the number of people entering our sport, the chance of those incidents happening again is a sure bet. Some people are new to the sport and do not have enough time on the stream to know what stream etiquette is, let alone apply it. You almost have to be sympathetic to those anglers. But there are avid anglers who know there are things they can do and things they shouldn't do and yet continue to defy logic and show no respect for other fishermen.

I would like to share with you an inventory of ideas on stream conduct for fly-fishermen to follow. Here are common questions and the answers:

- **How does a flyfisher approach another angler along a stream?**
A section of water belongs to the angler who starts fishing it first. Until that angler moves on to new water, it's very inconsiderate to crowd. If you must approach that person, move back from the bank so you don't disturb any water upstream or down. And watch your shadow, it can spook fish like crazy.

- **Is it appropriate to ask what fly is being used?**
Yes, but do it politely. Laws are not written saying you can't ask a fellow angler a question; just use common sense and be courteous. I always try to compliment an angler's efforts before I try to pry valuable information from him or her.

- **What should anglers bring to the stream every single time they fish?**
Courtesy, consideration, and common sense.

Here are a few ideas to adhere to and pass along to your fellow anglers:
- An angler owns a section of water if he or she is the first person to fish it.
- It is inconsiderate to crowd another angler.
- A slow moving or stationary fisherman has the right to remain where he is. If you are moving, leave the water and quietly walk around him.
- If a fisherman is resting a pool or planning his next move, it is still his water. Don't jump in without permission.
- A fisherman working upstream has the right of way over one coming downstream.
- Always yield to another angler who has a fish on his or her line.
- Don't enter the water directly across from a person fishing the opposite bank.
- Many streams flow though private property. Recognize that access is a privilege, not a right. If unsure about access, ask the landowner. Once permission is secured, don't trample crops, disturb livestock, or leave gates open.
- Try to use visible trails and paths.
- Wade only when necessary. The aquatic food chain is fragile.
- Don't litter. Pick up discarded monofilament, cans, used strike indicators, and tippet packages, and carry them out with you to be disposed of properly.
- Familiarize yourself with local and state fishing regulations.
- Drive slowly in dusty parking lots, foregoing loud music.

WaterTalk

Colorado Division of Water Resources has a unique system that allows access to data on the Satellite Monitoring system via telephone; no computer terminal is necessary. The system, named WaterTalk, provides a voice readout of current stream flows and reservoir storage.

The system is reliable and easy to use. The telephone number in Denver is 303-831-7135. Any call out of this calling area will be long distance.

After dialing in, there will be a welcome message and instructions; a touch tone telephone is necessary to access the system. The state is separated into divisions, and each division has stations on its water systems (see below); you'll use this information when calling WaterTalk. The voice readout will tell you the time of the last reading, a description of the area, and a flow rate in cubic feet per second. You can even check flows for several rivers during the same call.

After you become familiar with the WaterTalk messages, you don't need to wait for the voice to finish instructions; simply go ahead and enter the proper numbers. When you are finished, or should any confusion occur while in WaterTalk, just hang up.

The Colorado Division of Water Resources encourages the use of WaterTalk. There are four lines available, so they don't expect to have any overload on the phone lines. For more information or questions about WaterTalk, contact:

Office of the State Engineer
Division of Water Resources
1313 Sherman Street, Room 818
Denver, CO 80203
303-866-3581

A selective list of divisions and station numbers follows.

Division 1

2 Bear Creek, at Morrison
3 Bear Creek Reservoir
6 South Boulder Creek, below Gross Reservoir
8 Boulder Creek, at Boulder
10 Big Thompson River, above Lake Estes
11 Big Thompson River, below Lake Estes
12 North Fork Big Thompson River, near Drake
15 Chatfield Reservoir
16 Cheesman Reservoir
17 Cherry Creek Reservoir
19 Cache la Poudre River, at canyon mouth, Fort Collins
23 Clear Creek, near Lawson
24 Four Mile Creek, near Hartsel
29 Jefferson Creek, near Jefferson

32 Michigan Creek, above Jefferson
40 South Platte River, below Cheesman Reservoir
41 South Platte River, at Denver
42 North Fork South Platte River, at Grant
43 South Platte River, above Elevenmile
49 South Platte River, above Spinney Reservoir
51 South Platte River, below Strontia Springs
52 South Platte River, at Waterton
56 South Fork Platte River, above Antero Reservoir
58 Saint Vrain Creek, at Lyons
63 South Platte River, below Antero Reservoir
66 South Saint Vrain Creek, near Ward, Colorado
67 North Saint Vrain Creek, near Allens Park
68 South Platte River, below Chatfield Reservoir
71 Button Rock Reservoir
73 Laramie River, near Glendevy, Colorado
74 Tarryall Creek, below Tarryall Reservoir
78 South Platte River, near Lake George
79 North Fork South Platte River, near Bailey

Division 2
 8 Arkansas River, at Las Animas
11 Arkansas River, above Pueblo
12 Arkansas River, near Wellsville
30 John Martin Reservoir, at Caddoa
32 Lake Creek, below Twin Lakes
36 Lake Fork Creek, above Turquoise Reservoir
40 Pueblo Reservoir, near Pueblo
42 Purgatoire River, below Trinidad Reservoir
49 Twin Lakes Tunnel
59 Arkansas River, near Nathrop
60 Arkansas River, near Parkdale
61 Lake Creek, above Twin Lakes
63 Cottonwood Creek, near Buena Vista
64 Arkansas River, at Canyon City
65 Arkansas River, at Granite
67 Arkansas River, at Salida
69 Arkansas River, at Nathrop
70 Grape Creek, near West Cliff

Division 3
 3 Conejos River, near Mugote
 4 Conejos River, below Platoro Reservoir

5 Continental Reservoir, near Creede
9 Platoro Reservoir
12 Rio Grande River, near Del Norte
13 Rio Grande River, near Lobatos
14 Rio Grande River, at Thirty Mile Bridge
15 Rio Grande River, at Monte Vista
16 Rio Grande Reservoir
17 South Fork Rio Grande River, at South Fork
36 Trinchera Creek, below Smith Reservoir

Division 4

1 Blue Mesa Reservoir, Gunnison County
2 Cimarron River, near Cimarron, Gunnison County
5 East River, at Almont
6 Gunnison River, below East Portal Gunnison River
7 Gunnison River, at Delta, Delta County
9 Gunnison River, near Gunnison, Gunnison County
12 North Fork Gunnison River, near Somerset
15 Ridgway Reservoir, near Ridgway, Ouray County
17 San Miguel River, near Placerville
22 Taylor River, at Almont
23 Taylor Park Reservoir, Gunnison County
27 Uncompahgre River, below Ridgway Reservoir
30 Tomichi Creek, near Gunnison
31 Lake Fork, at Gateview, Colorado

Division 5

1 Blue River, below Dillon Reservoir, Summit County
2 Blue River, below Green Mountain Reservoir, Summit County
4 Colorado River, near Dotsero, Eagle County
5 Colorado River, below Grandby Reservoir, Grand County
6 Colorado River, below Glenwood Springs
7 Colorado River, near Kremmling
8 Colorado River, near Granby, Grand County
12 Crystal River, above Avalanche Creek, Redstone
13 Dillon Reservoir, Summit County
14 Eagle River, below Gypsum, Eagle County
16 Fraser River, near Windy Gap
17 Fryingpan River, near Ruedi, Eagle County
18 Fryingpan River, near Thomasville, Pitkin County
22 Green Mountain Reservoir, Summit County
26 Piney River, near State Bridge
30 Roaring Fork River, near Aspen

31 Roaring Fork River, below Maroon Creek
32 Roaring Fork River, at Glenwood Springs
33 Roaring Fork River, above Lost Man Creek
34 Ruedi Reservoir, near Basalt
35 Shadow Mountain Reservoir, Grand County
41 Williams Fork, below Williams Fork Reservoir, Grand County
42 Willow Creek Reservoir, Grand County
43 Willow Creek, below Willow Creek Reservoir
44 Williams Fork Reservoir
48 Muddy Creek, near Kremmling
50 Colorado River, at Chimney Rock
51 Colorado River, below Windy Gap
52 Colorado River, at Parshall
53 Troublesome Creek, near Kremmling
56 Tenmile Creek, below North Tenmile Creek, at Frisco

Division 6

 2 Elk River, near Milner
 3 Yampa River, at Steamboat Springs
 4 Illinois River
 8 Michigan Creek, near Gould
 9 North Platte River, near Gateway
11 White River, near Meeker
12 Yampa River, at Maybell
13 Yampa River, below Stagecoach Reservoir
14 Yampa River, above Stagecoach Reservoir
15 Yamcola Reservoir
16 North Fork White River, at Buford

Division 7

 2 Animas River, at Durango
 5 Dolores River, below McPhee Reservoir
 7 Dolores River, near Rico
 9 Florida River, above Lemon Reservoir
10 Florida River, below Lemon Reservoir
19 Pine River, below Vallecito Reservoir, Bayfield
22 San Juan River, at Pagosa Springs
23 Vallecito Reservoir

Whirling Disease

Portions reprinted from *Whirling Disease and Colorado's Trout* and Colorado
Division of Wildlife January 1996 update brochures

Whirling disease originated in Europe and was first observed in the United States in 1956. Between the 1960s and the 1990s, the spores spread to almost all western states and were first discovered in Colorado in the 1980s. Establishment of the disease in Colorado is believed to be the result of stocking trout imported from out of state by private aquaculturists.

Whirling disease (WD) is an infectious disease that attacks the cartilage of young trout and salmon; there is no known cure. It is caused by a microscopic parasite, *Myxobolus cerebralis*, so small that thousands of them could fit on the head of a pin.

Young fish are particularly susceptible to the disease. Spores from the parasite enter the fish's body and infest its soft cartilage before it turns to a bony skeleton, favoring the head and spinal column. When parasites reach a critical population in the body, the fish exhibits signs of the disease: skeletal deformities like sunken heads, bent backs, a possible black color, and the distinctive whirling and spinning motions that give the disease its name. If young trout absorb enough spores at the right time, the disease can be fatal. Trout larger than 4 inches can carry spores, but their hardened skeleton usually keeps them from being affected by the parasite.

Whirling disease is not spread directly from fish to fish, but through an intermediate host, the tubifex worm. The disease can also be spread by birds and mammals that consume infected fish and pass undigested spores through defecation in other waters. Unfortunately, the WD spore is resistant to freezing and other harsh environmental factors. Once it is established in a stream, the parasite may persist indefinitely.

Trout species vary in susceptibility to the disease. Brown trout, which evolved with the disease in Europe, appear to be less susceptible to the infection than other species. Conversely, rainbow trout, which are native to the western United States, did not evolve in the presence of whirling disease and haven't had a chance to develop much resistance to the parasite. The parasite's spores are very hardy and can easily reproduce in the wild, so it's likely that the parasite will continue to spread amongst rainbow populations. On a more fortunate note, WD has not been identified in any wild populations of the native Colorado cutthroat trout to this date. Birds, mammals, and humans cannot become infected.

The WD parasite now is found in 13 of Colorado's 15 major river drainages, including the Colorado, South Platte, Gunnison, Arkansas, and Rio Grande. However, many smaller streams in each drainage are free of the parasite.

Exhaustive research is being conducted by the Colorado Division of Wildlife in conjunction with other states. In February 1996, the DOW and the U.S. Fish and Wildlife service hosted a national conference of fishery biologists to share information on the disease and develop a strategy for future research. This cooperation will maximize all efforts, avoid duplication of research, and hopefully result in a better understanding of how to control the spread of the whirling disease parasite. Through public awareness and continued fish health programs, the impact of the whirling disease parasite and other pathogens may be minimized in many of the state's waters.

The Colorado Division of Wildlife is working to stop the spread of the disease and raise disease-free fish to release in the wild. A policy implemented in 1995 prevents stocking of trout from hatcheries testing positive into waters where whirling disease has not been found.

The DOW is developing a comprehensive policy to determine when and where stocking will occur. This policy is being developed by a group composed of anglers, federal land management agencies, business interests, tackle manufactures, private trout growers, and others. The goal is to protect the aquatic resource while continuing to provide quality recreational fishing for trout and other fish in Colorado.

By following a few simple rules, you can help in the effort to minimize the spread of WD. Don't transport any fish from one body of water to another; it is unlawful in Colorado to move and stock live fish without a special license. Don't dispose of fish entrails or other by-products into any body of water. Never transport aquatic plants. Remember that the tubifex worm may hold whirling disease spores; thoroughly wash off any mud from vehicles, boats, trailers, anchors, axles, waders, boots, and any fishing equipment that can hold these mud-dwelling worms. Please drain boats, equipment, coolers, and any water container away from rivers.

Food for Thought
Aquatic Insect Prey of Trout

The mechanics of flyfishing are easily taught, but the scientific aspect—learning what insects the trout feed on from day to day and the times of the day they feed on them—is a life-long endeavor. From the first day I attempted this sport, the big question was, "What fly do I use?" I find myself asking the very same question every day I'm on the water. As an instructor of the sport, this is one of the first questions I hear from the beginner. The key to being a successful flyfisher—in any part of the world, let alone Colorado—is to choose the fly that closely imitates the food source the fish are feeding on at that point in time.

As a commercial tier, I have been forced to learn the basics of entomology (the study of insects) simply to know what I'm attempting to tie. It has been a blessing in disguise. The more flies I tied and the more I studied about the life cycles of mayflies, caddis, stoneflies, damselflies, and midges, the more successful I became with a fly rod in my hand. The daunting task of choosing the right fly becomes easier when you have more information stored away in the memory banks. A working knowledge of the life histories and habitats of aquatic insects can add significantly to bringing more fish to the net. There are several sources including books, videos, word of mouth, and important personal experiences that will help you become more successful.

Aquatic insect forms are available to trout in two basic groups, depending on how they metamorphose after their eggs hatch. Caddisflies and midges, which have a complete metamorphosis, are food sources for trout as larvae, pupae, and winged adults. Mayflies, stoneflies, damselflies, and dragonflies have an incomplete metamorphosis and are eaten by trout as nymphs and adults. However, mayflies are often called emergers, as they float in the surface film trying to escape from their nymphal shuck.

Each type of insect is in a biological classification known as an order. An order is divided into families, genera and species. In the following sections, I list the aquatic insects of most interest to Colorado and Rocky Mountain flyfishers.

EPHEMEROPTERA / MAYFLIES

Adult mayflies rest with their large wings in an upright position and their long, slender bodies curved in a graceful arc, front to back. When floating on water they look like miniature sailboats. They are usually quiet and docile on the water, rarely fluttering, except for emergers that failed to shuck their nymphal casings. Mating swarms can be very busy and thick. The adults are literally "ephemeral." Few species live longer than a day.

The newly emerged adult is known as a *subimago*, or *dun*. Large mayfly duns are called *drakes*. Body color is dull and non-reflective, and the wings are opaque and grayish in color. After molting into the *imago*, or reproductive stage, body color is bright, and wings are clear or transparent. Males and females that complete the reproductive and egg-laying stage fall to the water with spent, outspread wings and are called *spinners*.

Nymphs can live 1 to 3 years under water, although a few species have two or three generations in a single season. The nymph goes through growth stages, called instars, where it shucks its exoskeleton each time it is outgrown, much like a snake sheds its skin every year. As it approaches the time when it is about to hatch, the wing pad on the back of the thorax becomes more dark and prominent.

The four categories of nymphs—swimmers, crawlers, clingers, and burrowers—reflect their habitats and habits. While a few species crawl ashore or up the stems of vegetation to emerge into adults, most nymphs float or swim to the surface as they shuck their exoskeletons and unfold their wings. Most fly off immediately. On cold or rainy days, their float on the water can be more prolonged, making them available to the trout longer as they try to dry their wings sufficiently for flight. The South Platte River is notorious for its incredible dry-fly fishing under adverse conditions.

Trout will grub for nymphs in their hiding places, move up into riffles to snatch nymphs or emergers, or wait in their feeding lanes to snare dislodged nymphs. Emergers and floating adults are taken as they pass down a feeding lane, flow over the lip of a riffle, or are swirled together in the backwaters of an eddy. When a multiple hatch occurs, trout will often key on a single species—and not always the larger one, but the one of most quantity.

Characteristics of mayfly species are reflected by the colors and other descriptive terms assigned to their common names and popular dry fly patterns.

Major mayfly hatches in Colorado include:

Baetidae

One of the most abundant and hardy families in the West, its many important species guarantee blue-ribbon action. Carpet hatches of blue-winged olive (BWO) are common. Baetis hatches overlap through the season from early spring into late fall. Expect these mayflies to hatch on every river in Colorado. Hatches on the South Platte, Arkansas, and Colorado Rivers are truly amazing.

Baetis / Blue-winged Olive

Habitat: Swimming nymphs prefer flowing waters. Mostly found in shallow riffles but also in rapids and eddies, they feed and find shelter in crevices and rock cobble of the stream bed, sometimes in weed beds. They emerge by floating or swimming to the surface to shed nymphal casing. Present dry flies that imitate the adults downstream and across.

Nymphs: Soft hackle and emerger patterns tied sparsely in olive, brown-olive, or tan, #14–#24. Pheasant tail nymphs, olive biot nymphs, and RS-2s are very popular.

Hatches/dry flies:

Baetis tricaudatus—blue-winged olive, AK's olive quill, iron blue quill, and Adams. Late March through mid-May, #16–#18; October through November, #18–#22.

Baetis bicaudatus—tiny blue-winged olive, #22–#24; July through August.

Baetis parvus—tiny brown dun and tiny blue quill, #20–#22; mid-July through October.

Pseudocloeon—tiny blue-winged olive.

Pseudocloeon edmundsi—tiny blue-winged olive, #22–#22; August through October. Important fall hatches on the South Platte and Fryingpan rivers.

Callibaetis / Speckle-wing Dun

Habitat: Very important species on lakes, ponds, and reservoirs, these are also found in slow, quiet waters of some mountain streams and spring creeks. Sporadic hatches occur throughout spring to autumn, but emergers and spinners offer most action. Swimming nymphs find food and shelter in weed beds, stands of aquatic vegetation, and debris of stream and lake beds. Nymphs are very active prior to emergence and rise swiftly to surface. There are excellent hatches on Spinney Mountain Reservoir and Delaney Butte Lakes.

Nymphs: Callibaetis nymph, parrot Callibaetis nymph, and ginger hare's ear, #12–#18. Sizes become smaller as season progresses; usually weighted and fished as rising emergers.

Hatches/dry flies:

Callibaetis coloradensis—speckled dun, rusty spinner, speckled biot spinner, light Cahill, comparadun or parachute Adams, #14–#16; mid-June to mid-August.

Callibaetis nigritus—speckled spinner, #14–#16; June through September.

Ephemerellidae

This family offers perhaps the two most productive patterns on western streams. Pale morning duns (PMD) are a class act throughout the summer, and giant green drakes elicit exciting midsummer action.

Drunella / Green Drake

Habitat: This genus is very important on the Fryingpan, Roaring Fork, Taylor, and Rio Grande rivers. Midsummer sparks the interest of anglers who seek big fish on big flies. Crawling nymphs are poor swimmers, preferring to find food and hide in haunts of streams with weedy, silty bottoms. Emergers are very vulnerable as they crawl to quiet waters or haphazardly rise slowly to surface. Adults equally vulnerable because of long floats after emerging.

Nymphs: Olive hare's ear, western green drake nymph, Zug bug, #8–#10.

Hatches/dry flies:

Drunella grandis, Drunella doddsi— Western green drake, AK's hair wing drake, green drake paradrake, green drake Wulff, great red spinner, #8–#12; late June to mid-August.

Drunella flavilinea—Flavs, small western drake, slate-winged olive, parachute olive hare's ear, #14–#16; July. The Cache la Poudre River has a fine hatch in July.

Drunella coloradensis—Slate-winged olive, parachute olive hare's ear, #14–#16; August.

Ephemerella / Pale Morning Dun

Habitat: Crawling nymphs are poor swimmers and prefer to find food and hide in haunts of streams with weedy, silty bottoms. Emergers are very vulnerable as they crawl to quiet waters or haphazardly rise slowly to surface. Colorado, Fryingpan, Eagle, and South Platte rivers host some of the best hatches in the state.

Nymphs: Biot pale morning dun nymph, pheasant tail nymph, dark hare's ear, yellow soft-hackle partridge, #16–#20.

Hatches/dry flies:

Ephemerella infrequens—pale morning dun, comparadun PMD, Lt. Cahill, parachute PMD, AK's pink quill, rusty spinner, #14–#18; June and early July.

Ephemerella inermis—pale morning dun, hair wing dun, comparadun PMD, parachute PMD, #16–#20; July through September.

Ephemeridae

Principal fly in this family is the brown drake, a large slow-water species which may overlap with the green drake hatch on some streams. It usually hatches in early summer.

Ephemera / Brown Drake

Habitat: Nymphs burrow into silty sand bottoms of streams and lakes and feed at night. The hatch occurs at twilight or at night, with emergers rapidly rising to the surface.

Nymphs: brown drake nymph, #10–#12.

Hatch/dry flies:

Ephemera simulans—brown drake, brown drake parachute, brown drake spinner, #10–#12; mid-June to early July.

Siphlonuridae

This family has only one major genus in Colorado, on the Laramie River, and in most of the West. The gray drake, a large mayfly, is somewhat rare but very important on streams where it occurs. Key hatches are in midsummer into fall.

Siphlonurus / Gray Drake

Habitat: Swimming nymphs prefer quiet pools and slack waters in streams, the edges and shallow waters of lakes and ponds. Nymphs find food and shelter in weed beds and around stems of aquatic vegetation. They emerge by crawling up stems of plants or onto logs, usually at night. The Laramie River has an incredible hatch right after runoff. Early evening spinner falls prove to be most exciting.

Nymphs: gray drake, black drake, #10–#14.

Hatch/dry fly:

Siphlonurus occidentals—Quill Gordon, gray drake dun, gray drake spinner, gray Wulff, Adams, #10–#12; midsummer to mid-October.

Leptophlebiidae

The principal fly in this family is the mahogany dun, a tiny fast-water species with a relatively long season. Late summer hatches are common.

Paraleptophlebia / Mahogany Dun

Habitat: Crawling nymphs prefer flowing waters, like fast riffles; they hide and feed in debris and gravel of streambed. Poor swimmers, they move to quieter waters prior to emerging.

Nymphs: Hare's ear nymph, #14–#18.

Hatch/dry flies:

Praraleptophlebia bicornuta—mahogany dun, mahogany spinner, #16–#18; late August through September.

Tricorythodidae

The very tiny flies of this family are a major feeding source for selective trout, mostly on streams but also on some lakes. Tricos are especially important on the South Platte and Colorado Rivers. Late summer hatches into September are common.

Tricorythodes / White-wing Black

Habitat: Nymphs prefer slow waters of streams; hide in bottom debris. Floating emerger and dun patterns work, but the spent female spinners are most vulnerable to slurping trout.

Nymphs: tan hare's ear nymphs, black or olive midge pupa, pheasant tail nymph, #20–#24.

Hatch/dry flies:

Tricorythodes minutus—white-wing black, parachute Trico, black or olive midges, Griffith's gnat, Trico spinner, #20–#26; August into September.

Heptageniidae

Common to fast mountain streams, species of this family prefer clear, cold water. The late summer hatch continues into fall.

Heptagenia / Pale Evening Dun

Habitat: These flattened, clinging nymphs prefer fast water. Referred to as the pale evening dun. Somewhat larger than the pale morning dun and cream in color.

Nymphs: Hare's ear nymph, olive-brown nymph, #14–#16.

Hatch/dry flies:

Heptagenia elegantula—pale evening dun, Lt. Cahill, cream comparadun. #14–#16; late afternoons and evenings.

Eperous / Pink Lady

Habitat: Nymphs cling to substrate of tumbling riffles and fast runs. Emergers and floating duns most vulnerable to quick-acting trout.

Nymphs: Soft hackle patterns and hare's ear nymph, #10–#16.

Hatch/dry flies:

Eperous albertea—pink lady, pink Cahill, cream dun, #14–#16; July to September.

TRICHOPTERA / CADDISFLIES

Few anglers bother to learn the Latin names of caddisflies. Almost none have common names, although on many streams they are more prolific than mayflies.

Popular caddis patterns are impressionistic but take tons of trout. Larval patterns are effective year-round because caddis are so common. Emerger patterns generally are more productive during a hatch than dry flies. A dry fly plays best when females return to deposit their eggs, but a dry fly is a good attractor pattern in spring and summer because caddis are on the water throughout their adult stage.

When resting, the two pairs of wings of the caddisfly slant back over the body in a tent-like position. In the air, caddis have an erratic, bouncing flight pattern. On the water, they often continue fluttering or swimming about. Their wings are not transparent, and coloration tends toward earth tones in shades of tan, brown, gray, or black. Body color can match the wings or be in shades of green or yellow. Adult caddisflies may live one to two weeks.

In the larval stage most caddis live in cases built from small grains of sand, sticks, strands of vegetation, or a combination of materials. Some live in a free-swimming form or construct a silken retreat with a web.

Caddis hibernate a week or more during pupation, like caterpillars, as they change into winged adults in their cases. When the transformation is complete, the pupae shuck their casings as they soar to the surface in a dash to freedom. Most adults fly off as soon as they hit the air.

Trout chasing caddis emergers often rocket fully out of the water in their pursuit. Their next best shot at caddis is when the females return to deposit their eggs. It is a busy affair, with lots of buzzing wings and swimming about, although a few dive straight to the bottom. With all that activity, trout hit caddis hard. Fishing strategies should follow suit.

Two most common families in Colorado are *Brachycentridae*, dark-gray and dark-brown caddis with wood-case larvae, and *Rhyacophilidae*, green caddis with free swimming larvae.

The most effective dry fly to cover the bases is the elk hair caddis in #12–#20 with green, tan, brown, or gray bodies. Other popular patterns include Colorado king, Goddard caddis, humpy, Henryville Special, CDC caddis, , Lawson's partridge caddis and balloon caddis.

Larval and pupa patterns in #10–#18 can include LaFontaine sparkle caddis, Macramé caddis, latex caddis, or soft hackle patterns like the green partridge, Charles Brooks' little green caddis and Lawson's caddis emerger.

PLECOPTERA / STONEFLIES

These prehistoric monsters of the aquatic insect world incite slashing, explosive rises by trophy trout during early-season hatches. But for wet flyfishers, the 2- to

3-inch nymphs of the largest species, *Pteronarcys californica*, are a standard pattern year-round.

The incredible "salmonfly" feeding frenzy can extend from mid-May through late-July in some of Colorado larger trout streams. The Colorado, Gunnison, Rio Grande, and Cache la Poudre have fine hatches. But Mother Nature doesn't always make it easy. Local weather or spring runoff conditions can speed up or slow a hatch dramatically. Elsewhere in the state, hatches can be very sporadic, and nymph patterns often perform better than dry flies.

Adult stoneflies look a lot like giant caddisflies, although their two pairs of heavily veined wings lie flat over their backs. Their flight is helicopter-like, with the long body hanging below the whirling wings. Nymphs follow the same life history as mayflies and live underwater 1 to 4 years. All species are found in swift, rocky waters, rich in oxygen.

Members of the *P. californica* species were dubbed salmonflies because of the bright-orange highlights on dark-brown bodies of nymphs and adult flying insects. A smaller species, the golden stonefly, *Acroneuria pacifica* or *Acroneuria californica*, are highlighted by golden-yellow markings on it light-brown body. Golden stones hatch toward the end of a salmonfly hatch. They also come in a wider variety of sizes and can be an effective dry-fly pattern for a longer duration.

Stoneflies do not emerge midstream. The nymphs crawl across the streambed to water's edge, climb a rock or bush and shuck their shells as they metamorphose into short-lived, flying insects.

Key to fishing salmonflies is staying at the front of the hatch as it moves upstream, usually about 5 miles a day. A hatch's head is determined by the point where only a few flying insects or nymph casings can be found. The best bet here is to cast nymphs toward the shoreline from a boat or parallel to it when wading.

Behind the vanguard of the emerging nymphs, dry flies come into play. Late afternoon flights of female salmonflies come back to the water to lay eggs into the swift currents. The large, black egg sacs are deposited like bombs in rocky, fast-water stretches of the stream to begin the cycle anew. Many females fall exhausted onto the water, and the bugs are often blown off streamside bushes by high winds.

There are hundreds of patterns, ranging from super realistic to plain buggy-looking impressions, and new ones are being created annually. Check with local fly tackle shops on what's hot.

A variety of salmonflies, #2–#8, is highly recommended. Golden stone patterns range from #8–#14. Popular dry flies include the sofa pillow, Bird's stonefly, golden stonefly, large yellow or orange stimulators and double humpies. Traditional nymph patterns include the halfback, twenty incher, Charles Brooks Montana stone, Bitch Creek nymph, black girdle bugs, and woolly bugger.

Small caddis-like insects on the water with wings resting flat over orange or yellow bodies are small species of brown or golden stoneflies. These are often called yellow Sallies, after the *Isogenus* species. Smaller yellow or orange stimulators and yellow Sally patterns are very effective, along with humpies, and yellow elk hair caddis, #10–#14.

Diptera / True Flies

Midges and mosquitoes are the two families in this order of most interest to flyfishers.

Chironomidae / Midges

Midges can be a dry-fly fishers' best friend in winter and early spring on streams open year-round. Tailwaters such as the South Platte, Fryingpan, Taylor, and Blue rivers can be outstanding. Float tubers often count on *Chironomid* emergers to ensure a good day on lakes and ponds.

Midge larva and pupa patterns are tied very sparsely with green, olive, light-olive, tan, brown, or black dubbing on #18–#26 hooks. Peacock or ostrich herl are used on the thorax of pupa patterns.

Flying midge patterns are tied very sparsely in colors to match a variety of hatches with only two or three turns of same-colored hackle for wings, #14–#26. The Griffith's gnat, tied with a grizzly hackle palmered over a peacock herl body, #18–#26, represents a clump of midges on the water. Palomino midges and biot midges are good single fly patterns for more selective trout.

Culicidae / Mosquitoes

This is the one fly everyone can identify.

Both larva and pupa patterns are tied to float in the surface film. Stripped hackle stems or peacock herl are used for the thin body, in #14–#18. The mosquito dry fly and Adams also work in #14–#18.

Odonata / Damselflies & Dragonflies

Dragonfly and damselfly hatches on lakes and ponds can rival the excitement of stonefly hatches on mountain streams. But even without a hatch, damsel nymphs, Charles Brooks' Assom dragon, small woolly buggers, crystal buggers, and Carey Special, #4–#12, should be part of a stillwater flyfisher's arsenal year-round.

Olive damsel nymphs, #8–#12, and woolly buggers and crystal buggers, #8–#10, are popular patterns on Delaney Buttes during the damselfly hatch from late June to mid-July.

Long-bodied dry flies also are available at some fly tackle shops.

Colorado Game Fish
CUTTHROAT TROUT: NATIVE SONS OF THE WEST

The favorite trout of dry fly purists and Colorado's state fish since 1994, the greenback cutthroat's lusty rises to fur-and-feather imitations gladden the hearts of novice and expert flyfishers. Along with the Colorado River cutthroat and the Rio Grande cutthroat, flyfishermen still have the opportunity to catch these wild species in the high country of Colorado.

Cutthroat stubbornly fight under water and use stream flows to their advantage, sometimes even rolling with the current and twisting the line around themselves. But it is often a short-lived fight if your terminal tackle is not too delicate and you are not forced to prolong it.

The greenback cutthroat, a native of Colorado's eastern drainages and the South Platte and the Arkansas rivers, is primarily found in Rocky Mountain National Park. However, other locations are being considered for recovery areas. The Colorado River cutthroat is native to the Colorado River drainage on the west slope. It is sad, but this trout is now found only in high country lakes and streams or special recovery areas. The Rio Grande cutthroat is native to the Rio Grande in the south central part of the state and is found in many of the high mountain lakes in the Rio Grande and Conejos River drainages. The Snake River fine-spotted cutthroat is a hearty implant from the Snake River drainage in Idaho and Wyoming and is found throughout the state. Spinney Mountain Reservoir is one of the best lakes for large Snake River cutts.

All species of Colorado cutthroat are considered at risk. Habitat is slowly being infringed upon, and their sensitivity to habitat change has reduced the range in which they can live.

Until other species were introduced in the late 1800s, the cutthroat was the only trout in much of the vast interior of the West, from the western slopes of the Sierras in California, north through Utah, Idaho, and Montana, and south to northern Mexico. The rainbow, the other native trout of the West, was historically a Pacific slope fish.

Originally, the cutthroat and rainbow were considered to be descendants of the Atlantic salmon, *Salmo salar*. But in 1990, taxonomy specialists agreed that western trout are more closely related to the Pacific salmon. Descendants of this genus are listed as *Oncorhynchus*, which means "hooked snout."

Ironically, the taxonomists only recently caught up with the 1804–1806 Corps of Discovery. Meriwether Lewis first recorded the cutthroat for science in 1805 in western Montana. The men of the Lewis and Clark Expedition and later mountain men referred to the fish as the "trout salmon" because of its rich, orange flesh. The greenback cutthroat is now known by biologists as *Oncorhynchus clarki stomias*. The Colorado River cutthroat's scientific name is *Oncorhynchus clarki pleuriticus*, while the Rio Grande River cutthroat is known as *Oncorhynchus clarki virginalis*.

The greenback cutthroat is a beautiful fish, with rouge-colored, sometimes bright red, gill plates. In larger fish, this bright coloring can extend under its body about midway. Large black spots, in contrast to those of other cutthroat species, are sparsely sprinkled across its back, with somewhat larger and more concentrated spots on its back near the tail.

Early on, the greenback cutthroat was mistaken for the Colorado River cutthroat. However, taxomonists have made distinctions in their differences. Aside from the real determining factor, the Continental Divide, the greenback has the largest spots, as well as more scales, of any cutthroat. Greenbacks were abundant until settlers started to occupy its range. Before their total destruction, five remnant populations were discovered and are now closed to angling. Reintroductions have been success-ful in 12 streams and 5 lakes, with populations stabilizing. This means the trout are reproducing naturally and developing several age classes.

The Colorado River cutthroat, like its native brother the greenback, is the most brilliantly colored of all cutthroat species. The bright reds, oranges, and yellows set these cutts apart from the rest.

In 1985, Colorado estimated it had at least 20 stable populations of pure Colorado River cutthroat in its historical range, which include the upper Colorado, Green, and San Juan River basins. Research has brought doubt to those claims and could mean the fate of *pleuriticus* could still be insecure.

The Rio Grande cutthroat is colored much like the Colorado River and greenback cutthroats, though not as brilliant. Spots are more oval in shape and are clustered primarily at the back of the body near the tail. Natives to the Rio Grande in Colorado and the Pecos River in New Mexico, *virginalis* is known to be the southernmost reaching cutthroat. There could be as many as 40 genetically pure populations of the Rio Grande cutthroat in New Mexico and as few as 10 in Colorado.

As an environmental barometer of the mountains, the cutthroat is like the canary in the mine—it is the first species to be eliminated. Most of the 15 subspecies of this colorful but vulnerable fish are now largely restricted to the uppermost, cold-est, headwater tributaries. A few that adapted to lower, warmer water conditions of the Utah and Nevada basin and range alkaline lakes and streams are largely gone or only shadows of their former glory.

Studies show the cutthroat can be easily overexploited by anglers. Even with light fishing pressure, their short growing season makes them susceptible to any food source, especially a well presented dry fly. Please handle all trout with care, especially our cutthroat.

Colorado's cutthroat were imperiled through indiscriminate stocking of nonna-tive species, particularly brook and rainbow trout, and habitat loss is a story repeated throughout the West. While steps are being taken to eliminate or reduce hybridiza-tion, the threat may now be here forever.

I have just read about certain organizations trying to introduce legislation to kill brook trout and other nonnative species in high mountain lakes in an attempt to restore habitat for the native cutthroats. I hate to say it, but with the popularity of fishing these days, it would be hard to see this happening. Fishing is a large revenue producer for the state, and to leave several of the best high mountain brook trout lakes barren would upset the majority of the fishing population. The state is having a difficult time restoring damage done by whirling disease without worrying about something like this. However, I will say it is a good idea with terribly bad timing.

Spawning normally occurs in April or May—the same period as the rainbow spawn, which accounts for the threat of hybridization. As the native trout that evolved in these waters, cutthroat grow at a better rate in a shorter period of time than their introduced brethren, including rainbow, brown, brook, and lake trout. Under wild trout management, cutthroat provide fish of remarkable size for the angler in all but the smallest streams. They have been known to live to 11 years, although 6 or 7 is more common. Twelve to 15 inches is considered a good-sized cutthroat, although occasional larger fish occur. Maximum growth is about 3 pounds, but it rarely exceeds 2 pounds because of its nonpiscivorous nature.

In lakes such as Spinney Mountain and Elevenmile reservoirs, the Snake River cutthroat averages 14 to 17 inches, with trout over 20 being common and a few reaching 10 pounds. Colorado's record cutthroat of 16 pounds was taken from Twin Lakes in 1964. The particular species was unrecorded; however, that is one big cutthroat.

Cutthroat are most active in water temperatures between 50 and 65° Fahrenheit. They can be found in both fast and slack water, although they are less fond of exceptionally fast waters than rainbows. Like all trout, they take advantage of whatever structural protection a stream provides, from overhanging, willow-lined banks to midstream boulders, logjams, streambed depressions and deep pools at the base of riffles.

Never pass a logjam or a bankside feeding lane protected by an overhanging tree without working it closely. Riffles also are prime feeding grounds of cutthroat and provide prodigious action, especially at the lip of a deep pool.

The cutthroat's reputation for eagerly rising to a dry fly remains paramount in most flyfishers' minds. Larger cutthroat will hit a stonefly or hopper pattern with slashing strikes rivaling the ferocity of rainbows or browns. Casting to the feeding frenzy on the lip of a riffle during a heavy caddis or mayfly hatch can bring a host of fish between 8 and 12 inches to the net. At the same time, a hit during selective, sipping rises to tiny mayflies will startle the angler who hooks a cutthroat lurking beneath the still waters.

A standard set of dry flies to attract cutthroat should include elk hair caddis, stimulators, yellow Sallies, humpies, Adams, pale morning duns, blue-winged olives, light Cahills, and parachute hare's ears. Nymph and emerger patterns for each of these can be equally effective, especially on riffles. Effective sizes for both dry and wet caddis and mayfly patterns can range from sizes 10 to 16 in spring and early summer. By late fall, you may have to go as small as sizes 18 to 22.

When all else fails, you can always fall back on standard attractor flies like the renegade, Royal Wulff, royal coachman, Royal Trude, orange humpy, or irresistible.

Cutthroat also succumb to the usual assortment of small streamers, muddlers, weighted nymphs, woolly buggers, and rubber-legged patterns. Sizes 8 to 14 generally work best.

Cutthroat can be the least shy of the trout family. Occasionally, you can get amazingly close to feeding fish. On some streams, they may even be right underfoot, feeding on nymphs your boots stir up from the gravel.

But never underestimate the cutthroat. It is not a brown trout with a lobotomy, as some would disparage this remarkable fish. It can be easy to catch and it can be exactingly selective as it keys in on a specific mayfly or caddis hatch with the resolute intensity of one of its so-called educated brethren.

Either way, cutthroat are a joy to catch and behold.

Cutthroat Trout Identification

Greenback Cutthroat Trout (*Oncorhynchus clarki stomias*)

The greenback cutthroat is a beautiful fish, with rouge-colored, sometimes bright red, gill plates. This bright coloring can extend under its body about midway, including the lower fins, in larger fish. Large black spots, in comparison to other cutthroat species, are sparsely sprinkled across its golden-olive back, with somewhat larger and more concentrated spots on its back near the tail. Very few spots occur under the midline of the fish.

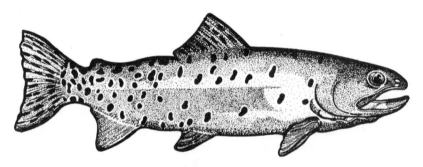

Greenback Cutthroat

Colorado River Cutthroat Trout (*Oncorhynchus clarki pleuriticus*)

The Colorado River cutthroat, as with its native brother the greenback, is the most brilliant of all cutthroat species. The bright reds, oranges, and yellows of a mature fish set these cutts apart from the rest. Spots are slightly smaller but are still distributed along the back with more concentration near the tail.

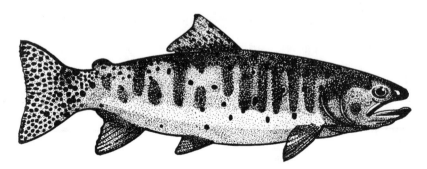

Colorado River Cutthroat

Rio Grande Cutthroat Trout (*Oncorhynchus clarki virginalis*)

The Rio Grande cutthroat is colored much like the Colorado River and greenback cutthroats but not as brilliant. Spots are more oval in shape and are clustered primarily at the back of the body near the tail. Small spots are distributed sparsely along the back. Natives to the Rio Grande in Colorado and the Pecos River in New Mexico, *virginalis* is known to be the southernmost reaching cutthroat.

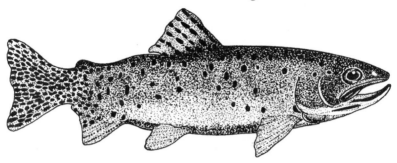

Rio Grande Cutthroat

Snake River Cutthroat Trout, fine-spotted cutthroat (*Oncorhynchus clarki sp.*)

The Snake River fine-spotted is similar to the Yellowstone cutthroat in body conformation and coloration. Its profuse spotting pattern is more similar to coastal species than interior cutthroat. Its many small spots concentrate toward the tail and extend below midbody. The tail and lower fins are sometimes darker orange. Found primarily in the upper Snake River in Jackson, Wyoming, and Palisades Reservoir in Idaho, fine-spotted cutthroat numbers are increasing in Colorado through stocking programs and natural spawning.

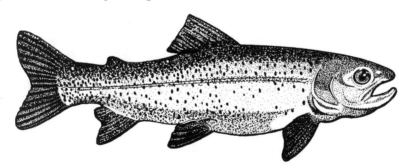

Snake River Cutthroat

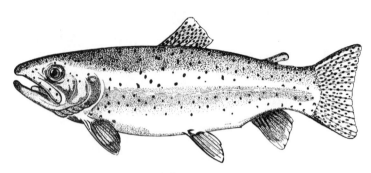

Rainbow Trout

RAINBOW TROUT: MIGHTY LEAPER

Far and away the most exciting fighter of the trout family, the rainbow always pulls something from its bag of tricks, from cartwheeling leaps to reel-sizzling runs to repeated dashes away from the net.

In waters containing other trout species, there's no doubt in an angler's mind when a rainbow is on the end of the line. A rainbow never hesitates in its frenzied quest for freedom. It often leaps more than once in its desperate panic to throw the hook. Even small fish offer a strong and agile fight. Large fish hooked on light tackle or a delicate leader tippet leave the angler only one option—give the fish its head and hope the line is long enough for the first run. Your prayers won't always be answered, even on the second or third run. A rainbow rarely comes to the net willingly.

Anglers should use the heaviest terminal tackle conditions permitted to make the fight as short as possible and not unduly tire out the fish. Always use a good-sized, soft-meshed net so you aren't inclined to manhandle the fish as you attempt to land it.

The feisty rainbow's acrobatic leaps and speckled, multihued beauty—described by a whimsical writer of the past as "sheened like a Kang Shi porcelain vase"—make it one of the most popular game fishes in the world. A native of coastal drainages of the northern Pacific, it has been transplanted throughout North America, South America, and Europe.

It gets its name from the crimson to pinkish-red band along the midline of its flanks. This reddish band may be absent in lake dwellers, which are generally more silver in total appearance. It is marked across its head, back, and upper flanks with many small, irregular black spots that are concentrated most heavily on its squarish tail.

The rainbow trout, *Oncorhynchus mykiss*, was reclassified as part of the western salmon genus *Oncorhynchus* in 1990; formerly it was classified with the Atlantic salmon genus, *Salmo*. Its former species name, *gairdneri irideus*, was replaced with *mykiss* because the Japanese description of the rainbow predated descriptions made in the western United States in the early 1800s.

The Kamloops, a landlocked steelhead from British Columbia, has been introduced into a few Colorado waters. Donaldson and Swedish steelhead are also favorites of private water owners. They do well under a wide range of temperatures in lakes, reservoirs, and streams.

The rainbow is also an important aquaculture species. A case can be made, however, that exploitation of the rainbow as a hatchery fish is overdone. Rainbows have been introduced in virtually every drainage in Colorado. Thus, on many reservoirs and smaller streams, the average rainbow taken by an angler is a hatchery-bred fish 8 to 12 inches in length. Its fins are ragged or deformed from rubbing against concrete hatchery raceways, its flesh pale and unsavory from its pellet-food diet.

But the modern trend toward wild fish management continues to gain acceptance in Colorado and is exhibiting promising results. A number of Colorado streams where past rainbow plantings have taken hold are producing remarkable fish under wild trout, quality, or trophy management policies. Cheesman Canyon on the South Platte River and the Taylor River are prime examples. By policy, no new plantings are made in these waters, and harvest is either strictly limited or catch-and-release only. Barring problems with whirling disease, we hope these policies continue.

The popularity of fishing for rainbows puts pressure on the Colorado Division of Wildlife to continue stocking them; however, and unfortunately this runs entirely contrary to efforts towards preservation of cutthroat species. Shifting hatchery rainbow plantings away from wild trout populations to designated "put-and-take" streams and reservoirs is a policy of appeasement. It helps spread out angling pressure by offering enhanced opportunities to the general public for the waters "negated" by the stricter regulations on wild trout streams.

However, discontinuing hatchery plants in restricted management streams is a biological decision, too. The disruptive effects of hatchery rainbows on wild populations is well documented. It is a bit like dumping the cast from "West Side Story" into the serenity of a classical ballet.

Generally, in streams where wild fish predominate or in lakes and reservoirs with good holdover potential for hatchery fish, the average rainbow is 12 to 16 inches, with the potential in nutrient-rich waters for fish over 24 inches. In trophy lakes, a rare rainbow can reach 15 pounds. Landlocked monsters approaching this size take on the appearance of a pot-bellied pig, totally opposite to the streamlined, typical rainbow characteristics necessitated by the fast moving streams they primarily inhabit.

Colorado's record fish is an 18-pound, 5-ounce slab caught in the South Platte River in 1972. The Taylor River below Taylor Park Reservoir holds a rainbow caught and released at an estimated weight of 22 pounds at an astounding length of 34 inches.

The rainbow, like the cutthroat, is a spring spawner, and this leads to hybridization when the species coexist. The rainbow also reaches sexual maturity earlier, at 2 or 3 years. In hatcheries, they often spawn at 1 year of age. The life span of the rainbow is fairly short; few live beyond 5 or 6 years.

Rainbow waters can be fast or slow, but chances are this trout will be found in faster moving and more turbulent waters than cutthroat or browns. Larger fish are found in the prime holding areas favored by all trout, like overhanging banks, obvious feeding lanes or sheer lines, in front of or behind midstream structures, or at the head of deep pools. While more active in morning or evening, they will move far up into a riffle, even at high noon, during a prime hatch, using the moving water as cover. Dark, cloudy days will set the fish on the prowl at any hour. The heaviest mayfly hatches regularly occur on these types of days, too.

The rainbow is most active in waters 45 to 65 degrees Fahrenheit. Peak activity is in waters around 60 degrees. They are highly aggressive fish and will vigorously defend a feeding territory, especially against other salmonids of equal size.

Rainbows eat anything they can catch and swallow. All sizes of rainbows depend heavily on aquatic and terrestrial insects. Larger fish prey on smaller fish, too, and are known to take small mammals like mice or meadow voles. While opportunistic, larger rainbows tend to be very selective and key in on a particular food source, especially during a multi-hatch of mayflies or caddisflies. They also may concentrate on a particular stage of a hatch, keying on the nymph, emerger, or adult flying form, or, later, the dead, spinner form. Lake dwellers tend to be more piscivorous.

The selective feeding nature of large rainbows requires more patience and skill of a flyfisher. For those willing to be patient, it boils down to approach and presentation. Approach a feeding fish slowly and quietly to present a fly into its feeding lane. The key is a short-as-possible cast and a drag-free float through that lane. Most rainbows will not move to intercept a fly outside their feeding paths, so keep trying to put your fly right on the mark. Often, presentation is more critical than a perfect hatch match. If a fish shows an interest, present the fly again immediately. If your first choice doesn't work, rest the fish and try a different pattern. Above all, don't let your expectations cloud your appreciation of the challenge. A day on the stream is valuable, no matter how many fish you net.

Of course, all bets are off during major fly hatches, like the salmon fly or western green drake. These "Big Macs" of the aquatic insect world bring up trout of all sizes. Wariness is abandoned. This also applies during prime grasshopper activity.

The standard set of dry flies to attract rainbows is much the same as for cutthroat, but again, presentation is more of a factor. It should include elk hair caddis, stimulators, yellow Sallies, humpies, Adams, pale morning duns, blue-winged olives, light Cahills, and any one of the many quill type patterns from A.K. Best. Nymph and emerger patterns for each of these can be equally effective, especially on riffles. Effective sizes for both dry and wet caddis and mayfly patterns can range from sizes 12 to 20 in spring and early summer. By late fall, when the tricos and tiny bluewings are out, you may have to go as small as a 26. Micro patterns of midges, Baetis, and tricos also produce amazing results when that's the action on a particular stream, such as the South Platte, Blue and Taylor rivers and other tailwaters. Sometimes small terrestrial patterns, like ants and beetles, work best, even during an aquatic insect hatch.

Standard attractor flies like the renegade, Royal Wulff, royal coachman, Royal Trude, humpy, or irresistible work as well, particularly in faster waters.

Larger streamers, muddlers, weighted nymphs, woolly buggers, halfbacks, and rubber-legged patterns can be very effective for rainbows. Waders fish them deep, dredging the bottom; float-boaters pound the banks. Leech, dragonfly nymph, woolly bugger, and freshwater shrimp patterns are effective in lakes. Sizes can range from 2 to 14.

Most often a rainbow will hook itself. Just hang on when your fly scores.

Rainbow Trout Identification

Rainbow Trout (*Oncorhynchus mykiss*)

The rainbow's common name comes from a broad swath of crimson to pinkish-red usually seen along the midline of its flanks. The reddish band may be much lighter in lake dwellers, which are generally more silver in appearance. River rainbow coloration ranges from olive to greenish-blue on back, with white to silvery belly. They are marked with many irregularly shaped black spots on the head, back, and tail that extend below the midline.

BROWN TROUT: CRAFTY BRUTES

The brown trout's well-deserved reputation for wariness demands a dedicated effort on the part of anglers seeking one of these crafty brutes.

Most flyfishers pursue browns with large, heavy nymphs or streamers, but they rise well to a dry fly when big flies like stoneflies or hoppers are present or a mayfly or caddis hatch is heavy enough to be profitable.

When hooked, browns run long and deep, although they will jump, especially in shallow-water runs or on riffles. They fight the hook with a bullheaded tenacity that can strip line from a singing reel more than once.

The brown's scientific name, *Salmo trutta*, declares it as the "true trout." It was introduced into the West in the late 1880s and in Colorado in 1887 from stocks originating in Scotland and Germany. Many anglers commonly refer to it as a German brown.

Its basic coloration is an overall golden-brown, with the back ranging from dark-brown to greenish-brown and its sides and belly ranging from light tan to lemon-yellow or white. The back and flanks are marked with many large black or brown spots. The few red spots on the lower flanks are surrounded by light blue-gray halos. There are very few or no spots on its squarish tail.

Brown trout are well established in Colorado. They can be caught in just about every stream in the state as well as in many lakes and reservoirs. Several river systems

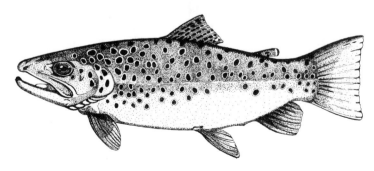

Brown Trout

at lower elevations in southern and central Colorado produce trophy fish. The largest fish are found in reservoirs.

Longer-lived than native North American species, browns have been known to exceed 30 pounds in the United States and grow up to 40 pounds in Europe. The U.S. record, 33 pounds, came from the Flaming Gorge Reservoir on the Green River on the southwestern Wyoming-northeastern Utah border. The Roaring Judy Ponds near Gunnison hold Colorado's official record of 30 pounds, 8 ounces for a 36½-inch fish caught in 1988.

The older the brown, the bigger and more wary it is. The trout normally grows about 4 to 6 inches a year during the first 3 years. Growth slows to about 2 inches a year after this. Browns have been known to live up to 15 years. However, depending on environmental variables such as water temperature and available food, size can range widely. Average fish on some streams may range from 10 to 12 inches and up to 2 pounds—still a respectable fish. On others, lunkers over 25 inches and 5 to 10 pounds may be common.

The preferred habitats of the brown are large rivers and lakes at lower elevations, although it can grow to remarkable size in small streams with adequate cover or deep pools—the meadow streams in North Park are prime examples. Undercut banks and corner pools are prime habitat for browns up to 20 inches. It is generally thought the brown is more able to adapt to warmer waters than are native North American species, but the brown's most active periods mirror those of the rainbow. It is active in waters ranging from 45 to 70 degrees Fahrenheit, with activity peaking at 60 degrees.

Cold water, in fact, spurs the brown's autumn spawning runs. Late October through December are the times trophy hunters most heavily flog the waters.

Browns first spawn at 3 or 4 years of age. They can spawn in lakes in shallow waters, but most move up into tributary streams. In rivers, browns are known to make long upstream runs to tributaries, but also spawn in shallow waters of their resident streams. In rivers with dams halting their upstream runs, they will go to extraordinary lengths to spawn, even to the extent of turning over cobble-sized rocks to create their redds.

A large spawning male can be distinguished from a female by its hooked lower jaw. This morphological adaptation is called a kype.

Browns rarely hybridize with brook trout, which also spawn in fall. One case was reported in California on a tributary to Lake Tahoe. The hybrids are called "tiger fish" and are sterile. Some Western states now stock a few streams with hatchery-bred hybrids. For the most part, though, anglers pursuing browns in Colorado will be going after wild fish. Once established in a stream, restocking is often unnecessary because they reproduce well and are difficult to catch.

In addition to the streams of North Park, significant wild brown rivers are distributed around the state and include the Colorado, Eagle, Gunnison, Lake Fork, Animas, and Arkansas.

The typical realm of larger browns can be summed up in a single phrase: Under the cover of darkness.

Small browns can be found in most waters common to other trout species. Larger browns prefer quieter waters than cutthroat or rainbows and hole up in areas where they feel safest and don't have to expend undue energy to feed.

By day, browns hide in the darker cover provided by deep pools, overhanging banks, and bankside or midstream structures like log jams and large boulders. The other essential element to a good brown hiding place is a steady supply of food streaming into or close by their hang-out.

A big brown will lay claim to the same prime spot for years. When it succumbs to old age or an angler, another large brown fills the vacancy.

Older browns are primarily nocturnal feeders but are very active during early-morning or evening hours and on heavily overcast days. At these times, they'll move out of the deeper waters of lakes to cruise the shallows, or come out of their stream-side haunts on feeding excursions.

An angler planning to linger into the night should scout out the area first, or only attempt it on well-known home waters. He needs to know the obstacles to avoid when casting to things that go plunk in the night, and, for his own safety, to prevent getting into a precarious situation.

Browns are known for their piscivorous nature, which contributes to their ability to obtain massive body weight. They even eat their own kind. However, they also feed on a large variety of other organisms, including aquatic and terrestrial insects, leeches, snails, and crayfish.

To entice them from their deeper hiding places, a lot of anglers resort to the chuck-and-duck technique of casting large nymphs to large trout. These heavy patterns in sizes 2 to 6 include large stonefly nymphs, woolly buggers, Zug bugs, and girdle bugs. They are bounced off the bottom or drifted just above it. Also effective in similar sizes are streamers, like marabou or bullet-head muddlers. Zonkers and spruce flies that imitate sculpin or other bait fish also are effective.

Both styles of wet flies can be used to pound the banks, too, by both drift boat and wading anglers. The same goes for large, buggy styles of dry fly patterns. In either case, hit the places with the thickest cover.

Stonefly hatches on the Colorado, Gunnison, and Rio Grande rivers bring large browns up in spring just like other trout. In midsummer, a hopper bounced off a grassy bank or tossed up under an overhanging tree can be deadly. Smaller dry flies, including large drakes, caddis patterns, and stimulators in sizes 10 to 14, occasionally bring up a good-sized fish if they float directly through a feeding lane. Browns will move the least of all the trout to intercept a fly. Still, under the right conditions, they will move up into a riffle to grub for nymphs or take emergers. And when there's a carpet hatch, they will slurp down huge quantities of microflies, like midges, tricos, and Callibaetis. Western anglers pursuing these cruisers call them gulpers and revel in the experience of taking a 20- to 25-inch fish on a size 20 to 22 hook.

Whether you use wet or dry patterns, you can expect to lose more than a few if you are getting them into the haunts where large browns reside. That is one of the costs of going after one. Also expect to spend more time on the water; studies show that for every 5 rainbow or brook trout taken, 1 brown is caught.

It is sometimes easier to tie into one during the fall spawning season, but some anglers frown on this practice because the fish are more vulnerable at this time and their redds can be damaged by waders. Colorado has closed seasons in the fall to protect redds on the Blue River above Dillon Reservoir. Other trophy hunters attempt to intercept large browns on the South Platte River above Elevenmile Reservoir on their upstream migrations. This is common of other tailwaters where dams block spawning runs. Autumn weather plays a major role in this pursuit. You can encounter conditions when weather is less than desirable, when days of spitting rain, or snow, prove to be the most rewarding. I was once told, "There is no such thing as bad weather, just bad gear!!!"

Any time of the year, a brown in the net is a flyfisher's reward earned the hard way.

Brown Trout Identification

Brown Trout (*Salmo trutta*)

The coloration of a brown trout is generally golden-brown with a dark-brown to greenish-brown back. The sides and belly range from light brown to lemon-yellow. There are well-spaced, large, black or brown spots mixed with a few red spots on the sides with light blue-gray halos. The adipose fin usually has an orange border. There are very few or no spots on the squarish tail.

The brown was introduced to the United States from Europe in the 1800s.

BROOK TROUT: HIGH COUNTRY BRAWLERS

The flamboyant brook trout is the painted porcelain doll of the trout world. A beautiful fish, it is almost birdlike in the brilliance of its colors.

Brookies offer stubborn, scrappy fights with leaps rivaling the rainbow's and frantic, line-tugging runs.

Native to East Coast and Canadian waters, the brook trout, *Salvelinus fortinalis*, is actually a char-like lake trout, bull trout, Dolly Varden, and Arctic char. Both trout and char belong to the same family, *Salmonidae*. The main difference between the two is that char have light spots on dark backgrounds; trout have dark spots on light backgrounds. Both prefer cold water environments, but char seek out the coldest water.

Introduced to the West in the 1880s, the brook trout is a resident of pure cold waters of headwater mountain streams and alpine lakes. To find brookies in Colorado, head for the high country. The Flat Tops Wilderness Area and the Gore Range are your best opportunities for larger than average brookies.

Unfortunately, its eastern reputation as a scrappy fighter is lost to most western anglers because it tends to overpopulate the waters in which it lives, thereby stunting its growth. The short growing seasons of alpine lakes also contribute to its diminutive size. But many high country hikers don't mind. They love to catch "plate-size" brookies because they are excellent table fare, often rated as the best among the trout species. Take advantage of it since Colorado provides anglers a very generous harvest limit on brook trout: 8, plus 10 fish under 8 inches.

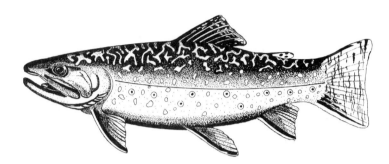

Brook Trout

Average size in most western waters is 8 to 12 inches, although its potential is much greater. Brook trout sometimes take up residence in lower lakes, reservoirs, and beaver ponds, where they may grow to a substantial size and provide a tussle worthy of their renown as excellent game fish. A 2- or 3-pounder taken from one of these waters is considered a good-sized fish.

Middle Cataract Lake in the Gore Range gave the state record of 7 pounds, 10 ounces back in 1947. A brook trout was caught and released in the Fryingpan River a couple years ago that could have been near 8 pounds. The world record, 14½ pounds and 31 inches, was taken from the Nipigon River in Ontario, Canada, in 1915.

The brook trout's most distinctive markings are white and black edges on the fronts of its lower fins. It is dark green or blue-black on its back, fading to white on the belly. Numerous wavy wormlike lines, or vermiculations, cover its back and dorsal fin. Scattered red spots surrounded by blue halos are seen on its flanks. The belly and lower fins of a spawning male are brilliant red in autumn.

The lake trout, *Salvelinus namaychush*, was introduced into the West in the late 1880s. Also called Mackinaw, it inhabits large, deep lakes. Its overall coloration is gray. It has no colored spots like the brook trout. The lake trout's tail is deeply forked. The tail of the brook trout is square.

Brook trout reach sexual maturity in 2 or 3 years. Their life span ranges from 6 to 10 years, although a fish over 5 is rare. It is a fall spawner and breeds in both streams and lakes.

Brook trout hybridize with other trout species. There is at least one record in California of brook trout naturally cross-breeding with the fall-spawning brown trout, an introduced European species. The two are crossbred in hatcheries. The hybrids are called "tiger trout" due to their yellowish coloration marked with dark, wavy stripes. Some states also cross brook trout with lake trout in hatcheries for introduction into a few lakes. These hybrids are called "splake."

Brook trout populations in Colorado are largely a product of earlier stockings. Wild fish populations are concentrated in upper elevation stretches of streams feeding down from the Continental Divide to both east and west, and in alpine lakes of the central and west central mesas.

The brook trout is the classic coldwater fish. Anglers who like to fish small waters can do well seeking it out in the churning pocket waters and small pools of Colorado's cascading mountain streams. In quieter waters, it can be found lurking under overhanging stream banks and under log jams. Beaver pond and lake haunts include the edges of weed beds near deep pools and along bushy banks. As the summer heats up, they often hang out in the cooler water at the mouths of tributary streams or spring inflows. Rarely found in waters with prolonged temperatures above 65 degrees Fahrenheit, it is most active in waters ranging from 45 to 65 degrees. Activity peaks at 58 degrees.

Its primary food base consists of aquatic insects and other small aquatic invertebrates, but brookies will also attack terrestrial insects with abandon. Larger brook trout eat small fish, including their own kind.

In fast waters, high-floating buggy patterns, like the Madam X or humpy, and easily seen attractor patterns, like the Royal Wulff or Royal Trude, work best. Standard nymphs can include the gold-ribbed hare's ear, Zug bug and caddis emergers. The new beadhead patterns eliminate the bother of dealing with split shot. Streamers also can be effective in streams and lakes. Leech and freshwater shrimp patterns, dragonfly nymphs, and woolly buggers are good producers in lakes and ponds.

Some consider the brook trout only slightly less gullible than the cutthroat. On small streams or alpine lakes where populations are profuse, brookies offer a good chance for young anglers to practice their flyfishing skills.

Brook trout can be overexploited like the cutthroat, particularly by hotspotting anglers going after big fish in a lake or pond. Most often, though, larger fish are more cautious, usually active only in the early morning or evening hours or on heavily overcast days. On quiet waters, such as smooth flowing streams and beaver ponds, they should be approached slowly and quietly, taking advantage of available cover.

Many flyfishers like to pursue brook trout with light tackle, like a 2-weight rod or one of the smaller backpacking models. A substantial brookie taken on one of these is a true challenge. Large or small, a brook trout in the hand is a portrait of beauty taken in a picture-postcard setting.

Brook Trout Identification

Brook Trout (*Salvelinus fontinalis*)

The most distinctive markings on a brook trout are the white and black edges on the front of the lower fins, the wavy or wormlike markings on the back, and scattered red spots surrounded by a blue halo on the flanks. Brook trout are dark green or blue-black on the back to white on the belly. The belly and lower fins turn brilliant red on spawning males in the fall. The tail is square.

Lake Trout Identification

Lake Trout (*Salvelinus namaychush*)

Lake trout are dark gray or gray-green on the head and upper flanks. The belly is slightly gray to white. They have irregularly shaped gray spots on the back, sides, dorsal fin, and tail; no pink or blue spots. The white border on the fins is less distinct than in brook trout. The tail is deeply forked. Lake trout are an introduced species.

MOUNTAIN WHITEFISH: UNHERALDED GAME FISH

One of the most abundant game fish in Colorado, the whitefish gets little respect from flyfishers on trout-rich waters.

There is almost a social stigma against taking whitefish in western Colorado. Fishing for whitefish is most popular in winter when they are more active than trout. There are winter whitefish seasons on many drainages, which often become *de facto* catch-and-release seasons for trout.

Some anglers scorn the whitefish because they presume it competes with trout; however, the two species evolved to occupy separate niches in a shared habitat. There is no biological evidence that high whitefish numbers harm trout populations.

While it is in the same family as trout, salmon, and char (*Salmonidae*), the whitefish's silvery body is slender and almost round in cross-section. It has a small head and tiny mouth, with a slightly overhanging snout. Its scales are large and coarse. Like its cousins, it has an adipose fin.

The most common species in the Northern Rockies, the mountain whitefish, *Prosopium williamsoni*, prefers clear, cool streams. The species was first recorded for science by the Lewis and Clark Expedition.

A similar species is the rare arctic grayling, *Thymallus arcticus*, whose trademark is its huge, colorful sail-like dorsal fin.

Mountain whitefish average 10 to 12 inches, but on nutrient-rich streams 18- to 20-inch fish are relatively common. The Colorado record, 5 pounds, 2 ounces, was taken from the Roaring Fork River in 1982.

Whitefish hang out in deep pools and shallow, slow-water runs. They feed actively in riffles on mayfly nymphs and caddis larvae. Surface feeding on adult insects occurs most often toward evening.

Among the best wet flies for whitefish are small green-colored nymphs, caddis larvae, and emergers. Beadhead patterns are very effective. Perhaps because of their

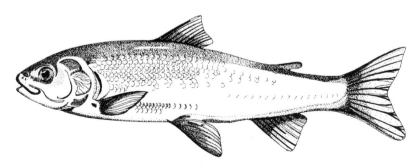

Mountain Whitefish

small mouths, many whitefish fail to take a dry fly when they strike. These misses can be frustrating, but they are also a sign that actively rising fish aren't trout.

Whitefish spawn in late fall and remain active through the winter. Midge patterns can be productive at this time.

Whitefish Identification

Mountain Whitefish (*Prosopium williamsoni*)

Light grayish-blue on back, silvery on sides, dull white belly. Scales large. Small mouth without teeth. Body almost round in cross-section. (Similar species, Arctic grayling, *Thymallus arcticus*: Dorsal fin large, sail-like and colorful. Dark spots on front half of silvery body.) They are native to the Western U.S.

BASS: PUGNACIOUS ACROBATS

Acrobatic leaps and a line-sizzling skirmish are guaranteed when tying into a smallmouth bass, considered by many to be the most dynamic fighter among freshwater game fish. Largemouth bass are husky brawlers that also rocket into the air before ripping off line in a run for cover.

By the early 1990s, most of the suitable waters of the state had received bass introductions, and management strategies switched to improving warmwater fisheries. Stricter regulations allow a bag limit of only 5 fish.

Unlike trout, bass have no adipose fin. The dorsal fin is long with two distinct parts: stiff spines in front and softer rays in back. Scales are large and obvious. The key difference between the two black bass species is the size of the mouth. The jaw of the largemouth extends behind the eye; the jaw of a smallmouth ends in front of the eye.

Largemouth bass, *Micropterus salmodies*, and smallmouth bass, *Micropterus dolomieui*, are members of the sunfish family, *Centrachidae*, which includes the sunfishes, crappies, and other basses. Native to North America, only one member of the family, the Sacramento perch, was originally found west of the Rocky Mountains. Many species have been introduced successfully all over the world.

The native range of largemouth and smallmouth bass overlapped from southeastern Canada south to Georgia and throughout the Great Lakes and Mississippi drainages.

The Florida strain of largemouth grow much larger than their northern cousins, and even in some Western waters may exceed 20 pounds. Most transplants to the West belong to the northern strain. Size can range from 1 to 12 pounds, although a 5-pounder is considered a good largemouth anywhere. The Colorado record, 10 pounds, 6 ounces, came from Stalker Lake in Yuma County in 1979.

Largemouth live in warmwater lakes and ponds and quiet backwaters and sloughs of streams. They prefer clear water with good cover like weed beds, reeds, lily pads, or flooded snags, but they also do well in somewhat barren irrigation reservoirs with radically fluctuating water levels.

Smallmouth bass inhabit cool, clear lakes and streams with rocky and gravel bottoms and shoals. Size averages 1 to 3 pounds. A 5-pounder is considered a trophy;

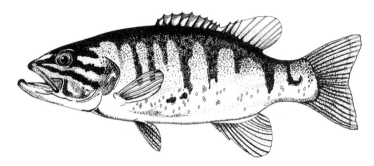

Smallmouth Bass

an 8-pounder, a monster. The Colorado record was set in 1993 with a 5-pound, 12-ounce bronzeback from Navajo Reservoir.

Both species are photosensitive and retreat to shadowy lays or deeper waters on bright days. They are more active at dawn and dusk, and in water temperatures above 50 degrees. Optimum water temperatures are 60 to 70 degrees.

The males of both species jealously guard egg nests and newly hatched young in spring. The determined defense of their progeny against predators makes them very vulnerable to anglers at this time.

Most of the quality bass lakes and reservoirs in Colorado are restricted with size restrictions, so please check current regulations. However, many fly anglers use catch-and-release habits for warmwater species as they do with trout.

Lakes and reservoirs that hold both bass and trout are called two-story fisheries. In summer, bass typically stick to the warmer waters closer to shore and trout retreat to the cooler depths. In streams, smallmouth orient toward the banks or along cliff walls and prefer slower and warmer holding areas than trout.

Black bass are voracious fish eaters, and can be instrumental in curbing population explosions of panfish and nongame species. They take both aquatic and terrestrial insects and other invertebrates. Smallmouth display a strong preference for crayfish. Largemouth are known to take frogs and mice—and other "things that go bump in the night."

Intrepid bass hunters pound reed lines and shoreline shallows after dark or before dawn with noisy popping bugs, hair-mice, hair frog patterns, diving bugs like the Dahlberg Diver, D's minnow, bunny flies, muddler minnows, and woolly buggers in large sizes 3/0 to 6. The same techniques are employed throughout the day, usually with slightly smaller flies.

Most flyfishers favor spun-hair or cork-bodied popping bugs with bushy tails and rubber legs. The theory is that the bass will hang on to soft-bodied patterns longer than plastic lures. Be wary of patterns with extra-stiff weed guards. They may push the fly away from the fish's mouth.

Because of the size and wind-resistance of the fly patterns, a rod in the 8-weight, 9-foot range is more effective for largemouth bass fishing. Lightweight rods and

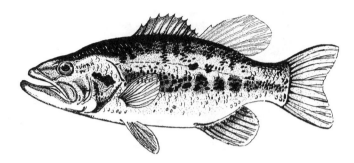

Largemouth Bass

smaller flies and streamers offer lots of fun on panfish, especially for children. Stay in the 4- to 6-weight range.

Generally, dry fly action on lakes is better with largemouth and panfish than smallmouth. Bronzebacks tend to hold deeper in lakes, around bottom structure and boulders.

Effective smallmouth flies in streams are weighted nymphs, brown woolly worms, crayfish imitations, white marabou muddlers, and Zonkers for pools and riffles. Cork or elk hair popping bugs and hair-wing dry flies produce when surface action occurs.

A 5- to 7-weight rod works for bronzebacks. Presentation can be less delicate than for trout, and leaders can be stouter—4 pounds or heavier.

The state's best largemouth bass enclaves are Cherry Creek Reservoir, John Martin Reservoir, the Rocky Mountain Arsenal, and Rifle Gap Reservoir. Several front range and plains lakes and ponds hold good largemouth populations. Check out Sawhill Ponds, Chatfield Ponds, and Bonny Reservoir.

Prime smallmouth bass waters are Pueblo, Chatfield, and Horsetooth reservoirs. Navajo and McPhee reservoirs in the southwest part of the state are also good smallmouth fisheries. Many small farm ponds and urban reservoirs also hold good populations of smallies in both the plains to the east of the mountains and the lowlands west of the Rockies.

Bass Identification

Largemouth Bass (*Micropterus salmoides*)

Dark green on back and flanks, belly white. Dark, irregular horizontal band along flanks. Upper jaw extends behind eye. Deep notch in dorsal fin.

Smallmouth Bass (*Micropterus dolomieui*)

Dark olive to brown on back, flanks bronze, belly white. Dark ventricle bands on flanks. Eyes reddish. Upper jaw ends in front of eye. Shallow notch in dorsal fin.

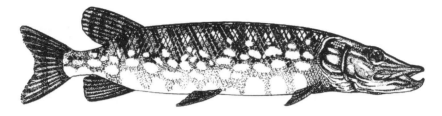

Northern Pike

NORTHERN PIKE: THE BIG BAD WOLF

The northern, also known as *Esox lucius* (water wolf) is one of a Colorado fly angler's best chances to hook and land a fish over 20 pounds. These awesome predatory fish can be readily available to the fly angler early in the season from late April to mid-July. They're also a great reason to stay on the water while trout fishing is slow due to heavily flowing and off-color rivers.

Northern pike are very aggressive and have a voracious appetite, which makes a good combination for any angler, especially the fly angler. Northerns have a period of time during pre- and post-spawn when they seek out the warm, shallow bays and shorelines of many of the state's lakes and reservoirs, making them accessible to the wading flyfisher. Shallow, dark-bottomed bays are the main points of interest for the pike hunter, due to the speed in which the water warms in the spring. Water temperatures between 58 and 68 seem to produce the best action. Feeding northerns may readily take flies of nearly 6 inches long when on the prowl.

With this in mind, a step up in equipment is a necessity. Rods of 9 feet with the ability to cast an 8- or 9-weight line are a must. Northerns are fast swimmers—some refer to them as sprinters—early in the battle after being hooked. Reels with good disk drag systems are needed to handle the initial flurry. Don't forget about the importance of a good fly line. A bass taper or a line especially designed for pike and muskie should be part of your rig. They are exaggerated weight-forward lines to aid in casting the big, heavy flies.

An assortment of flies including, black, chartreuse, and white bunny bugs in sizes 3/0 to 1/0 are the most productive patterns. Clouser's minnows, Lefty's deceivers, D's minnows, and strip minnows are other good choices.

As the hot summer months move in on us, the pike move out of the shallows back into the depths of cooler water. However, they may not be totally out of range for the fly angler. During the heat of the summer, fish for pike in the very early and the very late parts of the day. Pike still like to stay within range of the shallows until the water warms to something over 70. Breakfast and dinner become the two main meals to attend.

The new state record of nearly 31 pounds was taken in Williams Fork Reservoir in 1996. The previous record of 30 pounds, 1 ounce, taken out of Vallecito Reservoir, had held since 1971. Both impoundments are still highly rated as pike fisheries, as are Elevenmile, Spinney Mountain, and Stagecoach reservoirs. The real sleepers in the state are Taylor Park and Sanchez reservoirs. The Yampa River in the northwest part of the state can also be a memorable pike excursion for those of you who would like to try floating moving water.

Whichever body of water you may choose, you must be forewarned; as Barry Reynolds once said, "Just one pike on a fly rod may be enough to send you down the road to pike fishing madness."

Northern Pike Identification

Northern Pike (*Esox lucius*)

The northern pike, sometimes referred to as a "Gator," is a long, thin fish in its early stages of life, only gaining girth as it reaches 30 inches and greater. The back of a pike is a mixture of browns and greens with thin, light-colored, parallel markings along its side for camouflage. The belly is light in color ranging from pure white to creamy yellow. Some color variations may exist; however, this is the description most often found.

Northern pike are predatory fish with two distinctive features that make them great hunters. At one end we have a mouth full of razor sharp teeth that aid in grasping prey, and at the other end we have an upper and lower fin directly in front of a wide flat tail which makes them built for speed. Their ability to ambush prey is unmatched in the freshwater world.

TIGER MUSKIE: THE STUBBORN BAD BOY

Tiger muskie is a sterile hybrid comprised of a northern pike (*Esox lucius*) and a muskellunge (*Esox masquinongy*). Without anything better for the scientists to call it, they refer to the tiger as *Esox lucius x Esox masquinongy*.

This bad boy on the block is becoming very popular among fishery managers in the state. The population can be controlled due to its sterility. These fish grow to 40 inches (near 20 pounds) in as little as 4 or 5 years under ideal conditions and help control the panfish and rough fish populations.

Tigers do not spawn, but some of those urges may still exist. Their movement in the spring brings them into the shallow, dark-bottomed bays just as with pike; however, they are more interested in a meal ticket than shaking their tails. Tigers can be very stubborn in response to a fly. In a popular tiger lake just out my back door, Quincy Reservoir, they can be seen in groups in no more than 3 feet of water tucked under some sort of cover, but unlike a northern, refuse to jump on any fraudulent chunk of food. Why? A good question with no concrete answer. There could be several reasons, but the most simple would be to say, "Tigers are just more difficult to catch than northern pike!"

Tiger Muskie

Quincy Reservoir does stake claim to the state record tiger muskie of just over 40 pounds, caught in 1994!

Tigers do prefer slightly warmer water than northerns, which makes them ideal for lower elevation lakes. Aside from Quincy, tigers can be found in Evergreen Lake, Cherry Creek Reservoir, Bear Creek Reservoir, and Barr Lake, with Sterns Lake being an outstanding body of water for tigers.

Tackle and flies used for northern pike will do well for tigers, as do many of the same tactics. Show your fly to as many fish in a day as you possibly can. The more time you spend fishing for them, the more successful you will become. You must become as stubborn as they are!

Tiger Muskie Identification

Tiger Muskie (*Esox lucius x Esox masquinongy*)

The tiger muskie, like the northern pike, is a long, thin fish in its early stages of life, but grows somewhat faster. With beautiful, tigerlike stripes marking the sides of the fish, this hybrid is much lighter and brighter in color than the northern. The belly is light and lower fins and tail take on a reddish hue as the fish grows to trophy size.

Travel Tips

When traveling on a flyfishing trip, your biggest concern is to have fun. And a smooth trip takes planning, which is an integral part of a unique experience. You're in the wrong game if you don't like sitting around a map, plotting your course, or visiting the local fly shop to stock up on effective patterns and shoot the bull. Spending time prior to your trip, preparing for your Colorado adventure, will only escalate your opportunity to have a good time.

Before you walk out the door and head for the stream, you should consider such things as what stretch of river to fish, where to meet your fishing partner, what rod to take, which flies to take, what clothes you will need—not to mention what to bring for lunch. Chores, such as filling the fishing car with gas, checking the oil and tire pressure, and stocking up on mosquito repellent, are all part of that plan.

When a flyfishing trip takes you away for a weekend or more, extensive planning is a must. Motel reservations must be made or tent and camping gear packed. Check propane bottles for the camp stove, air the sleeping bags out from the last trip (you don't want a wet bag before your trip begins), and make sure the flashlight works. Ask yourself where those frying pans are. A couple cans of chili—and if that's the case, a roll of toilet tissue—might round out the weekend.

If you are traveling from other parts of the nation or from a different part of the world, a trip to Colorado becomes an episode that needs a masterfully thought out chain of events. The key to any travel is the way gear and clothing are packed, whether by car or plane. Take what is necessary, nothing more. Included with this guide is a checklist of items needed for an enjoyable experience on the streams and lakes of this colorful state.

Airlines

If you arrive by commercial airline, you will likely land at the Denver International Airport or Colorado Springs Municipal Airport. Connecting flights to other cities and towns across the state can be attained.

If you can carry any luggage on to the plane, do so. Four-piece rods in aluminum or hard plastic tubes, strapped to a carry-on type of bag, are one of the best options for your high dollar tools. However, two-piece rods up to 9 feet long (which makes the carrying case length 4.5 feet) can be strapped to a bag and fit into an overhead compartment. Often, a wink at the flight attendant lands your rod a safe place in the closet with personal attention.

Inside your carry-on bag, stow reels, extra spools, flies, a computer (I know some of us can't leave home without it) and camera equipment, if possible. Place some kind of identification on your baggage. This means all bags and rod tubes should be labeled. A secret from frequent fliers is to get on the plane as early as possible to reserve plenty of overhead space. If the plane is full and you are the last person to board, be prepared to have your bags checked.

Airlines are enforcing the basic rule that your carry-on luggage is limited to two bags that must fit under the seat in front of you or in overhead storage.

If you bring more luggage than can be carried on, a couple more tips may be of interest. First, reserve your tickets well in advance and make sure you get a seat assignment. Most major airlines have a service called "Skycap" where you can check your bags right at the curb outside the airport. Show the attendant your ticket and a photo ID, and your bags will be checked in. This will save time spent in the baggage check-in line. Receive your boarding pass well in advance to avoid the possibility of having a standby passenger procuring your seat. Thirty minutes prior to departure should be adequate.

When gearing up for a trip, pack only essential clothing. However, you will need to prepare for a variety of weather in Colorado. It has been said that predicting weather in Colorado is a fool's game, but with new technology relative accuracy can be expected. Spring trips to the high country can bring rain, sleet, wind, and snow. Some of the best early-season hatches happen in the midst of a heavy snowstorm, so be prepared for wet, cold weather. However, two hours later the sun might be beating down upon you, so also be prepared for warm weather.

Fishing conditions during summer can be hot and dry. It's not uncommon to have a "no fires" regulation in force during July and August. However, afternoons can be filled with thunderstorms that will drench the forest floor and make your favorite stream murky and barely fishable.

In my mind, the best time to enjoy the total beauty of Colorado extends from mid- to late September through mid-October. Aspens and scrub oak are in full color at that time, and you might even hear an occasional whistle from a rutting bull elk. Daytime temperature ranges from the low 70s to the mid-80s. At night, the temperature is crisp. Mornings bring the first frosts of the season. Best of all, fall hatches are excellent, and the fish are eager to munch them while fattening up for winter.

High Elevation

Colorado has more than 50 peaks that range to 14,000 feet or more. Much travel during any cold water fishing trip will mean crossing mountain passes in excess of 10,000 feet.

Eating your Wheaties and trying to get yourself into decent shape before attempting an excursion to the high country of Colorado is helpful, but anglers from lower elevations may experience a period of physical adjustment. The oxygen is about 40% to 45% less dense than at sea level. Effects will vary with each individual.

Acute mountain sickness (AMS) is the most common affliction from traveling the high country. Onset may be delayed, and symptoms can include a headache, nausea, loss of appetite, insomnia, strange dreams (some of which aren't too bad, I must say), and lethargy. Children may also have bouts of vomiting. Mild cases may last a few hours, but minor symptoms usually last a couple of days. Frequent breaks, liberal water intake, light eating, and decreased smoking are the best treatments for acute mountain sickness. Aspirin or Tylenol may help relieve symptoms. A prescription drug called Acetazolamide (Diamox) is known to help prevent AMS. Consult your doctor about acquiring a prescription if you have a history of problems.

Care must be taken if the affliction progresses to a more serious problem called high-altitude pulmonary edema (HAPE), a potentially fatal problem. If breathing becomes difficult, the headache continues with mental disturbance, coughing exists, or if staggering is apparent, a physician should be contacted. After rapid ascents to altitudes above 9,500 feet, symptoms may begin between 6 and 36 hours at high elevation and usually follow an episode of AMS. This could be the sign of a medical emergency.

When possible, preventative measures should be taken. Gradual ascents allow the body to adapt to changes in oxygen content. Drink lots of water on your way up. Try to limit elevation changes to 1,000 feet a day between 7,000 and 10,000 feet. Ascending to elevations between 10,000 and 14,000 feet should be limited to 500 feet a day. When this is not possible, pay close attention for symptoms mentioned earlier, and be prepared to backtrack to lower elevations.

People with lung or heart disease may be adversely affected by high elevation. Consult a doctor before traveling to the high country. Those people on medications, especially high blood pressure medicine, should discuss with their physician the possible effects of high elevations on those drugs.

Although not a medical problem, face, hands, and feet may swell at high elevation. The cause of the swelling is unknown, and it can persist for a day or two after returning to low elevation. A positive response may be found in a low sodium diet and diuretics.

The humidity in Colorado, on average, is less than 20 percent, which can cause dehydration. The dry mountain air and an increased respiratory rate due to the low oxygen content results in a loss of body fluids. Because of that, 1 to 2 quarts of water should be consumed each day to prevent dehydration. Low humidity also dries nasal membranes, which can cause a nosebleed. As with all bleeding, first aid for nosebleeds should consist of direct pressure on the nose or pinching the nose together. Five minutes of this pressure should stop the blood flow. Saline nose sprays can help hydrate the lining of the nose and prevent this common malady.

Camping

The state's national forests are filled with improved camping areas near or along major rivers, reservoirs, and in state parks. The National Forest Service has a reservation system that you can call 10 days in advance for reserving campsites; the number is 1-800-280-CAMP. They will need to know what campground you wish to stay in, so refer to the map of the area (located in this book) to which you are going. The campgrounds available through the reservation system will be marked. For further information on the reservation system, contact the Rocky Mountain regional office at 303-236-9431.

KOA Campgrounds are another outlet for those of you who enjoy a few amenities along with the great outdoors. Restrooms, showers, food stores, and an occasional pool table should help you feel a little bit more at home. A quick call to 1-800-KOA-7549 will help in locating a campground near your fishing destination.

Another source of information about camping and hiking in Colorado can be found on your computer via the Internet. Try:

- The Great Outdoor Recreation Pages: http://www.gorp.com
- All-In-One Web Directory: http://www.all-in-one.com
- Campground Online: http://www.channel1.com/users
- National Park Service: http://www.nps.gov

Blunders to Avoid

A few blunders, committed by some of the best flyfisherman I know, should be prevented at all cost.

First, carry your fishing license with you at all times. Fines for not having a license on your person can vary, but no one would like to spend another $50 on something quite this dumb.

Resident License Fees		Nonresident License Fees	
Annual	$20.25	Annual	$40.25
Five days	$18.25	Five days	$18.25
One day	$ 5.25	One day	$ 5.25

For more information call or write the Colorado Division of Wildlife at:

Colorado Division of Wildlife
6060 Broadway
Denver, CO 80216
303-297-1192

So you don't experience some painful dealings with a locksmith, you need to take care of your keys. The loss of keys, plainly said, can be a real pain in the ass and costly. Reverting to the old rock through the side window routine works, but car windows are pretty tough. Here are some suggestions on how not to lose or lock in your keys: first, designate a zippered pocket in your vest, one that is not in use on a regular basis, for your keys; second, have a key specifically made for your fly vest; third, leave the key there permanently and don't remove it until the "big unfortunate" occurs. Do not put your keys in the front pocket of your waders, in a sweater pocket, or leave them in a pair of pants in your fishing bag in the back of your vehicle.

Regarding motels, it's a good idea to keep all of your equipment with you. A little trick from some of the more traveled fishermen is to stack rod cases in a corner where there is not a chance of them being left behind. Do not lay them on the floor where they may get kicked under a bed. Another safety precaution for rod care is to put your rod together after you have dressed for the day so it's not leaning against a vehicle or tree. After a day of fishing, take the rod down and put it away before you take your gear off.

Travel Check List

____ Rod	____ Reel
____ Vest	____ Extra spool with sinking line
____ Fly boxes	____ Fly line
____ Nippers	____ Check and clean line
____ Hemostats	____ Check butt section connection
____ Tippet material, 2x to 7x	____ Check connection to backing
____ Leaders, 9–12 feet, 3x to 5x	____ Waders
____ Split shot (use nontoxic tin shot)	____ Boots
____ Seine	____ Wader repair kit (duct tape/aqua seal)
____ Fly floatant	____ Wading belt
____ Thermometer	____ Wading staff if needed
____ Strike indicators	____ Extra boot laces
____ Sunscreen	____ Rain gear
____ Insect repellent	____ Gloves
____ Landing net	____ Polarized sunglasses
____ Fishing license	____ Hat
____ Extra key to your vehicle	____ First aid kit
____ Camera and film	____ Flashlight
____ Flies	____ Small knife

Index

NOTES

WILDERNESS ADVENTURES GUIDE SERIES

If you would like to order additional copies of this book or our other Wilderness Adventures Press guidebooks, please fill out the order form below or call **1-800-925-3339** or **fax 800-390-7558.** Visit our website for a listing of over 2500 sporting books—the largest online: **www.wildadv.com**

Mail to: Wilderness Adventures Press, 45 Buckskin Road,
Belgrade, MT 59714

☐ **Please send me your quarterly catalog on hunting and fishing books.**

Ship to:
Name _____

Address _____

City _____State_____ Zip_____

Home Phone_____Work Phone_____

Payment: ☐ Check   ☐ Visa   ☐ Mastercard   ☐ Discover   ☐ American Express

Card Number _____ Expiration Date_____

Signature_____

Qty	Title of Book and Author	Price	Total
	Flyfisher's Guide to Colorado	$26.95	
	Flyfisher's Guide to Idaho	$26.95	
	Flyfisher's Guide to Montana	$26.95	
	Flyfisher's Guide to Northern California	$26.95	
	Flyfisher's Guide to Wyoming	$26.95	
	Flyfisher's Guide to Oregon	$26.95	
	Flyfisher's Guide to Washington	$26.95	
	Flyfisher's Guide to Northern New England	$26.95	
	Total Order + shipping & handling		

**Shipping and handling: $4.00 for first book,
$2.50 per additional book, up to $11.50 maximum**